ON VIOLENCE

ON

DUKE UNIVERSITY PRESS DURHAM AND LONDON 2007

VIOLENCE

A READER

Edited by Bruce B. Lawrence and Aisha Karim

© 2007 Duke University Press

All rights reserved. Printed in the United States of America
on acid-free paper ∞ Designed by Amy Ruth Buchanan.
Typeset in Minion and Meta by Keystone Typesetting, Inc.
Library of Congress Cataloging-in-Publication data appear
on the last printed page of this book.

Duke University Press gratefully acknowledges the support
of the Harry Frank Guggenheim Foundation, which
provided funds toward permission costs of this book.

FOR JAMES HESTER

AND KAREN COLVARD,

pillars and pioneers

of research on violence

CONTENTS

ACKNOWLEDGMENTS

A work of this scope and complexity covers many years in the life of an individual, and in the case of *On Violence* there were many stages from its inception as an idea to its completion as a book nearly fifteen years later.

We cannot begin to recapitulate all those who have assisted in the process. For Bruce Lawrence, the first editor, the chain of gratitude extends back to Bruce Kapferer, now a professor of anthropology at the University of Bergen. While Lawrence and Kapferer were serving on the board of advisors for the religion initiative at the Harry F. Guggenheim Foundation during the early 1990s, they conceived of this project and worked together on preliminary drafts. Graduate students at Duke University then stimulated and assisted the continuation of the project, and when Aisha Karim became fully committed to its completion, she also agreed to become a coeditor. Other graduate students at Duke University who worked on the project include Randy Styers, Scott Kugle, Ann Burlein, Youshaa Patel, and, especially in the final stages, Brett Wilson. Undergraduates have also done time in tracking down sources and proofreading, with Alex Barna and Sandra Hernandez deserving special mention. Another undergraduate student, now a professor in his own right, Louis Ruprecht Jr., provided the keen eye that led to the inclusion of the segment from Simone Weil, and to Lou the editors owe yet one more debt of gratitude.

On Violence would never have been possible without James Hester, president emeritus of the Harry Frank Guggenheim Foundation, and Karen Colvard, the foundation's senior program officer. Both helped in so many ways that the editors, happily and humbly, dedicate the book to them. Karen Colvard, in particular, had the intelligence, the energy, and the patience without which a project like this could never have been imagined, much less achieved its final apotheosis as a book. Both editors express an open, and deep, gratitude to her, as also to James Hester.

Bruce Lawrence has also been assisted by his partner, miriam cooke, at every stage. She has read and commented on parts of the manuscript. She has helped to make sense of gaps in its initial organization, and she has been a catalyst for many of the good ideas that appear in the introductions. Neither miriam nor anyone other than the editors, however, is responsible for the flaws that a book like this must, and always will, contain. The editors have struggled with a topic, an issue, and a problem that exceeds the bounds of both common sense and in-depth analysis, and they accept responsibility for whatever is lacking in the pages.

Ken Wissoker and Courtney Berger of Duke University Press made the final steps toward publication not only bearable but at times pleasant. They, too, deserve a token of gratitude, which we gladly extend to them.

General Introduction: Theorizing Violence in the Twenty-first Century

What is violence, and how is it calculated? September 11, 2001 has become the milestone of violence for the twenty-first century and for American citizens. On that day four U.S. commercial airliners were hijacked and transformed into weapons of mass destruction. One plane hit the Pentagon, destroying part of a major annex and exacting a high death toll. One plane crashed in a field in Pennsylvania, killing all on board. But the deadliest two planes were guided into the World Trade Center towers, major monuments of U.S. financial prowess located in New York City; both towers collapsed, and the lives of thousands were lost.

But how many thousands died? One day after the attack the U.S. media reported that 7,000 lives had been lost in the attacks on the World Trade Center and the Pentagon. The final count, tallied less than four months later, was 2,893.

Airplane wrecks can lead to indirect as well as direct carnage. In April 1994, following a plane crash that killed both the president of Burundi and the president of Rwanda, rumors abounded about the cause. Some suspected that the plane had been shot down due to ethnic rivalries and desires for vengeance. Riots flared in Rwanda. The estimated number of Tutsi and Hutu killed varied between 10,000 and 200,000! But, indisputably, the greater number of those killed were Hutu, so much so that the violence in Central Africa is now called Hutu genocide, albeit, outside of Rwanda, a faceless and nameless genocide.[1]

Not so the death of Amy Biehl. In August 1993 in South Africa, Biehl was dragged from her car in a black township near Capetown and beaten to death by three shantytown black youth. Her murder shocked. It, and the trial that followed, drew extensive media attention. Many black deaths also took place during 1993–1994, yet they "continued to be reported unceremoniously in South African newspapers as mere body counts, a persistent residue of the apartheid years. White deaths 'count'—the victims have names, personalities, histories and grieving family members." Black deaths do not, with "African murder victims . . . normally reported as 'faceless, unidentified bodies.' "[2]

Whether the goal is to count victims of violence or to represent them, the lesson is the same: context matters. Violence always has a context. Context shapes not just the actors or victims but also those who represent them. What is celebrated in one place may be mourned in another. Memory is never an equal balance, or a neutral lens, of human experience and history. What may be remembered and highlighted in New York may seem unimportant, even inconsequential, in Africa, but more often the reverse is true. The ongoing, massive violence in Central Africa, for instance, concerns almost no one outside of African aid agencies, or arms export merchants. It is as if "a thick curtain of silence" has descended on the blood-soaked landscape of Rwanda.[3]

One might say that the news media, whether dealing with Rwanda or some other crisis area, is just doing its job: telling prospective readers about the violence that defines their everyday lives. Yet the media also create and respond to expectations that news stories be shocking. In the early twenty-first century newspapers and magazines are confronting new rivals, having lost circulation nationally and worldwide to telejournalism and, since 1994, to the World Wide Web as well. Yet all media, from the oldest newspaper to the newest Web site, rely on the dramatic story that compels readers to buy or to tune in and turn on. Violent incidents still shock; their stories still sell. The chain of violence forged through image and narration thus cannot be broken by holding accountable the news media, whether print or visual or virtual. What is produced through the *New York Post* in the United States or the *Daily Mail* in London is magnified on MTV and CNN—and even, since the late 1990s, on Al-Jazeera. Market forces are driven in part by consumer interest, and violence sells.

On Violence projects violence as an element in the life stories of both editors, who are keenly aware of the shadow of violence that has claimed so many victims. It has made them both recognize how fragile and contingent is "ordinary," unviolated existence. Aisha's earliest memories go back to the Pakistani-Indian skirmishes in the early 1970s. There were frequent blackouts, and every evening, as Aisha and her family tried to sleep under the stairs of the apartment building, crammed in with the other four families that inhabited the same space, they wondered whether they would survive the night or whether they would be bombed out of existence. Many of those who shared that apartment building did not live to see the end of the last major war between India and Pakistan, which resulted in the formation of Bangladesh as an independent polity—but only after exacting a high human toll.

There is an ongoing sequel to the transnational violence of 1970s South Asia, with not just Muslim-Muslim but also Muslim-Hindu warfare scarring the Indian subcontinent at the outset of the new millennium. In March 2002 Hindu reprisals against Gujarati Muslims etched the world's headlines, but soon receded. No precise death toll was recorded: the Indian government wanted to reduce the magnitude of this politically induced tragedy, and so it became another "local," little-noted event. Most of the world press was riveted to the U.S.-led war on terror that was taking place elsewhere in the world. Even though the forces in western India that produced over 1,500 deaths in less than two months remain active and potentially lethal, they continue to be downplayed—

at least until the next bout of killing compels yet another brief but ineffectual round of media coverage.

Bruce experienced another kind of violence: he grew up during the so-called Cold War, under the shadow of potential nuclear holocaust. In the early 1960s, after he had been commissioned in the U.S. Navy, he served on board a battleship that took part in mock battle maneuvers. John F. Kennedy was president of the United States, Nikita Khrushchev his Soviet counterpart. In October 1962 Bruce's ship cruised south from Norfolk, Virginia. He and his fellow marine-corps combatants were certain that they would be invading Cuba, either to win victory via Gitmo (the U.S. naval base in Guantanamo Bay) or to be blown to bits by Fidel Castro's Russian-made bombs. Every night they went on watch fearing orders that would send their ship southward, propelling them into combat in the Caribbean, dooming many of them to watery graves.

The sequel to the Cuban Missile Crisis, which was defused by November 1962, seemed benign: the Vietnam War, a U.S.-led campaign fought to make the world safe for democracy. Ultimately, of course, the Vietnam War—waged for over a decade and costing the lives of over 55,000 Americans and nearly 4 million Vietnamese soldiers and civilians—was far from benign. The American dead have been memorialized by the Vietnam War Memorial in Washington, which names each one of them in a haunting marble sequence of inscribed walls and interlocking pathways. And the Vietnamese dead? No such memorial exists to remember by name the millions of Vietnamese who also died in that war. In death as in life the context of violence dictates both the range of public memory and political uses of the past, yet in every generation and in all parts of the world violence of some kind defines the experience, and limits the options, of humankind.

WHY VIOLENCE?

In 1989 the Cold War ended. The United States became the sole superpower, yet the world did not become a safer place. Instead, people now experience fear of violence as a daily reflex. Violence marks the new millennium; it registers as *the* sign of post–Cold War fever. After the 1989 fall of the Berlin Wall, both Americans and Europeans thought that a new moment had arrived, that peace seemed within the grasp of wise statesmen. But the Gulf War, the Bosnian War, and the collapse of the Oslo Accords suggested that sustainable peace was still remote, perhaps a mirage. Then came 11 September 2001 and the "war on terror." Peace plans, patchwork reforms, and diplomatic missions—all seemed doomed to fail. Each became merely a staging ground for the next episode of broad-scale violence.

The questions that drive *On Violence* have recurred throughout human history and contemporary experience: why is violence so intractable? Are human beings by nature ineluctably and irresistibly violent? No matter how socialized one is to resist the urges and reflexes of violence in one's personal and immediate circumstances, does one not remain enthralled by the spectacle of violence, its spiral and its logic, as inscribed in one's own life?

William James, perhaps the quintessential American philosopher of the last century, at least for the liberal minded, has argued just that: violence is constitutive of human nature. "The plain truth," according to James, "is that people *want* war. They want it anyhow; for itself and apart from each and every possible consequence. It is the final bouquet of life's fireworks. The born soldiers want it hot and actual. The non-combatants want it in the background, and always as an open possibility, to feed imagination on and keep excitement going. Its clerical and historical defenders fool themselves when they talk about it. What moves them is not the blessings it has won for us, but a vague religious exaltation. War is human nature at its uttermost. We are here to do our uttermost. It is a sacrament. Society would rot without the mystical blood-payment."[4]

James's paean to war heralded a new age of American expansionism. For most of the twentieth century, the U.S. government attempted to export its values and its products throughout the world. It controlled resistance where its presence was not welcomed, it engaged in wars big and small, and it succeeded in its principal goal: to keep war, international violence, away from American shores. But the beginning of the twenty-first century saw the end of U.S. immunity to war in its own territory. September 11 not only resulted in large-scale loss of life and property in New York City and Washington but also redefined war itself. September 11 became the cause and justification for a new war on terror abroad, at the same time as the "enemy" was recognized as being within, as well as beyond, U.S. borders, which led to new strictures on the civil liberties of immigrant Americans who might be deemed suspect by their nationality or religion or both. Was not the reality of violence once again a daily sacrament, a mystical blood-payment of American lives?

At the least, one might argue, Americans today are better able to imagine and understand violence in places like India and Rwanda because they have tasted the sacrament of violence at home. In *On Violence* we include selections from those who were both agents and victims of violence. India offers many historical examples of the dynamics of violence, including Gandhi's stand against British imperialism and, many years later, the consequences of the Shah Bano divorce case. With regard to the liberation of India, was not any actor, even the Gandhian actor, but one node in a chain of violent opposition to British colonial rule? While Gandhi did reject physical violence, he could not express his non-violence except by vilifying Western civilization as epitomized by British norms and values. Sublimated within Gandhi's embrace of Truth (*satyagraha*) is a hyper-rhetorical violence that must be highlighted if one is to understand the limits of his influence within the Asian subcontinent. The Shah Bano case foregrounds another kind of violence, one with implications that go far beyond its initial context. The Shah Bano case concerned the divorce of an upper-class Muslim woman, yet it became a prelude, and also a catalyst, to the Hindu-Muslim violence that erupted in the 1990s and continued into the twenty-first century. That violence was much more than religious or communal; it also involved the Indian government. Religion became a useful mask for pursuing ideological goals that had little to do with the noble teachings of Islam or the highest aims of Hinduism. It seems likely, for instance, that elected Indian officials colluded with Hindu nationalists to allow the destruction of a Muslim mosque in Ayodhya, then failed to assist Muslims victimized by the subsequent outbursts of violence throughout India in late 1992 and early 1993. The 2002 bloodlettings in Gujarat can be seen as a sequel to events set in motion by the Shah Bano case, then fueled by the Ayodhya mosque crisis. Our ultimate goal in this anthology is the commitment to heal, to go beyond the wounds of physical violence; yet structural violence persists, nowhere more so than in the sur-veillance instruments of national political groups and regional security forces.

THE ROLE OF THEORY

At its first eruption, violence is always experienced as unique. If given time and repetition, however, it becomes routine, part of the air, and one learns how to breathe it without being asphyxiated. One no longer seeks to eliminate it, nor even to understand it. Episodes of violence may flare up in different places, but each is contained in its local context, where it risks becoming normal.

In this anthology we try to break the quotidian hold of violence by bringing together reflections on both its origins and its persistence as process. Theories provide a deeper reflection on what otherwise seem to be but momentary aberrations in a well-oiled, economy-driven machine of global order. Theories provide a way of linking corporate scandals with inner-city gang wars, the war on drugs with the war on terror, civil wars with genocide. We begin with European theorists not because they are European but because they engage the topic of violence out of their own direct experiences of war and injustice.

The lesson from G. W. F. Hegel and Friedrich Engels, from Karl Marx and Frantz Fanon, is that violence is a structure. Violence is a fundamental force in the framework of the ordinary world and in the multiple processes of that world. Engels argues that the economic is a fundamental force for subjugation, that capital has a logic of its own that justifies the use of whatever means are available to achieve economic prosperity. The bourgeois revolution, suggests Engels, happened because the "political conditions in France had remained unaltered, while the economic conditions had outgrown them." The bourgeois revolution was needed to create political conditions in which "the new economic conditions could exist and develop." To illustrate this dialectical progression of history, Engels cites the history of warfare, suggesting that each military innovation is both instrumental for economic gain and threatened by it. Despite the seeming paradox of their interaction, economic and political and military forces elide with one another in subverting the very world they seem to be supporting and perpetuating.

If Engels allows too little room for human agency, liberal observers (such as James Scott, James Cone, and Elliott Leyton) foreground the role of the individual, assuming human nature as a constant frame and the politics of the center as defining all of society. While we agree that violence is always mediated through individuals, we challenge the notion that violence is intrinsic to the human condition or social structure. Violence is always and everywhere historically contingent; it can never be morally or politically neutral. In Part I: The Dialectics of Violence, we juxtapose Marx and Fanon in order to show how self and society are actually false oppositions. The state is neither the first nor the primary domain for exploring how self and society are complicit in each potential or actual expression of violence. In Part II: The Other of Violence, we include both actors and critics, placing Hitler in a subsection with Gandhi and Malcolm X in order to underscore how the latter two invoked the political rhetoric of the state even though they never controlled its structure, which Hitler did. Critics want to explore the multiple levels of power that resist or redefine the state, yet nonstate or quasi-state dimensions of violence recur in all three of the major social subsets: family, law, and religion (covered in Part III: The Institution of Violence).

In Part IV: The State of Violence, we highlight Michel Foucault, who asserts that violence begins in the conscious actions of human beings. Violence does not exist prior to structure or order but is created in human consciousness, indeed, in the very practices of human consciousness. The key concept for Foucault is subjectivity, not as an internal, voluntary, personal reflex, but rather as part of a larger nexus of texts, institutions, and discursive practices. Methodologically, what this means is a shift to archaeology and genealogy as cultural tools. Archaeology refers to a method of revealing how systems of knowing—or epistemes—organize a given text. Genealogy involves a reconstruction of the origins and evolution of discursive practices within a nexus of power relations. When combined and used in tandem, the archaeological-genealogical method foregrounds the necessity of reading a given text within its historical context, that is, within the networks of power that produce that text. What seems to be the liberal project is turned inside out: subjectivity becomes the basis for locating all the hidden assumptions of human identity marking difference as well as masking hierarchy.

It is because subjectivity is both marked and masked that violence seems to escape its own analysis: it lives in the shapes that it appears to subvert. Violence is not opposed to structure as something that exists external to structure; it is another form of structure, of processes, of practices. It is shadow to light, but without shadow how can one see light?

To bracket shadow with light, we explore violence through its practices. There is no general theory of violence apart from its practices. In other words, theories of violence must be as varied as the practices within which they occur; shadows abound, but rays of light also glimmer, and they, too, must be noted.

Our perspective is one that opposes and resists a natural theory of violence. We understand human beings as above all social agents who engage with like-minded beings, at the same time that they create technology, working to redirect nature and, through it, the world. Though violence exists at both levels—the social and the scientific—the orientation to violence develops, intensifies, and shifts in direct relation to the imaginative exercise of actual men and actual women. It is Engels who captures both the hierarchy and the entropy implicit in violence. At some point in the dynamic unfolding of the modern world, prophesies Engels, the true workers' revolution will take place. It will put an end to the traditional relationship between the subjugator and the subjugated, the proletariat and the bourgeoisie. Socialism will emerge the victor when "the armies of the princes become transformed into armies of the people; the machine refuses to work and militarism collapses by the dialectics of its evolution."

The collapse of militarism remains a remote, even utopian prospect, yet our theory of violence as inherent in certain day-to-day practices highlights the nature of those practices within which violence is revealed. Violence in marriage, for instance, must be framed within a theory of the structure of marriage, which Del Martin does in part III. Rape, too, must be analyzed within the structure of gender relations, sexuality, and society. Catharine MacKinnon criticizes early feminists for considering rape to be an exceptional and asexual form of male aggression; the more engaged feminist view, according to MacKinnon, is "one which derives from victims' experiences. The rape victim sees sexuality as a social sphere of male power of which forced sex is paradigmatic. Rape is not less sexual for being violent; to the extent that coercion has become integral to male sexuality, rape may be sexual to the degree that, and because, it is violent."[5]

A major goal of *On Violence* is to note both the achievements and the limits of Western European and, more recently, North American theories of violence. Some of the most significant theory was born at critical junctures of Western experience. Major zones where theory was transformed can and must be isolated; only then can one begin to see how they shaped discussions about the import of violence.

One obvious zone demarcating a theory of violence is that of the Manichaean position wherein order is opposed to, and valorized over, chaos. This position reflects the logic of colonialism that advocates violence as the legitimate mechanism of transformation, necessary to establish a new and "just" order. Nowhere is this more clear than in Algeria and in the experience of Frantz Fanon. The Algerian context of colonial violence produced its own anticolonial, and now postcolonial, upheavals. Both Fanon and Pierre Bourdieu, also a product of French Algerian experience, affirm our general thesis that violence can never be seen outside its own structure, which operates at multiple levels— historical, rhetorical, and practical.

The rhetorical level is the most difficult to decode. It is framed as taking sides, political partisanship, whether liberal or conservative, Left or Right, marginal or centrist. Violence viewed as a rhetorical instrumentality is common to both the Right and the Left in strikingly similar forms. Ideology becomes a secondary rather than a primary variable since both the Left and the Right, as totalizing strategies, see violence as "neutral," that is, it becomes merely another means of implicating the rest of humankind in their agendas.

The modern world brings forth several -isms, from nationalism and fundamentalism to communism and Maoism. All are linked to forms of intellectually created violence, which is distinct from mass forms of violence, yet the two are also related in Hitler and Nazism. Hitler's populist appeal masks some of his intellectual moves, for instance, his fondness for Wagner and his cooptation of Nietzsche.

No less implicated in rhetorical violence is the practice of cultural anthropologists who trace violence to primitive, non-Western antecedents, which they consider to be sources for the conditions of violence and thus for understanding and containing or overcoming its harmful effects. It is this vision of primitive or classical sources as the basis of the modern view that itself needs to be examined, as both Elliott Leyton and Michael Taussig argue (Part V: The Representation of Violence).

In theorizing violence Taussig challenges the unexamined "present-mindedness" or "presentism" of René Girard (see part III). Girard enacts the foundational fallacy, citing other sources as if they had a clear, unequivocal meaning without taking into account how his own status as modern critic informs both his selection of sources on sacrifice and their consequent use. By focusing exclusively on the sacrificial victim as an abstract, generic person, Girard begs the question, taken up so eloquently by Bourdieu and later by Taussig, of the violence of the "modes of domination" which produce the classes and marginalized groups from which Girard's victims are taken, specifically, the modes of racism, xenophobia, sexism, classism, homophobia, and ageism that are integral to systemic violence. Taussig, by contrast, embraces as his project "to radically rethink what it means to take an example or use some new symbolic theories or systems while also trying to remain 'nervous' about them, hoping to undermine the lust for order that provokes us all, including down under symbolic anthropologists of the post-colonial disorder."

The debate internal to *On Violence*, between Girard and Taussig, evokes a larger debate: the primitive-classical dichotomization. The primitive-classical break has too often been transformed into a system of thought that appropriates its visions in terms that may be at variance or even opposite to the structures of thought implicit in them. Too often it prizes accepted cultural-religious norms —in Girard's case, classical Christian notions of the Eucharist as supreme sacrifice—and regards them as superior to earlier forms of sacrifice, whether primitive or pagan or both.

Especially dubious is the notion that there is a sort of invisible fault line, a rite of passage called the Enlightenment, wherein magic is displaced with Science and superstition is overcome through Reason, thus enabling one to grasp other moments and understand other persons as they really were. By this logic, the past three hundred years supersede all prior history, for they have produced, even as they have privileged, a branch of humankind—specifically, Euro-American agents of the knowledge class—that is capable of decoding violence and human struggle as a universal map of social relations. While implicating ourselves in the critique of Enlightenment assumptions, we still want to make it more generally accessible to others.

QUESTIONS THAT WILL NOT GO AWAY

Why focus on violence? Are people inherently violent, and if so, are they more violent now than in prior periods?

We do not believe so, but it is impossible to review or to understand the cycles of history, including the present one, without engaging the construction and perpetuation of violence.

Where does violence come from? Does it come from individuals, groups, social structures, or some blind fate?

There is always a context, or a structure, to violence, and the reader-observer-participant must be alert to how her own life experience, location, and options frame the violence that seems to mark both her individual and collective existence.

What counts as violence? Can it be separated from technology or science, or does the very technology of communications replicate violence even while seeming to merely announce it? What is a sound-byte on violence? How does it function both to represent and also to falsify some quotient of violence?

No representation of violence exists apart from its rhetorical opposite or sublimated counterpart. The chimera or simulacrum of modernity has seemed to chart a time beyond history, or at the end of history, but this historical conceit must become part of the background—yes, the context—within which representations of violence are viewed and evaluated.

Who gets to speak about violence, whether in the academy, the media or in different parts of the globe? How do victim, perpetrator, agency, accountability, and victimization change, and why? Is violence private as well as public? Beyond war, terror, and persecution, does it also include internalized emotions, thoughts, and urges? What is the relationship between language, physical violence, and non-violence?

There has never been a period or a group or a place free from violence, whether defined as product or process, as internal or external to individuals and their worldview or experience, but the range of data can be and should be focused on specific questions, local projects, and collective strategies that neither ignore violence nor surrender to its inevitability.

The questions proliferate, and the answers provided are provisional. Not all questions will seem equally compelling to different readers, and each reader should ponder and produce her own answer to the issues they present, the prospects they suggest.

In our view, superseding all other questions and also informing them is the central question without which the focus on violence becomes a mere reflex of dominant stereotypes with no analytical advance: what is the relationship between knowledge about violence and action? That is, how does one speak about violence without replicating and perpetuating it? And how can one apply knowledge about violence to advocate strategies that either reduce its incidence or deflect its force?

OVERALL GOALS

In order to pursue the implications of this last question, one must first recognize that it cannot be answered. This question requires perpetual self-questioning and the daily practice of self-criticism, but one must also avoid the danger of overindulgence in self-doubt, namely, succumbing to individual or collective paralysis. The dilemma is also a hope: to understand, empathize, and advocate for others, one must first acknowledge one's spatial and circumstantial, if not one's substantive or essential, difference from them.

The epistemic lesson to be learned and relearned, then applied again and again, is the need to confront rhetorical violence. At the heart of rhetorical violence, which is also cognitive violence, is the assumption that Europeans— together with Americans, Australians, and other Anglos—are intrinsically superior to the rest of humankind. As a reflex, it is not limited to Euro-Americans; the selection from Gandhi's *Hind Swaraj* (part II), for example, indicates how mobile that assumption is among those who come within the orb of British or, more recently, U.S. imperial designs. All the more necessary is vigilance against presumptive notions of time: even though a post-Christian neo-imperial strategy of time marks the worldview of global elites, the dominant group cannot, and does not, subjugate all those who reckon time by another rhythm or an alternate calendar.

Unless one is aware of the distinctly European move to relocate time and to advocate a particular view of time as the sole valid view, one quickly becomes caught up in the snare of false dichotomization. The political theorist Benedict Anderson, for instance, fails to grasp the ambivalence of a distinctly European view of time in depicting the spirit of nationalism. For him, the notion of nation opposes linear time, which he lampoons as "homogeneous, empty time, measured by clock and calendar." Its opposite, embraced by nationalists of all stripes, is fractal time, that is, time as "a simultaneity of past and future in an instantaneous present."[6] Yet this argument is disingenuous, for the very persons positing the nation as an eternal essence are doing so with a visceral awareness of the linear stakes involved in their ideological reconfiguration of time. They invoke eternity even as they grasp the levers of temporal power. Their rhetoric must be separated from their action. Anderson, on this point as on others, shifts imperceptibly from describing the rhetoric of nationalist actors to embracing their views as "authentic," above further comment and therefore removed from criticism.

There is a deeper issue that goes beyond Anderson's rhetoric, and even beyond the critique of his rhetoric. *One must elect at the outset whether to view violence as product or to view it as process.* Violence as product is always depicted as a sporadic, singular episode or set of such episodes. When a violent episode occurs, it does so as the exception to the norm. It erupts at a specific time and in a particular place. It is both marked and limited by its temporal and spatial occurrence. Only later does the community that has been violated offer a variant account of the same moment, whether they be South Asians in British India, Jews in Nazi Germany, blacks in urban America, or resistors to Big Brother in post–World War II Great Britain (see part II). A product of violence is never just a single product with a seamless narrative or a fixed meaning.

Precisely because one must recognize the porous boundaries of each violent act, whether individual or group-specific, whether erupting in the private or in the public domain, violence is always and everywhere process. As process, violence is cumulative and boundless. It always spills over. It creates and recreates new norms of collective self-understanding. Violence as process is often not recorded because it is internalized; it becomes part of the expectation of the living, whether framed as revenge or as fear, but, most important, its creation must remain transparent, its instrumentality evident beyond all attempt to reify or essentialize both its origin and its function. That is the larger, and largest, theoretical goal of *On Violence*.

CONCLUSION: A SMALL STEP TOWARD BREAKING THE CHAIN OF VIOLENCE

Can any policy work to limit or reverse the effects of violence? We are doubtful that it can, for to break the cycle of violence would require more than a policy shift or a reliance on more effective policing and security measures. One would have to excise the persistent urge for revenge or the equally tenacious fear of further violence that too often elicits that which it most dreads. Such a strategy, moreover, presupposes that violence is a culturally created trait, capable of manipulation and containment.

It is the strategy of managing violence from the top down that we call into question at two crucial points. One point concerns the very move to predict a pattern of violence. Does one try to predict further patterns in order to control and manage violence, thus maintaining the present order and also benefiting those who are its current custodians? Does not such an effort to manage violence then presuppose a problematical ideology of stasis? For instance, since prediction too often relies on fixed labels rather than inchoate processes, it neglects mechanisms of social exchange that are neither rational nor routinized; only in retrospect do they become "evident."

The second demurral concerns the nature of violence. Precisely because it escapes both containment and curtailment, might it not be something intrinsic rather than extrinsic to the human psyche? If violence reappears again and again as a human reflex, might it not perhaps have a positive function that can only be realized by accepting its intrinsicality and responding to its energy rather than trying to remove it?

It was a child of Marxism, the Czech sociologist Mihailo Markovic, who once proclaimed: "Violence has always been present in human history both in individual behavior and in social life, in both the 'legitimate' form intended to preserve a given order and as a means to promote social change."[7] Markovic's dictum is more subtle than James's prescription, yet it raises a further question: how is violence, apart from warfare and the will to kill, ineluctably part of our lives? Though it may be permanent, is it not also permeable? Even though *On Violence*, and all its source citations, mark violence as inevitable, it is not inexorable as an evil force. Might we not be better served by limiting the harmful effects of violence, accenting but also transforming the ways in which it resembles Foucault's notion of power? Power pervades. In a Foucauldian worldview power becomes the single most significant index to human behavior. Omit or slight it and all social exchange escapes meaningful analysis.

Once violence is recognized as equivalent to power and endemic to the human condition, then one's attention is drawn to ways that one can respond to its outcomes. Whether one finds exemplary Gandhi, who broke strikes while sublimating his own erotic rage in satyagraha, or Malcolm X, who did not eschew violence but was also willing to work with anyone who would tackle racism head-on, one can hope to find, in the circumstances of one's own times and the opportunities of one's own life, creative ways to channel positively that lodestone of human creativity and energy which, if misdirected, becomes not just marked as violent but also perpetuated as recurrent, destructive violence.

Our hope is to have the violence announced in the headlines but often concealed from further analysis become at once more evident and more permeable, both in private and public, from the domestic to the political to the transnational. Whether one identifies violence in daily life or in global economic processes, one benefits by making it more transparent to those who, like us, live in its shadow.

One of the most hopeful indices of change has occurred within cultural anthropology during the past two decades. Many anthropological fieldworkers, including Elliott Leyton and Michael Taussig, whose works are excerpted in *On Violence*, no longer limit themselves to ethnographic observation but instead "deconstruct the insidious and pervasive effects and mechanisms of violence and terror, underscoring how it operates on the level of lived experience."[8] They augur a practical engagement with violence that makes the academy less remote from the real world and its many, too many victims of violence.

We intend this book to be accessible to students, whether they are studying culture within the social sciences, pursuing policy studies and global history, applying ethics to mediation conflict, examining case studies in legal theory, relating religion to its ideological uses, or surveying destruction art as an increment to peace building. While there is no escape from violence, there is also no limit to the contexts in which grappling with violence can be productive.

Many of the theorists whom we cite here will be known, others unknown. The selection could easily expand into a list twice as long, with more voices from the social sciences or from transnational perspectives. We have limited ourselves to one chain of violence. Why the metaphor of the chain? We project "chain" as a series of links that are neither fixed nor inevitable. Just as there are no necessary links to violence, so there are no predictable causes of violence. A chain is always a chain that is constructed. It can therefore be modified or adjusted or imagined anew. It is always contingent on specific structures and human agents situated in specific temporal-spatial contexts. Every chain of violence contains links that vary not only in everyday contexts but also in the interpretive lens of each observer of violence. Violence is best seen as a link-chain precisely because it is neither stable nor predictable. Violence is not a tree trunk, with roots and branches that naturalize both its existence and its recurrence. Nor is violence a scaled structure, a pyramid with related but variant layers, each indispensable to its design, construction, and function. Violence is always and everywhere a chain because chains are always and everywhere subject to change, whether from below or above, by actors or by observers.

On Violence does function in myriad ways and with unmapped consequences. Its function is restricted neither to one historical form nor to a predictive series of causes and outcomes. The several links in *On Violence* connect the dynamic of European precedents for violence with the experience of North America, but it also explores the nature of violence elsewhere, especially in South Asia. Violence remains a pervasive though elusive dynamic of all human social experience. What Allen Feldman observed about political violence in Northern Ireland—that it becomes "a residual and cultural institution . . . possessing its own symbolic and performative autonomy"—could be said about other forms of violence in many locations.[9] Conditions and relations of antagonism are often discontinuous. Neither formal ideological rationale nor prior contextual motivation explains chronic violence. What was true for Northern Ireland political protest between 1969 and 1986 applies as an analytical model to many of the cases in *On Violence*. Rather than blink at violence, that hidden face of modern and postmodern life, we remain confident that its exposure will help others to wrestle with its force and to find ways to transform its potential for destruction into options for growth, if not peace.

NOTES

1. Liisa H. Malkki, *Purity and Exile: Violence, Memory, and National Cosmology among Hutu Refugees in Tanzania* (Chicago: University of Chicago Press, 1995), 291–92. An engaged anthropologist, trying to take stock of the death toll, Malkki first estimated 10,000 to 20,000 dead, although other reports cited up to 100,000. When further

fighting between government and rival forces broke out in May, reports placed the rising number of deaths, both military and civilian, at 200,000.

2. Nancy Scheper-Hughes, "Small Wars and Invisible Genocides," *Social Science and Medicine* 43, no. 5: 898.

3. Malkki, *Purity and Exile*, 293.

4. William James, "Remarks at a Peace Banquet," in *The Philosophy of William James*, ed. Horace M. Kallen (New York: Modern Library, 1926), 258.

5. MacKinnon's views generate a mixed response. The British film critic Mandy Merck depicts MacKinnon herself as a Pavlovian subject ("MacKinnon's Dog: Anti-porn's Canine Conditioning," in *Talking Gender: Public Images, Personal Journeys, and Political Critiques*, ed. Nancy Hewitt, Jean O'Barr, and Nancy Rosebaugh [Chapel Hill: University of North Carolina Press, 1996], 65–82). Merck, along with others, criticizes MacKinnon for her reliance on a psychiatric reflexivity that essentializes a divided male subjectivity. Like MacKinnon's views, the arguments of most theorists cited in *On Violence* evoke a wide spectrum of responses. Despite the importance of such responses, we have opted to let theorists speak in their own voice, in order to reflect the diversity of contemporary approaches to violence.

6. Benedict Anderson, *Imagined Communities: Reflections on the Origin and Spread of Nationalism* (1983; repr., New York: Verso, 1991), 24.

7. Markovic, quoted in Philip Weiner and John Fisher, *Violence and Aggression in the History of Ideas* (New Brunswick, N.J.: Rutgers University Press, 1974), 234.

8. Linda Green, *Fear as a Way of Life: Mayan Widows in Rural Guatemala* (New York: Columbia University Press, 1999), 58. This reference, like many others in the introduction, was provided by one of the two outside readers commissioned by Duke University Press during the review process of *On Violence*.

9. Allen Feldman, *Formations of Violence: The Narrative of the Body and Political Terror in Northern Ireland* (Chicago: University of Chicago Press, 1991), 20–21.

PART I. THE DIALECTICS OF VIOLENCE

Force is the midwife of every old society

which is pregnant with a new one. It is

itself an economic power.

—Karl Marx, *Capital*

WHAT BINDS THE READINGS IN THIS SECTION is a vision of history as a dialectical unfolding through relations of domination and subordination that may, or may not, produce a degree of freedom from these relationships. Yet, as Marx suggests, the possibility of freedom in the form of a new or different society will still be marked by the violence that inaugurates it.

All four of the readings excerpted in this section reflect revolutionary moments in world history: Hegel belonged to the period of the French Revolution, while Marx and Engels belonged to the period which saw the ripening and elaboration of the working-class revolution, even though the 1848 European revolutions failed to secure for the working classes the social and economic gains that Marx and Engels had envisioned. Fanon belonged to the period that saw the widespread decolonization that followed World War II and also the rise of anti-European nationalisms.

These readings highlight the relationship between violence and the economic world orders of their respective historical junctures: violence and feudalism in Hegel, violence and capitalism in Marx and Engels, and violence and imperialism in Fanon. Not only do these selections represent the revolutions of their times, but they also encapsulate the dialectical nature of those historical revolutions.

Consider Hegel. For Hegel the establishment of self-consciousness in the bondsman involves two moments of fear. The first moment of fear entails a containment of self-consciousness in relational space (with respect to the lord), while the second moment results in a crystallization of that space into a nonrelational, independent space. It is in this second moment that the bondsman changes. He is no longer the bondsman in relation to the lord: because he labors, he achieves independence through the independence of the product of his labor. At both moments, he fears death, but with a difference: in the first moment his fear of death finds its mediating object in the lord, while in the second moment his fear is immediately of death itself.

The bondsman's fear of the lord is "the beginning of wisdom." It is wisdom because the bondsman recognizes that his self-consciousness needs another in order to exist. It is at this moment that fear becomes a means of containing self-consciousness in a relational space; and it is this containment in space that marks its existence. But once self-consciousness becomes arrested in this relational space, that is, servitude in relation to the lord, servitude becomes its essence. The first moment of fear not only forms the self-consciousness of the bondsman but also establishes servitude as the condition of being, of life itself, and not simply as a mode of living. He exists because he is a bondsman, and for that reason he seeks to preserve his status of bondsmanship, fearing that it is only through this status that he can preserve his life.

This anxiety to preserve his status, and thus his life, produces the second moment of fear, the fear of death, "the Absolute Lord." The bondsman responds to this fear of death by producing the thing that he works on, a thing that now becomes the essence of his self-consciousness. In other words, the bondsman becomes an independent consciousness through work. He no longer needs the lord to reaffirm his existence, for in this second moment he achieves bondsmanship, and thus existence, through production of the thing itself.

Further, the production of work entails the manufacturing of consent in and by the bondsman. The bondsman must give his consent for fear of his life. It is in the production of this thing that the continuation of his life lies; "thinghood is the essential characteristic" for his consciousness, Hegel argues, yet it is this very thing "which holds the bondsman in bondage; it is his chain from which he could not break free in the struggle." Existence means voluntary servitude.

The terror of death which the bondsman experiences and which becomes objectivized and exteriorized in the product of his work also becomes the mediatory force between absolute freedom, or anarchy, and government, which is "nothing else but the self-established focus . . . of the universal will." Freedom and control thus stand in direct opposition to each other in a life-and-death struggle. They constitute moments of a dialectical movement from the death of all distinction, of the individual self-consciousness and will in absolute freedom, to the reestablishment of the universal will through government. Such a movement is a halt, but it is a temporary halt, for as soon as this seizure of self-consciousness in its "allotted sphere" takes place, the dialectical movement begins all over again. There is no escape from that perpetual circularity through which social groups and classes move until they are again *arrested* into relational spaces of differentiation. Both movement and arrest must be preserved as negations of each other. "The negation coming from consciousness," argues Hegel, ". . . supersedes in such a way as to preserve and maintain what is superseded, and consequently survives its own supersession."

Absolute freedom, or anarchy, far from being an unqualified good, contains within itself its own death. For as soon as this "flat, commonplace monosyllable," which characterizes the universal will, is established, the unison fulfills itself in the establishment of the universal will through government, which, by definition, is a "victorious faction." Distinctions between this victorious faction and other factions are reconstituted, and with the return of these distinctions, individual self-consciousnesses also return to their state of containment in "allotted spheres." Universal will vanishes, and with it, absolute freedom.

Absolute freedom, then, is terrified of its own essence, its own work, or death. This "terror of death is the vision of this negative nature of itself." Stricken with terror at this vision of its own death, absolute freedom organizes itself into government, which results in its death by other means: since government is nothing "else but a faction," "victorious against other factions." The universal will passes into specific wills, and difference is reestablished. Terror thus becomes the force which drives the universal will first into arresting itself within a relational space of factions, then leads to its death in the reconstitution and recontainment of specific wills into "allotted spheres" marked by difference and distinctions. There is no escape from death, only from the choice of one means to death by the embrace of its opposite.

Despite its metaphysical pessimism, the Hegelian system does value the product of work and the social distinctions arising from division of labor. Only labor and its effects ward off the threat of a violence that lacks consciousness even of the self and of the violence done to one's whole being. Yet in the feudal schema, in bourgeois society, the threat of violence is seen to rest on production itself. It is this inversion of the Hegelian dialectic that appears prominent in Marxist thought. According to Engels, Marx turned the Hegelian dialectic "upon its head; or rather, turned off its head, on which it was standing, and placed upon its feet." Locating the origins of capital in the process that he dubs "so-called primitive accumulation," Marx points to violence as a historical necessity in the evolution of capital. Capital is the original sin that "comes [into the world] dripping from head to toe, from every pore, with blood and dirt."

Marx describes primitive accumulation as the "prehistory of capital"; it is not the "result of the capitalist mode of production but its point of departure." Look at the historical transformations in Britain in "the last third of the fifteenth century and the first few decades of the sixteenth," he observes, where one finds an example of the classic form taken by the process of primitive accumulation. It begins in England via "the rapid expansion of wool manufacture in Flanders and the corresponding rise in the price of wool." This prompts the new nobility, for whom "money was the power of all powers," to embrace with full force the transformation of communal arable land into sheep walks. They advocate the subsequent clearing of estates, which takes a most drastic form in the Scottish Highlands. Marx calls attention to the plight of Scottish clansmen who were deprived first of their land, then of their fishing rights, before being hurled into the labor market as free and rightless workers. The results were twofold: the concentration of the means of production—for instance, land, sheep, tools, money—in the hands of a few, and the creation of a mass of producers who had to work for the elite class in order to provide the barest minimum of subsistence for themselves.

It is not just in this forced clearing out of the people that the violent nature of primitive accumulation manifests itself; indeed, violence and force become necessary in order to compel these expropriated people to work and to conform to the discipline of the working day. Gradually, the worker is made to accept the discipline necessary for the capitalist mode of production. And in this process the elite makes use of the legal apparatus of the state and compels the workers through "grotesquely terrorist laws into accepting the discipline necessary for the system of wage-labor." Indeed, the emergent bourgeoisie uses the power of the state to regulate wages, effectively forcing workers into the limits suitable for making a profit while also lengthening the working day.

This creation of a proletariat, in Marx's view, requires comparison with the category of slavery. The workers' condition was effectively that of slaves. Marx paraphrases Isaac Le Chapelier, "rapporteur of the Committee" on the law in the French Penal Code, in order to advance his argument: "Every combination by the worker," noted Marx, "was 'an assault on liberty and the declaration of the rights of man.'" The former slave masters were now the entrepreneurs, while the workers were denied all but the fiction of liberty. They were not to be "permitted to inform themselves about their own interests, nor to act in common and thereby lessen their 'absolute dependence,' 'which is almost a state of slavery,' because by doing this they infringe 'the liberty of their former masters, who are the present entrepreneurs.'"

Indeed, the phenomenon of slavery is what makes primitive accumulation what it is. The compulsion to work created by the expropriation of these human beings finds its ultimate manifestation in precisely this analytic of slavery; it is not coincidental that Marx talks of wage labor as wage-slavery. Just as the process of primitive accumulation creates poverty, it transforms the poor into wage-slaves, actual slaves, and what Marx calls "slaves of the parish," comprising those poor people who could be employed by anyone "willing to give them food and drink and to find them work." Capitalist production from the fifteenth century on is like primitive accumulation, but it is worse. It is worse because the external force and violence of the latter are now internalized in the former: whereas during the stage of primitive accumulation, the worker has to be compelled, by circumstance, by law, or by violence, to work for another, the capitalist mode of production is characterized by the redundancy of this external use of force, for the worker has internalized the discipline necessary to earn wages; his dependence on the capitalist system itself becomes the driving force to work.

It is not coincidental that the simultaneous fostering of wage-labor and slavery in Europe, because of the growing demand for labor, is accompanied by the growth of slavery in the colonies. The capitalist mode of production corresponds to the emergence of the colonial mission; indeed, it could not have been made possible without the colonial era. In this sense, colonialism, by its very essence, reifies a form of primitive accumulation that is antecedent to the capitalist mode of production but is also instrumental to the success of the latter. That the colonial enterprise depended on an element of primitive accumulation becomes clear precisely in the role that it played in the slave trade and in the employment of slaves on plantations. While colonies such as India provided the grounds for loot and plunder, and later indentured labor to work on plantations in India itself and in Africa, the African colonies for a long time provided the labor power in the form of slaves, either kidnapped, or bought and sold by their own princes and chieftains, to work on the plantations in the Americas: "The treasures captured outside Europe by undisguised looting, enslavement, and murder flowed back to the mother-country and were turned into capital there." Although Marx is primarily occupied with the developed form that primitive accumulation takes in Britain, namely, the capitalist mode of production, he is nevertheless quite unambiguous that colonialism and slavery as its byproduct depend on, even as they demonstrate the power of, primitive accumulation.

While Marx speaks of slavery in the colonies as the "pedestal" on which wage slavery was built in Europe, Engels talks about the rise of slavery in Europe as a foundation for the Greek and Roman empires, and through these empires, for world civilization. Indeed, Engels makes the self-consciously "heretical" claim that slavery was "a great step forward" for world history, in the sense that at a certain juncture, "the advance to a society based on class antagonism could be accomplished only in the form of slavery," not simply because slavery meant that the prisoners of war who earlier would have been killed were now at least spared their lives to be incorporated as slaves into the labor power of the victorious faction, but also because the inception of the institution of slavery entailed an advance toward a society based on class antagonism, which was a step toward the anticipated and hoped-for Marxist ideal of the working-class revolution—the stage at which the worker would take control of the means of production.

In *Anti-Dühring*, written as a tirade against a then contemporary socialist, Eugen Dühring, Engels argues that the economic is a far more fundamental force for subjugation than the political (while Dühring had argued the reverse). Citing several historical examples, Engels asserts that capital has a logic of its own, that the use of force is merely the means to the ends, that is, economic power; speaking of the bourgeois revolution, Engels suggests that it happened because the "political conditions in France had remained unaltered, while the economic conditions had outgrown them." The bourgeois revolution was needed to create political conditions in which "the new economic conditions could exist and develop." As an illustration of the dialectical progression of history, Engels cites the history of warfare. He suggests that each innovation in the history of militarism had been effected because it was instrumental for economic gains. But, by the very same token, such innovations could take place only if a certain amount of economic power could be staked, which would "help force to victory without which force ceases to be force."

The prior necessity of economic power in effecting advances in military technology, however, becomes an economic burden on states. Engels suggests, first, that innovation in weaponry has created a situation wherein any "further progress which would have any revolutionizing influence is no longer possible." But second, and more important, he argues, militarism has reached a stage when it will collapse "by the dialectics of its own evolution," the weapons and their maintenance having become so expensive that they constitute an excessive economic burden on the states. Engels points to the modern warship, a "lavish waste of money," in his view, because it has been developed to such perfection that it is both "outrageously costly and unusable in war." The state now has to pay for one warship what it used to pay for a whole fleet of ships; hence, the cost of the production and the operation of warships has become prohibitively expensive. And what has happened in the navy is also happening in the army, with the result that it, too, is bound to fall into ruin.

The "bursting asunder from within of militarism" is only partially due to the financial collapse brought about by the extreme costs of running the army, the navy, or the weaponry in order to keep up with the competition between the individual states; it is also due to the reeducation of the populace at war, for militarized states must resort to universal compulsory military service, thereby "in the long run making the whole people familiar with the use of arms." Familiarity with the use of arms will, in turn, enable the people to "make their will prevail against the warlords in command." At such a point, prophesies Engels, the true workers' revolution will take place. It will put an end to the traditional relationship between the subjugator and the subjugated, the proletariat and the bourgeoisie. Socialism will emerge the victor when "the armies of the princes become transformed into armies of the people; the machine refuses to work and militarism collapses by the dialectics of its evolution."

If Engels's formula for ending this relationship of subordination and dominance between the workers and the bourgeoisie entails the necessary use of arms on the part of the workers, Frantz Fanon is even more forthright in recommending the use of violence in transforming the colonial relationship. In *The Wretched of the Earth* Fanon explores and explains the necessity of violence. Demonstrating the relationship between the universalizing mission of capital and historiography, Fanon suggests that the endeavor of the colonizer is to write the history of colonization in such a way that the history of the world makes evident not only the exploits of the colonizer but also the civilizing of colonized territories. The persons colonized become "condemned" to the passivity of inorganic material beings acted on by the historiographical gaze. When the settler writes the history of the colonies, he actually writes "not the history of the country which he plunders but the history of his own nation in regard to all she skims off, all she violates and starves." This culture of "immobility," this lack of history of which Fanon speaks, entails an arrest of those colonized into certain "compartments"—a state of arrest into which each of the colonized is conditioned through fear, for "[he] *learns*... to stay in his place, and not to go beyond certain limits." To make history, that is to say, to rewrite history, would be to transgress those boundaries.

It is precisely this making of history as a transgression of boundaries through a violent onslaught that Fanon prescribes. And, in a sense, it is in this prescription that Fanon himself could be seen to be rewriting history, rewriting the master-slave relationship, specifically rewriting and revolutionizing the Hegelian terrain of distinct masters and desperate slaves. For if the Hegelian framework, with its liberal historiographical project, disavows slavery in the name of freedom and independence, it does so with its "feet planted firmly in another paradigm, that of the ideology of wage slavery."[1] It is the distortion of this liberal historiography when viewed through colonial lenses that one sees in Fanon's illiberal discourse of terrorism—a discourse that provides the only avenue through which the native can rewrite history. What one finds in Fanon is not simply an inversion of the equation, through a reciprocal "terror, counter-terror, violence, counter-violence," but a suggestion that in the colonial situation everyone is always already a slave: first, because the fear that characterizes slavery is the lot both of colonial masters and of slaves in this situation; and second, because both dominance and resistance are modes of work, the product of which becomes the crystallizing of the slave consciousness. The fear of the other is embodied in Fanon's settler as fear of the colonized natives who want to appropriate the settler's place: "The colonized man is an envious man. And this the settler knows very well; when their glances meet he ascertains bitterly, always on the defensive, 'They want to take our place.'" It is the production of this terror in the settler—terror of usurpation of place, property, and life—through violence that becomes work for the native; it defines his self-consciousness. What in the Hegelian framework held the slave in thrall—namely, fear in the first moment and the thing, the product of work, in the second moment— becomes in Fanon precisely that which liberates the slave from his slavery. For in his framework, work itself becomes redefined as violence: "To work means to work for the death of the settler.... The colonized man finds his freedom in and through violence."

In Fanon's framework, the revolutionary activity of transforming violence into work can only be initiated by the lumpen proletariat, by what he refers to as the "workless, less than men": "In the colonial countries the peasants alone are revolutionary, for they have nothing to lose and everything to gain. The starving peasant, outside the class system, is the first among the exploited to discover that only violence pays." It is not until this first bout of violence has been given impetus by the peasants and the other "workless, less than men" that violence can then become the marker of an emerging national consciousness and a national culture that is based on a unity formed through violence. It is this unity, and only this unity, which "introduces into each man's consciousness the ideas of a common cause, of a national destiny, and of a collective history," as opposed to the "separatist and regionalist" tendencies of colonialism, which work precisely by dividing the colonized into tribes and clans that feud among themselves. The practice of violence on the part of colonized natives, on the other hand, not only "invests their characters with positive and creative quali-ties" but also "binds them together as a whole, since each individual forms a violent link in the great chain, a part of the great organism of violence which has surged upward in reaction to the settler's violence in the beginning."

The colonized native finds his freedom in violence not only because by his violent actions he has staked his own life and is not fearful of the settler and the threat of death that the settler's presence implies, but also because he has pro-duced that revolution in the master-slave relationships whereby the settler has become fearful of him. If the native finds freedom through violence, it is pre-cisely because through this violence the native is able to produce that terror in the settler that defines the settler's slavery. It is a new dialectic of terror, forged by the capitalist mode of production and its colonial lockstep. In it there is no way out for the settler but to work, since the colonies have become the market for goods produced in the mother country: "The colonial population is a customer who is ready to buy goods." If this is the case, Fanon concludes, domination by violence is not in the interest of these colonizing powers, since the colonies are a market for goods produced in the mother country. Even though the producers are themselves a "monopolistic group within this bourgeoisie," precisely for that reason they cannot and do "not support a government whose policy is solely that of the sword."

Fanon suggests that the capitalist countries must pay by racing ahead to the future problems that capital will have to contend with if a "redistribution of wealth" does not occur and if the newly independent countries are left to their own devices in "climbing out of the morass [and] catching up with the other nations using the only means at hand." The most dangerous of these problems, Fanon asserts, is that of the former colony ceasing to provide a market for the mother-country's goods. Suppose the young nation is left to its own devices in contending with the forces of poverty and underdevelopment. It might "decide to continue [its] evolution inside a collective autarky," with the result that in the capitalist countries "the machines will pile up their products in the warehouses." Not only will these products lose their colonial markets, but also the attendant unemployment "will force the European working class to engage in an open struggle against the capitalist regime. Then the monopolies will realize that their true interests lie in giving aid to underdeveloped countries." Otherwise, if "through lack of intelligence . . . the capitalist countries refuse to pay, the relentless dialectic of their system will smother them." The real threat is clear: it is the dying of capital through lack of circulation, for if capital is congealed and clotted in Europe, the capitalist countries will face collapse. Moreover, some triumphalists may dare to hope that by coming to the aid of the developing countries, Europe will help to end the centuries of slavery faced by the Third World and "to rehabilitate mankind, and make man victorious everywhere, once and for all."

Fanon's dialectic is at once Hegelian and far more nuanced than Hegel, or Marx or Engels. Fanon cites the need to find new outlets and passages for the circulation of capital, in order that it does not atrophy for want of circulation, as the primary motive for redistributing wealth and for capitalist countries coming to the aid of developing ones. What began as an illiberal discourse violating the harmony of "we" that Hegel spoke of is rehabilitated into the liberality of that very same "we," of rehabilitating mankind, the whole of mankind. The task of the creation of a nation and of a national culture becomes inextricably linked with, and directly proportional to, the fate of capital. Capital is not redeemed; it still lurks as Marx's original sin. Yet the mask of history produces a new kind of capital. European colonialism entails the historical rewriting which mobilizes the colonized native as both consumer and subject. The periphery is essential to the history of capital, if not the history of its putative center, Europe, and the hegemony of capital becomes the platform on which takes place exploitation, resistance to colonial rule, and also persistence beyond colonial rule.

NOTES

1. Ranajit Guha, "Dominance Without Hegemony and its Historiography," Subaltern Studies IV (Dehli: Oxford University Press), 221.

GEORG WILHELM FRIEDRICH HEGEL (1770–1831)

Born in Stuttgart to a civil servant, the German philosopher G. W. F. Hegel studied theology at Tübingen, then worked as a private tutor, newspaper editor (during the Napoleonic occupation), and rector of a Gymnasium at Nüremberg (1808–1816). He was appointed professor first at the University of Heidelberg (1816–1818) and then at the University of Berlin in 1818, where he lectured until he died.

Hegel's most famous contribution to philosophy is also his first major work: Phenomenology of Spirit *(1807), which has greatly influenced contemporary debates about class, race, and gender, and has also influenced social thinkers like Marx and Engels, Sartre, and Fanon. As the story goes,* Phenomenology *was written on the eve of the abolition of the Holy Roman Empire and just prior to the German Wars of Liberation. As such,* Phenomenology *is not only a child of the cultural and political revolutions that were under way in Europe at that time but also comprises a revolution in thinking about human relationships.* Phenomenology *traces the stages of* Geist, *or Spirit, and its development through a series of historical dialectics; it is the story of Spirit coming to know itself, of Spirit achieving self-consciousness, that, for Hegel, is the essence of all historical change and upheaval. Self-knowledge consists in nothing other than the Spirit's consciousness of its freedom, which, ironically, does not entail positing the individual in opposition to the collective or the state. On the other hand, this consciousness of freedom is brought about by the fruition of the rational individual for whom opposition to the state does not make any sense. Indeed, the final stage of Spirit coming to know itself is marked by the harmony of the individual and the collective, the " 'I' that is 'We' and 'We' that is 'I' " (*Phenomenology, *110). It is this stage, of the lack of the I-We distinction, that comprises the ideal toward which Spirit has been striving through history.*

Hegel also wrote Lectures on the Philosophy of History *(1830),* Elements of the Philosophy of Right *(1821), and* Science of Logic *(1812–1816). A summary of his philosophical framework is sketched out in his* Encyclopedia of the Philosophical Sciences in Outline *(1817).*

Phenomenology of Spirit

GEORG WILHELM FRIEDRICH HEGEL

SECTION B. SELF-CONSCIOUSNESS

Part I. Independence and Dependence of Self-Consciousness:
Lordship and Bondage

186. Self-consciousness is, to begin with, simple being-for-self, self-equal through the exclusion from itself of everything else. For it, its essence and absolute object is "I"; and in this immediacy, or in this [mere] being, of its being-for-itself, it is an *individual*. What is "other" for it is an unessential, negatively characterized object. But the "other" is also a self-consciousness; one individual is confronted by another individual. Appearing thus immediately on the scene, they are for one another like ordinary objects, *independent* shapes, individuals submerged in the being [or immediacy] of *Life*—for the object in its immediacy is here determined as Life. They are, *for each other*, shapes of consciousness which have not yet accomplished the movement of absolute abstraction, of rooting-out all immediate being, and of being merely the purely negative being of self-being, and of being merely the purely negative being of self-identical consciousness; in other words, they have not as yet exposed themselves to each other in the form of pure being-for-self, or as self-consciousnesses. Each is indeed certain of its won self, but not of the other, and therefore its own self-certainty still has no truth. For it would have truth only if its own being-for-self had confronted it as an indepen-dent object, or, what is the same thing, if the object had presented itself as this pure self-certainty. But according to the Notion of recognition this is possible only when each is for the other what the other is for it, only when each in its own self through its own action, and again through the action of the other, achieves this pure abstraction of being-for-self.

187. The presentation of itself, however, as the pure abstraction of self-consciousness consists in showing itself as the pure negation of its objective mode, or in showing that it is not attached to any specific *existence*, not to the individuality common to existence as such, that it is not attached to life. This presentation is a twofold action: action on the part of the other, and action on its own part. In so far as it is the action of the *other*, each seeks the death of the other. But in doing so, the second kind of action, action on its own part, is also involved; (for the former involves the staking of its own life). Thus the relation of the two self-conscious individuals is such that they prove themselves and each other through a life-and-death struggle. They must engage in this struggle, for

they must raise their certainty of being *for themselves* to truth, both in the case of the other and in their own case. And it is only through staking one's life that freedom is won; only thus is it proved that for self-consciousness, its essential being is not [just] being, not the *immediate* form in which it appears, not its submergence in the expanse of life, but rather that there is nothing present in it which could not be regarded as a vanishing moment, that it is only pure *being-for-self*. The individual who has not risked his life may well be recognized as a *person*, but he has not attained to the truth of this recognition as an independent self-consciousness. Similarly, just as each stakes his own life, so each must seek the other's death, for it values the other no more than itself; its essential being is present to it in the form of an "other," it is outside of itself and must rid itself of its self-externality. The other is an *immediate* consciousness entangled in a variety of relationships, and it must regard its otherness as a pure being-for-self or as an absolute negation.

188. This trial by death, however, does away with the truth which was supposed to issue from it, and so, too, with the certainty of self generally. For just as life is the *natural* setting of consciousness, independence without absolute negativity, so death is the *natural* negation of consciousness, negation without independence, which thus remains without the required significance of recognition. Death certainly shows that each staked his life and held it of no account, both in himself and in the other; but that is not for those who survived this struggle. They put an end to their consciousness in its alien setting of natural existence, that is to say, they put an end to themselves, and are done away with as *extremes* wanting to be *for themselves*, or to have an existence of their own. But with this there vanishes from their interplay the essential moment of splitting into extremes with opposite characteristics; and the middle term collapses into a lifeless unity which is split into lifeless, merely immediate, unopposed extremes; and the two do not reciprocally give and receive one another back from each other consciously, but leave each other free only indifferently, like things. Their act is an abstract negation, not the negation coming from consciousness, which supersedes in such a way as to preserve and maintain what is superseded, and consequently survives its own supersession.

189. In this experience, self-consciousness learns that life is as essential to it as pure self-consciousness. In immediate self-consciousness the simple "I" is absolute mediation, and has as its essential moment lasting independence. The dissolution of that simple unity is the result of the first experience; through this there is posited a pure self-consciousness, and a consciousness which is not purely for itself but for another, i.e. is a merely *immediate* consciousness, or consciousness in the form of *thinghood*. Both moments are essential. Since to begin with they are unequal and opposed, and their reflection into a unity has

not yet been achieved, they exist as two opposed shapes of consciousness; one is the independent consciousness whose essential nature is to be for itself, the other is the dependent consciousness whose essential nature is simply to live or to be for another. The former is lord, the other is bondsman.

190. The lord is the consciousness that exists for *itself*, but no longer merely the Notion of such a consciousness. Rather, it is a consciousness existing *for itself*, which is mediated with itself through another consciousness, i.e. through a consciousness whose nature it is to be bound up with an existence that is independent, or thinghood in general. The lord puts himself into relation with both of these moments, to a *thing* as such, the object of desire, and to the consciousness for which thinghood is the essential characteristic. And since he is (a) *qua* the Notion of self-consciousness an immediate relation of *being-for-self*, but (b) is now at the same time mediation, or a being-for-self which is for itself only through another, he is related (a) immediately to both, and (b) mediately to each through the other. The lord relates himself mediately to the bondsman through a being [a thing] that is independent, for it is just this which holds the bondsman in bondage; it is his chain from which he could not break free in the struggle, thus proving himself to be dependent, to possess his independence in thinghood. But the lord is the poser over this thing, for he proved in the struggle that it is something merely negative; since he is the power over this thing and this again is the power over the other [the bondsman], it follows that he holds the other in subjection. Equally, the lord relates himself mediately to the thing through the bondsman; the bondsman, *qua* self-consciousness in general, also relates himself negatively to the thing, and takes away its independence; but at the same time the thing is independent *vis-a-vis* the bondsman, whose negating of it, therefore, cannot go the length of being altogether done with it to the point of annihilation; in other words, he only *works* on it. For the lord, on the other hand, the *immediate* relation becomes through this mediation the sheer negation of the thing, or the enjoyment of it. What desire failed to achieve, he succeeds in doing, viz. to have done with the thing altogether, and to achieve satisfaction in the enjoyment of it. Desire failed to do this because of the thing's independence; but the lord, who has interposed the bondsman between it and himself, takes to himself only the dependent aspect of the thing and has the pure enjoyment of it. The aspect of its independence he leaves to the bondsman, who works on it.

191. In both of these moments the lord achieves his recognition through another consciousness; for in them, that other consciousness is expressly something unessential, both by its working on the thing, and by its dependence on a specific existence. In neither case can it be lord over the being of the thing and achieve absolute negation of it. Here, therefore, is present this moment of

recognition, viz. that the other consciousness sets aside its own being-for-self, and in so doing itself does what the first does to it. Similarly, the other moment too is present, that this action of the second is the first's own action; for what the bondsman does is really the action of the lord. The latter's essential nature is to exist only for himself; he is the sheer negative power for whom the thing is nothing. Thus he is the pure, essential action in this relationship, while the action of the bondsman is impure and unessential. But for recognition proper the moment is lacking, that what the lord does to the other he also does to himself, and what the bondsman does to himself he should also do to the other. The outcome is a recognition that is one-sided and unequal.

192. In this recognition the unessential consciousness is for the lord the object, which constitutes the truth of his certainty of himself. But it is clear that this object does not correspond to its Notion, but rather that the object in which the lord has achieved his lordship has in reality turned out to be something quite different from an independent consciousness. What now really confronts him is not an independent consciousness, but a dependent one. He is, therefore, not certain of *being-for-self* as the truth of himself. On the contrary, his truth is in reality the unessential consciousness and its unessential action.

193. The *truth* of the independent consciousness is accordingly the servile consciousness of the bondsman. This, it is true, appears at first *outside* of itself and not as the truth of self-consciousness. But just as lordship showed that its essential nature is the reverse of what it wants to be, so too servitude in its consummation will really turn into the opposite of what it immediately is; as a consciousness forced back into itself, it will withdraw into itself and be transformed into a truly independent consciousness.

194. We have seen what servitude is only in relation to lordship. But it is a self-consciousness, and we have not to consider what as such it is in and for itself. To begin with, servitude has the lord for its essential reality; hence the *truth* for it is the independent consciousness that is *for itself*. However, servitude is not yet aware that this truth is implicit in it. But it does in fact contain within itself this truth of pure negativity and being-for-self, for it has experienced this its own essential nature. For this consciousness has been fearful, not of this or that particular thing or just at odd moments, but its whole being has been seized with dread; for it has experienced the fear of death, the absolute Lord. In that experience it has been quite unmanned, has trembled in every fibre of its being, and everything solid and stable has been shaken to its foundations. But this pure universal movement, the absolute melting-away of everything stable, is the simple, essential nature of self-consciousness, absolute negativity, *pure being-for-self*, which consequently is *implicit* in this consciousness. This moment of pure being-for-self is also *explicit* for the bondsman, for in the lord it exists for

him as his *object*. Furthermore, his consciousness is not this dissolution of everything stable merely in principle; in his service he *actually* brings this about. Through his service he rids himself of his attachment to natural existence in every single detail; and gets rid of it by working on it.

195. However, the feeling of absolute power both in general, and in the particular form of service, is only implicitly this dissolution, and although the fear of the lord is indeed the beginning of wisdom, consciousness is not therein aware that it is a being-for-self. Through work, however, the bondsman becomes conscious of what he truly is. In the moment which corresponds to desire in the lord's consciousness, it did seem that the aspect of unessential relation to the thing fell to the lot of the bondsman, since in that relation the thing retained its independence. Desire has reserved to itself the pure negating of the object and thereby its unalloyed feeling of self. But that is the reason why this satisfaction is itself only a fleeting one, for it lacks the side of objectivity and permanence. Work, on the other hand, is desire held in check, fleetingness staved off; in other words, work forms and shapes the thing. The negative relation to the object becomes its *form* and something *permanent*, because it is precisely for the worker that the object has independence. This *negative* middle term or the formative *activity* is at the same time the individuality or pure being-for-self of consciousness which now, in the work outside of it, acquires an element of permanence. It is in this way, therefore, that consciousness, *qua* worker, comes to see in the independent being [of the object] its *own* independence.

196. But the formative activity has not only this positive significance that in it the pure being-for-self of the servile consciousness acquires an existence; it also has, in contrast with its first moment, the negative significance of *fear*. For, in fashioning the thing, the bondsman's own negativity, his being-for-self, becomes an object for him only through his setting at nought the existing *shape* confronting him. But this objective *negative* moment is none other than the alien being before which it has trembled. Now, however, he destroys this alien negative moment, posits *himself* as a negative in the permanent order of things, and thereby becomes *for himself*, someone existing on his own account. In the lord, the being-for-self is an "other" for the bondsman, or is only *for* him [i.e. is not his own]; in fear, the being-for-self is present in the bondsman himself; in fashioning the thing, he becomes aware that being-for-self belongs to *him*, that he himself exists essentially and actually in his own right. The shape does not become something other than himself through being made external to him; for it is precisely this shape that is his pure being-for-self, which in this externality is seen by him to be the truth. Through this rediscovery of himself by himself, the bondsman realizes that it is precisely in his work wherein he seemed to have only an alienated existence that he acquires a mind of his own. For this reflec-

tion, the two moments of fear and service as such, as also that of formative activity, are necessary, both being at the same time in a universal mode. Without the discipline of service and obedience, fear remains at the formal stage, and does not extend to the known real world of existence. Without the formative activity, fear remains inward and mute, and consciousness does not become explicitly *for itself*. If consciousness fashions the thing without that initial absolute fear, it is only an empty self-centered attitude; for its form or negativity is not negativity *per se*, and therefore its formative activity cannot give it a consciousness of itself as essential being. If it has not experienced absolute fear but only some lesser dread, the negative being has remained for it something external, its substance has not been infected by it through and through. Since the entire contents of its natural consciousness have not been jeopardized, determinate being still *in principle* attaches to it; having a "mind of one's own" is self-will, a freedom which is still enmeshed in servitude. Just as little as the pure form can become essential being for it, just as little is that form, regarded as extended to the particular, a universal formative activity, an absolute Notion; rather it is a skill which is master over some things, but not over the universal power and the whole of objective being.

. . . . .

SECTION C. SPIRIT

Part III. Absolute Freedom and Terror

582. Consciousness has found its Notion in Utility. But it is partly still an *object*, and partly, for that very reason, still an *End* to be attained, which consciousness does not find itself to possess immediately. Utility is still a predicate of the object, not itself a subject or the immediate and sole *actuality* of the object. It is the same thing that appeared before, when being-for-self had not yet shown itself to be the substance of the other moments, a demonstration which would have meant that the Useful was directly nothing else but the self of consciousness and that this latter was thereby in possession of it. This withdrawal from the form of objectivity of the Useful has, however, already taken place in principle and from this inner revolution there emerges the actual revolution of the actual world, the new shape of consciousness, *absolute freedom*.

583. In fact, what we have here is no more than an empty show of objectivity separating self-consciousness from possession. For, partly, all existence and validity of the specific members of the organization of the actual world and the world of faith have, in general, returned into this simple determination as into their ground and spiritual principle; partly, however, this simple determination

no longer possesses anything of its own, it is rather pure metaphysics, Pure Notion, or a pure knowing by self-consciousness. That is to say, of the *being-in-and-for-itself* of the Useful *qua* object, consciousness recognizes that its *being-in-itself* is essentially a *being-for-an-other*; being-in-itself, as *devoid of self*, is in truth a passive self, or that which is a self for another self. The object, however, exists for consciousness in this abstract form of pure being-in-itself, for consciousness is pure *insight* whose distinctions are in the pure form of Notions. But the *being-for-self* into which being-for-an-other returns, i.e. the self, is not a self belonging exclusively to what is called object and distinct from the "I"; for consciousness, *qua* pure insight, is not a *single* self which could be confronted by the object as equally having a self of its own, but is pure Notion, the gazing of the self into the self, the absolute seeing of *itself* doubled; the certainty of itself is the universal Subject, and its conscious Notion is the essence of all actuality. If, then, the Useful was merely the alternation of the moments, an alternation which did not return into its own unity, and hence was still an object for knowing, it now ceases to be this. For knowing is itself the movement of those abstract moments, it is the universal self, the self of itself as well as of the object and, as universal, is the self-returning unity of this movement.

584. Spirit thus comes before us as *absolute freedom*. It is self-consciousness which grasps the fact that its certainty of itself is the essence of all the spiritual "masses," or spheres, of the real as well as of the supersensible world, or conversely, that essence and actuality are consciousness's knowledge of *itself*. It is conscious of its pure personality and therein of all spiritual reality, and all reality is solely spiritual; the world is for it simply its own will, and this is a general will. And what is more, this will is not the empty thought of will which consists in silent assent, or assent by a representative, but a real general will, the will of all *individuals* as such. For will is in itself the consciousness of personality, or of each, and it is as this genuine actual will that it ought to be, as the self-conscious essence of each and every personality, so that each, undivided from the whole, always does everything, and what appears as done by the whole is the direct and conscious deed of each.

. . . . .

589. Just as the individual self-consciousness does not find itself in this *universal work* of absolute freedom *qua* existent Substance, so little does it find itself in the *deeds* proper and *individual* actions of the will of this freedom. Before the universal can perform a deed it must concentrate itself into the One of individuality and put at the head an individual self-consciousness; for the universal will is only an *actual* will in a self, which is a One. But thereby all other individuals are excluded from the entirety of this deed and have only a limited

share in it, so that the deed would not be a deed of the *actual universal* self-consciousness. Universal freedom, therefore, can produce neither a positive work nor a deed; there is left for it only *negative* action; it is merely the *fury* of destruction.

590. But the supreme reality and the reality which stands in the greatest antithesis to universal freedom, or rather the sole object that will still exist for that freedom, is the freedom and individuality of actual self-consciousness itself. For that universality which does not let itself advance to the reality of an organic articulation, and whose aim is to maintain itself in an unbroken continuity, at the same time creates a distinction within itself, because it is movement or consciousness in general. And, moreover, by virtue of its own abstraction, it divides itself into extremes equally abstract, into a simple, inflexible cold universality, and into the discrete, absolute hard rigidity and self-willed atomism of actual self-consciousness. Now that it has completed the destruction of the actual organization of the world, and exists now just for itself, this is its sole object, an object that no longer has any content, possession, existence, or outer extension, but is merely this knowledge of itself as an absolutely pure and free individual self. All that remains of the object by which it can be laid hold of is solely its *abstract* existence as such. The relation, then, of these two, since each exists indivisibly and absolutely for itself, and thus cannot dispose of a middle term which would link them together, is one of wholly *unmediated* pure negation, a negation, moreover, of the individual as a being *existing* in the universal. The sole work and deed of universal freedom is therefore *death*, a death too which has no inner significance or filling, for what is negated is the empty point of the absolutely free self. It is thus the coldest and meanest of all deaths, with no more significance than cutting off a head of cabbage or swallowing a mouthful of water.

591. In this flat, commonplace monosyllable is contained the wisdom of the government, the abstract intelligence of the universal will, in the fulfilling of itself. The government is itself nothing else but the self-established focus, or the individuality, of the universal will. The government, which wills and executes a specific order and action. On the one hand, it excludes all other individuals from its act, and on the other hand, it thereby stands opposed to the universal will; consequently, it is absolutely impossible for it to exhibit itself as anything else but a *faction*. What is called government is merely the *victorious* faction, and in the very fact of its being a faction lies the direct necessity of its overthrow; and its being government makes it, conversely, into a faction, and [so] guilty. When the universal will maintains that what the government has actually done is a crime committed against it, the government, for its part, has nothing specific and outwardly apparent by which the guilt of the will opposed to it could be

demonstrated; for what stands opposed to it as the *actual* universal will is only an unreal pure will, *intention*. *Being suspected*, therefore, takes the place, or has the significance and effect, of *being guilty*; and the external reaction against this reality that lies in the simple inwardness of intention consists in the cold, matter-of-fact annihilation of this existent self, from which nothing else can be taken away but its mere being.

592. In this its characteristic *work*, absolute freedom becomes explicitly objective to itself, and self-consciousness learns what absolute freedom in effect is. *In itself*, it is just this *abstract self-consciousness*, which effaces all distinction and all continuance of distinction within it. It is as such that it is objective to itself; the *terror* of death is the vision of this negative nature of itself. But absolutely free self-consciousness finds this its reality quite different from what its own Notion of itself was, viz. that the universal will is merely the *positive* essence of personality, and that this latter knows itself in it only positively, or as preserved therein. Here, however, this self-consciousness which, as pure insight, completely separates its positive and its negative nature—completely separates the predicateless Absolute as pure *Thought* and as pure *Matter*—is confronted with the absolute *transition* of the one into the other as a present reality. The universal will, *qua* absolutely *positive*, actual self-consciousness, because it is this self-conscious reality heightened to the level of *pure* thought or of *abstract* matter, changes round into its negative nature and shows itself to be equally that which *puts an end to the thinking of oneself*, or to self-consciousness.

593. Absolute freedom as *pure* self-identity of the universal will thus has within it *negation*; but this means that it contains *difference* in general, and this again it develops as an *actual* difference. For pure *negativity* has in the self-identical universal will the element of subsistence, or the *Substance* in which its moments are realized; it has the matter which it can utilize in accordance with its own determinateness; and in so far as this Substance has shown itself to be the negative element for the individual consciousness, the organization of spiritual "masses" or spheres to which the plurality of individual consciousnesses are assigned thus takes shape once more. These individuals who have felt the fear of death, of their absolute master, again submit to negation and distinctions, arrange themselves in the various spheres, and return to an apportioned and limited task, but thereby to their substantial reality.

594. Out of this tumult, Spirit would be thrown back to its starting-point, to the ethical and real world of culture, which would have been merely refreshed and rejuvenated by the fear of the lord and master which has again entered men's hearts. Spirit would have to traverse anew and continually repeat this cycle of necessity if the result were only the complete interpenetration of self-consciousness and Substance—an interpenetration in which self-consciousness,

which has experienced the negative power of its universal essence acting on it, would desire to know and find itself, not as this particular individual, but only as a universal, and therefore, too, would be able to endure the objective reality of universal Spirit, a reality excluding self-consciousness *qua* particular. But in absolute freedom there was no reciprocal action between a consciousness that is immersed in the complexities of existence, or that sets itself specific aims and thoughts, and a valid *external* world, whether of reality or thought; instead, the world was absolutely in the form of consciousness as a universal will, and equally self-consciousness was drawn together out of the whole expanse of existence or manifested aims and judgements, and concentrated into the simple self. The culture to which it attains in interaction with that essence is, therefore, the grandest and the last, is that of seeing its pure, simple reality immediately vanish and pass away into empty nothingness. In the world of culture itself it does not get as far as to behold its negation or alienation in this form of pure abstraction; on the contrary, its negation is filled with a content, either honour or wealth, which it gains in place of the self that it has alienated from itself; or the language of Spirit and insight which the disrupted consciousness acquires; or it is the heaven of faith, or the Utility of the Enlightenment. All these determinations have vanished in the loss suffered by the self in absolute freedom; its negation is the death that is without meaning, the sheer terror of the negative that contains nothing positive, nothing that fills it with a content. At the same time, however, this negation in its real existence is not something alien; it is neither the universal inaccessible *necessity* in which the ethical world perishes, nor the particular accident of private possession, nor the whim of the owner on which the disrupted consciousness sees itself dependent; on the contrary, it is the *universal will* which in this its ultimate abstraction has nothing positive and therefore can give nothing in return for the sacrifice. But for that very reason it is immediately one with self-consciousness, or it is the pure positive, because it is the pure negative; and the meaningless death, the unfilled negativity of the self, changes round in its inner Notion into absolutivity. For consciousness, the immediate unity of itself with the universal will, its demand to know itself as this specific point in the universal will, is changed round into the absolutely opposite experience. What vanishes for it in that experience is abstract *being* or the immediacy of that insubstantial point, and this vanished immediacy is the universal will itself which it now knows itself to be in so far as it is a pure knowing or pure will. Consequently, it knows that will to be itself, and knows itself to be essential being; but not essential being as an *immediate existence*, not will as revolutionary government or anarchy striving to establish anarchy, nor itself as the centre of this faction or the opposite faction; on the contrary, the *universal will* is its *pure knowing and willing* and *it* is the universal will *qua* this pure knowing and willing. It does not lose *itself* in that will, for pure knowing and willing is much more it than is that atomic point of consciousness. It is thus the interaction of pure knowing with itself; pure *knowing qua essential being* is the universal will; but this essential being is absolutely nothing else but pure knowing. Self-consciousness is, therefore, the pure knowing of essential being *qua* pure knowing. Further, as an *individual self*, it is only the form of the subject or of real action, a form which is known by it as *form*. Similarly, *objective* reality, *being*, is for it simply a selfless form; for that reality would be something that is not known. This knowing, however, knows knowing to be essential being.

595. Absolute freedom has thus removed the antithesis between the universal and the individual will. The self-alienated Spirit, driven to the extreme of its antithesis in which pure willing and the agent of that pure willing are still distinct, reduces the antithesis to a transparent form and therein finds itself. Just as the realm or the real world passes over into the realm of faith and insight, so does absolute freedom leave its self-destroying reality and pass over into another land of self-conscious Spirit where, in this unreal world, freedom has the value of truth. In the thought of this truth Spirit refreshes itself, in so far as *it is* and remains *thought*, and knows this being which is enclosed within self-consciousness to be essential being in its perfection and completeness. There has arisen the new shape of Spirit, that of the *moral* Spirit.

FRIEDRICH ENGELS (1820–1895)

The German social philosopher, businessman, and closest associate to Marx, Friedrich Engels became involved with the interests of the working classes while working at his father's textile mill in Manchester. He met Marx in 1844 while passing through Paris, and later introduced Marx to working-class movements and to political economy. His subsequent collaboration with Marx led to the production of the famous Communist Manifesto *in 1848. It was Engels's financial support that enabled Marx to work on the first volume of* Capital. *Engels retired at the age of forty-nine to dedicate himself solely to political writing and working-class organization. After Marx's death in 1883, Engels oversaw the posthumous publication of volumes 2 and 3 of* Capital. *He also authored books of his own and engaged in extensive correspondence with German political and intellectual leaders. He died from cancer in 1895.*

Engels's Anti-Dühring *(1878), written as a tirade against Eugen Dühring, a leading contemporary socialist, was the first attempt at a general exposition of scientific socialism and was instrumental in disseminating the Marxist agenda within the German Social Democratic Party. In the text, Engels accuses Dühring of completely misunderstanding the historical dialectic when he claims that the political gives rise to the economic; rather, Engels, along with Marx, asserts, the economic infrastructure underlies the political superstructure. In the changes in the mode of production and in the rapidly industrialization of the world, Engels espies signs of a time when the institution of war will become obsolete. "Militarism bears within itself the seeds of its own destruction," reasons Engels. As the cost of developing more refined weaponry escalates, and as people resist military conscription, states will no longer find it economically or socially feasible to wage war.*

Engels's other works include The Condition of the Working Class in England in 1844 *(1845),* Socialism: Utopian and Scientific *(1880),* The Origin of the Family, Private Property, and the State *(1884), and his final work,* Ludwig Feuerbach and the End of Classical German Philosophy *(1888).*

Anti-Dühring

FRIEDRICH ENGELS

PART II. POLITICAL ECONOMY

Chapter 2. Theory of Force

In my system, the relation between general politics and the forms of economic law is determined in so definite a way and at the same time a way *so original* that it would not be superfluous, in order to facilitate study, to make special reference to this point. The formation of *political* relationships is *historically the fundamental thing*, and instances of *economic* dependence are only *effects* or special cases, and are consequently always *facts of a second order*. Some of the newer socialists systems take as their guiding principle the conspicuous semblance of a completely reverse relationship, in that they assume that political phenomena are subordinate to and, as it were, grow out of the economic conditions. It is true that these effects of the second order do exist as such, and are most clearly perceptible at the present time; but the *primary* must be sought in *direct political force* and not in any indirect economic power.

This conception is also expressed in another passage, in which Herr Dühring starts from the principle that the political conditions are the decisive cause of the economic situation and that the reverse relationship represents only a reaction of a second order . . . so long as the political grouping is not taken for its own sake, as the starting-point, but is treated merely as a *stomach-filling agency*. One must have a portion of reaction stowed away in one's mind, however radical a socialist and revolutionary one may seem to be.

That is Herr Dühring's theory. In this and in many other passages it is simply set up, decreed, so to speak. Nowhere in the three fat tomes is there even the slightest attempt to prove it or to disprove the opposite point of view. And even if the arguments for it were as plentiful as blackberries, Herr Dühring would give us none of them, for the whole affair has been already proved through the famous original sin, when Robinson Crusoe made Friday his slave. That was an act of force, hence a political act. And inasmuch as this enslavement was the starting-point and the basic fact underlying all past history and inoculated it with the original sin of injustice, so much so that in the later periods it was only softened down and "transformed into the more indirect forms of economic dependence"; and inasmuch as "property founded on force," which has asserted itself right up to the present day, is likewise based on this original act of enslavement, it is clear that all economic phenomena must be explained by political causes, that is, by force. And anyone who is not satisfied with that is a reactionary in disguise.

We must first point out that only one with as much self-esteem as Herr Dühring could regard this view as so very "original," which it is not in the least. The idea that political acts, grand performances of state, are decisive in history is as old as written history itself, and is the main reason why so little material has been preserved for us in regard to the really progressive evolution of the peoples which has taken place quietly, in the background, behind these noisy scenes on the stage. This idea dominated all the conceptions of historians in the past, and the first blow against it was delivered only by the French bourgeois historians of the Restoration period; the only "original" thing about it is that Herr Dühring once again knows nothing of all this.

Furthermore, even if we assume for a moment that Herr Dühring is right in saying that all past history can be traced back to the enslavement of man by man, we are still very far from having got to the bottom of the matter. For the question then arises: how did Crusoe come to enslave Friday? Just for the fun of it? By no means. On the contrary, we see that Friday is compelled to render *economic* service as a slave or as "a mere tool" and is maintained also only as a tool. Crusoe enslaved Friday only in order that Friday should work for Crusoe's benefit. And how can he derive any benefit for himself from Friday's labour? Only through Friday producing by his labour more of the necessaries of life than Crusoe has to give him to keep him fit to work. Crusoe, therefore, in violation of Herr Dühring's express orders, "takes the political grouping" arising out of Friday's enslavement "not for its own sake, as the starting-point, but merely *as a stomach-filling agency*"; and now let him see to it that he gets along with his lord and master, Dühring.

The childish example especially selected by Herr Dühring in order to prove that force is "historically the fundamental thing," therefore, proves that force is only the means, and that the aim, on the contrary, is economic advantage. And more fundamental than the aim is the means used to secure it, more fundamental in history is the economic side of the relationship than the political side. The example therefore proves precisely the opposite of what it was supposed to prove. And as in the case of Crusoe and Friday, so in all cases of domination and subjection up to the present day. Subjugation has always been—to use Herr Dühring's elegant expression—a "stomach-filling agency" (taking stomach-filling in a very wide sense), but never and nowhere a political grouping established "for its own sake." It takes a Herr Dühring to be able to imagine that state taxes are only "effects of a second order," or that the present-day political grouping of the ruling bourgeoisie and the ruled proletariat has come into existence "for its own sake," and not as a "stomach-filling agency" for the ruling bourgeois, that is to say, for the sake of making profits and accumulating capital.

However, let us get back again to our two men. Crusoe, "sword in hand" [D. C. 23], makes Friday his slave. But in order to manage this, Crusoe needs something else besides his sword. Not everyone can make use of a slave. In order to be able to make use of a slave, one must possess two kinds of things: first, the instruments and material for his slave's labour; and secondly, the means of bare subsistence for him. Therefore, before slavery becomes possible, a certain level of production must already have been reached and a certain inequality of distribution must already have appeared. And for slave-labour to become the dominant mode of production in the whole of society, an even far higher increase in production, rate, and accumulation of wealth was essential. In the ancient primitive communities with common ownership of the land, slavery either did not exist at all or played only a very subordinate role. It was the same in the originally peasant city of Rome; but when Rome became a "world city" and Italic landownership came more and more into the hands of a numerically small class of enormously rich proprietors, the peasant population was supplanted by a population of slaves. If at the time of the Persian wars the number of slaves in Corinth rose to 460,000 and in Aegina to 470,000 and there were ten slaves to every freeman, something else besides "force" was required, namely, a highly developed arts and handicraft industry and an extensive commerce. Slavery in the United States of America was based far less on force than on the English cotton industry; in those districts where no cotton was grown or which, unlike the border states, did not breed slaves for the cotton-growing states, it died out of itself without any force being used, simply because it did not pay.

Hence, by calling property as it exists today property founded on force, and by characterizing it as "that form of domination *at the root of which lies* not merely the exclusion of fellow-men from the use of the natural means of subsistence, but also, what is far more important, the subjugation of man to make him do servile work," Herr Dühring is making the whole relationship stand on its head. The subjugation of a man to make him do servile work, in all its forms, presupposes that the subjugator has at his disposal the instruments of labour with the help of which alone he is able to employ the person placed in bondage, and in the case of slavery, in addition, the means of subsistence which enable him to keep his slave alive. In all cases, therefore, it presupposes the possession of a certain amount of property, in excess of the average. How did this property come into existence? In any case it is clear that it may in fact have been robbed, and therefore may be based on *force*, but that this is by no means necessary. It may have been got by labour, it may have been stolen, or it may have been obtained by trade or by fraud. In fact, it must have been obtained by labour before there was any possibility of its being robbed.

Private property by no means makes its appearance in history as the result of robbery or force. On the contrary. It already existed, though limited to certain objects, in the ancient primitive communities of all civilized peoples. It developed into the form of commodities within these communities, at first through barter with foreigners. The more the products of the community assumed the commodity form, that is, the less they were produced for their producers' own use and the more for the purpose of exchange, and the more the original spontaneously evolved division of labour was superseded by exchange also within the community, the more did inequality develop in the property owned by the individual members of the community, the more deeply was the ancient common ownership of the land undermined, and the more rapidly did the commune develop towards its dissolution and transformation into a village of smallholding peasants. For thousands of years Oriental despotism and the changing rule of conquering nomad peoples were unable to injure these old communities; the gradual destruction of their primitive home industry by the competition of products of large-scale industry brought these communities nearer and nearer to dissolution. . . . Even the formation of a primitive aristocracy, as in the case of the Celts, the Germans and the Indian Punjab, took place on the basis of common ownership of land, and at first was not based in any way on force, but on voluntariness and custom. Wherever private property evolved it was the result of altered relations of production and exchange, in the interest of increased production and in furtherance of intercourse—hence as a result of economic causes. Force plays no part in this at all. Indeed, it is clear that the institution of private property must already be in existence for a robber to be able to *appropriate* another person's property, and that therefore force may be able to change the possession of, but cannot create, private property as such.

Nor can we use either force or property founded on force in explanation of the "subjugation of man to make him do servile work" in its most modern form—wage-labour. We have already mentioned the role played in the dissolution of the ancient communities, that is, in the direct or indirect general spread of private property, by the transformation of the products of labour into commodities, their production not for consumption by those who produced them, but for exchange. Now in *Capital*, Marx proved with absolute clarity—and Herr Dühring carefully avoids even the slightest reference to this—that at a certain stage of development, the production of commodities becomes transformed into capitalist production, and that at this stage "the laws of appropriation" or of private property, laws that are based on the production and circulation of commodities, become by their own inner and inexorable dialectic changed into their opposite. The exchange of equivalents, the original operation with which we started, has now become turned round in such a way that there is only an apparent exchange. This is owing to the fact, first, that the capital which is exchanged for labour-power is itself but a portion of the product of others' labour appropriated without an equivalent; and, secondly, that this capital must not only be replaced by its producer, but replaced together with an added surplus. . . . At first property seemed to us to be based on a man's own labour.

"Now, however," (at the end of Marx's analysis), "property turns out to be the right, on the part of the capitalist, to appropriate the unpaid labour of others, and to be the impossibility, on the part of the labourer, of appropriating his own product. The separation of property from labour has become the necessary consequence of a law that apparently originated in their identity."

In other words, even if we exclude all possibility of robbery, force, and fraud, even if we assume that all private property was originally based on the owner's own labour, and that throughout the whole subsequent process there was only exchange of equal values for equal values, the progressive development of production and exchange nevertheless brings us of necessity to the present capitalist mode of production, to the monopolisation of the means of production and the means of subsistence in the hands of the one numerically small class, to the degradation into propertyless proletarians of the other class, constituting the immense majority, to the periodic alternation of speculative production booms and commercial crises and to the whole of the present anarchy of production. The whole process can be explained by purely economic causes; at no point whatever are robbery, force, the state, or political interference of any kind necessary. "Property founded on force" proves here also to be nothing but the phrase of a braggart intended to cover up his lack of understanding of the real course of things.

This course of things, expressed historically, is the history of the development of the bourgeoisie. If "political conditions are the decisive cause of the economic situation," then the modern bourgeoisie cannot have developed in struggle with feudalism, but must be the latter's voluntarily begotten child. Everyone knows that what took place was the opposite. Originally an oppressed estate liable to pay dues to the ruling feudal nobility, recruited from all manner of serfs and villains, the burghers conquered one position after another in their continuous struggle with the nobility, and finally, in the most highly developed countries, took power in its stead; in France, by directly overthrowing the nobility, in England, by making it more and more bourgeois and incorporating it as their own ornamental head. And how did they accomplish this? Simply through a change in the "economic situation," which sooner or later, voluntarily or as the outcome of combat, was followed by a change in the political conditions. The struggle of the bourgeoisie against the feudal nobility is the struggle of town against country, industry against landed property, money economy against natural economy; and the decisive weapon of the bourgeoisie in this struggle was its means of *economic* power, constantly increasing through the development of industry, first handicraft, and then, at a later stage, progressing to manufacture, and through the expansion of commerce. During the whole of this struggle political force was on the side of the nobility, except for a period when the Crown played the bourgeoisie against the nobility, in order to keep one estate in check by means of the other; but from the moment when the bourgeoisie, still politically powerless, began to grow dangerous owing to its increasing economic power, the Crown resumed its alliance with the nobility, and by so doing called for the bourgeois revolution, first in England and then in France. The "political conditions" in France had remained unaltered, while the "economic situation" had outgrown them. Judged by his political status the nobleman was everything, the burgher nothing; but judged by his social position the burgher now formed the most important class in the state, while the nobleman had been shorn of all his social functions and was now only drawing payment, in the revenues that came to him, for these functions which had disappeared.

Nor was that all. Bourgeois production in its entirety was still hemmed in by the feudal political forms of the Middle Ages, which this production—not only manufacture, but even handicraft industry—had long outgrown; it had remained hemmed in by all the thousandfold guild privileges and local and provincial customs barriers which had become mere irritants and fetters on production. The bourgeois revolution put an end to this. Not, however, by adjusting the economic situation to suit the political conditions, in accordance with Herr Dühring's precept—this was precisely what the nobles and the Crown had been vainly trying to do for years—but by doing the opposite, by casting aside the old mouldering political rubbish and creating political conditions in which the new "economic situation" could exist and develop. And in this political and legal atmosphere which was suited to its needs it developed brilliantly, so brilliantly that the bourgeoisie has already come close to occupying the position held by the nobility in 1789: it is becoming more and more not only socially superfluous, but a social hindrance; it is more and more becoming separated from productive activity, and, like the nobility in the past, becoming more and more a class merely drawing revenues; and it has accomplished this revolution in its own position and the creation of a new class, the proletariat, without any hocus-pocus of force whatever, in a purely economic way.

Even more: it did not in any way will this result of its own actions and activities—on the contrary, this result established itself with irresistible force, against the will and contrary to the intentions of the bourgeoisie; its own productive forces have grown beyond its control, and, as if necessitated by a law of nature, are driving the whole of bourgeois society towards ruin, or revolution. And if the bourgeois now make their appeal to force in order to save the collapsing "economic situation" from the final crash, this only shows that they are labouring under the same delusion as Herr Dühring: the delusion that "political conditions are the decisive cause of the economic situation"; this only shows that they imagine, just as Herr Dühring does, that by making use of "the primary," "the direct political force," they can remodel those "facts of the second order," the economic situation and its inevitable development; and that therefore the economic consequences of the steam-engine and the modern machinery driven by it, of world trade and the banking and credit developments of the present day, can be blown out of existence by them with Krupp guns and Mauser rifles.

· · · · ·

But let us look a little more closely at this omnipotent "force" of Herr Dühring's. Crusoe enslaved Friday "sword in hand." Where did he get the sword? Even on the imaginary island of the Robinson Crusoe epic, swords have not, up to now, been known to grow on trees, and Herr Dühring provides no answer to this question. If Crusoe could procure a sword for himself, we are equally entitled to assume that one fine morning Friday might appear with a loaded revolver in his hand, and then the whole "force" relationship is inverted. Friday commands, and it is Crusoe who has to drudge. We must apologize to readers for returning with such insistence to the Robinson Crusoe and Friday story, which properly belongs to the nursery and not to the field of science—but how can we help it? We are obliged to apply Herr Dühring's axiomatic method conscientiously, and it is not our fault if in doing so we have to keep all the time within the field of pure childishness. So, then, the revolver triumphs over the sword; and this will probably make even the most childish axiomatician comprehend that force is no mere act of the will, but requires the existence of very real preliminary conditions before it can come into operation, namely, *instruments*, the more perfect of which gets the better of the less perfect; moreover, that these instruments have to be produced, which implies that the producer of more perfect instruments of force, *vulgo* arms, gets the better of the producer of the less perfect instruments, and that, in a word, the triumph of force is based on the production of arms, and this in turn on production in general—therefore, on "economic power," on the "economic situation," on the *material* means which force has at its disposal.

Force, nowadays, is the army and navy, and both, as we all know to our cost, are "devilishly expensive." Force, however, cannot make any money; at most it can take away money that has already been made—and this does not help much either—as we have seen, also to our cost, in the case of the French milliards. In the last analysis, therefore, money must be provided through the medium of economic production; and so once more force is conditioned by the economic situation, which furnishes the means for the equipment and maintenance of the instruments of force. But even that is not all. Nothing is more dependent on economic prerequisites than precisely army and navy. Armament, composition, organization, tactics, and strategy depend above all on the stage reached at the time in production and on communications. It is not the "free creations of the mind" of generals of genius that have had a revolutionising effect here, but the invention of better weapons and the change in the human material, the soldiers; at the very most the part played by generals of genius is limited to adapting methods of fighting to the new weapons and combatants.

At the beginning of the fourteenth century, gunpowder came from the Arabs to Western Europe, and as every school child knows, completely revolutionised the methods of warfare. The introduction of gunpowder and fire-arms, however, was not at all an act of force, but a step forward in industry, that is, an economic advance. Industry remains industry, whether it is applied to the production or the destruction of things. And the introduction of fire-arms had a revolutionising effect not only on the conduct of war itself, but also on the political relationships of domination and subjection. The procurement of powder and fire-arms required industry and money, and both of these were in the hands of the burghers of the towns. From the outset, therefore, fire-arms were the weapons of the towns, and of the rising town-supported monarchy against the feudal nobility. The stone walls of the noblemen's castles, hitherto unapproachable, fell before the cannon of the burghers, and the bullets of the burghers' arquebuses pierced the armour of the knights. With the defeat of the nobility's armour-clad cavalry, the nobility's supremacy was broken; with the development of the bourgeoisie, infantry and artillery became more and more the decisive types of arms; compelled by the development of artillery, the military profession had to add to its organization a new and entirely industrial subsection, engineering.

The improvement of fire-arms was a very slow process. The pieces of artillery remained clumsy and the musket, in spite of a number of inventions affecting details, was still a crude weapon. It took over three hundred years for a weapon to be constructed that was suitable for the equipment of the whole body of infantry. It was not until the early eighteenth century that the flint-lock musket with a bayonet finally displaced the pike in the equipment of the infantry. The foot soldiers of that period were the mercenaries of princes; they consisted of the most demoralised elements of society, rigorously drilled but quite unreliable and only held together by the rod; they were often hostile prisoners of war who had been pressed into service. The only type of fighting in which these soldiers could apply the new weapons was the tactics of the line, which reached its highest perfection under Frederick II. The whole infantry of an army was drawn up in triple ranks in the form of a very long, hollow square, and moved in battle order only as a whole; at the very most, either of the two wings might move forward or keep back a little. This cumbrous mass could move in formation only on absolutely level ground, and even then only very slowly (seventy-five paces a minute); a change of formation during a battle was impossible, and once the infantry was engaged, victory or defeat was decided rapidly and at one blow.

In the American War of Independence, these unwieldy lines were met by bands of rebels, who although not drilled were all the better able to shoot from their rifled guns; they were fighting for their vital interests, and therefore did not desert like the mercenaries; nor did they do the English the favour of encountering them also in line and on clear, even ground. They came on in open formation, a series of rapidly moving troops of sharpshooters, under cover of the woods. Here the lines were powerless and succumbed to its invisible and inaccessible opponents. Skirmishing was reinvented—a new method of warfare which was the result of a change in the human war material.

What the American Revolution had begun the French Revolution completed, also in the military sphere. It also could oppose to the well-trained mercenary armies of the Coalition only poorly trained but great masses of soldiers, the levy of the entire nation. But these masses had to protect Paris, that is, to hold a definite area, and for this purpose victory in open mass battle was essential. Mere skirmishes would not achieve enough; a form had to be found to make use of large masses and this form was discovered in the *column*. Column formation made it possible for even poorly trained troops to move with a fair degree of order, and moreover with a greater speed (a hundred paces and more in a minute); it made it possible to break through the rigid forms of the old line formation; to fight on any ground, and therefore even on ground which was extremely disadvantageous to the line formation; to group the troops in any way if in the least appropriate; and, in conjunction with attacks by scattered bands of sharpshooters, to contain the enemy's lines, keep them engaged, and wear them out until the moment came for masses held in reserve to break through them at the decisive point in the position. This new method of warfare, based on the combined action of skirmishers and columns and on the partitioning of the army into independent divisions or army corps, composed of all arms of the service—a method brought to full perfection by Napoleon in both its tactical and strategical aspects—had become necessary primarily because of the changed personnel: the soldiery of the French Revolution. Beside, two very important technical prerequisites had been complied with: first, the lighter carriages for field guns constructed by Gribeauval, which alone made possible the more rapid movement now required of them; and secondly, the slanting of the butt, which had hitherto been quite straight, continuing the line of the barrel. Introduced in France in 1777, it was copied from hunting weapons and made it possible to shoot at a particular individual without necessarily missing him. But for this improvement it would have been impossible to skirmish with the old weapons.

The revolutionary system of arming the whole people was soon restricted o compulsory conscription (with substitution for the rich, who paid for their release), and in this form it was adopted by most of the large states on the Continent. Only Prussia attempted, through its *Landwehr* system, to draw to a greater extent on the military strength of the nation. Prussia was also the first state to equip its whole infantry—after the rifled muzzle-loader, which had been improved between 1830 and 1860 and found fit for use in war, had played a brief role—with the most up-to-date weapon, the rifled breech-loader. Its successes in 1866 were due to these two innovations.

The Franco-German War was the first in which two armies faced each other both equipped with breech-loading rifles, and moreover both fundamentally in the same tactical formations as in the time of the old smoothbore flint-locks. The only difference was that the Prussians had introduced the company column formation in an attempt to find a form of fighting which was better adapted to the new type of arms. But when, at St. Privat on August 18, the Prussian Guard tried to apply the company column formation seriously, the five regiments which were chiefly engaged lost in less than two hours more than a third of their strength (176 officers and 5,114 men). From that time on the company column, too, was condemned as a battle formation, no less than the battalion column and the line; all idea of further exposing troops in any kind of close formation to enemy gun-fire was abandoned, and on the German side all subsequent fighting was conducted only in those compact bodies of skirmishers into which the columns had so far regularly dissolved of themselves under a deadly hail of bullets, although this had been opposed by the higher commands as contrary to order; and in the same way the only form of movement when under fire from enemy rifles became the double. Once again the soldier had been shrewder than the officer; it was *he* who instinctively found the only way of fighting which has proved of service up to now under the fire of breech-loading rifles, and in spite of opposition from his officers he carried it through successfully.

The Franco-German War marked a turning-point of entirely new implications. In the first place the weapons used have reached such a stage of perfection that further progress which would have any revolutionising influence is no longer possible. Once armies have guns which can hit a battalion at any range at which it can be distinguished, and rifles which are equally effective for hitting individual men, while loading them takes less time than aiming, then all further improvements are of minor importance for field warfare. The era of evolution is therefore, in essentials, closed in this direction. And secondly, this war has compelled all continental powers to introduce in a stricter form the Prussian *Landwehr* system, and with it a military burden which must bring them to ruin within a few years. The army has become the main purpose of the state, and an end to itself; the peoples are there only to provide soldiers and feed them. Militarism dominates and is swallowing Europe.

But this militarism also bears within itself the seed of its own destruction. Competition among the individual states forces them, on the one hand, to spend more money each year on the army and navy, artillery, etc., thus more and more hastening their financial collapse; and, on the other hand, to resort to universal compulsory military service more and more extensively, thus in the long run making the whole people familiar with the use of arms, and therefore enabling them at a given moment to make their will prevail against the warlords in command. And this moment will arrive as soon as the mass of the people— town and country workers and peasants—*will have* a will. At this point the armies of the princes become transformed into armies of the people; the machine refuses to work and militarism collapses by the dialectics of its own evolution. What the bourgeois democracy of 1848 could not accomplish, just because it was *bourgeois* and not proletarian, namely, to give the labouring masses a will whose content would be in accord with their class position— socialism will infallibly secure. And this will mean the bursting asunder *from within* of militarism and with it all standing armies.

That is the first moral of our history of modern infantry. The second moral, which brings us back again to Herr Dühring, is that the whole organisation and method of warfare of the armies, and along with these victory or defeat, prove to be dependent on material, that is, economic conditions: on the human material and the armaments, and therefore on the quality and quantity of the population and on technical development. Only a hunting people like the Americans could rediscover skirmishing tactics—and they were hunters as a result of purely economic causes, just as now, as a result of purely economic causes, these same Yankees of the old States have transformed themselves into farmers, industrialists, seamen, and merchants who no longer skirmish in the primeval forests, but instead all the more effectively in the field of speculation, where they have likewise made much progress in making use of large masses. Only a revolution such as the French, which brought about the economic emancipation of the bourgeois and, especially, of the peasant, could find the mass armies and at the same time the free forms of movement which shattered the old rigid lines—the military counterparts of the absolutism which they were defending. And we have seen in case after case how advances in technique, as soon as they became applicable militarily and in fact were so applied, immediately and almost forcibly produced changes and even revolutions in the methods of warfare, often indeed against the will of the army command. And nowadays any zealous N.C.O. could explain to Herr Dühring how greatly, besides, the conduct of a war depends on the productivity and means of communication of the army's own hinterland as well as of the theatre of war. In short, always and everywhere it is the economic conditions and the instruments of economic power which help "force" to victory, without which force ceases to be force. And anyone who tried to reform methods of warfare from the opposite standpoint, on the basis of Dühringian principles, would certainly earn nothing but a beating.

If we pass now from land to sea, we find that in the last twenty years alone an even more complete revolution has taken place there. The warship of the Crimean War was the wooden two-and-three-decker of 60 to 100 guns; this was still mainly propelled by sail, with only a low-powered auxiliary steam-engine. The guns on these warships were for the most part 32-pounders, weighing approximately 50 centners, with only a few 68-pounders weighing 95 centners. Towards the end of the war, iron-clad floating batteries made their appearance; they were clumsy and almost immobile monsters, but to the guns of that period they were invulnerable. Soon warships, too, were swathed in iron armour-plating; at first the plates were still thin, a thickness of four inches being regarded as extremely heavy armour. But soon the progress made with artillery outstripped the armour-plating; each successive increase in the strength of the armour used was countered by a new and heavier gun which easily pierced the plates. In this way we have already reached armour-plating ten, twelve, fourteen, and twenty-four inches thick (Italy proposes to have a ship built with plates three feet thick) on the one hand, and on the other, rifled guns of 25, 35, 80, and even 100 tons (at 20 centners) in weight, which can hurl projectiles weighing 300, 400, 1,700, and up to 2,000 pounds to distances which were never dreamed of before. The warship of the present day is a giant armoured screw-driven steamer of 8,000 to 9,000 tons displacement and 6,000 to 8,000 horse power, with the revolving turrets and four or at most six heavy guns, the bow being extended under water into a ram for running down enemy vessels. It is a single colossal machine in which steam not only drives the ship at a high speed, but also works the steering-gear, raises the anchor, swings the turrets, changes the elevation of the guns and loads them, pumps out water, hoists and lowers the boats—some of which are themselves also steam-driven—and so forth. And the rivalry between armour-plating and the fire power of guns is so far from being at an end that nowadays a ship is almost always not up to requirements, already out of date, before it is launched. The modern warship is not a product, but at the same time it is a specimen of modern large-scale industry, a floating factory—producing mainly, to be sure, a lavish waste of money. The country in which large-scale industry is most highly developed has almost a monopoly of the construction of these ships. All Turkish, almost all Russian, and most German armoured vessels have been built in England; armour-plates that are at all serviceable are hardly made outside of Sheffield; of the three steelworks in Europe which alone are able to make the heaviest guns, two (Woolwich and Elswick) are in England, and the third (Krupp) in Germany. In this sphere it is most palpably evident that the "direct political force" which, according to Herr Dühring, is the "decisive cause of the economic situation," is on the contrary completely subordinate to the economic situation, that not only the construction but also the operation of the marine instrument of force, the warship, has itself become a branch of modern large-scale industry. And that this is so distresses no one more than force itself, that is, the state, which has now to pay for one ship as much as a whole small fleet used to cost; which has to resign itself to seeing these expensive vessels become obsolete, and therefore worthless, even before they slide into the water; and which must certainly be just as disgusted as Herr Dühring that the man of the "economic situation," the engineer, is now of far greater importance on board than the man of "direct force," the captain. We, on the contrary, have absolutely no cause to be vexed when we see that, in this competitive struggle between armour-plating and guns, the warship is being developed to a pitch of perfection which is making it both outrageously costly and unusable in war, and that this struggle makes manifest also in the sphere of naval warfare those inherent dialectical laws of motion on the basis of which militarism, like every other historical phenomenon, is being brought to its doom in consequence of its own development.

Here, too, therefore we see absolutely clearly that it is not by any means true that "the primary must be sought in direct political force and not in any indirect economic power." On the contrary. For what in fact does "the primary" in force itself prove to be? Economic power, the disposal of the means of power of large-scale industry. Naval political force, which reposes on modern warships, proves to be not at all "direct" but on the contrary *mediated* by economic power, highly developed metallurgy, command of skilled technicians, and highly productive coal-mines.

And yet what is the use of it all? If we put Herr Dühring in supreme command in the next naval war, he will destroy all fleets of armoured ships, which are the slaves of the economic situation, without torpedoes or any other artifices, solely by virtue of his "direct force."

. . . . .

Chapter 4. Theory of Force
Conclusion

It is a circumstance of great importance that as a matter of fact the domination over *nature*, generally speaking(!), only proceeded through the domination over *man*. The cultivation of landed property in tracts of considerable size never took place anywhere without the antecedent subjection of man in some form of slave-labour or corvée, the establishment of an economic domination of man over man. How could a large landed proprietor even be conceived without at once including in this idea also his domination over slaves, serfs, or others indirectly unfree? What could the efforts of an individual, at most supplemented by those of his family, have signified or signify in extensively practiced agriculture? The exploitation of the land, or the extension of economic control over it on a scale exceeding the natural capacities of the individual, was only made possible in previous history by the establishment, either before or simultaneously with the introduction of dominion over land, of the enslavement of man which this involves. In the later periods of development this servitude was mitigated . . . its present form in the more highly civilised states is wage-labour, to a greater or lesser degree carried on under police rule. Thus wage-labour provides the practical possibility of that form of contemporary wealth which is represented by dominion over wide areas of land (extensive landed property). It goes without saying that all other types of distributive wealth must be explained historically in a similar way, and the indirect dependence of man on man, which is now the essential feature of the conditions which economically are most fully developed, cannot be understood and explained by its own nature, but only as a somewhat transformed heritage of an earlier direct subjugation and expropriation.

Thus Herr Dühring.

Thesis: The domination of nature (by man) presupposes the domination of man (by man).

Proof: The cultivation of landed *property in tracts of considerable size* never took place anywhere except by use of bondmen.

Proof of the proof: How can there be large landowners without bondmen, as the large landowner, even with his family, could work only a tiny part of his property without the help of bondmen?

Therefore, in order to prove that man first had to subjugate man before he could bring nature under his control, Herr Dühring transforms "nature" without more ado into "landed property in tracts of considerable size," and then this landed property—ownership unspecified—is immediately further transformed into the property of a large landed proprietor, who naturally cannot work his land without bondmen.

In the first place "domination over nature" and the "cultivation of landed property" are by no means the same thing. In industry domination over nature is exercised on quite another and much greater scale than in agriculture, which is still subject to weather conditions instead of controlling them.

Secondly, if we confine ourselves to the cultivation of landed property consisting of tracts of considerable size, the question arises: whose landed property is it? And then we find in the early history of all civilized peoples, not the "large landed proprietors" whom Herr Dühring interpolates here with his customary sleight of hand, which he calls "natural dialectics," but tribal and village communities with common ownership of the land. From India to Ireland the cultivation of landed property in tracts of considerable size was originally carried on by such tribal and village communities; sometimes the arable land was tilled jointly for account of the community, and sometimes in separate parcels of land temporarily allotted to families by the community, while woodland and pastureland continued to be used in common. It is once again characteristic of "the most exhaustive specialized studies" made by Herr Dühring "in the domain of politics and law" that he knows nothing of all this; that all his works breathe total ignorance of Maurer's epoch-making writings on the primitive constitution of the German mark, the basis of all German law, and of the ever-increasing mass of literature, chiefly stimulated by Maurer, which is devoted to proving the primitive common ownership of the land among all civilised peoples of Europe and Asia, and to showing the various forms of its existence and dissolution. Just as in the domain of French and English law Herr Dühring "himself acquired all his ignorance," as great as it was, so it is with his even much greater ignorance in the domain of German law. In this domain the man who flies into such a violent rage over the limited horizon of university professors is himself today, at the very most, still where the professors were twenty years ago.

It is a pure "free creation and imagination" on Herr Dühring's part when he asserts that landed proprietors and bondmen were required for the cultivation of landed property in tracts of considerable size. In the whole of the Orient, where the village community or the state owns the land, the very term landlord is not to be found in the various languages, a point on which Herr Dühring can consult the English jurists, whose efforts in India to solve the question—who is the owner of the land?—were as vain as those of the late Prince Heinrich LXXII of Reuss-Greiz-Schleiz-Lobenstein-Eberwalde in his attempt to solve the question of who was the night-watchman. It was the Turks who first introduced a sort of feudal ownership of land in the countries conquered by them in the Orient. Greece made its entry into history, as far back as the heroic epoch, with a system of social estates which itself was evidently the product of a long but unknown prehistory; even there, however, the land is mainly cultivated by independent peasants; the larger estates of the nobles and tribal chiefs were the exception; moreover they disappeared soon after. Italy was brought under cultivation chiefly by peasants; when, in the final period of the Roman Republic, the great complexes of estates, the latifundia, displaced the small peasants and replaced them with slaves, they also replaced tillage with stockraising, and as Pliny already realized, brought Italy to ruin (*latifundia Italiam perdidere*). During the Middle Ages, peasant farming was predominant throughout Europe (especially in bringing virgin soil into cultivation); and in relation to the question we are now considering it is of no importance whether these peasants had to pay dues, and if so what dues, to any feudal lords. The colonists from Friesland, Lower Saxony, Flanders, and the Lower Rhine, who brought under cultivation the land east of the Elbe which had been wrested from the Slavs, did this as free peasants under very favourable quit-rent tenures, and not at all under "some form of corvée." In North America, by far the largest portion of the land was opened for cultivation by the labour of free farmers, while the big landlords of the South, with their slaves and their rapacious tilling of the land, exhausted the soil until it could grow only firs, so that the cultivation of cotton was forced further and further west. In Australia and New Zealand, all attempts of the British government to establish artificially a landed aristocracy came to nothing. In short, if we exclude the tropical and subtropical colonies, where the climate makes agricultural labour impossible for Europeans, the big landlord who subjugates nature by means of his slaves or serfs and brings the land under cultivation proves to be a pure figment of the imagination. The very reverse is the case. Where he makes his appearance in antiquity, as in Italy, he does not bring wasteland into cultivation, but transforms arable land brought under cultivation by peasants into stock pastures, depopulating and ruining whole countries. Only in a more recent period, when the increasing density of population had raised the value of land, and particularly since the development of agricultural science had made even poorer land more cultivable—it is only from this period that large landowners began to participate on an extensive scale in bringing wasteland and grass-land under cultivation—and this mainly through the robbery of common land from the peasants, both in England and in Germany. But there was another side even to this. For every acre of common land which the large landowners brought into cultivation in England, they transformed at least three acres of arable land in Scotland into sheep-runs and eventually even into mere big-game hunting-grounds.

We are concerned here only with Herr Dühring's assertion that the bringing into cultivation of tracts of land of considerable size and therefore of practically the whole area now cultivated, "never and nowhere" took place except through the agency of big landlords and their bondsmen—an assertion which, as we have seen, "presupposes" a really unprecedented ignorance of history. It is not necessary, therefore, for us to examine here either to what extent, at different periods, areas which were already made entirely or mainly cultivable were cultivated by slaves (as in the hey-day of Greece) or serfs (as in the manors of the Middle Ages); or what was the social function of the large landowners at various periods.

And after Herr Dühring has shown us this masterpiece of the imagination—in which we do not know whether the conjuring trick of deduction or the falsification of history is more to be admired—he exclaims triumphantly:

> It goes without saying that all other types of distributive wealth *must be explained historically in similar manner*!

This, of course, saves him the trouble of wasting even a single word more on the origin, for example, of capital.

If, with his domination of man by man as a prior condition for the domination of nature by man, Herr Dühring only wanted to state in a general way that the whole of our present economic order, the level of development now attained by agriculture and industry, is the result of a social history which evolved in class antagonisms, in relationships of domination and subjection, he is saying something which long ago, ever since the *Communist Manifesto*, became a commonplace. But the question at issue is how we are to explain the origin of classes and relations based on domination, and if Herr Dühring's only answer is the one word "force," we are left exactly where we were at the start. The mere fact that the ruled and exploited have at all times been far more numerous than the rulers and the exploiters, and that therefore it is in the hands of the former that the real force has reposed, is enough to demonstrate the absurdity of the whole force theory. Relationships based on dominion and subjection therefore still have to be explained.

They arose in two ways.

As men originally made their exit from the animal world—in the narrower sense of the term—so they made their entry into history: still half animal, brutal, still helpless in face of the forces of nature, still ignorant of their own strength; and consequently as poor as the animals and hardly more productive than they. There prevailed a certain equality in the conditions of existence, and for the heads of families also a kind of equality of social position—at least an absence of social classes—which continued among the primitive agricultural communities of the civilised peoples of a late period. In each such community there were from the beginning certain common interests the safeguarding of which had to be handed over to individuals, true, under the control of the community as a whole: adjudication of disputes; repression of abuse of authority by individuals; control of water supplies, especially in hot countries; and finally when conditions were still absolutely primitive, religious functions. Such offices are found in aboriginal communities of every period—in the oldest German marks and even today in India. They are naturally endowed with a certain measure of authority and are the beginnings of state power. The productive forces gradually increase; the increasing density of the population creates at one point common interests, at another conflicting interests, between the separate communities, whose grouping into larger units brings about in turn a new division of labour, the setting of organs to safeguard common interests and combat conflicting interests. These organs which, if only because they represent the common interests of the whole group, hold a special position in relation to each individual community—in certain circumstances even one of opposition—soon make themselves still more independent, partly through heredity of functions, which comes about almost as a matter of course in a world where everything occurs spontaneously, and partly because they become increasingly indispensable owing to the growing number of conflicts with other groups. It is not necessary for us to examine here how this independence of social functions in relation to society increased with time until it developed into domination over society; how he who was originally the servant, where conditions were favourable, changed gradually into the lord; how this lord, depending on the conditions, emerged as an Oriental despot or satrap, the dynast of a Greek tribe, chieftain of a Celtic clan, and so on; to what extent he subsequently had recourse to force in the course of this transformation; and how finally the individual rulers united into a ruling class. Here we are only concerned with establishing the fact that the exercise of a social function was everywhere the basis of political supremacy; and further that political supremacy has existed for any length of time only when it discharged its social functions. However great the number of despotisms which rose and fell in Persia and India, each was fully aware that above all it was the entrepreneur responsible for the collective maintenance of irrigation throughout the river valleys, without which no agriculture was possible there. It was reserved for the enlightened English to lose sight of this in India; they let the irrigation canals sluices fall into decay, and are now at last discovering, through the regularly recurring famines, that they have neglected the one activity which might have made their rule in India at least as legitimate as that of their predecessors.

But alongside this process of formation of classes another was also taking place. The spontaneously evolved division of labour within the family cultivating the soil made possible, at a certain level of well-being, the incorporation of one or more strangers as additional labour forces. This was especially the case in countries where the old common ownership of the land had already disintegrated or at least the former joint cultivation had given place to the separate cultivation of parcels of land by the respective families. Production had developed so far that the labour-power of a man could now produce more than was necessary for its mere maintenance; the means of maintaining additional labour forces existed; likewise the means of employing them; labour-power acquired a *value*. But the community itself and the association to which it belonged yielded no available, superfluous labour forces. On the other hand, such forces were provided by war, and war was as old as the simultaneous existence alongside each other of several groups of communities. Up to that time one had not known what to do with prisoners of war, and had therefore simply killed them; at an even earlier period, eaten them. But at the stage of "economic situation" which had now been attained the prisoners acquired a value; one therefore let them live and made use of their labour. Thus force, instead of controlling the economic situation, was on the contrary pressed into the service of the economic situation. *Slavery* had been invented. It soon became the dominant form of production among all peoples who were developing beyond the old community, but in the end was also one of the chief causes of their decay. It was slavery that first made possible the division of labour between agriculture and industry on a larger scale, and thereby also Hellenism, the flowering of the ancient world. Without slavery, no Greek state, no Greek art and science; without slavery, no Roman Empire. But without the basis laid by Hellenism and the Roman Empire, also no modern Europe. We should never forget that our whole economic, political, and intellectual development presupposes a state of things in which slavery was as necessary as it was universally recognised. In this sense we are entitled to say: without the slavery of antiquity no modern socialism.

It is very easy to inveigh against slavery and similar things in general terms, and to give vent to high moral indignation at such infamies. Unfortunately all that this conveys is only what everyone knows, namely, that these institutions of antiquity are no longer in accord with our present conditions and our sentiments, which these conditions determine. But it does not tell us one word as to how these institutions arose, why they existed, and what role they played in history. And when we examine these questions, we are compelled to say—however contradictory and heretical it may sound—that the introduction of slavery under the conditions prevailing at that time was a great step forward. For it is in fact that man sprang from the beasts, and had consequently to use barbaric and almost bestial means to extricate himself from barbarism. Where the ancient communities have continued to exist, they have for thousands of years formed the basis of the cruellest form of state, Oriental despotism, from India to Russia. It was only where these communities dissolved that the peoples made progress of themselves, and their next economic advance consisted in the increase and development of production by means of slave labour. It is clear that so long as human labour was still so little productive that it provided but a small surplus over and above the necessary means of subsistence, any increase of the productive forces, extension of trade, development of the state of law, or foundation of art and science, was possible only by means of a greater division of labour. And the necessary basis for this was the great division of labour between the masses discharging simple manual labour and the few privileged persons directing labour, conducting trade and public affairs, and, at a later stage, occupying themselves with art and science. The simplest and most natural form of this division of labour was in fact slavery. In the historical conditions of the ancient world, and particularly of Greece, the advance to a society based on class antagonisms could be accomplished only in the form of slavery. This was an advance even for the slaves; the prisoners of war, from whom the mass of the slaves was recruited, now at least saved their lives, instead of being killed as they had been before, or even roasted, as at a still earlier period.

We may add at this point that all historical antagonisms between exploiting and exploited, ruling and oppressed classes to this very day find their explanation in this same relatively undeveloped productivity of human labour. So long as the really working population were so much occupied with their necessary labour that they had no time left for looking after the common affairs of society—the direction of labour, affairs of state, legal matters, art, science, etc.— so long was it necessary that there should constantly exist a special class, freed from actual labour, to manage these affairs; and this class never failed, for its own advantage, to impose a greater and greater burden of labour on the working masses. Only the immense increase of the productive forces attained by modern industry has made it possible to distribute labour among all members of society without exception, and thereby to limit the labour-time of each individual member to such an extent that all have enough free time left to take part in the general—both theoretical and practical—affairs of society. It is only now, therefore, that every ruling and exploiting class has become superfluous and indeed a hindrance to social development, and it is only now, too, that it will be inexorably abolished, however much it may be in possession of "direct force."

When, therefore, Herr Dühring turns up his nose at Hellenism because it was founded on slavery, he might with equal justice reproach the Greeks with having had no steam-engines or electric telegraphs. And when he asserts that our modern wage bondage can only be explained as a somewhat transformed and mitigated heritage of slavery, and not by its own nature (that is, by the economic laws of modern society), this either means only that both wage-labour and slavery are forms of bondage and class domination, which every child knows to be so, or is false. For with equal justice we might say that wage-labour could only be explained as a mitigated form of cannibalism, which, it is now established, was the universal primitive form of utilisation of defeated enemies.

The role played in history by force as contrasted with economic development is therefore clear. In the first place, all political power is originally based on an economic, social function, and increases in proportion as the members of society, through the dissolution of the primitive community, become transformed into private producers, and thus become more and more divorced from the administrators of the common functions of society. Secondly, after the political force has made itself independent in relation to society, and has transformed itself from its servant into its master, it can work in two different directions. Either it works in a sense and in the direction of the natural economic development, in which case no conflict arises between them, the economic development being accelerated. Or it works against economic development, in which case, as a rule, with but few exceptions, force succumbs to it. These exceptions are isolated cases of conquest, in which the more barbarian conquerors exterminated or drove out the population of a country and laid waste or allowed to go to ruin productive forces which they did not know how to use. This was what the Christians in Moorish Spain did with the major part of the irrigation works on which the highly developed agriculture and horticulture of the Moors depended. Every conquest by a more barbarian people disturbs of course the economic development and destroys numerous productive forces. But in the immense majority of cases where the conquest is permanent, the more barbarian conqueror has to adapt himself to the higher "economic situation" as it emerges from the conquest; he is assimilated by the vanquished and in most cases he has even to adapt their language. But where—apart from cases of conquest—the internal state power of a country becomes antagonistic to its economic development, as at a certain stage occurred with almost every political power in the past, the contest always ended with the downfall of the political power.

Inexorably and without exception the economic development has forced its way through—we have already mentioned the latest and most striking example of this: the great French Revolution. If, in accordance with Herr Dühring's theory, the economic structure of a given country were dependent simply on political force, it is absolutely impossible to understand why Frederick William IV after 1848 could not succeed, in spite of his "magnificent army," ingrafting the mediaeval guilds and other romantic oddities on to the railways, the steam-engines, and the large-scale industry which was just then developing in his country; or why the tsar of Russia, who is possessed of even much more forcible means, is not only unable to pay his debts, but cannot even maintain his "force" without continually borrowing from the "economic situation" of Western Europe.

To Herr Dühring force is the absolute evil; the first act of force is to him the original sin; his whole exposition is a jeremiad on the contamination of all subsequent history consummated by this original sin; a jeremiad on the shameful perversion of all natural and social laws by this diabolical power, force. That force, however, plays yet another role in history, a revolutionary role; that, in the words of Marx it is the midwife of every old society pregnant with a new one, that it is the instrument with the aid of which social movement forces its way through and shatters the dead, fossilised political forms—of this there is not a word in Herr Dühring. It is only with sighs and groans that he admits the possibility that force will perhaps be necessary for the overthrow of an economic system of exploitation—unfortunately, because all use of force demoralises the person who uses it. And this in spite of the immense moral and spiritual impetus which has been given by every victorious revolution! And this in Germany, where a violent collision—which may, after all, be forced on the people—would at least have the advantage of wiping out the servility which has penetrated the nation's mentality following the humiliation of the Thirty Years' War. And this parson's mode of thought—dull, insipid, and impotent—presumes to impose itself on the most revolutionary party that history has known!

A Prussian revolutionary social philosopher, historian, and economist, Karl Marx was born of Jewish parents but was baptized in the Evangelical Established Church at the age of six. Karl matriculated at the University of Bonn in 1835 but stayed in Bonn for only a year before leaving for the University of Berlin, where he studied law and philosophy—and where he was introduced to the work of Hegel. He became an adherent member of the Young Hegelians. In January 1842 Marx began to contribute articles to an emergent newspaper, the Rheinische Zeitung, *associated with a group of liberal merchants, bankers, and industrialists. By October Marx had become the editor of the paper, which made him responsible for writing about the pressing economic and social issues of the time. Increasingly annoyed by Hegelian idealism, Marx found himself at odds with his Hegelian friends. He succeeded in making the newspaper one of the leading journals in Prussia, yet the newspaper was suspended by the authorities for being too outspoken. When this happened, Marx began to co-edit, with Arnold Ruge, a new review called the* Deutsche-Französische Jahrbucher *(German-French Yearbooks), to be published from Paris. It was through this publication that Marx was introduced to Friedrich Engels, who became a lifelong collaborator and the posthumous publisher of Marx's major work.*

In Paris Marx also began to associate with the communist societies of French and German workers—an association which produced and intensified his enduring preoccupation with the conditions of the working class, which, in turn, resulted in his revolutionary and groundbreaking Das Kapital. *Marx's stay in Paris was cut short, however, when the Prussian government intervened and forced him to be expelled from France. Followed by Engels, Marx left for Brussels in 1845, renouncing his Prussian nationality the same year. In 1847–1848 Marx and Engels collaborated on the* Communist Manifesto, *written as a program for the Communist League, which was composed mainly of emigrant German handicraftsmen.*

During the revolutionary months of 1848, Marx returned to Paris, then went to the Rhineland, where he pressed for a coalition between the working classes and the democratic bourgeoisie. He also supported a war with Russia and the establishment of a democratic constitution. When the King of Prussia dissolved the Prussian Assembly, Marx advocated armed resistance. He was indicted on several charges, but the jury acquitted him unanimously, agreeing with the defense argument that the Crown had attempted an unlawful counterrevolution. He was, nonetheless, banished in 1849 as an alien. He spent the remainder of his years in London.

His London years saw him turn to noncooperation with the bourgeois party. Only through such noncooperation, in his view, could the revolution be rendered perma-

nent. *The years 1850–1864 were also marked by intellectual isolation and utter pen-ury. He was persecuted by debtors, though Engels began to assist him substantially after becoming a partner in the firm of Erman and Engels at Manchester. What little money Marx earned himself came from journalism; in 1851 he became the European correspondent for the* New York Tribune, *to which he contributed about five hundred articles on social movements and issues in regions ranging from India and China to Britain and Spain.*

Marx's prolific writings include The Poverty of Philosophy *(1847),* Communist Manifesto *(1848),* The Eighteenth Brumaire of Louis Bonaparte *(1852), the three volumes of* Capital *(1867, 1885, and 1894, respectively); and* A Contribution to the Critique of Political Economy *(1859).*

Capital: A Critique of Political Economy

KARL MARX

CHAPTER 28. BLOODY LEGISLATION AGAINST THE EXPROPRIATED SINCE THE END OF THE FIFTEENTH CENTURY: THE FORCING DOWN OF WAGES BY ACT OF PARLIAMENT

The proletariat created by the breaking-up of the bands of feudal retainers and by the forcible expropriation of the people from the soil, this free and rightless proletariat could not possibly be absorbed by the nascent manufacturers as fast as it was thrown upon the world. On the other hand, these men, suddenly dragged from their accustomed mode of life, could not immediately adapt themselves to the discipline of their new condition. They were turned in massive quantities into beggars, robbers and vagabonds, partly from inclination, in the most cases under the force of circumstances. Hence at the end of the fifteenth and during the whole of the sixteenth centuries, a bloody legislation against vagabondage was enforced throughout Western Europe. The fathers of the present working class were chastised for their enforced transformation into vagabonds and paupers. Legislation treated them as "voluntary" criminals, and assumed that it was entirely within their power to go on working under the old conditions which in fact no longer existed.

In England this legislation began under Henry VIII.

Henry VIII, 1530: Beggars who are old and incapable of working receive a beg-gar's licence. On the one hand, whipping and imprisonment for sturdy vaga-bonds. They are to be tied to the cart-tail and whipped until the blood streams from their bodies, then they are to swear on oath to go back to their birthplace or to where they have lived the last three years and to "put themselves to labour." What grim irony! By Henry VIII the previous statute is repeated, but strengthened with new clauses. For the second arrest for vagabondage the whipping is to be repeated and half the ear sliced off; but for the third relapse the offender is to be executed as a hardened criminal and enemy of the common weal.

Edward VI: A statute of the first year of his reign, 1547, ordains that if anyone refuses to work, he shall be condemned as a slave to the person who has denounced him as an idler. The master shall feed his slave on bread and water, weak broth, and such refuse meat as he thinks fit. He has the right to force him to do any work, no matter how disgusting, with whip and chains. If the slave is absent for a fortnight, he is condemned to slavery for life and is to be branded on forehead or back with the letter S; if he runs away three times, he is to be executed as a felon. The master can sell him, bequeath him, let him out on hire as a slave, just as he can any other personal chattel or cattle. If the slaves attempt anything against the masters, they are also to be executed. Justices of the peace, on information, are to hunt the rascals down. If it happens that a vagabond has been idling about for three days, he is to be taken to his birthplace, branded with a red hot iron with the letter V on the breast, and set to work, in chains, on the roads or at some other labour. If the vagabond gives a false birthplace, he is then to become the slave for life of that place, of its inhabitants, or its corporation, and to be branded with an S. All persons have the right to take away the children of the vagabonds and keep them as apprentices, the young men until they are 24, the girls until they are 20. If they run away, they are to become, until they reach these ages, the slaves of their masters, who can put them in irons, whip them, etc. if they like. Every master may put an iron ring around the neck, arms, or legs of his slave, by which to know him more easily and to be more certain of him. The last part of this statute provides that certain poor people may be employed by a place or by persons who are willing to give them food and drink and to find them work. Slaves of the parish of this kind were still to be found in England in the mid nineteenth century under the name of "roundsmen."

Elizabeth, 1572: Unlicensed beggars above 14 years of age are to be severely flogged and branded on the left ear unless someone will take them into service for two years; in the case of a repetition of the offence, if they are over 18, they are to be executed, unless someone will take them into service for two years; but for the third offence they are to be executed without mercy as felons. Similar statutes include Elizabeth, 1597.

James I: Anyone wandering about and begging is declared a rogue and a vagabond. Justices of the peace in Petty Sessions are authorized to have them publicly whipped and to imprison them for six months for the first offence, and two years for the second. While in prison they are to be whipped as much and as often as the justices of the peace think fit. . . . Incorrigible and dangerous rogues are to be branded with an R on the left shoulder and set to hard labour, and if they are caught begging again, to be executed without mercy. These statutes were legally binding until the beginning of the eighteenth century; they were only repealed by Anne.

There were similar laws in France, where by the middle of the seventeenth century a kingdom of vagabonds had been established in Paris. Even at the beginning of the reign of Louis XVI, the Ordinance of 13 July 1777 provided that every man in good health from 16 to 60 years of age, if without means of subsistence and not practising a trade, should be sent to the galleys. The Statute of Charles V for the Netherlands (October 1537), the first Edict of the States and Towns of Holland (10 March 1614), and the *Plakaat* of the United Provinces (26 June 1649) are further examples of the same kind.

Thus were the agricultural folk first forcibly expropriated from the soil, driven from their homes, turned into vagabonds, and then whipped, branded, and tortured by grotesquely terroristic laws into accepting the discipline necessary for the system of wage-labour.

It is not enough that the conditions of labour are concentrated at one pole of society in the shape of capital, while at the other pole are grouped masses of men who have nothing to sell but their labour-power. Nor is it enough that they are compelled to sell themselves voluntarily. The advance of capitalist production develops a working class which by education, tradition, and habit looks upon the requirements of that mode of production as self-evident natural laws. The organization of the capitalist process of production, once it is fully developed, breaks down all resistance. The constant generation of a relative surplus population keeps the law of the supply and demand of labour, and therefore wages, within narrow limits which correspond to capital's valorization requirements. The silent compulsion of economic relations set the seal of the domination of the capitalist over the worker. Direct extra-economic force is still of course used, but only in exceptional cases. In the ordinary run of things, the worker can be left to the "natural laws of production," i.e., it is possible to rely on his dependence on capital, which springs from the conditions of production themselves, and is guaranteed in perpetuity by them. It is otherwise during the historical genesis of capitalist production. The rising bourgeoisie needs the power of the state, and uses it to "regulate" wages, i.e., to force them into the limits suitable for making a profit, to lengthen the working day, and to keep the worker himself at his normal level of dependence. This is an essential aspect of so-called primitive accumulation.

The class of wage-labourers, which arose in the latter half of the fourteenth century, formed then and in the following century only a very small part of the population, well protected in its position by the independent peasant proprietors in the countryside and by the organization of guilds in the towns. Masters and artisans were not separated by any great social distance either on the land or in the towns. The subordination of labour to capital was only formal, i.e., the mode of production itself had as yet no specifically capitalist character. The variable element in capital preponderated greatly over the constant element. The demand for wage-labour therefore grew rapidly with every accumulation of capital, while the supply only followed slowly behind. A large part of the national product which was later transformed into a fund for the accumulation of capital still entered at that time into the consumption-fund of the workers.

Legislation on wage-labour, which aimed from the first at the exploitation of the worker and, as it progressed, remained equally hostile to him, begins in England with the Statute of Labourers issued by Edward III in 1349. The Ordinance of 1350 in France, issued in the name of King John, corresponds to it. The English and French laws run parallel and are identical in content. Where these labour-statutes aim at a compulsory extension of the working day, I shall not return to them, as we discussed this point earlier.

The statute of Labourers was passed at the urgent insistence of the House of Commons. A Tory says naively: "Formerly the poor demanded such *high* wages as to threaten industry and wealth. Next, their wages are so *low* as to threaten industry and wealth equally and perhaps more, but in another way. A tariff of wages was fixed by law for town and country, for piece-work and day-work. The agricultural Labourers were to hire themselves out by the year, the urban workers were to do so "on the open market." It was forbidden, on pain of imprisonment, to pay higher wages than those fixed by the statute, but the taking of higher wages was more severely punished than the giving of them (similarly, in Sections 18 and 19 of Elizabeth's Statute of Apprentices, ten days' imprisonment is decreed for the person who pays the higher wages, but twenty-one days for the person who receives those wages). A statute of 1360 increased the penalties and authorized the masters to extort labour at the legal rate of wages by using corporal punishment. All combinations, contracts, oaths, etc. by which masons and carpenters reciprocally bound themselves were declared null and void. Workers' combinations are treated as heinous crimes from the fourteenth century until 1825, the year of the repeal of the laws against combinations. The spirit of the Statute of Labourers of 1349 and its offshoots shines out clearly in the fact that while the state certainly dictates a maximum of wages, it on no account fixes a minimum.

In the sixteenth century, as we know, the condition of the workers became much worse. The money wage rose, but not in proportion to the depreciation of money and the corresponding rise in the prices of commodities. Real wages therefore fell. Nevertheless, the laws for keeping them down remained in force, together with the ear-clipping and branding of those "whom no one was willing to take into service." By Elizabeth's Statute of Apprentices, the justices of the peace were given the power to fix certain wages and to modify them according to the time of the year and current prices of commodities. James I extended these labour regulations to weavers, spinners, and indeed to all other possible categories of worker. George II extended the laws against combinations of workers to all manufacturers.

In the period of manufacture properly so called, the capitalist mode of production had become sufficiently strong to render legal regulation of wages as impracticable as it was unnecessary; but the ruling classes were unwilling to be without the weapons of the old arsenal in case some emergency should arise. Hence, even in the eighteenth century, George I forbade a daily wage higher than 2s. 71/2d. for journeymen tailors in and around London, except in cases of general mourning; George III handed over to the justices of the peace the task of regulating the wages of silk-weavers; in 1796 it required two judgments of the higher courts to decide whether the orders made by justices of the peace as to wages also held good for non-agricultural workers; and in 1799 Parliament confirmed that the wages of mining workers in Scotland should continue to be regulated by a statute of Elizabeth and two Scottish Acts of 1661 and 1671. How completely the situation had been transformed in the meantime is proved by a hitherto unheard-of occurrence in the House of Commons. There, where for more than 400 years laws had been made for the maximum beyond which wages absolutely must not rise, Whitbread in 1796 proposed a legal minimum wage for agricultural labourers. Pitt opposed this, but conceded that the "condition of the poor was cruel." Finally, in 1813, the laws for the regulation of wages were repealed. They became an absurd anomaly as soon as the capitalist began to regulate his factory by his own private legislation, and was able to make up the wage of the agricultural labourer to the indispensable minimum by means of the poor-rate. The provisions of the statutes of labourers as to contracts between master and workman, regarding giving notice and the like, which allow only a civil action against the master who breaks his contract, but permit, on the contrary, a criminal action against the worker who breaks his contract, are still in full force at this moment.

The barbarous laws against combinations of workers collapsed in 1825 in the face of the threatening attitude of the proletariat. Despite this, they disappeared only in part. Certainly petty survivals of the old statutes did not vanish until 1859. Finally the Act of 29 June 1871 purported to remove the last traces of this class legislation by giving legal recognition to trade unions. But another Act, of the same date ("An act to amend the criminal law relating to violence, threats, and molestation"), in fact re-established the previous situation in a new form. This parliamentary conjuring-trick withdrew the means the workers could use in a strike or lock-out from the common law and placed them under exceptional penal legislation, the interpretation of which fell to the manufacturers themselves in their capacity of justices of the peace. Two years earlier, the same House of Commons, and the same Mr. Gladstone, in the customary honourable fashion, had brought in a bill for the removal of all exceptional penal legislation against the working class. But it was never allowed to go beyond the second reading, and the matter was drawn out in this way until at length the "great Liberal party," by an alliance with the Tories, found the courage to turn decisively against the very proletariat that had carried it into power. Not content with this betrayal, the "great Liberal party" allowed the English judges, ever ready to wag their tails for the ruling classes, to exhume the earlier laws against "conspiracy" and apply them to combinations of workers. It is evident that only against its will, and under the pressure of the masses, did the English Parliament give up the laws against strikes and trade unions, after it had itself, with shameless egoism, held the position of a permanent trade union of the capitalists against the workers throughout five centuries.

During the very first storms of the revolution, the French bourgeoisie dared to take away from the workers the right of association they had just acquired. By a decree of 14 June 1791, they declared that every combination by the workers was "an assault on liberty and the declaration of the rights of man," punishable by a fine of 500 livres, together with deprivation of the rights of an active citizen for one year. This law, which used state compulsion to confine the struggle between capital and labour within limits convenient for capital, has outlived revolutions and changes of dynasties. Even the terror left it untouched. It was only struck out of the Penal Code quite recently. Nothing is more characteristic than the pretext for this bourgeois *coup d' état*. "Granting," says Le Chapelier, the *rapporteur* of the Committee on this law, "that wages ought to be a little higher than they are . . . that they ought to be high enough for him that receives them to be free from that state of absolute dependence which results from the lack of the necessaries of life, and which is almost a state of slavery," granting this, the workers must nevertheless not be permitted to inform themselves about their own interests, nor to act in common and thereby lessen their "absolute dependence," "which is almost a state of slavery," because by doing this they infringe on "the liberty of their former masters, who are the present *entrepreneurs*," and because a combination against the despotism of the former masters of the corporation is—guess what!—a restoration of the corporations abolished by the French constitution!

· · · · ·

CHAPTER 31. THE GENESIS OF THE INDUSTRIAL CAPITALIST

The genesis of the industrial capitalist did not proceed in such a gradual way as that of the farmer. Doubtless many small guild-masters, and a still greater number of independent small artisans, or even wage-labourers, transformed themselves into small capitalists, and, by gradually extending their exploitation of wage-labour and the corresponding accumulation, into "capitalists" without qualification. In the period when capitalist production was in its infancy things often happened as they had done in the period of infancy of the medieval town, where the question as to which of the escaped serfs should be master and which servant was in great part decided by the earlier or later date of their flight. The snail's pace of adventure under this method by no means corresponded with the commercial requirements of the new world market, which had been created by the great discoveries of the end of the fifteenth century. But the Middle Ages had handed down two distinct forms of capital, which ripened in the most varied economic formations of society, and which, before the era of the capitalist mode of production, nevertheless functioned as capital-usurer's capital and merchant's capital.

At present, all the wealth of society goes first into the possession of the capitalist . . . he pays the landowner his rent, the labourer his wages, the tax and tithe gathered their claims, and keeps a large, indeed the largest, and a continually augmenting share, of the annual product of labour for himself. The capitalist may now be said to be the first owner of all the wealth of the community, though no law has conferred on him the right to this property . . . this change has been effected by the taking of interest on capital . . . and it is not a little curious that all the law-givers of Europe endeavoured to prevent this by statutes, viz., statutes against usury. . . . The power of the capitalist over all the wealth of the country is a complete change in the right of property, and by what law, or series of laws, was it effected? The author should have reminded himself that revolutions are not made with laws.

The money capital formed by means of usury and commerce was prevented from turning into industrial capital by the feudal organization of the countryside and the guild organization of the towns. These fetters vanished with the dissolution of the feudal bands of retainers, and the expropriation and partial eviction of the rural population. The new manufactures were established at seaports, or at points in the countryside which were beyond the control of the old municipalities and their guilds. Hence, in England, the bitter struggle of the corporate towns against these new seed-beds of industry.

The discovery of gold and silver in America, the extirpation, enslavement, and entombment in mines of the indigenous populations of that continent, the beginnings of the conquest and plunder of India, and the conversion of Africa into a preserve for the commercial hunting of black skins, are all things which characterize the dawn of the era of capitalist production. These idyllic proceedings are the chief moments of primitive accumulation. Hard on their heels follows the commercial war of the European nations, which has the globe as its battlefield. It begins with the revolt of the Netherlands from Spain, assumes gigantic dimensions in England's Anti-Jacobin War, and is still going on in the shape of the Opium Wars against China.

The different moments of primitive accumulation can be assigned in particular to Spain, Portugal, Holland, France and England, in more or less chronological order. These different moments are systematically combined together at the end of the seventeenth century in England; the combination embraces the colonies, the national debt, the modern tax system, and the system of protection. These methods depend in part on brute force, for instance, the colonial system. But they all employ the power of the state, the concentrated and organized force of society, to hasten, as in a hothouse, the process of transformation of the feudal mode of production into the capitalist mode, and to shorten the transition. Force is the midwife of every old society which is pregnant with a new one. It is itself an economic power.

W. Howitt, a man who specializes in being a Christian, says of the Christian colonial system, "The barbarities and desperate outrages of the so-called Christian race, throughout every region of the world, and upon every people they have been able to subdue, are not to be paralleled by those of any other race, however fierce, however untaught, and however reckless of mercy and of shame, in any age of the earth." The history of Dutch colonial administration—and Holland was the model capitalist nation of the seventeenth century—"is one of the most extraordinary relations of treachery, bribery, massacre, and meanness." Nothing is more characteristic than their system of stealing men in Celebes, in order to get slaves for Java. Man-stealers were trained for this purpose. The thief, the interpreter, and the seller were the chief agents in this trade, the native princes were the chief sellers. The young people thus stolen were hidden in secret dungeons on Celebes, until they were ready for sending to the slave-ships. An official report says: "This one town of Macassar, for example, is full of secret prisons, one more horrible than the other, crammed with unfortunates, victims of greed and tyranny fettered in chains, forcibly torn from their families." In order to get possession of Malacca, the Dutch bribed the Portuguese governor. He let them into the town in 1641. They went straight to his house and assassinated him, so as to be able to "abstain" from paying the £21,875 which was the amount of his bribe. Wherever they set foot, devastation and depopulation followed. Banjuwangi, a province of Java, numbered over 80,000 inhabitants in 1750 and only 18,000 in 1811. That is peaceful commerce!

The English East India Company, as is well known, received, apart from political control of India, exclusive monopoly of the tea trade, as well as of the Chinese trade in general, and the transport of goods to and from Europe. But the coasting trade round India and between the islands, as well as the international trade of India, was the monopoly of the higher officials of the Company. The monopolies of salt, opium, betel, and other commodities were inexhaustible mines of wealth. The officials themselves fixed the price and plundered the unfortunate Hindus at will. The Governor-General took part in this private traffic. His favourites received contracts under conditions whereby they, cleverer than the alchemists, made gold out of nothing. Great fortunes sprang up like mushrooms in a day; primitive accumulation proceeded without the advance of even a shilling. The trial of Warren Hastings swarms with such cases. He is an instance. A contract for opium was given to a certain Sullivan at the moment of his departure on an official mission to a part of India far removed from the opium district. Sullivan sold his contract to one Bill for £40,000; Bill sold it the same day for £60,000, and the ultimate purchaser who carried out the contract declared that he still extracted a tremendous profit from it. According to one of the lists laid before Parliament, the Company and its officials obtained £6,000,000 between 1757 and 1776 from the Indians in the form of gifts. Between 1769 and 1770, the English created a famine by buying up all the rice and refusing to sell it again, except at a fabulous price.

The treatment of the indigenous population was, of course, at its most frightful in plantation-colonies set up exclusively for the export trade, such as the West Indies, and in rich and well-populated countries, such as Mexico and India, that were given over to plunder. But even in the colonies properly so called, the Christian character of primitive accumulation was not belied. In 1703 those sober exponents of Protestantism, the Puritans of New England, by decrees of their assembly, set a premium of £40 on every Indian scalp and every captured redskin; in 1720, a premium of £100 was set on every scalp; in 1744, after Massachusetts Bay had proclaimed a certain tribe as rebels, the following prices were laid down: for a male scalp of 12 years and upwards, £100 in new currency, for a male prisoner £105, for women and children prisoners £50, for the scalps of women and children £50. Some decades later, the colonial system took its revenge on the descendants of the pious Pilgrim Fathers, who had grown seditious in the meantime. At English instigation, and for English money, they were tomahawked by the redskins. The British Parliament proclaimed bloodhounds and scalping as "means that God and Nature had given into its hand."

The colonial system ripened trade and navigation as in a hot-house. The "companies called Monopolia" (Luther) were powerful levers for the concentration of capital. The colonies provided a market for the budding manufactures, and a vast increase in accumulation which was guaranteed by the mother country's monopoly of the market. The treasures captured outside Europe, by undisguised looting, enslavement, and murder, flowed back to the mother-country, and were turned into capital there. Holland, which first brought the colonial system to its full development, already stood at the zenith of its commercial greatness in 1648. It was "in almost exclusive possession of the East Indian trade and the commerce between the south-east and the north-west of Europe. Its fisheries, its shipping, and its manufactures surpassed those of any other country. The total capital of the Republic was probably greater than that of all the rest of Europe put together." Gülich forgets to add that by 1648 the people of Holland were more over-worked, poorer, and more brutally oppressed than those of all the rest of Europe put together.

Today, industrial supremacy brings with it commercial supremacy. In the period of manufacture it is the reverse: commercial supremacy produces industrial predominance. Hence the preponderant role played by the colonial system at that time. It was the "strange God" who perched himself side by side with the old divinities of Europe on the altar, and one fine day threw them all overboard with a shove and a kick. It proclaimed the making of profit as the ultimate and the sole purpose of mankind.

The system of public credit, i.e., of national debts, the origins of which are to be found in Genoa and Venice as early as the Middle Ages, took possession of Europe as a whole during the period of manufacture. The colonial system, with its maritime trade and its commercial wars, served as a forcing-house for the credit system. Thus it first took root in Holland. The national debt, i.e., the alienation of the state—whether that state is despotic, constitutional, or republican—marked the capitalist era with its stamp. The only part of the so-called national wealth that actually enters into the collective possession of a modern nation is the national debt.

Hence, quite consistently with this, the modern doctrine that a nation becomes the richer the more deeply it is in debt. Public credit becomes the *credo* of capital. And with the rise of national debt-making, lack of faith in the national debt takes the place of the sin against the Holy Ghost, for which there is no forgiveness.

The public debt becomes one of the most powerful levers of primitive accumulation. As with the stroke of an enchanter's wand, it endows unproductive money with the power of creation and thus turns it into capital, without forcing it to expose itself to the troubles and risks inseparable from its employment in industry or even in usury. The state's creditors actually give nothing away, for the sum lent is transformed into public bonds, easily negotiable, which go on functioning in their hands just as would so much hard cash. But furthermore, and quite apart from the class of idle *rentiers* thus created, the improvised wealth of the financiers who play the role of middlemen between the government and the nation, and the tax-farmers, merchants, and private manufacturers, for whom a good part of every national loan performs the service of a capital fallen from heaven, apart from all these people, the national debt has given rise to joint-stock companies, to dealings in negotiable effects of all kinds, and to speculation: in a word, it has given rise to stock-exchange gambling and the modern bankocracy.

At their birth the great banks, decorated with national titles, were only associations of private speculators, who placed themselves by the side of governments and, thanks to the privileges they received, were in a position to advance money to those governments. Hence the accumulation of the national debt has no more infallible measure than the successive rise in the stocks of these banks, whose full development dates from the founding of the Bank of England in 1694. The Bank of England began by lending its money to the government at 8 percent; at the same time it was empowered by Parliament to coin money out of the same capital, by lending it a second time to the public in the form of bank-notes. It was allowed to use these notes for discounting bills, making advances on commodities, and buying the precious metals. It was not long before this credit-money, created by the bank itself, became the coin in which the latter made its loans to the state, and paid, on behalf of the state, the interest on the public debt. It was not enough that the bank gave with one hand and took back more with the other; it remained, even while receiving money, the eternal creditor of the nation down to the last farthing advanced. Gradually it became the inevitable receptacle of the metallic hoard of the country, and the centre of gravity of all commercial credit. The writings of the time (Bolingbroke's, for instance) show what effect was produced on their contemporaries by the sudden emergence of this brood of bankocrats, financiers, *rentiers*, brokers, and stock-jobbers.

Along with the national debt there arose an international credit system, which often conceals one of the sources of primitive accumulation in this or that people. Thus the villainies of the Venetian system of robbery formed one of the secret foundations of Holland's wealth in capital, for Venice in her years of decadence lent large sums of money to Holland. There is a similar relationship between Holland and England. By the beginning of the eighteenth century, Holland's manufactures had been far out-stripped. It had ceased to be the nation preponderant in commerce and industry. One of its main lines of business, therefore, from 1701 to 1776, was the lending out of enormous amounts of capital, especially to its great rival England. The same thing is going on today between England and the United States. A great deal of capital, which appears today in the United States without any birth-certificate, was yesterday, in England, the capitalized blood of children.

As the national debt is backed by the revenues of the state, which must cover the annual interest payments, etc. the modern system of taxation was the necessary complement of the system of national loans. The loans enable the government to meet extraordinary expenses without the taxpayers feeling it immediately, but they still make increased taxes necessary as a consequence. On the other hand, the raising of taxation caused by the accumulation of debts contracted one after another compels the government always to have recourse to new loans for new extraordinary expenses. The modern fiscal system, whose pivot is formed by taxes on the most necessary means of subsistence (and therefore by increases in their price), thus contains within itself the germ of automatic progression. Over-taxation is not an accidental occurrence, but rather a principle. In Holland, therefore, where this system was first inaugurated, the great patriot, De Witt, extolled it in his *Maxims* as the best system for making the wage-labourer submissive, frugal, industrious . . . and overburdened with work. Here, however, we are less concerned with the destructive influence it exercises on the situation of the wage-labourer than with the forcible expropriation, resulting from it, of peasants and artisans, in short, of all the constituents of the lower middle class. There are no two opinions about this, even among the bourgeois economists. Its effectiveness as an expropriating agent is heightened still further by the system of protection, which forms one of its integral parts.

The great part that the public debt and the fiscal system corresponding to it have played in the capitalization of wealth and the expropriation of the masses, has led many writers, like Cobbett, Doubleday, and others, to see here, incorrectly, the fundamental cause of the misery of the people in modern times.

The system of protection was an artificial means of manufacturing manufacturers, of expropriating independent workers, of capitalizing the national means of production and subsistence, and of forcibly cutting short the transition from a mode of production that was out of date to the modern mode of production. The European states tore each other to pieces to gain the patent of this invention, and, once they had entered into the service of the profit-mongers, they did not restrict themselves to plundering their own people, indirectly through protective duties, directly through export premiums, in the pursuit of this purpose. They also forcibly uprooted all industries in the neighbouring dependent countries, as for example England did with the Irish woollen manufacture. On the continent of Europe the process was much simplified, following the example of Colbert. The original capital for industry here came in part directly out of the state treasury. "Why," cries Mirabeau, "why go so far to seek the cause of the manufacturing glory of Saxony before the war? One hundred and eighty millions of debts contracted by the sovereigns!"

Colonial system, public debts, heavy taxes, protection, and commercial wars, these offshoots of the period of manufacture swell to gigantic proportions during the period of infancy of large-scale industry. The birth of the latter is celebrated by a vast, Herod-like slaughter of the innocents. Like the royal navy, the factories were recruited by means of the press-gang. Though Sir F. M. Eden is indifferent to the horrors of the expropriation of the agricultural population from the soil, from the last third of the fifteenth century up to his own time; though he shows great self-satisfaction in congratulating his country on this process, which was "essential" in order to establish capitalist agriculture and "the due proportion between arable and pasture land"; despite this, he does not show the same economic insight into the necessity of child-stealing and child-slavery for the transformation of manufacturing production into factory production and the establishment of the true relation between capital and labor power. He says: "It may perhaps be worthy the attention of the public to consider, whether any manufacture, which, in order to be carried on successfully, requires that cottages and workhouses should be ransacked for poor children; that they should be employed by turns during the greater part of the night and robbed of the rest which, though indispensable to all, is most required by the young; and that numbers of both sexes, of different ages and dispositions, should be collected together in such a manner that the contagion of example cannot lead to profligacy and debauchery, but will add to the sum of individual or national felicity?"

"In the counties of Derbyshire, Nottinghamshire, and more particularly in Lancashire," says Fielden, "the newly-invented machinery was used in large factories built on the sides of streams capable of turning the water-wheel. Thousands of hands were suddenly required in these places, remote from towns; and Lancashire, in particular, being, till then, comparatively thinly populated and barren, a population was all that she now wanted. The small and nimble fingers of little children being by very far the most in request, the custom instantly sprang up of procuring apprentices (!) from the different parish workhouses of London, Birmingham, and elsewhere. Many, many thousands of these little, hapless creatures were sent down into the north, being from the age of 7 to the age of 13 or 14 years old. The custom was for the master" (i.e., the child-stealer) "to clothe his apprentices and to feed and lodge them in an 'apprentice house' near the factory; overseers were appointed to see to the works, whose interest it was to work the children to the utmost, because their pay was in proportion to the quantity of work that they were exacted. Cruelty was, of course, the consequence. . . . In many of the manufacturing districts, but particularly, I am afraid, in the guilty county to which I belong (Lancashire), cruelties the most hard-rending were practiced upon the unoffending and friendless creatures who were thus consigned to the charge of master-manufacturers; they were harassed to the brink of death by excess of labour . . . were flogged, fettered, and tortured in the most exquisite refinement of cruelty; . . . they were in many cases starved to the bone while flogged to their work and . . . even in some instances . . . were driven to commit suicide. . . . The beautiful and romantic valleys of Derbyshire, Nottinghamshire, and Lancashire, secluded from the public eye, became the dismal solitudes of torture, and of many a murder. The profits of manufactures were enormous; but this only whetted the appetite that it should have satisfied, and therefore the manufacturers had recourse to an expedient that seemed to secure to them those profits without any possibility of limit; they began the practice of what is termed 'night-working,' that is, having tried one set of hands, by working them throughout the day, they had another set ready to go on working throughout the night; the day-set getting into the beds that the night-set had just quitted, and in their turn again, the night-set getting into the beds that the day-set quitted in the morning. It is a common tradition in Lancashire that the beds *never get cold*."

With the development of capitalist production during the period of manufacture, the public opinion of Europe lost its last remnant of shame and conscience. The nations bragged cynically of every infamy that served them as a means to the accumulation of capital. Read, for example, the native commercial annals of the worthy A. Anderson. Here it is trumpeted forth as a triumph of English statesmanship that, as at the Peace of Utrecht, England extorted from the Spaniards, by the Asiento Treaty, the privilege of being allow to ply the slave trade, not only between Africa and the English West Indies, which it had done until then, but also between Africa and Spanish America. England thereby acquired the right to supply Spanish America until 1743 with 4,800 Negroes a year. At the same time this threw an official cloak over British smuggling. Liverpool grew fat on the basis of the slave trade. This was its method of primitive accumulation. And even to the present day, the Liverpool "quality" have remained the Pindar of the slave trade, which—as noted in the work by Dr. Aiken we have just quoted—"has coincided with that spirit of bold adventures which has characterized the trade of Liverpool and rapidly carried it to its present state of prosperity; has occasioned vast employment for shipping and sailors, and greatly augmented the demand for the manufacturers of the country." In 1730 Liverpool employed 15 ships in the slave trade; in 1751, 53; in 1760, 74; in 1770, 96; and in 1792, 132.

While the cotton industry introduced child-slavery into England, in the United States it gave the impulse for transformation of the earlier, more or less patriarchal slavery into a system of commercial exploitation. In fact, the veiled slavery of the wage-labourers in Europe needed the unqualified slavery of the New World as its pedestal.

All this and more (tantae molis erat) helped to unleash the "eternal natural laws" of the capitalist mode of production, to complete the process of separation between the workers and the conditions of their labour, to transform, at one pole, the social means of production and subsistence into capital, and at the opposite pole, the mass of the population into wage-labourers, into the free "labouring poor," that artificial product of modern history. If money, according to Augier, "comes into the world with a congenital blood-stain on one cheek," capital comes dripping from head to toe, from every pore, with blood and dirt.

A Martinician theorist and psychologist trained in medicine and psychiatry in France after World War II, Frantz Fanon's involvement with the Algerian Nationalist Movement began when he was sent by the French colonial administration to a hospital in Algeria. When the Algerian War of Independence broke out, Fanon was there to analyze the debilitating effects of colonialism and war in the neuroses of both white soldiers and their black victims. He subsequently resigned from his position with the colonial administration to join hands with the Algerian revolutionaries and freedom-fighters. He became the most vocal critic of French rule in Algeria.

Fanon's The Wretched of the Earth *(1961) is perhaps the most powerful and comprehensive of his indictments of colonial rule. It also marks him as the foremost theorist of colonially derived violence. In this text, he advocates the use of violence on the part of the colonized as a necessary stage in the development of a national consciousness and a national culture. Although Fanon has time and again been called the "apostle of violence," he is not so much an apostle as a theorist of violence. The* Wretched of the Earth *provides an example of the chain reaction started by violence. It is precisely in reaction to the violence of the colonizer that Fanon prescribes counter-violence, arguing that the colonized can form a national consciousness, and facilitate independence, only through counterviolence. This prescription marks an attempt to correct the wrongs perpetrated by the colonizer. Fanon's position becomes an in-stantiation of the logic of violence: once it has been initiated, it takes its own course and produces more violence.*

Fanon provides the bridge between theory and praxis that seems to be lacking in an academic understanding of violence. The heavily theoretical first chapter ("Concern-ing Violence") in Wretched of the Earth *is accompanied by later chapters that deal specifically with case studies of Fanon's patients, both French soldiers and their colo-nized victims. He deals with prevalent stereotypes of the Negro-Algerian as lazy, violent, and criminal, demonstrating how these qualities entail resistance or non-cooperation to colonial rule. Indeed, Fanon's can be called a theory of praxis: it emerges out of a day-to-day involvement with the Algerian freedom-fighters and with the process of decolonization. Furthermore, he tries to provide a solution to a situation of injustice, theorizing about what is to be done, rather than simply about what has been done. In this respect, Fanon raises a most troubling and powerful question: is violence necessary at times, and if so, does it, or can it, put an end to further violence?*

Fanon's other titles include Black Skin, White Masks *(1952),* Toward the African Revolution *(1964), and* A Dying Colonialism *(trans., 1965).*

Concerning Violence

FRANTZ FANON

National liberation, national renaissance, the restoration of nationhood to the people, commonwealth: whatever may be the headings used or the new formulas introduced, decolonization is always a violent phenomenon. At whatever level we study it—relationships between individuals, new names for sports clubs, the human admixture at cocktail parties, in the police, on the directing boards of national or private banks—decolonization is quite simply the replacing of a certain "species" of men by another "species" of men. Without any period of transition, there is a total, complete, and absolute substitution. It is true that we could equally well stress the rise of a new nation, the setting up of a new state, its diplomatic relations, and its economic and political trends. But we have precisely chosen to speak of that kind of *tabula rasa* which characterizes at the outset all decolonization. Its unusual importance is that it constitutes, from the very first day, the minimum demands of the colonized. To tell the truth, the proof of success lies in a whole social structure being changed from the bottom up. The extraordinary importance of this change is that it is willed, called for, demanded. The need for this change exists in its crude state, impetuous and compelling, in the consciousness and in the lives of the men and women who are colonized. But the possibility of this change is equally experienced in the form of a terrifying future in the consciousness of another "species" of men and women: the colonizers.

Decolonization, which sets out to change the order of the world, is, obviously, a program of complete disorder. But it cannot come as a result of magical practices, nor of a natural shock, nor of a friendly understanding. Decolonization, as we know, is a historical process: that is to say that it cannot be understood, it cannot become intelligible nor clear to itself except in the exact measure that we can discern the movements which give it historical form and content. Decolonization is the meeting of two forces, opposed to each other by their very nature, which in fact owe their originality to that sort of substantification which results from and is nourished by the situation in the colonies. Their first encounter was marked by violence and their existence together—that is to say the exploitation of the native by the settler—was carried on by dint of a great array of bayonets and cannons. The settler and the native are old acquaintances. In fact, the settler is right when he speaks of knowing "them" well. For it is the settler who has brought the native into existence and who perpetuates his existence. The settler owes the fact of his very existence, that is to say, his property, to the colonial system.

Decolonization never takes place unnoticed, for it influences individuals and modifies them fundamentally. It transforms spectators crushed with their inessentiality into privileged actors, with the grandiose glare of history's floodlights upon them. It brings a natural rhythm into existence, introduced by new men, and with it a new language and new humanity. Decolonization is the veritable creation of new men. But this creation owes nothing of its legitimacy to any supernatural power; the "thing" which has been colonized becomes man during the same process by which it frees itself. In decolonization, there is therefore the need of a complete calling in question of the colonial situation. If we wish to describe it precisely, we might find it in the well-known words: "The last shall be first and the first last." Decolonization is the putting into practice of this sentence. That is why, if we try to describe it, all decolonization is successful.

The naked truth of decolonization evokes for us the searing bullets and bloodstained knives which emanate from it. For if the last shall be first, this will only come to pass after a murderous and decisive struggle between the two protagonists. That affirmed intention to place the last at the head of things, and to make them climb at a pace (too quickly, some say) the well-known steps which characterize an organized society, can only triumph if we use all means to turn the scale, including, of course, that of violence.

You do not turn any society, however primitive it may be, upside down with such a program if you have not decided from the very beginning, that is to say from the actual formulation of that program, to overcome all the obstacles that you will come across in so doing. The native who decides to put the program into practice, and to become its moving force, is ready for violence at all times. From birth it is clear to him that this narrow world, strewn with prohibitions, can only be called in question by absolute violence.

The colonial world is a world divided into compartments. It is probably unnecessary to recall the existence of native quarters and European quarters, of schools for natives and schools for Europeans; in the same way we need not recall apartheid in South Africa. Yet, if we examine closely this system of compartments, we will at least be able to reveal the lines of force it implies. This approach to the colonial world, its ordering, and its geographical layout will allow us to mark out the lines on which a decolonized society will be reorganized.

The colonial world is a world cut in two. The dividing line, the frontiers are shown by barracks and police stations. In the colonies it is the policeman and the soldier who are the official, instituted go-betweens, the spokesmen of the settler and his rule of oppression. In capitalist societies the educational system, whether lay or clerical, the structure of moral reflexes handed down from father to son, the exemplary honesty of workers who are given a medal after fifty years of good and loyal service, and the affection which springs from harmonious relations and good behavior—all these aesthetic expressions of respect for the established order serve to create around the exploited person an atmosphere of submission and of inhibition which lightens the task of policing considerably. In the capitalist countries a multitude of moral teachers, counselors, and "bewilderers" separate the exploited from those in power. In the colonial countries, on the contrary, the policeman and the soldier, by their immediate presence and their frequent and direct action maintain contact with the native and advise him by means of rifle butts and napalm not to budge. It is obvious here that the agents of government speak the language of pure force. The intermediary does not lighten the oppression, nor seek to hide the domination; he shows them up and puts them into practice with the clear conscience of an upholder of the peace; yet he is the bringer of violence into the home and into the mind of the native.

The zone where the natives live is not complementary to the zone inhabited by the settlers. The two zones are opposed, but not in the service of a higher unity. Obedient to the rules of pure Aristotelian logic, they both follow the principle of reciprocal exclusivity. No conciliation is possible, for of the two terms, one is superfluous. The settlers' town is a strongly built town, all made of stone and steel. It is a brightly lit town; the streets are covered with asphalt, and the garbage cans swallow all the leavings, unseen, unknown, and hardly thought about. The settler's feet are never visible, except perhaps in the sea; but there you're never close enough to see them. His feet are protected by strong shoes although the streets of his town are clean and even, with no holes or stones. The settler's town is a well-fed town, an easygoing town; its belly is always full of good things. The settlers' town is a town of white people, of foreigners.

The town belonging to the colonized people, or at least the native town, the Negro village, the medina, the reservation, is a place of ill fame, peopled by men of evil repute. They are born there, it matters little where or how; they die there, it matters not where, nor how. It is a world without spaciousness; men live there on top of each other, and their huts are built one on top of the other. The native town is a hungry town, starved of bread, of meat, of shoes, of coal, of light. The native town is a crouching village, a town on its knees, a town wallowing in the mire. It is a town of niggers and dirty Arabs. The look that the native turns on the settler's town is a look of lust, a look of envy; it expresses his dreams of possession—all manner of possession: to sit at the settler's table, to sleep in the settler's bed, with his wife if possible. The colonized man is an envious man. And this the settler knows very well; when their glances meet he ascertains bitterly, always on the defensive, "They want to take our place." It is true, for there is no native who does not dream at least once a day of setting himself up in the settler's place.

This world divided into compartments, this world cut in two is inhabited by two different species. The originality of the colonial context is that economic reality, inequality, and the immense difference of ways of life never come to mask the human realities. When you examine at close quarters the colonial context, it is evident that what parcels out the world is to begin with the fact of belonging to or not belonging to a given race, a given species. In the colonies the economic substructure is also a superstructure. The cause is the consequence; you are rich because you are white, you are white because you are rich. This is why Marxist analysis should always be slightly stretched every time we have to do with the colonial problem.

Everything up to and including the very nature of pre-capitalist society, so well explained by Marx, must here be thought out again. The serf is in essence different from the knight, but a reference to divine right is necessary to legitimize this statutory difference. In the colonies, the foreigner coming from another country imposed his rule by means of guns and machines. In defiance of his successful transplantation, in spite of his appropriation, the settler still remains a foreigner. It is neither the act of owning factories, nor estates, nor a bank balance which distinguishes the governing classes. The governing race is first and foremost those who come from elsewhere, those who are unlike the original inhabitants, "the others."

The violence which has ruled over the ordering of the colonial world, which has ceaselessly drummed the rhythm for the destruction of native social forms and broken up without reserve the systems of reference of the economy, the customs of dress and external life, that same violence will be claimed and taken over by the native at the moment when, deciding to embody history in his own person, he surges into the forbidden quarters. To wreck the colonial world is henceforward a mental picture of action which is very clear, very easy to understand, and which may be assumed by each one of the individuals which constitute the colonized people. To break up the colonial world does not mean that after the frontiers have been abolished lines of communication will be set up between the two zones. The destruction of the colonial world is no more and no less that the abolition of one zone, its burial in the depths of the earth or its expulsion from the country.

. . . . .

The problem of truth ought also to be considered. In every age, among the people, truth is the property of the national cause. No absolute verity, no discourse on the purity of the soul, can shake this position. The native replies to the living lie of the colonial situation by an equal falsehood. His dealings with his fellow-nationals are open; they are strained and incomprehensible with regard to the settlers. Truth is that which hurries on the break-up of the colonialist regime; it is that which promotes the emergence of the nation; it is all that protects the natives, and ruins the foreigners. In this colonialist context there is no truthful behavior, and the good is quite simply that which is evil for "them."

Thus we see that the primary Manicheanism which governed colonial society is preserved intact during the period of decolonization; that is to say that the settler never ceases to be the enemy, the opponent, the foe that must be overthrown. The oppressor, in his own sphere, starts the process, a process of domination, of exploitation, and of pillage, and in the other sphere, the coiled plundered creature which is the native provides fodder for the process as best he can, the process which moves uninterruptedly from the banks of the colonial territory to the palaces and the docks of the mother country. In this becalmed zone the sea has a smooth surface, the palm tree stirs gently in the breeze, the waves lap against the pebbles, and raw materials are ceaselessly transported, justifying the presence of the settler: and all the while the native, bent double, more dead than alive, exists interminably in an unchanging dream. The settler makes history; his life is an epoch, an Odyssey. He is the absolute beginning: "This land was created by us"; he is the unceasing cause: "If we leave, all is lost, and the country will go back to the Middle Ages." Over against him torpid creatures, wasted by fevers, obsessed by ancestral customs, form an almost inorganic background for the innovating dynamism of colonial mercantilism.

The settler makes history and is conscious of making it. And because he constantly refers to the history of his mother country, he clearly indicates that he himself is the extension of that mother country. Thus the history which he writes is not the history of the country which he plunders but the history of his own nation in regard to all that she skims off, all that she violates and starves.

The immobility to which the native is condemned can only be called in question if the native decides to put an end to the history of colonization—the history of pillage—and to bring into existence the history of the nation—the history of decolonization.

A world divided into compartments, a motionless, Manichean world, a world of statues: the statue of the general who carried out the conquest, the statue of the engineer who built the bridge: a world which is sure of itself, which crushes with its stones the backs flayed by whips; this is the colonial world. The native is a being hemmed in; apartheid is simply one form of the division into compartments of the colonial world. The first thing which the native learns is to stay in his place, and not to go beyond certain limits. This is why the dreams of the native are always of muscular prowess; his dreams are of action and of aggression. I dream I am jumping, swimming, running, climbing; I dream that I burst out laughing, that I span a river in one stride, or that I am followed by a flood of motorcars which never catch up with me. During the period of colonization, the native never stops achieving his freedom from nine in the evening until six in the morning.

The colonized man will first manifest this aggressiveness which has been deposited in his bones against his own people. This is the period when the niggers beat each other up, and the police and magistrates do not know which way to turn when faced with the astonishing waves of crime in North Africa. We shall see later how this phenomenon should be judged. When the native is confronted with the colonial order of things, he finds he is in a state of permanent tension. The settler's world is a hostile world, which spurns the native, but at the same time it is a world of which he is envious. We have seen that the native never ceases to dream of putting himself in the place of the settler—not of becoming the settler but of substituting himself for the settler. This hostile world, ponderous and aggressive because it fends off the colonized masses with all the harshness it is capable of, represents not merely a hell from which the swiftest flight possible is desirable, but also a paradise close at hand which is guarded by terrible watchdogs.

. . . . .

The peasantry is systematically disregarded for the most part by the propaganda put out by the nationalist parties. And is clear that in the colonial countries the peasants alone are revolutionary, for they have nothing to lose and everything to gain. The starving peasant, outside the class system, is the first among the exploited to discover that only violence pays. For him there is no compromise, no possible coming to terms; colonization and decolonization are simply a question of relative strength. The exploited man sees that his liberation implies the use of all means, and that of force first and foremost. When in 1956, after the capitulation of Monsieur Guy Mollet to the settlers in Algeria, the Front de Libération Nationale, in a famous leaflet, stated that colonialism only loosens its hold when the knife is at its throat, no Algerian really found these terms too violent. The leaflet only expressed what every Algerian felt at heart: colonialism is not a thinking machine, nor a body endowed with reasoning faculties. It is violence in its natural state, and it will only yield when confronted with greater violence.

At the decisive moment, the colonialist bourgeoisie, which up till then has remained inactive, comes into the field. It introduces that new idea which is in proper parlance a creation of the colonial situation: non-violence. In its simplest form this non-violence signifies to the intellectual and economic elite of the colonized country that the bourgeoisie has the same interests as they and that it is therefore urgent and indispensable to come to terms for the public good.

Non-violence is an attempt to settle the colonial problem around a green baize table, before any regrettable act has been performed or irreparable gesture made, before any blood has been shed. But if the masses, without waiting for the chairs to be arranged around the baize table, listen to their own voice and begin committing outrages and setting fire to buildings, the elite and the nationalist bourgeois parties will be seen rushing to the colonialists to exclaim, "This is very serious! We do not know how it will end; we must find a solution—some sort of compromise."

This idea of compromise is very important in the phenomenon of decolonization, for it is very far from being a simple one. Compromise involves the colonial system and the young nationalist bourgeoisie at one and the same time. The partisans of the colonial system discover that the masses may destroy everything. Blown-up bridges, ravaged farms, repressions, and fighting harshly disrupt the economy. Compromise is equally attractive to the nationalist bourgeoisie, who since they are not clearly aware of the possible consequences of the rising storm, are genuinely afraid of being swept away by this huge hurricane and never stop saying to the settlers: "We are still capable of stopping the slaughter; the masses still have confidence in us; act quickly if you do not want to put everything in jeopardy." One step more, and the leader of the nationalist party keeps his distance with regard to that violence. He loudly proclaims that he has nothing to do with these Mau-Mau, these terrorists, these throat-slitters. At best, he shuts himself off in a no man's land between the terrorists and the settlers and willingly offers his services as go-between; that is to say, that as the settlers cannot discuss terms with these Mau-Mau, he himself will be quite willing to begin negotiations. Thus it is that the rear guard of the national struggle, that very party of people who have never ceased to be on the other side in the fight, find themselves somersaulted into the can of negotiations and compromise—precisely because that party has taken very good care never to break contact with colonialism.

Before negotiations have been set afoot, the majority of nationalist parties confine themselves for the most part to explaining and excusing this "savagery." They do not assert that the people have to use physical force, and it sometimes even happens that they go so far as to condemn, in private, the spectacular deeds which are declared to be hateful by the press and public opinion in the mother country. The legitimate excuse for this ultra-conservative policy is the desire to see things in an objective light; but this traditional attitude of the native intellectual and of the leaders of the nationalist parties is not, in reality, in the least objective. For in fact they are not at all convinced that this impatient violence of the masses is the most efficient means of defending their own interests. Moreover, there are some individuals who are convinced of the ineffectiveness of violence methods; for them, there is no doubt about it, every attempt to break colonial oppression by force is a hopeless effort, an attempt at suicide, because in the innermost recesses of their brains the settler's tanks and airplanes occupy a huge place. When they are told "Action must be taken," they see bombs raining down on them, armored cars coming at them on every path, machine-gunning and police action . . . and they sit quiet. They are beaten from the start. There is no need to demonstrate their incapacity to triumph by violent methods; they take it for granted in their everyday life and in their political maneuvers. They have remained in the same childish position as Engels took up in his famous polemic with that monument of puerility, Monsieur Dühring:

> In the same way that Robinson [Crusoe] was able to obtain a sword, we can just as well suppose that [Man] Friday might appear one fine morning with a loaded revolver in his hand, and from then on the whole relationship of violence is reversed: Man Friday gives the orders and Crusoe is obliged to work. . . . Thus, the revolver triumphs over the sword, and even the most childish believer in axioms will doubtless form the conclusion that violence is not a simple act of will, but needs for its realization certain very concrete preliminary conditions, and in particular the implements of violence; and the more highly developed of those implements will carry the day against primitive ones. Moreover, the very fact of the ability to produce such weapons signifies that the producer of highly developed weapons, in every day speech, the arms manufacturer, triumphs over the producer of primitive weapons. To put it briefly, the triumph of violence depends upon the production of armaments, and this in its turn depends on production in general, and thus . . . on economic strength, on the economy of the State, and in the last resort on the material means which that violence commands. (Friedrich Engels, *Anti-Dühring*)

In fact, the leaders of reform have nothing else to say than: "With what are you going to fight the settlers? With your knives? Your shotguns?"

It is true that weapons are important when violence comes into play, since all finally depends on the distribution of these implements. But it so happens that the liberation of colonial countries throws new light on the subject. For example, we have seen that during the Spanish campaign, which was a very genuine colonial war, Napoleon, in spite of an army which reached in the offensives of the spring of 1810 the huge figure of 400,000 men, was forced to retreat. Yet the French army made the whole of Europe tremble by its weapons of war, by the bravery of its soldiers, and by the military genius of its leaders. Face to face with the enormous potentials of the Napoleonic troops, the Spaniards, inspired by an unshakeable national ardor, rediscovered the famous methods of guerilla warfare which, twenty-five years before, the American militia had tried out on the English forces. But the native's guerilla warfare would be of no value as opposed to other means of violence if it did not form a new element in the worldwide process of competition between trusts and monopolies.

In the early days of colonization, a single column could occupy immense stretches of country: the Congo, Nigeria, the Ivory Coast, and so on. Today, however, the colonized countries' national struggle crops up in a completely new international situation. Capitalism, in its early days, saw in the colonies a source of raw materials which, once turned into manufactured goods, could be distributed on the European market. After a phase of accumulation of capital, capitalism has today come to modify its conception of the profit-earning capacity of a commercial enterprise. The colonies have become a market. The colonial population is a customer who is ready to buy goods; consequently, if the garrison has to be perpetually reinforced, if buying and selling slackens off, that is to say if manufactured and finished goods can no longer be exported, there is clear proof that the solution of military force must be set aside. A blind domination founded on slavery is not economically speaking worthwhile for the bourgeoisie of the mother country. The monopolistic group within this bourgeoisie does not support a government whose policy is solely that of the sword. What the factory-owners and finance magnates of the mother country expect from their government is not that it should decimate the colonial peoples, but that it should safeguard with the help of economic conventions their own "legitimate interests."

Thus there exists a sort of detached complicity between capitalism and the violent forces which blaze up in colonial territory. What is more, the native is not alone against the oppressor, for indeed there is also the political and diplomatic support of progressive countries and peoples. But above all there is competition, that pitiless war which financial groups wage upon each other. A Berlin Conference was able to tear Africa into shreds and divide her up between three or four imperial flags. At the moment, the important thing is not whether such-and-such a region in Africa is under French or Belgian sovereignty, but rather that the economic zones are respected. Today, wars of repression are no longer waged against rebel sultans; everything is more elegant, less bloodthirsty; the liquidation of the Castro regime will be quite peaceful. They do all they can to strangle Guinea and they eliminate Mosaddeq. Thus the nationalist leader who is frightened of violence is wrong if he imagines that colonialism is going to "massacre all of us." The military will of course go on playing with tin soldiers which date from the time of the conquest, but higher finance will soon bring the truth home to them.

. . . . .

Let us return to considering the single combat between native and settler. We have seen that it takes the form of an armed and open struggle. There is no lack of historical examples: Indo-China, Indonesia, and of course North Africa. But what we must not lose sight of is that this struggle could have broken out anywhere, in Guinea as well as Somaliland, and moreover today it could break out in every place where colonialism means to stay on, in Angola, for example. The existence of an armed struggle shows that the people are decided to trust to violent methods only. He of whom *they* have never stopped saying that the only language he understands is that of force, decides to give utterance by force. In fact, as always, the settler has shown him the way he should take if he is to become free. The argument the native chooses has been furnished by the settler, and by an ironic turning of the tables it is the native who now affirms that the colonialist understands nothing but force. The colonial regime owes its legitimacy to force and at no time tried to hide this aspect of things. Every statue, whether of Faidherbe or of Lyautey, of Bugeaud or of Sergeant Blandan—all these conquistadors perched on colonial soil do not cease from proclaiming one and the same thing: "We are here by the force of bayonets . . ." (*This refers to Mirabeau's famous saying: "I am here by the will of the People; I shall leave only by the force of bayonets." —Trans.*) The sentence is easily completed. During the phase of insurrection, each settler reasons on a basis of simple arithmetic. This logic does not surprise the other settlers, but it is important to point out that it does not surprise the natives either. To begin with, the affirmation of the principle "It's them or us" does not constitute a paradox, since colonialism, as we have seen, is in fact the organization of a Manichean world, a world divided up into compartments. And when in laying down precise methods the settler asks each member of the oppressing minority to shoot down 30 or 100 or 200 natives, he sees that nobody shows any indignation and the whole problem is to decide whether it can be done all at once or by stages. (*It is evident that this vacuum cleaning destroys the very thing that they want to preserve. Sartre points this out when he says: "In short by the very fact of repeating them [concerning racist ideas] it is revealed that the simultaneous union of all against the natives is unrealizable. Such union only recurs from time to time and moreover it can only come into being as an active groupment in order to massacre the natives—an absurd though perpetual temptation to the settlers, which even if it was feasible would only succeed in abolishing colonization at one blow."*)

This chain of reasoning which presumes very arithmetically the disappearance of the colonized people does not leave the native overcome with moral indignation. He has always known that his duel with the settler would take place in the arena. The native loses no time in lamentations, and he hardly ever seeks for justice in the colonial framework. The fact is that if the settler's logic leaves the native unshaken, it is because the latter has practically stated the problem of his liberation in identical terms: "We must form ourselves into groups of two hundred or five hundred, and each group must deal with a settler." It is in this manner of thinking that each of the protagonists begins the struggle.

For the native, this violence represents the absolute line of action. The militant is also a man who works. The questions that the organization asks the militant bear the mark of this way of looking at things: "Where have you worked? With whom? What have you accomplished?" The group requires that each individual perform an irrevocable action. In Algeria, for example, where almost all the men who called on the people to join in the national struggle were condemned to death or searched for by the French police, confidence was proportional to the hopelessness of each case. You could be sure of a new recruit when he could no longer go back into the colonial system. This mechanism, it seems, had existed in Kenya among the Mau-Mau, who required that each member of the group should strike a blow at the victim. Each one was thus personally responsible for the death of that victim. To work means to work for the death of the settler. This assumed responsibility for violence allows both strayed and outlawed members of the group to come back again and to find their place once more, to become integrated. Violence is thus seen as comparable to a royal pardon. The colonized man finds his freedom in and through violence. This rule of conduct enlightens the agent because it indicates to him the means and the end. The poetry of Césaire takes on in this precise aspect of violence a prophetic significance. We may recall one of the most decisive pages of this tragedy where the Rebel (indeed!) explains his conduct:

> The Rebel (harshly): My name—an offense; my Christian name—humiliation; my status—a rebel; my age—the stone age.
> The Mother: My race—the human race. My religion—brotherhood.
> The Rebel: My race—that of the fallen. My religion . . . but it's not you that will show it to me with your disarmament . . . 'tis I myself, with my rebellion and my poor fists clenched and my wooly head. . . .
> (Very calm): I remember one November day; it was hardly six months ago . . . The master came into the cabin in a cloud of smoke like an April moon. He was flexing his short muscular arms—he was a very good master—and he was rubbing his little dimpled face with his fat fingers. His blue eyes were smiling and he couldn't get the honeyed words out of his mouth quick enough. "The kid will be a decent fellow," he said looking at me, and he said other pleasant things too, the master—that

you had to start very early, that twenty years was not too much to make a good Christian and a good slave, a steady, devoted boy, a good commander's chain-gang captain, sharp-eyed and strong-armed. And all that man saw of my son's cradle was that it was the cradle of a chain-gang captain. We crept in knife in hand . . .

The Mother: Alas, you'll die for it.

The Rebel: Killed . . . I killed him with my own hands. . . .

Yes, 'twas a fruitful death, a copious death. . . . It was night.

We crept among the sugar canes. The knives sang to the stars, but we did not heed the stars.

The sugar canes scarred our faces with streams of green blades.

The Mother: And I had dreamed of a son to close his mother's eyes.

The Rebel: But I chose to open my son's eyes upon another sun.

The Mother: O my son, son of evil and unlucky death—

The Rebel: Mother of living and splendid death,

The Mother: Because he has hated too much,

The Rebel: Because he has too much loved.

The Mother: Spare me, I am choking in your bonds. I bleed from your wounds.

The Rebel: And the world does not spare me. . . . There is not anywhere in the world a poor creature who's been lynched or tortured in whom I am not murdered and humiliated . . .

The Mother: God of Heaven, deliver him!

The Rebel: My heart, thou wilt not deliver me from all that I remember . . .

It was an evening in November . . .

And suddenly shouts lit up the silence;

We had attacked, we the slaves; we, the dung underfoot, we the animals with patient hooves,

We were running like madmen; shots rang out. . . . We were striking. Blood and sweat cooled and refreshed us. We were striking where the shouts came from, and the shouts became more strident and a great clamor rose from the east; it was the outhouses burning and the flames flickered sweetly on our cheeks.

Then was the assault made on the master's house.

They were firing from the windows.

We broke in the doors.

The master's room was wide open. The master's room was brilliantly lighted, and the master was there, very calm . . . and our people stopped dead . . . it was the master . . . I went in. "It's you," he said, very calm.

It was I, even I, and I told him so, the good slave, the faithful slave, the slave of slaves, and suddenly his eyes were like two cockroaches, frightened in the rainy season . . . I struck, and the blood spurted; that is the only baptism that I remember today. (Aimé Césaire, *Les Armes Miraculeuses*)

It is understandable that in this atmosphere, daily life becomes quite simply impossible. You can no longer be a fellah, a pimp, or an alcoholic as before. The violence of the colonial regime and the counter-violence of the native balance each other and respond to each other in an extraordinary reciprocal homogeneity. This reign of violence will be the more terrible in proportion to the size of the implantation from the mother country. The development of violence among the colonized people will be proportionate to the violence exercised by the threatened colonial regime. In the first phase of this insurrectional period, the home governments are the slaves of the settlers, and these settlers seek to intimidate the natives and their home governments at one and the same time. They use the same methods against both of them. The assassination of the Mayor of Evian, in its method and motivation, is identifiable with the assassination of Ali Boumendjel. For the settlers, the alternative is not between *Algérie algérienne* and *Algérie française* but between an independent Algeria and a colonial Algeria, and anything else is mere talk or attempts at treason. The settler's logic is implacable and one is only staggered by the counter-logic visible in the behavior of the native insofar as one has not clearly understood beforehand the mechanisms of the settler's ideas. From the moment that the native has chosen the methods of counter-violence, police reprisals automatically call forth reprisals on the side of the nationalists. However, the results are not equivalent, for machine-gunning from airplanes and bombardments from the fleet go far beyond in horror and magnitude any answer the natives can make. This recurring terror de-mystifies once and for all the most estranged members of the colonized race. They find out on the spot that all the piles of speeches on the equality of human beings do not hide the commonplace fact that the seven Frenchmen killed or wounded at the Col de Sakamody kindles the indignation of all civilized consciences, whereas the sack of the douars *(temporary village for the use of shepherds — Trans.)* of Guergour and of the dechras of Djerah and the massacre of whole populations—which had merely called forth the Sakamody ambush as a reprisal—all this is not of the slightest importance. Terror, counter-terror, violence, counter-violence: that is what observers bitterly record when they describe the circle of hate, which is so tenacious and so evident in Algeria.

· · · · ·

When the native is tortured, when his wife is killed or raped, he complains to no one. The oppressor's government can set up commissions of inquiry and of information daily if it wants to; in the eyes of the native, these commissions do not exist. The fact is that soon we shall have had seven years of crimes in Algeria and there has not yet been a single Frenchman indicted before a French court of justice for the murder of an Algerian. In Indo-China, in Madagascar, or in the colonies the native has always known that he need expect nothing from the other side. The settler's work is to make even dreams of liberty impossible for the native. The native's work is to imagine all possible methods for destroying the settler. On the logical plane, the Manicheanism of the settler produces a Manicheanism of the native. To the theory of the "absolute evil of the native" the theory of the "absolute evil of the settler" replies.

The appearance of the settler has meant in the terms of syncretism the death of the aboriginal society, cultural lethargy, and the petrification of individuals. For the native, life can only spring up again out of the rotting corpse of the settler. This then is the correspondence, term by term, between the two trains of reasoning.

But it so happens that for the colonized people this violence, because it constitutes their only work, invests their characters with positive and creative qualities. The practice of violence binds them together as a whole, since each individual forms a violent link in the great chain, a part of the great organism of violence which has surged upward in reaction to the settler's violence in the beginning. The groups recognize each other and the future nation is already indivisible. The armed struggle mobilizes the people; that is to say, it throws them in one way and in one direction.

The mobilization of the masses, when it arises out of the war of liberation, introduces into each man's consciousness the ideas of a common cause, of a national destiny, and of a collective history. In the same way the second phase, that of the building-up of the nation, is helped on by the existence of this cement which has been mixed with blood and anger. Thus we come to a fuller appreciation of the originality of the words used in these underdeveloped countries. During the colonial period the people are called upon to fight against oppression; after national liberation, they are called upon to fight against poverty, illiteracy, and underdevelopment. The struggle, they say, goes on. The people realize that life is an unending contest.

We have said that the native's violence unifies the people. By its very structure, colonialism is separatist and regionalist. Colonialism does not simply state the existence of tribes; it also reinforces it and separates them. The colonial system encourages chieftaincies and keeps alive the old Marabout confraternities. Violence is in action all-inclusive and national. It follows that it is closely involved in the liquidation of regionalism and of tribalism. Thus the national parties show no pity at all toward the caids and the customary chiefs. Their destruction is the preliminary to the unification of the people.

At the level of individuals, violence is a cleansing force. It frees the native from his inferiority complex and from his despair and inaction; it makes him fearless and restores his self-respect. Even if the armed struggle has been symbolic and the nation is demobilized through a rapid movement of decolonization, the people have the time to see that the liberation has been the business of each and all and that the leader has no special merit. From thence comes that type of aggressive reticence with regard to the machinery of protocol which young governments quickly show. When the people have taken violent part in the national liberation they will allow no one to set themselves up as "liberators." They show themselves to be jealous of the results of their action and take good care not to place their future, their destiny, or the fate of their country in the hands of a living god. Yesterday they were completely irresponsible; today they mean to understand everything and make all the decisions. Illuminated by violence, the consciousness of the people rebels against any pacification. From now on the demagogues, the opportunists, and the magicians have a difficult task. The action which has thrown them into a hand-to-hand struggle confers upon the masses a voracious taste for the concrete. The attempt at mystification becomes, in the long run, practically impossible.

VIOLENCE IN THE INTERNATIONAL CONTEXT

We have pointed out many times in the preceding pages that in underdeveloped regions the political leader is forever calling on his people to fight: to fight against colonialism, to fight against poverty and underdevelopment, and to fight against sterile traditions. The vocabulary which he uses in his appeals is that of a chief of staff: "mass mobilization"; "agricultural front"; "fight against illiteracy"; "defeats we have undergone"; "victories won." The young independent national evolves during the first years in an atmosphere of the battlefield, for the political leader of an underdeveloped country looks fearfully at the huge distance his country will have to cover. He calls to the people and says to them: "Let us gird up our loins and set to work," and the country, possessed by a kind of creative madness, throws itself into a gigantic and disproportionate effort. The program consists not only of climbing out of the morass but also of catching up with the other nations using the only means at hand. They reason that if the European nations have reached that stage of development, it is on account of their efforts: "Let us therefore," they seem to say, "prove to ourselves and to the whole world that we are capable of the same achievements." This manner of setting out the problem of the evolution of underdeveloped countries seems to us to be neither correct nor reasonable.

The European states achieved national unity at a moment when the national middle classes had concentrated most of the wealth in their hands. Shopkeepers and artisans, clerks and bankers monopolized finance, trade, and science in the national framework. The middle class was the most dynamic and prosperous of all classes. Its coming to power enabled it to undertake certain very important speculations: industrialization, the development of communications, and soon the search for outlets overseas.

In Europe, apart from certain slight differences (England, for example, was some way ahead) the various states were at a more or less uniform stage economically when they achieved national unity. There was no nation which by reason of the character of its development and evolution, caused affront to the others.

Today, national independence and the growth of national feeling in underdeveloped regions take on totally new aspects. In these regions, with the exception of certain spectacular advances, the different countries show the same absence of infrastructure. The mass of the people struggle against the same poverty, flounder about making the same gestures, and with their shrunken bellies, outline what has been called the geography of hunger. It is an underdeveloped world, a world inhuman in its poverty; but also it is a world without doctors, without engineers, and without administrators. Confronting this world, the European nations sprawl, ostentatiously opulent. This European opulence is literally scandalous, for it has been founded on slavery, it has been nourished with the blood of slaves, and it comes directly from the soil and from the subsoil of that underdeveloped world. The well-being and the progress of Europe have been built up with the sweat and the dead bodies of Negroes, Arabs, Indians, and the yellow races. We have decided not to overlook this any longer. When a colonialist country, embarrassed by the claims for independence made by a colony, proclaims to the nationalist leaders: "If you wish for independence, take it and go back to the Middle Ages," the newly independent people tend to acquiesce and to accept the challenge; in fact you may see colonialism withdrawing its capital and its technicians and setting up around the young State the apparatus of economic pressure. *(In the present international context, capitalism does not merely operate an economic blockade against African or Asiatic colonies. The United States with its anti-Castro operations is opening a new chapter in the long story of man's toiling advance toward freedom. Latin America, made up of new independent countries which sit at the United Nations and raise the wind there, ought to be an object lesson for Africa. These former colonies since their liberation have suffered the brazenfaced rule of Western capitalism in terror and destitution. The liberation of Africa and the growth of consciousness among man-kind have made it possible for the Latin American peoples to break with the old merry-go-round of dictatorships where each succeeding regime exactly resembled the preceding one. This heresy is felt to be a national scourge by the Yankees, and the United States now organizes counterrevolutionary brigades, puts together a provi-sional government, burns the sugar-cane crops, and generally has decided to stran-gle the Cuban people mercilessly. But this will be difficult. The people of Cuba will suffer, but they will conquer. The Brazilian president Jani Quadros has just an-nounced in a declaration of historic importance that his country will defend the Cuban revolution by all means. Perhaps even the United States may draw back when faced with the declared will of the peoples. When that day comes, we'll hang out the flags, for it will be a decisive moment for the men and women of the whole world. The almighty dollar, which when all is said or done is only guaranteed by slaves scattered all over the globe, in the oil wells of the Middle East, the mines of Peru, or of the Congo, and the United Fruit or Firestone plantations, will then cease to dominate with all its force these slaves which it has created and who continue, empty-headed and empty-bellied, to feed it from their substance.)* The apotheosis of independence is transformed into the curse of independence, and the colo-nial power through its immense resources of coercion condemns the young national to regression. In plain words, the colonial power says: "Since you want independence, take it and starve." The nationalist leaders have no other choice but to turn to their people and ask from them a gigantic effort. A regime of austerity is imposed on these starving men; a disproportionate amount of work is required from their atrophied muscles. An autarkic regime is set up and each state, with the miserable resources it has in hand, tries to find an answer to the nation's great hunger and poverty. We see the mobilization of a people which toils to exhaustion in front of a suspicious and bloated Europe.

Other countries of the Third World refuse to undergo this ordeal and agree to get over it by accepting the conditions of the former guardian power. These countries use their strategic position—a position which accords them privileged treatment in the struggle between the two blocs—to conclude treaties and give undertakings. The former dominated country becomes an economically depen-dent country. The ex-colonial power, which has kept intact and sometimes even reinforced its colonialist trade channels, agrees to provision the budget of the independent nation by small injections. Thus we see that the accession to inde-pendence of the colonial countries places an important question before the world, for the national liberation of colonized countries unveils their true eco-nomic state and makes it seem even more unendurable. The fundamental duel which seemed to be that between colonialism and anticolonialism, and indeed between capitalism and socialism, is already losing some of its importance.

What counts today, the question which is looming on the horizon, is the need for a redistribution of wealth. Humanity must reply to this question, or be shaken to pieces by it.

It might have been generally thought that the time had come for the world, and particularly for the Third World, to choose between the capitalist and socialist systems. The underdeveloped countries, which have used the fierce competition which exists between the two systems in order to assure the triumph of their struggle for national liberation, should however refuse to become a factor in that competition. The Third World ought not to be content to define itself in the terms of values which have preceded it. On the contrary, the underdeveloped countries ought to do their utmost to find their own particular values and methods and a style which shall be peculiar to them. The concrete problem we find ourselves up against is not that of a choice, cost what it may, between socialism and capitalism as they have been defined by men of other continents and of other ages. Of course, we know that the capitalist regime, in so far as it is a way of life, cannot leave us free to perform our work at home, nor our duty in the world. Capitalist exploitation and cartels and monopolies are the enemies of underdeveloped countries. On the other hand the choice of a socialist regime, a regime which is completely orientated toward the people as a whole and based on the principle that man is the most precious of all possessions, will allow us to go forward more quickly and more harmoniously, and thus make impossible that caricature of society where all economic and political power is held in the hands of a few who regard the nation as a whole with scorn and contempt.

But in order that this regime may work to good effect so that we can in every instance respect those principles which were our inspiration, we need something more than human output. Certain underdeveloped countries expend a huge amount of energy in this way. Men and women, young and old undertake enthusiastically what is in fact forced labor, and proclaim themselves the slaves of the nation. The gift of oneself, and the contempt for every preoccupation which is not in the common interest, bring into being a national morale which comforts the heart of man, gives him fresh confidence in the destiny of mankind, and disarms the most reserved observers. But we cannot believe that such an effort can be kept up at the same frenzied pace for very long. These young countries have agreed to take up the challenge after the unconditional withdrawal of the ex-colonial countries. The country finds itself in the hands of new managers; but the fact is that everything needs to be reformed and everything thought out anew. In reality the colonial system was concerned with certain forms of wealth and certain resources only—precisely those which provisioned her own industries. Up to the present no serious effort had been made to estimate the riches of the soil or of mineral resources. Thus the young independent nation sees itself obliged to use the economic channels created by the colonial regime. It can, obviously, export to other countries and other currency areas, but the basis of its exports is not fundamentally modified. The colonial regime has carved out certain channels and they must be maintained or catastrophe will threaten. Perhaps it is necessary to begin everything all over again: to change the nature of the country's exports, and not simply their destination, to re-examine the soil and mineral resources, the rivers, and—why not?—the sun's productivity. Now, in order to do all this other things are needed over and above human output—capital of all kinds, technicians, engineers, skilled mechanics, and so on. Let's be frank: we do not believe that the colossal effort which the underdeveloped peoples are called upon to make by their leaders will give the desired results. If conditions of work are not modified, centuries will be needed to humanize this world which has been forced down to animal level by imperial powers. *(Certain countries which have benefitted from a large European settlement come to independence with houses and wide streets, and these tend to forget the poverty-stricken, starving hinterland. By the irony of fate, they give the impression by a kind of complicit silence that their towns are contemporaneous with independence.)*

The truth is that we ought not to accept these conditions. We should flatly refuse the situation to which the Western countries wish to condemn us. Colonialism and imperialism have not paid their score when they withdraw their flags and their police forces from our territories. For centuries the capitalists have behaved in the underdeveloped world like nothing more than war criminals. Deportations, massacres, forced labor, and slavery have been the main methods used by capitalism to increase its wealth, its gold or diamond reserves, and to establish its power. Not long ago Nazism transformed the whole of Europe into a veritable colony. The governments of the various European nations called for reparations and demanded the restitution in kind and money of the wealth which had been stolen from them: cultural treasures, pictures, sculptures, and stained glass have been given back to their owners. There was only one slogan in the mouths of Europeans on the morrow of the 1945 V-day: "Germany must pay." Herr Adenauer, it must be said, at the opening of the Eichmann trial, and in the name of the German people, asked once more for forgiveness from the Jewish people. Herr Adenauer has renewed the promise of his people to go on paying to the state of Israel the enormous sums which are supposed to be compensation for the crimes of the Nazis. *(It is true that Germany has not paid all her reparations. The indemnities imposed on the vanquished nation have not been claimed in full, for the injured nations have included Germany in their anti-communist system of defense. This same preoccupation is the permanent motivation of the colonialist countries when they try to obtain from their former colonies, if not their inclusion in the Western system, at least military bases and enclaves. On the other hand they have decided unanimously to forget their demands for the sake of* NATO *strategy and to preserve the free world; and we have seen Germany receiving floods of dollars and machines. A Germany once more standing on its feet, strong and powerful, was a necessity for the Western Camp. It was in the understood interests of so-called free Europe to have a prosperous and reconstructed Germany which would be capable of serving as a first rampart against the eventual Red hordes. Germany has made admirable use of the European crisis. At the same time the United States and other European states feel a legitimate bitterness when confronted with this Germany, yesterday at their feet, which today metes out to them cutthroat competition in the economic field.)*

In the same way we may say that the imperialist states would make a great mistake and commit an unspeakable injustice if they contented themselves with withdrawing from our soil the military cohorts, and the administrative and managerial services whose function it was to discover the wealth of the country, to extract it, and to send it off to the mother countries. We are not blinded by the moral reparation of national independence; nor are we fed by it. The wealth of the imperial countries is our wealth too. On the universal plane this affirmation, you may be sure, should on no account be taken to signify that we feel ourselves affected by the creations of Western arts or techniques. For in a very concrete way Europe has stuffed herself inordinately with the gold and raw materials of the colonial countries: Latin America, China, and Africa. From all these continents, under whose eyes Europe today raises up her tower of opulence, there has flowed out for centuries toward that same Europe diamonds and oil, silk and cotton, wood and exotic products. Europe is literally the creation of the Third World. The wealth which smothers her is that which was stolen from the underdeveloped peoples. The ports of Holland, the docks of Bordeaux and Liverpool were specialized in the Negro slave trade, and owe their renown to millions of deported slaves. So when we hear the head of a European state declare with his hand on his heart that he must come to the aid of the poor underdeveloped peoples, we do not tremble with gratitude. Quite the contrary; we say to ourselves: "It's a just reparation which will be paid to us." Nor will we acquiesce in the help for underdeveloped countries being a program of "sisters of charity." This help should be the ratification of a double realization: the realization by the colonized peoples that *it is their due*, and the realization by the capitalist powers that in fact *they must pay*. For if, through lack of intelligence (we won't speak of lack of gratitude) the capitalist countries refuse to pay, then the relentless dialectic of their own system will smother them. It is a fact that young nations do not attract much private capital. There are many reasons which explain and render legitimate this reserve on the part of the monopolies. As soon as the capitalists know—and of course they are the first to know—that their government is getting ready to decolonize, they hasten to withdraw all their capital from the colony in question. The spectacular flight of capital is one of the most constant phenomena of decolonization.

Private companies, when asked to invest in independent countries, lay down conditions which are shown in practice to be unacceptable or unrealizable. Faithful to their principle of immediate returns which is theirs as soon as they go "overseas," the capitalists are very chary concerning all long-term investments. They are unamenable and often openly hostile to the prospective programs of planning laid down by the young teams which form the new government. At a pinch they willingly agree to lend money to the young states, but only on condition that this money is used to buy manufactured products and machines: in other words, that it serves to keep the factories in the mother country going. In fact, the cautiousness of the Western financial groups may be explained by their fear of taking any risk. They also demand political stability and a calm social climate which are impossible to obtain when account is taken of the appalling state of the population as a whole immediately after independence. Therefore, vainly looking for some guarantee which the former colony cannot give, they insist on garrisons being maintained or the inclusion of the young state in military or economic pacts. The private companies put pressure on their own governments to at least set up military bases in these countries for the purpose of assuring the protection of their interests. In the last resort these companies ask their government to guarantee the investments which they decide to make in such-and-such an underdeveloped region.

It happens that few countries fulfill the conditions demanded by the trusts and monopolies. Thus capital, failing to find a safe outlet, remains blocked in Europe, and is frozen. It is all the more frozen because the capitalists refuse to invest in their own countries. The returns in this case are in fact negligible and treasury control is the despair of even the boldest spirits.

In the long run the situation is catastrophic. Capital no longer circulates, or else its circulation is considerably diminished. In spite of the huge sums swallowed up by military budgets, international capitalism is in desperate straits.

But another danger threatens it as well. Insofar as the Third World is in fact abandoned and condemned to regression or at least to stagnation by the selfishness and wickedness of Western nations, the underdeveloped peoples will decide to continue their evolution inside a collective autarky. Thus the Western industries will quickly be deprived of their overseas markets. The machines will pile up their products in the warehouses and a merciless struggle will ensue on the European market between the trusts and the financial groups. The closing of factories, the paying off of workers, and unemployment will force the European working class to engage in an open struggle against the capitalist regime. Then the monopolies will realize that their true interests lie in giving aid to the underdeveloped countries—unstinted aid with not too many conditions. So we see that the young nations of the Third World are wrong in trying to make up to the capitalist countries. We are strong in our own right, and in the justice of our point of view. We ought, on the contrary, to emphasize and explain to the capitalist countries that the fundamental problem of our time is not the struggle between the socialist regime and them. The Cold War must be ended, for it leads nowhere. The plans for nuclearizing the world must stop, and large-scale investments and technical aid must be given to underdeveloped regions. The fate of the world depends on the answer that is given to this question.

Moreover, the capitalist regime must not try to enlist the aid of the socialist regime over "the fate of Europe" in the face of the starving multitudes of colored peoples. The exploit of Colonel Gargarin doesn't seem to displease General de Gaulle, for is it not a triumph which brings honor to Europe? For some time past the statesmen of the capitalist countries have adopted an equivocal attitude toward the Soviet Union. After having united all their forces to abolish the socialist regime, they now realize that they'll have to reckon with it. So they look as pleasant as they can, they make all kinds of advances, and they remind the Soviet people the whole time that they "belong to Europe."

They will not manage to divide the progressive forces which mean to lead mankind toward happiness by brandishing the threat of a Third World which is rising like the tide to swallow up all Europe. The Third World does not mean to organize a great crusade of hunger against the whole of Europe. What it expects from those who for centuries have kept it in slavery is that they will help it to rehabilitate mankind, and make man victorious everywhere, once and for all. But it is clear that we are not so naive as to think that this will come about with the cooperation and the good will of the European governments. This huge task, which consists of reintroducing mankind into the world, the whole of mankind, will be carried out with the indispensable help of the European peoples, who themselves must realize that in the past they have often joined the ranks of our common masters where colonial questions were concerned. To achieve this, the European peoples must first decide to wake up and shake themselves, use their brains, and stop playing the stupid game of Sleeping Beauty.

PART II. THE OTHER OF VIOLENCE

All reforms owe their origin to the initiation

of minorities in opposition to majorities.

—Mohandas K. Gandhi, *Hind Swaraj*

IN THIS SECTION, WE HAVE PIECED TOGETHER readings not only from political actors who have talked about the tension between violence and nonviolence but also from critics who have commented on this tension as well as on the difficulty of locating the concept of violence. In a sense, this section may be said to be about violence and resistance, especially resistance to violence that itself becomes a new form of violence, namely, political resistance or ethnic nationalism. In the first of the readings, from Mohandas K. Gandhi, resistance is Indian nationalism versus British colonialism; in the Malcolm X reading it is black nationalism versus white supremacy in America; in the Adolf Hitler reading it is a totalitarian Nazi Germany against the non-Aryan world.

Gandhi makes a distinction between so-called civilization and true civilization, and suggests that so-called civilization is a disease that is eating up England and, by extension, Europe. Such civilization is geared toward technological progress, toward making "bodily welfare the object of life," but "fails miserably even in doing so." It consists in traveling on trains or through the air at incredible speeds, as opposed to using older modes of commuting, such as bullock carts and wagons; it consists in getting work done by machinery rather than by manual labor; it consists in the ability to "take away thousands of lives by one man working behind a gun from a hill," rather than by older modes of fighting, which pit one man against another.

Opposed to this civilization is "true civilization," which is the legacy of India, and which consists in the performance of duty and in following the path of morality, which, in turn, entails "set[ting] limits to our indulgences." Settting such limits means avoiding the system of "life-corroding competition" which turns men into slaves of their wants and desires. This civilization, Gandhi claims, does still exist in India, where the newfangled notions of the other civilization have not infiltrated, that is, in "the interior that has yet not been polluted by the railways." Such a concept of civilization entails self-reliance, or what Gandhi means by home rule for India, and consists in a regime of self-denial, in refusing the technologies of desire and pleasure that the "so-called civilization" provides. This refusal means that India declines to be a market for European goods. Self-abnegation, Gandhi suggests, is what defines *swaraj*, or home rule; it is the ability to "rule ourselves," which becomes the founding principle for and makes possible Indian home rule.

The ability to "rule ourselves" involves refraining from violence as the means for freeing India. Gandhi's editor cites Giuseppe Garibaldi's Italy as an example of the inefficacy of violence as a means for freedom. Indeed, in the case of India, the use of violence would be an ineffective method not only because it would entail arming "thousands of Indians" against the already "splendidly armed" British—a course of action which could take years—but also because "to arm India on a large scale is to Europeanize it. Then her condition will be just as pitiable as that of Europe."

Furthermore, Gandhi shows through examples and analogies that the employment of violence unleashes a chain reaction that becomes impossible to stop and, in the long run, produces more harm than good. As an alternative to violence, Gandhi puts forth his doctrine of "love-force, soul-force, or . . . passive resistance," which is a "method of securing rights by personal suffering." Such love-force includes disobeying laws that one deems unjust, as well as being ready to endure the consequences of doing so.

If Gandhi's is a gospel of love and nonviolence delineating how spiritual freedom paves the way to freedom from the British, Malcolm X's is a gospel of reciprocity, of tit-for-tat. Although Malcolm X insists that he does not advocate violence, he states, "[We] should never be nonviolent unless [we] run into some nonviolence." Malcolm X asserts that the condition of the black populace in America is such that nonviolence will not and cannot work. His is not a gospel of self-restraint, but of lashing back. His political platform to promote the use of the black vote to wrest control over black communities, to take them back from the whites. He suggests that if voting practices are not encouraged, there will be an outbreak of violence: "If we don't do something real soon . . . we're going to be forced either to use the ballot or the bullet." He avows that the general trend is that the emergent black community refuses to continue being put down, and that there has appeared "the type of black man in America today . . . who just doesn't intend to turn the other cheek any longer."

According to Malcolm X, the "negroes" in America are faced not with a "segregationist conspiracy" but with a "government conspiracy," and in order to combat this, a new, "broader" interpretation of the struggle is needed: the struggle needs to be fought on the platform of human rights rather than civil rights. Malcolm X's logic for recoding this struggle involves generalizing it as a worldwide struggle that is not confined to the realm of the U.S. governmental affairs—it becomes the concern of the global community. When the struggle for racial emancipation is taken into the jurisdiction of the United Nations, the

United States will find itself answerable to the international community, "where our African brothers . . . our Asian brothers . . . our Latin American brothers . . . and 800 million Chinamen are sitting there waiting to throw their weight on our side."

Furthermore, Malcolm X suggests that government conspiracy is so pervasive that even the white politicians in Washington who profess to be on the side of racial emancipation for black Americans are actually in cahoots with the politicians who are against the civil-rights movement, playing the "same old giant con game that they call the filibuster." Malcolm X's project is one of edification—calling close attention to the details of the con game and to the power of the black vote. Malcolm X claims that it is two-faced white politicians who need to be exposed and replaced by black representatives in areas that have a black majority. He asserts that to elect black representatives from areas with a black majority is the only way that the black community can hope for decent housing, decent schools, and a decent living. He makes a distinction between separation and segregation, suggesting that while "separation means you're gone," due to the domination of white politicians and the white world, segregation means that "he puts you away from him, but not far enough for you to be out of his jurisdiction." For Malcolm X, segregation is the evil. It is segregation that prevents the black community from controlling its own politics and its own economy. It is segregation that allows people who live outside the confines of the segregated community, who have no interest in the welfare of this community, to control this community. Malcolm X vows, "We will work against the segregated school system because it's criminal, because it is absolutely destructive, in every way imaginable, to the minds of the children who have to be exposed to that type of crippling education."

While Malcolm X warns that violence may be the necessary outcome if the ballot is not used effectively, Hitler's outright appeal to violence, coming out of the catastrophic violence of World War I, suggests that "nations which lay down their arms without compelling reasons prefer in the ensuing period to accept the greatest humiliations and extortions." Such a nation is one "that has lost its character." He considers this to be the case with Germany after the war, but blames its state of affairs on the leadership, which was "quite openly furnished by Jews." In the paranoid vision of Hitler's Germany, conditions there were all considered part of a Jewish conspiracy; German leadership was "revealed as the subtlest, ice-cold logic in the service of the Jewish idea and struggle for world conquest."

Hitler portrays the contemporary history of the German state in the international scene as one of enduring carnage and violence at the hands of France and Britain. His language points specifically to the metaphor of violation: Germany and France had to "shatter the structure of the Reich"; England was victorious after the war because of the "annihilation of Germany as a colonial and commercial power and her reduction to the rank of a second-class state." In response Hitler advocates outright violence, not only for the preservation of the nation, but also for the preservation of its "honour." He deems passive resistance ineffective and suggests that "any so-called passive resistance has an inner meaning only if it is backed by determination to continue it if necessary in open warfare or guerrilla warfare." Indeed, Nazi Germany's reaction to Hitler's picture of victimization—at the hands of both internal traitors, like the German Jewry and Marxists, and international foes such as France and England—ironically exemplifies the points made by both Malcolm X and Gandhi. Malcolm X's statement "When you drop that violence on me, then you've made me go insane, and I'm not responsible for what I do" encapsulates the violence and insanity of Nazi Germany's program of concentration camps and annihilation of anything outside its totalitarian agenda as a reaction to a perceived violation. Such insanity also exemplifies what Gandhi terms the destructive effects of using violence against violence.

Whereas these political actors debate the appropriateness of using violence or nonviolence in their own political and social milieus, the critics in this section debate the various modalities of violence. Each selection in its own way emblematizes the impossibility not only of making a distinction between violence and nonviolence but also of defining what may be meant by the term *violence*. Antonio Gramsci, for instance, outspokenly discusses Gandhi's platform of nonviolence in terms of violence, calling it "a war of position, which at certain moments becomes a war of movement, and at others underground warfare." After giving a historical and theoretical overview of the differences between military and political struggle, Gramsci goes on to discuss the state and civil society and the role of each (though they elide as one and the same thing) in educating the individual so that the individual can become the "collective man," capable of participating in the process of production.

Gramsci disagrees with Hitler's logic as well as his politics, terming as "superficial and acritical" his dictum—a dictum that lay behind his persecution of the German Jewry—that "the founding or the destruction of a religion is an action of immeasurably greater importance than the founding or destruction of a state: not to speak of a party." For Gramsci, these three entities—state, religion, and party—are "indissoluble": the founding or destruction of one cannot take place without affecting the others, and the emergence of a state from a party requires the continuous reorganization of both. Such reorganization, Gramsci suggests, is nevertheless "hindered in its practical development by blind, unilateral 'party' fanaticism." One is left to guess if the finger points toward Hitler's Germany:

"The political life of today furnishes ample evidence of these mental limitations and deficiencies, which, besides, provoke dramatic struggles—for they are themselves the means by which historical development in practice occurs."

While Gramsci discusses Hitler and Gandhi specifically, Raymond Williams formulates violence on a general plane that has implications for both of these political actors without specifically naming them. Williams reviews the various historical usages of the term *violence*, only to end by declaring that it is "clearly a word that needs early specific definition, if it is not to be done violence to—to be wrenched from its meaning or significance." According to this formulation, even Gandhi's notion of passive resistance or nonviolence becomes a modality of violence, since such passive resistance or noncooperation is aimed at the total breakdown of the colonial machinery. Likewise, such nonviolence actually encapsulates a radical break from Western civilization, toward a reassertion of what Gandhi calls Indian civilization.

The question of social change preoccupies Williams in the selection titled "Marxism and Literature." He suggests that a sociohistorical formation may best be described as a lived hegemony which is "always a process," that it has "continually to be renewed, recreated, defended and modified. It is also continually resisted, limited, altered, and challenged by pressures not at all its own." Such change takes place due to the presence of oppositional elements within a dominant (or emergent or residual) historical formation, and it is in the interaction of these elements that breaks occur, sometimes gradual, sometimes radical, and at other times violently revolutionary.

While examining the differences between precapitalist and capitalist societies, Pierre Bourdieu, even more than Williams, focuses on dominant formations. Bourdieu suggests that relationships of domination and subordination are maintained by forms of violence, which he distinguishes as "overt (physical or economic) violence, or symbolic violence—censored, euphemized, i.e., unrecognizable, socially recognized violence." Bourdieu asserts that precapitalist societies depend heavily on symbolic violence because in such societies relationships of domination are maintained through the establishment of relationships of personal dependence, which must be misrecognized and "euphemized" so that the relationships of domination are not destroyed. He suggests that such symbolic violence, manifested in the debt or in the gift, coexists with overt violence; it is used whenever the maintenance of the relationships of domination becomes impossible merely through overt violence. This is applicable both to Gandhi's platform of the refusal of Western civilization and to Malcolm X's warning to beware the blue-eyed white man who patronizes the Negro. Just as Gandhi's refusal of Western civilization is a refusal of that very gift of civilization through which the colonial enterprise legitimated itself, and in that sense, a flat refusal of the colonial enterprise and of its legitimacy, so Malcolm X's refusal of the white man's patronization of the Negro is about independence from precisely that yoke which the symbolic violence of patronage maintains and restores.

Refusal can take many forms, and it is the concern of James Scott to identify major forms of political discourse and their implications for insuring domination or resisting subordination. Scott identifies four. The first is also "the safest and most public form . . . which takes as its basis the flattering self-image of elites." The second, what Scott calls the hidden transcript, concerns the behavior of the dominated when they are not under surveillance, when they can speak out the anger that "they must necessarily choke back when in the presence of the masters and mistresses." The third and more subversive form of political discourse is the "politics of disguise and anonymity that takes place in public but is designed to have a double meaning or to shield the identity of the actors. Rumour, gossip, folk tales, jokes, songs, rituals, codes, and euphemisms" are examples of this discourse. The most "explosive" form of discourse for Scott is the "rupture of the political cordon sanitaire between the hidden and the public transcript." In this instance the subordinate makes public the anger that is usually hidden from the dominant gaze.

It is only through the analytic of violence that one can see how these four levels are related. While the public transcript maintains its respectability and poise through the subordinates' fear of violence and punishment should they speak their minds, in the realm of the hidden transcript the subordinates are joined together precisely by a brotherhood of violence, which projects a fantasy of meting out to the master what is suffered by the dominated. It is this fantasy of violating the hierarchy that is taken to a further level in the third realm of disguise, where it becomes a form of organizing discontent into resistance, sometimes through rumor and gossip, sometimes through folktales and rituals. Such resistance evades the power that can punish, since it flourishes and accumulates force precisely because it cannot be localized and repressed. The fourth level may be seen as the stage where the fantasy of violating the master becomes an actuality, when the subordinate commits graphic violence, not only to the master or to the dominant in question but also to the very code of behavior set up by the public transcript. Both Malcolm X and Gandhi belong to this fourth stage. Malcolm X, addressing both friends and enemies, publicly warns about the necessity of violence if the black community does not become politically, economically, and socially independent, while Gandhi advocates nonviolence so as to dismiss the British colonizers from India, thereby doing violence to the codes of subordination and obedience that the colonizer-colonized relationship has set up.

An Indian freedom-fighter and political philosopher best known for his theory of noncooperation and nonviolence as a means to gaining independence from British colonial rule, Mohandas K. Gandhi began his career as a lawyer in South Africa, after having obtained his degree in England. It was in South Africa, while working for the rights of the South Asian merchant and working-class communities, that he began what he called his "experiments with truth." His application to work as an advocate for the supreme court was vehemently opposed by the Law Society of Natal on the grounds that he was a colored man, but the chief justice rejected the opposition demands and accepted Gandhi's application, enabling him to practice as a lawyer in South Africa. Gandhi then set to work intensively, among other projects, on the plight of indentured laborers, trying to set them legally free from abusive masters and help them to find new employment.

While in South Africa, Gandhi also formulated his renowned philosophy, denoted by the term satyagraha *(satya meaning truth, graha meaning standing firm or grasping). It became the rallying cry for Indian freedom-fighters and later influenced the American civil-rights movement via proponents such as Martin Luther King Jr. In* An Autobiography *Gandhi describes how the term* passive resistance *did not approximate his philosophy and how satyagraha was an active, energizing outlook. Gandhi also examines the evolution of his philosophy, which hinges on the dual notions of* ahimsa *(nonviolence) and* brahmacharya *(self-restraint). Gandhi goes on to explain how he employs these two notions in his own life and daily dealings with colonial officers and with fellow Indians: in his strict vegetarian diet and refusal of Western medicine, in his abstinence from sex, and in his self-restraint in confrontational situations. He describes how these two notions come together in the embodiment of the spinning wheel, as a way to* swaraj *(self-rule) and as a "panacea for the growing pauperism of India."*

Indeed, the spinning wheel became a most powerful symbol of the nationalist movement: through the handloom, every Indian could spin his or her own material, a crude cloth called khadi, *which could be used for clothing. Both khadi and the spinning wheel stood for self-reliance and noncooperation. Manufacturing one's own clothing represented the refusal to buy European-manufactured cloth, and it was also a step toward refusing to allow one's country to be a market for European goods. Because it is this philosophy that the spinning wheel symbolized, it is the topic of the selection from* Hind Swaraj *included in this anthology.*

Decisive moments in Gandhi's life shaped the emergence of modern India, from his defiant organization of the Salt March (1930) to his crusade on behalf of the parity for

Muslims that led to his own murder by a Hindu fanatic in 1948. An indefatigable speaker, letter writer, and essayist, Gandhi left An Autobiography: The Story of My Experiments with Truth *(1957) and a mountainous literary legacy posthumously edited in the ninety-eight volumes of* The Collected Works of Mahatma Gandhi *(1958).*

Hind Swaraj, or Indian Home Rule

MOHANDAS K. GANDHI

CHAPTER 13. WHAT IS TRUE CIVILIZATION?

Reader: You have denounced railways, lawyers, and doctors, I can see that you will discard all machinery. What, then, is civilization?

Editor: The answer to that question is not difficult. I believe that the civilization India has evolved is not to be beaten in the world. Nothing can equal the seeds sown by our ancestors. Rome went, Greece shared the same fate; the might of the Pharaohs was broken; Japan has become westernized; of China nothing can be said; but India is still, somehow or other, sound at the foundation. The people of Europe learn their lessons from the writings of the men of Greece or Rome, which exist no longer in their former glory. In trying to learn from them, the Europeans imagine that they will avoid the mistakes of Greece and Rome. Such is their pitiable condition. In the midst of all this India remains immovable and that is her glory. It is a charge against India that her people are so uncivilized, ignorant, and stolid, that it is not possible to induce them to adopt any changes. It is a charge really against our merit. What we have tested and found true on the anvil of experience, we dare not change. Many thrust their advice upon India, and she remains steady. This is her beauty: it is the sheet-anchor of our hope.

Civilization is that mode of conduct which points out to man the path of duty. Performance of duty and observance of morality are convertible terms. To observe morality is to attain mastery over our mind and our passions. So doing, we know ourselves. The Gujarati equivalent for civilization means "good conduct."

If this definition be correct, then India, as so many writers have shown, has nothing to learn from anybody else, and this is as it should be. We notice that the mind is a restless bird; the more it gets the more it wants, and still remains unsatisfied. The more we indulge in our passions the more unbridled they become. Our ancestors, therefore, set a limit to our indulgences. They saw that happiness was largely a mental condition. A man is not necessarily happy because he is rich, or unhappy because he is poor. The rich are often seen to be unhappy, the poor to be happy. Millions will always remain poor. Observing all this, our ancestors dissuaded us from luxuries and pleasures. We have managed with the same kind of plough as existed thousands of years ago. We have retained the same kind of cottages that we had in former times and our indigenous education remains the same as before. We have no system of life-corroding competition. Each followed his own occupation or trade and charged a regulation wage. It was not that we did not know how to invent machinery, but our forefathers knew that, if we set our hearts after such things, we would become slaves and lose our moral fibre. They, therefore, after due deliberation decided that we should only do what we could with our hands and feet. They saw that our real happiness and health consisted in a proper use of our hands and feet. They further reasoned that large cities were a snare and a useless encumbrance and that people would not be happy in them, that there would be gangs of thieves and robbers, prostitution and vice flourishing in them and that poor men would be robbed by rich men. They were, therefore, satisfied in small villages. They saw that kings and their swords were inferior to the sword of ethics, and they, therefore, held the sovereigns of the earth to be inferior to the Rishis and the Fakirs. A nation with a constitution like this is fitter to teach others than to learn from others. This nation had courts, lawyers, and doctors, but they were all within bounds. Everybody knew that these professions were not particularly superior; moreover, these vakils and qaids did not rob people; they were considered people's dependants, not their masters. Justice was tolerably fair. The ordinary rule was to avoid courts. There were no touts to lure people into them. This evil, too, was noticeable only in and round capitals. The common people lived independently and followed their agricultural occupation. They enjoyed true Home Rule.

And where this cursed modern civilization has not reached, India remains as it was before. The inhabitants of that part of India will very properly laugh at your new-fangled notions. The English do not rule over them, nor will you ever rule over them. Those in whose name we speak we do not know, nor do they know us. I would certainly advise you and those like you who love the motherland to go into the interior that has yet been not polluted by the railways and to live there for six months; you might then be patriotic and speak of Home Rule.

Now you see what I consider to be real civilization. Those who want to change conditions such as I have described are enemies of the country and are sinners.

Reader: It would be all right if India were exactly as you described it, but it is also India where there are hundreds of child widows, where two-year-old babies are married, where twelve-year-old girls are mothers and housewives, where women practice polyandry, where the practice of Niyoga obtains, where, in the name of religion, girls dedicate themselves to prostitution, and in the name of religion sheep and goats are killed. Do you consider these also symbols of the civilization that you described?

Editor: You make a mistake. The defects that you have shown are defects. Nobody mistakes them for ancient civilization. They remain in spite of it. Attempts have always been made and will be made to remove them. We may utilize the new spirit that is born in us for purging ourselves of these evils. But what I have described to you as emblems of modern civilization are accepted as such by its votaries. The Indian civilization, as described by me, has been so described by its votaries. In no part of the world, and under no civilization, have all men attained perfection. The tendency of the Indian civilization is to elevate the moral being, that of the Western civilization is to propagate immorality. The latter is godless, the former is based on a belief in God. So understanding and so believing, it behooves every lover of India to cling to the old Indian civilization even as a child clings to the mother's breast.

CHAPTER 14. HOW CAN INDIA BECOME FREE?

Reader: I appreciate your views about civilization. I will have to think over them. I cannot take them in all at once. What, then, holding the views you do, would you suggest for freeing India?

Editor: I do not expect my views to be accepted all of a sudden. My duty is to place them before readers like yourself. Time can be trusted to do the rest. We have already examined the conditions for freeing India, but we have done so indirectly; we will now do so directly. It is a world-known maxim that the removal of the cause of a disease results in the removal of the disease itself. Similarly if the cause of India's slavery be removed, India can become free.

Reader: If Indian civilization is, as you say, the best of all, how do you account for India's slavery?

Editor: This civilization is unquestionably the best, but it is to be observed that all civilizations have been on their trial. The civilization which is permanent outlives it. Because these sons of India were found wanting, its civilization has been placed in jeopardy. But its strength is to be seen in its ability to survive the shock. Moreover, the whole of India is not touched. Those alone who have been affected by Western civilization have become enslaved. We measure the universe by our own miserable foot-rule. When we are slaves, we think that the whole universe is enslaved. Because we are in an abject condition, we think that the whole of India is in that condition. As a matter of fact, it is not so, yet it is as well to impute our slavery to the whole of India. But if we bear in mind the above fact, we can see that if we become free, India is free. And in this thought you have a definition of Swaraj. It is Swaraj when we learn to rule ourselves. It is, therefore, in the palm of our hands. Do not consider this Swaraj to be like a dream. There is no idea of sitting still. The Swaraj that I wish to picture is such that, after we have once realized it, we shall endeavor to the end of our life-time to persuade others to do likewise. But such Swaraj has to be experienced, by each one for himself. One drowning man will never save another. Slaves ourselves, it would be a mere pretension to think of freeing others. Now you will have seen that it is not necessary for us to have as our goal the expulsion of the English. If the English become Indianized, we can accommodate them. If they wish to remain in India along with their civilization, there is no room for them. It lies with us to bring about such a state of things.

Reader: It is impossible that Englishmen should ever become Indianized.

Editor: To say that is equivalent to saying that the English have no humanity in them. And it is really beside the point whether they become so or not. If we keep our own houses in order, only those who are fit to live in it will remain. Others will leave of their own accord. Such things occur within the experience of all of us.

Reader: But it has not occurred in history.

Editor: To believe that what has not occurred in history will not occur at all is to argue disbelief in the dignity of man. At any rate, it behooves us to try what appeals to our reason. All countries are not similarly conditioned. The condition of India is unique. Its strength is immeasurable. We need not, therefore, refer to the history of other countries. I have drawn attention to the fact that, when other civilizations have succumbed, the Indian has survived many a shock.

Reader: I cannot follow this. There seems little doubt that we shall have to expel the English by force of arms. So long as they are in the country we cannot rest. One of our poets says that slaves cannot even dream of happiness. We are day by day becoming weakened owning to the presence of the English. Our greatness is gone; our people look like terrified men. The English are in the country like a blight which we must remove by every means.

Editor: In your excitement, you have forgotten all we have been considering. We brought the English, and we keep them. Why do you forget that our adoption of their civilization makes their presence in India at all possible? Your hatred against them ought to be transferred to their civilization. But let us assume that we have to drive away the English by fighting, how is that to be done?

Reader: In the same way as Italy did it. What was possible for Mazzini and Garibaldi is possible for us. You cannot deny that they were very great men.

Editor: It is well that you have instanced Italy. Mazzini was a great and good man; Garibaldi was a great warrior. Both are adorable; from their lives we can learn much. But the condition of Italy was different from that of India. In the first instance, the difference between Mazzini and Garibaldi is worth noting. Mazzini's ambition was not and has not yet been realized regarding Italy. Mazzini has shown in his writings on the duty of man that every man must learn to rule himself. This has not happened in Italy. Garibaldi did not hold this view of Mazzini's. Garibaldi gave, and every Italian took arms. Italy and Austria had the same civilization; they were cousins in this respect. It was a matter of tit for tat. Garibaldi simply wanted Italy to be free from the Austrian yoke. The machinations of Minister Cavour disgrace that portion of the history of Italy. And what has been the result? If you believe that because Italians rule Italy the Italian nation is happy, you are groping in darkness. Mazzini has shown conclusively that Italy did not become free. Victor Emanuel gave one meaning to the expression; Mazzini gave another. According to Emanuel, Cavour, and even Garibaldi, Italy meant the King of Italy and his henchmen. According to Mazzini, it meant the whole of the Italian people, that is, its agriculturists. Emanuel was only its servant. The Italy of Mazzini still remains in a state of slavery. At the time of the so-called national war, it was a game of chess between two rival kings and the people of Italy as pawns. The working classes in that land are still unhappy. They, therefore, indulge in assassination, rise in revolt, and rebellion on their part is always expected. What substantial gain did Italy obtain after the withdrawal of the Austrian troops? The gain was only nominal. The reforms for the sake of which the war was supposed to have been undertaken have not yet been granted. The condition of the people in general still remains the same. I am sure you do not wish to reproduce such a condition in India. I believe that you want the millions of India to be happy, not that you want the reins of Government in your hands. If that be so, we have to consider only one thing: how can the millions obtain self-rule? You will admit that people under several Indian princes are being ground down. The latter mercilessly crush them. Their tyranny is greater than that of the English, and if you want such tyranny in India, then we shall never agree. My patriotism does not teach me that I am to allow people to be crushed under the heel of Indian princes if only the English retire. If I have the power, I should resist the tyranny of Indian princes just as much as that of the English. By patriotism I mean the welfare of the whole people, and if I could secure it at the hands of the English, I should bow down my head to them. If any Englishman dedicated his life to securing the freedom of India, resisting tyranny, and serving the land, I should welcome that Englishman as an Indian.

Again, India can fight like Italy only when she has arms. You have not considered this problem at all. The English are splendidly armed; that does not frighten me, but it is clear that, to pit ourselves against them in arms, thousands of Indians must be armed. If such a thing be possible, how many years will it take? Moreover, to arm India on a large scale is to Europeanize it. Then her condition will be just as pitiable as that of Europe. This means, in short, that India must accept European civilization, and if that is what we want, the best thing is that we have among us those who are so well trained in that civilization. We will fight for a few rights, will get what we can and so pass our days. But the fact is that the Indian nation will not adopt arms, and it is well that it does not.

Reader: You are over-stating the facts. All need not be armed. At first, we shall assassinate a few Englishmen and strike terror; then, a few men who will have been armed will fight openly. We may have to lose a quarter of a million men, more or less, but we shall regain our land. We shall undertake guerilla warfare, and defeat the English.

Editor: That is to say, you want to make the holy land of India unholy. Do you not tremble to think of freeing India by assassination? What we need to do is to sacrifice ourselves. It is a cowardly thought, that of killing others. Whom do you suppose to free by assassination? The millions of India do not desire it. Those who are intoxicated by the wretched modern civilization think these things. Those who will rise to power by murder will certainly not make the nation happy. Those who believe that India has gained by Dhingra's act and other similar acts in India make a serious mistake. Dhingra was a patriot, but his love was blind. He gave his body in the wrong way; its ultimate result can only be mischievous.

Reader: But you will admit that the English have been frightened by these murders, and that Lord Morley's reforms are due to fear.

Editor: The English are both a timid and a brave nation. England is, I believe, easily influenced by the use of gunpowder. It is possible that Lord Morley has granted the reforms through fear, but what is granted under fear can be retained only so long as the fear lasts.

CHAPTER 16. BRUTE FORCE

Reader: This is a new doctrine, that what is gained through fear is retained only while the fear lasts. Surely, what is given will not be withdrawn?

Editor: Not so. The Proclamation of 1857 was given at the end of a revolt, and for the purpose of preserving peace. When peace was secured and people became simple-minded its full effect was toned down. If I cease stealing for fear of punishment, I would recommence the operation as soon as the fear is withdrawn from me. This is almost a universal experience. We have assumed that we can get men to do things by force and, therefore, we use force.

Reader: Will you not admit that you are arguing against yourself? You know that what the English obtained in their own country they obtained by using brute force. I know you have argued that what they have obtained is useless, but that does not affect my argument. They wanted useless things and they got them. My point is that their desire was fulfilled. What does it matter what means they adopted? Why should we not obtain our goal, which is good, by any means whatsoever, even by using violence? Shall I think of the means when I have to deal with a thief in the house? My duty is to drive him out anyhow. You seem to admit that we have received nothing, and that we shall receive nothing by petitioning. Why, then, may we not do so by using brute force? And to retain what we may receive we shall keep up by the fear by using the same force to the extent that it may be necessary. You will find fault with a continuance of force to prevent a child from thrusting its foot into the fire. Somehow or other we have to gain our end.

Editor: Your reasoning is plausible. It has deluded many. I have used similar arguments before now. But I think I know better now, and I shall endeavour to undeceive you. Let us first take the agreement that we are justified in gaining our end by using brute force because the English gained theirs by using similar means. It is perfectly true that they used brute force and that it is possible for us to do likewise, but by using similar means we can get only the same thing that they got. You will admit that we do not want that. Your belief that there is no connection between the means and the end is a great mistake. Through that mistake even men who have been considered religious have committed grievous crimes. Your reasoning is the same as saying that we can get a rose through planting a noxious weed. If I want to cross the ocean, I can do so only by means of a vessel; if I were to use a cart for that purpose, both the cart and I would soon find the bottom. "As is the God, so is the votary," is a maxim worth considering. Its meaning has been distorted and men have gone astray. The means may be likened to a seed, the end to a tree; and there is just the same inviolable connection between the means and the end as there is between the seed and the tree. I am not likely to obtain the result flowing from the worship of God by laying myself prostrate before Satan. If, therefore, anyone were to say: "I want to worship God; it does not matter that I do so by means of Satan," it would be set down as ignorant folly. We reap exactly as we sow. The English in 1833 obtained greater voting power by violence. Did they by using brute force better appreciate their duty? They wanted the right of voting, which they obtained by using physical force. But real rights are a result of performance of duty; these rights they have not obtained. We, therefore, have before us in England the force of everybody wanting and insisting on his rights, nobody thinking of his duty. And, where everybody wants rights, who shall give them to whom? I do not wish to imply that they do no duties. They don't perform the duties corresponding to those rights; and as they do not perform that particular duty, namely, acquire fitness, their rights have proven a burden to them. In other words, what they have obtained is an exact result of the means they adopted. They used the means corresponding to the end. If I want to deprive you of your watch, I shall certainly have to fight for it; if I want to buy your watch, I shall have to pay you for it; and if I want a gift I shall have to plead for it; and, according to the means I employ, the watch is stolen property, my own property, or a donation. Thus we see three different results from three different means. Will you still say that means do not matter?

Now we shall take the example given by you of the thief to be driven out. I do not agree with you that the thief may be driven out by any means. If it is my father who has come to steal I shall use one kind of means. If it is an acquaintance I shall use another; and in case of a perfect stranger I shall use a third. If it is a white man, you will perhaps say you will use means different from those you will adopt with an Indian thief. If it is a weakling, the means will be different from those to be adopted for dealing with an equal in physical strength; and if the thief is armed from top to toe, I shall simply remain quiet. Thus we have a variety of means between the father and the armed man. Again, I fancy that I should pretend to be sleeping whether the thief was my father or that strong armed man. The reason for this is that my father would also be armed and I should succumb to the strength possessed by either and allow my things to be stolen. The strength of my father would make me weep with pity; the strength of the armed man would rouse in me anger and we should become enemies. Such is the curious situation. From these examples we may not be able to agree as to the means to be adopted in each case. I myself seem clearly to see what should be done in all these cases, but the remedy may frighten you. I therefore hesitate to place it before you. For the time being I will leave you to guess it, and if you cannot, it is clear you will have to adopt different means in each case. You will also have seen that any means will not avail to drive away the thief. You will have to adopt means to fit each case. Hence it follows that your duty is *not* to drive away the thief by any means you like.

Let us proceed a little further. That well-armed man has stolen your property; you have harboured the thought of his act; you are filled with anger; you argue that you want to punish that rogue, not for your own sake, but for the good of your neighbours; you have collected a number of armed men, you want to take his house by assault; he is duly informed of it, he runs away; he too is incensed. He collects his brother robbers, and sends you a defiant message that he will commit robbery in broad daylight. You are strong, you do not fear him, you are prepared to receive him. Meanwhile, the robber pesters your neighbours. They complain before you. You reply that you are doing all for their sake, yet you do not mind that your own goods have been stolen. Your neighbours reply that the robber never pestered them before, and that he commenced his depredations only after you declared hostilities against him. You are between Scylla and Charybdis. You are full of pity for the poor men. What they say is true. What are you to do? You will be disgraced if you now leave the robber alone. You, therefore, tell the poor men: "Never mind. Come, my wealth is yours, I will give you arms, I will teach you how to use them, you should belabour the rogue; don't you leave him alone." And so the battle grows; the robbers increase in numbers; your neighbours have deliberately put themselves to inconvenience. Thus the result of wanting to take revenge upon the robber is that you have disturbed your own peace; you are in perpetual fear of being robbed and assaulted; your courage has given place to cowardice. If you will patiently examine the argument, you will see that I have not overdrawn the picture. This is one of the means. Now let us examine the other. You set this armed robber down as an ignorant brother; you intend to reason with him at a suitable opportunity; you argue that he is, after all, a fellow-man; you do not know what prompted him to steal. You, therefore, decide that, when you can, you will destroy the man's motive for stealing. Whilst you are thus reasoning with yourself the man comes again to steal. Instead of being angry with him you take pity on him. You think that this stealing habit must be a disease with him. Henceforth, you, therefore, keep your doors and windows open, you change your sleeping-place, and you keep your things in a manner most accessible to him. The robber comes again and is confused as all this is new to him; nevertheless, he takes away your things, but his mind is agitated. He inquires about you in the village, he comes to learn about your broad and loving heart, he repents, he begs your pardon, he returns you your things, and he leaves off the stealing habit. He becomes your servant, and you find for him honourable employment. This is the second method. Thus, you see, different means have brought about totally different results. I do not wish to deduce from this that robbers will act in the above manner or that all will have the same pity and love like you, but I only wish to show that fair means alone can produce fair results, and that, at least in the majority of cases, if not indeed in all, the force of love and pity is infinitely greater than the force of arms. There is harm in the exercise of brute force, never in that of pity.

Now we will take the question of petitioning. It is a fact beyond dispute that a petition, without the backing of force, is useless. However, the late Justice Ranade used to say that petitions served a useful purpose because they were a means of educating people. They give the latter an idea of their condition and warn the rulers. From this point of view, they are not altogether useless. A petition of equal is a sign of courtesy; a petition from a slave is a symbol of his slavery. A petition backed by force is a petition from an equal and, when he transmits his demand in the form of a petition, it testifies to his nobility. Two kinds of force can back petitions. "We shall hurt if you do not give this," is one kind of force; it is the force of arms, whose evil results we have already examined. The second kind of force can thus be stated: "If you do not concede our demand, we shall be no longer your petitioners. You can govern us only so long as we remain the governed; we shall no longer have any dealings with you." The force implied in this may be described as love-force, soul-force, or, more popularly but less accurately, passive resistance. This force is indestructible. He who uses it perfectly understands his position. We have an ancient proverb which literally means: "One negative cures thirty-six diseases." The force of arms is powerless when matched against the force of love or the soul.

Now we shall take your last illustration, that of the child thrusting its foot into fire. It will not avail you. What do you really do to the child? Supposing that it can exert so much physical force that it renders you powerless and rushes into fire, then you cannot prevent it. There are only two remedies open to you— either you must kill it in order to prevent it from perishing in the flames, or you must give your own life because you do not wish to see it perish before your very eyes. You will not kill it. If your heart is not quite full of pity, it is possible that you will not surrender yourself by preceding the child and going into the fire yourself. You, therefore, helplessly allow it to go into the flames. Thus, at any rate, you are not using physical force. I hope you will not consider that it is still physical force, though of a low order, when you would forcibly prevent the child from rushing towards the fire if you could. That force is of a different order and we have to understand what it is.

Remember that, in thus preventing the child, you are minding entirely its own interest; you are exercising authority for its sole benefit. Your example does not apply to the English. In using brute force against the English you consult entirely your own, that is the national, interest. There is no question here either of pity or of love. If you say that the actions of the English, being evil, represent fire, and that they proceed to their actions through ignorance, and that therefore they occupy the position of a child and that you want to protect such a child, then you will have to overtake every evil action of that kind by whomsoever committed and, as in the case of the evil child, you will have to sacrifice yourself. If you are capable of such immeasurable pity, I wish you well in its exercise.

CHAPTER 17. PASSIVE RESISTANCE

Reader: Is there any historical evidence as to the success of what you have called soul-force or truth-force? No instance seems to have happened of any nation having risen through soul-force. I still think that the evil-doers will not cease doing evil without physical punishment.

Editor: The poet Tulsidas has said: "Of religion, pity, or love, is the root, as egotism of the body. Therefore, we should not abandon pity so long as we are alive." This appears to me to be a scientific truth. I believe in it as much as I believe in two and two being four. The force of love is the same as the force of the soul or truth. We have evidence of its working at every step. The universe would disappear without the existence of that force. But you ask for historical evidence. It is, therefore, necessary to know what history means. The Gujarati equivalent means: "It so happened." If that is the meaning of history, it is possible to give copious evidence. But, if it means the doings of kings and emperors, there can be no evidence of soul-force or passive resistance in such history. You cannot expect silver ore in a tin mine. History, as we know it, is a record of the wars of the world, and so there is a proverb among Englishmen that a nation which has no history, that is, no wars, is a happy nation. How kings played, how they became enemies of one another, how they murdered one another, is found accurately recorded in history, and if this were all that happened in the world, it would have been ended long ago. If the story of the universe had commenced with wars, not a man would have been found alive today. Those people who have been warred against have disappeared as, for instance, the natives of Australia of whom hardly a man was left alive by the intruders. Mark, please, that these natives did not use soul-force in self-defence, and it does not require much foresight to know that the Australians will share the same fate as their victims. "Those that take the sword shall perish by the sword." With us the proverb is that professional swimmers will find a watery grave.

The fact that there are so many men still alive in the world shows that it is based not on the force of arms but on the force of truth or love. Therefore, the greatest and most unimpeachable evidence of the success of this force is to be found in the fact that, in spite of the wars of the world, it still lives on.

Thousands, indeed tens of thousands, depend for their existence on a very active working of this force. Little quarrels of millions of families in their daily lives disappear before the exercise of this force. Hundreds of nations live in peace. History does not and cannot take note of this fact. History is really a record of every interruption of the even working of the force of love of the soul.

Two brothers quarrel; one of them repents and re-awakens the love that was lying dormant in him; the two again begin to live in peace; nobody takes note of this. But if the two brothers, through the intervention of solicitors or some other reason, take up arms or go to law—which is another form of exhibition of brute force,—their doings would be immediately noticed in the press, they would be the talk of their neighbours and would probably go down to history. And what is true of families and communities is true of nations. There is no reason to believe that there is one law for families and another for nations. History, then, is a record of an interruption of the course of nature. Soul-force, being natural, is not noted in history.

Reader: According to what you say, it is plain that instances of this kind of passive resistance are not to be found in history. It is necessary to understand this passive resistance more fully. It will be better, therefore, if you enlarge upon it.

Editor: Passive resistance is a method of securing rights by personal suffering; it is the reverse of resistance by arms. When I refuse to do a thing that is repugnant to my conscience, I use soul-force. For instance, the Government of the day has passed a law which is applicable to me. I do not like it. If by using violence I force the Government to repeal the law, I am employing what may be termed body-force. If I do not obey the law and accept the penalty for its breach, I use soul-force. It involves sacrifice of self.

Everybody admits that sacrifice of self is infinitely superior to sacrifice of others. Moreover, if this kind of force is used in a cause that is unjust, only the person using it suffers. He does not make others suffer for his mistakes. Men have before now done many things which were subsequently found to have been wrong. No man can claim that he is absolutely in the right or that a particular thing is wrong because he thinks so, but it is wrong for him so long as that is his deliberate judgement. It is therefore meet that he should not do that which he knows to be wrong, and suffer the consequence whatever it may be. This is the key to use of soul-force.

Reader: You would then disregard laws—this is rank disloyalty. We have always been considered a law-abiding nation. You seem to be going even beyond the extremists. They say that we must obey the laws that have been passed, but that if the laws be bad, we must drive out the law-givers even by force.

Editor: Whether I go beyond them or whether I do not is a matter of no consequence to either of us. We simply want to find out what is right and to act accordingly. The real meaning of the statement that we are a law-abiding nation is that we are passive resisters. When we do not like certain laws, we do not break the heads of the law-givers but we suffer and do not submit to the laws. That we should obey laws whether good or bad is a new-fangled notion. There was no such thing in former days. The people disregarded those laws they did not like and suffered the penalties for their breach. It is contrary to our manhood if we obey laws repugnant to our conscience. Such teaching is opposed to religion and means slavery. If the Government were to ask us to go about without any clothing, should we do so? If I were a passive resister, I would say to them that I would have nothing to do with their law. But we have so forgotten ourselves and become so compliant that we do not mind any degrading laws.

A man who realized his manhood, who fears only God, will fear no one else. Man-made laws are not necessarily binding on him. Even the Government does not expect any such thing from us. They do not say: "You must do such and such a thing," but they ask "If you do not do it, we will punish you." We are sunk so low that we fancy that it is our duty and our religion to do what the law lays down. If man will only realize that it is unmanly to obey laws that are unjust, no man's tyranny will enslave him. This is the key to self-rule or home-rule.

It is a superstition and ungodly thing to believe that an act of a majority binds a minority. Many examples can be given in which acts of majorities will be found to have been wrong and those minorities have been right. All reforms owe their origin to the initiation of minorities in opposition to majorities. If among a band of robbers knowledge of robbing is obligatory, is a pious man to accept the obligation? So long as the superstition that men should obey unjust laws exists, so long will their slavery exist. And a passive resister alone can remove such a superstition.

To use brute-force, to use gunpowder, is contrary to passive resistance, for it means that we want our opponent to do by force that which we desire but he does not. And if such a use of force is justifiable, surely he is entitled to do likewise by us. And so we should never come to an agreement. We may simply fancy, like the blind horse moving in a circle round a mill, that we are making progress. Those who believe that they are not bound to obey laws which are repugnant to their conscience have only the remedy of passive resistance open to them. Any other must lead to disaster.

Reader: From what you say I deduce that passive resistance is a splendid weapon of the weak, but that when they are strong they may take up arms.

Editor: This is gross ignorance. Passive resistance, that is, soul-force, is matchless. It is superior to the force of arms. How, then, can it be considered only a weapon of the weak? Physical-force men are strangers to the courage that is requisite in a passive resister. Do you believe that a coward can ever disobey a law that he dislikes? Extremists are considered to be advocates of brute force. Why do they, then, talk about obeying laws? I do not blame them. They can say nothing else. When they succeed in driving out the English and they themselves become governors, they will want you and me to obey their laws. And that is a fitting thing for their constitution. But a passive resister will say he will not obey a law that is against his conscience, even though he may be blown to pieces at the mouth of a cannon.

What do you think? Wherein is courage required—in blowing others to pieces from behind a cannon, or with a smiling face to approach a cannon and be blown to pieces? Who is the true warrior—he who keeps death always as a bosom-friend, or he who controls the death of others? Believe me that a man devoid of courage and manhood can never be a passive resister.

This, however, I will admit: that even a man weak in body is capable of suffering this resistance. One man can offer it just as well as millions. Both men and women can indulge in it. It does not require the training of an army; it needs no jiu-jitsu. Control over the mind is alone necessary, and when that is attained, man is free like the king of the forest and his very glance withers the enemy.

Passive resistance is an all-sided sword; it can be used anyhow; it blesses him who uses it and him against whom it is used. Without drawing a drop of blood, it produces far-reaching results. It never rusts and cannot be stolen. Competition between passive resisters does not exhaust. The sword of passive resistance does not require a scabbard. It is strange indeed that you should consider such a weapon to be a weapon merely in the weak.

Reader: You have said that passive resistance is a specialty of India. Have cannons never been used in India?

Editor: Evidently, in your opinion, India means its few princes. To me it means its teeming millions on whom depends the existence of its princes and our own.

Kings will always use their kingly weapons. To use force is bred in them. They want to command, but those who have to obey commands do not want guns; and these are in a majority throughout the world. They have to learn either body-force or soul-force. Where they learn the former, both the rulers and the ruled become like so many madmen; but where they learn soul-force the commands of the rulers do not go beyond the point of their swords, for true men disregard unjust commands. Peasants have never been subdued by the sword and never will be. They do not know the use of the sword, and they are not frightened by the use of it by others. That nation is great which rests its head upon death as its pillow. Those who defy death are free from all fear. For those who are labouring under the delusive charms of brute-force, this picture is not overdrawn. The fact is that, in India, the nation at large has generally used passive resistance in all departments of life. We cease to co-operate with our rulers when they displease us. This is passive resistance.

I remember an instance .when, in a small principality, the villagers were offended by some command issued by the prince. The former immediately began vacating the village. The prince became nervous, apologized to his subjects, and withdrew his command. Many such instances can be found in India. Real Home Rule is possible only where passive resistance is the guiding force of the people. Any other rule is foreign rule.

Reader: Then you will say that it is not all necessary for us to train the body?

Editor: I will certainly not say any such thing. It is difficult to become a passive resister unless the body is trained. As a rule, the mind, residing in a body that has become weakened by pampering, is also weak, and where there is no strength of mind there can be no strength of soul. We shall have to improve our physique by getting rid of infant marriages and luxurious living. If I were to ask a man with a shattered body to face a cannon's mouth I should make a laughing-stock of myself.

Reader: From what you say, then, it would appear that it is not a small thing to become a passive resister and, if that is so, I should like you to explain how a man may become one.

Editor: To become a passive resister is easy enough but it is also equally difficult. I have known a lad of fourteen years become a passive resister; I have known also sick people do likewise; and I have also known physically strong and otherwise happy people unable to take up passive resistance. After a great deal of experience it seems to me that those who want to become passive resisters for the service of the country have to observe perfect chastity, adopt poverty, follow truth, and cultivate fearlessness.

Chastity is one of the greatest disciplines without which the mind cannot attain requisite firmness. A man who is unchaste loses stamina, becomes emasculated and cowardly. He whose mind is given over to animal passions is not capable of any great effort. This can be proved by innumerable instances. What, then, is a married person to do is the question that arises naturally; and yet it need not. When a husband and wife gratify the passions, it is no less an animal indulgence on that account. Such an indulgence, except for perpetuating the race, is strictly prohibited. But a passive resister has to avoid even that very limited indulgence because he can have no desire for progeny. A married man, therefore, can observe perfect chastity. This subject is not capable of being treated at greater length. Several questions arise: How is one to carry one's wife with one, what are her rights, and other similar questions. Yet those who wish to take part in a great work are bound to solve these puzzles.

Just as there is necessity for chastity, so is there for poverty. Pecuniary ambition and passive resistance cannot well go together. Those who have money are not expected to throw it away, but they *are* expected to be indifferent about it. They must be prepared to lose every penny rather than give up passive resistance.

Passive resistance has been described in the course of our discussion as truth-force. Truth, therefore, has necessarily to be followed and that at any cost. In this connection, academic questions such as whether a man may not lie in order to save a life, etc., arise, but these questions occur only to those who wish to justify lying. Those who want to follow truth every time are not placed in such a quandary; and if they are, they are still saved from a false position.

Passive resistance cannot proceed a step without fearlessness. Those alone can follow the path of passive resistance who are free from fear, whether as to their possessions, false honour, their relatives, the government, bodily injuries, or death.

These observances are not to be abandoned in the belief that they are difficult. Nature has implanted in the human breast the ability to cope with any difficulty or suffering that may come to man unprovoked. These qualities are worth having, even for those who do not wish to serve the country. Let there be no mistake, as those who want to train themselves in the use of arms are also obligated to have these qualities more or less. Everybody does not become a warrior for the wish. A would-be warrior will have to observe chastity and to be satisfied with poverty as his lot. A warrior without fearlessness cannot be conceived of. It may be thought that he would not need to be exactly truthful, but that quality follows real fearlessness. When a man abandons truth, he does so owing to fear in some shape or form. The above four attributes, then, need not frighten anyone. It may be as well here to note that a physical-force man has to have many other useless qualities which a passive resister never needs. And you will find that whatever extra effort a swordsman needs is due to lack of fearlessness. If he is an embodiment of the latter, the sword will drop from his hand that very moment. He does not need its support. One who is free from hatred requires no sword. A man with a stick suddenly came face to face with a lion and instinctively raised his weapon in self-defence. The man saw that he had only prated about fearlessness when there was none in him. That moment he dropped the stick and found himself free from all fear.

The dictator of Nazi Germany, Adolf Hitler was born in Austria-Hungary and grew up in Linz. He spent his early life fantasizing about becoming an artist. He tried twice to get into the Academy of Fine Arts, with no success. In 1913 he moved to Munich only to be recalled to Austria so that he could be recruited for military service. Although he was deemed unfit for military service in the Austrian army, when World War I broke out, he joined the German army. He earned a name for his bravery and was awarded the Iron Cross twice. He was wounded in 1916, and two years later he was gassed, as a result of which he was hospitalized until the end of the war. He joined the German Workers' Party in Munich in 1919, and later left the army to devote his time to reorganizing the party that in 1920 became the Nationalsozialistische Deutsche Arbeiterpartei, or the National Socialist German Workers Party. He became president of the party in 1921. In 1923 the party tried unsuccessfully to seize governmental power and to declare a revolution. As a result of this failed attempt, Hitler was sentenced to five years in prison, but he served only nine months. It was in prison that he wrote the first volume of Mein Kampf.

Once out of prison, Hitler set out to regain his position in party politics and to build the membership of the party. Aided by Germany's postwar atmosphere of general demoralization and of discontent with the peace treaty and with the Weimar Republic, the National Socialist Party's propaganda, with its terrorist tactics and show of strength, succeeded in making the party the second largest, garnering more than 6,000,000 votes in the 1930 election. In 1933 Hitler was invited to be the Chancellor of Germany. In 1934 the chancellorship and the presidency were merged, with Hitler being planted as the head of the armed forces of the Reich. What followed was the Nazi regime's aggressive campaign of expansion, which ended only as a result of its defeat in World War II. When Germany was defeated, Hitler and his longtime mistress, Eva Braun, committed suicide. (Some neofascists and others, however, claim that his death by suicide was a ruse and that Hitler lives on.)

Mein Kampf, *or* My Struggle, *details Hitler's youth, the events of World War I, and what Hitler calls the "betrayal" of Germany in 1918. The worst enemies of Germany were the Marxists and the Jews, the only solution for which was mass extermination. Hitler viewed inequality between different races as the natural order of things and claimed the superiority of the Aryan race; he also declared the preservation of the purity of this race as his ultimate goal. He regarded the existence of the state as justifiable only insofar as it fulfilled its function of preserving and acting in the interest of the German Volk. It was for this reason that the Weimar Republic and all democratic state formations were doomed to failure: they assumed an equality of the races that betrayed the interest of the German Volk. Indeed, the only state formation that could act in accordance with the interest of the Volk was the one led by the Führer, who was the embodiment of a unified Volk. The second volume of* Mein Kampf *is dedicated to outlining the program of the party in bringing this kind of state, a people's state, into being and to using any kind of violence and terrorism necessary to preserve this state.*

The following selection is from chapter 15, "The Right of Emergency Defense," in Mein Kampf.

The Right of Emergency Defense

ADOLF HITLER

The Armistice of November 1918 ushered in a policy which in all human probability was bound to lead gradually to total submission. Historical examples of a similar nature show that nations which lay down their arms without compelling reasons prefer in the ensuing period to accept the greatest humiliations and extortions rather than attempt to change their fate by a renewed appeal to force.

This is humanly understandable. A shrewd victor will, if possible, always present his demands to the vanquished in installments. And then, with a nation that has lost its character—and this is the case of everyone which voluntarily submits—he can be sure that it will not regard one more of these individual oppressions as an adequate reason for taking up arms again. The more extortions are willingly accepted in this way, the more unjustified it strikes people finally to take up the defensive against a new, apparently isolated, though constantly recurring, oppression, especially when, all in all, so much more and greater misfortune has already been borne in patient silence.

The fall of Carthage is the most horrible picture of such a slow execution of a people through its own desserts.

That is why Clausewitz in his *Drei Bekenntnisse* incomparably singles out this idea and nails it fast for all time, when he says: "That the stain of a cowardly submission can never be effaced; that this drop of poison in the blood of a people is passed on to posterity and will paralyze and undermine the strength of later generations"; that, on the other hand, "even the loss of this freedom after a bloody and honorable struggle assures the rebirth of a people and is the seed of life from which some day a new tree will strike fast roots."

Of course, a people that has lost all honor and character will not concern itself with such teachings. For no one who takes them to heart can sink so low;

only he who forgets them, or no longer wants to know them, collapses. There-fore, we must not expect those who embody a spineless submission suddenly to look into their hearts and, on the basis of reason and all human experience, begin to act differently than before. On the contrary, it is these men in particular who will dismiss all such teachings until either the nation is definitely ac-customed to its yoke of slavery or until better forces push to the surface, to wrest the power from the hands of the infamous spoilers. In the first case these people usually do not feel so badly, since not seldom they are appointed by the shrewd victors to the office of slave overseer, which these spineless natures usually wield more mercilessly over their people than any foreign beast put in by the enemy himself.

The development since 1918 shows us that in Germany the hope of winning the victor's favor by voluntary submission unfortunately determines the politi-cal opinions and the actions of the broad masses in the most catastrophic way. I attach special importance to emphasizing the *broad masses*, because I cannot bring myself to profess the belief that the commissions and omissions of our people's *leaders* are attributable to the same ruinous lunacy. As the leadership of our destinies has, since the end of the War, been quite openly furnished by Jews, we really cannot assume that faulty knowledge alone is the cause of our misfor-tune; we must, on the contrary, hold the conviction that conscious purpose is destroying our nation. And once we examine the apparent madness of our nation's leadership in the field of foreign affairs from this standpoint, it is revealed as the subtlest, ice-cold logic, in the service of the Jewish idea and struggle for world conquest.

And thus, it becomes understandable that the same time-span, which from 1806 to 1813 sufficed to imbue a totally collapsed Prussia with new vital energy and determination for struggle, today has not only elapsed unused, but, on the contrary, has led to an every-greater weakening of our state.

Seven years after November 1918, the Treat of Locarno was signed.[1]

The course of events was that indicated above: Once the disgraceful armistice had been signed, neither the energy nor the courage could be summoned sud-denly to oppose resistance to our foes' repressive measures, which subsequently were repeated over and over. Our enemies were too shrewd to demand too much at once. They always limit their extortions to the amount which, in their opinion—and that of the German leadership—would at the moment be bear-able enough so that an explosion of popular feeling need not be feared. But the more of these individual dictates had been signed, the less justified it seemed, because of a *single* additional extortion or exacted humiliation, to do the thing that had not been done because of so many others: to offer resistance. For this is the "drop of poison" of which Clausewitz speaks: the spinelessness which once begun must increase more and more and which gradually becomes the foulest heritage, burdening every future decision. It can become a terrible lead weight, a weight which a nation is not likely to shake off, but which finally drags it down into the existence of a slave race.

Thus, in Germany edicts of disarmament alternated with edicts of enslavement, political emasculation with economic pillage, and finally created that moral spirit which can regard the Dawes Plan as a stroke of good fortune and the Treaty of Locarno as success.[2] Viewing all this from a higher vantage-point, we can speak of one single piece of good fortune in all this misery, which is that, though men can be befuddled, the heavens cannot be bribed. For their blessing remained absent: since then hardship and care have been the constant companions of our people, and our one faithful ally has been misery. Destiny made no exception in this case, but gave us what we deserved. Since we no longer knew how to value honor, it teaches us at least to appreciate freedom in the matter of bread. By now people have learned to cry out for bread, but one of these days they will pray for freedom.

Bitter as was the collapse of our nation in the years after 1918, and obvious at that time, every man who dared prophesy even then what later always materialized was violently and resolutely persecuted. Wretched and bad as the leaders of our nation were, they were equally arrogant, and especially when it came to ridding themselves of undesired, because unpleasant, prophets. We were treated to the spectacle (as we still are today!) of the greatest parliamentary thick-heads, regular saddlers and glove-makers—and not only by profession, which in itself means nothing—suddenly setting themselves on the pedestal of statesmen, from which they could lecture down at plain ordinary mortals. It had and has nothing to do with the case that such a "statesman" by the sixth month of his activity is shown up as the most incompetent windbag, the butt of everyone's ridicule and contempt, that he doesn't know which way to turn and has provided unmistakable proof of his total incapacity! No, that makes no difference, on the contrary: the more lacking the parliamentary statesmen of this Republic are in real accomplishment, the more furiously they persecute those who expect accomplishments from them, who have the audacity to point out the failure of their previous activity and predict the failure of their future moves. But if once you finally pin down one of these parliamentary honorables, and this political showman really cannot deny the collapse of his whole activity and its results any longer, they find thousands and thousands of grounds for excusing their lack of success, and there is only one that they will not admit, namely, that they themselves are the main cause of all evil.

· · · · ·

By the winter of 1922–23, at the latest, it should have been generally under-stood that even after the conclusion of peace France was still endeavoring with iron logic to achieve the war aim she had originally had in mind. For no one will be likely to believe that France poured out the blood of her people—never too rich to begin with—for four and a half years in the most decisive struggle of her history, only to have the damage previously done made good by subsequent reparations. Even Alsace-Lorraine in itself would not explain the energy with which the French carried on the War, if it had not been a part of French foreign policy's really great political program for the future. And this goal is: the dis-solution of Germany into a hodge-podge of little states. That is what chauvinis-tic France fought for, though at the same time in reality it sold its people as mercenaries to the international world Jew.

This French war aim would have been attainable by the War alone if, as Paris had first hoped, the struggle had taken place on German soil. Suppose that the bloody battles of the World War had been fought, not on the Somme, in Flan-ders, in Artois, before Warsaw, Nijni-Novgorod, Kovno, Riga, and all the other places, but in Germany, on the Ruhr and the Main, on the Elbe, at Hanover, Leipzig, Nuremberg, etc., and you will have to agree that this would have offered a possibility of breaking up Germany. It is very questionable whether our young federative state could for four and a half years have survived the same test of strain as rigidly centralized France, oriented solely toward her uncontested center in Paris. The fact that this gigantic struggle of nations occurred outside the borders of our fatherland was not only to the immortal credit of the old army, it was also the greatest good fortune for the German future. It is my firm and heartfelt conviction, and sometimes almost a source of anguish to me, that otherwise there would long since have been no German Reich, but only "Ger-man states." And this is the sole reason why the blood of our fallen friends and brothers has at least not flowed entirely in vain.

Thus everything turned out differently! True, Germany collapsed like a flash in November, 1918. But when the catastrophe occurred in the homeland, our field armies were still deep in enemy territory. The first concern of France at that time was not the dissolution of Germany, but: How shall we get the German armies out of France and Belgium as quickly as possible? And so the first task of the heads of state in Paris for concluding the World War was to disarm the German armies and if possible drive them back to Germany at once; and only after that could they devote themselves to the fulfillment of their real and original war aim. In this respect, to be sure, France was already paralyzed. For England the War had really been victoriously concluded with the annihilation of Germany as a colonial and commercial power and her reduction to the rank of a second-class state. Not only did the English possess no interest in the total extermination of the German state; they even had every reason to desire a rival against France in Europe for the future. Hence the French political leaders had to continue with determined peacetime labor what the War had begun, and Clemenceau's utterance, that for him the peace was only the continuation of the War, took on an increased significance.

Persistently, on every conceivable occasion, they had to shatter the structure of the Reich. By the imposition of one disarmament note after another, on the one hand, and by the economic extortion thus made possible, on the other hand, Paris hoped slowly to disjoint the Reich structure. The more rapidly national honor withered away in Germany, the sooner could economic pressure and unending poverty lead to destructive political effects. Such a policy of political repression and economic plunder, carried on for ten or twenty years, must gradually ruin even the best state structure and under certain circumstances dissolve it. And thereby the French war aim would finally be achieved.

By the winter of 1922–23 this must long since have been recognized as the French intent. Only two possibilities remained: We might hope gradually to blunt the French will against the tenacity of the German nation, or at long last to do what would have to be done in the end anyway, to pull the helm of the Reich ship about on some particularly crass occasion, and ram the enemy. This, to be sure, meant a life-and-death struggle, and there existed a prospect of life only if previously we succeeded in isolating France to such a degree that this second war would not again constitute a struggle of Germany against the world, but a defense of Germany against a France which was constantly disturbing the world and its peace.

I emphasize the fact, and I am firmly convinced of it, that this second eventuality must and will some day occur; whatever happens, I never believe that France's intentions toward us could ever change, for in the last analysis they are merely in line with the self-preservation of the French nation. If I were a Frenchman, and if the greatness of France were as dear to me as that of Germany is sacred, I could not and would not act any differently from Clemenceau. The French national, slowly dying out, not only with regard to population, but particularly with regard to its best racial elements, can in the long run retain its position in the world only if Germany is shattered. French policy may pursue a thousand détours; somewhere in the end there will be this goal, false to believe, that a purely *passive* will, desiring only to preserve itself, can for any length of time resist a will that is no less powerful, but proceeds *actively. As long as the eternal conflict between Germany and France is carried on only in the form of a German defense against French aggression, it will never be decided, but from year to year, from century to century, Germany will lose one position after another.* Follow the movements of the German language frontier beginning with the twelfth century until today, and you will hardly be able to count on the success of an attitude and a development which has done us so much damage up till now.

Only when this is fully understood in Germany, so that the vital will of the German nation is no longer allowed to languish in purely passive defense, but is pulled together for a final active reckoning with France and thrown into a last decisive struggle with the greatest ultimate aims on the German side—only then will we be able to end the eternal and essentially so fruitless struggle between ourselves and France; presupposing, of course, that Germany actually regards the destruction of France as only a means which will afterward enable her finally to give our people the expansion made possible elsewhere. Today we count eighty million Germans in Europe! This foreign policy will be acknowledged as correct only if, after scarcely a hundred years, there are two hundred and fifty million Germans on this continent, and not living penned in as factory coolies for the rest of the world, but as peasants and workers, who guarantee each other's livelihood by their labor.

In December 1922, the situation between Germany and France again seemed menacingly exacerbated. France was contemplating immense new extortions, and needed pledges for them. The economic pillage had to be preceded by a political pressure and it seemed to the French that only a violent blow at the nerve center of our entire German life would enable them to subject our "re-calcitrant" people to a sharper yoke. With the *occupation of the Ruhr*, the French hoped not only to break the moral backbone of Germany once and for all, but to put us into an embarrassing economic situation in which, whether we liked it or not, we would have to assume every obligation, even the heaviest.[3]

It was a question of bending and breaking. Germany bent at the very outset, and ended up by breaking completely later.

With the occupation of the Ruhr, Fate once again held out a hand to help the German people rise again. For what at the first moment could not but seem a great misfortune embraced on closer inspection an infinitely promising opportunity to terminate all German misery.

From the standpoint of foreign relations, the occupation of the Ruhr for the first time really alienated England basically from France, and not only in the circles of British diplomacy which had concluded, examined, and maintained the French alliance as such only with the sober eye of cold calculators, but also in the broadest circles of the English people. The English economy in particular viewed with ill-concealed displeasure this new and incredible strengthening of French continental power. For not only that France, from the purely politico-military point of view, now assumed a position in Europe such as previously not even Germany had possessed, but, economically as well, she now obtained economic foundations which almost combined a position of economic monopoly with her capacity for political competition. The largest iron mines and coal fields in Europe were thus united in the hands of a nation which, in sharp contrast to Germany, had always defended its vital interests with equal determination and activism, and which in the Great War had freshly reminded the whole world of its military reliability. With the occupation of the Ruhr coal fields by France, England's entire gain through the War was wrested from her hands, and the victor was no longer British diplomacy so industrious and alert, but Marshal Foch and the France he represented.

In Italy, too, the mood against France, which, since the end of the War, had been by no means rosy to begin with, shifted to a veritable hatred. It was the great, historical moment in which the allies of former days could become the enemies of tomorrow. If things turned out differently and the allies did not, as in the second Balkan War, suddenly break into a sudden feud among themselves, this was attributable only to the circumstance that Germany simply had no Enver Pasha, but a Reich Chancellor Cuno.

Yet not only from the standpoint of foreign policy, but of domestic policy as well, the French assault on the Ruhr held great future potentialities for Germany. A considerable part of our people which, thanks to the incessant influence of our lying press, still regarded France as the champion of progress and liberalism, was abruptly cured of this lunatic delusion. Just as the year 1914 had dispelled the dreams of international solidarity between peoples from the heads of our German workers and led them suddenly back into the world of eternal struggle, throughout which one being feeds on another and the death of the weaker means the life of the stronger, the spring of 1923 did likewise.

When the Frenchman carried out his threats and finally, though at first cautiously and hesitantly, began to move into the lower German coal district, a great decisive hour of destiny had struck for Germany. If in this moment our people combined a change of heart with a shift in their previous attitude, the Ruhr could become a Napoleonic Moscow for France. There were only *two possibilities: Either we stood for this offense and did nothing, or directing the eyes of the German people to this land of glowing smelters and smoky furnaces, we inspired them with a glowing will to end this eternal disgrace and rather take upon themselves the terrors of the moment than bear an endless terror one moment longer.*

To have discovered a third way was the immortal distinction of Reich Chancellor Cuno, to have admired it and gone along, the still more glorious distinction of our German bourgeois parties.

Here I shall first examine the second course as briefly as possible.

With the occupation of the Ruhr, France had accomplished a conspicuous breach of the Versailles Treaty. In doing so, she had also put herself in conflict with a number of signatory powers, and especially with England and Italy.

France could no longer hope for any support on the part of these states, for her own selfish campaign of plunder. She herself, therefore, had to bring the adventure—and that is what it was at first—to some happy conclusion. For a national German government there could be but a single course, that which honor prescribed. It was certain that for the present France could not be opposed by active force of arms; but we had to realize clearly that any negotiations, unless backed by power, would be absurd and fruitless. Without the possibility of active resistance, it was absurd to adopt the standpoint: "We shall enter into no negotiations"; but it was even more senseless to end by entering into negotiations after all, without having meanwhile equipped ourselves with power.

Not that we could have prevented the occupation of the Ruhr by *military means.* Only a madman could have advised such a decision. But utilizing the impression made by this French action and while it was being carried out, what we absolutely should have done was, without regard for the Treaty of Versailles which France herself had torn up, to secure the military resources with which we could later have equipped our negotiators. For it was clear from the start that one day the question of this territory occupied by France would be settled at some conference table. But we had to be equally clear on the fact that even the best negotiators can achieve little success, as long as the ground on which they stand and the chair on which they sit is not the shield arm of their nation. A feeble little tailor cannot argue with athletes, and a defenseless negotiator has always suffered the sword of Brennus on the opposing side of the scale, unless he had his own to throw in as a counterweight. Or has it not been miserable to watch the comic-opera negotiations which since 1918 have always preceded the repeated dictates? This degrading spectacle presented to the whole world, first inviting us to the conference table, as though in mockery, then presenting us with decisions and programs prepared long before, which, to be sure, could be discussed, but which from the start could only be regarded as unalterable. It is true that our negotiators, in hardly a single case, rose above the most humble average, and for the most part justified only too well the insolent utterance of Lloyd George, who contemptuously remarked, *à propos* of former Reich Minister Simon, "that the Germans didn't know how to choose men of intelligence as their leaders and representatives." But even geniuses, in view of the enemy's determined will to power and the miserable defenselessness of our own people in every respect, would have achieved but little.

But anyone who in the spring of 1923 wanted to make France's occupation of the Ruhr an occasion for reviving our military implements of power had first to give the nation its spiritual weapons, strengthen its will power, and destroy the corrupters of this most precious national strength.

Just as in 1918 we paid with our blood for the fact that in 1914 and 1915 we did not proceed to trample the head of the Marxist serpent once and for all, we would have to pay most catastrophically if in the spring of 1923 we did not avail ourselves of the opportunity to halt the activity of the Marxist traitors and murderers of the nation for good.

Any idea of real resistance to France was utter nonsense if we did not declare war against those forces which five years before had broken German resistance on the battlefields from within. Only bourgeois minds can arrive at the incredible opinion that Marxism might now have changed, and that the scoundrelly leaders of 1918, who then coldly trampled two million dead underfoot, the better to climb into the various seats of government, now in 1923 were suddenly ready to render their tribute to the national conscience. An incredible and really insane idea, the hope that the traitors of former days would suddenly turn into fighters of a German freedom. It never entered their heads. *No more than a hyena abandons carrion does a Marxist abandon treason*. And don't annoy me, if you please, with the stupidest of all arguments, that, after all, so many workers bled for Germany. German workers, yes, but then they were no longer international Marxists. If in 1914 the German working class in their innermost convictions had still consisted of Marxists, the War would have been over in three weeks. Germany would have collapsed even before the first soldier set foot across the border. No, the fact that the German people were still fighting proved that the Marxist delusion had not yet been able to gnaw its way into the bottommost depths. But in exact proportion as, in the course of the War, the German worker and the German soldier fell back into the hands of the Marxist leaders, in exactly that proportion he was lost to the fatherland. If at the beginning of the War and during the War twelve or fifteen thousand of these Hebrew corrupters of the people had been held under poison gas, as happened to hundreds of thousands of our very best German workers in the field, the sacrifice of millions at the front would not have been in vain. On the contrary: twelve thousand scoundrels eliminated in time might have saved the lives of a million real Germans, valuable for the future. But it just happened to be in the line of bourgeois "statesmanship" to subject millions to a bloody end on the battlefield without batting an eyelash, but to regard ten or twelve thousand traitors, profiteers, usurers, and swindlers as a sacred national treasure and openly proclaim their inviolability. We never know which is greater in this bourgeois world, the imbecility, weakness, and cowardice, or their deep-dyed corruption. It is truly a class doomed by Fate, but unfortunately, however, it is dragging a whole nation with it into the abyss.

And in 1923 we faced exactly the same situation as in 1918. Regardless what type of resistance was decided on, the first requirement was always the elimination of the Marxist poison from our national body. And in my opinion, it was then the very first task of a truly national government to seek and find the forces which were resolved to declare a war of annihilation on Marxism, and then to give these forces a free road; it was their duty not to worship the idiocy of "law and order" at a moment when the enemy without was administering the most annihilating blow to the fatherland and at home treason lurked on every street corner. No, at that time a really national government should have desired disorder and unrest, provided only that amid the confusion a basic reckoning with Marxism at last became possible and actually took place. If this were not done, any thought of resistance, regardless of what type, was pure madness.

Such a reckoning of real world-historical import, it must be admitted, does not follow the schedules of a privy councilor or some dried-up old minister, but the eternal laws of life on this earth, which are the struggle for this life and which remain struggle. It should have been borne in mind that the bloodiest civil wars have often given rise to a steeled and healthy people, while artificially cultivated states of peace have more than once produced a rottenness that stank to high Heaven. You do not alter the destinies of nations in kid gloves. And so, in the year 1923, the most brutal thrust was required to seize the vipers that were devouring our people. Only if this were successful did the preparation of active resistance have meaning.

At that time I often talked my throat hoarse, attempting to make it clear, at least to the so-called national circles, what was now at stake, and that, if we made the same blunders as in 1914 and the years that followed, the end would inevitably be the same as in 1918. Again and again, I begged them to give free rein to Fate, and to give our movement an opportunity for a reckoning with Marxism; but I preached to deaf ears. They all knew better, including the chief of the armed forces, until at length they faced the most wretched capitulation of all time.

Then I realized in my innermost soul that the German bourgeois was at the end of its mission and is destined for no further mission. Then I saw how all these parties continued to bicker with the Marxists only out of competitor's envy, without any serious desire to annihilate them; at heart they had all of them long since reconciled themselves to the destruction of the fatherland, and what moved them was only grave concern that they themselves should be able to partake in the funeral feast. That is all they were still "fighting" for.

In this period—I openly admit—I conceived the profoundest admiration for the great man south of the Alps, who, full of ardent love for his people, made no pacts with the enemies of Italy, but strove for their annihilation by all ways and means. What will rank Mussolini among the great men of this earth is his determination not to share Italy with the Marxists, but to destroy internationalism and save the fatherland from it.

How miserable and dwarfish our German would-be statesmen seem by comparison, and how one gags with disgust when these nonentities, with boorish arrogance, dare to criticize this man who is a thousand times greater than they; and how painful it is to think that this is happening in a land which barely half a century ago could call a Bismarck its leader.

In view of this attitude on the part of the bourgeoisie and the policy of leaving the Marxists untouched, the fate of any active resistance in 1923 was decided in advance. To fight France with the deadly enemy in our own ranks would have been sheer idiocy. What was done after that could at most be shadow-boxing, staged to satisfy the nationalistic element in Germany in some measure, or in reality to dupe the "seething soul of the people." If they had seriously believed in what they were doing, they would have had to recognize that the strength of a nation lies primarily, not in its weapons, but in its will, and that, before foreign enemies are conquered, the enemy within must be annihilated; otherwise God help us if victory does not reward our arms on the very first day. Once so much as the shadow of a defeat grazes a people that is not free of internal enemies, its force of resistance will break and the foe will be the final victor.

This could be predicted as early as February, 1923. Let no one mention the questionableness of a military success against France! For if the result of the German action in the face of the invasion of the Ruhr had only been the destruction of Marxism at home, by that fact alone success would have been on our side. A Germany saved from these mortal enemies of her existence and her future would possess forces which the whole world could no longer have stifled. *On the day when Marxism is smashed in Germany, her fetters will in truth be broken forever.* For never in our history have we been defeated by the strength of our foes, but always by our own vices and by the enemies in our own camp.

Since the leaders of the German state could not summon up the courage for such a heroic deed, logically they could only have chosen the first course, that of doing nothing at all and letting things slide.

But in the great hour Heaven sent the German people a great man, Herr von Cuno. He was not really a statesman or a politician by profession, and of course still less by birth; he was a kind of political hack, who was needed only for the performance of certain definite jobs; otherwise he was really more adept at business. A curse for Germany, because this businessman in politics regarded politics as an economic enterprise and acted accordingly.

"France has occupied the Ruhr; what is in the Ruhr? Coal. Therefore, France has occupied the Ruhr on account of coal." What was more natural for Herr Cuno than the idea of striking in order that the French should get no coal, whereupon, in the opinion of Herr Cuno, they would one day evacuate the Ruhr when the enterprise proved unprofitable. Such, more or less, was this "eminent" "national" "statesman," who in Stuttgart and elsewhere was allowed to address *his people*, and whom the people gaped at in blissful admiration.

But for a strike, of course, the Marxists were needed, for it was primarily the *workers* who would have to strike. Therefore, it was necessary to bring the worker (and in the brain of one of these bourgeois statesman he is always synonymous with the Marxist) into a united front with all the other Germans. The way these moldy political party cheeses glowed at the sound of such a brilliant slogan was something to behold! Not only a product of genius, it was national at the same time—there at last they had what at heart they had been seeking the whole while. The bridge to Marxism had been found, and the national swindler was enabled to put on a Teutonic face and mouth German phrases while holding out a friendly hand to the international traitor. And the traitor seized it with the utmost alacrity. For just as Cuno needed the Marxist leaders for his *"united front,"* the Marxist leaders were just as urgently in need of Cuno's money. So it was a help to both parties. Cuno obtained his united front, formed of national windbags and anti-national scoundrels, and the international swindlers received state funds to carry out the supreme mission of their struggle—that is, to destroy the national economy, and this time actually at the expense of the state. An immortal idea, to save the nation by buying a general strike; in any case a slogan in which even the most indifferent good-for-nothing could join with full enthusiasm.

It is generally known that a nation cannot be made free by prayers. But maybe one could be made free by sitting with folded arms, and that had to be historically tested. If at that time Herr Cuno, instead of proclaiming his subsidized general strike and setting it up as the foundation of the "united front," had only demanded two more hours of work from every German, the "united front" swindle would have shown itself up on the third day. Peoples are not freed by doing nothing, but by sacrifices.

To be sure, this so-called passive resistance as such could not be maintained for long. For only a man totally ignorant of warfare could imagine that occupying armies can be frightened away by such ridiculous means. And that alone could have been the sense of an action the costs of which ran into billions and which materially helped to shatter the national currency to its very foundations.

Of course, the French could make themselves at home in the Ruhr with a certain sense of inner relief as soon as they saw the resisters employing such methods. They had in fact obtained from us the best directions for bringing a recalcitrant civilian population to reason when its conduct represents a serious menace to the occupation authorities. With what lightning speed, after all, we had routed the Belgian *franc-tireur* bands nine years previous and made the seriousness of the situation clear to the civilian population when the German armies ran the risk of incurring serious damage from their activity. As soon as the passive resistance in the Ruhr had grown really dangerous to the French, it would have been child's play for the troops of occupation to put a cruel end to the whole childish mischief in less than a week. For the ultimate question is always this: What do we do if the passive resistance ends by really getting on an adversary's nerves and he takes up the struggle against it with brutal strong-arm methods? Are we then resolved to offer further resistance? If so, we must for better or worse invite the gravest, bloodiest persecutions. But then we stand exactly where the active resistance would put us—face to face with struggle. Hence any so-called passive resistance has an inner meaning only if it is backed by determination to continue it if necessary in open struggle or in undercover guerrilla warfare. In general, any such struggle will depend on a conviction that success is possible. As soon as a besieged fortress under heavy attack by the enemy is forced to abandon the last hope of relief, for all practical purposes it gives up the fight, especially when in such a case the defender is lured by the certainty of life rather than the probability of death. Rob the garrison of a surrounded fortress of faith in a possible liberation, and all the forces of defense will abruptly collapse.

Therefore, a passive resistance in the Ruhr, in view of the ultimate consequences it could and inevitably would produce in case it were actually successful, only had meaning if an active front were built up behind it. Then, it is true, there is no limit to what could have been drawn from our people. If every one of these Westphalians had known that the homeland was setting up an army of eighty or a hundred divisions, the Frenchmen would have found it thorny going. There are always more courageous men willing to sacrifice themselves for success than for something that is obviously futile.

It was a classical case which forced us National Socialists to take the sharpest position against a so-called national slogan. And so we did. In these months I was attacked by little men whose whole national attitude was nothing but a mixture of stupidity and outward sham, all of whom joined in the shouting only because they were unable to resist the agreeable thrill of suddenly being able to put on national airs without any danger. I regarded this most lamentable of all united fronts as a most ridiculous phenomenon, and history has proved me right.

As soon as the unions had filled their treasuries with Cuno's funds, and the passive resistance was faced with the decision of passing from defense with folded arms to active attack, the Red hyenas immediately bolted from the national sheep herd and became again what they had always been. Quietly and ingloriously Herr Cuno retreated to his ships, and Germany was richer by one experience and poorer by one great hope.

Down to late midsummer many officers, and they were assuredly not the worst, had at heart not believed in such a disgraceful development. They had all hoped that, if not openly, in secret at least, preparations had been undertaken to make this insolent French assault a turning point in German history. Even in our ranks there were many who put their confidence at least in the Reichswehr. And this conviction was so alive that it decisively determined the actions and particularly the training of innumerable young people.

But when the disgraceful collapse occurred and the crushing, disgraceful capitulation followed, the sacrifice of billions of marks and thousands of young Germans—who had been stupid enough to take the promises of the Reich's leaders seriously—indignation flared into a blaze against such a betrayal of our unfortunate people. In millions of minds the conviction suddenly arose bright and clear that only a radical elimination of the whole ruling system could save Germany.

Never was the time riper, never did it cry out more imperiously for such a solution than in the moment when, on the one hand, naked treason shamelessly revealed itself, while, on the other hand, a people was economically delivered to slow starvation. Since the state itself trampled all laws of loyalty and faith underfoot, mocked the rights of its citizens, cheated millions of its truest sons of their sacrifices, and robbed millions of others of their last penny, it has no further right to expect anything but hatred of its subjects. And in any event, this hatred against the spoilers of people and fatherland was pressing toward an explosion. In this place I can only point to the final sentence of my last speech in the great trial of spring, 1924:

"The judges of this state may go right ahead and convict us for our actions at that time, but History, acting as the goddess of a higher truth and a higher justice, will one day smilingly tear up this verdict, acquitting us of all guilt and blame."

And then she will call all those before her judgment seat, who today, in possession of power, trample justice and law underfoot, who have led our people into misery and ruin and amid the misfortune of the fatherland have valued their own ego above the life of the community.

In this place I shall not continue with an account of those events which led to and brought about the 8th of November 1923. I shall not do so because in doing so I see no promise for the future, and because above all it is useless to reopen wounds that seem scarcely healed; moreover, because it is useless to speak of guilt regarding men who in the bottom of their hearts, perhaps were all devoted to their nation with equal love, and who only missed or failed to understand the common road.

In view of the great common misfortune of our fatherland, I today no longer wish to wound and thus perhaps alienate those who one day in the future will have to form the great united front of those who are really true Germans at heart against the common front of the enemies of our people. For I know that some day the time will come when even those who then faced us with hostility will think with veneration of those who traveled the bitter road of death for their German people.

NOTES

1. The treaties signed at Locarno attempted to normalize relations between European states and Germany in the period between the world wars. Moreover, they forbade Germany to place troops in the Rhineland. Additionally, France signed treaties with Poland and Czechoslovakia vowing to offer mutual assistance in any altercation with Germany.

2. The Dawes Plan (1924) created a strategy for the payment of Germany's enormous war reparation debts incurred from the Treaty of Versailles. The payments required by the plan were burdensome to the German economy, and the plan was replaced by the less cumbersome Young Plan in 1929. However, Hitler refused to pay these reparations.

3. The Ruhr is the German equivalent for the Rhineland, the land on both sides of the Rhine, or Ruhr, River in West Germany, which European states decided to demilitarize in the Treaty of Versailles (1919) and the Treaty of Locarno (1926) after World War I, to act as a buffer zone between Germany on one side and France, Belgium, Luxembourg, and the Netherlands on the other.

A black militant, Muslim spokesman, and popular icon, Malcolm X grew up Malcolm Little in Lansing, Michigan, where he saw his house burnt down by the Ku Klux Klan, his father murdered two years later, and his mother put in a mental institution. He was imprisoned for burglary, and while in prison, in 1946, he converted to Islam through his contact with the Nation of Islam, a black separatist organization proclaiming black superiority. It was also while he was at the Norfolk Prison Colony that he acquired what he calls his "homemade education." He first learned words from the dictionary, then progressed to "serious reading" of books from the Parkhurst collection at the prison library. He recalls how outraged he was when the prison lights went out at 10:00 p.m. each night: it "always seemed to catch [him] right in the middle of something engrossing." He began to read after that time by sitting on the floor in his room, squinting at pages in the corridor light that "cast a glow" into his room.

When Malcolm was released from prison in 1952, he went to Chicago to meet and apprentice himself to the Nation of Islam leader, Elijah Muhammad. Malcolm became an active speaker and organizer for the Nation of Islam, going on speaking tours around the country. He founded Muhammad Speaks, *the official journal for the Nation of Islam. Finally he became the minister of Mosque Number Seven in Harlem, New York City.*

Malcolm X emerged as one of Nation of Islam's most influential members. In accordance with the teachings of Elijah Muhammad, he conceived of the white man as the harbinger of evil. In his Autobiography *he details the injustice of colonial oppression in India and Africa, and of China's opium war, to point to the ravages of white oppression. Though he began his career as an apostle of hatred against whites, Malcolm later diverged from the group's separatist philosophy when he went to Mecca on a pilgrimage and realized that everyone "snored in the same language." He subsequently came to believe in human equality. Opposing Elijah Muhammad's insistence on black supremacy, he observed how "orthodox Islam . . . had given [him] the insight and the perspective to see that the black men and white men truly could be brothers." He was assassinated in 1965, yet his preachings about human equality influenced Elijah Muhammad's son, Wallace. Changing his name to Warith Deen, Wallace also disavowed his father's teachings, and after the latter's death, he opted to lead the Nation of Islam, now the American Muslim Community, toward mainstream Islam, with its emphasis on human equality and brotherhood.*

*The following excerpt is from a speech that Malcolm X gave in Cleveland, Ohio, at a meeting of the Congress of Racial Equality (*CORE*), on 3 April 1964, shortly after he had broken away from the Nation of Islam. It was included in the volume* Malcolm X

Speaks: Selected Speeches and Statements, *edited by George Breitman, a journalist, author, and editor who has written extensively on Malcolm X.*

The Ballot or the Bullet

MALCOLM X

If we don't do something real soon, I think you'll have to agree that we're going to be forced either to use the ballot or the bullet. It's one or the other in 1964. It isn't that time is running out—time has run out! 1964 threatens to be the most explosive year America has ever witnessed. The most explosive year. Why? It's also a political year. It's the year when all of the white politicians will be back in the so-called Negro community jiving you and me for some votes. The year when all of the white political crooks will be right back in your and my community with their false promises, building up our hopes for a letdown, with their trickery and their treachery, with their false promises which they don't intend to keep. As they nourish these dissatisfactions, it can only lead to one thing, an explosion; and now we have the type of black man on the scene in America today—I'm sorry, Brother Lomax—who just doesn't intend to turn the other cheek any longer.

· · · · ·

It was the black man's vote that put the present administration in Washington, D.C. Your vote, your dumb vote, your ignorant vote, your wasted vote put in an administration in Washington, D.C., that has seen fit to pass every kind of legislation imaginable, saving you until last, then filibustering on top of that. And your and my leaders have the audacity to run around clapping their hands and talking about how much progress we're making. And what a good president we have. If he wasn't good in Texas, he sure can't be good in Washington, D.C. Because Texas is a lynch state. It is in the same breath as Mississippi, not different; only they lynch you in Texas with a Texas accent and lynch you in Mississippi with a Mississippi accent. And these Negro leaders have the audacity to go and have some coffee in the White House with a Texan, a Southern cracker—that's all he is—and then come out and tell you and me that he's going to be better for us because, since he's from the South, he knows how to deal with southerners. What kind of logic is that? Let Eastland be president, he's from the South too.[1] He should be better able to deal with them than Johnson.

In this present administration they have in the House of Representatives 257

Democrats to only 177 Republicans. They control two-thirds of the House vote. Why can't they pass something that will help you and me? In the Senate there are 67 senators who are of the Democratic Party. Only 33 of them are Republicans. Why, the Democrats have got the government sewed up, and you're the one who sewed it up for them. And what have they given you for it? Four years in office, and just now getting around to some civil-rights legislation. Just now, after everything else is gone, out of the way, they're going to sit down now and play with you all summer long—the same old giant con game that they call filibuster. All those are in cahoots together. Don't you ever think they're not in cahoots together, for the man that is heading the civil-rights filibuster is a man from Georgia named Richard Russell. When Johnson became president, the first man he asked for when he got back to Washington, D.C., was "Dicky"—that's how tight they are. That's his boy, that's his pal, that's his buddy. But they're playing that old con game. One of them makes believe he's for you, and he's got it fixed where the other one is so tight against you, he never has to keep his promise.

So it's time in 1964 to wake up. And when you see them coming up that kind of conspiracy, let them know your eyes are open. And let them know you got something else that's wide open too. It's got to be the ballot or the bullet. The ballot or the bullet. If you're afraid to use an expression like that, you should get on out of the country, you should get back in the cotton patch, you should get back in the alley. They get all the Negro vote, and after they get it, the Negro gets nothing in return. All they did when they got to Washington was give a few big Negroes big jobs. Those big Negroes didn't need big jobs, they already had jobs. That's camouflage, that's trickery, that's treachery, window-dressing. I'm not trying to knock out the Democrats for the Republicans, we'll get to them in a minute. But it is true—you put the Democrats first and the Democrats put you last.

Look at it the way it is. What alibis do they use, since they control Congress and the Senate? What alibi do they use when you and I ask, "Well, when are you going to keep your promise?" They blame the Dixiecrats. What is a Dixiecrat? A Democrat. A Dixiecrat is nothing but a Democrat in disguise. The titular head of the Democrats is also the head of the Dixiecrats, because the Dixiecrats are a part of the Democratic Party. The Democrats have never kicked the Dixiecrats out of the party. The Dixiecrats bolted themselves once, but the Democrats didn't put them out. Imagine, these lowdown southern segregationists put the Northern Democrats down. But the Northern Democrats have never put the Dixiecrats down. No, look at that thing the way it is. They have got a con game going on, a political con game, and you and I are in the middle. It's time for you and me to wake up and start looking at it like it is, and trying to understand it like it is; and then we can deal with it like it is.

The Dixiecrats in Washington, D.C., control the key committees that run the government. The only reason the Dixiecrats control these committees is because they have seniority. The only reason they have seniority is because they come from states where Negroes can't vote. This is not even a government that's based on democracy. It is not a government that is made up of representatives of the people. Half of the people in the South can't even vote. Eastland is not even supposed to be in Washington. Half of the senators and congressmen who occupy these key positions in Washington, D.C., are there illegally, they are there unconstitutionally.

I was in Washington, D.C., a week ago Thursday, when they were debating whether or not they should let the bill come onto the floor. And in the back of the room where the Senate meets, there's a huge map of the United States, and on that map it shows the location of Negroes throughout the country. And it shows that the Southern section of the country, the states that are most heavily concentrated with Negroes, are the ones that have senators and congressmen standing up filibustering and doing all other kinds of trickery to keep the Negro from being able to vote. This is pitiful. But it's not pitiful for us any longer; it's actually pitiful for the white man, because soon now, as the Negro awakens a little more and sees the vise that he's in, sees the bag that he's in, sees the real game that he's in, then the Negro's going to develop a new tactic.

These senators and congressmen actually violate the constitutional amendments that guarantee the people of that particular state or county the right to vote. And the constitution itself has within it the machinery to expel any representative from a state where the voting rights of the people are violated. You don't even need new legislation. Any person in Congress right now who is there from a state or a district where the voting rights of the people are violated, that particular person should be expelled from Congress. And when you expel him, you've removed one of the obstacles in the path of any real meaningful legislation in this country. In fact, when you expel them, you don't need new legislation, because they will be replaced by black representatives from counties and districts where the black man is in the majority, not in the minority.

If the black man in these southern states had his full voting rights, the key Dixiecrats in Washington, D.C., which means the key Democrats in Washington, D.C., would lose their seats. The Democratic Party itself would lose its power. It would cease to be powerful as a party. When you see the amount of power that would be lost by the Democratic Party if it were to lose the Dixiecrat wing, or branch, or element, you can see where it's against the interests of the Democrats to give voting rights to Negroes in states where the Democrats have been in complete power and authority ever since the Civil War. You just can't belong to that party without analyzing it.

I say again, I'm not anti-Democrat, I'm not anti-Republican, I'm not anti-anything. I'm just questioning their sincerity and some of the strategy that they've been using on our people by promising them promises that they don't intend to keep. When you keep the Democrats in power, you keep the Dixiecrats in power. I doubt that my good Brother Lomax will deny that. A vote for a Democrat is a vote for a Dixiecrat. That's why, in 1964, it's time now for you and me to become more politically mature and realize what the ballot is for; what we're supposed to get when we cast a ballot; and that if we don't cast a ballot, it's going to end up in a situation where we're going to have to cast a bullet. It's either a ballot or a bullet.

In the North, they do it a different way. They have a system that's known as gerrymandering, whatever that means. It means when Negroes become too heavily concentrated in a certain area, and begin to gain too much political power, the white man comes along and changes the district lines. You may say, "Why do you keep saying white man?" Because it's the white man who does it. I haven't ever seen any Negro changing any lines. They don't let him get near the line. It's the white man who does this. And usually, it's the white man who grins at you the most, and pats you on the back, and is supposed to be your friend. He may be friendly, but he's not your friend.

So, what I'm trying to impress upon you, in essence, is this: you and I in America are faced not with a segregationist conspiracy, we're faced with a government conspiracy. Everyone who's filibustering is a senator—that's the government. Everyone who's finagling in Washington, D.C., is a congressman—that's the government. You don't have anybody putting blocks in your path but people who are part of the government. The same government that you go abroad to fight for and die for is the government that is in a conspiracy to deprive you of your voting rights, deprive you of your economic opportunities, deprive you of decent housing, deprive you of decent education. You don't need to go to the employer alone, it is the government itself, the government of America, that is responsible for the oppression and exploitation and degradation of black people in this country. And you should drop it in their lap. This government has failed the Negro. This so-called democracy has failed the Negro. And all these white liberals have definitely failed the Negro.

So, where do we go from here? First, we need some friends. We need some new allies. The entire civil-rights struggle needs a new interpretation, a broader interpretation. We need to look at this civil-rights thing from another angle—from the inside as well as from the outside. To those of us whose philosophy is black nationalism, the only way you can get involved in the civil-rights struggle is give it a new interpretation. That old interpretation excluded us. It kept us out. So, we're giving a new interpretation to the civil-rights struggle, an interpretation that will enable us to come into it, take part in it. And these handker-chief-heads who have been dillydallying and pussyfooting and compromising—we don't intend to let them pussyfoot and dillydally and compromise any longer.

How can you thank a man for giving you what's already yours? How then can you thank him for giving you only part of what's already yours? You haven't even made progress, if what's being given to you, you should have had already. That's not progress. And I love my Brother Lomax, the way he pointed out we're right back where we were in 1954. We're not even as far up as we were in 1954. We're behind where we were in 1954. There's more segregation now than there was in 1954. There's more racial animosity, more racial hatred, more racial violence today in 1964, than there was in 1954. Where is the progress?

And now you're facing a situation where the young Negro's coming up. They don't want to hear that "turn-the-other-cheek" stuff, no. In Jacksonville, those were teenagers, they were throwing Molotov cocktails. Negroes have never done that before. But it shows you there's a new deal coming in. There's new thinking coming in. There's new strategy coming in. It'll be Molotov cocktails this month, hand grenades the next month, and something else next month. It'll be ballots, or it'll be bullets. It'll be liberty, or it will be death. The only difference about this kind of death—it'll be reciprocal. You know what is meant by "reciprocal"? That's one of Brother Lomax's words, I stole it from him. I don't usually deal with those big words because I don't usually deal with big people. I deal with small people. I find you can get a whole lot of small people and whip hell out of a whole lot of big people. They haven't got anything to lose, and they've got everything to gain. And they'll let you know in a minute: "It takes two to tango; when I go, you go."

The black nationalists, those whose philosophy is black nationalism, in bringing about this new interpretation of the entire meaning of civil rights, look upon it as meaning, as Brother Lomax has pointed out, equality of opportunity. Well, we're justified in seeking civil rights, if it means equality of opportunity, because all we're doing there is trying to collect for our investment. Our mothers and fathers invested sweat and blood. Three hundred and ten years we worked in this country without a dime in return—I mean without a *dime* in return. You let the white man walk around here talking about how rich this country is, but you never stop to think how it got rich so quick. It got rich because you made it rich.

You take the people who are in this audience right now. They're poor, we're all poor as individuals. Our weekly salary individually amounts to hardly anything. But if you take the salary of everyone in here collectively, it'll fill up a whole lot of baskets. It's a lot of wealth. If you can collect the wages of just these people right here for a year, you'll be rich—richer than rich. When you look at it like that, think how rich Uncle Sam had to become, not with this handful, but millions of black people. Your and my mother and father, who didn't work an eight-hour shift, but worked from "can't see" in the morning until "can't see" at night, and worked for nothing, making the white man rich, making Uncle Sam rich.

This is our investment. This is our contribution—our blood. Not only did we give of our free labor, we gave of our blood. Every time he had a call to arms, we were the first ones in uniform. We died on every battlefield the white man had. We have made a greater sacrifice than anybody who's standing up in America today. We have made a greater contribution and have collected less. Civil rights, for those of us whose philosophy is black nationalism, means: "Give it to us now. Don't wait for next year. Give it to us yesterday, and that's not fast enough."

I might stop right here to point out one thing. Whenever you're going after something that belongs to you, anyone who's depriving you of the right to have it is a criminal. Understand that. Whenever you are going after something is yours, you are within your legal rights to lay claim to it. And anyone who puts forth any effort to deprive you of that which is yours, is breaking the law, is a criminal. And this was pointed out by the Supreme Court decision. It outlawed segregation. Which means segregation is against the law. Which means segregation is breaking the law. A segregationist is a criminal. You can't label him as anything other than that. And when you demonstrate against segregation, the law is on your side. The Supreme Court is on your side.

Now, who is it that opposes you in carrying out the law? The police department itself, with police dogs and clubs. Whenever you demonstrate against segregation, whether it is segregated education, segregated housing, or anything else, the law is on your side, and anyone who stands in the way is not the law any longer. They are breaking the law, they are not representatives of the law. Any time you demonstrate against segregation and a man has the audacity to put a police dog on you, kill that dog, kill him, I'm telling you, kill that dog. I say it, if they put me in jail tomorrow, kill—that—dog. Then you'll put a stop to it. Now, if these white people in here don't want to see that kind of action, get down and tell the mayor to tell the police department to pull the dogs in. That's all you have to do. If you don't do it, someone else will.

If you don't take this kind of stand, your little children will grow up and look at you and think "shame." If you don't take an uncompromising stand—I don't mean go out and get violent; but at the same time you should never be non-violent unless you run into some nonviolence. I'm nonviolent with those who are nonviolent with me. But when you drop that violence on me, then you've made me go insane, and I'm not responsible for what I do. And that's the way every Negro should get. Any time you know you're within the law, within your legal rights, within your moral rights, in accord with justice, then die for what you believe in. But don't die alone. Let your dying be reciprocal. This is what is meant by equality. What's good for the goose is good for the gander.

When we begin to get in this area, we need new friends, we need new allies. We need to expand the civil-rights struggle to a higher level—to the level of human rights. Whenever you are in a civil-rights struggle, whether you know it or not, you are confining yourself to the jurisdiction of Uncle Sam. No one from the outside world can speak out in your behalf as long as your struggle is a civil-rights struggle. Civil rights comes within the domestic affairs of this country. All of our African brothers and our Asian brothers and our Latin-American brothers cannot open their mouths and interfere in the domestic affairs of the United States. And as long as it's civil rights, this comes under the jurisdiction of Uncle Sam.

But the United Nations has what's known as the charter of human rights, it has a committee that deals in human rights. You may wonder why all of the atrocities that have been committed in Africa and in Hungary and in Asia and in Latin America are brought before the UN, and the Negro problem is never brought before the UN. This is part of the conspiracy. This old, tricky, blue-eyed liberal who is supposed to be your and my friend, supposed to be in our corner, supposed to be acting in the capacity of an adviser, never tells you anything about human rights. They keep you wrapped up in civil rights. And you spend so much time barking up the civil-rights tree, you don't even know there's a human-rights tree on the same floor.

When you expand the civil-rights struggle to the level of human rights, you can then take the case of the black man in this country before the nations in the UN. You can take it before the General Assembly. You can take Uncle Sam before a world court. But the only level you can do it on is the level of human rights. Civil rights keeps you under his restrictions, under his jurisdiction. Civil rights keeps you in his pocket. Civil rights means you're asking Uncle Sam to treat you right. Human rights are something you were born with. Human rights are your God-given rights. Human rights are the rights that are recognized by all nations of this earth. And any time anyone violates your human rights, you can take them to the world court. Uncle Sam's hands are dripping with blood, dripping with the blood of the black man in this country. He's the earth's number-one hypocrite. He has the audacity—yes, he has—imagine him posing as the leader of the free world. The free world!—and you over here singing "We Shall Overcome." Expand the civil-rights struggle to the level of human rights, take it into the United Nations, where our African brothers can throw their weight on our side, where our Asian brothers can throw their weight on our side, where our Latin-American brothers can throw their weight on our side, and where 800 million Chinamen are sitting there waiting to throw their weight on our side.

Let the world know how bloody his hands are. Let the world know the hypocrisy that's practiced over here. Let it be the ballot or the bullet. Let him know that it must be the ballot or the bullet.

When you take your case to Washington, D.C., you're taking it to the criminal who's responsible; it's like running from the wolf to the fox. They're all in cahoots together. They all work political chicanery and make you look like a chump before the eyes of the world. Here you are walking around in America, getting ready to be drafted and sent abroad, like a tin soldier, and when you get over there, people ask you what are you fighting for, and you have to stick your tongue in your cheek. No, take Uncle Sam to court, take him before the world.

By ballot I only mean freedom. Don't you know—I disagree with Lomax on this issue—that the ballot is more important than the dollar? Can I prove it? Yes. Look in the UN. There are poor nations in the UN; yet those poor nations can get together with their voting power and keep the rich nations from making a move. They have one nation—one vote, everyone has an equal vote. And when those brothers from Asia, and Africa and the darker parts of this earth get together, their voting power is sufficient to hold Sam in check. Or Russia in check. Or some other section of the earth in check. So, the ballot is most important.

· · · · ·

I would like to say, in closing, a few things concerning the Muslim Mosque, Inc., which we established recently in New York City. It's true we're Muslims and our religion is Islam, but we don't mix our religion with our politics and our economics and our social and civil activities—not anymore. We keep our religion in our mosque. After our religious services are over, then as Muslims we become involved in political action, economic action, and social and civic action. We become involved with anybody, anywhere, any time, and in any manner that's designed to eliminate the evils, the political, economic, and social evils that are afflicting the people of our community.

The political philosophy of black nationalism means that the black man should control the politics and the politicians in his own community; no more. The black man in the black community has to be re-educated into the science of politics so he will know what politics is supposed to bring him in return. Don't be throwing out any ballots. A ballot is like a bullet. You don't throw your ballots until you see a target, and if that target is not within your reach, keep your ballot in your pocket. The political philosophy of black nationalism is being taught in the Christian church. It's being taught in the NAACP. It's being taught in CORE meetings. It's being taught in SNCC [Student Nonviolent Coordinating Committee] meetings. It's being taught in Muslim meetings. It's being taught where nothing but atheists and agnostics come together. It's being taught everywhere.

Black people are fed up with the dillydallying, pussyfooting, compromising approach that we've been using toward getting our freedom. We want freedom *now*, but we're not going to get it saying "We Shall Overcome." We've got to fight until we overcome.

The economic philosophy of black nationalism is pure and simple. It only means that we should control the economy of our community. Why should white people be running all the stores in our community? Why should white people be running the banks of our community? Why should the economy of our community be in the hands of the white man? Why? If a black man can't move his store into a white community, you tell me why a white man should move his store into a black community. The philosophy of black nationalism involves a re-education program in the black community in regards to economics. Our people have to be made to see that any time you take your dollar out of your community and spend it in a community where you don't live, the community where you live will get poorer and poorer, and the community where you spend your money will get richer and richer. Then you wonder why where you live is always a ghetto or a slum area. And where you and I are concerned, not only do we lose it when we spend it out of the community, but the white man has got all our stores in the community tied up; so that though we spend it in the community, at sundown the man who runs the store takes it over across town somewhere. He's got us in a vise.

So the economic philosophy of black nationalism means in every church, in every civic organization, in every fraternal order, it's time now for our people to become conscious of the importance of controlling the economy of our community. If we own the stores, if we operate the businesses, if we try and establish some industry in our own community, then we're developing to the position where we are creating employment for our own kind. Once you gain control of the economy of your own community, then you don't have to picket and boycott and beg some cracker downtown for a job in his business.

The social philosophy of black nationalism only means that we have to get together and remove the evils, the vices, alcoholism, drug addiction, and other evils that are destroying the moral fiber of our community. We ourselves have to lift the level of our community, the standard of our community to a higher level, make our own society beautiful so that we will be satisfied in our own social circles and won't be running around here trying to knock our way into a social circle where we're not wanted.

So I say, in spreading a gospel such as black nationalism, it is not designed to make the black man re-evaluate the white man—you know him already—but to make the black man re-evaluate himself. Don't change the white man's mind—you can't change his mind, and that whole thing about appealing to the moral conscience of America—America's conscience is bankrupt. She lost all conscience a long time ago. Uncle Sam has no conscience. They don't try and eliminate an evil because it's evil, or because it's illegal, or because it's immoral; they eliminate it only when it threatens their existence. So you're wasting your time appealing to the moral conscience of a bankrupt man like Uncle Sam. If he had a conscience, he'd straighten this thing out with no more pressure being put upon him. So it is not necessary to change the white man's mind. We have to change our own mind. You can't change his mind about us. We've got to change our own minds about each other. We have to see each other with new eyes. We have to see each other as brothers and sisters. We have to come together with warmth so we can develop unity and harmony that's necessary to get this problem solved ourselves. How can we do this? How can we avoid jealousy? How can we avoid the suspicion and the divisions that exist in the community? I'll tell you how.

I have watched how Billy Graham comes into a city, spreading what he calls the gospel of Christ, which is only white nationalism. That's what he is. Billy Graham is a white nationalist; I'm a black nationalist. But since it's the natural tendency for leaders to be jealous and look upon a powerful figure like Graham with suspicion and envy, how is it possible for him to come into a city and get all the cooperation of the church leaders? Don't think because they're church leaders that they don't have weaknesses that make them envious and jealous—no, everybody's got it. It's not an accident that when they want to choose a cardinal [as Pope] over there in Rome, they get in a closet so you can't hear them cussing and fighting and carrying on.

Billy Graham comes in preaching the gospel of Christ, he evangelizes the gospel, he stirs everybody up, but he never tries to start a church. If he came in trying to start a church, all the churches would be against him. So, he just comes in talking about Christ and tells everybody who gets Christ to go to any church where Christ is; and in this way the church cooperates with him. So we're going to take a page from his book.

Our gospel is black nationalism. We're not trying to threaten the existence of any organization, but we're spreading the gospel of black nationalism. Anywhere there's a church that is also preaching and practicing the gospel of black nationalism, join the NAACP. If CORE is spreading and practicing the gospel of black nationalism, join CORE. Join any organization that has a gospel that's for the uplift of the black man. And when you get into it and see them pussyfooting or compromising, pull out of it because that's not black nationalism. We'll find another one.

And in this manner, the organizations will increase in number and in quantity and in quality, and by August, it is then our intention to have a black nationalism convention which will consist of delegates from all over the country who are interested in the political, economic, and social philosophy of black nationalism. After these delegates convene, we will listen to everyone. We want to hear new ideas and new solutions and new answers. And at that time, if we see fit then to form a black nationalist party. If it's necessary to form a black nationalist army, we'll form a black nationalist army. It'll be the ballot or the bullet. It'll be liberty or it'll be death.

It's time for you and me to stop sitting in this country, letting some cracker senators, Northern crackers and Southern crackers, sit there in Washington, D.C., and come to a conclusion in their mind that you and I are supposed to have civil rights. There's no white man going to tell me anything about *my* rights. Brothers and sisters, always remember, if it doesn't take senators and congressmen and presidential proclamations to give freedom to the white man, it is not necessary for legislation or proclamation or Supreme Court decisions to give freedom to the black man. You let that white man know, if this is a country of freedom, let it be a country of freedom; and if it's not a country of freedom, change it.

We will work with anybody, anywhere, at any time, who is genuinely interested in tackling the problem head-on, nonviolently as long as the enemy is nonviolent, but violent when the enemy gets violent. We'll work with you on the voter-registration drive, we'll work with you on rent strikes, we'll work with you on school boycotts—I don't believe in any kind of integration; I'm not even worried about it because I know you're not going to get it anyway; you're not going to get it because you're afraid to die; you've got to be ready to die if you try and force yourself on the white man, because he'll get just as violent as those crackers in Mississippi, right here in Cleveland. But we will still work with you on the school boycotts because we're against a segregated school system. A segregated school system produces children who, when they graduate, graduate with crippled minds. But this does not mean that a school is segregated because it's all black. A segregated school means a school that is controlled by people who have no real interest in it whatsoever.

Let me explain what I mean. A segregated district or community is a community in which people live, but outsiders control the politics and the economy of that community. They never refer to the white section as a segregated community. It's the all-Negro section that's a segregated community. Why? The white man controls his own school, his own bank, his own economy, his own politics, his own everything, his own community—but he also controls yours. When you're under someone else's control, you're segregated. They'll always give you the lowest or the worst that there is to offer, but it doesn't mean you're segregated just because you have your own. You've got to *control* your own. Just like the white man has control of his, you need to control yours.

You know the best way to get rid of segregation? The white man is more afraid of separation than he is of integration. Segregation means that he puts you away from him, but not far enough for you to be out of his jurisdiction; separation means you're gone. And the white man will integrate faster than he'll let you separate. So we will work with you against the segregated school system because it's criminal, because it is absolutely destructive, in every way imaginable, to the minds of the children who have to be exposed to that type of crippling education.

Last but not least, I must say this concerning the great controversy over rifles and shotguns. The only thing that I've ever said is that in areas where the government has proven itself either unwilling or unable to defend the lives and the property of Negroes, it's time for Negroes to defend themselves. Article number two of the constitutional amendments provides you and me the right to own a rifle or a shotgun. It is constitutionally legal to own a shotgun or a rifle. This doesn't mean you're going to get a rifle and form battalions and go out looking for white folks, although you'd be within your rights—I mean, you'd be justified; but that would be illegal and we don't do anything illegal. If the white man doesn't want the black man buying rifles and shotguns, then let the government do its job. That's all. And don't let the white man come to you and ask you what you think about what Malcolm says—why, you old Uncle Tom. He would never ask you if he thought you were going to say, "Amen!" No, he is making a Tom out of you.

So, this doesn't mean forming rifle clubs and going out looking for people, but it is time, in 1964, if you are a man, to let that man know. If he's not going to do his job in running the government and providing you and me with the protection that our taxes are supposed to be for, since he spends all those billions for his defense budget, he certainly can't begrudge you and me spending $12 or $15 for a single-shot, or double-action. I hope you understand. Don't go out shooting people, but any time, brothers and sisters, and especially the men in this audience—some of you wearing Congressional Medals of Honor, with shoulders this wide, chests this big, muscles that big—any time you and I sit around and read where they bomb a church and murder in cold blood, not some grownups, but four little girls while they were praying to the same god the white man taught them to pray to, and you and I see the government go down and can't find who did it.

Why, this man—he can find Eichmann hiding down in Argentina somewhere. Let two or three American soldiers, who are minding somebody else's business way over in South Vietnam, get killed, and he'll send battleships, sticking his nose in their business. He wanted to send troops down to Cuba and make them have what he calls free elections—this old cracker who doesn't have free elections in his own country. No, if you never see me another time in your life, if I die in the morning, I'll die saying one thing: the ballot or the bullet, the ballot or the bullet.

If a Negro in 1964 has to sit around and wait for some cracker senator to filibuster when it comes to the rights of black people, why, you and I should hang our heads in shame. You talk about a march on Washington in 1963, you haven't seen anything. There's some more going down in '64. And this time they're not going like they went last year. They're not going singing "We Shall Overcome." They're not going with white friends. They're not going with round-trip tickets. They're going with one-way tickets.

And if they don't want that non-nonviolent army going down there, tell them to bring the filibuster to a halt. The black nationalists aren't going to wait. Lyndon B. Johnson is the head of the Democratic Party. If he's for civil rights, let him go into the Senate next week and declare himself. Let him go in there right now and take a moral stand—right now, not later. Tell him, don't wait until election time. If he waits too long, brothers and sisters, he will be responsible for letting a condition develop in this country which will create a climate that will bring seeds up out of the ground with vegetation on the end of them looking like something these people never dreamed of. In 1964, it's the ballot or the bullet. Thank you.

NOTE

1. James Eastland (1904–1986) was a U.S. senator from Mississippi who opposed civil-rights legislation, supported Jim Crow laws, denounced the Supreme Court's *Brown v. Board of Education* decision, denied the existence of the Ku Klux Klan in Mississippi, and was an unabashed racist. He addressed a rally of the White Citizens Council in 1956: "When in the course of human events it becomes necessary to abolish the Negro race, proper methods should be used. Among these are guns, bows and arrows, slingshots and knives. . . . All whites are created equal with certain rights, among these are life, liberty, and the pursuit of dead niggers" (http://encyclopedia .thefreedictionary.com).

ANTONIO GRAMSCI (1891–1937)

A Sardinian Marxist, political activist, and social theorist, Antonio Gramsci suffered from various ailments as a young child, including a malformation of the spine; because in their attempt to cure him his doctors had him suspended from a beam in the ceiling for long periods of time, he grew up hunchbacked. Gramsci spent his formative years in Turin, a thriving industrial center and the base for the Fiat industry, which manufactured tractors, armored cars, and airplanes. By the time the proletarian uprisings wreaked havoc on the city, between 1912 and 1920, Gramsci had already been introduced to the workers' cause, initially through his elder brother, then through his association with the Communist Party of Italy. Gramsci led the party from 1924 until 1926, when he was arrested, along with other dissidents, by the Mussolini regime. Gramsci had at first supported Mussolini and had even written an article defending the dictator's position, but by the time Gramsci was arrested he had become keenly aware of the dangers of fascism. Even though he could have fled and thus avoided arrest, he remained in Italy, explaining in a note from prison that "a captain must be the last to abandon his vessel in a shipwreck; that he must leave only when everybody else on board is safe."

During Gramsci's trial, the prosecutor ended his speech by declaring, "We must stop this brain working for twenty years." Of course, they could not, for it was while Gramsci was in prison that he wrote the Prison Notebooks, *which filled more than thirty notebooks and took up 2,350 pages in print! The* Prison Notebooks *had to be smuggled out of the prison and out of Italy, and were published later. In the* Prison Notebooks *Gramsci stresses the problematic of praxis, a philosophy that is actively engaged in the political life of a culture. Gramsci redefines the role of the intellectual, putting forth the idea of "organic intellectuals," whose task it is to direct the aspirations of their class in the dynamics of the class struggle. Education, or learning, becomes a mode of work which helps funnel the revolutionary energies of the working class. Education seen in this light becomes a means of "actively participat[ing] in natural life in order to transform and socialize it." Closely tied to the question of education and work is Gramsci's concept of hegemony, whereby a social group achieves the consent of the other classes, a consent that is a necessary precondition for gaining political power. And thus Gramsci comes close to answering his question about how fascism can be overthrown and the working class into its own: through creating material conditions which will lead to the hegemony of the working class and, consequently, to government by this class.*

Selections from the *Prison Notebooks*

ANTONIO GRAMSCI

POLITICAL STRUGGLE AND MILITARY WAR

In military war, when the strategic aim—destruction of the enemy's army and occupation of his territory—is achieved, peace comes. It should also be observed that for war to come to an end, it is enough that the strategic aim should simply be achieved potentially: it is enough in other words that there should be no doubt that an army is no longer able to fight, and that the victorious army "could" occupy the enemy's territory. Political struggle is enormously more complex: in a certain sense, it can be compared to colonial wars or to old wars of conquest in which the victorious army occupies, or proposes to occupy, permanently all or a part of the conquered territory. Then the defeated army is disarmed and dispersed, but the struggle continues on the terrain of politics and of military "preparation."

Thus India's political struggle against the English (and to a certain extent that of Germany against France, or of Hungary against the Little Entente) knows three forms of war: war of movement, war of position, and underground warfare. Gandhi's passive resistance is a war of position, which at certain moments becomes a war of movements, and at others underground warfare. Boycotts are a form of war of position, strikes of war of movement and the secret preparation of weapons and combat troops belongs to underground warfare. A kind of commando tactics is also to be found, but it can only be utilised with great circumspection. If the English believed that a great insurrectional movement was being prepared, destined to annihilate their present strategic superiority (which consists, in a certain sense, in their ability to manoeuvre through control of the internal lines of communication, and to concentrate their forces at the "sporadically" most dangerous spot) by mass suffocation—i.e. by compelling them to spread out their forces over a theatre of war which had simultaneously become generalised—then it would suit them to *provoke* a premature out-break of the Indian fighting forces, in order to identify them and decapitate the general movement. Similarly it would suit France if the German Nationalist Right were to be involved in an adventurist *coup d'état*; for this would oblige the suspected illegal military organisation to show itself prematurely, and so permit an intervention which from the French point of view would be timely. It is thus evident that in the forms of mixed struggle—fundamentally of a military character, but mainly fought on the political plane (though in fact every political struggle always has a military substratum)—the use of commando squads requires an original tactical development, for which the experience of war can only provide a stimulus, and not a model.

The question of the Balkan *comitadjis* requires separate treatment; they are related to particular conditions of the region's geophysical environment, to the particular formation of the rural classes, and also to be real effectiveness of the governments there. The same is true with the Irish bands, whose form of warfare and of organisation was related to the structure of Irish society. The *commitadjis*, the Irish, and the other forms of partisan warfare have to be separated from the question of commandos, although they appear to have points of contact. These forms of struggle are specific to weak, but restive, minorities confronted by well-organised majorities: modern commandos on the contrary presuppose a large reserve-force, immobilised for one reason or another but potentially effective, which gives them support and sustenance in the form of individual contributions.

The relationship which existed in 1917–18 between the commando units and the army as a whole can lead, and has led, political leaders to draw up erroneous plans of campaign. They forget: 1. that the commandos are simple tactical units, and do indeed presuppose an army which is not very effective—but not one which is completely inert. For even though discipline and fighting spirit have slackened to the point where a new tactical deployment has become advisable, they still do exist to a certain degree—a degree to which the new tactical formation precisely corresponds. Otherwise there could only be rout, and headlong flight; 2. that the phenomenon of commandos should not be considered as a sign of the general combativity of the mass of the troops, but, on the contrary, as a sign of their passivity and relative demoralisation. But in saying all this, the general criterion should be kept in mind that comparisons between military art and politics, if made, should always be taken *cum grano salis* [with a pinch of salt]—in other words, as stimuli to thought, or as terms in a *reductio ad absurdum*. In actual fact, in the case of the political militia there is neither any implacable penal sanction for whoever makes a mistake or does not obey an order exactly, nor do court-martials exist—quite apart from the fact that the line-up of political forces is not even remotely comparable to the line-up of military forces.

In political struggle, there also exist other forms of warfare—apart from the war of movement and siege warfare or the war of position. True, i.e. modern, commandos belong to the war of position, in its 1914–18 form. The war movement and siege warfare of the preceding periods also had their commandos, in a certain sense. The light and heavy cavalry, crack rifle corps, etc.—and indeed, mobile forces in general—partly functioned as commandos. Similarly the art of organising patrols contained the germ of modern commandos. This germ was contained in siege warfare more than in the war of movement: more extensive use of patrols, and particularly the art of organising sudden sorties and surprise attacks with picked men.

Another point to be kept in mind is that in political struggle one should not ape the methods of the ruling classes, or one will fall into easy ambushes. In the current struggles this phenomenon often occurs. A weakened State structure is like a flagging army; the commandos—i.e. the private armed organisations— enter the field and they have two tasks: to make use of illegal means, while the State appears to remain within legality, and thus to reorganise the State itself. It is stupid to believe that when one is confronted by illegal private action one can counterpose to it another similar action—in other words, combat commando tactics by means of commando tactics. It means believing that the State remains perpetually inert, which is never the case—quite apart from all the other conditions which differ. The class factor leads to a fundamental difference: a class which has to work fixed hours every day cannot have permanent and specialised assault organisations—as can a class which has ample financial resources and all of whose members are not tied down by fixed work. At any hour of day or night, these by now professional organisations are able to strike decisive blows, and strike them unawares. Commando tactics cannot therefore have the same importance for some classes as for others. For certain classes a war of movement and manoeuvre is necessary—because it is the form of war which belongs to them; and this, in the case of political struggle, may include a valuable and perhaps indispensable use of commando tactics. But to fix one's mind on the military model is the mark of a fool: politics, here too, must have priority over its military aspect, and only politics creates the possibility for manoeuvre and movement.

From all that has been said it follows that in the phenomenon of military commandos, it is necessary to distinguish between the technical function of commandos and a special force linked to the modern war of position, and their politico-military function. As a special force commandos were used by all armies in the World War. But they have only had a politico-military function in those countries which are politically enfeebled and non-homogeneous, and which are therefore represented by a not very combative national army, and a bureaucratised General Staff, grown rusty in the service.

On the subject of parallels between on the one hand the concepts of war of manoeuvre and war of position in military science, and on the other the corresponding concepts in political science, Rosa [Luxemburg]'s little book, translated (from French) into Italian in 1919 by C. Alessandri, should be recalled.

In this book, Rosa—a little hastily, and rather superficially too—theorised the historical experiences of 1905. She in fact disregarded the "voluntary" and organisational elements which were far more extensive and important in those events than—thanks to a certain "economistic" and spontaneist prejudice—she tended to believe. All the same, this little book (like others of the same author's essays) is one of the most significant documents theorizing the war manoeuvre in relation to political science. The immediate economic element (crises, etc.) is seen as the field artillery which in war opens a breach in the enemy's defences—a breach sufficient for one's own troops to rush in and obtain a definitive (strategic) victory, or at least an important victory in the context of the strategic line. Naturally the effects of immediate economic factors in historical science are held to be far more complex than the effects of heavy artillery in a war of manoeuvre, since they are conceived of as having a double effect: 1. they breach the enemy's defences, after throwing him into disarray and causing him to lose faith in himself, his forces, and his future; 2. in a flash they organise one's own troops and create the necessary cadres—or at least in a flash they put the existing cadres (formed, until that movement, by the general historical process) in positions which enable them to encadre one's scattered forces; 3. in a flash they bring about the necessary ideological concentration on the common objective to be achieved. This view was a form of iron economic determinism, with the aggravating factor that it was conceived of as operating with lightning speed in time and in space. It was thus out and out historical mysticism, the awaiting of a sort of miraculous illumination.

General Krasnov asserted (in his novel) that the Entente did not wish for the victory of Imperial Russia (for fear that the Eastern Question would be definitively resolved in favour of Tsarism), and therefore obliged the Russian General Staff to adopt trench warfare (absurd, in view of the enormous length of the Front from the Baltic to the Black Sea, with vast marshy and forest zones), whereas the only possible strategy was a war of manoeuvre. This assertion is merely silly. In actual fact, the Russian Army did attempt a war of manoeuvre and sudden incursion, especially in the Austrian sector (but also in East Prussia), and won successes which were as brilliant as they were ephemeral. The truth is that one cannot choose the form of war one wants, unless from the start one has a crushing superiority over the enemy. It is well known what losses were caused by the stubborn refusal of the General Staffs to recognise that a war of position was "imposed" by the overall relation of the forces in conflict. A war of position is not, in reality, constituted simply by the actual trenches, but by the whole organisational and industrial system of the territory which lies to the rear of the army in the field. It is imposed notably by the rapid fire-power of cannons, machine-guns, and rifles, by the armed strength which can be concentrated at a particular spot, as well as by the abundance of supplies which make possible the swift replacement of material lost after an enemy breakthrough or a retreat. A further factor is the great mass of men under arms; they are of very unequal calibre, and are precisely only able to operate as a mass force. It can be seen how on the Eastern Front it was one thing to make an incursion in the Austrian Sector, and quite another in the German Sector; and how even in the Austrian Sector, reinforced by picked German troops and commanded by Germans, incursion tactics ended in disaster. The same thing occurred in the Polish campaign of 1920; the seemingly irresistible advance was halted before Warsaw by General Weygand, on the line commanded by French officers. Even those military experts whose minds are now fixed on the war of position, just as they were previously on that of manoeuvre, naturally do not maintain that the latter should be considered and expunged from military science. They merely maintain that, in wars among the more industrially and socially advanced States, the war of manoeuvre must be considered as reduced to more of a tactical than a strategic function; that it must be considered as occupying the same position as siege warfare used to occupy previously in relation to it.

The same reduction must take place in the arts and sciences of politics, at least in the case of the most advanced States, where "civil society" has become a very complex structure and one which is resistant to the catastrophic "incursions" of the immediate economic element (crises, depressions, etc.). The superstructures of civil society are like the trench-systems of modern warfare. In war it would sometimes happen that a fierce artillery attack seemed to have destroyed the enemy's entire defensive system, whereas in fact it had only destroyed the outer perimeter; and at the moment of their advance and attack the assailants would find themselves confronted by a line of defence which was still effective. The same thing happens in politics, during the great economic crises. A crisis cannot give the attacking forces the ability to organise with lightning speed in time and in space; still less can it endow them with fighting spirit. Similarly, the defenders are not demoralised, nor do they abandon their positions, even among the ruins, nor do they lose faith in their own strength or their own future. Of course, things do not remain exactly as they were; but it is certain that one will not find the element of speed of accelerated time, of the definitive forward march expected by the strategists of political Cadornism.[1]

The last occurrence of this kind in the history of politics was the events of 1917. They marked a decisive turning-point in the history of the art and science of politics. Hence it is a question of studying "in depth" which elements of civil society correspond to the defensive systems in a war of position. The use of the phrase "in depth" is intentional, because 1917 has been studied—but only either from superficial and banal viewpoints, as when certain social historians study the vagaries of women's fashions, or from a "rationalistic" viewpoint—in other words, with the conviction that certain phenomena are destroyed as soon as they are "realistically" explained, as if they were popular superstitions (which anyway are not destroyed either merely by being explained).

The question of the meagre success achieved by new tendencies in the trade-union movement should be related to this series of problems. One attempt to begin a revision of the current tactical methods was perhaps that outlined by L. Dav. Br. [Trotsky] at the fourth meeting, when he made a comparison between the Eastern and Western fronts.[2] The former had fallen at once, but unprecedented struggles had then ensued; in the case of the latter, the struggles would take place "beforehand." The question, therefore, was whether civil society resists before or after the attempt to seize power, where the latter takes place, etc. However, the question was outlined only in a brilliant, literary form, without directives of a practical character.

It should be seen whether Bronstein's famous theory about the permanent character of the movement is not the political reflection of the theory of war of manoeuvre (recall the observation of the Cossack general Krasnov)—i.e. in the last analysis, a reflection of the general-economic-cultural-social conditions in a country in which the structures of national life are embryonic and loose, and incapable of becoming "trench or fortress." In this case one might say that Bronstein, apparently "Western," was in fact a cosmopolitan—i.e. superficially national and superficially Western or European. Ilitch [Lenin] on the other hand was profoundly national and profoundly European.

Bronstein in his memoirs recalls being told that his theory had been proved true . . . fifteen years later, and replying to the epigram with another epigram. In reality his theory, as such, was good neither fifteen years earlier nor fifteen years later. As happens to the obstinate, of whom Guicciardini speaks, he guessed more or less correctly; that is to say, he was right in his more general practical prediction. It is as if one were to prophesy that a little four-year-old girl would become a mother, and when at twenty she did so one said: "I guessed then she would"—overlooking the fact, however, that when she was four years old one had tried to rape the girl, in the belief that she would become a mother even then. It seems to me that Ilitch understood that a change was necessary from the war of manoeuvre applied victoriously in the East in 1917, to a war of position which was the only form possible in the West—where, as Krasnov observes, armies could rapidly accumulate endless quantities of munitions, and where the social structures were of themselves still capable of becoming heavily-armed fortifications. This is what the formula of the "United Front" seems to me to mean, and it corresponds to the conception of a single front for the Entente under the sole command of Foch.

Ilitch, however, did not have time to expand his formula—though it should be borne in mind that he could only have expanded it theoretically, whereas the fundamental task was a national one; that is to say it required a reconnaissance of the terrain and identification of the elements of trench and fortress represented by the elements of civil society, etc. In Russia the State was everything, civil society was primordial and gelatinous; in the West, there was a proper relation between State and civil society, and when the State trembled a sturdy structure of civil society was at once revealed. The State was only an outer ditch, behind which there stood a powerful system of fortresses and earthworks: more or less numerous from one State to the next, it goes without saying—but this precisely necessitated an accurate reconnaissance of each individual country.

Bronstein's theory can be compared to that of certain French syndicalists on the General Strike, and to Rosa [Luxemburg]'s theory in the work translated by Alessandri. Rosa's book and theories anyway influenced the French syndicalists, as is clear from some of Rosmer's articles on Germany in Vie Ouvière (first series in pamphlet form). It partly depends too on the theory of spontaneity.

THE TRANSITION FROM THE WAR OF MANOEUVRE (FRONTAL ATTACK) TO THE WAR OF POSITION IN THE POLITICAL FIELD AS WELL

This seems to me to be the most important question of political theory that the post-war period has posed, and the most difficult to solve correctly. It is related to the problems raised by Bronstein [Trotsky], who in one way or another can be considered the political theorist of frontal attack in a period in which it only leads to defeats. This transition in political science is only indirectly (mediately) related to that which took place in the military field, although certainly a relation exists and an essential one. The war of position demands enormous sacrifices by infinite masses of people. So an unprecedented concentration of hegemony is necessary, and hence a more "interventionist" government, which will take the offensive more openly against the oppositionists and organise permanently the "impossibility" of internal disintegration—with controls of every kind, political, administrative, etc., reinforcement of the hegemonic "positions" of the dominant group, etc. All this indicates that we have entered a culminating phase in the political-historical situation, since in politics the "war of position," once won, is decisive definitively. In politics, in other words, the war of manoeuvre subsists so long as it is a question of winning positions which are not decisive, so that all the resources of the State's hegemony cannot be mobilised. But when, for one reason or another, these positions have lost their value and only the decisive positions are at stake, then one passes over to siege warfare; this is concentrated, difficult, and requires exceptional qualities of patience and inventiveness. In politics, the siege is a reciprocal one, despite all appearances, and the mere fact that the ruler has to muster all his resources demonstrates how seriously he takes his adversary.

"A resistance too long prolonged in a besieged camp is demoralising in itself. It implies suffering, fatigue, loss of rest, illness and the continual presence not of the acute danger which tempers but of the chronic danger which destroys." ...

. . . . .

Problem of the "Collective Man" or of "Social Conformism"

(Consider) education and the formative role of the State. Its aim is always that of creating new and higher types of civilisation; of adapting the "civilisation" and the morality of the broadest popular masses to the necessities of the continuous development of the economic apparatus of production; hence the evolving of even physically new types of humanity. But how will each single individual succeed in incorporating himself into the collective man, and how well can educative pressure be applied to single individuals so as to obtain their consent and their collaboration, turning necessity and coercion into "freedom"? Question of the "Law": this concept will have to be extended to include those activities which are at present classified as "legally neutral," and which belong to the domain of civil society; the latter operates without "sanctions" or compulsory "obligations," but nevertheless exerts a collective pressure and obtains objective results in the form of an evolution of customs, ways of thinking and acting, morality, etc.

The political concept of the so-called "Permanent Revolution" emerged before 1848 as a scientifically evolved expression of the Jacobin experience from 1789 to Thermidor.[3] The formula belongs to a historical period in which the great mass of political parties and the great economic trade unions did not yet exist, and society was still, so to speak, in a state of fluidity from many points of view: greater backwardness of the countryside, and almost complete monopoly of political and State power by a few cities or even by a single one (Paris in the case of France); a relatively rudimentary State apparatus, and greater autonomy of civil society from State activity; a specific system of military forces and of national armed services; greater autonomy of a national economics from the economic relations of the world market, etc. In the period after 1870, with the colonial expansion of Europe, all these elements change: the internal and international organisational relations of the State become more complex and massive, and the Forty-Eightist formula of the "Permanent Revolution" is expanded and transcended in political science by the formula of "civil hegemony." The same thing happens in the art of politics as happens in military art: war of movement increasingly becomes war of position, and it can be said that a State will win a war in so far as it prepares for it minutely and technically in peacetime. The massive structures of the modern democracies, both as State organisations, and as complexes of association in civil society, constitute for the art of politics as it were the "trenches" and the permanent fortifications of the front in the war of position: they render merely "partial" the element of movement which before used to be "the whole" of war, etc.

This question is posed for the modern States, but not for backward countries or for colonies, where forms which elsewhere have been superseded and have become anachronistic are still in vigour. The question of the value of ideologies must also be studied in a treatise of political science.

Sociology and Political Science

The rise of sociology is related to the decline of the concept of political science and the art of politics which took place in the nineteenth century (to be more accurate, in the second half of that century, with the success of evolutionary and positivist theories). Everything that is of real importance in sociology is nothing other than political science. "Politics" became synonymous with parliamentary politics or the politics of personal cliques. Conviction that the constitutions and parliaments had initiated an epoch of "natural" "evolution," that society had discovered its definitive, because rational, foundations, etc. And, lo and behold, society can now be studied with the methods of the natural sciences! [Consider the] impoverishment of the concept of the State which ensued from such views! If political science means science of the State, and the State is the entire complex of practical and theoretical activities with which the ruling class not only justifies and maintains its dominance, but manages to win the active consent of those over whom it rules, then it is obvious that all the essential questions of sociology are nothing other than the questions of political science. If there is a residue, this can only be made up of false problems, i.e. frivolous problems. The question therefore which faced Bukharin when he wrote his *Popular Manual* was that of determining what status could be accorded to political science in relation to the philosophy of praxis: whether the two are identical (something impossible to maintain, except from the most crudely positivist viewpoint); or whether political science is the body of empirical or practical principles which are deduced from a vaster conception of the world or philosopher properly speaking; or whether this philosophy is only the science of the concepts or general categories created by political science, etc.

If it is true that man cannot be conceived of except as historically determined man—i.e. man who has developed, and who lives, in certain conditions, in a particular social complex or totality of social relations—is it then possible to take sociology as meaning simply the study of these conditions and the laws which regulate their development? Since the will and initiative of men themselves cannot be left out of account, this notion must be false. The problem of what "science" itself is has to be posed. Is not science itself "political activity" and political thought, in as much as it transforms men, and makes them different from what they were before? If everything is "politics," then it is necessary —in order to avoid lapsing into a wearisome and tautological catalogue of platitudes—to distinguish by means of new concepts between on the one hand the politics which corresponds to that science which is traditionally called "philosophy," and on the other the politics which is called political science in the strict sense. If science is the "discovery" of formerly unknown reality, is this reality not conceived of in a certain sense as transcendent? And is it not thought that there still exists something "unknown" and hence transcendent? And does the concept of science as "creation" not then mean that it too is "politics"? Everything depends on seeing whether the creation involved is "arbitrary," or whether it is rational—i.e. "useful" to men in that it enlarges their concept of life, and raises to a higher level (develops) life itself.

HEGEMONY (CIVIL SOCIETY) AND SEPARATION OF POWER

The separation of powers, together with all the discussion provoked by its realisation and the legal dogmas which its appearance brought into being, is a product of the struggle between civil society and political society in a specific historical period. This period is characterised by a certain unstable equilibrium between the classes, which is a result of the fact that certain categories of intellectuals (in the direct service of the State, especially the civil and military bureaucracy) are still too closely tied to the old dominant classes. In other words, there takes place within the society what Croce calls the "perpetual conflict between Church and State," in which the Church is taken as representing the totality of civil society (whereas in fact it is only an element of diminishing importance within it), and the State as representing every attempt to crystallise permanently a particular state of development, a particular situation. In this sense, the Church itself may become State, and the conflict may occur between on the one hand secular (and secularising) civil society, and on the other State/Church (when the Church has become an integral part of the State, of political society monopolised by a specific privileged group, which absorbs the Church in order the better to preserve its monopoly with the support of that zone of "civil society" which the Church represents).

Essential importance of the separation of powers for political and economic liberalism; the entire liberal ideology, with its strengths and its weaknesses, can be encapsulated in the principle of the separation of powers, and the source of liberalism's weakness then becomes apparent: it is the bureaucracy—i.e. the crystallisation of the leading personnel—which exercises coercive power, and at a certain point it becomes a caste. Hence the popular demand for making all posts elective—a demand which is extreme liberalism, and at the same time its dissolution (principle of the permanent Constituent Assembly, etc.; in Republics, the election at fixed intervals of the Head of State gives the illusion of satisfying this elementary popular demand).

Unity of the State in the differentiation of powers: Parliament more closely linked to civil society; the judiciary power, between government and Parliament, represents the continuity of the written law (even against the government). Naturally all three powers are also organs of political hegemony, but in different degrees: 1. Legislature; 2. Judiciary; 3. Executive. It is to be noted how lapses in the administration of justice make an especially disastrous impression on the public: the hegemonic apparatus is more sensitive in this sector, to which arbitrary actions on the part of the police and political administration may also be referred.

The Conception of Law

A conception of the Law which must be an essentially innovatory one is not to be found, integrally, in any pre-existing doctrine (not even in the doctrine of the so-called positive school, and notably that of Ferri). If every State tends to create and maintain a certain type of civilisation and of citizen (and hence the collective life and of individual relations), and to eliminate certain customs and attitudes and to disseminate others, then the Law will be its instrument for this purpose (together with the school system, and other institutions and activities). It must be developed so that it is suitable for such a purpose—so that it is maximally effective and productive of positive results.

The conception of law will have to be freed from every residue of transcendentalism and from every absolute; in practice, from every moralistic fanaticism. However, it seems to me that one cannot start from the point of view that the State does not "punish" (if this term is reduced to its human significance), but only struggles against social "dangerousness." In reality, the State must be conceived of as an "educator," in as much as it tends precisely to create a new type of level of civilisation. Because one is acting essentially on economic forces, reorganising and developing the apparatus of economic production, creating a new structure, the conclusion must not be drawn that superstructural factors should be left to themselves, to develop spontaneously, to a haphazard and sporadic germination. The State, in this field, too, is an instrument of "rationalisation," of acceleration and of Taylorisation.[4] It operates according to a plan, urges, incites, solicits, and "punishes"; for once the conditions are created in which a certain way of life is "possible," then "criminal action or omission" must have a punitive sanction, with moral implications, and not merely be judged generically as "dangerous." The Law is the repressive and negative aspect of the entire positive, civilising activity undertaken by the State. The "prize-giving" activities of individuals and groups, etc., must also be incorporated in the conception of the Law; praiseworthy and meritorious activity is rewarded, just as criminal actions are punished (and punished in original ways, bringing in "public opinion" as a form of sanction).

The State

In the new "juridical" tendencies represented by the *Nuovi Studi* of Volpicelli and Spirito, the confusion between the concept of class-State and the concept of regulated society should be noted, as a critical point of departure. This confusion is especially noteworthy in the paper on Economic Freedom presented by Spirito at the Nineteenth Congress of the Society for Scientific Progress held at Bolzano in September 1930 and published in *Nuovi Studi* in the 1930 September–October issue.

As long as the class-State exists the regulated society cannot exist, other than metaphorically—i.e. only in the sense that the class-State too is a regulated society. The utopians, in as much as they expressed a critique of the society that existed in their day, very well understood that the class-State could not be the regulated society. So much is this true that in the types of society which the various utopias represented, economic equality was introduced as a necessary basis for the projected reform. Clearly in this the utopians were not utopians, but concrete political scientists and consistent critics. The utopian character of some of them was due to the fact that they believed economic equality could be introduced by arbitrary laws, by an act of will, etc. But the idea that complete and perfect political equality cannot exist without economic equality (an idea to be found in other political writers, too, even right-wing ones—i.e. among the critics of democracy, in so far as the latter makes use of the Swiss or Danish model to claim that the system is a reasonable one for all countries) nevertheless remains correct. This idea can be found in the writers of the seventeenth century too, for example in Ludovico Zuccolo and in his book *Il Belluzzi*, and I think in Machiavelli as well. Maurras believes that in Switzerland that particular form of democracy is possible precisely because there is a certain common averageness of economic fortunes, etc.

The confusion of class-State and regulated society is peculiar to the middle classes and petty intellectuals, who would be glad of any regularisation that would prevent sharp struggles and upheavals. It is a typically reactionary and regressive conception.

In my opinion, the most reasonable and concrete thing that can be said about the ethical State is this: every State is ethical in as much as one of its most important functions is to raise the great mass of the population to a particular cultural and moral level, a level (or type) which corresponds to the needs of the productive forces for development, and hence to the interests of the ruling classes. The school as a positive educative function, and the courts as a repressive and negative educative function, are the most important State activities in this sense: but, in reality, a multitude of other so-called private initiatives and activities tend to the same end—initiatives and activities which form the apparatus of the political and cultural hegemony of the ruling classes. Hegel's conception belongs to a period in which the spreading development of the bourgeoisie could seem limitless, so that its ethnicity or universality could be asserted: all mankind will be bourgeois. But, in reality, only the social group that poses the end of the State and its own end as the target to be achieved can create an ethical State—i.e. one which tends to put an end to the internal divisions of the ruled, etc., and to create a technically and morally unitary social organism.

Hegel's doctrine depicts parties and associations as the "private" domain of the State. This derived historically from the political experiences of the French Revolution, and was to serve to give a more concrete character to constitutionalism. Government with the consent of the governed—but with this consent organised, and not generic and vague as it is expressed in the instant of elections. The State does have and request consent, but it also "educates" this consent by means of the political and syndical associations; these, however, are private organisms, left to the private initiative of the ruling class. Hegel, in a certain sense, thus already transcended pure constitutionalism and theorised the parliamentary State with its party system. But his conception of association could not help still being vague and primitive, halfway between the political and the economic; it was in accordance with the historical experience of the time, which was very limited and offered only one perfected example of organisation —the "corporative" (a political grafted directly on the economy). Marx was not able to have historical experiences superior (or at least much superior) to those of Hegel; but, as a result of his journalistic and agitational activities, he had a sense for the masses. Marx's concept of organisation remains entangled amid the following elements: craft organisation; Jacobin clubs; secret conspiracies by small groups; journalistic organisation.

The French Revolution offered two prevalent types. There were the "clubs"— loose organisations of the "popular assembly" type, centralised around individual political figures. Each had its newspaper, by means of which it kept alive the attention and interest of a particular clientèle that had no fixed boundaries. This clientèle then upheld the theses of the paper in the club's meetings. Certainly, among those who frequented the clubs, there must have existed tight, select groupings of people who knew each other, who met separately and prepared the climate of the meetings, in order to support one tendency or another—depending on the circumstances and also on the concrete interests in play.

The secret conspiracies, which subsequently spread so widely in Italy prior to 1848, must have developed in France after Thermidor among the second-rank followers of Jacobinism; with great difficulty in the Napoleonic period on account of the vigilant control of the police; with greater facility from 1815 to 1830 under the Restoration, which was fairly liberal at the base and was free from certain preoccupations. In this period, from 1815 to 1830, the differentiation of the popular political camp was to occur. This already seemed considerable during the "glorious days" of 1830, when the formations which had been cystallising during the preceding fifteen years now came to the surface. After 1830 and up to 1848, this process of differentiation became perfected, and produced some quite highly-developed specimens in Blanqui and Filippo Buonarroti.

It is unlikely that Hegel could have had first-hand knowledge of these historical experiences, which are, however, more vivid in Marx.

The revolution which the bourgeois class had brought into the conception of law, and hence into the function of the State, consists especially in the will to conform (hence the ethicity of the law and of the State). The previous ruling classes were essentially conservative in the sense that they did not tend to construct an organic passage from the other classes into their own, i.e. to enlarge their class sphere "technically" and ideologically: their conception was that of a closed caste. The bourgeois class poses itself as an organism in continuous movement, capable of absorbing the entire society, assimilating it to its own cultural and economic level. The entire function of the State has been transformed; the State has become an "educator," etc.

How does this process come to a halt, with the return to a conception of the State as pure force? The bourgeois class is "saturated": it not only does not expand—it starts to disintegrate; it not only does not assimilate new elements, it loses part of itself (or at least its losses are enormously more numerous than its assimilations). A class claiming to be capable of assimilating the whole of society, and which was at the same time really able to express such a process, would perfect this conception of the State and of law, so as to conceive the end of the State and of law—rendered useless since they will have exhausted their function and will have been absorbed by civil society.

That the everyday concept of State is unilateral and leads to grotesque errors can be demonstrated with reference to Daniel Halévy's recent book *Décadence de la Liberté*, of which I have read a review in *Nouvelles Littéraires*. For Halévy, "State" is the representative apparatus; and he discovers that the most important events of French history from 1870 until the present day have not been due to initiatives by political organisms deriving from universal suffrage, but to those either of private organisms (capitalist firms, General Staffs, etc.), or of great civil servants unknown to the country at large, etc. But what does that signify if not that by "State" should be understood not only the apparatus of government, but also the "private" apparatus of "hegemony" or civil society? It should be noted how from this critique of the State which does not intervene, which trails behind events, etc., there is born the dictatorial ideological current of the Right, with its reinforcement of the executive, etc. However, Halévy's book should be read to see whether he too has taken this path: it is not likely in principle, given his antecedents (sympathies for Sorel, for Maurras, etc.).

Curzio Malaparte, in the introduction to his little volume on the *Technique of the Coup d' Etat*, seems to assert the equivalence of the formula: "Everything within the State, nothing outside the State, nothing against the State" with the proposition: "Where there is freedom, there is no State." In the latter proposition, the term "freedom" cannot be taken in its ordinary meaning of "political freedom, freedom of the press, etc.," but as counterposed to "necessity"; it is related to Engels' proposition on the passage from the rule of necessity to the rule of freedom. Malaparte has not caught even the faintest whiff of the significance of the proposition.

In the (anyway superficial) polemic over the functions of the State (which here means the State as a politico-juridical organisation in the narrow sense), the expression "the State as watchman of the night" corresponds to the Italian expression "the State as policeman" and means a State whose functions are limited to the safeguarding of public order and of respect for the laws. The fact is glossed over that in this form of régime (which anyway has never existed except on paper, as a limiting hypothesis), hegemony over its historical development belongs to private forces, to civil society—which is "State" too, indeed is the State itself.

It seems that the expression "watchman of the night," which should have a more sarcastic ring than "the State as policeman," comes from Lassalle. Its opposite should be "ethical State" or "interventionist State" in general, but there are differences between the two expressions. The concept of ethical State is of philosophical and intellectual origin (belonging to the intellectuals: Hegel), and in fact could be brought into conjunction with the concept of State-*veilleur de nuit*; for it refers rather to the autonomous, educative, and moral activity of the secular State, by contrast with the cosmopolitanism and the interference of the religious-ecclesiastical organisation as a mediaeval residue. The concept of interventionist State is of economic origin, and is connected on the one hand with tendencies supporting protection and economic nationalism, and on the other with the attempt to force a particular State personnel, of landowning and feudal origin, to take on the "protection" of the working classes against the excesses of capitalism (policy of Bismarck and of Disraeli).

These diverse tendencies may combine in various ways, and in fact have so combined. Naturally liberals ("economists") are for the "State as watchman of the night," and would like the historical initiative to be left to civil society and to the various forces which spring up there—with the "State" as guardian of "fair play" and of the rules of the game. Intellectuals draw very significant distinctions as to when they are liberals and when they are interventionists (they may be liberals in the economic field and interventionists in the cultural field, etc.). The catholics would like the State to be interventionist one hundred per cent in their favor; failing that, or where they are in a minority, they call for a "neutral" State, so that it should not support their adversaries.

The following argument is worth reflecting upon: is the conception of the *gendarme*-nightwatchman State (leaving aside the polemical designation: *gendarme*, nightwatchman, etc.) not in fact the only conception of the State to transcend the purely "economic-corporate" stages?

We are still on the terrain of the identification of State and government—an identification which is precisely a representation of the economic-corporate form, in other words of the confusion between civil society and political society. For it should be remarked that the general notion of State includes elements which need to be referred back to the notion of civil society (in the sense that one might say the State = political society + civil society, in other words hegemony protected by the armour of coercion). In a doctrine of the State which conceives the latter as tendentially capable of withering away and of being subsumed into regulated society, the argument is a fundamental one. It is possible to imagine the coercive element of the State withering away by degrees, as ever-more conspicuous elements of regulated society (or ethical State or civil society) make their appearance.

The expressions "ethical State" or "civil society" would thus mean that this "image" of a State without a State was present to the greatest political and legal thinkers, in so far as they placed themselves on the terrain of pure science (pure utopia, since based on the premise that all men are really equal and hence equally rational and moral, i.e. capable of accepting the law spontaneously, freely, and not through coercion, as imposed by another class, as something external to consciousness).

It must be remembered that the expression "nightwatchman" for the liberal State comes from Lassalle, i.e. from a dogmatic and non-dialectical statalist (look closely at Lassalle's doctrines on this point and on the State in general, in contrast with Marxism). In the doctrine of the State as regulated society, one will have to pass from a phase in which "State" will be identified with "civil society," to a phase of the State as nightwatchman—i.e. of a coercive organisation which will safeguard the development of the continually proliferating elements of regulated society, and which will therefore progressively reduce its own authoritarian and forcible interventions. Nor can this conjure up the idea of a new "liberalism," even though the beginning of an era of organic liberty be imminent.

If it is true that no type of State can avoid passing through a phase of economic-corporate primitivism, it may be deduced that the content of the political hegemony of the new social group which has founded the new type of State must be predominantly of an economic order: what is involved is the reorganisation of the structure of the real relations between men on the one hand and the world of the economy or of production on the other. The superstructural elements will inevitably be few in number, and have a character of foresight and of struggle, but as yet few "planned" elements. Cultural policy will above all be negative, a critique of the past; it will be aimed at erasing from the memory and at destroying. The lines of construction will as yet be "broad lines," sketches, which might (and should) be changed at all times, so as to be consistent with the new structure as it is formed. This precisely did not happen in the period of the mediaeval communes; for culture, which remained a function of the Church, was precisely anti-economic in character (i.e. against the nascent capitalist economy); it was not directed towards giving hegemony to the new class, but rather to preventing the latter from acquiring it. Hence Humanism and the Renaissance were reactionary, because they signalled the defeat of the new class, the negation of the economic world which was proper to it, etc.

Another element to examine is that of the organic relations between the domestic and foreign policies of a State. Is it domestic policies which determine foreign policy, or vice versa? In this case too, it will be necessary to distinguish: between great powers, with relative international autonomy, and other powers; also, between different forms of government (a government like that of Napoleon III had two policies, apparently—reactionary internally, and liberal abroad).

[What are the] conditions in a State before and after a war? It is obvious that, in an alliance, what counts are the conditions in which a State finds itself at the moment of peace. Therefore it may happen that whoever has exercised hegemony during the war ends up by losing it as a result of the enfeeblement suffered in the course of the struggle, and is forced to see a "subordinate" who has been more skilful or "luckier" become hegemonic. This occurs in "world wars" when the geographic situation compels a State to throw all its resources into the crucible: it wins through its alliances, but victory finds it prostrate, etc. This is why in the concept of "great power" it is necessary to take many elements into account, and especially those which are "permanent"—i.e. especially "economic and financial potential" and population.

ORGANIZATION OF NATIONAL SOCIETIES

I have remarked elsewhere that in any given society nobody is disorganised and without party, provided that one takes organisation and party in a broad and not a formal sense. In this multiplicity of private associations (which are of two kinds: natural, and contractual or voluntary) one or more predominates relatively or absolutely—constituting the hegemonic apparatus of one social group over the rest of the population (or civil society): the basis for the State in the narrow sense of the governmental-coercive apparatus.

It always happens that individuals belong to more than one private association, and often to associations which are objectively in contradiction to one another. A totalitarian policy is aimed precisely: 1. at ensuring that the members of a particular party find in that party all the satisfactions that they formerly found in a multiplicity of organisations, i.e. at breaking all the threads that bind these members to extraneous cultural organisms; 2. at destroying all other organisations or at incorporating them into a system of which the party is the sole regulator. This occurs: 1. when the given party is the bearer of a new culture—then one has a progressive phase; 2. when the given party wishes to prevent another force, bearer of a new culture, from becoming itself "totalitarian"—then one has an objectively regressive and reactionary phase, even if that reaction (as invariably happens) does not avow itself, and seeks itself to appear as the bearer of a new culture.

. . . . .

Who Is a Legislator?

The concept of "legislator" must inevitably be identified with the concept of "politician." Since all men are "political beings," all are also "legislators." But distinctions will have to be made. "Legislator" has a precise juridical and official meaning—i.e. it means those persons who are empowered by the law to enact laws. But it can have other meanings too.

Every man, in as much as he is active, i.e. living, contributes to modifying the social environment in which he develops (to modifying certain of its characteristics or to preserving others); in other words, he tends to establish "norms," rules of living and of behaviour. One's circle of activity may be greater or smaller, one's awareness of one's own actions and aims may be greater or smaller; furthermore, the representative power may be greater or smaller, and will be put into practice to a greater or lesser extent in its normative, systematic expression by the "represented." A father is a legislator for his children, but the paternal authority will be more or less conscious, more or less obeyed and so forth.

In general, it may be said that the distinction between ordinary men and others who are more specifically legislators is provided by the fact that this second group not only formulates directives which will become a norm of conduct for the others, but at the same time creates the instruments by means of which the directives themselves will be "imposed," and by means of which it will verify their execution. Of this second group, the greatest legislative power belongs to the State personnel (elected and career officials), who have at their disposal the legal coercive powers of the State. But this does not mean that the leaders of "private" organisms and organisations do not have coercive sanctions at their disposal too, ranging even up to the death penalty. The maximum of legislative capacity can be inferred when a perfect formulation of directives is matched by a perfect arrangement of the organisms of execution and verification, and by a perfect preparation of the "spontaneous" consent of the masses who must "live" those directives, modifying their own habits, their own will, their own convictions to conform with those directives and with the objectives which they propose to achieve. If everyone is a legislator in the broadest sense of the concept, he continues to be a legislator even if he accepts directives from others—if, as he carries them out, he makes certain that others are carrying them out too; if, having understood their spirit, he propagates them as though making them into rules specifically applicable to limited and definite zones of living.

Religion, State, Party

In *Mein Kampf*, Hitler writes: "the founding or the destruction of a religion is an action of immeasurably greater importance than the founding or the destruction of a State: not to speak of a party. . . ." Superficial and acritical [is this assertion since] the three elements—religion (or "active" conception of the world), State, party—are indissoluble, and in the real process of historico-political development there is a necessary passage from one to the other.

In Machiavelli, in the ways and language of the time, an understanding of this necessary homogeneity and interrelation of the three elements can be observed. To lose one's soul in order to save one's country or State is an element of absolute laicism, or positive and negative conception of the world (against religion, or the dominant conception). In the modern world, a party is such— integrally, and not, as happens, a fraction of a larger party—when it is conceived, organised, and led in ways and in forms such that it will develop integrally into a State (an integral State, and not into a government technically understood) and into a conception of the world. The development of the party into a State reacts upon the party and requires of it a continuous reorganisation and development, just as the development of the party and State into a conception of the world, i.e. into a total and molecular (individual) transformation of ways of thinking and acting, reacts upon the State and the party, compelling them to reorganise continually and confronting them with new and original problems to solve. It is evident that such a conception of the world is hindered in its practical development by blind, unilateral "party" fanaticism (in this case that of a sect, of a fraction of a larger party, within which the struggle takes place), i.e. by the absence either of a State conception or of a conception of the world capable of developing because historically necessary.

The political life of today furnishes ample evidence of these mental limitations and deficiencies, which, besides, provoke dramatic struggles—for they are themselves the means by which historical development in practice occurs. But the past, and the Italian past which interests us most, from Machiavelli onwards, is no less rich in experiences, for all of history bears witness to the present.

NOTES

1. " 'Cadornism' is coined after Luigi Cadorna, commander-in-chief of the Italian armed forces until the defeat and retreat at Caporetto (September 1917), for which he was held responsible. Cadorna epitomized for Gramsci the kind of military (and, by analogy, political) strategist who forces reality into a preconceived schema, even if this means demoralizing his army, sacrificing troops in battle, and provoking a mutiny. Gramsci elsewhere defines Cadornism as 'the conviction that a thing will be done because the leader considers it just and reasonable that it should be done; if it is not done, the blame is put on those who "ought to have" ' " (http://www.marxists.org/archive/gramsci).

2. Lev Davidovich Bronstein (1879–1940) was a Marxist thinker, author, and activist. He adopted the pseudonym "Trotsky" while fleeing to Europe to escape persecution. He worked with Lenin in the formation of the Soviet Union, served on the Politburo, and is credited with establishing the Red Army of the Bolsheviks. Later he opposed Stalin's regime and became a vociferous critic of the Soviet Union. He was assassinated in 1940 during his exile in Mexico. See the selection from André Breton and Leon Trotsky in part V herein.

3. Thermidor was the eleventh month of the French Revolutionary calendar and marked the fall in 1794 of Maximilien Robespierre and the Jacobins, who had controlled France after the revolution and instituted the wave of political executions (often using the guillotine) known as the Reign of Terror.

4. This term refers to a system outlined by Fredrick Taylor in *The Principle of Scientific Management* (1911). Taylor sought to increase industrial output by rationaliz-

ing the production process, using increased observation of workers by management and analyzing meticulously the stages of production. Taylorism thus diminished the autonomy of the workers and increased the role of management. This business approach became very influential in the United States because of its economic efficiency and profitability (see http://college.hmco.com/history).

The British novelist and literary and social critic Raymond Williams was born to working-class parents in Pandy, where his father worked as a railway signalman. He was educated at Abergavenny Grammar School and at Trinity College, Cambridge. While at Cambridge, he joined the student faction of the Communist Party. During World War II, he served in the Guards Armored Division (1941–1945); after the war, he finished his degree in English at Cambridge and subsequently accepted an appointment at the Oxford University Extra-Mural Delegacy (1946–1961) while turning down a senior scholarship at Trinity College. Around this time he began to participate actively in the Workers' Educational Association. His postwar activities catapulted him directly into his career as a politically committed critic and as an exemplary public intellectual. Williams's publications, totaling more than 650 by the time of his death in 1988, were instrumental in shaping and directing the relatively new discipline of cultural studies, which found its first institutionalized form in the University of Birmingham Centre for Contemporary Cultural Studies, directed by such luminaries as Richard Hoggart and Stuart Hall.

Williams's early writings dealt with the concept of culture in its anthropological sense as a whole way of life. However, by the 1970s he moved on to theorizing culture as a process of production, whereby the arts, literature, and cultural practices were viewed in terms of their use value for the material means of production—a position that was identified as Williams's "cultural materialism." Perhaps one of Williams's most significant and original contributions to cultural studies was the concept of "structure of feeling": a component of the lived experience of a community that is above and beyond its experience of social institutions and ideology—an experience which resides primarily in things such as everyday, seemingly mundane personal interactions and relationships. In Marxism and Literature Williams redefined "structure of feeling" as a structure of social experience that lies somewhere between the articulated and the lived experience of a community. It is this concept that constituted Williams's attack on the structuralist and poststructuralist paradigms that posited language as the distillation of cultural experience such that culture could only be experienced through language and that cultural experience was limited to the articulated. In the first selection from Keywords, Williams reviews the various historical usages of the term violence.

Other texts by Williams include Culture and Society, 1780–1950 (1958), The Long Revolution (1961), Communications (1962), Modern Tragedy (1966), The Country and the City (1973), and Problems in Materialism and Culture: Selected Essays (1981).

Keywords

RAYMOND WILLIAMS

Violence is often now a difficult word, because its primary sense is of physical assault, as in "robbery with *violence*," yet it is also used more widely in ways that are not easy to define. If we take physical assault as sense (i) we can take a clear general sense (ii) as the use of physical force, including the distant use of weapons or bombs, but we have then to add that this seems to be specialized to "unauthorized" uses: the *violence* of a "terrorist" but not, except by its opponents, of an army, where "force" is preferred and most operations of war and preparation for war are described as "defence"; or the similar partisan range between "putting under restraint" or "restoring order," and "police *violence*." We can note also a relatively simple sense (iii), which is not always clearly distinguished from (i) and (ii), as in "*violence* on television," which can include the reporting of violent physical events but indicates mainly the dramatic portrayal of such events.

The difficulty begins when we try to distinguish sense (iv), *violence* as threat, and sense (v), *violence* as unruly behavior. Sense (iv) is clear when the threat is of physical *violence*, but it is often used when the real threat, or the real practice, is unruly behaviour. The phenomenon known as "student *violence*" included cases in senses (i) and (ii), but it clearly also included cases of sense (iv) and sense (v). The emotional power of the word can then be very confusing.

It is a longstanding complexity. There has been obvious interaction between *violence* and *violation*, the breaking of some custom or some dignity. . . . This is part of the complexity. But *violence* has also been used in English, as in the Latin for intensity or vehemence; "marke me with what *violence* she first lov'd the Moore" (Othello, II, i); "*violence* of party spirit" (Coleridge, 1818). There was an interesting note in 1696: "*violence* . . . figuratively spoken of Human Passions and Designs, when unruly, and not to be govern'd." It is the interaction of this sense with the sense of physical force that underlies the real difficulties of senses (iv) and (v); a sense (vi), as in "violently in love," is never in practice misunderstood. But if it is said that the State uses force, not only in senses (i) and (ii) but more critically in sense (iv)—the threat implied as the consequence of any breach of "law and order" as at any time or in any one place defined—it is objected that *violence* is the wrong word for this, not only because of the sense of "authorized" force but because it is not "unruly." At the same time, questions of what it is to be "unruly" or "not to be govern'd" can be side-stepped. It is within the assumption of "unruly," and not, despite the transfer in the word, of physical force, that loud or vehement (or even very strong and persistent) verbal criticism has been commonly described as violent, and the two steps beyond that—threat to some existing arrangement, threat of actual force—sometimes become a moving staircase to the strong meanings of *violence* in senses (i) and (ii).

It is then clearly a word that needs early specific definition, if it is not (as in yet another sense), (vii) to be done *violence* to—to be wrenched from its meaning or significance.

Marxism and Literature

The traditional definition of "hegemony" is political rule or domination, especially in relations between states. Marxism extended the definition of rule or domination to relations between social classes, and especially to definitions of a ruling class. "Hegemony" then acquired a further significant sense in the work of Antonio Gramsci, carried out under great difficulties in a Fascist prison between 1927 and 1935. Much is still uncertain in Gramsci's use of the concept, but his work is one of the major turning-points in Marxist cultural theory.

Gramsci made a distinction between "rule" (dominio) and "hegemony." "Rule" is expressed in directly political forms and in times of crisis by direct or effective coercion. But the more normal situation is a complex interlocking of political, social, and cultural forces, and "hegemony," according to different interpretations, is either this or the active social and cultural forces which are its necessary elements. Whatever the implications of the concept for Marxist political theory (which has still to recognize many kinds of direct political control, social class control, and economic control, as well as this more general formation), the effects on cultural theory are immediate. For "hegemony" is a concept which at once includes and goes beyond two powerful earlier concepts: that of "culture" as a "whole social process," in which men define and shape their whole lives; and that of "ideology," in any of its Marxists senses, in which a system of meanings and values is the expression or projection of a particular class interest.

"Hegemony" goes beyond "culture," as previously defined, in its insistence on relating the "whole social process" to specific distributions of power and influence. To say that "men" define and shape their whole lives is true only in abstraction. In any actual society there are specific inequalities in means and therefore in capacity to realize this process. In a class society there are primarily inequalities between classes. Gramsci therefore introduced the necessary recognition of dominance and subordination in what has still, however, to be recognized as a whole process.

It is in just this recognition of the wholeness of the process that the concept of "hegemony" goes beyond "ideology." What is decisive is not only the conscious system of ideas and beliefs, but the whole lived social process as practically organized by specific and dominant meanings and values. Ideology, in its normal senses, is a relatively formal and articulated system of meanings, values, and beliefs, of a kind that can be abstracted as a "world-view" or a "class outlook." This explains its popularity as a concept in retrospective analysis (in base-superstructure models or in homology), since a system of ideas can be abstracted from that once living social process and represented, usually by the selection of "leading" or typical "ideologists" or "ideological features," as the decisive form in which consciousness was at once expressed and controlled (or, as in Althusser, was in effect unconscious, as an imposed structure). The relatively mixed, confused, incomplete, or inarticulate consciousness of actual men in that period and society is thus overridden in the name of this decisive generalized system, and indeed in structural homology is procedurally excluded as peripheral or ephemeral. It is the fully articulate and systematic forms which are recognizable as ideology, and there is a corresponding tendency in the analysis of art to look only for similarly fully articulate and systematic expressions of this ideology in the content (base-superstructure) or form (homology) of actual works. In less selective procedures, less dependent on the inherent classicism of the definition of form as fully articulate and systematic, the tendency is to consider works as variants of, or as variably affected by, the decisive abstracted ideology.

More generally, this sense of "an ideology" is applied in abstract ways to the actual consciousness of both dominant and subordinated classes. A dominant class "has" this ideology in relatively pure and simple forms. A subordinate class has, in one version, nothing but this ideology as its consciousness (since the production of all ideas is, by axiomatic definition, in the hands of those who control the primary means of production) or, in another version, has this ideology imposed on its otherwise different consciousness, which it must struggle to sustain or develop against "ruling-class ideology."

The concept of hegemony often, in practice, resembles these definitions, but it is distinct in its refusal to equate consciousness with the articulate formal system which can be and ordinarily is abstracted as "ideology." It of course does not exclude the articulate and formal meanings, values, and beliefs which a dominant class develops and propagates. But it does not equate these with consciousness, or rather it does not reduce consciousness to them. Instead it sees the relations of domination and subordination, in their forms as practice consciousness, as in effect a saturation of the whole process of living—not only of political and economic activity, nor only of manifest social activity, but of the whole substance of lived identities and relationships, to such a depth that the pressures and limits of what can ultimately be seen as a specific economic, political, and cultural system seem to most of us the pressures and limits of simple experience and common sense. Hegemony is then not only the articulate upper level of "ideology," nor are its forms of control only those ordinarily seen as "manipulation" or "indoctrination." It is a whole body of practices and expectations, over the whole of living: our senses and assignments of energy, our shaping perceptions of ourselves and our world. It is a lived system of meanings and values—constitutive and constituting—which as they are experienced as practices appear as reciprocally confirming. It thus constitutes a sense of reality for most people in the society, a sense of absolute because experienced reality beyond which it is very difficult for most members of the society to move, in most areas of their lives. It is, that is to say, in the strongest sense a "culture," but a culture which has also to be seen as the lived dominance and subordination of particular classes.

There are two immediate advantages in this concept of hegemony. First, its forms of domination and subordination correspond much more closely to the normal processes of social organization and control in developed societies than the more familiar projections from the idea of a ruling class, which are usually based on much earlier and simpler historical phases. It can speak, for example, to the realities of electoral democracy, and to the significant modern areas of "leisure" and "private life," more specifically and more actively than older ideas of domination, with their trivializing explanations of simple "manipulation," "corruption," and "betrayal." If the pressures and limits of a given form of domination are to this extent experienced and in practice internalized, the whole question of class rule, and of opposition to it, is transformed. Gramsci's emphasis on the creation of an alternative hegemony, by the practical connection of many different forms of struggle, including those not easily recognizable as and indeed not primarily "political" and "economic," thus leads to a much more profound and more active sense of revolutionary activity in a highly developed society than the persistently abstract models derived from very different historical situations. The sources of any alternative hegemony are indeed difficult to define. For Gramsci they spring from the working class, but not this class as an ideal or abstract construction. What he sees, rather, is a working people which has, precisely, to become a class, and a potentially hegemonic class, against the pressures and limits of an existing and powerful hegemony.

Second, and more immediately in this context, there is a whole different way of seeing cultural activity, both as tradition and as practice. Cultural work and activity are not now, in any ordinary sense, a superstructure: not only because of the depth and thoroughness at which any cultural hegemony is lived, but because cultural tradition and practice are seen as much more than superstructural expressions—reflections, mediations, or typifications—of a formed social and economic structure. On the contrary, they are among the basic processes of the formation itself and, further, related to a much wider area of reality than the abstractions of "social" and "economic" experience. People seeing themselves and each other in directly personal relationships; people seeing the natural world and themselves in it; people using their physical and material resources for what one kind of society specializes to "leisure" and "entertainment" and "art": all these active experiences and practices, which make up so much of the reality of a culture and its cultural production, can be seen as they are, without reduction to other categories of content, and without the characteristic straining to fit them (directly as reflection, indirectly as mediation or typification or analogy) to other and determining manifest economic and political relationships. Yet they can still be seen as elements of a hegemony: an inclusive social and cultural formation which indeed to be effective has to extend to and include, indeed to form and be formed from, the whole area of lived experience.

Many difficulties then arise, both theoretically and practically, but it is important to recognize how many blind alleys we may now be saved from entering. If any lived culture is necessarily so extensive, the problems of domination and subordination on the one hand, and of the extraordinary complexity of any actual cultural tradition and practice on the other, can at last be directly approached.

There is of course the difficulty that domination and subordination, as effective descriptions of cultural formation, will, by many, be refused; that the alternative language of co-operative shaping, of common contribution, which the traditional concept of "culture" so notably expressed, will be found preferable. In this fundamental choice there is no alternative, from any socialist position, to recognition and emphasis on the massive historical and immediate experience of class domination and subordination, in all their different forms. This becomes, very quickly, a matter of specific experience and argument. But there is a closely related problem within the concept of "hegemony" itself. In some uses, though not I think in Gramsci, the totalizing tendency of the concept, which is significant and indeed crucial, is converted into an abstract totalization, and in this form it is readily compatible with sophisticated senses of "the superstructure" or even "ideology." The hegemony, that is, can be seen as more uniform, more static, and more abstract than in practice, if it is really understood, it can ever actually be. Like any other Marxist concept, it is particularly susceptible to epochal as distinct from historical definition, and to categorical as distinct from substantial description. Any isolation of its "organizing principles," or of its "determining features," which have indeed to be grasped in experience and by analysis, can lead very quickly to a totalizing abstraction. And then the problems of the reality of domination and subordination, and of their relations to co-operative shaping and common contribution, can be quite falsely posed.

A lived hegemony is always a process. It is not, except analytically, a system or a structure. It is a realized concept of experiences, relationships, and activities, with specific and changing pressures and limits. In practice, that is, hegemony can never be singular. Its internal structures are highly complex, as can readily be seen in any concrete analysis. Moreover (and this is crucial, reminding us of the necessary thrust of the concept), it does not just passively exist as a form of dominance. It has continually to be renewed, recreated, defended, and modified. It is also continually resisted, limited, altered, challenged by pressures not at all its own. We have then to add to the concept of hegemony the concepts of counter-hegemony and alternative hegemony, which are real and persistent elements of practice.

One way of expressing the necessary distinction between practical and abstract senses within the concept is to speak of "the hegemonic" rather than the "hegemony," and of "the dominant" rather than simple "domination." The reality of any hegemony, in the extended political and cultural sense, is that, while by definition it is always dominant, it is never either total or exclusive. At any time, forms of alternative or directly oppositional politics and culture exist as significant elements in the society. We shall need to explore their conditions and their limits, but their active presence is decisive, not only because they have to be included in any historical (as distinct from epochal) analysis, but as forms which have had significant effect on the hegemonic process itself. That is to say, alternative political and cultural emphases, and the many forms of opposition and struggle, are important not only in themselves but as indicative features of what the hegemonic process has in practice had to work to control. A static hegemony, of the kind which is indicated by abstract totalizing definitions of a dominant "ideology" or "world-view," can ignore or isolate such alternatives and opposition, but to the extent that they are significant the decisive hegemonic function is to control or transform or even incorporate them. In this active process the hegemonic has to be seen as more than the simple transmission of an (unchanging) dominance. On the contrary, any hegemonic process must be especially alert and responsive to the alternatives and opposition which question or threaten its dominance. The reality of cultural process must then always include the efforts and contributions of those who are in one way or another outside or at the end of the terms of the specific hegemony.

Thus it is misleading, as a general method, to reduce all political and cultural initiatives and contributions to the terms of the hegemony. That is the reductive consequence of the radically different concept of "superstructure." The specific functions of "the hegemonic," "the dominant," have always to be stressed, but not in ways which suggest any a priori totality. The most interesting and difficult part of any cultural analysis, in complex societies, is that which seeks to grasp the hegemonic in its active and formative but also its transformational processes. Works of art, by their substantial and general character, are often especially important as sources of this complex evidence.

The major theoretical problem, with immediate effect on methods of analysis, is to distinguish between alternative and oppositional initiatives and contributions which are made within or against a specific hegemony (which then sets certain limits to them or which can succeed in neutralizing, changing, or actually incorporating them) and other kinds of initiative and contribution which are irreducible to the terms of the original or the adaptive hegemony, and are in that sense independent. It can be persuasively argued that all or nearly all initiatives and contributions, even when they take on manifestly alternative or oppositional forms, are in practice tied to the hegemonic: that the dominant culture, so to say, at once produces and limits its own forms of counter-culture. There is more evidence for this view (for example in the case of the Romantic critique of industrial civilization) than we usually admit. But there is evident variation in specific kinds of social order and in the character of the consequent alternative and oppositional formations. It would be wrong to overlook the importance of works and ideas which, while clearly affected by hegemonic limits and pressures, are at least in part significant breaks beyond them, which may again in part be neutralized, reduced, or incorporated, but which in their most active elements nevertheless come through as independent and original.

Thus cultural process must not be assumed to be merely adaptive, extensive, and incorporative. Authentic breaks within and beyond it, in specific social conditions which can vary from extreme isolation to pre-revolutionary breakdowns and actual revolutionary activity, have often in fact occurred. And we are better able to see this, alongside more general recognition of the insistent pressures and limits of the hegemonic, if we develop modes of analysis which instead of reducing works to be finished products, and activities to fixed positions, are capable of discerning, in good faith, the finite but significant openness of many actual initiatives and contributions. The finite but significant openness of many works of art, as signifying forms making possible but also requiring persistent and variable signifying responses, is then especially relevant.

The French sociologist and cultural historian Pierre Bourdieu was born in Denguin, France, and educated at École Normale Supérieure, where he specialized in philosophy. His early career included a period on the faculty of letters at the University of Algiers in Algeria (1958–1960), after which he returned to Paris, where he was a member of the École des Hautes Études, Paris, and a director of studies from 1964 until his death. In 1981 he was also elected to the prestigious Collège de France, Paris.

His writings are wide-ranging and numerous, and many of them have been translated into English. Several have relevance to the study of violence, but perhaps none more than Esquisse d'une théorie de la pratique: Précédé de trois études d'ethnologie kabyle (Droz, 1972), which was translated into English and published as Outline of a Theory of Practice (Cambridge University Press, 1977). Bourdieu's attention to "modes of domination" and "symbolic capital" helps theorize the institutionalization of violence. Bourdieu understands "modes of domination" to exist on a continuum. They are constructed through practices, institutions, and social spaces, and must be analyzed precisely because they are not rational and, insofar as they "overflow" the bounds of language, cannot be articulated. In Outline of a Theory of Practice, Bourdieu "reads" material artifacts and practices as other theorists read texts, stories, or words. While he clearly draws on Marxist theory and uses and develops a materialist approach in this work, he also attempts to avoid the overdetermination of which some Marxist theory is guilty.

In Bourdieu's view, all aspects of social life are infused with power relations, so the central question is not about the existence of "violence" in those aspects, but about the degree to which they participate in, or foster, "violence." With his focus on institutions and on the habitus (the range of practices which both group us together and differentiate us from each other), Bourdieu makes it possible to account for agency but also to avoid scapegoating in reductive ways.

Yet to assert that one learns everything from habitus and practices which are limited by the ineffable doxa makes it very difficult to account for change or innovation. In the same way that Michel Foucault's work could be strengthened by attention to a subject's location on multiple axes of networks of power relations, the possibility of participation in multiple "habitus" would open up new avenues for the work that Bourdieu began in Outline of a Theory of Practice.

Other texts by Bourdieu include: Algerie 60 (translated as Algeria 1960, Cambridge University Press, 1979); La Distinction: Critique sociale du jugement (translated as Distinction: A Social Critique of the Judgement of Taste, Harvard Univer-

sity Press, 1984); Homo academicus *(Stanford University Press, 1988);* In Other Words: Essays Towards a Reflexive Sociology *(Stanford University Press, 1990); and* The Field of Cultural Production: Essays on Art and Literature *(edited and introduced by Randal Johnson, Columbia University Press, 1993).*

Outline of a Theory of Practice

PIERRE BOURDIEU

The habitus is the product of the work of inculcation and appropriation necessary in order for those products of collective history, the objective structures (e.g. of language, economy, etc.) to succeed in reproducing themselves more or less completely, in the form of durable dispositions, in the organisms (which one can, if one wishes, call individuals) lastingly subjected to the same conditionings, and hence placed in the same material conditions of existence. Therefore sociology treats as identical all the biological individuals who, being the product of the same objective conditions, are the supports of the same habitus: social class, understood as a system of objective determinations, must be brought into relation not with the individual or with the "class" as a *population*, i.e. as an aggregate of enumerable, measurable biological individuals, but with the class habitus, the system of dispositions (partially) common to all products of the same structures. Thought it is impossible for *all* members of the same class (or even two of them) to have had the same experiences, in the same order, it is certain that each member of the same class is more likely than any member of another class to have been confronted with the situations most frequent for the members of that class. The objective structures which science apprehends in the form of statistical regularities (e.g. employment rates, income curves, probabilities of access to secondary education, frequency of holidays, etc.) inculcate, through the direct or indirect but always convergent experiences which give a social environment its *physiognomy*, with its "closed doors," "dead ends," and limited "prospects," that "art of assessing likelihoods," as Leibniz put it, of anticipating the objective future, in short, the sense of reality or realities which is perhaps the best-concealed principle of their efficacy.

In order to define the relations between class, habitus, and the organic individuality which can never entirely be removed from sociological discourse, inasmuch as, being given immediately to immediate perception (*intuitus personae*), it is also socially designated and recognized (name, legal identity, etc.) and is defined by a *social trajectory* strictly speaking irreducible to any other, the habitus could be considered as a subjective but not individual system of inter-nalized structures, schemes of perception, conception, and action common to all members of the same group or class and constituting the precondition for all objectification and apperception; and the objective coordination of practices and the sharing of a world-view could be found on the perfect impersonality and interchangeability of singular practices and views. But this would amount to regarding all the practices or representations produced in accordance with identical schemes as impersonal and substitutable, like singular intuitions of space which, according to Kant, reflect none of the peculiarities of the individ-ual ego. In fact, it is in a relation of homology, of diversity within homogeneity reflecting the diversity within homogeneity characteristic of their social condi-tions of production, that the singular habitus of the different members of the same class are united; the homology of world-views implies the systematic differences which separate singular world-views, adopted from singular but concerted standpoints. Since the history of the individual is never anything other than a certain specification of the collective history of his group or class, *each individual system of dispositions* may be seen as a *structural variant* of all the other group or class habitus, expressing the difference between trajectories and positions inside or outside the class. "Personal" style, the particular stamp marking all the products of the same habitus, whether practices or works, is never more than a *deviation* in relation to the *style* of a period or class so that it relates back to the common style not only by its conformity—like Phidias, who, according to Hegel, had no "manner"—but also by the difference which makes the whole "manner."

The principle of these individual differences lies in the fact that, being the product of a chronologically ordered series of structuring determinations, the habitus, which at every moment structures in terms of the structuring experi-ences which produced it the structuring experiences which affect its structure, brings about a unique integration, dominated by the earliest experiences, of the experiences statistically common to the members of the same class. Thus, for example, the habitus acquired in the family underlies the structuring of school experiences (in particular the reception and assimilation of the specifically pedagogic message), and the habitus transformed by schooling, itself diversi-fied, in turn underlies the structuring of all subsequent experiences (e.g. the reception and assimilation of the messages of the culture industry or work experiences), and so on, from restructuring to restructuring.

Springing from the encounter in an integrative organism of relatively inde-pendent causal series, such as biological and social determinisms, the habitus makes coherence and necessity out of accident and contingency: for example, the equivalences it establishes between positions in the division of labour and positions in the division between the sexes are doubtless not peculiar to societies in which the division of labour and the division between the sexes coincide almost perfectly. In a class society, all the products of a given agent, by an essential *overdetermination*, speak inseparably and simultaneously of his class—or, more, precisely, his position in the social structure and his rising or falling trajectory— and of his (or her) body—or, more precisely, all the properties, always socially qualified, of which he or she is the bearer—sexual properties of course, but also physical properties, praised, like strength or beauty, or stigmatized.

· · · · ·

So, it is in the degree of objectification of the accumulated social capital that one finds the basis of all the pertinent differences between the modes of domination: that is, very schematically, between, on the one hand, social universes in which relations of domination are made, unmade, and remade in and by the interactions between persons, and on the other hand, social formations in which, mediated by objective, institutionalized mechanisms, such as those producing and guaranteeing the distribution of "titles" (titles of nobility, deeds of possession, academic degrees, etc.), relations of domination have the opacity and permanence of things and escape the grasp of individual consciousness and power. Objectification guarantees the permanence and cumulativity of material and symbolic acquisitions which can then subsist without the agents having to recreate them continuously and in their entirety by deliberate action; but, because the profits of these institutions are the object of differential appropriation, objectification also and inseparably ensures the reproduction of the structure of the distribution of the capital which, in its various forms, is the precondition for such appropriation, and in so doing, reproduces the structure of the relations of domination and dependence.

Paradoxically, it is precisely because there exist relatively autonomous fields, functioning in accordance with rigorous mechanisms capable of imposing their necessity on the agents, that those who are in a position to command these mechanisms and to appropriate the material and/or symbolic profits accruing from their functioning are able to *dispense with* strategies aimed *expressly* (which does not mean manifestly) and directly (i.e. without being mediated by the mechanisms) at the domination of individuals, a domination which in this case is the condition of the appropriation of the material and symbolic profits of their labour. The saving is a real one, because strategies designed to establish or maintain lasting relations of dependence are generally very expensive in terms of material goods (as in the potlatch or in charitable acts), services, or simply *time*;

which is why, by a paradox constitutive of this mode of domination, the means eat up the end, and the actions necessary to ensure the continuation of power themselves help to weaken it.

. . . . .

Just as economic wealth cannot function as capital until it is linked to an economic apparatus, so cultural competence in its various forms cannot be constituted as cultural capital until it is inserted into the objective relations between the system of economic production and the system producing the producers (which is itself constituted by the relation between the school system and the family). When a society lacks both the literacy which would enable it to preserve and accumulate in objectified form the cultural resources it has inherited from the past, and also the educational system which would give its agents the aptitudes and dispositions required for the symbolic reappropriation of those resources, it can only preserve them *in their incorporated state*. Consequently, to ensure the perpetuation of cultural resources which would otherwise disappear along with the agents who bear them, it has to resort to systematic inculcation, a process which, as is shown by the case of the bards, may last as long as the period during which the resources are actually used. The transformations made possible by an instrument of cultural communication such as writing have been abundantly described: by detaching cultural resources from persons, literacy enables a society to move beyond immediate human limits—in particular those of individual memory—and frees it from the constraints implied by mnemonic devices such as poetry, the preservation technique par excellence in non-literate societies; it enables a society to accumulate culture hitherto preserved in embodied form, and correlatively enables particular groups to practise *primitive accumulation of cultural capital*, the partial or total monopolizing of the society's symbolic resources in religion, philosophy, art, and science, by monopolizing the instruments for appropriation of those resources (writing, reading, and other decoding techniques) henceforward preserved not in memories but in texts.

But the objectification effects of literacy are nothing in comparison with those produced by the educational system. Without entering into detailed analysis, it must suffice to point out that academic qualifications are to cultural capital what money is to economic capital. By giving the same value to all holders of the same certificate, so that any one of them can take the place of any other, the educational system minimizes the obstacles to the free circulation of cultural capital which result from its being incorporated in individual persons (without, however, sacrificing the advantages of the charismatic ideology of the irreplaceable individual); it makes it possible to relate all qualification-holders (and also, negatively, all unqualified individuals) to a single standard, thereby setting up a *single market* for all cultural capacities and guaranteeing the convertibility of cultural capital into money, at a determinate cost in labour and time. Academic qualifications, like money, have a conventional, fixed value which, being guaranteed by law, is freed from local limitations (in contrast to scholastically uncertified cultural capital) and temporal fluctuations: the cultural capital which they in a sense guarantee once and for all does not constantly need to be proved. The objectification accomplished by academic degrees and diplomas and, in a more general way, by all forms of credentials, is inseparable from the objectification which the law guarantees by defining *permanent positions* which are distinct from the biological individuals holding them, and may be occupied by agents who are biologically different but interchangeable in terms of the qualifications required. Once this state of affairs is established, relations of power and domination no longer exist directly between individuals; they are set up in pure objectivity between institutions, i.e. between socially guaranteed qualifications and socially defined positions, and through them, between the social mechanisms which produce and guarantee both the social value of the qualifications and the positions and also the distribution of these social attributes among biological individuals.

Law does no more than symbolically consecrate—by *recording* it in a form which renders it both eternal and universal—the structure of the power relation between groups and classes which is produced and guaranteed practically by the functioning of these mechanisms. For example, it records and legitimates the distinction between the position and the person, the power and its holder, together with the relationship obtaining at a particular moment between qualifications and jobs (reflecting the relative bargaining power of the buyers and sellers of qualified, i.e. scholastically guaranteed, labour power) which appears concretely in a particular distribution of the material and symbolic profits assigned to the holders (or non-holders) of qualifications. The law thus contributes its own (specifically symbolic) force to the action of the various mechanisms which render it superfluous constantly to reassert power relations by overtly resorting to force.

Thus the task of legitimating the established order does not fall exclusively to the mechanisms traditionally regarded as belonging to the order of ideology, such as law. The system of symbolic goods production and the system producing the producers fulfill in addition, i.e. by the very logic of their normal functioning, ideological functions, by virtue of the fact that the mechanisms through which they contribute to the reproduction of the established order and to the perpetuation of domination remain hidden. The educational system helps to provide the dominant class with what Max Weber terms "a theodicy of its own privilege," not so much through the ideologies it produces or inculcates (as those who speak of "ideological apparatuses" would have it); but rather through the practical justification of the established order which it achieves by using the overt connection between qualifications and jobs as a smokescreen for the connection—which it *records surreptitiously*, under cover of formal equality —between the qualifications people obtain and the cultural capital they have inherited—in other words, through the legitimacy it confers on the transmission of this form of heritage. The most successful ideological effects are those which have no need of words, and ask no more than complicitous silence. It follows, incidentally that any analysis of ideologies, in the narrow sense of "legitimating discourses," which fails to include an analysis of the corresponding institutional mechanisms, is liable to be no more than a contribution to the efficacy of those ideologies: this is true of all internal (semiological) analyses of political, educational, religious, or aesthetic ideologies which forget that the political function of these ideologies may in some cases be reduced to the effect of displacement and diversion, camouflage and legitimation, which they produce by reproducing—through their oversights and omissions, and in their deliberately or involuntarily complicitous silences—the effects of the objective mechanisms.

It has been necessary at least to sketch an analysis of the objective mechanisms which play a part both in setting up and in concealing lasting relations of domination, in order to understand fully the radical difference for conservation characteristic of social formations whose accumulated social energy is unequally objectified in mechanisms. On the one side there are social relations which, not containing within themselves the principle of their own reproduction, must be kept up through nothing less than a process of continuous creation; on the other side, a social world which, containing within itself the principle of its own continuation, frees agents from the endless work of creating or restoring social relations. This opposition finds expression in the history or prehistory of sociological thought. In order to "ground social being in nature," as Durkheim puts it, it has been necessary to break with the propensity to see it as founded on the arbitrariness of individual wills, or, with Hobbes, on the arbitrariness of a sovereign will: "For Hobbes," writes Durkheim, "it is an act of will which gives birth to the social order and it is a perpetually renewed act of will which upholds it." And there is every reason to believe that the break with this artificialist vision, which is the precondition for scientific apprehension, could not be made before the constitution, in reality, of objective mechanisms like the self-regulating market, which, as Polyani points out, was intrinsically conducive to belief in determinism. But social reality had another trap in store for science: the existence of mechanisms capable of reproducing the political order, independently of any deliberate intervention, makes it possible to recognize as political, amongst the different types of conduct directed towards gaining or keeping power, only such practices as tacitly exclude control over the reproduction mechanisms from the area of legitimate competition. In this way, social science, taking for its object the sphere of legitimate politics (as so-called "political science" does nowadays), adopted the preconstructed object which reality foisted upon it.

The greater the extent to which the task of reproducing the relations of domination is taken over by objective mechanisms, which serve the interests of the dominant group without any conscious effort on the latter's part, the more indirect and, in a sense, impersonal, become the strategies objectively oriented towards reproduction: it is not by lavishing generosity, kindness, or politeness on his charwoman (or on any other "socially inferior" agent), by choosing the best investment for his money, or the best school for his son, that the possessor of economic or cultural capital perpetuates the relationship of domination which objectively links him with his charwoman and even her descendants. Once a system of mechanisms has been constituted capable of objectively ensuring the reproduction of the established order by its own motion (*apo tou automatou*, as the Greeks put it), the dominant class have only to *let the system they dominate take its own course* in order to exercise their domination; but until such a system exists, they have to work directly, daily, personally, to produce and reproduce conditions of domination which are even then never entirely trustworthy. Because they cannot be satisfied with appropriating the profits of a social machine which has not yet developed the power of self-perpetuation, they are obliged to resort to *the elementary forms of domination*, in other words, the direct domination of one person by another, the limiting case of which is appropriation of persons, i.e. slavery. They cannot appropriate the labour, services, goods, homage, and respect of others without "winning" them personally, "tying" them—in short, creating a bond between persons.

Thus this system contains only two ways (and they prove in the end to be just one way) of getting and keeping a lasting hold over someone: gifts or debts, the overtly economic obligations of debt, or the "moral," "affective" obligations created and maintained by exchange, in short, overt (physical or economic) violence, or symbolic violence—*censored, euphemized*, i.e. unrecognizable, socially recognized violence. There is an intelligible relation—not a contradiction —between these two forms of violence, which coexist in the same social formation and sometimes in the same relationship: when domination can only be exercised in its *elementary form*, i.e. directly, between one person and another, it cannot take place overtly and must be disguised under the veil of enchanted relationships, the official model of which is presented by relations between kinsmen; in order to be socially recognized it must get itself misrecognized. The reason for the pre-capitalist economy's great need for symbolic violence is that the only way in which relations of domination can be set up, maintained, or restored, is through strategies which, being expressly oriented towards the establishment of relations of personal dependence, must be disguised and transfigured lest they destroy themselves by revealing their true nature; in a word, they must be *euphemized*. Hence the *censorship* to which the overt manifestation of violence, especially in its naked economic form, is subjected by the logic characteristic of an economy in which interests can only be satisfied on condition that they be disguised in and by the strategies aiming to satisfy them. It would be a mistake to see a contradiction in the fact that violence is here both more present and more hidden. Because the pre-capitalist economy cannot count on the implacable, hidden violence of objective mechanisms, it resorts *simultaneously* to forms of domination which may strike the modern observer as more brutal, more primitive, more barbarous, or at the same time, as gentler, more humane, more respectful of persons. This coexistence of overt physical and economic violence and of the most refined symbolic violence is found in all the institutions characteristic of this economy, and at the heart of every social relationship: it is present both in the debt and in the gift, which, in spite of their apparent opposition, have in common the power of founding either dependence (and even slavery) or solidarity, depending on the strategies within which they are deployed. The fundamental ambiguity of all the institutions which modern taxonomies tend to present as economic is evidence that contrary strategies, which, as we have also seen in the case of the master-*khammes* (slave) relationship, may coexist under the same name, are *interchangeable* ways of performing the same function, with the "choice" between overt violence and gentle, hidden violence depending on the relative strengths of the two parties at a particular time, and on the degree of integration and ethical integrity of the arbitrating group. In a society in which overt violence, the violence of the usurer or the merciless master, meets with collective reprobation and is liable either to provoke a violent riposte from the victim or to force him to flee (that is to say, in either case, in *the absence of any other recourse*, to provoke the annihilation of the very relationship which was intended to be exploited), symbolic violence, the gentle, invisible form of violence, which is never recognized as such, and is not so much undergone as chosen, the violence of credit, confidence, obligation, personal loyalty, hospitality, gifts, gratitude, piety—in short, all the virtues honoured by the code of honour—cannot fail to be seen as the most economical mode of domination, i.e. the mode which best corresponds to the economy of the system.

. . . . .

The endless reconversion of economic capital into symbolic capital, at the cost of a wastage of social energy which is the condition for the permanence of domination, cannot succeed without the complicity of the whole group: the work of denial which is the source of social alchemy is, like magic, a collective undertaking. As Mauss puts it, the whole society pays itself in the false coin of its dream. The collective misrecognition which is the basis of the ethic of honour, a collective denial of the economic reality of exchange, is only possible because, when the group lies to itself in this way, there is neither deceiver nor deceived: the peasant who treats his *khammes* as an associate, because that is the custom and because honour requires him to do so, deceives himself as much as he deceives his *khammes*, since the *only* form in which he can serve his interest is the euphemistic form presented by the ethic of honour; and nothing suits the *khammes* better than to play his part in an interested fiction which offers him an honourable representation of his condition. Thus the mechanisms responsible for reproducing the appropriate habitus are here an integral part of an apparatus of production which could not function without them. Agents lastingly "bind" each other, not only as parents and children, but also as creditor and debtor, master and *khammes*, only through the dispositions which the group inculcates in them and continuously reinforces, and which render *unthinkable* practices which would appear as legitimate and even be taken for granted in the disenchanted economy of "naked self-interest."

The official truth produced by the collective work of euphemization, an elementary form of the labour of objectification which eventually leads to the juridical definition of acceptable behaviour, is not simply the group's means of saving its "spiritualistic point of honour"; it also has a practical efficacy, for, even if it were contradicted by everyone's behaviour, like a rule to which every case proved an exception, it would still remain a true description of such behaviour as is intended to be acceptable. The code of honour weighs on each agent with the weight of all the other agents, and the disenchantment which leads to the progressive unveiling of repressed meanings and functions can only result from a collapse of the social conditions of the *cross-censorship* to which each agent submits with impatience but which he imposes on all the others.

If it be true that symbolic violence is the gentle, hidden form which violence takes when overt violence is impossible, it is understandable why symbolic forms of domination should have progressively withered away as objective mechanisms came to be constituted which, in rendering superfluous the work of euphemization, tended to produce the "disenchanted" dispositions their development demanded. It is equally clear why the progressive uncovering and neutralization of the ideological and practical effects of the mechanisms assuring the reproduction of the relations of domination should determine a return to forms of symbolic violence again based on dissimulation of the mechanisms of reproduction through the conversion of economic into symbolic capital: it is through legitimacy-giving redistribution, public ("social" policies) and private (financing of "disinterested" foundations, grants to hospitals and to academic and cultural institutions), which they make possible, that the efficacy of the mechanisms of reproduction is exerted.

To these forms of legitimate accumulation, through which the dominant groups or classes secure a capital of "credit" which seems to owe nothing to the logic of exploitation, must be added another form of accumulation of symbolic capital, the collection of luxury goods attesting the taste and distinction of their owner. The denial of economy and of economic interest, which in pre-capitalist societies at first took place on a ground from which it had to be expelled in order for economy to be constituted as such, thus finds its favourite refuge in the domain of art and culture, the site of pure consumption—money, of course, but also of time convertible into money. The world of art, a sacred island systematically and ostentatiously opposed to the profane, everyday world of production, a sanctuary for gratuitous, disinterested activity in a universe given over to money and self-interest, offers, like theology in a past epoch, an imaginary anthropology obtained by denial of all the negations really brought about by the economy.

A renowned political scientist and theoretical comparativist, James C. Scott was born in New Jersey and educated at Williams College. Scott did graduate study in Burma, then France, before returning to the United States and earning a master's degree (1963) and Ph.D. (1967) from Yale University. After teaching at University of Wisconsin, Madison (1967–1976), he returned to Yale, where he has been a professor of political science since 1976.

Scott's commitment to the persons and issues about whom he writes is epitomized in the dedication of his most theoretically ambitious work to date, Domination and the Arts of Resistance, *which he dedicated to Moorestown Friends' School—fittingly, for it is issues of individual dignity and cultural autonomy that inform most of Scott's work. Among his theoretical predecessors, his greatest debt is to Antonio Gramsci for his writings on hegemony and resistance and to Barrington Moore Jr., the Harvard historical sociologist. It is Moore whose eclectic style of moralistic inquiry prefigures Scott's more than does any other, and of Moore's corpus the most significant work for Scott's own formulations is without doubt* Injustice: The Social Bases of Obedience and Revolt *(1978).*

Above all, personal terror, the riveting anxiety of the individual faced with her or his powerlessness, preoccupies Scott. It is terror of this sort that, in his view, informs all relationships of domination and subordination. It informs the dominators who must construct public personae and offers a "public transcript" that makes their domination seem natural, even inevitable. But it also informs the subordinate. In the face of powerlessness, they devise strategies for creating their own social space, becoming proficient in the arts of political disguise and thus perpetuating an infrapolitics of resistance. Out of the ordeal of their domination they forge a hidden transcript, and it is this "hidden transcript" that becomes the key phrase for Scott's analysis, signaling what is most distinctive about his approach to the issue of violence. The hidden transcript functions as "a critique of power spoken behind the back of the dominant," and sometimes, although rarely, it can be spoken directly and publicly "in the teeth of power." When it is proclaimed publicly for the first time, it is its prehistory that "explains its capacity to produce political breakthroughs." Even should it fail to spark immediate change, it is "likely to be noted, admired and even mythologized in stories of bravery, social banditry, and noble sacrifice (that) themselves become part of the hidden transcript."

Scott's major books include Political Ideology in Malaysia: Reality and the Beliefs of an Elite *(1968),* The Moral Economy of the Peasant: Rebellion and Subsistence in Southeast Asia *(1976),* Weapons of the Weak: Everyday Forms of Peasant Resistance

(1985), Domination and the Arts of Resistance: Hidden Transcripts *(1990)*, *and* Seeing Like a State: How Certain Schemes to Improve the Human Condition Have Failed *(1998)*.

Domination and the Arts of Resistance

JAMES C. SCOTT

The public transcript is, to put it crudely, the *self*-portrait of dominant elites as they would have themselves seen. Given the usual power of dominant elites to compel performances from others, the discourse of the public transcript is a decidedly lopsided discussion. While it is unlikely to be merely a skein of lies and misrepresentations, it is designed to be impressive, to affirm and naturalize the power of dominant elites, and to conceal or euphemize the dirty linen of their rule.

If, however, this flattering self-portrait is to have any rhetorical force among subordinates, it necessarily involves some concessions to their presumed interests. That is, rulers who aspire to hegemony in the Gramscian sense of that term must make out an ideological case that they rule, to some degree, on behalf of their subjects. This claim, in turn, is always highly tendentious but seldom completely without resonance among subordinates.

The distinction between the hidden and the public transcripts, together with the hegemonic aspirations of the public transcript allows us to distinguish at least four varieties of political discourse among subordinate groups. They vary according to how closely they conform to the official discourse and according to who comprises their audience.

The safest and most public form of political discourse is that which takes as its basis the flattering self-image of elites. Owing to the rhetorical concessions that this self-image contains, it offers a surprisingly large arena for political conflict that appeals to these concessions and makes use of the room for interpretation within any ideology. For example, even the ideology of white slave owners of the antebellum U.S. South incorporated certain paternalist flourishes about the care, feeding, housing, and clothing of slaves and their religious instruction. Practices, of course, were something else. Slaves were, however, able to make political use of this small rhetorical space to appeal for garden plots, better food, humane treatment, freedom to travel to religious services, and so forth. Thus, some slave interests could find representation in the prevailing ideology without appearing in the least seditious.

A second and sharply contrasting form of political discourse is that of the hidden transcript itself. Here, offstage, where subordinates may gather outside the intimidating gaze of power, a sharply dissonant political culture is possible. Slaves in the relative safety of their quarters can speak the words of anger, revenge, self-assertion that they must normally choke back when in the presence of masters and mistresses.

A central argument of this book is that there is a third realm of subordinate group politics that lies strategically between the first two. This is a politics of disguise and anonymity that takes place in public view but is designed to have a double meaning or to shield the identity of the actors. Rumor, gossip, folktale, jokes, songs, rituals, codes, and euphemisms—a good part of the folk culture of subordinate groups—fit this description. As a case in point, consider the Brer Rabbit stories of slaves, and trickster tales more generally. At one level these are nothing but innocent stories about animals; at another level they appear to celebrate the cunning wiles and vengeful spirit of the weak as they triumph over the strong. I argue that a partly sanitized, ambiguous, and coded version of the hidden transcript is always present in the public discourse of subordinate groups. Interpreting these texts which, after all, are designed to be evasive is not a straightforward matter. Ignoring them, however, reduces us to an understanding of historical subordination that rests either on those rare moments of open rebellion or on the hidden transcript itself, which is not just evasive but often altogether inaccessible. The recovery of the nonhegemonic voices and practices of subject peoples requires, I believe, a fundamentally different form of analysis than the analysis of elites, owing to the constraints under which they are produced.

Finally, the most explosive realm of politics is the rupture of the political *cordon sanitaire* between the hidden and public transcript. When Mrs. Poyser has her "say," she obliterates the distinction by making the hitherto hidden transcript public. In her case, the squire fled, but such moments of challenge and open defiance typically provoke either a swift stroke of repression or, if unanswered, often lead to further words and acts of daring. We will examine such moments for the insights they offer into certain forms of charisma and the dynamic of political breakthroughs.

· · · · ·

The difference in power relations toward the hidden transcript segment of the continuum is that they are generated among those who are mutually subject, often as peers, to a larger system of domination. Although the slave may be freer vis-à-vis the master in this setting, it does not follow that relations of domination do not prevail among the slaves. Power relations among subordinates are not necessarily conducted along democratic lines at all. Among the inmates of prisons, who are all subject to a common domination from the institution and its officers, there frequently develops a tyranny as brutal and exploitive as anything the guards can devise. In this domination within domination the subordinate prisoner must measure his words and conduct perhaps more carefully before dominant prisoners than he does before prison officials.

Even if relations among subordinates may be characterized by symmetry and mutuality, the hidden transcript that develops in this case may be experienced as no less tyrannical despite the fact that all have had a hand in shaping it. Consider, for example, the ethos that often prevails among workers which penalizes any laborer who would go out of his way to curry the favor of the bosses. The words used from below to describe such behavior (today, ass-kisser, rate-buster, bootlicker) are designed to prevent it. These may be supplemented by glares, shunning, and perhaps even beatings.

The power relations generated among subordinate groups are often the only countervailing power to the determination of behavior from above. Tenant farmers in the Malaysian village I studied had developed a strong norm among themselves condemning anyone who might try to secure or enlarge his acreage by offering the landlord a higher seasonal rent than the current local tenant paid. Fifteen years ago someone apparently defied the norm; since then the family is poorly regarded and has not been spoken to or invited to feasts by any kin or friends of the offended family. In a comparable case no Andalusian farmworkers were said to take work for less than the minimum wage. If they did, they would be given the cold shoulder, ostracized, or branded "low" or a "creeper." The strength of the sanctions deployed to enforce conformity depends essentially on the cohesiveness of the subordinate group and on how threatening they view the defection. In nineteenth-century rural Ireland when a tenant broke a rent boycott by paying the land agent, he was likely to find his cow "houghed" in the morning: its Achilles tendon severed so that the tenant would have to destroy it himself. All such cases are instances of the more or less coercive pressure that can be generated to monitor and control deviance among a subordinate group. This pressure serves not only to suppress dissent among subordinates but may also place limits on the temptation to compete headlong with one another—at the expense of all—for the favor of the dominant.

. . . The dialectical relationship between the public and hidden transcript is obvious. By definition, the hidden transcript represents discourse—gesture, speech, practices—that is ordinarily excluded from the public transcript of subordinates by the exercise of power. The practice of domination, then, *creates* the hidden transcript. If the domination is particularly severe, it is likely to produce a hidden transcript of corresponding richness. The hidden transcript of subordinate groups, in turn, reacts back on the public transcript by engendering a subculture and by opposing its own variant form of social domination against that of the dominant elite. Both are realms of power and interests.

The hidden transcript of the dominant is similarly an artifact of the exercise of power. It contains that discourse—gestures, speech, practices—which is excluded from the public transcript by the ideological limits within which domination is cast. It too is a realm of power and interests. . . . [If] we instead took the perspective of the slave master and [ranged] from audiences of his family and closest friends all the way to his interaction on ceremonial occasions with the slaves assembled, [that perspective] would yield a spectrum of discursive realms of the dominant. Here too, as with a diplomat whose discourse varies enormously depending on whether he is talking formally with his own negotiating team or formally with the chief negotiator of a threatening enemy power, is a realm of masks. The masks may get thicker or thinner, they may be crude or subtle, depending on the nature of the audience and the interests involved, but they are nevertheless performances, as are all social actions.

POWER AND ACTING

> Your presence frightens any common man
> From saying things you would not care to hear
> But in dark corners I have heard them say
> How the whole town is grieving for this girl
> Unjustly doomed if ever woman was
> To die in shame for glorious action done. . . .
> This is the undercover speech in town.
> —Haemon to Creon, *Antigone*

On a daily basis, the impact of power is more readily observed in acts of deference, subordination, and ingratiation. The script and stage directions for subordinate groups are generally far more confining than for the dominant. Putting it in terms of "paying respect" to status, Hochschild observes, to have higher status is to have a stronger claim to rewards, including emotional rewards. It is also to have greater access to the means of enforcing claims. The deferential behavior of servants and women—the encouraging smiles, the attentive listening, the appreciative laughter, the comments of affirmation, admiration, or concern—comes to seem normal even built into personality rather than inherent in the kinds of exchange that low-status people commonly enter into.

A convincing performance may require both the suppression of control of feelings that would spoil the performance and the simulation of emotions that are necessary to the performance. Practical mastery through repetition may make the performance virtually automatic and apparently effortless. In other cases, it is a conscious strain, as when Old Tiennon said that when he met his father's ex-landlord, "I forced myself to be amiable." We often talk in this schizophrenic way as if our tactical self exercises control over our emotional self, which threatens to spoil the performance. The performance, as I shall continually emphasize, comprises not only speech acts but conformity in facial expression and gesture as well as practical obedience to commands that may be distasteful or humiliating.

More of the public life of subordinates than of the dominant is devoted to "command" performances. The change in the posture, demeanor, and apparent activity of an office workforce when the supervisor suddenly appears is an obvious case. The supervisor, though she too is constrained, can typically be more relaxed about her manner, less on guard, for it is the supervisor, after all, who sets the tone of the encounter. Power means not *having* to act or, more accurately, the capacity to be more negligent and casual about any single performance. So close was this association between power and acting in the French royal court that the slightest trace of an increase in servility could be taken as evidence of declining status and power: "Let a favorite pay close heed to himself for if he does not keep me waiting as long in his antechamber, if his face is more open, if he frowns less, if he listens to me a little further while showing me out, I shall think he is beginning to fall, and I shall be right." The haughtiness associated with the bearing of power may, in a physical sense, contain more of the unguarded self, while servility virtually by definition requires an attentive watchfulness and attuning of response to the mood and requirements of the powerholder. Less of the unguarded self is ventured because the possible penalties for a failure or misstep are severe; one must be constantly on one's "best behavior."

The influence that the powerful exercise on public discourse is apparent in the findings of sociolinguists about language use and power. These findings indicate how hierarchies of gender, race, caste, and class are encoded in the domination of talk.

In her study of contemporary language-use differences between women and men, Robin Lakoff emphasizes that the history of male dominance has meant that women increasingly use men's language—imitating the higher status dialect —while the reverse is rarely the case. In a face-to-face encounter the tone, grammar, and dialect of the dominant male is likely to prevail, not to mention that, as in other asymmetrical power relations, the dominant is typically the one who initiates the conversation, controls its direction, and terminates it. The fact of subordination can be read in the use of linguistic forms shaped so as to reflect and anticipate the response of the dominant. Thus Lakoff notes the far more widespread use by women of what linguists call the "tag question formation"—an "isn't it so?" Or a rising tone at the end of what would otherwise be a declarative sentence, which indicates a request for reassurance and approval before continuing. Other linguistic marks of subordination include the greater use of hyper-polite forms ("Would you be so kind as to please . . ." in place of a command), of hyper-correct grammar, linguistic hedges ("sort of," "kind of") that weaken a declarative phrase, and a disinclination to tell jokes in public. When the subordination is extreme, as in slavery and racism, it is often observed that stammering is common, a stammering that reflects not a speech defect, since the stammerers can speak fluently in other contexts, but a fear-induced hesitation over producing the correct formula. One can, I think, read in these patterns a consistent risk-averse use of language by the powerless—an attempt to venture as little as possible, to use stock formulas when available, and to avoid taking liberties with language that might give offense. As a high-caste anthropologist conducting interviews among untouchable Chamars in Lucknow discovered, "The triter the inquiry the 'better' the Chamar's response. In less trodden areas, evasive devices —deflection, postponement, containment, cliché, rhetorical questions, and feigned ignorance—were deftly employed." Such performances require practice, mastery, and their own kind of improvisation if they are to be exercised successfully, but they are nevertheless all damage-control maneuvers in the face of power. As Lakoff concludes in the case of women's speech and dress conformity, "Her overattention to appearance and appearances (including perhaps overcorrectness and overgentility of speech and etiquette) is merely the result of being forced to exist only as a reflection in the eyes of others."

Societies with long-established court cultures develop elaborate codes for speech-levels which in extreme cases can nearly constitute a separate language. Here the hyper-correctness of subordinates is institutionalized linguistically. Strong traces of such codes persist in the differences between Saxon and Norman English: The Saxon commoners ate while the Norman conquerors dined. In Malaysia a host of special verbs distinguish quite ordinary actions when the sultan is undertaking them: commoners bathe, the sultan sprinkles himself; commoners walk, the sultan progresses (implying a smooth, gliding motion); commoners sleep, the sultan reclines. Pronouns also change, as they do in most highly stratified societies, depending on the relative status of the speakers. When a commoner is addressing the sultan, he uses the term *hamba*, which translates roughly as "your slave," and he traditionally approaches the throne in a posture of abject humility. Every encounter that brings together people of different statuses in such societies is designed to underline and reinforce those differences by rules about language, gesture, tone, and dress.

Terms of address, perhaps because they lend themselves to historical analysis, have been the object of considerable research by sociolinguists. In the past, the polite and the familiar forms of the second person pronoun (*vous* and *tu* in French respectively) were used asymmetrically in a semantic of power. The dominant class used tu when addressing commoners, servants, peasants and received back the more polite, dignified vous. No one who prudently used the formula could avoid thereby seeming to endorse the distinctions of worth and status inscribed in its use. Inasmuch as there was a determined effort by the revolutionaries in France immediately after 1789 to ban the use of vous, we can take it for granted that this semantic of power was not a matter of popular indifference. To this day, at socialist and communist gatherings, Europeans who are strangers will use the familiar form with one another to express equality and comradeship. In ordinary usage vous is not used *reciprocally* to express not status, but lack of close acquaintance.

A function equivalent to this nonreciprocity of address is the use of *boy* or first names by ruling groups when speaking with inferiors, and the latters' use of *Mister* to address their superiors. Common in systems of stratification by class and by race, this usage has not by any means disappeared in the West, though it is decidedly less universal today than fifty years ago. (It also survives as a kind of curiosity in the French *garçon*, for waiter, although *monsieur* is now increasingly favored.) Afrikaans, significantly, retains today both the asymmetrical use of the second person pronoun by the boy–mister pattern.

We are in danger of missing much of their significance if we see linguistic deference and gestures of subordination merely as performances extracted by power. The fact is they serve also as a barrier and a veil that the dominant find difficult or impossible to penetrate. A striking example is the usually futile effort by sociolinguists to record "pure," "authentic" versions of lower-class dialect. Since the recorder is almost inevitably someone of higher status and education, a kind of linguistic Heisenberg effect takes place which drives out the more stigmatized forms of the dialect. The only way the semantics of power can be breached is by a highly unethical, surreptitious taping of conversations without the subject's knowledge or permission. From one perspective this fact is merely an example of how power distorts communication. But from another perspective, it also preserves a sequestered site where a more autonomous discourse may develop. How are we to interpret the fact, for example, that lower-caste men in the pluralistic culture of the Punjab are likely to use any of several names, depending upon whom they are speaking to? Confronted with a Hindu, they called themselves Ram Chand, with a Sikh they called themselves Ram Singh, and with a Christian, John Samuel. The frustrated British census taker wrote of the "fickleness" of the lower castes with respect to religion, but it is not hard to recognize the evasive adoption of protective cover. We also learn that black miners in Southern Rhodesia had several names which arose not simply from the confusion of languages but because the confusion could plausibly excuse a delay in responding to a summons or an otherwise unexplained absence. The appearances that power requires are, to be sure, imposed forcefully on subordinate groups. But this does not preclude their active use as a means of resistance and evasion. The evasion, it must be noted, however, is purchased at the considerable cost of contributing to the production of a public transcript that *apparently* ratifies the social ideology of the dominant. Subordinates appear deferential, they bow and scrape, they seem amiable, they appear to know their place and to stay in it, thereby indicating that they also know and recognize the place of their superiors.

When the script is rigid and the consequences of a mistake large, subordinate groups may experience their conformity as a species of manipulation. Insofar as the conformity is tactical it is surely manipulative. This attitude again requires a division of the self in which one self observes, perhaps cynically and approvingly, the performance of the other self. Many of the accounts given by untouchables (notice how the term *untouchable* assumes a high-caste perspective) are frank in this respect. Noting that vital goods and services—sugar, kerosene, work, grain, loans—can be procured only by being on the good side of a member of the dominant castes, one observes, "We actually have to encounter, appease, and cajole the caste Hindus in a hundred different ways to secure our share." Thus, conformity is far too lame a word for the active manipulation of rituals of subordination to turn them to good personal advantage; it is an art form in which one can take some pride at having successfully misrepresented oneself. Another untouchable emphasizes the tactical side of concealment: "We must also tactfully disguise and hide, as necessary, our true aims and intentions from our social adversaries. To recommend it is not to encourage falsehood but only to be tactical in order to survive."

Blacks in the South, both before and after emancipation, had to thread their way among dangerous whites in much the same fashion. Thus it was possible for a black man speaking to a white abolitionist audience before the Civil War to explain, "Persons live and die in the midst of Negroes and know comparatively little of their real character. They are one thing before the whites and another before their own color. Deception towards the former is characteristic of them, whether bond or free, throughout the whole U.S." This sense of achievement is a successful performance *and* the massive realities of power that make it necessary are each evident in this account of a black sharecropper between the wars:

I've joked with white people, in a nice way. I've had to play dumb sometimes—I knowed not to go too far and let them know what I knowed, because they taken exception of it too quick. I had to humble down and play shut-mouthed in many cases to get along, I've done it all—they didn't know what it was all about, it's just a plain fact. . . . And I could go to 'em a heap of times for a favor and get it. . . . They'd give you good name if you was obedient to 'em, acted nice when you met 'em, and didn't question 'em 'bout what they said they had against you. You begin to cry about your rights and the mistreatin' of you and they'd murder you.

Nate Shaw reminds us eloquently that the theater of power can, by artful practice, become an actual political resource of subordinates. Thus we get the wrong impression, I think, if we visualize actors perpetually wearing fake smiles and moving with the reluctance of a chain gang. To do so is to see the performance as totally determined from above and to miss the agency of the actor in appropriating the performance for his own ends. What may look from above like the extraction of a required performance can easily look from below like the artful manipulation of deference and flattery to achieve its own ends. The slaves who artfully reinforced their master's stereotyped view of them as shiftless and unproductive may well have thereby lowered the work norms expected of them. By their artful praise at celebrations and holidays, they may have won better food rations and clothing allowances. The performance is often collective, as subordinates collude to create a piece of theater that serves their superior's view of the situation but that is maintained in their own interests. In fact, the stereotypes of the dominant are, from this perspective, a resource as well as an oppression to the subordinate, as Richard Hoggart's observation of the British working-class's use of deference makes plain: "the kind of obvious 'fiddling' of someone from another class which accompanies an overreadiness to say 'Sir,' but assumes . . . that it is all a contemptuous game, that one can depend on the middle class distaste for a scene to allow one to cheat easily." Rituals of subordination, then, may be deployed both for purposes of manipulation and concealment. What was often called Uncle Tom behavior, from this angle, may be no more than a label for someone who has mastered the theater arts of subordination. Deference and a smile may be what a poacher habitually deploys before the gentry to avoid suspicion, rather like the normal walk of the fleeing suspect when he encounters a cop on the beat. This achievement is considerable, but we should not forget that it is won on a stage on which the usual performances, no matter how artful, must reinforce the appearances approved by the dominant.

Such performances are seldom, of course, entirely successful. Dominant elites may well not know what lies behind the façade, but it is rare that they merely take what they see and hear at face value. An ancient text from Buddhist India seeks to instruct the master on what the façade conceals:

> O Bhante, our slaves . . . do another thing with their bodies, say another with their speech, and have a third in their mind.
>
> On seeing the master, they rise up, take things from his hands, discarding this and talking that; others show a seat, fan him with a hand fan, wash his feet, thus doing all that needs to be done. But in his absence, they do not even look if oil is being spilled, they do not turn to look even if there were a loss of hundreds or thousands to the master. (This is how they behave differently with the body). . . . Those who in the masters' presence praise him by saying, "our master, our Lord," say all that is unutterable, all that they feel like saying once he is away. (This is how they behave differently in speech.)

The white slave master is always wary of being put on by his slaves; an eighteenth-century Japanese landlord can wonder, "Does anyone lie as much as a peasant?" What is notable here, I believe, is not that the dominant should assume that wily subordinates will try to get around them. To believe this is not to be paranoid; it is merely to perceive reality. They attribute such behavior, however, not to the effect of arbitrary power but rather to the inborn characteristics of the subordinate group itself. In the ersatz science of race at the turn of the century the characteristics of subordination became traits of culture, gender, or ethnicity. Accounting for what he termed the negative and superficial quality of women's speech, Schopenhauer explained, "It arises immediately from the want of reason and reflection above alluded to, and is *assisted* by the fact that they, as the weaker, are driven by nature to have recourse not to force but to cunning: hence their instinctive treachery, and their irremediable tendency to lying." Otto Weininger, who wrote a widely read study called *Sex and Character* not long after, made much the same point: "The impulse to lie is much stronger in women, because, unlike that of a man, her memory is not continuous, whilst her life is discrete, unconnected, discontinuous, swayed by the sensations and perceptions of the moment instead of dominating them." Each author gives some evidence here of understanding the structural position of women that might account for the character of their observed speech; but each ultimately explains the difference by gender. In Weininger's case, the argument is extended to cover the "speech-character" of another subordinate group: the Jews. Both groups stood accused of the misuse of language and were "to be identified by the false, manipulative tone of their discourse." The logic of the argument is marvelously perverse. Patterns of speech that are adaptations to inequalities in power are depicted as natural characteristics of the subordinate group, a move that has, in turn, the great advantage of underlining the innate inferiority of its members when it comes to logic, truth, honesty, and reason and thereby justifying their continued domination by their betters.

CONTROL AND FANTASY—THE BASIS OF THE HIDDEN TRANSCRIPT

When vengeance is tabled, it turns into an illusion, a personal religion, a myth which records day by day from its cast of characters, who remakes the same in the myth of vengeance.
—Milan Kundera, *The Joke*

It is plain enough thus far that the prudent subordinate will ordinarily conform by speech and gesture to what he knows is expected of him—even if that conformity masks a quite different offstage opinion. What is not perhaps plain enough is that, in any established system of domination, it is not just a question of masking one's feelings and producing the correct speech acts and gestures in their place. Rather it is often a question of controlling what would be a natural impulse to rage, insult, anger, and the violence that such feelings prompt. There is no system of domination that does not produce its own routine harvest of insults and injury to human dignity—the appropriation of labor, public humiliations, whippings, rapes, slaps, leers, contempt, ritual denigration, and so on. Perhaps the worst of these, many slaves narratives agree, was not personal sufferings but rather the abuse of one's child or spouse while one had little choice but to look on helplessly. This inability to defend oneself or members of one's family (that is, to act as mother, father, husband, or wife) against the abuses of domination is simultaneously an assault on one's physical body and one's personhood or dignity. The cruelest result of human bondage is that it transforms the assertion of personal dignity into a moral risk. Conformity in the face of domination is thus occasionally—and unforgettably—a question of suppressing a violent rage in the interest of oneself and loved ones.

We may capture the existential dilemma at work here by contrasting it briefly with Hegel's analysis of the duelist. A person challenges another to a duel because he judges that his honor and standing (including often that of his family) has been mortally insulted. He demands an apology or retraction, failing which his honor can be satisfied only by a duel to the death. What the challenge to a duel says, symbolically, is that to accept this insult is to lose standing, without which life is not worth living (the ideal code, seldom rigorously followed, of the warrior aristocrat). Who wins the duel is symbolically irrelevant; it is the challenge that restores honor. If the challenger loses, he paradoxically wins his point by demonstrating that he was willing to wager his physical life in order to preserve his honor, his name. The very logic of the duel makes its status as an ideal apparent; any code that preaches the assertion of standing and honor at the expense of life itself is likely to have many lukewarm adherents in a pinch.

For most bondsmen through history, whether untouchables, slaves, serfs, captives, minorities held in contempt, the trick to survival, not always mastered by any means, has been to swallow one's bile, choke back one's rage, and conquer the impulse to physical violence. It is this systematic *frustration of reciprocal action* in relations of domination which, I believe, helps us understand much of the content of the hidden transcript. At its most elementary level the hidden transcript represents an acting out in fantasy—and occasionally in secretive practice—of the anger and reciprocal aggression denied by the presence of domination. Without the sanctions imposed by power relations, subordinates would be tempted to return a blow with a blow, an insult with an insult, a whipping with a whipping, a humiliation with a humiliation. It is as if the "voice," to use Albert Hirschman's term, they are refused in the public transcript finds its full-throated expression backstage. The frustration, tension, and control necessary in public give way to unbridled retaliation in a safer setting, where the accounts of reciprocity are, symbolically at least, finally balanced.

Later in this analysis I will want to move beyond the elementary, individual, and psychologistic view of the hidden transcript to its cultural determinants, its elaboration, and the forms in which it is expressed. For the moment, however, it is crucial to recognize that there is an important wish-fulfillment component to the hidden transcript.

The greater part of Richard Wright's account, the *Black Boy*, of his youth in Mississippi is infused with his attempt to control his anger when in the presence of whites and, in turn, to give vent to that anger in the safety of black company. His effort at stifling his anger is a daily, conscious effort—one that does not always succeed:

> Each day in the store I watched the brutality with a growing hate, yet trying to keep my feelings from registering in my face. When the boss looked at me I would avoid his eyes.
>
> I feared that if I clashed with whites I would lose control of my emotions and spill out the words that would be my sentence of death.

Among his friends during work breaks, the talk frequently turned to fantasies of retaliation and revenge. The fantasies are explicit and often take the forms of rumors about what has happened elsewhere. For example,

> Yeah, if they hava race riot around here, I'm gonna kill all the white folks with position.

My mamma, that old white woman where she works talked about slapping her and ma said, "Miz Green, if you slaps me, I'll kill you and go to hell to pay for it."

They say a white man hit a colored man up north and that colored man hit that white man, knocked him cold, and nobody did a damned thing.

Wright explains that a "latent sense of violence" surrounded all the offstage talk about whites and that such talk was the "touchstone of fraternity" among the black boys who gathered at the crossroads.

Further evidence for the like between the practical need to control anger and its reflection in fantasy may be illustrated by the findings of a remarkable, if deeply flawed, study of the psychological consequences of racial domination on blacks written in the 1940s: Abram Kardiner and Lionel Ovesey's *The Mark of Oppression*. As they understand it, any response to an all-powerful other will be some combination of idealization and hatred. The inventiveness and originality of these fantasies lie in the artfulness with which they reverse and negate a particular domination. No one recognized this more fully than W. E. B. Du Bois, who wrote of the double-consciousness of the American Black arising from racial domination: "such a double life with double thoughts, double duties, and double social classes, must give rise to double words and double ideals, and *tempt the mind to pretense or revolt, to hypocrisy or radicalism.* Occasionally, Du Bois thought of individual blacks as representing one or the other consciousness. Those given to "revolt" or "radicalism" were those who "stood ready to curse God and die," while those given to "pretense" and "hypocrisy" had forgotten that "life is more than meat and the body more than raiment." We can, I think, more usefully think of the former as a hidden transcript and the latter as the public transcript embodied in the same individual; the former being the site of the rage and anger generated by the necessity of preserving a deferential or obsequious public demeanor despite humiliations. If Du Bois associated the radicalism more with the North and the hypocrisy with the South, this was probably because blacks were somewhat freer to speak their mind in the North.

At this point in the argument, a skeptic might wonder if the official, or public, transcript of power relations serves any purpose at all. Who takes it seriously? We have seen that subordinate groups are generally careful to comport themselves in ways that do not breach the etiquette of power relations determined largely from above. Even then, however, they are quite capable of tactically manipulating appearances for their own ends or using a show of servility to wall off a world beyond direct power relations where sharply divergent views may prevail. Dominant elites, for their part, are unlikely to be completely taken in by outward shows of deference. They expect that there is more here than meets the eye (and ear) and that part of all of the performance is in bad faith. They sense that they are being "jockeyed" even if the harness is of their own devising. If, then, this is all a gigantic shell game in which there is no real dupe, why bother with the pretence?

PART III. THE INSTITUTION OF VIOLENCE: THREE CONNECTIONS

Women experience rape most often
by men we know.
—Catharine MacKinnon, "Feminism,
Marxism, Method, and the State"

HAVING EXPLORED THE DIALECTIC OF VIOLENCE and sketched the other of violence, we are now prepared to examine the institutional face of violence. It is a face too often hidden. It depends less on rhetoric, as in pursuing dialectics, or on imagination, as in naming "violent" others, and more on the starkest examination of what is most ordinary and most taken-for-granted. On close inspection it turns out that what one might have assumed was natural and beneficent is also deeply implicated in the genesis, as well as the persistence, of violence.

FAMILIAL

Sigmund Freud uses the very notion of love and love relationships as the entry point into discussing what has become the benchmark of contemporary psychoanalysis: neurosis. Freud warns that his enquiry is not for the fainthearted. He exposes what had been hidden, at least until his time, namely, the connection between love, eros, and sexuality—a connection that redefines the structure of all groups and institutions, beginning with the family. What has been termed "love," in fact, encodes a spectrum of instincts. In Freud's view one cannot separate self-love from love for parents and children, or from friendship, or from love for humanity in general. "All these tendencies," he observes, "are an expression of the same instinctual impulses; in relations between the sexes these impulses force their way towards sexual union, but in other circumstances they are diverted from this aim or are prevented from reaching it, though always preserving enough of their original nature to keep their identity recognizable."

It has become almost a trope of psychoanalytic wisdom that love for parents and children, the core of familial devotion, is itself another register for self-love, and like self-love, it is characterized not as the stable sediment of human social exchange but rather as a kind of longing or neurosis. Love-eros-sexuality can never be stable nor can it ever be satisfied. At the same time that it provides the basis for intimacy, it can also be the catalyst for alienation, for rivalry, for contention. Why does one not recognize this fault line at the very heart of the human condition? Because, in Freud's mind, repression works to hide what is most closely held, yet what is keenly antagonistic in the human personality. "Almost every intimate emotional relation between two people that lasts for some time—marriage, friendship, the relations between parents and children— contains a sediment of feelings of aversion and hostility, which only escapes perception as a result of *repression*. . . . Every time two families become connected by marriage, each of them thinks itself superior to or of better birth than the other. Of two neighboring towns each is the other's most jealous rival. . . . Closely related races keep one another at arm's length; the South German cannot endure the North German, the Englishman casts every kind of aspersion upon the Scot, the Spaniard despises the Portuguese . . . and greater differences lead to an almost insuperable repugnance, such as the Gallic people feel for the German, the Aryan for the Semite, and the white races for the colored!"

If the impossibility of avoiding conflict seems to portend its inevitability, Freud also allows for human freedom to control urges that will otherwise result in hostile relations and destructive outcomes. Yet the mechanism of hope is once again repression. It is repression, and repression alone, which provides the mechanism to keep aversions in check, for "the sediment of feelings of aversion and hostility" pervades the human race; it is the irreducible sine qua non of private and public exchange, within the nuclear family or within the larger family, whether group, society, or the state.

Linda Gordon elaborates on Freud's insights and confirms his diagnostic pessimism about the human condition. Her specific concerns are the struggle against family violence and the interpretation of its history. Alert to the difficulties in defining family violence, she also acknowledges the critiques of social control and the welfare state. She harbors no illusions that gender, class, and race biases will be eliminated by top-down interventionist strategies and practices. Yet she remains alert to the need for finding more nuanced approaches to the tension between state intervention and family autonomy. "I want to insist," she concludes, "that an accurate view of this 'outside' intervention into the family must consider, as the clients so often did in their strategic decisions, both external and familial forms of domination." In other words, one cannot revert to the family as a safe harbor from violence. "There is no returning to an old or newly romanticized 'family autonomy,'" and whatever answers there may be to problems of family violence, for Gordon, they must wrestle with, not seek to eradicate, the tension between state agencies and family actors.

Central to Gordon's search for a middle point between the intrusive state and the independent family is the matter of battered wives. Gordon is aware that battered wives are one of the vulnerable units in the violent affections that Freud diagnosed and that modern societies have witnessed in painstaking detail. Dorothy (Del) Martin, however, feels that wives bear a disproportionate share of the battering that expressive male neuroses have shown in multiple modern contexts. She focuses on late-twentieth-century American society as the test case for a general hypothesis that places the principal burden, and blame, on men.

Marriage, from Martin's perspective, legalizes a form of patriarchal ownership, implicitly if not explicitly, and with catastrophic results. Men who feel that they own women become the perpetrators of the most extreme forms of violence between husband and wife: violence that is located within and, as it were, sanctioned by marriage. The eminent sociologist Richard Gelles, in Martin's view, demonstrates her thesis, even though he has not himself advanced the radical hypothesis that governs her work.

While one may quibble with the general accent of Gordon and the particular data of Martin, it is difficult to avoid Freud's persistent, and ominous, insight: close relationships do not insure intimacy or safety so much as they allow the possibility of greater violence that is the greater for being under cover, since it is a violence legitimated by social norms as "private" and "autonomous," hence beyond the purview of any outsiders or the control of any outside agency.

LEGAL

In the same way that the family is not an innocent construct, but embeds tensions, conflicts, and hostilities that portend violence, so the law is more than a mere arbitrator of others' problems. The law is neither an objective nor a neutral path to the solution of problems raised by social agents, and particular contexts reveal how the law itself can be an instrument of structural violence.

One major instance of law as a structural violence, with institutional support, is Muslim Personal Law in India. Dating back to the colonial period of British rule in the Asian subcontinent, it reflects two levels of conflict, one often denied, the other much publicized. The first has to do with the distance between the ideals of Islamic judicial oversight and the realities of Muslim women's legal status. Though both property inheritance and dowry rights are supposedly guaranteed to Muslim wives, customary practice has often undermined their implementation. The British, bearing the burden of a legacy for civil equity, felt obliged to protect all their subjects under a common code, both in India and in other colonial domains.

Yet equity itself became a codeword for the exercise of instrumental power: in the name of equity, violence was done both to the notion of Muslim autonomy and to the separation of secular from religious norms. The compromise that came into play immediately after Indian Independence in 1948, but increasingly after 1972, when the All India Muslim Personal Law Board was formed to adjudicate cases for Muslim women solely in Muslim law courts. In other words, the double identity of some women as both Muslim and Indian complicated their judicial rights. Precisely because Muslim women were also Indian citizens, they could appeal an unfair verdict in a civil court, and non-Muslim judges would be given the right to make judgments that either confirmed or super-ceded those of their Muslim compatriots. But what did such judgments say about the putative autonomy of Muslims within the Republic of India?

The Shah Bano case exposed the underside of legal compromises. It made evident the inequitable nature of Indian constitutional practice in a secular state presiding over many religions. Just how complicated the reasoning on both sides can be is evident from the language of the case analyzed in this volume by Bruce B. Lawrence. By detailing the plight of one Muslim woman, the Shah Bano case offers a litmus test for measuring structural violence, carried out in the name of judicial justice, within the contemporary Republic of India.

Walter Benjamin has taken the argument about law and violence in an entirely different direction from MacKinnon. He is concerned with demonstrat-ing how artificial has been the general argument for legal or illegal uses of violence. He accepts the notion that violence pervades, but wonders how it is approved, or disapproved, according to certain, mostly suppressed, codes of persuasion. Rejecting the distinction between violence used for just and unjust ends, Benjamin wonders how one can legitimate violence *in any circumstance*. To maintain that natural ends meet the standard of justice, while individual ends do not, simply begs the question. The criterion of permissibility applies not to the individual who commits violence, but rather to the system that adjudicates. In Benjamin's words, "Violence, when not in the hands of the law, threatens it not by the ends that it may pursue but by its mere existence outside the law." Consider the figure of the " 'great' " criminal: "However repellent his ends may have been, he has aroused the secret admiration of the public. This cannot result from his deed, but only from the violence to which it bears witness, (for) even in defeat he arouses the sympathy of the mass against law."

Also highlighting women as the marker for virtue and violence in contempo-rary society is Catharine MacKinnon. Her approach is more abstract than that of Lawrence's study of the Shah Bano case, because MacKinnon is primarily con-cerned with how language justifies systems of power—above all, patriarchal power—through the abuse of key terms, chiefly *rape*. In her line of reasoning, all sexual intercourse is a form of rape, since the law still reflects the sexual norms of its original framers, heterosexual men. Her reasoning is at once provocative and speculative: she comments that "because women experience rape most often by men we know," "sometimes I think women and men live in different cultures." The generalized truth of her assertion depends on the level of internal repression, going back to Freud, which marks the line between friendship and hostility. MacKinnon, familiar with psychoanalysis as well as with law and feminist theory, concludes that all violence is sexually driven and that its interpretation must be sorted out on a gender spectrum, from liberated woman to dominating man.

Robert M. Cover also believes that the law conceals as much as it reveals, but he does not attribute all the causes of structural violence to a war of the sexes, as MacKinnon does, nor to the monopolistic jurisdiction of violence by jurists, as Benjamin does. Rather, he begins with a thoroughly Freudian premise that violence is intrinsic to the human condition. It can be manipulated, either extolled or limited, but it can never be removed. Thus it is no surprise that law instantiates violence; instead, it is interesting to see how law provides for a way of both marking violence and claiming to limit its exercise. Cover at once defends violence as inevitable and pleads for its careful monitoring. "Almost all people," he observes, "are fascinated and attracted by violence, even though they are at the same time repelled by it." Moreover, he continues, "in almost all people social cues may overcome or suppress the revulsion to violence under certain circumstances. These limitations do not deny the force of inhibitions against violence. Indeed, both together create the conditions without which law would either be unnecessary or impossible. Were the inhibition against violence perfect, law would be unnecessary; were it not capable of being overcome through social signals, law would not be possible." And so law in general, and judges in particular, do authorize violence, even though "interpretations which occasion violence are distinct from the violent acts they occasion. In order to understand the violence of a judge's interpretive act, we must also understand the way in which it is transformed into a violent deed despite general resistance to such deeds; in order to comprehend the meaning of the violent deed, we must also understand in what way the judge's interpretive act authorizes and legitimizes it." In other words, Cover argues, context is central to evaluating juridical violence. He strips from the law any pretense to arbitration and fairness, and instead analyzes how its very agents, judges, serve as "virtual triggers for action" in routinizing violent behavior. The focus here is on pragmatic processes, not on the underlying deep structures that rivet both MacKinnon and Benjamin.

Chandra Muzaffar is even more drawn to the actual operation of law and its way of binding parties to preconceptions that have no objective parallel in universal notions of justice. Because Muzaffar has worked and written in Southeast Asia, he argues for a different playing field from the macroconcepts that occupy too many Euro-American theorists of violence. He takes as his major topic for concern and critique the United Nations's Universal Declaration of Human Rights. In Muzaffar's view it fails on two counts: major polities, such as the United States and its European allies, have a disproportionate influence in setting the agenda and pursuing policies of the UN; and, even more important, what is highlighted as human rights applies in the political and military domains, where Euro-American interests are prevalent, rather than in economic and social issues of major concern to the so-called newly developing, or underdeveloped, nations of the Third World. These reflect structural inequities in the new world order, according to Muzaffar, but their real, truly lethal result is to perpetuate a system of asymmetry and violence that projects the power of colonial regimes into a postcolonial, or neocolonial, montage of global norms and values. It is not the clash of civilizations, but the hegemony of the old order disguised as the new that is his major concern.

RELIGIOUS

The religious is often assumed to be the opposite of violence, the holy and sacred versus the profane and secular. Yet religious structures are above all social; they are embedded in the same maze of human motives and competitive interests as their secular "opposites."

The religious element to structural violence may seem obscure, as religion is taken to be a bulwark of hope against the violence of worldly assailants. Yet for René Girard, violence is inseparable from religion, and religion from obscurity. In fact, Girard specifically links these two seemingly disparate traits—violence and obscurity—in his definition of religion: "Religion, in its broadest sense . . . must be another term for that obscurity that surrounds man's efforts to defend himself by curative or preventive means against his own violence." The one "curative or preventive means" against the intrinsic human will to violence, for Girard, is sacrifice. It is sacrifice that stands as a rite of substitution for the community, protecting members against their limitless proclivity to violence. It is sacrifice that restores harmony to the community. It is sacrifice that acts as a restraining, policing force in primitive societies where law is absent, and it is the modern judicial system that performs for civilized societies a function similar to sacrifice among primitives.

Yet religion, even in advanced societies, cannot escape its close link to sacrifice and, therefore, to violence. Girard skirts the edge of a paradox when he postulates that "religious and moral authorities in a community attempt to instill nonviolence, as an active force into daily life and as a mediating force into ritual life, through the application of violence." In other words, selective violence, by being restricted and directed to specific objects or victims, channels violent instincts into nonviolent ends.

While Freud would applaud this display of casuistic artistry, he would also agree with James Cone and Sharon Welch that the edge of religion is not just in the obscure genuflections or ritual devotions of the powerful but also in the appropriation of religious symbols by the marginal and oppressed. For African Americans, resistance to the institutional violence of patriarchal theology is crucial, and their sense of oppression has been etched by Cone. In a brilliant inversion of the usual theological ploy, which quotes scripture as if it were self-evident justification for the status quo, Cone shows how the status quo has itself concealed questions that scriptural narrative, and early Christian experience, would insist on raising. If Cone is right, then theology becomes "the Church's reflection upon the meaning of its faith-claim that God's revelation is identical with the historical freedom of the weak and the helpless." But that theology always has ethical implications, for just as Christian theology asks, "Who is God?" ethics asks, "What must we do?" In Cone's view, "The answer to the theological question about God includes in it the answer to the ethical question about human behavior."

And it is not just a broad set of reflections that Cone raises; he also wants to revisit past moments where the question of the status quo has been too neatly lodged beneath the seamless narrative of the powers that be, colluding church and state under the canopy of a single juridical monopoly. In the past, it was too easy to minimize the connection between theology and ethics. "The black answer to the God-question focuses on the divine liberation of the oppressed, and thus includes in it God's election of the oppressed for participation with him in the struggle for freedom." And all theologies that do not side with the oppressed, which do not make common cause with them in the struggle for freedom, must themselves be radically questioned. Especially the ethics of the fourth-century Fathers must be judged to be unbiblical. "Instead of standing unquestionably with the outcasts and downtrodden, as the God of the Bible does, their ethics did more to preserve the status quo than to change it. *Whatever else the gospel of Jesus might be, it can never be identified with the established power of the state.* Thus whatever else Christian ethics might be, it can never be identified with the actions of people who conserve the status quo. This was the essential error of the early Church. By becoming the religion of the Roman state, replacing the public state sacrifices [with the Eucharist], Christianity became the opposite of what Jesus intended."

Welch constructs a view of religiously structured violence almost opposite to Girard's. For her the central issue is not sacrifice but liberation. On what grounds and through what means do those marginal to dominant groups express their commitment to escape, to self-expression, to freedom? She reasons that the path to liberation lies through recuperated knowledge. "Liberation theology" she defines as "an insurrection of subjugated knowledges. It means that the discourse of liberation theology represents the resurgence of knowledges suppressed by a dominant theology and a dominant culture." It always attempts to preserve, then communicate repressed memories of conflict and exclusion. It uses these recuperated memories as the basis for an ongoing strategic struggle against dominant culture and its "natural" knowledge of the past.

By constructing its own genealogy, it denies the single, seamless genealogy of the dominant theology and provides an alternative path to authenticity and power.

The source of inspiration for Welch is Michel Foucault, but the bridge to Foucault is of enormous import. It stresses recuperating the past not as a form of bygone moments, but as an active resource for present and future struggles. Memory includes memories of conflict and exclusion, which, by being remembered and brought into contemporary discussions, make it possible to discover and explore contents excluded, meanings ignored. For feminists, trying to find their way back to a goddess of the future who will also empower them as autonomous subjects, the move against the institutional violence of patriarchal theology is pivotal.

Revisiting the church Fathers and strategizing their God as different from the God of Moses, Amos, and Jesus is akin to the project of another radical reformulater of divine discourse, Simone Weil. Weil struggled to understand God as the force of history but not the duplicitous agent of war. It was a tough juggling act, and she performed it most powerfully and poignantly in her meditation on Homer's *Iliad*. In her view, this classic Greek epic is a lofty poem because it depicts all the horrors of war, and yet it is also a brutal jeremiad because it reflects how few are the warriors, either Greek or German, ancient or modern, who can be like Patroclus, "displaying god-like generosity" even toward their foes. In extolling the Christian hope of a reprieve from war's horror and the human capitulation to slavery it entails, Weil almost seems to tilt against the windmills of time and human destiny. Christian tradition, like contemporary post-Christian European—and American—polities, seem to have forgotten the lesson of the *Iliad*, or perhaps, in the vision of Freud, it is not a lesson to simply remember, but one to announce, again and again, as each generation wrestles with the levels of repression that are as intrinsic to human nature as they are generative of violence.

FAMILIAL

SIGMUND FREUD (1856–1939)

The Viennese physician and founder of psychoanalysis Sigmund Freud was born to Jewish parents in Moravia, which was then part of Austria-Hungary. Freud claimed that his Jewish parentage, and the isolation that came with it, caused a trend of independent thinking in him. Although he grew up under impecunious circumstances, his father saw his potential and prioritized his education. A nine-year-old Sigmund managed to secure a place in the Gymnasium; he later entered Vienna University as a medical student. Freud's career, which began with neuropathology, took a turn toward psychopathology after his work with Jean-Martin Charcot and then in association with Josef Breuer, on hysteria and hypnosis. He ultimately diverged from Breuer's practice of hypnosis, instead formulating the technique of free-association. Further distancing himself from Breuer, Freud began to use the concepts of repression and defense, hypothesizing that the cause of neuroses lay in the conflict between the ego and the libido.

Freud also used the concept of neurosis as an ego-libido conflict to explain group psychology when he turned to larger sociological and sociopsychological concerns near the end of his career. In his later works, such as Totem and Taboo *(1913),* Group Psychology and the Analysis of the Ego *(1922),* Future of an Illusion *(1927), and* Civilization and Its Discontents *(1930), Freud applied the technique of psycho-analysis, which he had developed in relation to individual neuroses, to explain group conflicts, wars, and social upheavals. The category of the unconscious which Freud uses to analyze individuals becomes operative with collective life; it is through repression of instinctual violent drives that human beings can live in a collective. Social life is possible, according to Freud, precisely through the repressive mechanisms that civilization imposes on individuals. Specifically, the dual mechanisms of work and love channel individual impulses to death and destruction into meaningful activity. It is no wonder that by the end of his career, Freud became preoccupied with social "neuroses," since his final illness and death coincided with Hitler's invasion of Austria. Earlier, in 1933, Freud's books had been publicly burned in Berlin, and after the Nazi invasion in 1938, he managed to escape to London, where he spent the last year of his life.*

Other works by Freud include The Interpretation of Dreams *(1913),* A General Introduction to Psychoanalysis *(1920),* Beyond the Pleasure Principle *(1922),* Repression *(1925), and* The Unconscious *(1925). Freud's writings have been collected and translated in the standard edition of* The Complete Psychological Works of Sigmund Freud *(1953–74).*

Group Psychology and the Analysis of the Ego

SIGMUND FREUD

CHAPTER 4. SUGGESTIONS OF LIBIDO

Libido is an expression taken from the theory of the emotions. We call by that name the energy, regarded as a quantitative magnitude (though not at present actually measurable), of those instincts which have to do with all that may be comprised under the word "love." The nucleus of what we mean by love naturally consists (and this is what is commonly called love, and what the poets sing of) in sexual love with sexual union as its aim. But we do not separate from this—what in any case has a share in the name "love"—on the one hand, self-love, and on the other, love for parents and children, friendship, and love for humanity in general, and also devotion to concrete objects and to abstract ideas. Our justification lies in the fact that psycho-analytic research has taught us that all these tendencies are an expression of the same instinctual impulses; in relations between the sexes these impulses force their way towards sexual union, but in other circumstances they are diverted from this aim or are prevented from reaching it, though always preserving enough of their original nature to keep their identity recognizable (as in such features as the longing for proximity, and self-sacrifice).

We are of opinion, then, that language has carried out an entirely justifiable piece of unification in creating the word "love" with its numerous uses, and that we cannot do better than take it as the basis of our scientific discussions and expositions as well. By coming to this decision, psycho-analysis has let loose a storm of indignation, as though it had been guilty of an act of outrageous innovation. Yet it has done nothing original in taking love in our "wider" sense. In its origin, function, and relation to sexual love, the "Eros" of the philosopher Plato coincides exactly with the love-force, the libido of psycho-analysis, as has been shown in detail by Nachmansohn (1915) and Pfister (1921); and when the apostle Paul, in his famous epistle to the Corinthians, praises love above all else, he certainly understands it in the same "wider" sense. But this only shows that men do not always take their great thinkers seriously, even when they profess most to admire them.

Psycho-analysis, then, gives these love instincts the name of sexual instincts, *a potiori* and by reason of their origin. The majority of "educated" people have regarded this nomenclature as an insult, and have taken their revenge by retorting upon psycho-analysis with the approach of "pan-sexualism." Anyone who considers sex as something mortifying and humiliating to human nature is at liberty to make use of the more genteel expressions "Eros" and "erotic." I might have done so myself from the first and thus have spared myself much opposition. But I did not want to, for I like to avoid concessions to faintheartedness. One can never tell where that road may lead one; one gives way first in words, and then little by little in substance too. I cannot see any merit in being ashamed of sex; the Greek word "Eros," which is to soften the affront, is in the end nothing more than a translation of our German work *Liebe* [love]; and finally, he who knows how to wait need make no concessions.

We will try our fortune, then, with the supposition that love relationships (or, to use a more neutral expression, emotional ties) also constitute the essence of the group mind. Let us remember that the authorities make no mention of any such relations. What would correspond to them is evidently concealed behind the shelter, the screen, of suggestion. Our hypothesis finds support in the first instance from two passing thoughts. First, that a group is clearly held together by a power of some kind: and to what power could this feat be better ascribed than Eros, which holds together everything in the world? Secondly, that if an individual gives up his distinctiveness in a group and lets its other members influence him by suggestion, it gives one the impression that he does it because he feels the need of being in harmony with them rather than in opposition to them—so that perhaps after all he does it "*ihnen zu Liebe.*"

CHAPTER 5. TWO ARTIFICIAL GROUPS: THE CHURCH AND THE ARMY

We may recall from what we know of the morphology of groups that it is possible to distinguish very different kinds of groups and opposing lines in their development. There are very fleeting groups and extremely lasting ones; homogeneous ones, made up of the same sorts of individuals, and unhomogeneous ones; natural groups, and artificial ones, requiring an external force to keep them together; primitive groups, and highly organized ones with a definite structure. But for reasons which remain to be explained we should like to pay particular stress upon a distinction to which writers on the subject have been inclined to give too little attention; I refer to that between leaderless groups and those with leaders. And, in complete opposition to the usual practice, we shall not choose a relatively simple group formation as our point of departure, but shall begin with highly organized, lasting, and artificial groups. The most interesting example of such structures are Churches—communities of believers—and armies.

A Church and an army are artificial groups—that is, a certain external force is employed to prevent them from disintegrating and to check alterations in their structure. As a rule a person is not consulted, or is given no choice, as to whether he wants to enter such a group; any attempt at leaving it is usually met with persecution or with severe punishment, or has quite definite conditions attached to it. It is quite outside our present interest to enquire why these associations need such special safeguards. We are only attracted by one circumstance, namely that certain facts, which are far more concealed in other cases, can be observed very clearly in those highly organized groups which are protected from dissolution in the manner that has been mentioned.

In a Church (and we may with advantage take the Catholic Church as a type) as well as in an army, however different the two may be in other respects, the same illusion holds good of there being a head—in the Catholic Church Christ, in an army its Commander-in-Chief—who loves all the individuals in the group with an equal love. Everything depends upon this illusion; if it were to be dropped, then both Church and army would dissolve, so far as the external force permitted them to. This equal love was expressly enunciated by Christ: "Inasmuch as ye have done it unto one of the least of these my brethren, ye have done it unto me." He stands to the individual members of the group of believers in the relation of a kind elder brother; he is their substitute father. All the demands come from this love of Christ's. A democratic strain runs through the Church, for the very reason that before Christ everyone is equal, and that everyone has an equal share in his love. It is not without a deep reason that the similarity between the Christian community and a family is invoked, and that believers call themselves brothers in Christ, that is, brothers through the love which Christ has for them. There is no doubt that the tie which unites each individual with Christ is also the cause of the tie which unites them with one another. The like holds good of an army. The Commander-in-Chief is a father who loves all soldiers equally, and for that reason they are comrades among themselves. The army differs structurally from the Church in being built up of a series of such groups. Every captain is, as it were, the Commander-in-Chief and the father of his company, and so is every non-commissioned officer of his company, and so is every non-commissioned officer of his section. It is true that a similar hierarchy has been constructed in the Church, but it does not play the same part in it economically; for more knowledge and care about individuals may be attributed to Christ than to a human Commander-in-Chief.

An objection will justly be raised against this conception of the libidinal structure of an army on the ground that no place has been found in it for such ideas as those of one's country, of national glory, etc., which are of such importance in holding an army together. The answer is that that is a different instance of a group tie, and no longer such a simple one; for the examples of great generals, like Caesar, Wallenstein, or Napoleon, show that such ideas are not indispensable to the existence of an army. We shall presently touch upon the possibility of a leading idea being substituted for a leader and upon the relations between the two. The neglect of this libidinal factor in an army, even when it is not the only factor operative, seems to be not merely a theoretical omission but also a practical danger. Prussian militarism, which was just as unpsychological as German science, may have had to suffer the consequences of this in the [First] World War. We know that the war neuroses which ravaged the German army have been recognized as being a protest of the individual against the part he was expected to play in the army; and according to the communication of Simmel (1918), the hard treatment of the men by their superiors may be considered as foremost among the motive forces of the disease. If the importance of the Libido's claims on this score had been better appreciated, the fantastic promises of the American President's Fourteen Points would probably not have been believed so easily, and the splendid instrument would not have broken in the hands of the German leaders.

It is to be noticed that in these two artificial groups each individual is bound by libidinal ties on the one hand to the leader (Christ, the Commander-in-Chief) and on the other hand to the other members of the group. How these two ties are related to each other, whether they are of the same kind and the same value, and how they are to be described psychologically—these questions must be reserved for subsequent enquiry. But we shall venture even now upon a mild reproach against earlier writers for not having sufficiently appreciated the importance of the leader in the psychology of the group, while our own choice of this as a first subject for investigation has brought us into a more favourable position. It would appear as though we were on the right road towards an explanation of the principal phenomenon of group psychology—the individual's lack of freedom in a group. If each individual is bound in two directions by such an intense emotional tie, we shall find no difficulty in attributing to that circumstance the alteration and limitation which have been observed in his personality.

A hint to the same effect, that the essence of a group lies in the libidinal ties existing in it, is also to be found in the phenomenon of panic, which is best studied in military groups. A panic arises if a group of that kind becomes disintegrated. Its characteristics are that none of the orders given by superiors are any longer listened to, and that each individual is only solicitous on his own account, and without any consideration for the rest. The mutual ties have ceased to exist, and a gigantic and senseless fear is set free. At this point, again, the objection will naturally be made that it is rather the other way around; and that the fear has grown so great as to be able to disregard all ties and all feelings of consideration for others. McDougall has even made use of panic (though not of military panic) as a typical instance of that intensification of emotion by contagion ("primary induction") on which he lays so much emphasis. But nevertheless this rational method of explanation is here quite inadequate. The very questions that needs explanation is why the fear has become so gigantic. The greatest of the danger cannot be responsible, for the same army which now falls a victim to panic may previously have faced equally great or greater danger with complete success; it is of the very essence of panic that it bears no relation to the danger that threatens, and often breaks out on the most trivial occasions. If an individual in panic fear begins to be solicitous only on his own account, he bears witness in so doing to the fact that the emotional ties, which have hitherto made the danger seem small to him, have ceased to exist. Now that he is by himself in facing the danger, he may surely think it greater. The fact is, therefore, that panic fear presupposes a relaxation in the libidinal structure of the group and reacts to that relaxation in a justifiable manner, and the contrary view—that the libidinal ties of the group are destroyed owing to fear in the face of the danger—can be refuted.

The contention that fear in a group is increased to enormous proportions through induction (contagion) is not in the least contradicted by these remarks. McDougall's view meets the case entirely when the danger is a really great one and when the group has no strong emotional ties—conditions which are fulfilled, for instance, when a fire breaks out in a theatre or a place of amusement. But the truly instructive case and the one which can be best employed for our purposes is that mentioned above, in which a body of troops breaks into a panic although the danger has not increased beyond a degree that is usual and has often been previously faced. It is not to be expected that the usage of the word "panic" should be clearly and unambiguously determined. Sometimes it is used to describe any collective fear, sometimes even fear in an individual when it exceeds all bounds, and often the name seems to be reserved for cases in which the outbreak of fear is not warranted by the occasion. If we take the word "panic" in the sense of collective fear, we can establish a far-reaching analogy. Fear in the individual is provoked either by the greatness of a danger or by the cessation of emotional ties (libidinal cathexes); the latter is the case of neurotic fear or anxiety. In just the same way panic arises either owing to an increase of the common danger or owing to the disappearance of the emotional ties which hold the group together; and the latter case is analogous to that of neurotic anxiety.

Anyone who, like McDougall, describes a panic as one of the plainest functions of the "group mind," arrives at the paradoxical position that this group mind does away with itself in one of its most striking manifestations. It is impossible to doubt that panic means the disintegration of a group; it involves the cessation of all the feelings of consideration which the members of the group otherwise show one another.

The typical occasion of the outbreak of a panic is very much as it is represented in Nestroy's parody of Hebbel's play about Judith and Holofernes. A soldier cries out: "The general has lost his head!" and thereupon all the Assyrians take to flight. The loss of the leader in some sense or other, the birth of misgivings about him, brings on the outbreak of panic, though the danger remains the same; the mutual ties between the members of the group disappear, as a rule, at the same time as the tie with their leader. The group vanishes in dust, like a Prince Rupert's drop when its tail is broken off.

The dissolution of a religious group is not so easy to observe. A short time ago there came into my hands an English novel of Catholic origin, recommended by the Bishop of London, with the title *When It Was Dark*. It gave a clever and, as it seems to me, a convincing picture of such a possibility and its consequences. The novel, which is supposed to relate to the present day, tells how a conspiracy of enemies of the person of Christ and of the Christian faith succeed in arranging for a sepulchre to be discovered in Jerusalem. In this sepulchre is an inscription, in which Joseph of Arimathaea confesses that for reasons of piety he secretly removed the body of Christ from its grave on the third day after the entombment and buried it in this spot. The resurrection of Christ and his divine nature are by this means disproved, and the result of this archaeological discovery is a convulsion in European civilization and an extraordinary increase in all crimes and acts of violence, which only ceases when the forgers' plot has been revealed.

The phenomenon which accompanies the dissolution that is here supposed to overtake a religious group is not fear, for which the occasion is wanting. Instead of it ruthless and hostile impulses toward other people make their appearance, which owing to the equal love of Christ, they had previously been unable to do. But even during the kingdom of Christ those people who do not belong to the community of believers, who do not love him, and whom he does not love, stand outside this tie. Therefore a religion, even if it calls itself the religion of love, must be hard and unloving to those who do not belong to it. Fundamentally indeed every religion is in this same way a religion of love for all those whom it embraces; while cruelty and intolerance towards those who do not belong to it are natural to every relation. However difficult we may find it personally, we ought not to reproach believers too severely on this account; people who are unbelieving or indifferent are much better off psychologically in this matter [of cruelty and intolerance]. If today that intolerance no longer shows itself so violent and cruel as in former centuries, we can scarcely conclude that there has been a softening in human manners. The cause is rather to be found in the undeniable weakening of religious feelings and the libidinal ties which depend upon them. If another group tie takes the place of the religious one—and the socialistic tie seems to be succeeding in doing so—then there will be the same intolerance towards outsiders as in the age of the Wars of Religion; and if differences between scientific opinions could ever attain a similar significance for groups, the same result would again be repeated with this new motivation.

CHAPTER 6. FUTURE PROBLEMS AND LINES OF WORK

We have hitherto considered two artificial groups and have found that both are dominated by emotional ties of two kinds. One of these, the tie with the leader, seems (at all events for these cases) to be more of a ruling factor than the other, which holds between the members of the group.

Now much else remains to be examined and described in the morphology of groups. We should have to start from the ascertained fact that a mere collection of people is not a group, so long as these ties have not been established in it; but we should have to admit that in any collection of people the tendency to form a psychological group may very easily come to the fore. We should have to give our attention to the different kinds of groups, more or less stable, that arise spontaneously, and to study the conditions of their origin and of their dissolution. We should above all be concerned with the distinction between groups which have a leader and leaderless groups. We should consider whether groups with leaders may not be the more primitive and complete, whether in the others an idea, an abstraction, may not take the place of the leader (a state of things to which religious groups, with their invisible head, form a transitional stage), and whether a common tendency, a wish in which a number of people can have a share, may not in the same way serve as a substitute. This abstraction again might be more or less completely embodied in the figure of what we might call a secondary leader, and interesting varieties would arise from the relation between the idea and the leader. The leader or the leading idea might also, so to speak, be negative; hatred against a particular person or institution might operate in just the same unifying way, and might call up the same kind of emotional ties as positive attachment. Then the question would also arise whether a leader is really indispensable to the essence of a group—and other questions besides.

But all these questions, which may, moreover, have been dealt with in part in the literature of group psychology, will not succeed in diverting our interest from the fundamental psychological problems that confront us in the structure of a group. And our attention will first be attracted by a consideration which promises to bring us in the most direct way to a proof that libidinal ties are what characterize a group.

Let us keep before our eyes the nature of the emotional relations which hold between men in general. According to Schopenhauer's famous simile of the freezing porcupines, no one can tolerate a too intimate approach to his neighbour.

The evidence of psycho-analysis shows that almost every intimate emotional relation between two people which lasts for some time—marriage, friendship, the relations between parents and children—contains a sediment of feelings of aversion and hostility, which only escapes perception as a result of repression. This is less disguised in the common wrangles between business partners or in the grumbles of a subordinate at his superior. The same thing happens when men come together in larger units. Every time two families become connected by marriage, each of them thinks itself superior to or of better birth than the other. Of two neighbouring towns each is the other's most jealous rival; every little canton looks down upon the others with contempt. Closely related races keep one another at arm's length; the South German cannot endure the North German, the Englishman casts every kind of aspersion upon the Scot, the Spaniard despises the Portuguese. We are no longer astonished that greater differences should lead to an almost insuperable repugnance, such as the Gallic people feel for the German, the Aryan for the Semite, and the white races for the colored.

When this hostility is directed against people who are otherwise loved we describe it as ambivalence of feeling; and we explain the fact, in what is probably far too rational a manner, by means of the numerous occasions for conflicts of interest which arise precisely in such intimate relations. In the undisguised antipathies and aversions which people feel towards strangers with whom they have to do we may recognize the expression of self-love—of narcissism. This self-love works for the preservation of the individual, and behaves as though the occurrence of any divergence from his own particular lines of development involve a criticism of them and a demand for their alteration. We do not know why such sensitiveness should have been directed to just these details of differentiation; but it is unmistakable that in this whole connection men give evidence of a readiness for hatred, an aggressiveness, the source of which is known, and to which one is tempted to ascribe an elementary character.

But when a group is formed the whole of this intolerance vanishes, temporarily or permanently, within the group. So long as a group formation persists or so far as it extends, individuals in the group behave as though they were uniform, tolerate the peculiarities of its other members, equate themselves with them, and have no feeling of aversion towards them. Such a limitation of narcissism can, according to our theoretical views, only be produced by one factor, a libidinal tie with other people. Love for oneself knows only one barrier —love for others, love for objects. The question will at once be raised whether community of interest in itself, without any addition of libido, must not necessarily lead to the toleration of other people and to considerateness for them. This objection may be met by the reply that nevertheless no lasting limitation of narcissism is effected in this way, since this tolerance does not persist longer than the immediate advantage gained from the other people's collaboration. But the practical importance of this discussion is less than might be supposed, for experience has shown that in cases of collaboration libidinal ties are regularly formed between the fellow-workers which prolong and solidify the relation between them to a point beyond what is merely profitable. The same thing occurs in men's social relations as has become familiar to psycho-analytic research in the course of the development of the individual libido. The libido attaches itself to the satisfaction of the great vital needs, and chooses as its first objects the people who have a share in that process. And in the development of mankind as a whole, just as in individuals, love alone acts as the civilizing factor in the sense that it brings a change from egoism to altruism. And this is true both of sexual love for women, with all the obligations which it involves of not harming the things that are dear to women, and also of desexualized, sublimated homosexual love for other men, which springs from work in common.

If therefore in groups narcissistic self-love is subject to limitations which do not operate outside them, that is cogent evidence that the essence of a group formation consists in new kinds of libidinal ties among the members of the group.

Our interest now leads us on to the pressing question as to what may be the nature of these ties which exist in groups. In the psycho-analytic study of neuroses we have hitherto been occupied almost exclusively with ties with objects made by love instincts which still pursue directly sexual aims. In groups there can evidently be no question of sexual aims of that kind. We are concerned here with love instincts which have been diverted from their original aims, though they do not operate with less energy on that account. Now, within the range of the usual sexual object-cathexis, we have already observed phenomena which represent a diversion of the instinct from it sexual aim. We have described them as degrees of being in love, and have recognized that they involve a certain encroachment upon the ego. We shall now turn our attention more closely to these phenomena of being in love, in the firm expectation of finding in them conditions which can be transferred to the ties that exist in groups. But we should also like to know whether this kind of object-cathexis, as we know it in sexual life, represents the only manner of emotional tie with other people, or whether we must take other mechanisms of the sort into account. As a matter of fact we learn from psycho-analysis that there do exist other mechanisms for emotional ties, the so called *identifications*, insufficiently-known processes and hard to describe, the investigation of which will for some time keep us away from the subject of group psychology.

CHAPTER 7. IDENTIFICATION

Identification is known to psycho-analysis as the earliest expression of an emotional tie with another person. It pays a part in the early history of the Oedipus complex. A little boy will exhibit a special interest in his father; he would like to grow like him and be like him, and take his place everywhere. We may say simply that he takes his father as his ideal. This behaviour has nothing to do with a passive or feminine attitude towards his father (and towards males in general); it is on the contrary typically masculine. It fits in very well with the Oedipus complex, for which it helps to prepare the way.

At the same time as this identification with his father, or a little later, the boy has begun to develop a true object-cathexis towards his mother according to the attachment [anaclitic] type. He then exhibits, therefore, two psychologically distinct ties: a straightforward sexual object-cathexis towards his mother and an identification with his father which takes him as his model. The two subsist side by side for a time without any mutual influence or interference. In consequence of the irresistible advance towards an unification of mental life, they come together, at last; and the normal Oedipus complex originates from their confluence. The little boy notices that his father stands in his way with his mother. His identification with his father then takes on a hostile colouring and becomes identical with the wish to replace his father in regard to his mother as well. Identification, in fact, is ambivalent from the very first; it can turn into an expression of tenderness as easily as into a wish for someone's removal. It behaves like a derivative of the first, *oral* phase of the organization of the libido, in which the object that we long for and prize is assimilated by eating and is in that way annihilated as such. The cannibal, as we know, has remained at this standpoint; he has a devouring affection for his enemies and only devours people of whom he is fond.

The subsequent history of this identification with the father may easily be lost sight of. It may happen that the Oedipus complex becomes inverted, and that the father is taken as the object of a feminine attitude, an object from which the directly sexual instincts look for satisfaction; in that event the identification with the father has become the precursor of an object-tie with the father. The same holds good, with the necessary substitutions, of the baby daughter as well.

It is easy to state in a formula the distinction between an identification with the father and the choice of the father as an object. In the first case one's father is what one would like to object. In the first case one's father is what one would like to *be*, and in the second he is what one would like to *have*. The distinction, that is, depends upon whether the tie attaches to the subject or to the object of the ego. The former kind of tie is therefore already possible before any sexual object-choice has been made. It is much more difficult to give a clear metapsychological representation of the distinction. We can only see that identification endeavours to mould a person's own ego after the fashion of the one that has been taken as a model.

Let us disentangle identification as it occurs in the structure of a neurotic symptom from its rather complicated connections. Supposing that a little girl (and we will keep to her for the present) develops the same painful symptom as her mother—for instance, the same tormenting cough. This may come about in various ways. The identification may come from the Oedipus complex; in that case it signifies a hostile desire on the girl's part to take her mother's place, and the symptom expresses her object-love towards her father, and brings about a realization, under the influence of a sense of guilt, of her desire to take her mother's place: "You wanted to be your mother, and now you *are*—anyhow so far as your sufferings are concerned." This is the complete mechanism of the structure of a hysterical symptom. Or, on the other hand, the symptom may be the same as that of the person who is loved; so, for instance, Dora imitated her father's cough. In that case we can only describe the state of things by saying *that identification has appeared instead of object-choice, and that object-choice has regressed to identification*. We have heard that identification is the earliest and original form of emotional tie; it often happens that under the conditions in which symptoms are constructed, that is, where there is repression and where the mechanisms of the unconscious are dominant, object-choice is turned back into identification—the ego assumes the characteristics of the object. It is noticeable that in these identifications the ego sometimes copies the person who is not loved and sometimes the one who is loved. It must also strike us that in both cases the identification is a partial and extremely limited one and only borrows a single trait from the person who is its object.

There is a third particularly frequent and important case of symptom formation, in which the identification leaves entirely out of account any object-relation to the person who is being copied. Supposing, for instance, that one of the girls in a boarding school has had a letter from someone with whom she is secretly in love which arouses her jealousy, and that she reacts to it with a fit of hysterics; then some of her friends who know about it will catch a fit, as we say, by mental infection. The mechanism is that of identification based upon the possibility or desire of putting oneself in the same situation. The other girls would like to have a secret love affair too, and under the influence of a sense of guilt they also accept the suffering involved in it. It would be wrong to suppose that they take on the symptom out of sympathy. On the contrary, the sympathy only arises out of the identification, and this is proved by the fact that infection or imitation of this kind takes place in circumstances where even less pre-existing sympathy is to be assumed than usually exists between friends in a girls' school. One ego has perceived a significant analogy with another upon one point—in our example upon openness to a similar emotion; an identification is thereupon constructed on this point, and, under the influence of the pathogenic situation, is displaced on to the symptom which the one ego has produced. The identification by means of the symptom has thus become the mark of a point of coincidence between the two egos which has to be kept repressed.

What we have learned from these three sources may be summarized as follows. First, identification is the original form of emotional tie with an object; secondly, in a regressive way it becomes a substitute for a libidinal object-tie, as it were by means of introjection of the object into the ego; and thirdly, it may arise with any new perception of a common quality shared with some other person who is not an object of the sexual instinct. The more important this common quality is, the more successful may this partial identification become, and it may thus represent the beginning of a new tie.

We already begin to divine that the mutual tie between members of a group is in the nature of an identification of this kind, based upon an important emotional common quality; and we may suspect that this common quality lies in the nature of the tie with the leader. Another suspicion may tell us that we are far from having exhausted the problem of identification, and that we are faced by the process which psychology calls "empathy [*Einfühlung*]" and which plays the largest part in our understanding of what is inherently foreign to our ego in other people. But we shall here limit ourselves to the immediate emotional effects of identification, and shall leave on one side its significance for our intellectual life.

Psycho-analytic research, which has already occasionally attacked the more difficult problems of the psychoses, has also been able to exhibit identification to us in some other cases which are not immediately comprehensible. I shall treat two of these cases in detail as material for our further consideration.

The genesis of male homosexuality in a large class of cases is as follows. A young man has been unusually long and intensely fixated upon his mother in the sense of the Oedipus complex, but at last, after the end of puberty, the time comes for exchanging his mother for some other sexual object. Things take a sudden turn: the young man does not abandon his mother, but identifies himself with her; he transforms himself into her, and now looks about for objects which can replace his ego for him, and on which he can bestow such love and care as he has experienced from his mother. This is a frequent process, which can be confirmed as often as one likes, and which is naturally quite independent of any hypothesis that may be made as to the organic driving force and the motives of the sudden transformation. A striking thing about this identification is its ample scale; it remoulds the ego in one of its important features—in its sexual character—upon the model of what has hitherto been the object. In this process the object itself is renounced—whether entirely or in the sense of being preserved only in the unconscious is a question outside the present discussion. Identification with an object that is renounced or lost, as a substitute for that object—introjection of it into the ego—is indeed no longer a novelty to us. A process of the kind may sometimes be directly observed in small children. A short time ago an observation of this sort was published in the *Internationale Zeitschrift für Psychoanalyse*. A child who was unhappy over the loss of a kitten declared straight out that now he himself was the kitten, and accordingly crawled about on all fours, would not eat at table, etc.

Another such instance of introjection of the object has been provided by the analysis of melancholia, an affection which counts among the most notable of its exciting causes the real or emotional loss of a loved object. A leading characteristic of these cases is a cruel self-depreciation of the ego combined with relentless self-criticism and bitter self-reproaches. Analyses have shown that this disparagement and these reproaches apply at bottom to the object and represent the ego's revenge upon it. The shadow of the object has fallen upon the ego, as I have said elsewhere. The introjection of the object is here unmistakably clear.

But these melancholias also show us something else, which may be of importance for our later discussions. They show us the ego divided, fallen apart into two pieces, one of which rages against the second. This second piece is the one which has been altered by introjection and which contains the lost object. But the piece which behaves so cruelly is not unknown to us either. It comprises the conscience, a critical agency within the ego, which even in normal times takes up a critical attitude towards the ego, though never so relentlessly and so unjustifiably. On previous occasions we have been driven to the hypothesis that some such agency develops in our ego which may cut itself off from the rest of the ego and come into conflict with it. We have called it the "ego ideal," and by way of functions we have ascribed to it self-observation, the moral conscience, the censorship of dreams, and the chief influence in repression. We have said that it is the heir to the original narcissism in which the childish ego enjoyed self-sufficiency; it gradually gathers up from the influences of the environment the demands which that environment makes upon the ego and which the ego cannot always rise to; so that a man, when he cannot be satisfied with his ego itself, may nevertheless be able to find satisfaction in the ego ideal which has been differentiated out of the ego. In delusions of observation, as we have further shown, the disintegration of this agency has become patent, and has thus revealed its origin in the influence of superior powers, and above all of parents. But we have not forgotten to add that the amount of distance between this ego ideal and the real ego is very variable from one individual to another, and that with many people this differentiation within the ego does not go further than with children.

. . . . .

What appears later on in society in the shape of *Gemeingeist, esprit de corps,* "group spirit," etc., does not belie its derivation from what was originally envy. No one must want to put himself forward; every one must be the same and have the same. Social justice means that we deny ourselves many things so that others may have to do without them as well, or, what is the same thing, may not be able to ask for them. This demand for equality is the root of social conscience and the sense of duty. It reveals itself unexpectedly in the syphilitic's dread of infecting other people, which psycho-analysis has taught us to understand. The dread exhibited by these poor wretches corresponds to their violent struggles against the unconscious wish to spread their infection on to other people; for why should they alone be infected and cut off from so much? Why not other people as well? And the same germ is to be found in the apt story of the judgement of Solomon. If one woman's child is dead, the other shall not have alive one either. The bereaved woman is recognized by this wish.

Thus social feeling is based upon the reversal of what was first a hostile feeling into a positively-toned tie in the nature of an identification. So far as we have hitherto been able to follow the course of events, this reversal seems to occur under the influence of a common affectionate tie with a person outside the group. We do not ourselves regard our analysis of identification as exhaustive, but it is enough for our present purpose that we should revert to this one feature—its demand that equalization shall be consistently carried through. We have already heard in the discussion of the two artificial groups, Church and army, that their necessary precondition is that all their members should be loved in the same way by one person, the leader. Do not let us forget, however, that the demand for equality in a group applies only to its members and not to the leader. All the members must be equal to one another, but they all want to be ruled by one person. Many equals, who can identify themselves with one another, and a single person superior to them all—that is the situation that we find realized in groups which are capable of subsisting. Let us venture, then, to correct Trotter's pronouncement that man is a herd animal and assert that he is rather a horde animal, an individual creature in a horde led by a chief.

The Group and the Primal Horde

In 1912 I took up a conjecture of Darwin's to the effect that the primitive form of human society was that of a horde ruled over despotically by a powerful male. I attempted to show that the fortunes of this horde have left indestructible traces upon the history of human descent; and, especially, that the development of totemism, which comprises in itself the beginnings of religion, morality, and social organization, is connected with the killing of the chief by violence and the transformation of the paternal horde into a community of brothers. To be sure, this is only a hypothesis, like so many others with which archaeologists endeavour to lighten the darkness of prehistoric times—a "Just-So Story," as it was amusingly called by a not unkind English critic; but I think it is creditable to such a hypothesis if it proves able to bring coherence and understanding into more and more new regions.

Human groups exhibit once again the familiar picture of an individual of superior strength among a troop of equal companions, a picture which is also contained in our idea of the primal horde. The psychology of such a group, as we know it from the descriptions to which we have so often referred—the dwindling of the conscious individual personality, the focusing of thoughts and feelings into a common direction, the predominance of the affective side of the mind and of unconscious psychical life, the tendency to the immediate carrying out of intentions as they emerge—all this corresponds to a state of regression to a primitive mental activity, of just such a sort as we should be inclined to ascribe to the primal horde.

Thus the group appears to us as a revival of the primal horde. Just as primitive man survives potentially in the every individual, so the primal horde may arise once more out of any random collection; in so far as men are habitually under the sway of group formation we recognize in it the survival of the primal horde. We must conclude that the psychological group is the oldest human psychology; what we have isolated as individual psychology, by neglecting all traces of the group, has only since come into prominence out of the old group psychology, by a gradual process which may still, perhaps, be described as incomplete. We shall later venture upon an attempt at specifying the point of departure of this development.

Further reflection will show us in what respect this statement requires correction. Individual psychology must, on the contrary, be just as old as group psychology, for from the first there were two kinds of psychologies, that of the individual members of the group and that of the father, chief, or leader. The members of the group were subject to ties just as we see them today, but the father of the primal horde was free. His intellectual acts were strong and independent even in isolation, and his will needed no reinforcement from others. Consistency leads us to assume that his ego had few libidinal ties; he loved no one but himself, or other people only in so far as they served his needs. To objects his ego gave away no more than was barely necessary.

He, at the very beginning of the history of mankind, was the "superman" whom Nietzsche only expected from the future. Even to-day the members of a group stand in need of the illusion that they are equal and justly loved by their leaders; but the leader himself need love no one else, he may be of a masterful nature, absolutely narcissistic, self-confident, and independent. We know that love puts a check upon narcissism, and it would be possible to show how, by operating in this way, it became a factor of civilization.

The primal father of the horde was not yet immortal, as he later became by deification. If he died, he had to be replaced; his place was probably taken by a youngest son, who had up to then been a member of the group like any other. There must therefore be a possibility of transforming group psychology into individual psychology; a condition must be discovered under which such a transformation is easily accomplished, just as it is possible for bees in case of necessity to turn a larva into a queen instead of into a worker. One can imagine only one possibility: the primal father had prevented his sons from satisfying their directly sexual impulsions; he forced them into abstinence and consequently into the emotional ties with him and with one another which could arise out of those of their impulsions that were inhibited in their sexual aim. He forced them, so to speak, into group psychology. His sexual jealousy and intolerance became in the last resort the causes of group psychology.

Whoever became his successor was also given the possibility of sexual satisfaction, and was by that means offered a way out of the conditions of group psychology. The fixation of the libido to woman and the possibility of satisfaction without any need for delay or accumulation made an end of the importance of those of his sexual impulsions that were inhibited in their aim, and allowed his narcissism always to rise to its full height. We shall return in a postscript to this connection between love and character formation.

We may further emphasize, as being especially instructive, the relation that holds between the contrivance by means of which an artificial group is held together and the construction of the primal horde. We have seen that with an army and a Church this contrivance is the illusion that the leader loves all of the individuals equally and justly. But this is simply an idealistic remodelling of the state of affairs in the primal horde, where all of the sons knew that they were equally *persecuted* by the primal father, and *feared* him equally. The same recasting upon which all social duties are built up is already presupposed by the next form of human society, the totemic clan. The indestructible strength of the family as a natural group formation rests upon the fact that this necessary presupposition of the father's equal love can have a real application in the family.

But we expect even more of this derivation of the group from the primal horde. It ought also to help us to understand what is still incomprehensible and mysterious in group formations—all that lies hidden behind the enigmatic words "hypnosis" and "suggestion." And I think it can succeed in this too. Let us recall that hypnosis has something positively uncanny about it; but the characteristic of uncanniness suggests something old and familiar that has undergone repression. Let us consider how hypnosis is induced. The hypnotist asserts that he is in possession of a mysterious power that robs the subject of his own will; or, which is the same thing, the subject believes it of him. This mysterious power (which is even now often described popularly as "animal magnetism") must be the same power that is looked upon by primitive people as the source of taboo, the same that emanates from kings and chieftains and makes it dangerous to approach them (*mana*). The hypnotist, then, is supposed to be in possession of this power; and how does he manifest it? By telling the subject to look him in the eyes; his most typical method of hypnotizing is by his look. But it is precisely the *sight* of the chieftain that is dangerous and unbearable for primitive people, just as later that of the Godhead is for mortals. Even Moses had to act as an intermediary between his people and Jehovah, since the people could not support the sight of God; and when he returned from the presence of God his face shone—some of the *mana* had been transferred on to him, just as happens with the intermediary among primitive people.

It is true that hypnosis can also be evoked in other ways, for instance by fixing the eyes upon a bright object or by listening to a monotonous sound. This is misleading and has given occasion to inadequate physiological theories. In point of fact these procedures merely serve to divert conscious attention and to hold it riveted. The situation is the same as if the hypnotist had said to the subject: "Now concern yourself exclusively with my person; the rest of the world is quite uninteresting." It would of course be technically inexpedient for a hypnotist to make such a speech; it would tear the subject away from his unconscious attitude and stimulate him to conscious opposition. The hypnotist avoids directing the subject's conscious thoughts towards his own intentions, and makes the person upon whom he is experimenting sink into an activity in which the world is bound to seem uninteresting to him; but at the same time the subject is in reality unconsciously concentrating his whole attention upon the hypnotist, and is getting into an attitude of *rapport*, of transference on him. Thus the indirect methods of hypnotizing, like many of the technical procedures used in making jokes, have the effect of checking certain distributions of mental energy which would interfere with the course of events in the unconscious, and they lead eventually to the same result as the direct method of influence by means of staring or stroking.

Ferenczi has made the true discovery that when a hypnotist gives the command to sleep, which is often done at the beginning of hypnosis, he is putting himself in the place of the subject's parents. He thinks that two sorts of hypnotism are to be distinguished: one coaxing and soothing, which he considers is derived from the father. Now the command to sleep in hypnosis means nothing more nor less than an order to withdraw all interest from the world and to concentrate it on the person of the hypnotist. And it is so understood by the subject; for in his withdrawal of interest from the external world lies the psychological characteristic of sleep, and the kinship between sleep and the state of hypnosis is based on it.

The uncanny and coercive characteristics of group formations, which are shown in the phenomena of suggestion that accompany them, may therefore with justice be traced back to the fact of their origin from the primal horde. The leader of the group is still the dreaded primal father; the group still wishes to be governed by unrestricted force; it has an extreme passion for authority; in Le Bon's phrase, it has a thirst for obedience. The primal father is the group ideal, which governs the ego in the place of the ego ideal. Hypnosis has a good claim to being described as a group of two. There remains as a definition for suggestion a conviction which is not based upon perception and reasoning but upon an erotic tie.

An American historian, Linda Gordon received an undergraduate degree from Swarthmore College in 1961, a master's from Yale University in 1963, and a Ph.D., also from Yale, in 1970. She taught for many years at the University of Wisconsin, Madison, where she was the Florence Kelley Professor of History and Vilas Distinguished Research Professor. She now teaches at New York University.

A Leftist and feminist historian, Gordon's first book was Woman's Body, Woman's Right: A Social History of Birth Control in America (1976); it has been reissued in a revised version as The Moral Property of Women (2003). Among her other books are Heroes of Their Own Lives: The Politics and History of Family Violence, Boston, 1880–1960 (1988); Pitied but Not Entitled: Single Mothers and the Origins of Welfare (1994); and The Great Arizona Orphan Abduction (1999), which won the Bancroft prize for the best book in U.S. history and the Beveridge prize for the best book on the history of the Americas.

The following excerpt is from her theoretically nuanced and broad gauged book on family violence, Heroes of Their Own Lives, which reflects her singular ability to bring historical contexts to bear on contemporary, critical issues.

Social Control and the Powers of the Weak

LINDA GORDON

> Whether I shall turn out to be the hero of my own life, or whether that station will be held by anybody else, these pages must show.
> —Charles Dickens, *David Copperfield*

Most of this book is sad. Most of the individual stories had bad endings. Family violence has not been stopped. Moreover, there is more wretchedness than heroism in this study. There has been a tendency, in telling the histories of the poor, to render survivors as heroes, to romanticize forbearance. The family-violence stories do not allow this because in them many who did not survive were equally brave, including the alcoholic, the delinquent, the depressed. Few of the victims were without some moment of complicity or resignation that lessened their resistance, at least temporarily. And many who were victims were also aggressors.

But this history is not finished. Both the struggle against family violence, and the interpretation of its history, are continuing. In the short period since the end of this study—in the 1960s and 1970s—the situation has changed markedly. In recent years, rediscovery of family violence was accomplished in part by pressure from the victims themselves. A much greater proportion of the contemporary response to family violence has been empowering to its victims, notably through battered women's shelters and other self-help groups. Moreover, as better histories of women, children, and social policy are written, they will reveal, I think, that these recent developments were built on earlier achievements: the original exposure of crimes against women and children, including previously denied and unspeakable sexual crimes; the campaigns that focused on child welfare, such as pensions for single mothers, anti-child-labor legislation, laws against the adulteration of milk and other foods, for example. These accomplishments, all critical to the protection of women and children, have been obscured by the long period of the quiescence of feminism between 1920 and 1960.

The rediscovery of family violence in the last two decades is no evidence that the problem is actually increasing. No one can know the *per capita* occurrence of family violence prior to the last few decades. The potential of publicity to increase reports of such problems is great. The definitions of what constitutes family violence suggest that less violence is tolerated as acceptable punishment today.

Moreover, even in the worst times, there were many family-violence victims attempting to become the heroes of their own lives, as Charles Dickens put it. Using the "powers of the weak," to cite Elizabeth Janeway again, attempting to replace with creativity and stubbornness what they lacked in resources, they manipulated every device at their disposal to free themselves from abuse. The people I knew from these case records were often isolated, poor, and sick, depressed and angry, but they did not appear to have done worse than I might have done under the same circumstances.

In exercising these powers of the weak, the family-violence clients contribute to an understanding of the dilemmas of all social control and social helping. Conflicts between privacy and social control, between individual rights and public responsibility, affect not only family violence but many aspects of "personal" life. In this study, despite the fact that I considered only cases in which criminal violence or neglect was proved, the violent families seemed ordinary, not alien.

Moreover, the very definition of family violence is by no means established. Ultimately we may all have to define for ourselves, for our own lives, the border between acceptable and unacceptable attempts to coerce. In Jean Thompson's extraordinary short story "The People of Color," a woman comes to question her own marriage from listening to beatings and screams from the next apartment. Considering the violence of others, instead of congratulating herself on the superiority of her relationship, she begins to question what might be called the institutionalized violence of her own marriage, a relationship that "works" only because of her acquiescence to her husband's infantile need for domination and ego support. The boundaries of family violence are openly in dispute among child-abuse experts, some of whom would declare all physical punishment to be abusive, although the majority of Americans use it.

This study made the variability of definitions of family violence a central part of its subject. It also encompassed, moreover, not only the changing experience of family violence, but also the strategies of both its participants and social control agents in responding to it. It has been necessary to show that family violence is not the unilateral expression of one person's violent temperament, but is cooked up jointly—albeit not equally—by several individuals in the pot of the family. There are no objects, only subjects, in this study. Out of this complex perspective, three general conclusions have emerged. First, family violence is a political issue. It has been defined and policies about it formed under the influence of changing political contexts since the 1870s. Second, domestic violence itself, as experienced by its participants, was also affected by historical change as it entered gender and generational relations. Third, the participants in family violence, both victims and assailants, were by no means passive recipients of social-control policies. Rather, they struggled actively to get help they considered useful from charity and social-work agencies as well as kin and neighbors.

Awareness of family violence has been shaped by several reform movements, of which the most important was feminism. It promoted critique of the conventional family and social responsibility for the welfare of children. During the period of this study, before 1960, it legitimated state intervention on behalf of children, but not for women. Nevertheless, the close connection, in ideology and in material circumstances, between women's and children's well-being meant that women gained much from child-protection agencies. Indeed, the inadequacy of means of caring for children outside their original families has meant that women may well have gained more, because children gained so little, from child work.

The decline of feminist influence in social work, particularly after World War I, meant not only the decreased visibility of family-violence problems altogether but also their redefinition in ways that were disadvantageous to victims. For example, the definitions of child neglect from the Progressive era tended to hold women exclusively responsible for the welfare of children; to emphasize economic deprivation but not gender-domination; and, through the maintenance of a punitive approach without complementary social services, to intensify poor women's vulnerability to neglect allegations and to loss of their children. When child-welfare workers lost their familiarity with critiques of male domination as an overall social problem, they also lost their ability to "see" the particularly male types of family violence, wife-beating, and sexual abuse. A more continuous feminist influence might have encouraged a search for alternative responses to child abuse other than removal of children. Only in the past few decades has a woman's movement been again strong enough to direct attention to wife-beating and incest; there is need for a stronger feminist influence in the analysis of child abuse and neglect.

Family violence has been political not only in its definitions but also in its causes. It usually emerged from power struggles in which family members were contesting for material, and often scarce, benefits. Moreover, the goals of the individuals were affected by historical change, particularly that influencing the aspirations of women and children, or frustrating the expectations of men. This study encountered less evidence of the contribution of individual, psychological factors to these struggles, but we know they were there. Structural, "social" analyses do not contradict the importance of individual temperament. (The psychological categories for personality and mental disorders have been so shifting over the years that it is best to remain here for vernacular categories such as "temperament.") But very few of the victims or assailants in these family-violence cases were mentally ill. Moreover, to call family violence political is not to deny that each subjective experience of it is wholly personal and unique.

Despite psychological and social disabilities, many agency clients were far from despairing or resigned. The women clients, whether victims or assailants, were not only resourceful in seeking help for themselves and their families but also self-critical about their own behavior. Their aspirations thus contributed to social definitions of their own deviance. In these efforts they helped others beyond themselves, because they collectively influenced the responses of individual social workers and, ultimately, the policy of the agencies.

SOCIAL CONTROL

These conclusions, especially with respect to the activity of clients of child-protection agencies, call into question much of the legacy of scholarship about social control. Ever since E. A. Ross first used the phrase "social control" in 1901, two traditions have dominated appraisals of the growing social regulatory side of the state. One, the liberal interpretation, that of Ross himself and Talcott Parsons after him in the 1940s and 1950s, considered such intervention a sign of progress. They viewed the replacement of family functions—such as socialization—by professionals as beneficial. A contrasting, more pessimistic interpretation of social control has been advanced since the 1930s by both Marxists and conservatives, from the Frankfurt School to Ortega y Gasset. The former were concerned with the suppression of class consciousness, the latter with individual autonomy, but both joined in a condemnation of professional intervention. These condemnations, not only of regulatory agencies, but also of the controlling aspects of much of the apparatus of the modern welfare state, were continued by scholars influenced by the New Left in the 1960s and 1970s.

Neither positive nor negative appraisals of social control had gender or generational analyses. Both, in fact, continued a patriarchal usage in identifying "the family" that was being invaded with a male-dominated, father-dominated form of family. If one uses family violence as the key instance of social control, an issue that contained an inherent critique of patriarchal domination, then new questions arise and the evaluation of intervention must be more complex.

For example, the critique of social control, both left and right, frequently points to the violation of civil liberties as evidence of the dangers of intervention into family privacy. We have seen many instances of such violations in this book, but before condemning the very enterprise of intervening into the family, one must ask: Whose privacy? Whose liberties? The conception of liberties dominant in the nineteenth century was one of individual rights against the state, which was in fact an attribution of rights to heads of households. These rights functioned to enshrine the home as private and inviolable, and the champions of these rights were naturally adult men, particular those with the privilege and wealth to maintain independent households. (Many poor and working-class people were not able to achieve these independent households.) Such rights did not protect subordinate members of families against intrafamily oppression or violence. On the contrary, privacy rights have been invoked to remove some individuals from the public guarantees of these liberties. Until recently it was customary for law enforcement officials to decline to guarantee such liberties to battered women, for example. Children did not usually even get as far as telling their story to law officers, so removed were they from access to their "rights." Thus one man's loss of privacy was often another's (frequently a woman's) gain in rights.

Of course, the control of family violence guaranteed no victories for victims, and may often have hurt them further. Once social-control agents, whether public or private, entered families, all family members lost their privacy. The victims often had their "rights" defined for them in ways that they did not always recognize, let alone want. Yet what privacy or control did they have without these interventions? The clients' problems were defined not only by their own faults, not only by their interaction with the large economy and social structure, but also by a range of very personal and very invasive other relationships. A family-violence case is constructed by children and their parents, in-laws and grandparents and cousins, caseworkers, judges, probation officers, relief officials, school counselors, doctors, psychologists. Behind the fear of invasion of privacy is also the myth of an isolated nuclear family.

Nor is it true, as several scholars have argued, that these interventions by "outsiders" are a modern piece of deviltry destroying a traditional family autonomy. On the contrary, no family relations have been immune from social regulation. Certainly the modern form of social control exercised by child-protection agencies is qualitatively and quantitatively different from that of traditional societies. The child protectors were "outsiders," lacking investment in local community values and traditions, uncaring about the individuals involved. But traditional forms of social control—community gossip or private interventions—were no more tolerant of individual liberty or deviance than the modern bureaucratic state and its professionals.

Furthermore, we have seen that clients often wanted this intervention. While the definitions of family violence and its remedies have reflected the biases of dominant groups—have been unfair, discriminatory, and oppressive—family violence remains as a problem experienced *by its participants*. The clients did not consider their sufferings inevitable. The power of labeling, the representation of poor people's behavior by experts whose status is defined through their critique of the problematic behavior of others, coexists with real family oppressions. In one case an immigrant father who sexually molested his thirteen-year-old daughter told a social worker that was the way it was done in the old country! He was not only lying but also trying to manipulate a social worker, perhaps one he recognized as guilt-ridden over her privileged role, using his own fictitious cultural relativism. His daughter's victimization by incest was not the result of oppression by professionals.

The "interventions" of professionals, bureaucrats, or even upper-class charity workers were, as often as not, really invitations by family members. This does not mean that the inviters kept control of the relationships, or got what they wanted. The guests did not usually leave upon request. Moreover, collectively the interveners and the establishment they represented had much more power than the clients individually or collectively. But it is a mistake to see the flow of initiative in these social-control relationships in only one direction, from top to bottom, from professionals to clients, from elite to subordinate. In fact, the clients were not usually passive but, rather, active in arguing for what they wanted. And sometimes they got what they wanted: single mothers got relief, battered wives got separations, abused children got, at least, attention. More frequently, the clients did not get what they wanted, but their cumulative pressure affected the agencies' definitions of problems and proposals for help.

In historical fact, most of the invitations for intervention came from women and secondarily children. In other words, the inviters were the weaker members of family power structures. Social work intervention has not been a process that can be expressed simply in class terms, as the rich against the poor. In their struggles to escape the control of a patriarchal family, women not only use the professions and the state but helped build them. The social worker/social control establishment did not arise out of the independent agenda of the ruling class, or even of the middle class. Rather it developed out of conflicts that had gender and generational as well as class "sides."

When critics of social control perceive social work simply as unwanted intervention, and fail to recognize the active role of agency, clients, it is in large part because they conceive of the family as a homogeneous unit. This is an intellectual reification here, which expresses itself in sentence structure, particularly in academic language. The family is in decline, "threats to the family," "the family responds to industrialization." Shorthand expressions attributing behavior to an aggregate such as the family would be harmless except that they often impose particular cultural norms about what "the family" is, and mask intrafamily differences and conflicts of interest. Usually "the family" becomes a representation of the interests of the family head, if it is a man, carrying an assumption that all family members share his interests. (Families without a married male head, like single-parent or grandparent-headed families, are, in the common usage, broken, deformed, or incomplete families.) Among the clients in family-violence cases, outrage over the intervention into the family was frequently an outrage over a territorial violation, a challenge to male authority; or expressed differently, an outrage at the exposure of intrafamily conflict and of the family head's lack of control. Indeed, the interventions actually *were* more substantive, more invasive, when their purpose was to change the status quo than if they had been designed to reinforce it. The effect of social workers' involvement was to change existing family power relations, usually in the interest of the weaker family members.

In the legitimation of charitable and professional intervention into domestic problems, an important political leadership was contributed by the women's rights movement. Feminist consciousness was largely responsible, not only for the several waves of sensitivity to women's and children's domestic victimization, but also for public assumption of responsibility for defending them against abusive husbands and parents. Indeed, the whole welfare state, including particularly its regulatory organizations, derived to a significant degree from the feminist agenda of the late nineteenth and early twentieth centuries. The influence of these women activists and their vision is only slowly being recognized. Their vision reflected, of course, their class as well as their sex position, and most of them were elite. Feminist influence as well as male leadership and professional social work were guilty of disdain for non-Wasp cultures, arrogance toward the poor, failure to understand the impact of structural unemployment, and refusal to defend the rights of single mothers, to name but a few examples.

But that enthusiasm for state regulation was not strictly a middle-class maneuver, nor was it on balance disadvantageous to poor women. Furthermore, many family oppressions were problems shared by women across class lines. Opposition to wife-beating did not need to be taught to the working class by middle-class women; poor mothers did not lag behind prosperous mothers in their desire for kindness, safety, education, and nutrition for their children; and the rebellion of both women and children against paternal tyranny was easily as sharp in the working class as elsewhere. In other words, family violence was not a middle-class or "bourgeois" issue. The women who called upon the child protectors knew the risks they were taking. Despite the fact that fathers were more often outraged at being investigated and possibly maligned, the mothers had more to lose: by far the most common outcome of agency action was the removal of children, an action dreaded least by fathers and most by mothers. But these fears did not stop women from attempting to manipulate social workers in their own interest—both because they had confidence in their own purposes and because they wanted help so badly. Nor was it only victims who appealed: abusive and neglectful mothers, distressed that they were not able to raise their children according to their own standards, were among the complainants. These people were finding the traditional informal methods of social controls, which may have prevailed in agrarian societies, inadequate to their needs in modern, impersonal urban society.

The usual critique of social-control-as-domination also ignores the fact that the controllers often preferred not to act. Chronically under-funded and under-staffed, agencies frequently disregarded complaints and repelled requests for help. Most cases led to no action; indeed caseworkers more often disappointed clients by their inactivity than by their activism.

Despite patterns of class and cultural domination, family casework agencies were often helpful to clients. This was mainly because individual caseworkers were usually better (although sometimes worse) than the official agency policies they were supposed to follow. This superiority, in turn, came in part from the casework approach itself, and the attention paid to all aspects of clients' family context. Even more it came from the fact that individuals brought flexibility, creativity, and empathy beyond the strictures of agency policy. The most helpful caseworkers were those who understood family-violence problems to be simultaneously social/cultural and personal in origin, and who therefore offered help in both dimensions. Good caseworkers might help a family get relief, or medical care, or a better apartment, and build a woman's or child's self-esteem by legitimating their complaints and aspirations.

Social work interventions in family-violence cases rarely changed assailants' behavior, but they had a greater impact on victims. The main factor determining the usefulness of casework was the activity of clients: those who sought help and knew what they wanted were more likely to get it. This is why, ironically, the child-protection agencies contributed more to help battered women, defined as outside their jurisdiction, than abused children. Modern urban society gave women some opportunity to leave abusive men because they could earn their own living. In these circumstances, even a bit of material help—a referral to a relief agency, a positive recommendation to the courts regarding child custody—could turn their aspirations for autonomy into reality. Moreover, women could get this help despite class and ethnic prejudices against them. Italian-American women might reap this benefit even from social workers who held derogatory views of Italians; single mothers might get help in establishing independent households despite charity workers' suspicions of their morals. Children would need more than money to escape abusive parents.

At the same time, in this society of great inequality, interventions against family violence have been and continue to be discriminatory. Class privilege brings with it immunity from discovery and/or intervention. Not only have poor, working-class, immigrant, and black people been discriminated against, but so too have women, despite the feminist influence in stimulating anti-family violence intervention. The disrespect and victim-blaming of many professionals toward clients was the worst, because they were proffered by those defined as "helping." Loss of control was a debilitating experience for many clients, including those who may have gained some material aid. Often the main beneficiaries of professionals' interventions hated them most, because in wrestling with them one rarely gets what one really wants but, rather, is asked to submit to another's interpretation of one's needs.

In these complexities, anti-family-violence work is emblematic of the entire welfare state. Its unfairness is true of every aspect of the welfare state, from which, despite much popular myth to the contrary, the rich and privileged benefit more than the poor. But the abolition of such interventions would not better protect the subordinate groups from discrimination. The dichotomous argument, between those who applaud the welfare state as a sign of progress and those who condemn its oppressiveness, is not useful. The very inequalities of power that make the state oppressive create the need for state responsibility for welfare, and these inequalities include gender and age as well as class. Integrating gender and generational conflicts along with class and economic conflicts in our understanding of the welfare state will demonstrate the need for a more complex appraisal.

I do not wish to discard the cumulative insights offered by many critiques of social control, and by contemporary revelations of the unfairness and violence of many accusations of family violence. Rather, I want to insist that an accurate view of this "outside" intervention into the family must consider, as the clients so often did in their strategic decisions, both external and familial forms of domination. This is a complexity that women particularly faced, struggling as they so often were not only for themselves but also for children. But I do not see any way to circumvent this contradiction. There is no returning to an old or newly romanticized "family autonomy." An answer to problems of family violence, indeed to the whole question of public responsibility for private welfare, must contain and wrestle with, not seek to eradicate, this tension.

Del Martin is a feminist activist with special concerns about the American family as traditionally defined. Her major work is Battered Wives, *though she also wrote* Lesbian/Woman *with her longtime lover, Phyllis Lyon (1972). Also with Lyon she founded the 1950s lesbian organization Daughters of Bilitis, and together they published the* Ladder, *one of the first lesbian magazines in the United States. Martin's and Lyon's unapologetic stance as lesbians who were also public intellectuals institutionalized the change propounded by feminist and lesbian and gay liberation movements from the 1960s. They insisted on equality on lesbian terms, promoting "a society that will recognize and adjust to the diversity and humanness of all its citizens."*

Battered Wives

DEL MARTIN

THE GREAT AMERICAN FAMILY

The door behind which the battered wife is trapped is the door to the family home. The white-picket-fence stereotype of the American family home still persists from the days of Andy Hardy. The privacy of the home supposedly protects a comfortable space within which intimate and affectionate relationships among spouses, parents and children, and siblings become richer and deeper with each passing year. Loyalty, constancy, and protectiveness are demonstrated by the parents and learned by the children. If you modernize the picture by adding some self-deprecating humor gleaned from television's situation comedies, the image of the ideal American family will be complete.

In one sense, the family home is supposed to provide refuge from the stormy turbulence of the outside world. In another, it is a family factory, designed to perpetuate its own values and to produce two or three replicas of itself as the children in the family marry—whether or not they are ready for or suited for marriage. The nuclear family is the building block of American society, and the social, religious, educational, and economic institutions of society are designed to maintain, support, and strengthen family ties even if the people involved can't stand the sight of one another.

Until very recently, no acceptable alternatives to the family home existed in the United States. People who chose to live alone or to share their homes with non-relatives, those who chose to set up same-sex households, or who married but chose not to have children—all were seen as outcasts, failures, or deviants. This attitude is changing, albeit very slowly, possibly more as a result of over-population than of growing openmindedness and tolerance. But even now, the stereotype of the happy, harmonious family persists in American society. Compared with this ideal, most actual families composed of real people appear to be tragic failures, and in many cases they are.

In reality, the glowing image of the American family is a myth. The privacy that protects the family can also muffle the blows and stifle the yells of a violent home. People who would not otherwise consider striking anyone sometimes act as if establishing a household together gives them the right to abuse each other. "From our interviews," Richard Gelles says in *The Violent Home*, "we are still convinced that in most cases a marriage license also functions as a hitting license." In his research, which admittedly was limited to eighty subjects who were legally married, Gelles found that numerous incidents of violence between married partners were considered by them to be normal, routine, and generally acceptable. He also found a high incidence of violence in his control group and only one instance in which violence had occurred before the couple married. Furthermore, in the case of two couples in his sample who dated, married, divorced, dated again, and remarried, violence occurred *only* when these couples were *legally* married. These findings indicate to Gelles the possibility that violence between a couple is considered acceptable within, but not outside of, marriage.

Unmarried women who have been beaten by their mates undoubtedly would take exception to Gelles's interpretation. It may well be that the shared home, not the marriage vow, is the key element here. Some men may feel that they have the right to exercise power over the women they live with whether or not they are legally married to them.

Our patriarchal system allows a man the right of ownership to some degree over the property *and* people that comprise his household. A feminist friend learned this lesson in an incident in Oakland, California. She witnessed a street fight in which a husband was hitting his pregnant wife in the stomach (a recurring theme in stories of wife-abuse). She saw the fight as she was driving by, stopped her car, and jumped out to help the woman. When she tried to intervene, the male bystanders who stood idly by watching the spectacle shouted at her, "You can't do that! She's his wife!" and "You shouldn't interfere; it's none of your business." Although the wife had begged the gathered crowd to call the police, no one did so until my friend was struck by the furious husband. (I have heard of a similar incident where a man interfered and *he* was the one who was arrested and charged with assault!)

Sociologist Howard Erlanger of the University of Wisconsin found that 25 percent of his sample of American adults actually approved of husband-wife battles. What is more surprising was that the greater the educational level, the greater was the acceptance of marital violence. Approval ranged from 17 percent of grade-school graduates to 32 percent of college postgraduate students, with a slightly lower 30 percent for those who had completed just four years of college. The study also showed that, contrary to popular belief, low-income respondents were no more prone to nor more readily accepting of violence in the home than were middle- or upper-income respondents.

The popular assumption by the middle class that marital violence occurs more frequently in the ghetto and among lower-class families reflects the inability of middle-class investigators to face the universality of the problem. Evidence of wife-beating exists wherever one cares to look for it. Fairfax County, Virginia, for instance, is a suburb of the District of Columbia and considered to be one of the wealthiest counties in the United States. Police there received 4,073 family disturbance calls in 1974. They estimated that thirty assault warrants are sought by Fairfax County wives each week.

Morton Bard's study of New York's 30th Precinct, a West Harlem community of about 85,000 people, is another example. This socially stable residential community consists mostly of working-class Blacks, with a sprinkling of Latin Americans (8 percent) and whites (2 percent). Bard found that the number of wife-abuse cases reported in the 30th precinct was roughly the same as that reported in another study conducted in Norwalk, Connecticut—a white, upper-middle-class area with approximately the same population.

A survey conducted for the National Commission on the Causes and Prevention of Violence by Louis Harris and Associates bears out Erlanger's conclusions that a great many people approve of husband-wife battles. The Harris poll in October 1968, consisting of 1,176 interviews with a representative national sample of American adults, showed that one-fifth approved of slapping one's spouse on "appropriate" occasions. In this survey, 16 percent of those with eight years of schooling or less approved, and 25 percent of college-educated people approved of a husband slapping his wife.

Rodney Stark and James McEvoy III further analyzed the Harris data and found that 25 percent of the Blacks, 20 percent of the whites, 25 percent of the males, and 16 percent of the females interviewed "could approve of a husband's slapping his wife's face." The percentage points rose in all of these categories (from 1 to 3 percent) when the question was reversed and subjects were asked if they "could approve of a wife's slapping her husband's face." Analyzed by regions of the country, persons from the West rated highest and the South lowest in approval of either action. Those with an income of $5,000 or less were considerably less approving than those in other income brackets. Persons under thirty years old were most approving, and those sixty-five years or older were least approving of husband-wife slappings.

A slap in the face could be construed as a fairly innocent gesture compared with a full-fledged beating. But a friend of mine told me this story. Three months after her mother and stepfather were married, they had an argument and he gave her a sound "slapping." A few months later he "slapped" her again; this time the woman wound up in the hospital with her jaws wired together. When she came home from the hospital, her husband was contrite and conciliatory. He did his best to please her so that she wouldn't leave him. The woman stayed, though she never really forgave her husband. They still had their fights, but he never laid a hand on her again. However, two years later, when the couple got into a particularly heated argument in the kitchen, he grabbed a knife and killed her.

Later, my daughter was slapped by a friend's violent husband when she responded to the wife's call for help. He just slapped her on the cheek, but with such force that her head snapped back and pain shot through her head to the top of her skull. He struck her twice in this heavy-handed manner. Her face was sore for several days, though there were no bruises; she also suffered the effects of a minor whiplash. "I didn't think he would hit *me*. He was my friend," she said. "And I certainly didn't realize that a man would exert so much force with his open hand. It was just a short slap. He didn't need to take a long swing."

In the Harris poll cited above, if the word had been "hit" instead of "slap" would the results of the poll have been the same? Would 25 percent of the males and 16 percent of the females interviewed approve of a husband hitting his wife in the face? The answer to that question is anybody's guess. But there is a good chance that the interviewees would have considered the question an invasion of privacy had the word been "hit" rather than "slap." I cite this possibility to underscore the subtlety of the problem and the difficulty of interpreting the significance of the data.

Even agreeing on a definition of "violence" may be a problem for some people. Police, for instance, seem to think that few domestic disturbances are really violent. They tend to define violence in terms of its effect. Unless blood is drawn and injuries are visible, they are apt to discount the report of violence and call the incident merely a "family spat." To me, any physical attack by one person upon another is a violent act and an instance of illegal aggression, even if no visible injury results. Still, Gelles noted that after the bruises had healed, some of his subjects called even the most severe beatings they received "non-violent."

However the terms are defined, though, sufficient evidence of serious injury and homicide exists to show that domestic violence is a critical problem. In *The Violent Home*, Gelles determined where and when violence is most likely to occur. The "typical location of family violence was the kitchen. The bedroom and the living room are the next most likely scenes of violence. Some respondents are unable to pinpoint exact locations because their battles begin in one room and progress through the house. The *only* room in the house where there was *no violence* was the bathroom."

Alex D. Pokorny says that murder seldom occurs in public places. The usual site is the home, though the car is the setting in a fair number of cases. Other studies of homicides show that the bedroom is the deadliest room in the house and that the victims there are usually female. The next most likely place for family murders is the kitchen; in these cases the women are more frequently the offenders.

According to Gelles, couples get into violent fights most often after dinner, between 8 and 11:30 p.m. The second most frequent time is during dinner (5 to 8 p.m.), and the third is late evening to early morning. The same time-table applies to those acts of violence that result in death. Also violence of either variety occurs most frequently on weekends. Kansas City police cite Monday as another day of reckoning.

Bruce B. Lawrence is a coeditor of this book. The excerpt below comes from his monograph, Shattering the Myth: Islam Beyond Violence *(1998), in which he explores not only the nature of the violence ascribed to Muslim norms and actors but also the role of the nation-state and the modern media in representing multiple forms of violence.*

The Shah Bano Case

BRUCE B. LAWRENCE

Nowhere have the contradictions posed by an Islamist solution become more evident than in the case of a South Asian Muslim divorcee who sought support from her husband through the court system. To examine the case of Shah Bano is to call attention to the pivotal yet problematic role of one mode of governance, the judiciary, as it functions in the three major Muslim states of South Asia: India, Pakistan, and Bangladesh. I will argue two points that emerge when one looks at women as an independent category and the judiciary as a crucial dimension of governance. The first is that women are made to represent the cultural norms shared by men and women alike throughout Muslim South Asia. The second is that court cases involving women's legal rights not only reflect boundary markings between Muslim and other communities, they also heighten tensions about their maintenance, even as they complicate notions of what it is to be both Asian and Muslim in the late twentieth century of the common era.

Shah Bano was the daughter of a police constable. At an early age she had been married to her first cousin, Muhammad Ahmad Khan. During more than forty years of marriage she had borne him five children. Then one day in 1975, according to her account, he evicted her from their home. At first he paid her a maintenance sum, as was required by Islamic law, but he ceased payment after some two and a half years. When she applied to the district court for redress, he divorced her. Uttering the formula disapproved by the Prophet but authorized by the Hanafi school of law, he declared: "I divorce you, I divorce you, I divorce you."

At that point they were fully divorced, but, complying with a further provision of Islamic law, Muhammad Ahmad Khan repaid Shah Bano the dower of about three hundred dollars that he had set aside at the time of their marriage. Legally he had fulfilled all his responsibilities to her.

Shah Bano, however, was left impoverished. She had no means to support herself, having worked only as a housewife for over forty years in the domicile from which she was now debarred. She sued her former husband by going to the magistrate of a provincial court. The magistrate ruled that Muhammad Ahmad Khan, having violated the intent of Muslim Personal Law, was obliged to continue paying Shah Bano her maintenance. The court awarded her the sum of roughly two dollars a month. She appealed the amount of that award, and two years later, in 1980, the High Court of her state (Madhya Pradesh) awarded Shah Bano approximately twenty-three dollars a month.

It was at that point that Muhammad Ahmad Khan appealed the High Court's decision. A lawyer himself, he took the case to the Indian Supreme Court, arguing that he had fulfilled all the provisions of Muslim Personal Law and hence had no more financial obligations toward his former spouse.

The Shah Bano case dragged on for another five years. Without the financial support of "fairly well-off male family members (in this case, Shah Bano's sons)," she could not have pursued her appeal. Finally, in 1985, seven years after she had begun litigation in the lower courts, Shah Bano was vindicated: The Indian Supreme Court upheld the Madhya Pradesh High Court judgment, and her former husband had to comply with its verdict. The Supreme Court justices, in dismissing Muhammad Ahmad Khan's appeal, cited the Criminal Procedure Code of 1973, one section of which referred to "the maintenance of wives, children, and parents."

None of the above narratives makes Shah Bano exceptional. Neither her plight nor the length of her legal battles lacks precedents. Numerous are the studies of South Asian women that underscore the discrimination they continue to experience even after the attention drawn to Third World women during the International Women's Decade (1975–1985). It is no small irony that Shah Bano's legal vindication came just as the International Women's Decade was ending, but the favorable outcome of her case had more to do with a legislative act than with public advocacy of women's rights: it was a change in the Code of Criminal Procedure, enacted in 1973, that made possible the reconsideration of provisions for divorced Muslim women. Under this code, two Muslim women had been awarded maintenance—in 1979 and again in 1980—and it was their cases, though reviewed and modified in the Shah Bano judgment, that provided the precedent with reference to which the Supreme Court opted to rule in favor of Shah Bano.

The legal drama and its political consequence are dense. Often the case seems to remain only a watershed for identity politics in the continuing struggle for inclusive norms within postcolonial India. What needs to be stressed alternatively is the nature of the legal system that made all three cases possible. All three women resided neither in Bangladesh nor in Pakistan, the two majoritarian Muslim nations of the subcontinent, but in the Republic of India. As Indian citizens, they lived under an ad hoc system evolved since British colonial rule. It was a system that tended to separate criminal law from Muslim personal law. Throughout the nineteenth and the early twentieth centuries there was no uniform manner of applying Muslim family law within the lower courts. On the one hand, the number of rules applied to questions of marriage and inheritance were restricted, while on the other hand, they were enforced through a strict hierarchical structure where appeals moved haltingly from a subordinate district judge to a state high court to the London Privy Council, replaced after 1947 by the Indian Supreme Court.

Due to the omissions and excesses of this system, it is not surprising that customary law, unfavorable to women, was often applied instead of the more favorable terms of Islamic law. Muslim women in the western and northern regions of India were especially vulnerable to facing the denial of property inheritance and dowry settlements, both provided to them under the *shari a* or Islamic law. Finally, in 1937, under pressure from Muslim elites, the Shariat Law was passed. It required all Indian Muslims to be governed solely by Islamic juridical norms in family matters, namely, in marriage, divorce, maintenance, adoption, succession, and inheritance. But at independence ten years later, Parliament passed an All India Criminal Procedure Code that applied, as its title suggests, to all Indian citizens, whatever their religious affiliations; one of its provisions stipulated "the maintenance of wife, children, and parents." It was that provision which the Supreme Court justices cited in the 1979 and 1980 cases again in 1985 when they ruled in favor of Shah Bano and against Muhammad Ahmad Khan.

Personal law, in effect, acquired a double tracking, one pertaining to the Muslim community, the other to the common Indian citizenship. While that double tracking created tension between secular and religious authorities after independence, such tension was nonetheless successfully negotiated prior to 1985. Were the issue itself a sufficient provocation, then both the 1979 and the 1980 cases should have set off a nationwide row. In fact, they did not.

The case of Shah Bano became decisive for one reason: its timing. It did not occur in the mid-1970s, when Mrs. Gandhi's declaration of a state of emergency had muzzled the court system, nor will it occur again in the mid-1990s, for reasons what will be made clear below. It was the changed climate of religious identity in the mid-1980s that set the stage for the Shah Bano debacle. There were several necessary conditions, but the one sufficient condition was Muslim Personal Law, that is, law that applied to the personal status of each Muslim within the family domain. Personal law becomes the litmus test of Indian Muslim collective identity, its fragility underscored by the creation in 1972 of an All India Muslim Personal Law Board to maintain and defend its application.

Even so, personal law by itself would not have created the Shah Bano debacle. The case came to public attention in the aftermath of Indira Gandhi's assassination at the hands of Sikh extremists. Riots in Delhi and elsewhere had shredded the myth of communal harmony in the Republic of India. Everyone had become more aware and more worried about his or her markings as a Hindu or a Muslim or a Sikh or a tribal. When Sikhs, not Muslims, had been the primary targets of the Delhi riots, Muslims still felt vulnerable.

It was in this charged atmosphere that demagogues sought pretexts to "prove" that the ruling party was but a front for furthering Hindu hegemony, at the expense of all minorities but especially the largest, which was the Muslim, minority. The Shah Bano case provided Muslim ideologues, supported and abetted by the All India Muslim Personal Law Board, with "clear" evidence that there was a juridical slide toward uniform civil codes, codes that would enforce majoritarian Hindu values on all Indians. Rajiv Gandhi's Congress-I was then the ruling party. When Congress-I supported the Supreme Court decision, an incensed Muslim politician ran against the Congress-I candidate (who also happened to be a Muslim). The demagogue won, lambasting the anti-Muslim impact of the Shah Bano judgment. How could Muslims preserve their separate identity, he argued, if even their personal laws were subject to arbitration in the higher, "secular" courts of India? The Muslim Personal Law Board, having won a victory at the regional level, ratcheted its claims to the next level. Its members pressed on the national front, appealing to legislators, ministers, and, of course, journalists. They were abetted by Muhammad Ahmad Khan, a barrister arguing his own case! Together the aggrieved former spouse and representatives of the Muslim Personal Law Board carried the banner of Muslim juridical autonomy to several members of Parliament, their every move broadcast by the press.

The role of the press in dramatizing the Shah Bano case has been considerable. In volume of print and decibels of emotion it exceeds all other tragedy-laced spectacles, even the storming of the Sikh golden temple in Amritsar, even the assassination of Mrs. Gandhi and later her son, Rajiv. It exceeds even the Rushdie affair, with which it has sometimes been linked, notably by Gayatri Spivak. The Shah Bano case exceeds all these because it concerns a process that has tapped into communal fears, and drawn out appeals to communal loyalty, not witnessed since independence. Its only competitor for sustained media attention is the Ayodhya mandir/Babri masjid dispute. The dispute erupted in

1986 as a politically motivated effort to reclaim all of India as "Hindu" by pinpointing, with scant historical evidence, one pilgrimage site as the birthplace of the god Ram and then alleging that sixteenth-century Mughal invaders built a mosque on this same site in order to affirm their superiority over Hinduism.

Important though the Ayodhya dispute is, in a real sense it occupies adjacent space on the same spectrum of communally marked confrontation as Shah Bano. Ayodhya becomes the sequel to Shah Bano since it was the latter that pushed Muslim-Hindu antagonism to new levels. Unlike the local protagonists of previous communal riots, the India-wide Hindu protagonists of Ayodhya's sacral purity were used in the media to stage a grievance identical to that of the Shah Bano case, namely, that Muslim and Hindu worldviews were finally incommensurate and that the Republic of India could not grant both equal representation.

In such a charged atmosphere the value of religious identity is heightened, and appeals to creedal shibboleths abound. The ideological weapon wielded on both sides quickly became identified as fundamentalism. It was fundamentalism Indian-style, but it was still the bugbear of fundamentalism. The challenge was thrown down by the demagogue who used Shah Bano as the rallying cry for his own election to Parliament in 1985. Syed Shahabuddin decried the Supreme Court decision as "clear" evidence of Hindu contempt for Muslim law. He opposed it not only for himself and for his Muslim constituents but also for all believing Muslims who, like himself, were fundamentalists. Fundamentalists? Yes, fundamentalists, because to be a true Muslim, in his view, was to bind oneself to the literal revelation of the Qur'an. "Historically," declared Syed Shahabuddin, "the Qur'an was revealed to the Prophet 1400 years ago but it is the final message of God to mankind. Not one syllable is subject to change. . . . It is in this sense that the Muslim is by definition a fundamentalist."

There are, of course, enormous contradictions in this assertion, since the Qur'an itself is subject to variant interpretations *within* the believing community of Muslims. Despite the consensus shared by all Muslims that the Qur'an is the final message of God's final messenger, its rare legal passages engender multiple interpretations, arising as they do in a myriad of human circumstances. When Syed Shahabuddin and his followers appeal to Qur'anic finality, they are really staking out a claim for themselves as the sole valid interpreters of what they take to be the simple, singular meaning mandated by Qur'anic verses. Yet other, equally devout Muslims can challenge those claims and offer in their stead equally valid alternative readings of both the Holy Qur'an and Islamic history.

In a time of crisis, to those who perceive themselves at risk, a dispassionate view of the Qur'an may be less plausible than the unequivocal reading claimed by Syed Shahabuddin and other "fundamentalists." The mid-1980s were such a time of crisis for many Indians. India's Muslim "fundamentalists" challenged the Shah Bano ruling at a moment when the center seemed to be unraveling. Their appeal to Parliament to reverse the Shah Bano decree seemed implausible, and the uproar about Shah Bano would have quickly subsided had their appeal failed. But for a variety of political considerations both the Congress-I and Prime Minister Rajiv Gandhi perceived themselves as vulnerable to "the Muslim vote." Out of expediency the Indian Parliament in 1986 passed a bill often referred to as the Muslim Women's Bill. That bill withdrew the right of Muslim women to appeal for maintenance under the Criminal Procedure Code. In other words, after 1986 Shah Bano could have no successors, for the Muslim Women (Protection of Rights on Divorce) Bill, in fact, discriminated against Muslim women: it removed the right of any Muslim woman to juridical appeal for redress of the award made to her under Muslim Personal Law.

Damaging though the outcome may be to the invisible seam of multiculturalism without which Indian democracy cannot function, its most dire consequences may yet be muted by the logic of its initial success. Rather than closing debate on the Shah Bano case, the legislative reversal of the Supreme Court ruling raised new questions about who has the right to speak on behalf of the Muslim community. The Supreme Court judge who read the majority decision made his own claim to best understand Muslim interests when in concluding his argument for the court's ruling he justified it as "more in keeping with the Qur'an than the traditional interpretation by Muslim of the Shariat." His move to separate the purity of Qur'anic principles from the obfuscation of Muslim jurists was followed by others, including a score of journalists. In an exchange that enlivened the *Illustrated Weekly of India* during early March 1986, a Hindu journalist, Arun Shouri, argued that "while there was much oppression of women under Islamic law, the Qur'an, rightly interpreted, would make possible the removal of the injustices they suffered." But, according to his respondent, the Islamic scholar Rafiq Zakaria, Shouri only seemed to be concerned about true Islam; his stated concern actually masked a contempt for Muslims and a not so subtle attempt to undermine Muslim religious identity. Nor did the debate disappear once the Muslim Women Bill became law: women's groups opposed the government's stand in favor of the bill, with the result that leading Muslims spoke out on *both* sides of the issue. Seldom before had religious identity and gender parity been so publicly framed in antithetical, competing terms. No wonder that Shah Bano subsequently rejected the court verdict in her favor, and occasioned still another round of debate about the meaning of her subjectivity as a Muslim woman.

A German philosopher, Walter Benjamin became one of the most influential literary and cultural theorists of the twentieth century. He was born into an affluent Jewish family in Berlin, then studied philosophy in Berlin, Freiburg im Breisgau, Munich, and Bern. After settling in Berlin in 1920, Benjamin embarked on a career of literary criticism and translation. His first major article, "Goethe's Elective Affinities" (1925), led to further work on German literary criticism, more specifically, his unconventional doctoral dissertation, The Origin of German Tragic Drama (1928; English trans., 1988). But any hopes that Benjamin might have had for an academic career were dashed when the University of Frankfurt rejected his dissertation.

After the Nazis came to power in 1933, Benjamin left Germany for Paris. He fled again in 1940 when the Nazis occupied France. Heading toward Spain, he intended to escape to the United States, but was captured; on finding out that he would be turned over to the Gestapo, he killed himself at the Franco-Spanish border.

Benjamin's position on art suggests not only that art and social life are inextricable but also that to the extent that social life is characterized by technology and class, the intellectual-cum-artist faces the obligation to take political action consistent with his or her artistic ideals. This conviction developed later into a larger critique of fascism and any other form of reactionary political stance.

His other works include Illuminations *(English trans., 1969),* Reflections: Essays, Aphorisms, Autobiographical Writings *(English trans., 1978),* The Arcades Project *(English trans., 1991), and* Understanding Brecht *(English trans., 1998). His impressions on the newly emergent Soviet Union, written during a visit to Moscow in 1926– 27, are recorded in the* Moscow Diaries *(English trans., 1986). The following essay is taken from* Reflections.

Critique of Violence

WALTER BENJAMIN

The task of a critique of violence can be summarized as that of expounding its relation to law and justice. For a cause, however effective, becomes violent, in the precise sense of the word, only when it bears on moral issues. The sphere of these issues is defined by the concepts of law and justice. With regard to the first of these, it is clear that the most elementary relationship within any legal system is that of ends to means, and, further, that violence can first be sought only in the realm of means, not of ends. These observations provide a critique of violence with more—and certainly different—premises than perhaps appears. For if violence is a means, a criterion for criticizing it might seem immediately available. It imposes itself in the question whether violence, in a given case, is a means to a just or an unjust end. A critique of it would then be implied in a system of just ends. This, however, is not so. For what such a system, assuming it to be secure against all doubt, would contain is not a criterion for violence itself as a principle, but, rather, the criterion for cases of its use. The question would remain open whether violence, as a principle, could be a moral means even to just ends. To resolve this question a more exact criterion is needed, which would discriminate within the sphere of means themselves, without regard for the ends they serve.

The exclusion of this more precise critical approach is perhaps the predominant feature of a main current of legal philosophy: natural law. It perceives in the use of violent means to just ends no greater problem than a man sees in his "right" to move his body in the direction of a desired goal. According to this view (for which the terrorism in the French Revolution provided an ideological foundation), violence is a product of nature, as it were a raw material, the use of which is in no way problematical, unless force is misused for unjust ends. If, according to the theory of state of natural law, people give up all their violence for the sake of the state, this is done on the assumption (which Spinoza, for example, states explicitly in his *Tractatus Theologico-Politicus*) that the individual, before the conclusion of this rational contract, has *de jure* the right to use at will the violence that is *de facto* as his disposal. Perhaps these views have been recently rekindled by Darwin's biology, which, in a thoroughly dogmatic manner, regards violence as the only original means, besides natural selection, appropriate to all the vital ends of nature. Popular Darwinistic philosophy has often shown how short a step it is from this dogma of natural history to the still cruder one of legal philosophy, which holds that the violence that is, almost alone, appropriate to natural ends is thereby also legal.

This thesis of natural law that regards violence as a natural datum is diametrically opposed to that of positive law, which sees violence as a product of history. If natural law can judge all existing law only in criticizing its ends, so positive law can judge all evolving law only in criticizing its means. If justice is the criterion of ends, legality is that of means. Notwithstanding this antithesis, however, both schools meet in their common basic dogma: just ends can be attained by justified means, justified means used for just ends. Natural law attempts, by the justness of the ends, to "justify" the means, positive law to "guarantee" the justness of the ends through the justification of the means. This antinomy would prove insoluble if the common dogmatic assumption were false, if justified means on the one hand and just ends on the other were in irreconcilable conflict. No insight into this problem could be gained, however, until the circular argument had been broken, and mutually independent criteria both of just ends and of justified means were established.

The realm of ends, and therefore also the question of a criterion of justness, is excluded for the time being from this study. Instead, the central place is given to the question of the justification of certain means that constitute violence. Principles of natural law cannot decide this question, but can only lead to bottomless casuistry. For if positive law is blind to the absoluteness of ends, natural law is equally so to the contingency of means. On the other hand, the positive theory of law is acceptable as a hypothetical basis at the outset of this study, because it undertakes a fundamental distinction between kinds of violence independently of cases of their application. This distinction is between historically acknowledged, so-called sanctioned violence, and unsanctioned violence. If the following considerations proceed from this it cannot, of course, mean that given forms of violence are classified in terms of whether they are sanctioned or not. For in a critique of violence, a criterion for the latter in positive law cannot concern its uses but only its evaluation. The question that concerns us is, what light is thrown on the nature of violence by the fact that such a criterion or distinction can be applied to it at all, or, in other words, what is the meaning of this distinction? That this distinction supplied by positive law is meaningful, based on the nature of violence, and irreplaceable by any other, will soon enough be shown, but at the same time light will be shed on the sphere in which alone such a distinction can be made. To sum up: if the criterion established by positive law to assess the legality of violence can be analyzed with regard to its meaning, then the sphere of its application must be criticized with regard to its value. For this critique a standpoint outside positive legal philosophy but also outside natural law must be found. The extent to which it can only be furnished by a historico-philosophical view of law will emerge.

The meaning of the distinction between legitimate and illegitimate violence is not immediately obvious. The misunderstanding in natural law by which a distinction is drawn between violence used for just and unjust ends must be emphatically rejected. Rather, it has already been indicated that positive law demands of all violence a proof of its historical origin, which under certain conditions is declared legal, sanctioned. Since the acknowledgment of legal violence is most tangibly evident in a deliberate submission to its ends, a hypothetical distinction between kinds of violence must be based on the presence or absence of a general historical acknowledgment of its ends. Ends that lack such acknowledgment may be called natural ends, the other legal ends. The differing function of violence, depending on whether it serves natural or legal ends, can be most clearly traced against a background of specific legal conditions. For the sake of simplicity, the following discussion will relate to contemporary European conditions.

Characteristic of these, as far as the individual as legal subject is concerned, is the tendency not to admit the natural ends of such individuals in all those cases in which such ends could, in a given situation, be usefully pursued by violence. This means: this legal system tries to erect, in all areas where individual ends could be usefully pursued by violence, legal ends that can only be realized by legal power. Indeed, it strives to limit by legal ends even those areas in which natural ends are admitted in principle within wide boundaries, like that of education, as soon as these natural ends are pursued with an excessive measure of violence, as in the laws relating to the limits of educational authority to punish. It can be formulated as a general maxim of present-day European legislation that all the natural ends of individuals must collide with legal ends if pursued with a greater or lesser degree of violence. (The contradiction between this and the right of self-defense will be resolved in what follows.) From this maxim it follows that law sees violence in the hands of individuals as a danger undermining the legal system. As a danger nullifying legal ends and the legal executive? Certainly not; for then violence as such would not be condemned, but only that directed to illegal ends. It will be argued that a system of legal ends cannot be maintained if natural ends are anywhere still pursued violently. In the first place, however, this is a mere dogma. To counter it one might perhaps consider the surprising possibility that the law's interest in a monopoly of violence vis-à-vis individuals is not explained by the intention of preserving legal ends, but, rather, by that of preserving the law itself; that violence, when not in the hands of the law, threatens it not by the ends that it may pursue but by its mere existence outside the law. The same may be more drastically suggested if one reflects how often the figure of the "great" criminal, however repellent his ends may have been, has aroused the secret admiration of the public. This cannot result from his deed, but only from the violence to which it bears witness. In this case, therefore, the violence of which present-day law is seeking in all areas of activity to deprive the individual appears really threatening, and arouses even in defeat the sympathy of the mass against law. By what function violence can with reason seem so threatening to law, and be so feared by it, must be especially evident where its application, even in the present legal system, is still permissible.

This is above all the case in the class struggle, in the form of the workers' guaranteed right to strike. Organized labor is, apart from the state, probably today the only legal subject entitled to exercise violence. Against this view there is certainly the objection that an omission of actions, a nonaction, which a strike really is, cannot be described as violence. Such a consideration doubtless made it easier for a state poser to conceive the right to strike, once this was no longer avoidable. But its truth is not unconditional, and therefore not unrestricted. It is true that the omission of an action, or service, where it amounts simply to a "severing of relations," can be an entirely nonviolent, pure means. And as in the view of the state, or the law, the right to strike conceded to labor is certainly not a right to exercise violence but, rather, to escape from a violence indirectly exercised by the employer, strikes conforming to this may undoubtedly occur from time to time and involve only a "withdrawal" or "estrangement" from the employer. The moment of violence, however, is necessarily introduced, in the form of extortion, into such an omission, if it takes place in the context of a conscious readiness to resume the suspended action under certain circumstances that either have nothing whatever to do with this action or only superficially modify it. Understood in this way, the right to strike constitutes in the view of labor, which is opposed to that of the state, the right to use force in attaining certain ends. The antithesis between the two conceptions emerges in all its bitterness in face of a revolutionary general strike. In this, labor will always appeal to its right to strike, and the state will call this appeal an abuse, since the right to strike was not "so intended," and take emergency measures. For the state retains the right to declare that a simultaneous use of strike in all industries is illegal, since the specific reasons for strike admitted by legislation cannot be prevalent in every workshop. In this difference of interpretation is expressed the objective contradiction in the legal situation, whereby the state acknowledges a violence whose ends, as natural ends, it sometimes regards with indifference, but in a crisis (the revolutionary general strike) confronts inimically. For, however paradoxical this may appear at first sight, even conduct involving the exercise of a right can nevertheless, under certain circumstances, be described as violent. More specifically, such conduct, then active, may be called violent if it exercises a right in order to overthrow the legal system that has conferred it; when passive, it is nevertheless to be so described if it constitutes extortion in the sense explained above. It therefore reveals an objective contradiction in the legal situation, but not a logical contradiction in the law, if under certain circumstances the law meets the strikers, as perpetrators of violence, with violence. For in a strike the state fears above all else that function of violence which it is the object of this study to identify as the only secure foundation of its critique. For if violence were, as first appears, merely the means to secure directly whatever happens to be sought, it could fulfill its end as predatory violence. It would be entirely unsuitable as a basis for, or a modification to, relatively stable conditions. The strike shows, however, that it can be so, that it is able to found and modify legal conditions, however offended the sense of justice may find itself thereby. It will be objected that such a function of violence is fortuitous and isolated. This can be rebutted by a consideration of military violence.

The possibility of military law rests on exactly the same objective contradiction in the legal situation as does that of strike law, that is to say, on the fact that legal subjects sanction violence whose ends remain for the sanctioners natural ends, and can therefore in a crisis come into conflict with their own legal or natural ends. Admittedly, military violence is in the first place used quite directly, as predatory violence, toward its ends. Yet it is very striking that even—or, rather, precisely—in primitive conditions that know hardly the beginnings of constitutional relations, and even in cases where the victor has established himself in invulnerable possession, a peace ceremony is entirely necessary. Indeed, the word "peace," in the sense in which it is the correlative to the word "war" (for there is also a quite different meaning, similarly unmetaphorical and political, the one used by Kant in talking of "Eternal Peace"), denotes this a priori, necessary sanctioning, regardless of all other legal conditions, of every victory. This sanction consists precisely in recognizing the new conditions as a new "law," quite regardless of whether they need *de facto* any guarantee of their continuation. If, therefore, conclusions can be drawn from military violence, as being primordial and paradigmatic of all violence used for natural ends, there is inherent in all such violence a lawmaking character. We shall return later to the implications of this insight. It explains the above-mentioned tendency of modern law to divest the individual, at least as a legal subject, of all violence, even that directed only to natural ends. In the great criminal this violence confronts the law with the threat of declaring a new law, a threat that even today, despite its impotence, in important instances horrifies the public as it did in primeval times. The state, however, fears this violence simply for its lawmaking character, being obliged to acknowledge it as lawmaking whenever external powers force it to concede them the right to conduct warfare, and classes the right to strike.

If in the last war the critique of military violence was the starting point for a passionate critique of violence in general—which taught at least one thing, that violence is no longer exercised and tolerated naively—nevertheless, violence was not only subject to criticism for its lawmaking character, but was also judged, perhaps more annihilatingly, for another of its functions. For a duality in the function of violence is characteristic of militarism, which could only come into being through general conscription. Militarism is the compulsory, universal use of violence as a means to the ends of the state. This compulsory use of violence has recently been scrutinized as closely as, or still more closely than, the use of violence itself. In it violence shows itself in a function quite different from its simple application for natural ends. For the subordination of citizens to laws—

in the present case, to the law of general conscription—is a legal end. If that first function of violence is called the lawmaking function, this second will be called the law-preserving function. Since conscription is a case of law-preserving violence that is not in principle distinguished from others, a really effective critique of it is far less easy than the declamations of pacifists and activists suggest. Rather, such a critique coincides with the critique of all legal violence—that is, with the critique of legal or executive force—and cannot be performed by any lesser program. Nor, of course—unless one is prepared to proclaim a quite childish anarchism—is it achieved by refusing to acknowledge any constraint toward persons and declaring, "What pleases is permitted." Such a maxim merely excludes reflection on the moral and historical spheres, and thereby on any meaning in action, and beyond this on any meaning in reality itself, which cannot be constituted if "action" is removed from its sphere. More important is the fact that even the appeal, so frequently attempted, to the categorical imperative, with its doubtless incontestable minimum program—act in such a way that at all times you use humanity both in your person and in the person of all others as an end, and never merely as a means—is in itself inadequate for such a critique. (One might, rather, doubt whether the famous demand does not contain too little, that is, whether it is permissible to use, or allow to be used, oneself or another in any respect as a means. Very good grounds for such doubt could be adduced.) For positive law, if conscious of its roots, will certainly claim to acknowledge and promote the interest of mankind in the person of each individual. It sees this interest in the representation and preservation of an order imposed by fate. While this view, which claims to preserve law in its very basis, cannot escape criticism, nevertheless all attacks that are made merely in the name of a formless "freedom," without being able to specify this higher order of freedom, remain impotent against it. And most impotent of all when, instead of attacking the legal system root and branch, they impugn particular laws or legal practices that the law, of course, takes under the protection of its power, which resides in the fact that there is only one fate and that what exists, and in particular what threatens, belongs inviolably to its order. For law-preserving violence is a threatening violence. And its threat is not intended as the deterrent that uninformed liberal theorists interpret it to be. A deterrent in the exact sense would require a certainty that contradicts the nature of a threat and is not attained by any law, since there is always hope of eluding its arm. This makes it all the more threatening, like fate, which depends on whether the criminal is apprehended. The deepest purpose of the uncertainty of the legal threat will emerge from the later consideration of the sphere of fate in which it originates. There is a useful pointer to it in the sphere of punishments. Among them, since the validity of positive law has been called into question, capital punishment has provoked more criticism than all others. However superficial the arguments may in most cases have been, their motives were and are rooted in principle. The opponents of these critics felt, perhaps without knowing why and probably involuntarily, that an attack on capital punishment assails, not legal measure, not laws, but law itself in its origin. For if violence, violence crowned by fate, is the origin of law, then it may be readily supposed that where the highest violence, that over life and death, occurs in the legal system, the origins of law jut manifestly and fearsomely into existence. In agreement with this is the fact that the death penalty in primitive legal systems is imposed even for such crimes as offenses against property, to which it seems quite out of "proportion." Its purpose is not to punish the infringement of law but to establish new law. For in the exercise of violence over life and death more than in any other legal act, law reaffirms itself. But in this very violence something rotten in law is revealed, above all to a finer sensibility, because the latter knows itself to be infinitely remote from conditions in which fate might imperiously have shown itself in such a sentence. Reason must, however, attempt to approach such conditions all the more resolutely, if it is to bring to a conclusion its critique of both lawmaking and law-preserving violence.

In a far more unnatural combination than in the death penalty, in a kind of spectral mixture, these two forms of violence are present in another institution of the modern state, the police. True, this is violence for legal ends (in the right of disposition), but with the simultaneous authority to decide these ends itself within wide limits (in the right of decree). The ignominy of such an authority, which is felt by few simply because its ordinances suffice only seldom for the crudest acts, but are therefore allowed to rampage all the more blindly in the most vulnerable areas and against thinkers, from whom the state is not protected by law—this ignominy lies in the fact that in this authority the separation of lawmaking and law-preserving violence is suspended. If the first is required to prove its worth in victory, the second is subject to the restriction that it may not set itself new ends. Police violence is emancipated from both conditions. It is lawmaking, for its characteristic function is not the promulgation of laws but the assertion of legal claims for any decree, and law-preserving, because it is at the disposal of these ends. The assertion that the ends of police violence are always identical or even connected to those of general law is entirely untrue. Rather, the "law" of the police really marks the point at which the state, whether from impotence or because of the immanent connections within any legal system, can no longer guarantee through the legal system the empirical ends that it desires at any price to attain. Therefore the police intervene "for security reasons" in countless cases where no clear legal situation exists, when they are not merely, without the slightest relation to legal ends, accompanying the citizen as a brutal encumbrance through a life regulated by ordinances, or simply supervising him. Unlike law, which acknowledges in the "decision" determined by place and time a metaphysical category that gives it a claim to critical evaluation, a consideration of the police institution encounters nothing essential at all. Its power is formless, like its nowhere tangible, all-pervasive, ghostly presence in the life of civilized states. And though the police may, in particulars, everywhere appear the same, it cannot finally be denied that their spirit is less devastating where they represent, in absolute monarchy, the power of a ruler in which legislative and executive supremacy are united, than in democracies where their existence, elevated by no such relation, bears witness to the greatest conceivable degeneration of violence.

All violence as a means is either lawmaking or law-preserving. If it lays claim to neither of these predicates, it forfeits all validity. It follows, however, that all violence as a means, even in the most favorable case, is implicated in the problematic nature of law itself. And if the importance of these problems cannot be assessed with certainty at this stage of the investigation, law nevertheless appears, from what has been said, in so ambiguous a moral light that the question poses itself whether there are no other than violent means for regulating conflicting human interests. We are above all obligated to note that a totally nonviolent resolution of conflicts can never lead to a legal contract. For the latter, however peacefully it may have been entered into by the parties, leads finally to possible violence. It confers on both parties the right to take recourse to violence in some form against the other, should he break the agreement. Not only that; like the outcome, the origin of every contract also points toward violence. It need not be directly present in it as lawmaking violence, but is represented in it insofar as the power that guarantees a legal contract is in turn of violent origin even if violence is not introduced into the contract itself. When the consciousness of the latent presence of violence in a legal institution disappears, the institution falls into decay. In our time, parliaments provide an example of this. They offer the familiar, woeful spectacle because they have not remained conscious of the revolutionary forces to which they owe their existence. Accordingly, in Germany in particular, the last manifestation of such forces bore no fruit for parliaments. They lack the sense that a lawmaking violence is represented by themselves; no wonder that they cannot achieve decrees worthy of this violence, but cultivate in compromise a supposedly nonviolent manner of dealing with political affairs. This remains, however, a "product situated within the mentality of violence, no matter how it may disdain all open violence, because the effort toward compromise is motivated not internally but from outside, by the opposing effort, because no compromise, however freely accepted, is conceivable without a compulsive character. 'It would be better otherwise' is the underlying feeling in every compromise." Significantly, the decay of parliaments has perhaps alienated as many minds from the ideal of a nonviolent resolution of political conflicts as were attracted to it by the war. The pacifists are confronted by the Bolsheviks and Syndicalists. These have effected an annihilating and on the whole apt critique of present-day parliaments. Nevertheless, however desirable and gratifying a flourishing parliament might be by comparison, a discussion of means of political agreement that are in principle nonviolent cannot be concerned with parliamentarianism. For what parliament achieves in vital affairs can only be those legal decrees that in their origin and outcome are attended by violence.

Is any nonviolent resolution of conflict possible? Without doubt. The relationships of private persons are full of examples of this. Nonviolent agreement is possible wherever a civilized outlook allows the unalloyed means of agreement. Legal and illegal means of every kind that are all the same violent may be confronted with nonviolent ones as unalloyed means. Courtesy, sympathy, peaceableness, trust, and whatever else might here be mentioned, are their subjective preconditions. Their objective manifestation, however, is determined by the law (the enormous scope of which cannot be discussed here) that unalloyed means are never those of direct, but always those of indirect solutions. They therefore never apply directly to the resolution of conflict between man and man, but only to matters concerning objects. The sphere of nonviolent means opens up in the realm of human conflicts relating to goods. For this reason technique in the broadest sense of the word is their most particular area. Its profoundest example is perhaps the conference, considered as a technique of civil agreement. For in it not only is nonviolent agreement possible, but also the exclusion of violence in principle is quite explicitly demonstrable by one significant factor: there is no sanction for lying. Probably no legislation on earth originally stipulated such a sanction. This makes clear that there is a sphere of human agreement that is nonviolent to the extent that it is wholly inaccessible to violence: the proper sphere of "understanding," language. Only late and in a peculiar process of decay has it been penetrated by legal violence in the penalty placed on fraud. For whereas the legal system at its origin, trusting to its victorious power, is content to defeat lawbreaking wherever it happens to show itself and deception, having itself no trace of power about it, was on the principle *ius civile vigilantibus scriptum est*, exempt from punishment in Roman and ancient Germanic law, the law of a later period, lacking confidence in its own violence, no longer felt itself a match for that of all others. Rather, fear of the latter and mistrust of itself indicate its declining vitality. It begins to set itself ends, with the intention of sparing law-preserving violence more taxing manifestations. It turns to fraud, therefore, not out of moral considerations, but for fear of the violence that it might unleash in the defrauded party. Since such fear conflicts with the violent nature of law derived from its origins, such ends are inappropriate to the justified means of law. They reflect not only the decay of its own sphere, but also a diminution of pure means. For, in prohibiting fraud, law restricts the use of wholly nonviolent means because they could produce reactive violence. This tendency of law has also played a part in the concession of the right to strike, which contradicts the interests of the state. It grants this right because it forestalls violent actions the state is afraid to oppose. Did not workers previously resort at once to sabotage and set fire to factories? To induce men to reconcile their interests peacefully without involving the legal system, there is, in the end, apart from all virtues, one effective motive that often enough puts into the most reluctant hands pure instead of violent means; it is the fear of mutual disadvantages that threaten to arise from violent confrontation, whatever the outcome might be. Such motives are clearly visible in countless cases of conflict of interests between private persons. It is different when classes and nations are in conflict, since the higher orders that threaten to overwhelm equally victor and vanquished are hidden from the feelings of most, and from the intelligence of almost all. Space does not here permit me to trace such higher orders and the common interests corresponding to them, which constitute the most enduring motive for a policy of pure means. We can therefore only point to pure means in politics as analogous to those which govern peaceful intercourse between private persons.

As regards class struggles, in them strike must under certain conditions be seen as a pure means. Two essentially different kinds of strike, the possibilities of which have already been considered, must now be more fully characterized. Sorel has the credit—from political, rather than purely theoretical, considerations—of having first distinguished them. He contrasts them as the political and the proletarian general strike. They are also antithetical in their relation to violence. Of the partisans of the former he says: "The strengthening of state power is the basis of their conceptions; in their present organizations the politicians (viz. the moderate socialists) are already preparing the ground for a strong centralized and disciplined power that will be impervious to criticism from the opposition, capable of imposing silence, and of issuing its mendacious decrees." "The political general strike demonstrates how the state will lose none of its strength, how power is transferred from the privileged to the privileged, how the mass of producers will change their masters." In contrast to this political general strike (which incidentally seems to have been summed up by the abortive German revolution), the proletarian general strike sets itself the sole task of destroying state power. It "nullifies all the ideological consequences of every possible social policy; its partisans see even the most popular reforms as bourgeois." "This general strike clearly announces its indifference toward material gain through conquest by declaring its intention to abolish the state; the state was really . . . the basis of the existence of the ruling group, who in all their enterprises benefit from the burdens borne by the public." While the first form of interruption of work is violent since it causes only an external modification of labor conditions, the second, as a pure means, is nonviolent. For it takes place not in readiness to resume work following external concessions and this or that modification to working conditions, but in the determination to resume only a wholly transformed work, no longer enforced by the state, an upheaval that this kind of strike not so much causes as consummates. For this reason, the first of these undertakings is lawmaking but the second anarchistic. Taking up occasional statements by Marx, Sorel rejects every kind of program, of utopia—in a word, of lawmaking—for the revolutionary movement: "With the general strike all these fine things disappear; the revolution appears as a clear, simple revolt, and no place is reserved either for the sociologists or for the elegant amateurs of social reforms or for the intellectuals who have made it their profession to think for the proletariat." Against this deep, moral, and genuinely revolutionary conception, no objection can stand that seeks, on grounds of its possibly catastrophic consequences, to brand such a general strike as violent. Even if it can rightly be said that the modern economy, seen as a whole, resembles much less a machine that stands idle when abandoned by its stoker than a beast that goes berserk as soon as its tamer turns his back, nevertheless the violence of an action can be assessed no more from its effects than from its ends, but only from the law of its means. State power, of course, which has eyes only for effects, opposes precisely this kind of strike for its alleged violence, as distinct from partial strikes which are for the most part actually extortionate. The extent to which such a rigorous conception of the general strike as such is capable of diminishing the incidence of actual violence in revolutions, Sorel has explained with highly ingenious arguments. By contrast, an outstanding example of violent omission, more immoral and cruder than the political general strike, akin to a blockade, is the strike by doctors, such as several German cities have seen. In this is revealed at its most repellent an unscrupulous use of violence that is positively depraved in a professional class that for years, without the slightest attempts at resistance, "secured death its prey," and then at the first opportunity abandoned life of its own free will. More clearly than in recent class struggles, the means of nonviolent agreement have developed in thousands of years of the history of states. Only occasionally does the task of diplomats in their transactions consist of modifications to legal systems. Fundamentally they have, entirely on the analogy of agreement between private persons, to resolve conflicts case by case, in the names of their states, peacefully and without contracts. A delicate task that is more robustly performed by referees, but a method of solution that in principle is above that of the referee because it is beyond all legal systems, and therefore beyond violence. Accordingly, like the intercourse of private persons, that of diplomats has engendered its own forms and virtues, which were not always mere formalities, even though they have become so.

Among all the forms of violence permitted by both natural law and positive law, there is not one that is free of the gravely problematic nature, already indicated, of all legal violence. Since, however, every conceivable solution to human problems, not to speak of deliverance from the confines of all the world-historical conditions of existence obtaining hitherto, remains impossible if violence is totally excluded in principle, the question necessarily arises as to the other kinds of violence than all those envisaged by legal theory. It is at the same time the question of the truth of the basic dogma common to both theories: just ends can be attained by justified means, justified means used for just ends. How would it be, therefore, if all the violence imposed by fate, using justified means, were of itself in irreconcilable conflict with just ends, and if at the same time a different kind of violence came into view that certainly could be either the justified or the unjustified means to those ends, but was not related to them as means at all but in some different way. This would throw light on the curious and at first discouraging discovery of the ultimate insolubility of all legal problems (which in its hopelessness is perhaps comparable only to the possibility of conclusive pronouncements on "right" and "wrong" in evolving languages). For it is never reason that decides on the justification of means and the justness of ends, but fate-imposed violence on the former and God on the latter. And insight that is uncommon only because of the stubborn prevailing habit of conceiving those just ends as ends of a possible law, that is, not only as generally valid (which follows analytically from the nature of justice), but also capable of generalization, which, as could be shown, contradicts the nature of justice. For ends that for one situation are just, universally acceptable, and valid, are so for no other situation, no matter how similar it may be in other respects. The nonmediate function of violence at issue here is illustrated by everyday experience. As regards man, he is impelled by anger, for example, to the most visible outbursts of a violence that is not related as a means to a preconceived end. It is not a means but a manifestation. Moreover, this violence has thoroughly objective manifestations in which it can be subjected to criticism. These are to be found, most significantly, above all in myth.

Mythical violence in its archetypal form is a mere manifestation of the gods. Not a means to their ends, scarcely a manifestation of their will, but first of all a manifestation of their existence. The legend of Niobe contains an outstanding example of this. True, it might appear that the action of Apollo and Artemis is only a punishment. But their violence establishes a law far more than it punishes for the infringement of one already existing. Niobe's arrogance calls down fate upon itself not because her arrogance offends against the law but because it challenges fate—to a fight in which fate must triumph, and can bring to light a law only in its triumph. How little such divine violence was to the ancients the law-preserving violence of punishment is shown by the heroic legends in which the hero—for example, Prometheus—challenges fate with dignified courage, fights it with varying fortunes, and is not left by the legend without hope of one day bringing a new law to men. It is really this hero and the legal violence of the myth native to him that the public tries to picture even now in admiring the miscreant. Violence therefore bursts upon Niobe from the uncertain, ambiguous sphere of fate. It is not actually destructive. Although it brings a cruel death to Niobe's children, it stops short of the life of their mother, whom it leaves behind, more guilty than before through the death of the children, both as an eternally mute bearer of guilt and as a boundary stone on the frontier between men and gods. If this immediate violence in mythical manifestations proves closely related, indeed identical to lawmaking violence, it reflects a problematic light on lawmaking violence, insofar as the latter was characterized above, in the account of military violence, as merely a mediate violence. At the same time this connection promises further to illuminate fate, which in all cases underlies legal violence, and to conclude in broad outline the critique of the latter. For the function of violence in lawmaking is twofold, in the sense that lawmaking pursues as its end, with violence as the means, *what* is to be established as law, but at the moment of instatement does not dismiss violence; rather, at this very moment of lawmaking, it specifically establishes as law not an end unalloyed by violence, but one necessarily and intimately bound to it, under the title of power. Lawmaking is power making, and, to that extent, an immediate manifestation of violence. Justice is the principle of all divine end making, power the principle of all mythical lawmaking.

An application of the latter that has immense consequences is to be found in constitutional law. For in this sphere the establishing of frontiers, the task of "peace" after all the wars of the mythical age, is the primal phenomenon of all lawmaking violence. Here we see most clearly that power, more than the most extravagant gain in property, is what is guaranteed by all lawmaking violence. Where frontiers are decided the adversary is not simply annihilated; indeed, he is accorded rights even when the victor's superiority in power is complete. And these are, in a demonically ambiguous way, "equal" rights: for both parties to the treaty it is the same line that may not be crossed. Here appears, in a terribly primitive form, the same mythical ambiguity of laws that may not be "infringed," to which Anatole France refers satirically when he says, "Poor and rich are equally forbidden to spend the night under the bridges." It also appears that Sorel touches not merely on a cultural-historical but also on a metaphysical truth in surmising that in the beginning all right was the prerogative of the kings or the nobles—in short, of the mighty; and that, *mutatis mutandis*, it will remain so as long as it exists. For from the point of view of violence, which alone can guarantee law, there is no equality, but at the most equally great violence. The act of fixing frontiers, however, is also significant for an understanding of law in another respect. Laws and unmarked frontiers remain, at least in primeval times, unwritten laws. A man can unwittingly infringe upon them and thus incur retribution. For each intervention of law that is provoked by an offense against the unwritten and unknown law is called, in contradistinction to punishment, retribution. But however unluckily it may befall its unsuspecting victim, its occurrence is, in the understanding of the law, not chance, but fate showing itself once again in its deliberate ambiguity. Hermann Cohen, in a brief reflection on the ancients' conception of fate, has spoken of the "inescapable realization" that it is "fate's orders themselves that seem to cause and bring about this infringement, this offense." To this spirit of law even the modern principle that ignorance of a law is not protection against punishment testifies, just as the struggle over written law in the early period of the ancient Greek communities is to be understood as a rebellion against the spirit of mythical statutes.

Far from inaugurating a purer sphere, the mythical manifestation of immediate violence shows itself fundamentally identical with all legal violence, and turns suspicion concerning the latter into certainty of the perniciousness of its historical function, the destruction of which thus becomes obligatory. This very task of destruction poses again, in the last resort, the question of a pure immediate violence that might be able to call a halt to mythical violence. Just as in all spheres God opposes myth, mythical violence is confronted by the divine. And the latter constitutes its antithesis in all respects. If mythical violence is lawmaking, divine violence is law-destroying; if the former sets boundaries, the latter boundlessly destroys them; if mythical violence brings at once guilt and retribution, divine power only expiates; if the former threatens, the latter strikes; if the former is bloody, the latter is lethal without spilling blood. The legend of Niobe may be confronted, as an example of this violence, with God's judgment on the company of Korah. It strikes privileged Levites, strikes them without warning, without threat, and does not stop short of annihilation. But in annihilating it also expiates, and a deep connection between the lack of bloodshed and the expiatory character of this violence is unmistakable. For blood is the symbol of mere life. The dissolution of legal violence stems, as cannot be shown in detail here, from the guilt of more natural life, which consigns the living, innocent, and unhappy, to a retribution that "expiates" the guilt of mere life—and doubtless also purifies the guilty, not of guilt, however, but of law. For with mere life the rule of law over the living ceases. Mythical violence is bloody power over mere life for its own sake, divine violence pure power over all life for the sake of the living. The first demands sacrifice, the second accepts it.

This divine power is attested not only by religious tradition but is also found in present-day life in at least one sanctioned manifestation. The educative power, which in its perfected form stands outside the law, is one of its manifestations. These are defined, therefore, not by miracles directly performed by God, but by the expiating moment in them that strikes without bloodshed and, finally, by the absence of all lawmaking. To this extent it is justifiable to call this violence, too, annihilating; but it is so only relatively, with regard to goods, right, life, and suchlike, never absolutely, with regard to the soul of the living. The premise of such an extension of pure or divine power is sure to provoke, particularly today, the most violent reactions, and to be countered by the argument that taken to its logical conclusion it confers on men even lethal power against one another. This, however, cannot be conceded. For the question "May I kill?" meets its irreducible answer in the commandment "Thou shalt not kill." This commandment precedes the deed, just as God was "preventing" the deed. But just as it may not be fear of punishment that enforces obedience, the injunction becomes inapplicable, incommensurable once the deed is accomplished. No judgment of the deed can be derived from the commandment. And so neither the divine judgment, nor the grounds for this judgment, can be known in advance. Those who base a condemnation of all violent killing of one person by another on the commandment are therefore mistaken. It exists not as a criterion of judgment, but as a guideline for the actions of persons or communities who have to wrestle themselves the responsibility of ignoring it. Thus it was understood by Judaism, which expressly rejected the condemnation of killing in self-defense. But those thinkers who take the opposed view refer to a more distant theorem, on which they possibly propose to base even the commandment itself. This is the doctrine of the sanctity of life, which they either apply to all animal or even vegetable life, or limit to human life. Their argumentation, exemplified in an extreme case by the revolutionary killing of the oppressor, runs as follows: "If I do not kill I shall never establish the world dominion of justice . . . that is the argument of the intelligent terrorist. . . . We, however, profess that higher even than the happiness and justice of existence stands existence itself." As certainly as this last proposition is false, indeed ignoble, it shows the necessity of seeking the reason for the commandment no longer in what the deed does to the victim, but in what it does to God and the doer. The proposition that existence stands higher than a just existence is false and ignominious, if existence is to mean nothing other than mere life—and it has this meaning in the argument referred to. It contains a mighty truth, however, if existence, or, better, life (words whose ambiguity is readily dispelled, analogously to that of freedom, when they are referred to two distinct spheres), means the irreducible, total condition that is "man"; if the proposition is intended to mean that the nonexistence of man is something more terrible than the (admittedly subordinate) not-yet-attained condition of the just man. To this ambiguity the proposition quoted above owes its plausibility. Man cannot, at any price, be said to coincide with the mere life in him, no more than with any other of his conditions and qualities, not even with the uniqueness of his bodily person. However sacred man is (or that life in him that is identically present in earthly life, death, and afterlife), there is no sacredness in his condition, in his bodily life vulnerable to injury by his fellow men. What, then, distinguishes it essentially from the life of animals and plants? And even if these were sacred, they could not be so by virtue only of being alive, of being in life. It might be well worthwhile to track down the origin of the dogma of the sacredness of life. Perhaps, indeed probably, it is relatively recent, the last mistaken attempt of the weakened Western tradition to seek the saint it has lost in cosmological impenetrability. (The antiquity of all religious commandments against murder is no counter argument, because these are based on other ideas than the modern theorem.) Finally, this idea of man's sacredness gives grounds for reflection that what is here pronounced sacred was according to ancient mythical thought the marked bearer of guilt: life itself.

The critique of violence is the philosophy of its history—the "philosophy" of this history, because only the idea of its development makes possible a critical, discriminating, and decisive approach to its temporal data. A gaze directed only at what is close at hand can at most perceive a dialectical rising and falling in the lawmaking and law-preserving formations of violence. The law governing their oscillation rests on the circumstance that all law-preserving violence, in its duration, indirectly weakens the lawmaking violence represented by it, through the suppression of hostile counter-violence. (Various symptoms of this have been referred to in the course of this study.) This lasts until either new forces or those earlier suppressed triumph over the hitherto lawmaking violence and thus found a new law, destined in its turn to decay. On the breaking of this cycle maintained by mythical forms of law, on the suspension of law with all the forces on which it depends as they depend on it, finally therefore on the abolition of state power, a new historical epoch is founded. If the rule of myth is broken occasionally in the present age, the coming age is not so unimaginably remote that an attack on law is altogether futile. But if the existence of violence outside the law, as pure immediate violence, is assured, this furnishes the proof that revolutionary violence, the highest manifestation of unalloyed violence by man, is possible, and by what means. Less possible and also less urgent for humankind, however, is to decide when unalloyed violence has been realized in particular cases. For only mythical violence, not divine, will be recognizable as such with certainty, unless it be in incomparable effects, because the expiatory power of violence is not visible to men. Once again all the eternal forms are open to pure divine violence, which myth bastardized with law. It may manifest itself in a true war exactly as in the divine judgment of the multitude on a criminal. But all mythical, lawmaking violence, which we may call executive, is pernicious. Pernicious, too, is the law-preserving, administrative violence that serves it. Divine violence, which is the sign and seal but never the means of sacred execution, may be called sovereign violence.

Lawyer, legal scholar, educator, author, and political activist, Catharine MacKinnon was educated at Smith College, where she received her undergraduate degree in 1969; she earned her law degree in 1977 and her Ph.D. in 1987, both from Yale University. She was a visiting professor of law at numerous institutions before becoming in 1989 a professor of law at the University of Michigan, where she remains.

MacKinnon is an original and controversial social theorist. She broke new legal ground in the late 1970s by arguing that the sexual harassment of women in the workplace constituted a form of sex discrimination in violation of existing civil-rights statutes. Her thesis became an important weapon in fighting the mistreatment of working women. Equally passionate and effective has been her opposition to pornography, which she defines as the sexual subordination of women to men. She goes on to argue that as the vehicle for perpetuating male dominance throughout society, pornography becomes a form of sex-based discrimination. For MacKinnon, outlawing pornography is thus not an issue of art or morality, but one of protecting and respecting women as equals. MacKinnon's contributions to feminist and social theory have not been limited to her opposition to pornography. The speeches in Feminism Unmodified *also address issues of abortion, rape, women's athletics, sexual harassment, and the rights of Native American women, while* Toward a Feminist Theory of the State *outlines a unified political-social-sexual theory of male domination. The second section from the 1991 article excerpted here outlines her views on the conjunction of sexual and social practices.*

Her major writings include Sexual Harassment of Working Women: A Case of Sex Discrimination *(1979),* Feminism Unmodified: Discourses on Life and Law *(1987), (with Andrea Dworkin)* Pornography and Civil Rights: A New Day for Women's Equality, Organizing against Pornography *(1988), and* Toward a Feminist Theory of the State *(1989).*

Feminism, Marxism, Method, and the State:

An Agenda for Theory

CATHARINE MACKINNON

Feminists have reconceived rape as central to women's condition in two ways. Some see rape as an act of violence, not sexuality, the threat of which intimidates all women. Others see rape, including its violence, as an expression of male sexuality, the social imperatives of which define all women. The first, formally in the liberal tradition, comprehends rape as a displacement of power based on physical force onto sexuality, a preexisting natural sphere to which domination is alien. Thus, Susan Brownmiller examines rape in riots, wars, pogroms, and revolutions; rape by police, parents, prison guards; and rape motivated by racism—seldom rape in normal circumstances, in everyday life, in ordinary relationships, by men as men. Women are raped by guns, age, white supremacy, the state—only derivatively by the penis. The more feminist view to me, one which derives from victims' experiences, sees sexuality as a social sphere of male power of which forced sex is paradigmatic. Rape is not less sexual for being violent; to the extent that coercion has become integral to male sexuality, rape may be sexual to the degree that, and because, it is violent.

The point of defining rape as "violence not sex" or "violence against women" has been to separate sexuality from gender in order to affirm sex (heterosexuality) while rejecting violence (rape). The problem remains what it has always been: telling the difference. The convergence of sexuality with violence, long used at law to deny the reality of women's violation, is recognized by rape survivors, with a difference; where the legal system has seen the intercourse in rape, victims see the rape in intercourse. The uncoerced contexts for sexual expression become as elusive as the physical acts come to feel indistinguishable. Instead of asking, what is the violation of rape, what if we ask, what is the nonviolation of intercourse? To tell what is wrong with rape, explain what is right about sex. If this, in turn, is difficult, the difficulty is as instructive as the difficulty men have in telling the difference when women see one. Perhaps the wrong of rape has proven so difficult to articulate because the unquestionable starting point has been that rape is definable as distinct from intercourse, when for women it is difficult to distinguish them under conditions of male dominance.

Like heterosexuality, the crime of rape centers on penetration. The law to protect women's sexuality from forcible violation/expropriation defines the protected in male genital terms. Women do resent force penetration. But penile invasion of the vagina may be less pivotal to women's sexuality, pleasure, or violation, than it is to male sexuality. This definitive element of rape centers upon a male-defined loss, not coincidentally also upon the way men define loss of exclusive access. In this light, rape, as legally defined, appears more a crime against female monogamy than against female sexuality. Property concepts fail fully to comprehend this, however, not because women's sexuality is not, finally, a thing, but because it is never ours. The moment we "have" it—"have sex" in the dual sexuality/gender sense—it is lost as ours. This may explain the male incomprehension that, once a woman has had sex, she loses anything when raped. To them we *have nothing* to lose. Dignitary harms, because nonmaterial, are remote to the legal mind. But women's loss through rape is not only less tangible, it is less existent. It is difficult to avoid the conclusion that penetration itself is known to be a violation and that women's sexuality, our gender definition, is itself stigmatic. If this is so, the pressing question for explanation is not why some of us accept rape but why any of us resent it.

The law of rape divides the world of women into spheres of consent according to how much "say" we are legally presumed to have over sexual access to us by various categories of men. Little girls may not consent; wives must. If rape laws existed to enforce women's control over our own sexuality, as the consent defense implies, marital rape would not be a widespread exception, nor would statutory rape proscribe all sexual intercourse with underage girls regardless of their wishes. The rest of us fall into parallel provinces: good girls, like children, are unconsenting, virginal, rapable; bad girls, like wives, are consenting, whores, unrapable. The age line under which girls are presumed disabled from withholding consent to sex rationalizes a condition of sexual coercion women never outgrow. As with protective labor laws for women only, dividing and protecting the most vulnerable becomes a device for not protecting everyone. Risking loss of even so little cannot be afforded. Yet the protection is denigrating and limiting (girls may not choose to be sexual) as well as perverse (girls are eroticized as untouchable; now reconsider the data on incest).

If the accused knows us, consent is inferred. The exemption for rape in marriage is consistent with the assumption underlying most adjudications of forcible rape: to the extent the parties relate, it was not really rape, it was personal. As the marital exemptions erode, preclusions for cohabitants and voluntary social companions may expand. In this light, the partial erosion of the marital rape exemption looks less like a change in the equation between women's experience of sexual violation and men's experience of intimacy, and more like a legal adjustment to the social fact that acceptable heterosexual sex is increasingly not limited to the legal family. So although the rape law may not now always assume that the woman consented simply because the parties are legally one, indices of closeness, of relationship ranging from nodding acquaintance to living together, still contraindicate rape. Perhaps this reflects men's experience that women they know meaningfully consent to have sex with them. That cannot be rape; rape must be by someone else, someone unknown. But *women* experience rape most often by men we know. Men believe that it is less awful to be raped by someone one is close to: "The emotional trauma suffered by a person victimized by an individual with whom sexual intimacy is shared as a normal part of an ongoing marital relationship is not nearly as severe as that suffered by a person who is victimized by one with whom that intimacy is not shared." But women feel as much, if not more, traumatized by being raped by someone we have known or trusted, someone we have shared at least an illusion of mutuality with, than by some stranger. In whose interest is it to believe that it is not so bad to be raped by someone who has fucked you before as by someone who has not? Disallowing charges of rape in marriage may also "remove a substantial obstacle to the resumption of normal marital relations." Depending upon your view of normal. Note that the obstacle to normalcy here is not the rape but the law against it. Apparently someone besides feminists finds sexual victimization and sexual intimacy not all that contradictory. Sometimes I think women and men live in different cultures.

Having defined rape in male sexual terms, the law's problem, which becomes the victim's problem, is distinguishing rape from sex in specific cases. The law does this by adjudicating the level of acceptable force starting just above the level set by what is seen as normal male sexual behavior, rather than at the victim's, or women's, point of violation. Rape cases finding insufficient force reveal that acceptable sex, in the legal perspective, can entail a lot of force. This is not only because of the way specific facts are perceived and interpreted but because of the way the injury itself is defined as illegal. Rape is a sex crime that is not a crime when it looks like sex. To seek to define rape as violent, not sexual, is understandable in this context, and often seems strategic. But assault that is consented to is still assault; rape consented to is intercourse. The substantive reference point implicit in existing legal standards is the sexually normative level of force. Until this norm is confronted as such, no distinction between violence and sexuality will prohibit more instances of women's experienced violation than does the existing definition. The question is what is *seen as* force, hence as violence, in the sexual arena. Most rapes, as women live them, will not be seen to violate women until sex and violence are confronted as mutually definitive. It is not only men convicted of rape who believe that the only thing they did different from what men do all the time is get caught.

The line between rape and intercourse commonly centers on some measure of the woman's "will." But from what should the law know woman's will? Like much existing law, Brownmiller tends to treat will as a question of consent and consent as a factual issue of the presence of force. Proof problems aside, force and desire are not mutually exclusive. So long as dominance is eroticized they never will be. Women are socialized to passive receptivity; may have or perceive no alternative to acquiescence; may prefer it to the escalated risk of injury and the humiliation of a lost fight; submit to survive. Some eroticize dominance and submission; it beats feeling forced. Sexual intercourse may be deeply unwanted —the woman would never have initiated it—yet no force may be present. Too, force may be used, yet the woman may want the sex—to avoid more force or because she, too, eroticizes dominance. Women and men know this. Calling rape violence, not sex, thus evades, at the moment it most seems to confront, the issue of who controls women's sexuality and the dominance/submission dynamic that has defined it. When sex is violent, women may have lost control over what is done to us, but absence of force does not ensure the presence of that control. Nor, under conditions of male dominance, does the presence of force make an interaction nonsexual. If sex is normally something men do to women, the issue is less whether there was force and more whether consent is a meaningful concept.

To explain women's gender status as a function of rape, Brownmiller argues that the threat of rape benefits all men. She does not specify in what way. Perhaps it benefits them sexually, hence as a gender: male initiatives toward women carry the fear of rape as support for persuading compliance, the resulting appearance of which has been called consent. Here the victims' perspective grasps what liberalism applied to women denies: that forced sex as sexuality is not exceptional in relations between the sexes but constitutes the social meaning of gender: "Rape is a man's act, whether it is male or a female man and whether it is a man relatively permanently or relatively temporarily; and being raped is a woman's experience, whether it is a female or a male woman and whether it is a woman relatively permanently or relatively temporarily." To be *rapable*, a position which is social, not biological, defines what a woman *is*.

Most women get the message that the law against rape is virtually unenforceable as applied to them. Our own experience is more often delegitimized by this than the law is. Women radically distinguish between rape and experiences of sexual violation, concluding that we have not "really" been raped if we have ever seen or dated or slept with or been married to the man, if we were fashionably dressed or are not provably virgin, if we are prostitutes, if we put up with it or tried to get it over with, if we were force-fucked over a period of years. If we probably couldn't prove it in court, it wasn't rape. The distance between most sexual violations of women and the legally perfect rape measures the imposition of someone else's definition upon women's experiences. Rape, from women's point of view, is not prohibited; it is regulated. Even women who know we have been raped do not believe that the legal system will see it the way we do. We are often not wrong. Rather than deterring or avenging rape, the state, in many victims' experiences, perpetuates it. Women who charge rape say they were raped twice, the second time in court. If the state is male, this is more than a figure of speech.

The law distinguishes rape from intercourse by the woman's lack of consent coupled with a man's (usually) knowing disregard of it. A feminist distinction between rape and intercourse, to hazard a beginning approach, lies instead in the *meaning* of the act from women's point of view. What is wrong with rape is that it is an act of the subordination of women to men. Seen this way, the issue is not so much what rape "is" as the way its social conception is shaped to interpret particular encounters. Under conditions of sex inequality, with perspective bound up with situation, whether a contested interaction is rape comes down to whose meaning wins. If sexuality is relational, specifically if it is a power relation of gender, consent is a communication under conditions of inequality. It transpires somewhere between what the woman actually wanted and what the man comprehended she wanted. Instead of capturing this dynamic, the law gives us linear, static entities face to face. Nonconsent in law becomes a question of the man's force or the woman's resistance or both. Rape, like many crimes and torts, requires that the accused possess a criminal mind (*mens rea*) for his acts to be criminal. The man's mental state refers to what he actually understood at the time or to what a reasonable man should have understood under the circumstances. The problem is this: the injury of rape lies in the meaning of the act to its victims, but the standard for its criminality lies in the meaning of the same act to the assailants. Rape is only an injury from women's point of view. It is only a crime from the male point of view, explicitly including that of the accused. Thus the crime of rape is defined and adjudicated from the male standpoint, that is, presuming that (what feminists see as) forced sex is sex.

One of the most brilliant jurists of his generation, Robert Cover taught at Yale Law School during the 1970s and early 1980s. His early death did not prevent him from founding a tradition of legal scholarship that does not stop short of seeing how the judicial process itself may pervert justice. His defining book was Justice Accused: Antislavery and the Judicial Process *(Yale University Press, 1975). It explored how passive acquiescence afflicted judges as well as politicians and hieratic functionaries. It exposed the space between law and morality. It explained institutional evil, describing why a group of judges could—and did—pursue a mechanistic interpretation of the fugitive slave law and of law itself in direct opposition to their original moral intentions. He even coined a neologism that, alas, has not found popular acceptance:* jurispathic *depicts the power and practice of a government that rules by displacing, suppressing, or exterminating values that run counter to its own.*

Cover once described himself as an anarchist who loved law. Educated at Princeton, he still volunteered as a Student Nonviolent Coordinating Committee volunteer, and when arrested for participating in a hunger strike, he was beaten up by his fellow prisoners in the Albany, Georgia, jail. Later, as a law student at Columbia, he produced an important jurisdictional theory on behalf of welfare recipients. He continued as a judicial activist while teaching first at Columbia Law School and then at Yale Law School.

Yet he often took sides that were anything but liberal. He did not oppose capital punishment in all instances, and he once defended a Yale student who had been accused of homophobic expression at a public rally on the Yale campus.

It was his passionate engagement with Judaism that occupied the last years of his life and produced singularly original and pathbreaking articles. Paradox was at the center of Cover's vision, etched for him by the verse of Wallace Stevens, who once wrote,

> *A. A violent order is disorder; and*
> *B. A great order is an order. These*
> *Two things are one. (Pages of Illustrations).*

Following the razor edge of Stevens's paradox, in his landmark essay "Nomos and Narrative" Cover laid bare the limits of order and privilege, even while affirming their necessity. Likewise, in "Violence and the Word," which is excerpted below, he laments the pain and death inherent in the judicial process, with "judges sitting atop a pyramid of violence," yet finds instances in which capital punishment may be necessary.

Among his other significant publications are Narrative, Violence, and the Law: The Essays of Robert Cover *(1993);* Procedure, *which he wrote with Owen M. Fiss and Judith Resnick (1988); and* The Federal Procedural System: A Rule and Statu-tory Source Book, *which he co-edited with Owen M. Fiss and Judith Resnick (1989).*

Violence and the Word

ROBERT M. COVER

I. INTRODUCTION: THE VIOLENCE OF LEGAL ACTS

Legal interpretation takes place in a field of pain and death. This is true in several senses. Legal interpretive acts signal and occasion the imposition of violence upon others: A judge articulates her understanding of a text, and as a result, somebody loses his freedom, his property, his children, even his life. Interpretations in law also constitute justifications for violence which has al-ready occurred or which is about to occur. When interpreters have finished their work, they frequently leave behind victims whose lives have been torn apart by these organized social practices of violence. Neither legal interpretation nor the violence it occasions may be properly understood apart from one another. This much is obvious, though the growing literature that argues for the centrality of interpretive practices in law blithely ignores it.

Taken by itself, the word "interpretation" may be misleading. "Interpreta-tion" suggests a social construction of an interpersonal reality through lan-guage. But pain and death have quite other implications. Indeed, pain and death destroy the world that "interpretation" calls up. That one's ability to construct interpersonal realities is destroyed by death is obvious, but in this case, what is true of death is true of pain also, for pain destroys, among other things, lan-guage itself. Elaine Scarry's brilliant analysis of pain makes this point:

> [F]or the person, in pain, so incontestably and unnegotiably present is it that "having pain" may come to be thought of as the most vibrant example of that it is to "have certainty," while for the other person it is so elusive that hearing about pain may exist as the primary model of what it is "to have doubt." Thus pain comes unshareably into our midst as at once that which cannot be denied and that which cannot be confirmed. Whatever pain achieves, it achieves in part through its unshareability, and it ensures this unshareability in part through its resistance to language.... Prolonged pain does not simply resist language but actively destroys it, bringing about an immediate reversion to a state anterior to language, to the sounds and cries a human being makes before language is learned.

The deliberate infliction of pain in order to destroy the victim's normative world and capacity to create shared realities we call torture. The interrogation that is part of torture, Scarry points out, is rarely designed to elicit information. More commonly, the torturer's interrogation is designed to demonstrate the end of the normative world of the victim—the end of what the victim values, the end of the bonds that constitute the community in which the values are grounded. Scarry thus concludes that "in compelling confession, the torturers compel the prisoner to record and objectify the fact that intense pain is world-destroying." That is why torturers almost always require betrayal—a demonstration that the victim's intangible normative world has been crushed by the material reality of pain and its extension, fear. The torturer and victim do end up creating their own terrible "world," but this world derives its meaning from being imposed upon the ashes of another. The logic of that world is complete domination, though the objective may never be realized.

Whenever the normative world of a community survives fear, pain, and death in their more extreme forms, that very survival is understood to be literally miraculous both by those who have experienced and by those who vividly imagine or recreate the suffering. Thus, of the suffering of sainted Catholic martyrs it was written:

> We must include also . . . the deeds of the saints in which their triumph blazed forth through the many forms of torture that they underwent and their marvelous confession of the faith. For what Catholic can doubt that they suffered more than is possible for human beings to bear, and did not endure this by their own strength, but by the grace and help of God?

And Jews, each year on Yom Kippur, remember

> Rabbi Akiba . . . chose to continue teaching in spite of the decree [of the Romans forbidding it]. When they led him to the executioner, it was time for reciting the Sh'ma. With iron combs they scraped away his skin as he recited *Sh'ma Yisrael*, freely accepting the yoke of God's Kingship. "Even now?" his disciples asked. He replied: "All my life I have been troubled by a verse": 'Love the Lord your God with all your heart and with all your soul,' which means even if He take your life. I often wondered if I would ever fulfill that obligation. And now I can." He left the world while uttering, "The Lord is One."

Martyrdom, for all its strangeness to the secular world of contemporary American Law, is a proper starting place for understanding the nature of legal interpretation. Precisely because it is so extreme a phenomenon, martyrdom helps us see what is present in lesser degree whenever interpretation is joined with the practice of violent domination. Martyrs insist in the face of over-whelming force that if there is to be a continuing life, it will not be on the terms of the tyrant's law. Law is the projection of an imagined future upon reality. Martyrs require that any future they possess will be on the terms of the law to which they are committed, even in the face of world-destroying pain. Their triumph—which may well be partly imaginary—is the imagined triumph of the normative universe—of Torah, Nomos—over the material world of death and pain. Martyrdom is an extreme form of resistance to domination. As such it reminds us that the normative world-building which constitutes "Law" is never just a mental or spiritual act. A legal world is built only to the extent that there are commitments that place bodies on the line. The torture of the martyr is an extreme and repulsive form of the organized violence of institutions. It reminds us that the interpretive commitments of officials are realized, indeed, in the flesh. As long as that is so, the interpretive commitments of a community which resists official law must also be realized in the flesh, even if it be the flesh of its own adherents.

Martyrdom is not the only possible response of a group that has failed to adjust to or accept domination while sharing a physical space. Rebellion and revolution are alternative responses when conditions make such acts feasible and when there is a willingness not only to die but also to kill for an understanding of the normative future that differs from that of the dominating power.

Our own constitutional history begins with such an act of rebellion. The act was, in form, an essay in constitutional interpretation affirming the right of political independence from Great Britain:

> We therefore the representatives of the United States of America in General Congress assembled, appealing to the supreme judge of the world for the rectitude of our intentions, do in the name, and by the authority of the good people of these colonies, solemnly publish and declare that these United Colonies are and of right ought to be free and independent states; that they are absolved from all allegiance to the British crown, and that all political connection between them and the State of Great Britain is, and ought to be, totally dissolved.

But this interpretive act also incorporated an awareness of the risk of pain and death that attends so momentous an interpretive occasion:

> We mutually pledge to each other our lives, our fortunes and our sacred honour.

Life, fortune, and sacred honour were, of course, precisely the price that would have been exacted from the conspirators were their act unsuccessful. We too often forget that the leaders of the rebellion had certainly committed treason from the English constitutional perspective. A conviction of treason carried with it a horrible and degrading death, forfeiture of estate, and corruption of the blood. Great issues of constitutional interpretation that reflect fundamental questions of political allegiance—the American Revolution, the secession of the States of the Confederacy, or the uprising of the Plains Indians—clearly carry the seeds of violence (pain and death) at least from the moment that the understanding of the political texts becomes embedded in the institutional capacity to take collective action. But it is precisely this embedding of an understanding of political text in institutional modes of action that distinguishes *legal* interpretation from the interpretation of literature, from political philosophy, and from constitutional criticism. Legal interpretation is either played out on the field of pain and death or it is something less (or more) than law.

Revolutionary constitutional understandings are commonly staked in blood. In them, the violence of the law takes its most blatant form. But the relationship between legal interpretation and the infliction of pain remains operative even in the most routine of legal acts. The act of sentencing a convicted defendant is among these most routine of acts performed by judges. Yet it is immensely revealing of the way in which interpretation is distinctively shaped by violence. First, examine the event from the perspective of the defendant. The defendant's world is threatened. But he sits, usually quietly, as if engaged in a civil discourse. If convicted, the defendant customarily walks—escorted—to prolonged confinement, usually without significant disturbance to the civil appearance of the event. It is, of course, grotesque to assume that the civil facade is "voluntary" except in the sense that it represents the defendant's autonomous recognition of the overwhelming array of violence ranged against him, and of the hopelessness of resistance or outcry.

There are societies in which contrition or shame control defendants' behavior to a greater extent than does violence. Such societies require and have received their own distinctive form of analysis. But I think it is unquestionably the case in the United States that most prisoners walk into prison because they know they will be dragged or beaten into prison if they do not walk. They do not organize force against being dragged because they know that if they wage this kind of battle they will lose—very probably lose their lives.

If I have exhibited some sense of sympathy for the victims of this violence, it is misleading. Very often the balance of terror in this regard is just as I would want it. But I do not wish us to pretend that we talk our prisoners into jail. The "interpretations" or "conversations" that are the reconditions for violent incarceration are themselves implements of violence. To obscure this fact is precisely analogous to ignoring the background screams or visible instruments of torture in an inquisitor's interrogation. The experience of the prisoner is, from the outset, an experience of being violently dominated, and it is colored from the beginning by the fear of being violently treated.

The violence of the act of sentencing is most obvious when observed from the defendant's perspective. Therefore, any account which seeks to downplay the violence or elevate the interpretive character or meaning of the event within a community of shared values will tend to ignore the prisoner or defendant and focus upon the judge and the judicial interpretive act. Beginning with broad interpretive categories such as "blame" or "punishment," meaning is created for the event which justifies the judge to herself and to others with respect to her role in the acts of violence. I do not wish to downplay the significance of such ideological functions of law. But the function of ideology is much more significant in justifying an order to those who principally benefit from it and who must defend it than it is in hiding the nature of the order from those who are its victims.

The ideology of punishment is not, of course, the exclusive property of judges. The concept operates in the general culture and is intelligible to and shared by prisoners, criminals, and revolutionaries as well as judges. Why, then, should we not conclude that interpretation *is* the master concept of law, that the interpretive work of understanding "punishment" may be seen as mediating or making sense of the opposing acts and experiences of judge and defendant in the criminal trial? Naturally, one who is to be punished may have to be coerced. And punishment, if it is "just," supposedly legitimates the coercion or violence applied. The ideology of punishment may, then, operate successfully to justify our practices of criminal law to ourselves and, possibly, even to those who are or may come to be "punished" by the law.

There is, however, a fundamental difference between the way in which "punishment" operates as an ideology in popular or professional literature, in political debate, or in general discourse, and the way in which it operates in the context of the legal acts of trial, imposition of sentence, and execution. For as the judge interprets, using the concept of punishment, she also acts—through others—to restrain, hurt, render helpless, even kill the prisoner. Thus, any commonality of interpretation that may or may not be achieved is one that has its common meaning destroyed by the divergent experiences that constitute it. Just as the torturer and victim achieve a "shared" world only by virtue of their diametrically opposed experiences, so the judge and prisoner understand "punishment" through their diametrically opposed experiences of the punishing act. It is ultimately irrelevant whether the torturer and his victim share a common theoretical view on the justifications for torture—outside the torture room. They still have come to the confession through destroying in the one case and through having been destroyed in the other. Similarly, whether or not the judge and the prisoner share the same philosophy of punishment, they arrive at the particular act of punishment having dominated and having been dominated with violence, respectively.

II. THE ACTS OF JUDGES: INTERPRETATION, DEEDS, AND ROLES

We begin, then, not with what the judges say, but with what they do.

The judges deal pain and death.

That is not all that they do. Perhaps that is not what they usually do. But they *do* deal death, and pain. From John Winthrop through Warren Burger they have sat atop a pyramid of violence. . . .

In this they are different from poets, from critics, from artists. It will not do to insist on the violence of strong poetry, and strong poets. Even the violence of weak judges is utterly real—a naive but immediate reality, in need of no interpretation, no critic to reveal it. Every prisoner displays its mark. Whether or not the violence of judges is justified is not now the point—only that it exists in fact and differs from the violence that exists in literature or in the metaphoric characterizations of literary critics and philosophers. I have written elsewhere that judges of the state are jurispathic—that they kill the diverse legal traditions that compete with the State. Here, however, I am not writing of the jurispathic quality of the office, but of its homicidal potential.

The dual emphasis on the *acts* of judges and on the violence of these acts leads to consideration of three characteristics of the interpretive dimension of judicial behavior. Legal interpretation is (1) a practice activity, (2) designed to generate credible threats and actual deeds of violence, (3) in an effective way. In order to explore the unseverable connection between legal interpretation and violence, each of these three elements must be examined in turn.

A. Legal Interpretation as a Practical Activity

Legal interpretation is a form of practical wisdom. At its best it seeks to "impose *meaning* on the institution . . . and then to restructure it in light of that meaning." There is, however, a persistent chasm between thought and action. It is one thing to understand what ought to be done, quite another thing to do it. Doing entails an act of will and may require courage and perseverance. In the case of an individual's actions, we commonly think such qualities are functions of motivation, character, or psychology.

Legal interpretation is practical activity in quite another sense, however. The judicial word is a mandate for the deeds of others. Were that not the case, the practice objectives of the deliberative process could be achieved, if at all, only through more indirect and risky means. The context of a judicial utterance is institutional behavior in which others, occupying preexisting roles, can be expected to act, to implement, or otherwise to respond in a specified way to the judge's interpretation. Thus, the institutional context ties the language act of practical understanding to the physical acts of others in a predictable, though not logically necessary, way. These interpretations, then, are not only "practice," they are, themselves, practices.

Formally, on both a normative and descriptive level, there are or may be rules and principles which describe the relationship between the interpretive acts of judges and the deeds which may be expected to follow from them. These rules and principles are what H. L. A. Hart called "secondary rules." At least some secondary rules and principles identify the terms of cooperation between interpretation specialists and other actors in a social organization. Prescriptive secondary materials purport to set the norms for what those relations ought to be; descriptive secondary rules and principles would generate an accurate prediction of what the terms of cooperation actually will be. Of course, in any given system there need be no particular degree of correspondence between the two sets of rules.

Secondary rules and principles provide the template for transforming language into action, word into deed. As such they occupy a critical place in the analysis of legal interpretation proposed here. The legal philosopher may hold up to us a model of a hypothetical judge who is able to achieve a Herculean understanding of the full body of legal and social texts relevant to a particular case, and from this understanding to arrive at the single legally correct decision. But that mental interpretive act cannot give itself effect. The practice of interpretation requires an understanding of what others will do with such a judicial utterance and, in many instances, an adjustment to that understanding, regardless of how misguided one may think the likely institutional response will be. Failing this, the interpreter sacrifices the connection between understanding what ought to be done and the deed itself. But bridging the chasm between thought and action in the legal system is never simply a matter of will. The gap between understanding and action roughly corresponds to differences in institutional roles and to the division of labor and of responsibility that these roles represent. Thus, what may be described as a problem of will with respect to the individual becomes, in an institutional context, primarily a problem in social organization. Elsewhere I have labeled the specialized understanding of this relation, between the interpretation of the judge and the social organization required to transform it into a reality, the hermeneutic of the tests of jurisdiction. This specialized understanding must lie at the heart of official judging.

B. Interpretation within a System Designed to Generate Violence

The gulf between thought and action widens wherever serious violence is at issue, because for most of us, evolutionary, psychological, cultural, and moral considerations inhibit the infliction of pain on other people. Of course, these constraints are neither absolute nor universal. There are some deviant individuals whose behavior is inconsistent with such inhibitions. Furthermore, almost all people are fascinated and attracted by violence, even though they are at the same time repelled by it. Finally, and most important for our purposes, in almost all people social cues may overcome or suppress the revulsion to violence under certain circumstances. These limitations do not deny the force of inhibitions against violence. Indeed, both together create the conditions without which law would either be unnecessary or impossible. Were the inhibition against violence perfect, law would be unnecessary; were it not capable of being overcome through social signals, law would not be possible.

Because legal interpretation is as a practice incomplete without violence—because it depends upon the social practice of violence for its efficacy—it must be related in a strong way to the cues that operate to bypass or suppress the psycho-social mechanisms that usually inhibit people's actions causing pain and death. Interpretations which occasion violence are distinct from the violent acts they occasion. When judges interpret the law in an official context, we expect a close relationship to be revealed or established between their words and the acts that they mandate. That is, we expect the judges' words to serve as virtual triggers for action. We would not, for example, expect contemplations or deliberations on the part of jailers and wardens to interfere with the action authorized by judicial words. But such a routinization of violent behavior requires a form of organization that operates simultaneously in the domains of action and interpretation. In order to understand the violence of a judge's interpretive act, we must also understand the way in which it is transformed into a violent deed despite general resistance to such deeds; in order to comprehend the meaning of the violent deed, we must also understand in what way the judge's interpretive act authorizes and legitimizes it.

While it is hardly possible to suggest a comprehensive review of the possible ways in which the organization of the legal system operates to facilitate overcoming inhibitions against intraspecific violence, I do wish to point to some of the social codes which limit these inhibitions. Here the literature of social psychology is helpful. The best-known study and theory of social codes and their role in overcoming normal inhibitions against inflicting pain through violence is Milgram's *Obedience to Authority*. In the Milgram experiments, subjects administered what they thought were actually painful electric shocks to persons who they thought were the experimental subjects. This was done under the direction or orders of supposed experimenters. The true experimental subjects—those who administered the shocks—showed a disturbingly high level of compliance with authority figures despite the apparent pain evinced by the false experimental subjects. From the results of his experiment, Milgram has formulated a theory that is in some respects incomplete. The most developed part of the theory relies heavily on the distinction he draws between acting in an "autonomous" state and acting in an "agentic" state. Milgram posits the evolution of a human disposition to act "agentically" within hierarchies, since the members of organized hierarchies were traditionally more likely to survive than were members of less organized social groups. Concurrently, the "conscience" or "superego" evolved in response to the need for autonomous behavior or judgment given the evolution of social structures. It is this autonomous behavior which inhibits the infliction of pain on others. But the regulators for individual autonomous behavior had to be capable of being suppressed or subordinated to the characteristics of agentic behavior when individuals acted within a hierarchical structure. In addition to his theories of species-specific evolutionary mechanisms, Milgram also points to the individual-specific and culture-specific forms of learning and conditioning for agentic behavior within hierarchical structures. Thus, in Milgram's explanation of the "agentic state," "institutional systems of authority" play a key role in providing the requisite cues for causing the shift from autonomous behavior to the agentic behavior cybernetically required to make hierarchies work. According to Milgram, the cues for overcoming autonomous behavior or "conscience" consist of the institutionally sanctioned commands, orders, or signals of institutionally legitimated authorities characteristic of human hierarchical organization.

There are, of course, a variety of alternative ways to conceptualize the facilitation of violence through institutional roles. One could point, for example, to the theory that human beings have a natural tendency, an instinctual drive, to aggression, and that a variety of learned behaviors keep aggression within bounds. The institutionally specified occasions for violence may then be seen as outlets for the aggression that we ordinarily would seek to exercise but for the restraints. Some scholars have, from a psychoanalytic perspective, hypothesized that formal structures for the perpetration of violence permit many individuals to deny themselves the fulfillment of aggressive wishes by "delegating" the violent activity to others.

There is an enormous difference between Milgram's theory of institutionalized violence and Anna Freud's or Konrad Lorenz's, and between the assumptions about human nature which inform them. But common to all of these theories is a behavioral observation in need of explanation. Persons who act within social organizations that exercise authority act violently without experiencing the normal inhibitions or the normal degree of inhibition which regulates the behavior of those who act autonomously. When judges interpret, they trigger agentic behavior within just such an institution or social organization. On one level judges may appear to be, and may in fact be, offering their understanding of the normative world to their intended audience. But on another level they are engaging a violent mechanism through which a substantial part of their audience loses its capacity to think and act autonomously.

C. Interpretation and the Effective Organization of Violence

A third factor separates the authorization of violence as a deliberative, interpretive exercise from the deed. Deeds of violence are rarely suffered by the victim apart from a setting of domination. That setting may be manifestly coercive and violent or it may be the product of a history of violence which conditions the expectations of the actors. The imposition of violence depends upon the satisfaction of the social preconditions for its effectiveness. Few of us are courageous or foolhardy enough to *act* violently in an uncompromisingly principled fashion without attention to the likely responses from those upon whom we would impose our wills.

If legal interpretation entails action in a field of pain and death, we must expect, therefore, to find in the act of interpretation attention to the *conditions of effective domination*. To the extent that effective domination is not present, either our understanding of the law will be adjusted so that it will require only that which can reasonably be expected from people in conditions of reprisal, resistance, and revenge, or there will be a crisis of credibility. The law may come over time to bear only an uncertain relation to the institutionally implemented deeds it authorizes. Some systems, especially religious ones, can perpetuate and even profit from a dichotomy between an ideal law and a realizable one. But such a dichotomy has immense implications *if built into* the law. In our own secular legal system, one must assume this to be an undesirable development.

D. Legal Interpretation as Bonded Interpretation

Legal interpretation, therefore, can never be "free," it can never be the function of an understanding of the text or word alone. Nor can it be a simple function of what the interpreter conceives to be merely a reading of the "social text," a reading of all relevant social data. Legal interpretation must be capable of transforming itself into action; it must be capable of overcoming inhibitions against violence in order to generate its requisite deeds; it must be capable of massing a sufficient degree of violence to deter reprisal and revenge.

In order to maintain these critical links to effective violent behavior, legal interpretation must reflexively consider its own social organization. In so reflecting, the interpreter thereby surrenders something of his independence of mind and autonomy of judgment, since the legal meaning that some hypothetical Hercules (Hyporcules) might construct out of the sea of our legal and social texts is only one element in the institutional practice we call law. Coherent legal meaning is an element in legal interpretation. But it is an element potentially in tension with the need to generate effective action in a violent context. And neither effective action nor coherent meaning can be maintained, separately or together, without an entire structure of social cooperation. Thus, legal interpretation is a form of bonded interpretation, bound at once to practical application (to the deeds it implies) and to the ecology of jurisdictional roles (the conditions of effective domination). The bonds are reciprocal. For the deeds of social violence as we know them also require that they be rendered intelligible—that they be both subject to interpretation and to the specialized and constrained forms of behavior that are "roles." And the behavior within roles that we expect can neither exist without the interpretations which explain the otherwise meaningless patterns of strong action and inaction, nor be intelligible without understanding the deeds they are designed to effectuate.

Legal interpretation may be the act of judges or citizens, legislators or presidents, draft resisters or right-to-life protesters. Each kind of interpreter speaks from a distinct institutional location. Each has a differing perspective on factual and moral implications of any given understanding of the Constitution. The understanding of each will vary as roles and moral commitments vary. But consideration of word, deed, and role will always be present in some degree. The relationships among these three considerations are created by the practical, violent context of the practice of legal interpretation, and therefore constitute the most significant aspect of the legal interpretive process.

III. INTERPRETATION AND EFFECTIVE ACTION:
THE CASE OF CRIMINAL SENTENCING

The bonded character of legal interpretation can be better appreciated by further unpacking a standard judicial act—the imposition of a sentence in a criminal case—this time from the judge's perspective. Such an act has few of the problematic remedial and role complications that have occupied commentators on the judicial role with regard to affirmative relief in institutional reform litigation or complex "political questions" cases. In imposing sentences in criminal cases, judges are doing something clearly within their province. I do not mean to suggest that there are not disagreements about how the act should be carried out—whether with much or little discretion, whether attending more to objective and quantifiable criteria or to subjective and qualitative ones. But the act is and long has been a judicial one, and one which requires no strange or new modes of interaction with other officials or citizens.

Taken for granted in this judicial act is the structure of cooperation that ensures, we hope, the effective domination of the present and prospective victim of state violence—the convicted defendant. The role of judge becomes dangerous, indeed, whenever the conditions for domination of the prisoner and his allies are absent. Throughout history we have seen the products of ineffective domination in occasional trials in our country and in many instances in other nations. The imposition of a sentence thus involves the roles of police, jailers, or other enforcers who will restrain the prisoner (or set him free subject to effective conditions for future restraint) upon the order of the judge, and guards who will secure the prisoner from rescue and who will protect the judge, prosecutors, witnesses, and jailers from revenge.

The judge in imposing a sentence normally takes for granted the role structure which might be analogized to the "transmission" of the engine of justice. The judge's interpretive authorization of the "proper" sentence can be carried out as a deed only because of these others; a bond between word and deed obtains only because a system of social cooperation exists. That system guarantees the judge massive amounts of force—the conditions of effective domination —if necessary. It guarantees—or is supposed to—a relatively faithful adherence to the word of the judge in the deeds carried out against the prisoner.

A. Revealing Latent Role Factors

If the institutional structure—the system of roles—gives the judge's understanding its effect, thereby transforming understanding into "law," so it confers meaning on the deeds which effect this transformation, thereby legitimating them as "lawful." A central task of the legal interpreter is to attend to the problematic aspects of the integration of role, deed, and word, not only where the violence (i.e., enforcement) is lacking for meaning, but also where meaning is lacking for violence.

In a nation like ours, in which the conditions of state domination are rarely absent, it is too easy to assume that there will be faithful officials to carry out what the judges decree, and judges available to render their acts lawful. Just how crucial this taken-for-granted structure is may be appreciated by examining a case in which it is lacking. The decisions by Judge Herbert Stern in *United States v. Tiede* display an unusually lucid appreciation of the significance of the institutional connections between the judicial world and the violent deeds it authorizes.

Judge Stern was (and is) a federal district judge in New Jersey. In 1979 he was appointed an Article II judge for the United States Court for Berlin. This unique event, the only convening of the Court for Berlin, was a response to the reluctance of West Germany to prosecute two skyjackers who had used a toy gun to threaten the crew of a Polish airliner en route from Gdansk to East Berlin and had forced it to land in West Berlin. The formal status of Berlin as an "occupied" city enabled the Germans to place responsibility for prosecution of the skyjacker-refugees upon the Americans.

Stern wrote a moving account of the unusual trial which ensued, including his long struggle with the United States government over the general question of whether the Constitution of the United States would govern the proceedings. After a jury trial, opposed by the prosecution, and a verdict of guilty on one of the charges, Stern was required to perform the "simple" interpretive act of imposing the appropriate sentence. As a matter of interpreting the governing materials on sentencing it might indeed have been a "simple" act—one in which relatively unambiguous German law was relatively unambiguously to be applied by virtue of American law governing a court of occupation.

Stern brilliantly illuminated the defects in such a chain of reasoning. The judicial interpretive act in sentencing issues is a deed—the actual performance of the violence of punishment upon a defendant. But these two—judicial word and punitive deed—are connected only by the social cooperation of many others, who in their roles as lawyers, police, jailers, wardens, and magistrates perform the deeds which judicial words authorize. Cooperation among these officials is usually simply assumed to be present, but, of course, the conditions which normally ensure the success of this cooperation may fail in a variety of ways.

This is Judge Stern's account of his sentencing of the defendant, Hans Detlef Alexander Tiede:

> Gentlemen [addressing the State Department and Justice Department lawyers], I will not give you this defendant. . . . I have kept him in your custody now for nine months, nearly. . . . You have persuaded me. I believe, now, that you recognize no limitations of due process. . . .
>
> I don't have to be a great prophet to understand that there is probably not a great future for the United States Court for Berlin here. [Stern had just been officially "ordered" not to proceed with a civil case brought against the United States in Stern's Court. The case was a last ditch attempt in a complicated proceeding in which the West Berlin government had acquired park land—allegedly in violation of German law—for construction of a housing complex for the United States Army Command in Berlin. The American occupation officials had refused to permit the German courts to decide the case as it affected the interests of the occupation

authority. American Ambassador Walter Stroessel had officially written Stern on the day before the sentencing that "your appointment as a Judge of the United States Court for Berlin does not extend to this matter."]. . . .

Under those circumstances, who will be here to protect Tiede if I give him to you for four years? Viewing the Constitution as non-existent, considering yourselves not restrained in any way, who will stand between you and him? What independent magistrate will you permit here?

When a judge sentences, he commits a defendant to the custody—in the United States he says, "I commit to the custody of the Attorney General of the United States"—et cetera. Here I suppose he says, I commit to the custody of the Commandant, or the Secretary of State, or whatever. . . . I will not do it. Not under these circumstances. . . .

I sentence this defendant to time served. You are a free man right now.

Herbert Stern's remarkable sentence is not simply an effective, moving plea for judicial independence, a plea against subservience which Stern's government tried to impose. It is a dissection of the anatomy of criminal punishment in a constitutional system. As such, it reveals the interior role of the judicial word in sentencing. It reveals the necessity of a latent role structure to render the judicial utterance morally intelligible. And it proclaims the moral unintelligibility of routine judicial utterance when the structure is no longer there. Almost all judicial utterance becomes deed through the acts of others—acts embedded in roles. The judge must see, as Stern did, that the meaning of her words may change when the roles of these others change. We tend overwhelmingly to assume that constitutional violence is always performed within institutionally sanctioned limits and subject to the institutionally circumscribed, role-bound action of others. Stern uncovered the unreliability of that assumption in the Berlin context and "reinterpreted" his sentence accordingly.

B. The Death Sentence as an Interpretive Act of Violence

The questions of whether the death sentence is constitutionally permissible and, if it is, whether to impose it, are among the most difficult problems a judge encounters. While the grammar of the capital sentence may appear to be similar to that of any other criminal sentence, the capital sentence as interpretive act is unique in at least three ways. The judge must interpret those constitutional and other legal texts which speak to the question of the proper or permissible occasions for imposition of a capital sentence. She must understand the texts in the context of an application that prescribes the killing of another person. And she must act to set in motion the acts of others which will in the normal course of events end with someone else killing the convicted defendant. Our judges do not *ever* kill the defendants themselves. They do not witness the execution. Yet, they are intensely aware of the deed their words authorize.

The confused and emotional situation which now prevails with respect to capital punishment in the United States is in several ways a product of what I have described as the bonded character of legal interpretation—the complex structure of relationships between word and deed. To any person endowed with the normal inhibitions against the imposition of pain and death, the deed of capital punishment entails a special measure of the reluctance and abhorrence which constitute the gulf that must be bridged between interpretation and action. Because in capital punishment the action or *deed* is extreme and irrevocable, there is pressure placed on the *word*—the interpretation that establishes the legal justification for the act. At the same time, the fact that capital punishment constitutes the most plain, the most deliberate, and the most thoughtful manifestation of legal interpretation as violence makes the imposition of the sentence an especially powerful test of the faith and commitment of the interpreters. Not even the facade of civility, where it exists, can obscure the violence of a death sentence.

Capital cases, thus, disclose far more of the structure of judicial interpretation than do other cases. Aiding this disclosure is the agonistic character of law: The defendant and his counsel search for and exploit any part of the structure that may work to their advantage. And they do so to an extreme degree in a matter of life and death.

Thus, in the typical capital case in the United States, the judge is constantly reminded of that which the defense constantly seeks to exploit: The structure of interdependent roles that Judge Stern found to be potentially lacking in Berlin in the *Tiede* case. Consider. Not only do the actors in these roles carry out the judicial decision—they await it! All of them know that the judges will be called upon, time and again, to consider exhaustively all interpretive avenues that the defense counsel might take to avoid the sentence. And they expect that no capital sentence will in fact be carried out without several substantial delays during which judges consider some defense not yet fully decided by that or other courts. The almost stylized action of the drama requires that the jailers stand visibly ready to receive intelligence of the judicial act—even if it be only the act of deciding to take future action. The stay of execution, though it be nothing—literally nothing—as an act of *textual* exegesis, nonetheless constitutes an important form of constitutional interpretation. For it shows the violence of the warden and executioner to be linked to the judge's deliberative act of understanding. The stay of execution, the special line open, permits, or more accurately, requires the inference to be drawn from the failure of the stay of execution. That too is the visible tie between word and deed. These wardens, these guards, these doctors, jump to the judge's tune. If the deed is done, it is a constitutional deed—one integrated to and justifiable under the proper understanding of the word. In short, it is the stay, the drama of the possibility of the stay, that renders the execution constitutional violence, that makes the deed an act of interpretation.

For, after all, executions I can find almost anywhere. If people disappear, if they die suddenly and without ceremony in prison, quite apart from any articulated justification and authorization for their demise, then we do not have constitutional interpretation at the heart of this deed, nor do we have the deed, the death at the heart of the Constitution. The problem of incapacity or unwillingness to ensure a strong, virtually certain link between judicial utterance and violent deed in this respect characterizes certain legal systems at certain times. It characterized much of the American legal system well into the twentieth century; lynching, for example was long thought to be a peculiarly American scandal. It was a scandal which took many forms. Often it entailed taking the punishment of alleged offenders out of the hands of courts entirely. But sometimes it entailed the carrying out of death sentences without abiding by ordered process of appeals and post-conviction remedies. Such was the outcome, for example, of the notorious "Leo Frank" case.

The plain fact is that we have come a good way since 1914 with respect to our expectations that persons accused of capital crimes will be given a trial, will be sentenced properly, and will live to see the appointed time of the execution of their sentence. In fact, we have come to expect near perfect coordination of those whose role it is to inflict violence subject to the interpretive decisions of the judges. We have even come to express coordinated cooperation in securing all plausible judicial interpretations on the subject.

Such a well-coordinated form of violence is an achievement. The careful social understandings designed to accomplish the violence that is capital punishment, or to refrain from that act, are not fortuitous or casual products of circumstance. Rather, they are the products of design, tied closely to the secondary rules and principles which provide clear criteria for the recognition of these and other interpretive acts as, first and foremost, *judicial* acts. Their "meaning" is always secondary to their provenance. No wardens, guards, or executioners wait for a telephone call from the latest constitutional law scholar, jurisprude, or critic before executing prisoners, no matter how compelling the interpretations of these others may be. And, indeed, they await the word of judges only insofar as that word carries with it the formal indicia of having been spoken in the judicial capacity. The social cooperation critical to the constitutional form of cooperation in violence is, therefore, also predicated upon the recognition of the judicial role and the recognition of the one whose utterance performs it.

There are, of course, some situations in which the judicial role is not well-defined but is contested. Nonetheless, social cooperation in constitutional violence as we know it requires at least that it be very clear who speaks as a judge and when. The hierarchical ordering among judicial voices must also be clear or subject to clarification. We have established, then, the necessity for rules and principles that locate authoritative interpreters and prescribe action on the basis of what they say. The rules and principles that locate authoritative voices for the purposes of action point to the defect in a model of judicial interpretation that centers around a single coherent and consistent mind at work. For here in the United States there is no set of secondary rules and principles more fundamental than those which make it impossible for any single judge, however Herculean her understanding of the law, ever to have the last word on legal meaning as it affects real cases. In the United States—with only trivial exceptions—no judge sitting alone on a significant legal issue is immune from appellate review. Conversely, whenever any judge sits on the court of last resort on a significant legal issue, that judge does not sit alone. A complex of secondary rules determines this situation. These rules range from the statutes which generally give a right to at least one appeal from final judgments of trial courts, to special statutes which require that there be appellate review of death sentences, to the constitutional guarantee that the writ of habeas corpus not be suspended. Final appellate courts in the United States have always had at least three judges. Some state constitutions specify the number. No explicit provision in the United States Constitution defines the Supreme Court in such a way that requires that it be made up of more than a single judge. But both invariant practice and basic understandings since 1789 have made the idea of a single-Justice Supreme Court a practical absurdity. Given the clarity of the expectation that Supreme Court judicial bodies be plural, it seems doubtful to me whether such an imaginary Court should be held to satisfy the constitutional requirement that there be a Supreme Court.

If some hypothetical Herculean judge should achieve an understanding of constitutional and social texts—an interpretation—such that she felt the death penalty to be a permissible and appropriate punishment in a particular case, she would be confronted at once with the problem of translating that conviction into a deed. Her very understanding of the constitutionality of the death penalty and the appropriateness of its imposition would carry with it—as part of the understanding—the knowledge that she could not carry out the sentence herself. The most elementary understanding of our social practice of violence ensures that a judge know that she herself cannot actually pull the switch. This is not a trivial convention. For it means that someone else will have the duty and opportunity to pass upon what the judge has done. Were the judge a trial judge, and should she hand down an order to execute, there would be another judge to whom application could be made to stay or reverse her decision. The fact that *someone else* has to carry out the execution means that this someone else may be confronted with two pieces of paper: let us say a warrant for the execution of the sentence of death at a specified time and place and a stay of execution from an appellate tribunal. The someone else—the warden, for simplicity's sake—is expected to determine which of these two pieces of paper to act upon according to some highly arbitrary, hierarchical principles which have nothing to do with the relative merits or demerits of the arguments which justify the respective substantive positions.

It is crucial to note here that if the warden should cease paying relatively automatic heed to the pieces of paper which flow in from the judges according to these arbitrary and sometimes rigid hierarchical rules and principles, the judges would lose their capacity to do violence. They would be left with only the opportunity to persuade the warden and his men to do violence. Conversely, the warden and his men would lose their capacity to shift to the judge primary moral responsibility for the violence which they themselves carry out. They would have to pass upon the justifications for violence in every case themselves, thereby turning the trial into a sort of preliminary hearing. There are, indeed, many prisons in this world that bear some resemblance to this hypothetical situation. There are systems in which the most significant punishment decisions are made by those who either perform or have direct supervisory authority over the performance of the violence itself.

We have done something strange in our system. We have rigidly separated the act of interpretation—of understanding what ought to be done—from the carrying out of this "ought to be done" through violence. At the same time we have, at least in the criminal law, rigidly linked the carrying out of judicial orders to the act of judicial interpretation by relatively inflexible hierarchies of judicial utterances and firm obligations on the part of penal officials to heed them. Judges are both separated from, and inextricably linked to, the acts they authorize.

This strange yet familiar attribute of judging in America has the effect of ensuring that no judge *acts* alone. Ronald Dworkin's "Judge as Hercules" may appear to be a useful construct for understanding how a judge's mind ought to work. But it is misleading precisely because it suggests, if it does not require, a context which, in America, is never present. There may or may not be any sense in thinking about a judicial understanding of the law apart from its application. But one thing is near certain. The application of legal understanding in our domain of pain and death will always require the active or passive acquiescence of other judicial minds. It is possible to wear this point down to the most trite observation of professional practice. A judge who wishes to transform her understanding into deed must, if located on a trial court, attend to ensuring that her decision not be reversed. If on an appellate court, she must attend to getting at least one other judge to go along. It is commonplace that many "majority" opinions bear the scars or marks of having been written primarily to keep the majority. Many a trial court opinion bears the scars of having been written primarily to avoid reversal.

Now the question arises, which is the true act of legal interpretation? The hypothetical understanding of a single mind placed in the admittedly hypothetical position of being able to render final judgments sitting alone? Or the actual products of judges acting under the constraint of potential group oversight of all decisions that are to be made real through collective violence? The single decision of a hypothetical Hercules is likely to be more articulate and coherent than the collective decision of many judges who may make compromises to arrive at that decision. But Hercules does not and cannot carry the force of collective violence. This defect is intrinsic to the definition of legal interpretation as a mental activity of a person rather than the violent activity of an organization of people.

So let us be explicit. If it seems a nasty thought that death and pain are at the center of legal interpretation, so be it. It would not be better were there only a community of argument, of readers and writers of texts, of interpreters. As long as death and pain are part of our political world, it is essential that they be at the center of the law. The alternative is truly unacceptable—that they be within our polity but outside the discipline of the *collective* decision rules and the individual efforts to achieve outcomes through those rules. The fact that we require many voices is not, then, an accident or peculiarity of our jurisdictional rules. It is intrinsic to whatever achievement is possible in the domesticating of violence.

CONCLUSION

There is a worthy tradition that would have us hear the judge as a voice of reason; see her as the embodiment of principle. The current academic interest in interpretation, the attention to community of meaning and commitment, is apologetic neither in its intent or effect. The trend is, by and large, an attempt to hold a worthy ideal before what all would agree is an unredeemed reality. I would not quarrel with the impulse that leads us to this form of criticism.

There is, however, danger in forgetting the limits which are intrinsic to this activity of legal interpretation; in exaggerating the extent to which any interpretation rendered as part of the act of the state violence can ever constitute a common and coherent meaning. I have emphasized two rather different kinds of limits to the commonality and coherence of meaning that can be achieved. One kind of limit is a practical one which follows from the social organization of legal violence. We have seen that in order to do that violence safely and effectively, responsibility for the violence must be shared; law must operate as a system of cues and signals to many actors who would otherwise be unwilling, incapable, or irresponsible in their violent acts. This social organization of violence manifests itself in the secondary rules and principles which generally ensure that no single mind and no single will can generate the violent outcomes that follow from interpretive commitments. No single individual can render any interpretation operative as law—as authority for the violent act. While a convergence of understandings on the part of all relevant legal actors is not necessarily impossible, it is, in fact, very unlikely. And, of course, we cannot flee from the multiplicity of minds and voices that the social organization of law-as-violence requires to some hypothetical decision process that would aggregate the many voices into one. We know that—aside from dictatorship—there is no aggregation rule that will necessarily meet elementary conditions for rationality in the relationships among the social choices made.

While our social decision rules cannot guarantee coherence and rationality of meaning, they can and do generate violent action which may well have a distinct coherent meaning for at least one of the relevant actors. We are left, then, in this actual world of the organization of law-as-violence with decisions whose meaning is not likely to be coherent if it is common, and not likely to be common if it is coherent.

This practical, contingent limit upon legal interpretation is, however, the less important and less profound of the two kinds of limits I have presented. For if we truly attend to legal interpretation as it is practiced on the field of fear, pain, and death, we find that the principal impediment to the achievement of common and coherent meaning is a necessary limit, intrinsic to the activity. Judges, officials, resisters, martyrs, wardens, convicts, may or may not share common texts; they may or may not share a common vocabulary, a common cultural store of gestures and rituals; they may or may not share a common philosophical framework. There will be in the immense human panorama a continuum of degrees of commonality in all of the above. But as long as legal interpretation is constitutive of violent behavior as well as meaning, as long as people are committed to using or resisting the social organizations of violence in making their interpretations real, there will always be a tragic limit to the common meaning that can be achieved.

The perpetrator and victim of organized violence will undergo achingly disparate significant experiences. For the perpetrator, the pain and fear are remote, unreal, and largely unshared. They are, therefore, almost never made a part of the interpretive artifact, such as the judicial opinion. On the other hand, for those who impose the violence, the justification is important, real, and carefully cultivated. Conversely, for the victim, the justification for the violence recedes in reality and significance in proportion to the overwhelming reality of the pain and fear that is suffered.

Between the idea and the reality of common meaning falls the shadow of the violence of law itself.

Born into a small rural community in Kedah (northwest Malaysia) in 1947, Chandra Muzaffar was the only son in a family with three sisters. From a very early age he learned to understand and empathize with the other sex. He himself has two daughters and no sons; more nieces than nephews; more sisters-in-law than brothers-in-law. Afflicted with polio at the age of four, Chandra experiences physical immobility, which, combined with a feminine acculturation, seems to have made him acutely sensitive to human suffering and human misery.

A political-science major at the University of Singapore in the late 1960s, he became disenchanted with mainstream, mostly U.S. political science, and though he became a political-science lecturer at the Sciences University of Malaysia in Penang in the early 1970s, he sought to understand the meaning and purpose of politics and how it related to moral values and life, and it was this intellectual and spiritual quest which took him closer and closer to Islam, to which he converted in early 1974. He returned to Singapore to do his doctorate in 1975. He became increasingly critical of Western intellectual and cultural dominance, more committed to nurturing and nourishing the spiritual and moral roots of his own philosophical tradition. He saw the importance of developing an alternative vision of human civilization, one which would do justice to the weak and powerless majority.

After earning his Ph.D. in 1977, he returned to Penang, and with a few of his friends established a social reform group, Aliran, to address issues of political transformation in Malaysia from a spiritual-moral perspective. Throughout the 1980s, Muzaffar wrote and spoke extensively about the problems of authoritarianism, corruption, disparities in wealth and opportunity, communalism and religious bigotry. He eventually gave up his academic career to concentrate on developing Aliran and its monthly magazine.

In 1987 he was arrested by the Malaysian government for his crusading efforts, and while he was in detention, the Singapore government issued a ban that prevented him from entering the island republic. Though he was never informed of the reason for the ban, which remains in effect, it is believed that his criticism of the Singapore government's parajudicial arrest of social activists and professionals in May 1987 earned him the displeasure of the authorities.

After his release from detention in December 1987, Muzaffar continued to campaign for various causes, especially those pertaining to inter-ethnic integration. However, in November 1991, he stepped down as Aliran president in order, he said, to emphasize the shared values of Malaysia's multireligious population and to develop a common spiritual and moral bond transcending communal boundaries in the fight against materialistic development.

Since September 1992, Muzaffar has focused on global concerns: the erosion of universal spiritual and moral values; the concentration of global wealth and global power with a minority; the ubiquitous impact of the West on the rest of the world. To address these concerns, he helped set up the international nongovernmental organization Just World Trust, which champions the victims of dominant power, positioning itself as the voice of the other and challenging powerful and entrenched interests both in Malaysia and throughout the political-economic centers of Asia and Euro-America.

His writings include numerous essays in edited volumes and periodicals. The following excerpt is taken from his most notable—and notorious—book, Human Rights and the New World Order *(1993).*

Human Rights and the New World Order

CHANDRA MUZAFFAR

This study will focus upon the role of the United Nations in promoting human rights since the adoption of the Universal Declaration of Human Rights (UDHR) in 1948.

It is divided into three sections. The first evaluates the UN's achievements in the field of human rights since 1948, while the second examines some of the obstacles it faces as it attempts to promote human rights. In the third and final section, we explore ways and means of overcoming these obstacles.

HOW MUCH PROGRESS?

Instruments and Institutions

Since the UDHR, the UN has developed an impressive array of instruments and institutions dedicated to the protection and promotion of human rights. The International Covenant on Economic, Social, and Cultural Rights and the International Covenant on Civil and Political Rights would be among the most prominent of the instruments. The International Convention on the Elimination of All Forms of Racial Discrimination, the International Convention on the Suppression and Punishment of the Crime of Apartheid, the Convention on the Elimination of All Forms of Discrimination Against Women, the Convention Against Torture and Other Cruel, Inhuman, and Degrading Treatment or Punishment, and the Convention on the Rights of the Child would be some of the other better known instruments adopted by the UN.

Among UN institutions concerned with human rights, one should of course include the General Assembly and the Security Council. However, in terms of concrete human rights work, the Economic and Social Council is much more important. The Commission on Human Rights is one of its subsidiary bodies. So are the Sub-Commission on Prevention of Discrimination and Protection of Minorities and the Commission on the Status of Women. Then we have the Trusteeship Council, the International Court of Justice, otherwise known as the World Court, and the Centre for Human Rights. The last named is part of the UN secretariat. They are also Treaty-monitoring bodies like the Committee on the Elimination of Racial Discrimination, the Committee on the Elimination of Discrimination Against Women, the Committee Against Torture, the Committee on Economic, Social, and Cultural Rights, and so on. Some of the specialized agencies of the UN like the International Labour Organization (ILO), the Food and Agricultural Organization (FAO), the United National Educational, Scientific, and Cultural Organization (UNESCO) and the World Health Organization (WHO) are also concerned with human rights issues. Last, but by no means least, there are also consultative Non-Governmental Organizations (NGOs) that also help to promote the cause of human rights.

Impact

What has been the impact of all these institutions and instruments upon human rights? To start with, they have helped to broaden and deepen our understanding of human rights. It is partly through the work of the UN that human rights, at least in theory, have gone beyond civil and political liberties to encompass such challenging concerns as the right to development and the right to peace. In a sense, the UN instruments have done more than just refining and expanding the ideas embodied in the UDHR. They have explored new areas which the UDHR as the inheritor of a liberal-democratic tradition revolving around the rights of the individual could not possibly envisage. In the process, not just human rights though but political philosophy itself has been enriched. Indeed, the new dimensions of human rights have forced some of us to adopt a more holistic, integrated approach to human rights.

At the same time, for the over 150 states which became independent after the UDHR, the various UN declarations and conventions have been a huge reservoir of ideas on human rights, the rule of law, the independence of the judiciary, public accountability and so on. Some of these ideas have taken the form of specific rights enshrined in national constitutions. Malaya, the predecessor of Malaysia, as a case in point, took into cognizance the UN Charter and the UDHR in formulating various constitutional provisions on civil liberties when it attained independence in 1957. So did Ghana and Nigeria, Kenya and Tanzania. By absorbing rights and principles from UN documents, these new states sought to establish their credentials as members of the international community.

It is not just states—meaning by which their ruling elites—which find support in UN documents. Dissidents in many parts of the world have often tried to reinforce their struggle for human rights through the moral and intellectual authority of UN declarations and covenants. This is what the student movement in Myanmar did in September 1988 when it challenged the military junta in power. This is what elements in the Thai middle-class did in their successful protest against the military elite in May 1992. For dissidents, universal human rights have become criteria for judging the performance of their governments.

What this shows is that UN instruments and UN institutions have succeeded, to some extent, in evolving universally acceptable human rights standards. Human rights standard-setting then is one of the outstanding achievements of the UN. In other words, there are certain norms of conduct in the arena of human rights applicable to human beings everywhere, irrespective of their ethnic or religious, ideological or national backgrounds.

As a result of these universal standards, and by virtue of the UN's role as the most representative international forum in the world today, the UN's human rights activities have contributed toward the emergence of a global moral climate. It is because there is such a climate that people in most places are revolted by certain gross violations of human rights. The brutal suppression of the black majority by a white minority in South Africa in the heyday of apartheid evoked a lot of moral revulsion everywhere. Similarly, the barbaric ethnic pogrom being conducted by the Serbs against the Bosnians in the former Yugoslavia is producing the sort of moral outrage among ordinary men and women which we have not witnessed for a long while. It is doubtful if there would have been such a reaction if there were no global moral climate.

These then are the five areas where the UN's human rights work since 1948 appears to have made some impact. There are of course other areas too where the UN's role has been commendable. They are however more specific. But whether specific or general, we must acknowledge that the world body, important though its contribution is, has not been the principal force behind progress in the human rights field since the UDHR.

Decolonialization

Right from the beginning, the UN was concerned with the struggle of colonized peoples from freedom, with their quest for political independence and national sovereignty. The General Assembly recognized the right of peoples and nations to self-determination "as a fundamental human right in resolution 421

D (v) of 4 December 1950." A more important step was taken on 14 December 1960 when the General Assembly proclaimed "the necessity of bringing to a speedy and unconditional end colonialism in all its forms and manifestations." It then adopted the Declaration on the Granting of Independence to Colonial Countries and Peoples. The Declaration states, *inter alia*, "The subjection of peoples to alien subjugation, domination, and exploitation constitutes a denial of fundamental human rights, is contrary to the Charter of the United Nations, and is an impediment to the promotion of world peace and co-operation."

Following the Declaration, a Special Committee on Decolonization was established whose main task was to monitor the implementation of the Declaration. The Special Committee, it should be noted, played a fairly prominent role in expediting the independence of Namibia.

The UN also created a Trusteeship system in 1947 under which a number of territories ruled by various colonial powers were brought within the purview of the world body. In this way, the UN provided active encouragement to colonized peoples to pursue their goal of independence through peaceful, non-violent means.

For all its excellent work, however, it is doubtful if the UN on its own could have made much progress in decolonizing the globe. By the time the UN came into being in 1945, there was already a powerful clamor for independence in a number of countries in Asia. Significant changes within the colonies—notably the growth of an intelligentsia conscious of the importance of freedom (Indonesia in 1946; India in 1947)—and this inspired other nationalists in other parts of the continent and even in Africa to fight for their freedom. Besides, colonialism itself had lost its potency following the Second World War. Colonial powers like Britain and France, though victorious in war, were too exhausted in peace to re-impose their authority upon all and sundry. In any case, the political atmosphere itself had changed so much that classical colonialism with direct control over land and administration was no longer acceptable to most people.

Revolution

Like the struggle against colonialism which had a tremendous impact upon the human rights and human dignity of a huge segment of humanity, the democratic revolution in Eastern Europe in 1989 also has far-reaching implications for political freedom and civil liberties. There is no doubt that the rights and principles contained in the UDHR and in the two main covenants served as valuable signposts for those committed, courageous activists in Solidarity and the Civic Forum in their long and arduous march to freedom.

Nevertheless, UN instruments and institutions had a very limited role in the Eastern European revolution. Popular aversion to state regimentation and authoritarianism, the rise of a middle-class conscious of individual rights, the failure of a rigid, centralized production system to respond to the changing consumer demands of an expanding middle-class, and constant exposure to Western media and culture over a period of time all contributed to the collapse of communist rule in Eastern Europe.

Our brief reflections on specific human rights situations and general trends since the UDHR suggest that the UN's contribution should be seen within the larger context of political and social changes affecting human rights. The UN, it is apparent, has been able to coax and cajole, even persuade and pressurize human rights transgressions. But it is in no position to transform the circumstances and structures that are responsible for the transgressions. Once the UN's role in determining the pace of progress in the human rights arena is put in proper perspective, it will be possible to locate the obstacles that lie in its path.

OBSTACLES

Sovereignty

National sovereignty, it is often argued, is a formidable barrier. No international body can ensure the faithful observance of human rights within a particular state as long as the principle and practice of national sovereignty remains central to international law. The UN charter itself recognizes the fundamental importance of national sovereignty. A state which may be a gross violator of the basic rights of its people can always claim that the well-being of its citizens is its own responsibility and no international institution should interfere in its domestic affairs. It is only the state, in other words, which has complete and absolute jurisdiction over the human rights of its people. In adopting such a position a state can, as it often does, seek sanctuary within the precincts of the UN Charter.

In the last forty odd years, a number of countries, both big and small, and of different ideological orientations, have used the cloak of national sovereignty to protect themselves from criticisms of their human rights records by the UN. Israel and South Africa, China and Indonesia, Turkey and Iraq, Kenya and Uganda, Chile and Argentina, among many others, have at different times accused various UN organs and agencies, including the Security Council and the Commission on Human Rights of interfering in their domestic affairs. This has often placed the UN in a dilemma. How does it reconcile its commitment to the human rights and human dignity of human beings everywhere, so lucidly articulated in the UDHR, with its pledge not "to intervene in matters which are essentially within the domestic jurisdiction of any state" as enshrined in the UN Charter? The first reflects an ideal the UN must pursue; the second represents a reality it must accept.

Its dilemma notwithstanding, the UN has, on occasions, criticized the violation of human rights by particular member-states. The General Assembly, for instance, has adopted numerous resolutions censuring Israel for suppressing the rights of the Palestinian people. However, these resolutions have not been acted upon. This is mainly because the United States has invariably used its veto in the Security Council—the UN organ which has the power to act against a transgressor of the UN charter—to kill any move against Israel.

When the US or some other superstate in the UN provides leave or license, the world body has been able to go beyond rhetoric. It has, through the Commission on Human Rights, carried out investigations into alleged human rights violations committed by certain member-states. A Special Rapporteur of the Commission prepares a report which is then presented to the General Assembly. Iran was investigated in this manner two years ago. This goes to show that the principle of domestic jurisdiction—however much a state may insist upon it—is not really an obstacle if the UN is determined to act.

Domestic jurisdiction has not been allowed to stand in the way of yet another type of UN action. The UN has, now and then, authorized massive humanitarian assistance to victims of famine, drought, and civil war. These would undoubtedly be human rights operations since they involve the most basic of all human rights: the right to life. These operations ensure that people have adequate food, clothing, and medicines. What is happening in Somalia today would be an example of UN intervention on behalf of a humanitarian cause. The humanitarian factor has also been the principal consideration in the UN's intervention in the former Yugoslavia.

In one recent instance, however, the humanitarian factor has served as a justification for a much broader human rights role for the UN. Following the exodus of tens of thousands of Kurds from northern Iraq, in the aftermath of the suppression of the Kurdish rebellion by the Baghdad government at the end of the Gulf War last year, the US and some of its Western allies decided to establish "safe havens" for the Kurds in northern Iraq. These "safe havens" are supposed to provide protection for the political, economic and cultural rights of the Kurds. They have the blessings of the UN: a Security Council resolution which demands that Iraq respect the rights of its people has been used to legitimize their establishment.

The UN's role in Iraq shows that national sovereignty as such is not as insurmountable a hurdle as it is made out to be. If certain powers which exercise immense influence upon the decision-making process within the UN want to enforce human rights in a particular country, there is no force on earth which can stop them.

It is this determination to enforce human rights in some situations, and yet ignore human rights in other situations, which is the real problem. It is a far more difficult problem to handle than national sovereignty. Indeed, as events are now beginning to reveal, the lack of consistency in the enforcement of human rights by the UN is having certain effects upon national sovereignty itself. . . . The UN Security Council has not only been totally inconsistent in its responses to human rights transgressions but has also been terribly unfair. Iraq is punished. Libya is penalized. But not Turkey. Nor Israel. Never the United States. For some reason this selective approach to justice is not difficult to comprehend. Turkey and Israel are allies of the US. The US controls and dominates the Security Council. And therefore nations like Iraq and Libya which are not prepared to acquiesce with US power and influence over the Arab world invariably earn the ire of the Security Council.

Gulf Crisis: Gulf War

Nothing in the entire history of the Security Council demonstrates more dramatically the power of the US over the body than the Gulf crisis of August 1990, which later became the Gulf War in January 1991. That is why it is important to examine the Gulf crisis in some detail in order to develop a proper understanding of how US domination of the Security Council resulted in the most blatant display ever of selective justice, of biased morality, of double standards in the annals of international relations.

When Iraq invaded Kuwait on 2 August 1990, the UN Security Council condemned the invasion and demanded that Iraqi forces withdraw immediately from Kuwaiti territory. This was the right thing to do since Iraq had committed a flagrant violation of the UN charter. From 2 August to 28 November 1990, the Council adopted a series of 10 resolutions on Iraq—from one imposing a trade and financial embargo on Iraq and occupied Kuwait to one condemning Iraq's attempt to change Kuwait's demographic composition. Then on 29 November, the Council authorized UN members "to use all necessary means" to bring about an Iraqi withdrawal. This was understood by everyone as a resolution which gave the UN the right to go to war.

It is significant that the war resolution—Resolution 678—was adopted without evaluating the impact of the Council's earlier economic embargo. This amounted to utter disregard for the UN Charter. For "according to Article 42, military measures can only be taken if the Security Council has found that other measurers have failed. In other words, before the vote on Resolution 678 on 29 November a formal decision should have been made that sanctions and diplomacy had been tried for a significant period of time and had not worked."

But the United States was not really interested in resolving the Gulf crisis in any other way, except through the use of military force. This is why it spurned all attempts to achieve an Iraqi withdrawal through negotiations and dialogue. There were a number of peace initiatives from within and without the region. In fact, the Iraqi government itself decided it would withdraw on 5 August and some Arab heads of government had already planned a meeting which would have endorsed a peace proposal formulated by the Palestinian leader Yasser Arafat. The proposal would have established a basis for resolving Iraqi-Kuwaiti disputes over oil, money, and territory. The United States, needless to say, sabotaged the proposal. It was because the US did not want a peaceful settlement that it did not allow the Security Council to initiate negotiations between the main protagonists. By its inaction, the Council had failed to uphold Chapter VI of the UN Charter which emphasizes the importance of "the Pacific Settlement of Disputes." . . .

Once the war began on 15th January 1991, the real motives behind US action became even clearer. It was not just to get Iraq out of Kuwait. The US, with the solid support of Israel, was determined to destroy Iraq's industrial and military strength. Only in this way could the US and Israel hope to preserve and perpetuate a power structure in the Arab world which ensured US dominance and Israeli supremacy. Besides, the US, argues Richard Falk, a distinguished American International Relations expert, wanted to demonstrate in the post-Cold War era that it "was able and willing to guarantee the interest of world capitalism" and uphold the security concerns of the industrialized world. Geopolitically the Gulf War can be seen as the first resource war of the new international era. It also finessed the perceived "danger" that the end of the Cold War would produce a so-called "peace dividend" that would weaken the Pentagon and the military in American society and lead to a shift in international relations from security to economics—that is, the area where the United States is weak in relation to Japan and Europe. While the United States has always sought to coax or coerce the Security Council to refrain from any action which is inimical to US interests, the Gulf War was perhaps the first occasion in UN history when the Security Council became an active agent of US foreign policy. As we have shown, it was not just one but a number of foreign policy objectives which the US tried to achieve. . . .

Even after the war ended, the Security Council continued to display its utter impotence in ensuring that justice and fair play prevailed. Though the Iraqi armed forces had been evicted from Kuwait, the Council refused to lift the economic sanctions against Iraq. After all, Iraq's invasion and occupation of Kuwait was the sole reason for the imposition of a trade and financial embargo via Resolution 661 in August 1990. Instead of abrogating the sanctions, the Council imposed new conditions . . . , requiring what is undoubtedly the most stringent regime of economic sanctions against any country in this century.

The determination of the Western powers to keep their tight grip upon Iraq is most vividly reflected in their manipulation of the issue of the elimination of Iraq's weapons of mass destruction. Immediately after the war, in March 1991, the UN began sending inspection teams to supervise the elimination of Iraq's weapons of mass destruction. Now after 18 months and "more than 40 UN inspection missions there is little, if any, evidence Baghdad is capable of firing Scud missiles, building an atomic bomb or using chemical or biological weapons." Though even some members of UN inspection teams have admitted openly that Iraq is in no position today to challenge anyone, the US and its allies continue to project Iraq as a major military threat to the stability of the Middle East . . . and by perpetuating this myth of a military threat and by using that as the rationale for maintaining economic sanctions against Iraq, the US has, with the help of the Security Council, brought death and disease to thousands and thousands of Iraqis. While it is difficult to provide accurate figures, it has been estimated that "in the first seven months of 1991, about 46,900 more children died in Iraq than would have been expected based on averages from the six years preceding the war." The number of deaths among adults has also increased by leaps and bounds. It is ironic that so many thousands of human beings should be deprived of the right to life—the most fundamental of human rights—by an organization which has pledged to protect the right to life. . . .

For Arabs and Muslims the crucial comparison is this: why has the UN not taken stern action against Israel which has been occupying Palestinian and Arab lands for the last 25 years? Why has the UN not gone beyond pious platitudes in dealing with the callous slaughter, the cruel massacre of thousands of Palestinians since the creation of Israel in 1948? Why has the UN made no attempt to inspect Israel's nuclear arsenal, its colossal military machine—more powerful, more devastating than that of any other nation in the Middle East? Why the double standards? Why this lop-sided justice?

And when ordinary Arabs and Muslims compare the UN's actions in Iraq with its lukewarm response to the situation in Bosnia-Herzegovina, their disillusionment is total. Though there are significant differences in the two situations, they cannot understand why the UN Security Council has done so little to check Serbian aggression against Bosnian Muslims in particular—aggression which seeks to wipe out a whole community, aggression which is nothing less than an ethnic pogrom. Once again, they conclude—and rightly—that the UN is neither willing nor capable of protecting human rights qua human rights. There is no universal application or implementation of human rights. The UN is selective, it is biased in its response to human rights violations. The UN—and this is not a perception confined to Arabs and Muslims—will act only when it is allowed to act. The UN, in other words, is nothing more than an instrument of the US and other Western powers. The UN, in the eyes of a lot of people, has no credibility. It has no integrity.

UN Failure and National Sovereignty

Because a lot of people and many states in the South have little faith in the UN's ability to apply human rights standards in a just and fair manner, they have begun to argue that national sovereignty should be protected at all costs—since national sovereignty is the only way of safeguarding the human rights of the masses which are now threatened by a powerful state in a unipolar world. All that they have to do is to point to the plight of Iraq and Libya as they try to defend their sovereignty in the face of the US's superpower expressed through the UN's most important organ.

National sovereignty is thus becoming a protective armour for the states of the South trapped within an international system where the strong do what they will and the weak suffer what they must. It is an armour which, from a human rights angle, could have a positive effect just as it could have negative consequences. There are times when it will be used for the protection of the collective rights of communities and peoples. But there will also be occasions when ruling elites in the South will use the armour to ward off legitimate criticisms from foreign governments and international organizations about gross violations of fundamental human rights—especially civil and political rights—within their nation-states. More often than not, however, the same ruling elite uses national sovereignty for both purposes: to defend the rights of its people as a collectivity within an unjust global order and, at the same time, to suppress dissent within its own boundaries with impunity. There is perhaps no better example of this than Iraq. While Iraq is a tragic victim of blatant authoritarianism in international politics, its government is an unrepentant dictatorship which has, over the years, imposed some of the severest political curbs upon its own people.

But dictatorships like Iraq, as it should be obvious, derive part of their sustenance from an unjust international system which oppresses them. As long as the United States as the sole military superpower within this system bullies and harasses small states which refuse to submit to her will, it will always be possible for the leaders of these states to persuade their people to give them total support. This enables the leaders to exercise maximum control over their citizens, to monopolize power in the name of defending the integrity of the nation and the sovereignty of the people.

The International System

This does not mean that if the international system was just and equitable, there would be no dictatorships. The desire to dominate and control, the tendency to accumulate and centralize power, has been part and parcel of the saga of government and politics since the beginning of time. Besides, there are forces in society, outside the parameters of state power, which are also sometimes responsible for the deprivation of the rights of certain groups. Why women have been denied their rights as human beings in certain societies is a complex issue, which is linked to tradition and culture and rooted in patriarchal structures. A change in the international power structure is not going to guarantee equality for all women. Similarly, caste attitudes and caste practices which challenge the most basic rights of millions and millions of downtrodden Hindus in India will not disappear the moment an equitable international system emerges. Nonetheless, if the international system was just and fair to each and every nation and community, if human rights standards and principles were applied equitably to each and every human being, it would be so much easier for people everywhere to combine their energies to fight against dictatorial regimes and authoritarian practices. There is no denying that the selective justice, the biased morality of the strong so prevalent today prevents people from South and North, East and West from joining forces, from working together, for the triumph of human rights in every nook and corner of the globe. This is why a just and equitable international system is so important for the success of the UDHR and other related covenants, declarations and conventions.

Conversely, what this implies is that the present unjust, iniquitous international system is one of the major obstacles in the way of a holistic, universal realization of human rights; it is a system which concentrates effective power in the hands of the dominant elites of a few nations in the North. These are the elites who direct, decide, and determine the political, economic, cultural, and intellectual life of the people of this planet. They have created a system which ensures that the interests of the strong and the powerful take precedence over the welfare of the weak and the powerless.

What does all this mean for human rights? It means that while a minority of the world's population enjoys the privileges of ease and affluence, the vast majority of humanity continues to be deprived of their most basic rights. Isn't it a matter of some significance that in 1990 over one billion people lived in absolute poverty, about a billion adults could not read or write, one and a half billion people were deprived of primary health care? What human rights are we talking about when human beings cannot even fulfill the fundamental conditions for being human? How can we espouse the cause of a common humanity, advocate the concept of "one world" when the rich-poor gap, the North-South divide is so formidable?

The report of the South Commission puts the matter in proper perspective when it says, "Were all humanity a single nation-state, the present North-South divide would make it an unviable, semi-feudal entity, split by internal conflicts. Its small part is advanced, prosperous, powerful; its much bigger part is under-developed, poor, powerless. A nation so divided within itself would be recognized as unstable. A world so divided should likewise be recognized as inherently unstable. And the position is worsening, not improving."

An international system which is so palpably unjust and unfair to human-kind cannot be expected to protect human rights and human dignity. This is why the United Nations, a product of this unjust international system, has failed to live up to its own expectations—of translating into reality the ideals of the UDHR. Indeed, the UN will act only if the strong and powerful who control the international system allow it to act. They have structured the UN and pro-grammed its activities in such a way that the world body will, first and foremost, reflect their interests and aspirations.

Security Council

This is mirrored in the structure and composition of the UN Security Coun-cil. The military superpower of our time—the United States—and its two West-ern allies, Britain and France, together with Russia and China are permanent members of the Council. Each of them has the right to veto any decision of the Council. Permanent membership, and what is worse, the right to veto, repudiate every known principle of democratic participation. They create a special class of UN members with extraordinary powers at their command. Their presence and their vote have much greater weight and value than that of other member-states which negates the idea of one nation, one vote. Besides, the veto can be used—as it has been used—to nullify a majority decision of the Security Council which may well be aimed at protecting the human rights of an oppressed people. How can the UN, with such an undemocratically structured Security Council at its vortex, campaign for universal human rights as envisaged in the UDHR? Cynics may be tempted to hurl that ancient adage at the UN: physician, heal thyself!

Restricting the Meaning of Human Rights

That the US and its Western allies wield tremendous influence over the UN system is demonstrated in yet another way. Though the UDHR, and more so, the two covenants and later conventions and declarations try to articulate a truly holistic, integrated concept of human rights, the UN Commission of Human Rights has, through its work and activities, restricted human rights to civil, political, and cultural rights. When the Commission investigates the alleged violation of human rights it is, more often than not, some political freedom or civil liberty which some government somewhat has trampled upon. It has never investigated the violation of some economic rights, rights which have to be monitored over a period of time before one can come to some definite conclusions. An execution, or torture, or detention without trial amount to human rights violations which can be judged immediately and acted upon. Nevertheless, the fact remains that neither the Commission nor the Centre for Human Rights has developed mechanisms and strategies for evaluating a member-state's performance in the protection of the economic and social rights of its citizens.

Part of the reason for this lies in the way in which the dominant segment of Western society perceives human rights. Invariably, human rights are equated with individual civil and political rights. This has a lot to do with the history and evolution of human rights within the Western political and intellectual tradition. There is no doubt that this tradition has shaped thinking with the UN on human rights.

More than that, major Western powers, like the US and its allies, have an interest in ensuring that human rights are equated to individual civil and political rights—period. It is an equation which, within the arena of international politics, keeps the spotlight on countries of the South—more precisely, on their summary execution of dissidents, their torture of political prisoners, their detention without trial of social critics, and so on. At the same time, "the human rights equal to civil and political rights" approach pushes into the background the success of certain Southern countries in looking after the economic and social rights of their people. To put it differently, it is an approach which allows Western governments and Western human rights groups to condemn China for suppressing human rights—a condemnation which ignores the fact that the same China has succeeded in securing one of the most basic human rights of all, the right of food, of more than a billion human beings. Because economic rights are not quite human rights within mainstream Western thinking no attempt is made to distinguish the suppression of political rights from the protection of economic rights. It is a measure of the inordinate power of the dominant West that it has succeeded in narrowing, and indeed, distorting the UN's own balanced, universal concept of human rights.

Economic Agenda

Just as Western domination has had an adverse impact upon the UN's political role (via the Security Council) and its human rights activities (via the Human Rights Commission), it has also generated a negative effect upon the UN's economic agenda. Though the UN, through its Economic and Social Council and through various agencies, had, right from the outset, sought to promote the economic and social rights of the less developed nations in particular, the major Western powers were never really keen on allowing the UN to assume a significant role in economic and social affairs. . . . .

This is most apparent in one particular area—debt. Many countries of the South, caught in the web of prevailing financial and economic relationships, are heavily indebted to lending agencies and institutions in the North. In order to service their debts, governments are often forced to cut back upon the basic needs of the populace. . . . What is sad is that faced with a problem like the debt which has such a devastating impact upon the most fundamental of all rights—the right to life—the UN appears to be totally helpless. The powers that dictate the international affairs have made sure that the UN will have no role. It is very likely the UN's already negligible role in the world economy will be further circumscribed once the current restructuring of the UN is completed. . . .

The downgrading of the UN's economic and social programmes is a grievous blow to the South in particular. For it was the South which fought so hard to strengthen this dimension of the UN, Southern states used their numerical power in the UN General Assembly, especially in the late sixties and seventies, to create various social and economic programmes which are now being closed down. This was also the time that they managed to establish the United Nations Conference on Trade and Development (UNCTAD), otherwise known as the Group of 77. UNCTAD was the South's attempt to protect its interests vis-à-vis commodity prices, trade, investments and technology through the UN. Today, it has become totally irrelevant in global trade negotiations. By the same token, the South's New International Economic Order (NIEO), with its promise of justice and equality, proclaimed by the UN General Assembly in 1974, has faded into oblivion.

Information Flow

This goes to show that in the post-Cold War era, the major Western and Industrial powers led by the US are more determined than ever to re-shape and restructure the UN in the interest of their sectarian aims and objectives. In fact, even before the end of the Cold War, they had destroyed yet another Southern idea—the New International Information Order (NIIO)—which sought to give a voice to the voiceless millions of Asia, Africa and Latin America through a more just and equitable flow of news and information. The US and its allies launched a vigorous campaign against the proposed NIIO and its advocates especially those with the UN system. They feared that if the South gained equitable access to the main information arteries of the world, their tight grip upon global communication would be threatened. After all, more than 90 percent of the world news is controlled by four news agencies, all located in the North. Today, there are very few individuals, within or without the UN system, who would even whisper about a New International Information Order.

The death of the NIIO proved once again that for the nations and peoples of the South, the UDHR's "freedom of opinion and expression" and freedom "to receive and impart information and ideas" would remain unfulfilled hopes. Indirectly, the UN had not only helped to perpetuate the domination of the South by the North in the sphere of news and information, but it had also, perhaps unwittingly, contributed to the continuing intellectual bondage of the South.

Weapons and War

The UN has failed the people of the South in yet another sense. It has failed to save them from "the scourge of war." While there has been relative peace in the North since the end of the Second World War, there have been at least 145 armed conflicts in the South which have claimed 30 million lives. In many of these wars, Northern powers, usually the United States, sometimes the former Soviet Union, have been involved in one way or another. Invariably, the arms come from the North.

The UN has not been able to prevent wars of this sort from breaking out. To put it in another way, it has not been able to maintain peace, to protect human life—which is the primary purpose of its very existence.

Part of the explanation for this would lie in the overwhelming power of the United States and, to a much lesser extent, the former Soviet Union vis-à-vis the UN. They could ignore the UN as they pursued their imperial goal of expanding and enhancing their power and influence over all the world. They produced and developed weapons as they liked. They sold weapons to whomever they wanted.

One would have thought that a world today established to prevent war would, as a matter of priority, seek to exercise some form of control over the production and sale of weapons. The UN should have been equipped with the authority to check, nay to curb, the manufacture and proliferation of all weapons of mass destruction. But this was not possible during the long years of the Cold War since armed might was a vital element in superpower competition and conflict. Now the Cold War is over. There is only one superpower left. And yet, the UN is in no position to bring arms production and sales under its control.

This, in fact, underscores the real challenge facing the UN today. The UN has to be reformed and restructured so that it can maintain peace and prevent war, protect human rights and enhance human dignity.

Report

A restructured UN, it goes without saying, could deal with the violation of every type of human right—and not just civil and political rights. As a first step towards this end, the Centre for Human Rights should prepare an annual or at least a triennial report on the human rights situation within each member-state and within the international system. The report would thus contain sections which address the economic, social, cultural, civil, and political rights of individuals and communities within a state during a certain period of time. It would, besides, discuss the impact of a global system upon the economic or political, civil or cultural rights of the people. . . .

Given the importance of human rights in both the charter and the UDHR and its significance in today's world, a substantial sum of money should be allocated for human rights monitoring and investigations, for human rights education and training. In fact, UN personnel will have to be specially trained to handle the complex challenge arising from greater emphasis upon a holistic, integrated approach to human rights.

The UN human rights report should be widely publicized. It should be given maximum coverage in both national and international print and electronic media. The UN's annual (or triennial) human rights report should be regarded by all as the most authoritative statement on the human rights situation in each country and within the international community. For the report to attain such a high level of credibility, it should be fair and balanced. This is possible only if national interests—especially the interests of powerful states—are not allowed to influence the content and character of the report.

Within the UN system itself, the report should be presented to the General Assembly. The General Assembly should debate the recommendations contained in the report. It is only the Assembly that should have the power to decide whether action should be taken against a particular state or even a particular commercial or industrial corporation which is guilty of misconduct. Whenever gross violation of a fundamental human right on a massive scale has been proven—the industrial genocide committed by Union Carbide against thousands of people in Bhopal, India, in December 1984 would be an outstanding example—the General Assembly should not hesitate to act. Action can take various forms, from compensation to the victims, to economic sanctions against the violator, to military intervention by the UN. But whatever the action, the important point to remember is that only the Assembly—and not the Security Council—should have the right to authorize action in the defence of human rights. Indeed, the right to use force even in dire circumstances should be the exclusive prerogative of the Assembly.

The General Assembly

The intention is clear: reform of the UN must lead to the strengthening of the General Assembly. The General Assembly should also have the authority over those areas in international relations which impinge directly upon human rights.

One of the most crucial of these areas is, of course, the production and sale of weapons—an issue which we have examined in some detail. The General Assembly should perhaps create an agency under its jurisdiction which will oversee the production and sale of all weapons of mass destruction in particular . . . for if the General Assembly can control arms it would be a boon to the human rights struggle. If it can also bring the major international economic institutions and arrangements under its direction, it would be an even greater blessing for human dignity. . . . Since the General Assembly is dominated numerically by states with meagre to modest national incomes, it is quite conceivable that it will—given a chance—undertake to reform existing economic institutions and arraignments so that they will benefit the poor and powerless masses. The issues that are so often espoused by UNCTAD provide some inkling of the sort of economic reforms that a General Assembly endowed with power and authority could be expected to pursue. Debt alleviation, apart from more trade opportunities and technology transfer in favour of the South, would undoubtedly be high on the agenda of such an Assembly. An effective General Assembly then offers some hope for the protection of the economic and social rights of the majority of the human race.

A strong General assembly is important for yet another reason. For the Assembly includes all member-states, big and small, rich and poor. Since it observes the principle of one-nation, one-vote it equalizes everyone, at least in theory. It is, in that sense, a truly democratic forum. It reflects, more than most other organs within the UN system, some of the values and principles underlying the UDHR.

Security Council

By strengthening the General Assembly, we are in fact endowing it with greater importance than the Security Council. This is as it should be. For the Council, as we have seen, is an undemocratic institution structured to preserve and perpetuate the dominance of the US and its Western allies. This is why there is an urgent need to reform the Council. The veto should be abolished. There should be no permanent members. Membership of the Council should be based upon the concept of regional representation. Each region should be given a certain number of seats on the Council, calculated on the basis of its total population. Thus, East Asia covering China, Japan and the two Koreas with more than 1.4 billion human beings will be given more seats than Western Europe or North America. The restructured Council will of course be bigger than the present Security Council. It may even have 30 to 40 members. . . . What is important is that the proposed Council will be genuinely representative of humankind. In composition it will be truly democratic. Such a Council can stand up and fight for human rights with a clear conscience. No one will be able to point a finger at its composition and accuse the Council of hypocrisy.

The restructured Council that we envisage here—unlike the present Security Council—will be concerned largely with the implementation of policies and decisions made by the General Assembly. It will be a body which executes, which implements, but which does not determine policy. Properly speaking, it should be known as the Executive Council of the General Assembly, assisted by the Secretary-General. The Secretary-General will continue to play a pivotal role within the UN system and will even submit proposals direct to the General Assembly for its consideration.

It does not require much insight to realize that democratization of the UN will be opposed by those very nations which today parade the world stage as the greatest champions of human rights. They will fight tooth and nail to preserve the existing undemocratic order. At the very most, they may be willing to make some meaningless concessions which will not affect the status quo.

The organized opposition of the powerful to the reform of the UN should not deter those of us who are committed to human rights and human dignity from continuing our just struggle for an equitable international system. For we must remember that only a restructured UN will be able to protect the Universal Declaration of Human Rights (UDHR). Only a reformed UN will be able to realize the rights of all human beings everywhere.

A major Franco-American literary theorist of the late twentieth century, René Girard is Hammond Professor of French Language, Literature, and Civilization at Stanford University. He belongs to a long list of theorists who view violence as grounded in notions of universal and essential human nature. He is best known for his scapegoat theory and his exploration of the cyclical nature of vengeance. In his oft-cited work, Violence and the Sacred *(1977), he articulates a notion of substitionary sacrifice as crucial to breaking the cycle of vengeance and so preventing broader scale, and less containable, forms of violence. Yet Girard bifurcates primitive from judicial social forms and focuses exclusively on the sacrificial victim as a judicially prescribed but otherwise abstract person. He begs the question, taken up so eloquently by Pierre Bourdieu, of the violence of the "modes of domination." It is the latter—specifically, the modes of racism, xenophobia, sexism, classism, homophobia, and ageism that are integral to systemic violence—which produce the classes and marginalized groups from which Girard's victims are taken. If the danger of Bourdieu's work is to frame all humankind as potential victims, the danger of Girard's is to define violence so narrowly that most of our lived experiences of violence fall beyond the realm of his definition. All of this is particularly ironic: despite Girard's assertions that the nature and existence of violence is only revealed from the position of the victim, it is just this position which Girard himself, at least within a theoretical text such as* Violence and the Sacred, *occludes.*

Though he also has written on more strictly literary topics (such as A Theatre of Envy: William Shakespeare *[1991]), Girard's reputation rests on his theoretically sophisticated, but sociologically thin, reworking of major arguments about religion and violence. His other works include* The Scapegoat *(1986) and* Things Hidden since the Foundation of the World *(1987).*

Violence and the Sacred

RENÉ GIRARD

Sacrifice plays a very real role in these societies, and the problem of substitution concerns the entire community. The victim is not a substitute for some particularly endangered individual, nor is it offered up to some individual of particularly bloodthirsty temperament. Rather, it is a substitute for all the members of the community, offered up by the members themselves. The sacrifice serves to protect the entire community from its *own* violence; it prompts the entire community to choose victims outside itself. The elements of dissension scattered throughout the community are drawn to the person of the sacrificial victim and eliminated, at least temporarily, by its sacrifice.

If we turn our attention from the theological superstructure of the act—that is, from an interpretive version of the event that is often accepted as the final statement on sacrifice—we quickly perceive yet another level of religious discourse, in theory subordinated to the theological dimension, but in reality quite independent of it. This has to do with the social function of the act, an aspect far more accessible to the modern mind.

It is easy to ridicule a religion by concentrating on its more eccentric rites, rites such as the sacrifices performed to induce rain or bring fine weather. There is in fact no object or endeavor in whose name a sacrifice cannot be made, especially when the social basis of the act has begun to blur. Nevertheless, there is a common denominator that determines the efficacy of all sacrifices and that becomes increasingly apparent as the institution grows in vigor. This common denominator is internal violence—all the dissensions, rivalries, jealousies, and quarrels within the community that the sacrifices are designed to suppress. The purpose of the sacrifice is to restore harmony to the community, to reinforce the social fabric. Everything else derives from that. If once we take this fundamental approach to sacrifice, choosing the road that violence opens before us, we can see that there is no aspect of human existence foreign to the subject, not even material prosperity. When men no longer live in harmony with one another, the sun still shines and the rain falls, to be sure, but the fields are less well tended, the harvests less abundant.

The classic literature of China explicitly acknowledges the propitiatory function of sacrificial rites. Such practices "pacify the country and make the people settled. . . . It is through the sacrifices that the unity of the people is strengthened" (CH'U YU II, 2). The *Book of Rites* affirms that sacrificial ceremonies, music, punishments, and laws have one and the same end: to unite society and establish order.

In attempting to formulate the fundamental principles of sacrifice without reference to the ritualistic framework in which the sacrifice takes place, we run the risk of appearing simplistic. Such an effort smacks strongly of "psychologizing." Clearly it would be inexact to compare the sacrificial act to the spontaneous gesture of the man who kicks his dog because he dares not kick his wife or boss. However, there are Greek myths that are hardly more than colossal variants of such gestures. Such a one is the story of Ajax. Furious at the leaders of the Greek army, who refused to award him Achilles' weapons, Ajax slaughters the herd of sheep intended as provisions for the army. In his mad rage he mistakes these gentle creatures for the warriors on whom he means to vent his rage. The slaughtered animals belong to a species traditionally utilized by the Greeks for sacrificial purposes; but because the massacre takes place outside the ritual framework, Ajax is taken for a madman. The myth is not, strictly speaking, about the sacrificial process; but it is certainly not irrelevant to it. The institution of sacrifice is based on effects analogous to those produced by Ajax's anger—but structured, channeled, and held in check by fixed laws.

In the ritualistic societies most familiar to us—those of the Jews and of the Greeks of the classical age—the sacrificial victims are almost always animals. However, there are other societies in which human victims are substituted for the individuals who are threatened by violence.

Even in fifth century Greece—the Athens of the great tragedians—human sacrifice had not, it seems, completely disappeared. The practice was perpetuated in the form of the pharmakos, maintained by the city at its own expense and slaughtered at the appointed festivals as well as at a moment of civic disaster. If examined closely for traces of human sacrifice, Greek tragedy offers some remarkable revelations. It is clear, for example, that the story of Medea parallels that of Ajax on the sacrificial level, although here we are dealing with human rather than with animal sacrifice. In Euripides' *Medea* the principle of human substitution of one victim for another appears in its most savage form. Frightened by the intensity of Medea's rage against her faithless husband, Jason, the nurse begs the children's tutor to keep his charges out of their mother's way:

> I am sure her anger will not subside until it has found a victim.
> Let us pray that the victim is at least one of our enemies!

Because the object of her hatred is out of reach, Medea substitutes her own children. It is difficult for us to see anything resembling a religious act in Medea's insane behavior. Nonetheless, infanticide has its place among ritualistic practices; the practice is too well documented in too many cultures (including the Jewish and the ancient Greek) for us to exclude it from consideration here. Medea's crime is to ritual infanticide what the massacre of sheep in the *Ajax* is to animal sacrifice. Medea prepares for the death of her children like a priest preparing for a sacrifice. Before the fateful act, she issues the traditional ritual announcement: all those whose presence might in any way hinder the effectiveness of the ceremony are requested to remove themselves from the premises.

Medea, like Ajax, reminds us of a fundamental truth about violence; if left unappeased, violence will accumulate until it overflows its confines and floods the surrounding area. The role of sacrifice is to stop this rising tide of indiscriminate substitutions and redirect violence into "proper" channels.

Ajax has details that underline the close relationship between the sacrificial substitution of animals and of humans. Before he sets upon the flock of sheep, Ajax momentarily contemplates the sacrifice of his own son. The boy's mother does not take this threat lightly; she whisks the child away.

In a general study of sacrifice there is little reason to differentiate between human and animal victims. When the principle of the substitution is *physical resemblance* between the vicarious victim and its prototypes, the mere fact that both victims are human beings seems to suffice. Thus, it is hardly surprising that in some societies whole categories of human beings are systematically reserved for sacrificial purposes in order to protect other categories.

I do not mean to minimize the gap that exists between the societies that practice human sacrifice and those that do not. However, this gap should not prevent us from perceiving what they have in common. Strictly speaking, there is no essential difference between animal sacrifice and human sacrifice, and in many cases one is substituted for the other. Our tendency to insist on differences that have little reality when discussing the institution of sacrifice—our reluctance, for example, to equate animal with human sacrifice—is undoubtedly a factor in the extraordinary misunderstandings that still persist in that area of human culture.

This reluctance to consider all forms of sacrifice as a single phenomenon is nothing new. Joseph de Maistre, having defined the principal of sacrificial substitution, makes the bold and wholly unsubstantiated assertion that this principle does not apply to human sacrifice. One cannot, he insists, kill a man to save a man. Yet this assertion is repeatedly contradicted by Greek tragedy, implicitly in a play like *Medea*, and explicitly elsewhere in Euripides.

In Euripides' *Electra*, Clytemnestra explains that the sacrifice of her daughter Iphigenia would have been justified if it had been to save human lives. The tragedian thus enlightens us, by way of Clytemnestra, on the "normal" function of human sacrifice—the function de Maistre had refused to acknowledge. If, says Clytemnestra, Agamemnon had permitted his daughter to die:

> ... in order to prevent the sack of the city, to help his home, to rescue his children, sacrificing one to save the others, I could then have pardoned him. But for the sake of brazen Helen ... !

Without ever expressly excluding the subject of human sacrifice from their research—and indeed, on what grounds could they do so?—modern scholars, notably Hubert and Mauss, mention it but rarely in their theoretical discussions. On the other hand, the scholars who do concern themselves with human sacrifice tend to concentrate on it to the exclusion of everything else, dwelling at length on the "sadistic" or "barbarous" aspects of the custom. Here, again, one particular form of sacrifice is isolated from the subject as a whole.

This dividing of sacrifice into two categories, human and animal, has itself a sacrificial character, in a strictly ritualistic sense. The division is based in effect on a value judgement, on the preconception that one category of victim—the human being—is quite unsuitable for sacrificial purposes, while another category—the animal—is eminently sacrificeable. We encounter here a survival of the sacrificial mode of thinking that perpetuates a misunderstanding about the institution as a whole. It is not a question of rejecting the value judgment on which this misunderstanding is based, but of putting it, so to speak, in parentheses, of recognizing that as far as the institution is concerned, such judgments are purely arbitrary. All reduction into categories, whether implicit or explicit, must be avoided; all victims, animal or human, must be treated in the same fashion if we wish to apprehend the criteria by which victims are selected (if indeed such criteria exist) and discover (if such a thing is possible) a universal principle for their selection.

We have remarked that all victims, even the animal ones, bear a certain *resemblance* to the object they replace; otherwise the violent impulse would remain unsatisfied. But this resemblance must not be carried to the extreme of complete assimilation, or it would lead to disastrous confusion. In the case of animal victims the difference is always clear, and no such confusion is possible. Although they do their best to empathize with their cattle, the Nuers never quite manage to mistake a man for a cow—the proof being that they always sacrifice the latter, never the former. I am lapsing into the trap of Lévy-Bruhl's "primitive mentality." I am not saying that primitive man is less capable of making distinctions than we moderns.

In order for a species or category of living creature, human or animal, to appear suitable for sacrifice, it must bear a sharp resemblance to the *human* categories excluded from the ranks of the "sacrificeable," while still maintaining a degree of difference that forbids all possible confusion. As I have said, no mistake is possible in the case of animal sacrifice. But it is quite another case with human victims. If we look at the extremely wide spectrum of human victims sacrificed by various societies, the list seems heterogeneous, to say the least. It includes prisoners of war, slaves, small children, unmarried adolescents, and the handicapped; it ranges from the very dregs of society, such as the Greek pharmakos, to the king himself.

Is it possible to detect a unifying factor in this disparate group? We notice at first glance beings who are either outside or on the fringes of society: prisoners of war, slaves, pharmakos. In many primitive societies children who have not yet undergone the rites of initiation have no proper place in the community; their rights and duties are almost nonexistent. What we are dealing with, therefore, are exterior or marginal individuals, incapable of establishing or sharing the social bonds that link the rest of the inhabitants. Their status as foreigners or enemies, their servile condition, or simply their age prevents these future victims from fully integrating themselves into the community.

But what about the king? Is he not at the very heart of the community? Undoubtedly—but it is precisely his position at the center that serves to isolate him from his fellow men, to render him casteless. He escapes from society, so to speak, via the roof, just as the pharmakos escapes through the cellar. The king has a sort of foil, however, in the person of his fool. The fool shares his master's status as an outsider—an isolation whose literal truth is often of greater significance than the easily reversible symbolic values often attributed to it. From every point of view the fool is eminently "sacrificeable," and the king can use him to vent his own anger. But it sometimes happens that the king himself is sacrificed, and that (among certain African societies) in a thoroughly regulated and highly ritualistic manner.

It is clearly legitimate to define the difference between sacrificeable and nonsacrificeable individuals in terms of their degree of integration, but such a definition is not yet sufficient. In many cultures women are not considered full-fledged members of their society; yet women are never, or rarely, selected as sacrificial victims. There may be a simple explanation for this fact. The married woman retains her ties with her parents' clan even after she has become in some respects the property of her husband and his family. To kill her would be to run the risk of one of the two groups' interpreting her sacrifice as an act of murder committing it to the reciprocal act of revenge. The notion of vengeance casts a new light on the matter. All our sacrificial victims, whether chosen from one of the human categories enumerated above or, *a fortiori*, from the animal realm, are invariably distinguishable from the nonsacrificeable beings by one essential characteristic: between these victims and the community a crucial social link is missing, so they can be exposed to violence without fear of reprisal. Their death does not automatically entail an act of vengeance.

The considerable importance this freedom from reprisal has for the sacrificial process makes us understand that sacrifice is primarily an act of violence without risk of vengeance. We also understand the paradox—not without its comic aspects on occasion—of the frequent references to vengeance in the course of sacrificial rites, the veritable obsession with vengeance when no chance of vengeance exists:

> For the act they were about to commit elaborate excuses were offered; they shuddered at the prospect of the sheep's death, they wept over it as though they were its parents. Before the blow was struck, they implored the beast's forgiveness. They then addressed themselves to the species to which the

beast belonged, as if addressing a large family clan, beseeching it not to seek vengeance for the act that was about to be inflicted on one of its members. In the same vein the actual murderer was punished in some manner, either beaten or sent into exile.

It is the entire species *considered as a large family clan* that the sacrificers beseech not to seek vengeance. By incorporating the element of reprisal into the ceremony, the participants are hinting broadly at the true function of the rite, the kind of action it was designed to circumvent and the criteria that determined the choice of victim. The desire to commit an act of violence on those near us cannot be suppressed without a conflict; we must divert that impulse, therefore, toward the sacrificial victim, the creature we can strike down without fear of reprisal, since he lacks a champion.

Like everything that touches on the essential nature of the sacrificial act, the true distinction between the sacrificeable and the nonsacrificeable is never clearly articulated. Oddities and inexplicable anomalies confuse the picture. For instance, some animal species will be formally excluded from sacrifice, but the exclusion of members of the community is never mentioned. In constantly drawing attention to the truly maniacal aspects of sacrifice, modern theorists only serve to perpetuate an old misunderstanding in new terms. Men can dispose of their violence more efficiently if they regard the process not as something emanating from within themselves, but as a necessity imposed from without, a divine decree whose least infraction calls down terrible punishment. When they banish sacrificial practices from the "real," everyday world, modern theorists continue to misrepresent the violence of sacrifice.

The function of sacrifice is to quell violence within the community and to prevent conflicts from erupting. Yet societies like our own, which do not, strictly speaking, practice sacrificial rites, seem to get along without them. Violence undoubtedly exists within our society, but not to such an extent that the society itself is threatened with extinction. The simple fact that sacrificial practices, and other rites as well, can disappear without catastrophic results should in part explain the failure of ethnology and theology to come to grips with these cultural phenomena, and explain as well our modern reluctance to attribute a real function to them. After all, it is hard to maintain that institutions for which, as it seems, we have no need are actually indispensable.

It may be that a basic difference exists between a society like ours and societies imbued with religion—a difference that is partially hidden from us by rites, particularly by rites of sacrifice, that play a compensatory role. This difference would help explain why the actual function of sacrifice still eludes us.

When internal strife, previously sublimated by means of sacrificial practices, rises to the surface, it manifests itself in interfamily vendettas or blood feuds. This kind of violence is virtually nonexistent in our own culture. And perhaps it is here that we should look for the fundamental difference between primitive societies and our own; we should examine the specific ailments to which we are immune and which sacrifice manages to control, if not to eliminate.

Why does the spirit of revenge, wherever it breaks out, constitute such an intolerable menace? Perhaps because the only satisfactory revenge for spilt blood is spilling the blood of the killer; and in the blood feud there is no clear distinction between the act for which the killer is being punished and the punishment itself. Vengeance professes to be an act of reprisal, and every reprisal calls for another reprisal. The crime to which the act of vengeance addresses itself is almost never an unprecedented offense; in almost every case it has been committed in revenge for some prior crime.

Vengeance, then, is an interminable, infinitely repetitive process. Every time it turns up in some part of the community, it threatens to involve the whole social body. There is the risk that the act of vengeance will initiate a chain reaction whose consequences will quickly prove fatal to any society of modest size. The multiplication of reprisals instantaneously puts the very existence of a society in jeopardy, and that is why it is universally proscribed.

Curiously enough, it is in the very communities where the proscription is most strictly enforced that vengeance seems to hold sway. Even when it remains in the background, its role in the community unacknowledged, the specter of vengeance plays an important role in shaping the relationships among individuals. That is not to say that the prohibition against acts of vengeance is taken lightly. Precisely because murder inspires horror and because men must be forcibly restrained from murder, vengeance is inflicted on all those who commit it. The obligation never to shed blood cannot be distinguished from the obligation to exact vengeance on those who shed it. If men wish to prevent an interminable outbreak of vengeance (just as today we wish to prevent nuclear war), it is not enough to convince their fellows that violence is detestable—for it is precisely because they detest violence that men make a duty of vengeance.

In a world still haunted by the specter of vengeance, it is difficult to theorize about vengeance without resorting to equivocations or paradoxes. In Greek tragedy, for instance, there is not—and cannot be—any consistent stand on the subject. To attempt to extract a coherent theory of vengeance from the drama is to miss the essence of tragedy. For in tragedy each character passionately embraces or rejects vengeance depending on the position he occupies at any given moment in the scheme of the drama.

Vengeance is a vicious circle whose effect on primitive societies can only be surmised. For us the circle has been broken. We owe our good fortune to one of our social institutions above all: our judicial system, which serves to deflect the menace of vengeance. The system does not suppress vengeance; rather, it effectively limits it to a single act of reprisal, enacted by a sovereign authority specializing in this particular function. The decisions of the judiciary are invariably presented as the final word on vengeance.

Vocabulary is perhaps more revealing here than judicial theories. Once the concept of interminable revenge has been formally rejected, it is referred to as *private* vengeance. The term implies the existence of a *public* vengeance, a counterpart never made explicit. By definition, primitive societies have only private vengeance. Thus, public vengeance is the exclusive property of well-policed societies, and our society calls it the judicial system.

Our penal system operates according to principles of justice that are in no real conflict with the concept of revenge. The same principle is at work in all systems of violent retribution. Either the principle is just, and justice is therefore inherent in the idea of vengeance, or there is no justice to be found anywhere. He who exacts his own vengeance is said to "take the law into his own hands." There is no difference of principle between private and public vengeance; but on the social level, the difference is enormous. Under the public system, an act of vengeance is no longer avenged; the process is terminated, the danger of escalation averted.

The absence of a judicial system in primitive societies has been confirmed by ethnologists. Malinowski concludes that "the 'criminal' aspect of law in savage communities is perhaps even vaguer than the civil one; the idea of 'justice' in our sense [is] hardly applicable and the means of restoring a disturbed tribal equilibrium [are] slow and cumbersome."

Radcliffe-Brown's conclusions are identical, and summon up, as such conclusions must, the specter of perpetual vengeance: "Thus, though the Andaman Islanders had a well-developed social conscience, that is, a system of moral notions as to what is right and wrong, there was no such thing as punishment of a crime by the society. If one person injured another it was left to the injured one to seek vengeance if he wished and if he dared. There were probably always some who would side with the criminal, their attachment to him overcoming their disapproval of his actions."

The anthropologist Robert Lowie speaks of the "administering of justice" in reference to primitive societies. He distinguishes two types of societies, those that possess a "central authority," and those that do not. Among the latter it is the parental group, he declares, that exercises the judicial power, and *this group confronts the other group in the same way that a sovereign state confronts the outside world*. There can be no true "administering of justice," no judicial system without a superior tribunal capable of arbitrating between even the most powerful groups. Only that superior tribunal can remove the possibility of blood feud or perpetual vendetta. Lowie himself recognizes that this condition is not always met: "From the supreme law of group solidarity it follows that when an individual has injured a member of another group, his own group shield him while the opposing group support the injured man's claims for compensation or revenge. Thence there may develop blood-feuds and civil wars. . . . The Chukchi generally make peace after the first act of retribution, but among the Ifugao, the struggle may go on almost interminably. . . ."

To speak here of the "administering of justice" is to abuse the meaning of the words. The desire to find in primitive societies virtues equal or superior to our own as regards the control of violence must not lead us to minimize the differences. Lowie's terminology simply perpetuates a widely accepted way of thinking by which the right to vengeance *takes the place* of a judicial system wherever such a system is lacking. This theory, which seems securely anchored to common sense, is in fact erroneous and gives rise to an infinite number of errors. Such thinking reflects the ignorance of a society—our own—that has been the beneficiary of a judicial system for so many years that it is no longer conscious of the system's real achievements.

If vengeance is an unending process it can hardly be invoked to restrain the violent impulses of society. In fact, it is vengeance itself that must be restrained. Lowie bears witness to the truth of this proposition every time he gives an example of the "administering of justice," even in those societies that, according to him, possess a "central authority." It is not the lack of any abstract principle of justice that is important, but the fact that the so-called legal reprisals are always in the hands of the victims themselves and those near to them. As long as there exists no sovereign and independent body capable of taking the place of the injured party and taking upon itself the responsibility for revenge, the danger of interminable escalation remains. Efforts to modify the punishment or to hold vengeance in check can only result in a situation that is precarious at best. Such efforts ultimately require a spirit of conciliation that may indeed be present, but may equally well be lacking. As I have said, it is inexact to speak of the administering of justice, even in connection with such institutional concepts as "an eye for an eye" or the various forms of trial by combat. In such cases it seems wise to adhere to Malinowski's conclusion: "The means of restoring a disturbed tribal equilibrium [are] slow and cumbersome. . . . We have not found any arrangement or usage which could be classed as a form of 'administration of justice,' according to a code and by fixed methods."

If primitive societies have no tried and true remedies for dealing with an outbreak of violence, no certain cure once the social equilibrium has been upset, we can assume that *preventive* measures will play an essential role. Here again I return to the concept of sacrifice as I earlier defined it: an instrument of prevention in the struggle against violence.

In a universe where the slightest dispute can lead to disaster—just as a slight cut can prove fatal to a hemophiliac—the rites of sacrifice serve to polarize the community's aggressive impulses and redirect them toward victims that may be actual or figurative, animate or inanimate, but that are always incapable of propagating further vengeance. The sacrificial process furnishes an outlet for those violent impulses that cannot be mastered by self-restraint; a partial outlet, to be sure, but always renewable, and one whose efficacy has been attested by an impressive number of reliable witnesses. The sacrificial process prevents the spread of violence by keeping vengeance in check.

In societies that practice sacrifice there is no critical situation to which the rites are not applicable, but there are certain crises that seem to be particularly amenable to sacrificial mediation. In these crises the social fabric of the community is threatened; dissension and discord are rife. The more critical the situation, the more "precious" the sacrificial victim must be.

It is significant that sacrifice has languished in societies with a firmly established judicial system—ancient Greece and Rome, for example. In such societies the essential purpose of sacrifice has disappeared. It may still be practiced for a while, but in diminished and debilitated form. And it is precisely under such circumstances that sacrifice usually comes to our notice, and our doubts as to the "real" function of religious institutions are only reinforced.

Our original proposition stands: ritual in general, and sacrificial rites in particular, assume essential roles in societies that lack a firm judicial system. It must not be assumed, however, that sacrifice simply "replaces" a judicial system. One can scarcely speak of replacing something that never existed to begin with. Then, too, a judicial system is ultimately irreplaceable, short of a unanimous and entirely voluntary renunciation of all violent actions.

When we minimize the dangers implicit in vengeance we risk losing sight of the true function of sacrifice. Because revenge is rarely encountered in our society, we seldom have occasion to consider how societies lacking a judicial system of punishment manage to hold it in check. Our ignorance engages us in a false line of thought that is seldom, if ever, challenged. Certainly we have no need of religion to help us solve a problem, runaway vengeance, whose very existence eludes us. And because we have no need for it, religion itself appears senseless. The efficiency of our judicial solution conceals the problem, and the elimination of the problem conceals from us the role played by religion.

The air of mystery that primitive societies acquire for us is undoubtedly due in large part to this misunderstanding. It is undoubtedly responsible for our extreme views of these societies, our insistence on portraying them alternately as vastly superior or flagrantly inferior to our own. One factor alone might well be responsible for our oscillation between extremes, our radical evaluations: the absence in such societies of a judicial system. No one can assess with certainty the amount of violence present in another individual, much less in another society. We can be sure, however, that in a society lacking a judicial system the violence will not appear in the same places or take the same forms as in our own. We generally limit our area of inquiry to the most conspicuous and accessible aspects of these societies. Thus, it is not unnatural that they should seem to us either horribly barbarous or blissfully utopian.

In primitive societies the risk of unleashed violence is so great and the cure so problematic that the emphasis naturally falls on prevention. The preventive measures naturally fall within the domain of religion, where they can on occasion assume a violent character. Violence and the sacred are inseparable. But the covert appropriation by sacrifice of certain properties of violence—particularly the ability of violence to move from one object to another—is hidden from sight by the awesome machinery of ritual.

Primitive societies are not given over to violence. Nor are they necessarily less violent or less "hypocritical" than our own society. Of course, to be truly comprehensive we ought to take into consideration *all* forms of violence, more or less ritualized, that divert a menace from nearby objects to more distant objects. We ought, for instance, to consider war. War is clearly not restricted to one particular type of society. Yet the multiplication of new weapons and techniques does not constitute a fundamental difference between primitive and modern warfare. On the other hand, if we compare societies that adhere to a judicial system with societies that practice sacrificial rites, the difference between the two is such that we can indeed consider the absence or presence of these institutions as a basis for distinguishing primitive societies from "civilized" ones. These are the institutions we must scrutinize in order to arrive, not at some sort of value judgment, but at an objective knowledge of the respective societies to which they belong.

In primitive societies the exercise of preventive measures is not confined exclusively to the domain of religion. The way in which these measures are made manifest in normal social intercourse made a lasting impression on the minds and imaginations of the first European observers and established a prototype of "primitive" psychology and behavior which, if not universally applicable, is still not wholly illusory.

When the least false step can have dire consequences, human relationships may well be marked by a prudence that seems to us excessive and accompanied by precautions that appear incomprehensible. It is in this sense that we must understand the lengthy palavers that precede any undertaking not sanctified by custom, in this sense that we must understand primitive man's reluctance to engage in nonritualized games or contests. In a society where every action or gesture may have irreparable consequences it is not surprising that the members should display a "noble gravity" of bearing beside which our own demeanor appears ridiculous. The commercial, administrative, or ideological concerns that make such overwhelming demands on our time and attention seem utterly frivolous in comparison to primitive man's primary concerns.

Primitive societies do not have built into their structure an automatic brake against violence; but we do, in the form of powerful institutions whose grip grows progressively tighter as their role grows progressively less apparent. The constant presence of a restraining force allows modern man safely to transgress the limits imposed on primitive peoples without even being aware of the fact. In "policed" societies the relationships between individuals, including total strangers, is characterized by an extraordinary air of informality, flexibility, and even audacity.

Religion invariably strives to subdue violence, to keep it from running wild. Paradoxically, the religious and moral authorities in a community attempt to instill nonviolence, as an active force into daily life and as a mediating force into ritual life, through the application of violence. Sacrificial rites serve to connect the moral and religious aspects of daily life, but only by means of a lengthy and hazardous detour. Moreover, it must be kept in mind that the efficacy of the rites depends on their being performed in the spirit of *pietas*, which marks all aspects of religious life. We are beginning to understand why the sacrificial act appears as both sinful and saintly, an illegal as well as a legitimate exercise of violence. However, we are still far from a full understanding of the act itself.

Primitive religion tames, trains, arms, and directs violent impulses as a defensive force against those forms of violence that society regards as inadmissible. It postulates a strange mixture of violence and nonviolence. The same can perhaps be said of our own judicial system of control.

There may be a certain connection between all the various methods employed by man since the beginning of time to avoid being caught up in an interminable round of revenge. They can be grouped into three general categories: (1) preventive measures in which sacrificial rites divert the spirit of revenge into other channels; (2) the harnessing or hobbling of vengeance by means of compensatory measures, trials by combat, etc., whose curative effects remain precarious; (3) the establishment of a judicial system—the most efficient of all curative procedures.

We have listed the methods in ascending order of effectiveness. The evolution from preventive to curative procedures is reflected in the course of history or, at any rate, in the course of the history of the Western world. The initial curative procedures mark an intermediary stage between a purely religious orientation and the recognition of a judicial system's superior efficiency. These methods are inherently ritualistic in character, and are often associated with sacrificial practices.

The curative procedures employed by primitive societies appear rudimentary to us. We tend to regard them as fumbling efforts to improvise a judicial system. Certainly their pragmatic aspects are clearly visible, oriented as they are not toward the guilty parties, but toward the victims—since it is the latter who pose the most immediate threat. The injured parties must be accorded a careful measure of satisfaction, just enough to appease their own desire for revenge but not so much as to awaken the desire elsewhere. It is not a question of codifying good and evil or of inspiring respect for some abstract concept of justice; rather it is a question of securing the safety of the group by checking the impulse for revenge. The preferred method involves a reconciliation between parties based on some sort of mutual compensation. If reconciliation is impossible, however, an armed encounter can be arranged in such a manner that the violence is wholly self-contained. This encounter can take place within an enclosed space and can involve prescribed regulations and specifically designated combatants. Its purpose is to cut violence short.

To be sure, all these curative measures are steps in the direction of a legal system. But the evolution, if indeed evolution is the proper term, is not continuous. The break comes at the moment when the intervention of the independent legal authority becomes *constraining*. Only then are men freed from the terrible obligations of vengeance. Retribution in its judicial guise loses its terrible urgency. Its meaning remains the same, but this meaning becomes increasingly indistinct or even fades from view. In fact, the system functions best when everyone concerned is least aware that it involves retribution. The system can—and as soon as it can it will—reorganize itself around the accused and the concept of guilt. In fact, retribution still holds sway, but forged into a principle of abstract justice that all men are obliged to uphold and respect.

We have seen that the "curative" measures, ostensibly designed to temper the impulse toward vengeance, become increasingly mysterious in their workings as they progress in efficiency. As the focal point of the system shifts away from religion and the preventive approach is translated into judicial retribution, the aura of misunderstanding that has always formed a protective veil around the institution of sacrifice shifts as well, and becomes associated in turn with the machinery of the law.

As soon as the judicial system gains supremacy, its machinery disappears from sight. Like sacrifice, it conceals—even as it also reveals—its resemblance to vengeance, differing only in that it is not self-perpetuating and its decisions discourage reprisals. In the case of sacrifice, the designated victim does not become the object of vengeance because he is a replacement, is not the "right" victim. In the judicial system the violence does indeed fall on the "right" victim; but it falls with such force, such resounding authority, that no retort is possible.

It can be argued that the function of the judicial system is not really concealed; and we can hardly be unaware that the judicial process is more concerned with the general security of the community than with any abstract notion of justice. Nonetheless, we believe that the system is founded on a unique principle of justice unknown to primitive societies. The scholarly literature on the subject seems to bear out this belief. It has long been assumed that a decisive difference between primitive and civilized man is the former's general inability to identify the guilty party and to adhere to the principle of guilt. Such an assumption only confuses the issue. If primitive man insists on averting his attention from the wrongdoer, with an obstinacy that strikes us as either idiotic or perverse, it is because he wishes above all to avoid fueling the fires of vengeance.

If our own system seems more rational, it is because it conforms more strictly to the principle of vengeance. Its insistence on the punishment of the guilty party underlines this fact. Instead of following the example of religion and attempting to forestall acts of revenge, to mitigate or sabotage its effects or to redirect them to secondary objects, our judicial system *rationalizes* revenge and succeeds in limiting and isolating its effects in accordance with social demands. The system treats the disease without fear of contagion and provides a highly effective technique for the cure and, as a secondary effect, the prevention of violence.

This rationalistic approach to vengeance might seem to stem from a particularly intimate relationship between the community and the judicial system. In fact, it is the result not of any familiar interchange between the two, but of the recognition of the sovereignty and independence of the judiciary, whose decisions no group, not even the collectivity as a body, can challenge (at least, that is the principle). The judicial authority is beholden to no one. It is thus at the disposal of everyone, and it is universally respected. The judicial system never hesitates to confront violence head on, because it possesses a monopoly on the means of revenge. Thanks to this monopoly, the system generally succeeds in stifling the impulse to vengeance rather than spreading or aggravating it, as a similar intervention on the part of the aggrieved party would invariably do.

In the final analysis, then, the judicial system and the institution of sacrifice share the same function, but the judicial system is infinitely more effective. However, it can only exist in conjunction with a firmly established political power. And like all modern technological advances, it is a two-edged sword, which can be used to oppress as well as to liberate. Certainly that is the way it is seen by primitive cultures, whose view on the matter is indubitably more objective than our own.

If the function of the system has now become apparent, that is because it no longer enjoys the obscurity it needs to operate effectively. A clear view of the inner workings indicates a crisis in the system; it is a sign of disintegration. No matter how sturdy it may seem, the apparatus that serves to hide the true nature of legal and illegal violence from view eventually wears thin. The underlying truth breaks through, and we find ourselves face to face with the specter of reciprocal reprisal. This is not a purely theoretical concept belonging to the intellectual and scholarly realm, but a sinister reality; a vicious circle we thought we had escaped, but one we find has tightened itself, all unsuspected, around us.

The procedures that keep men's violence in bounds have one thing in common: they are no longer strangers to the ways of violence. There is reason to believe that they are all rooted in religion. As we have seen, the various forms of prevention go hand in hand with religious practices. The curative procedures are also imbued with religious concepts—both the rudimentary sacrificial rites and the more advanced judicial forms. *Religion* in its broadest sense, then, must be another term for that obscurity that surrounds man's efforts to defend himself by curative or preventative means against his own violence. It is the enigmatic quality that pervades the judicial system when that system replaces sacrifice. This obscurity coincides with the transcendental effectiveness of a violence that is holy, legal, and legitimate successfully opposed to a violence that is unjust, illegal, and illegitimate.

In the same way that sacrificial victims must in principle meet the approval of the divinity before being offered as a sacrifice, the judicial system appeals to a theology as a guarantee of justice. Even when this theology disappears, as has happened in our culture, the transcendental quality of the system remains intact. Centuries can pass before men realize that there is no real difference between their principle of justice and the concept of revenge.

Only the transcendental quality of the system, acknowledged by all, can assure the prevention or cure of violence. This is the case no matter what the consecrating institution may be. Only by opting for a sanctified, legitimate form of violence and preventing it from becoming an object of disputes and recriminations can the system save itself from the vicious circle of revenge.

A unique generative force exists that we can only qualify as religious in a sense deeper than the theological one. It remains concealed and draws it strength from this concealment, even as its self-created shelter begins to crumble. The acknowledgment of such a force allows us to assess our modern ignorance—ignorance in regard to violence as well as religion. Religion shelters us from violence just as violence seeks shelter in religion. If we fail to understand certain religious practices, it is not because we are outside their sphere of influence but because we are still to a very real extent enclosed within them. The solemn debates on the death of God and of man are perhaps beside the point. They remain theological at bottom, and by extension sacrificial; that is, they draw a veil over the subject of vengeance, which threatens to become quite real once again, in the form not of a philosophical debate but of unlimited violence, in a world with no absolute values. As soon as the essential quality of transcendence—religious, humanistic, or whatever—is lost, there are no longer any terms by which to define the legitimate form of violence and to recognize it among the multitude of illicit forms. The definition of legitimate and illegitimate forms then becomes a matter of mere opinion, with each man free to reach his own decision. In other words, the question is thrown to the winds. Henceforth there are as many legitimate forms of violence as there are men to implement them; legitimacy as a principle no longer exists. Only the introduction of some transcendental quality that will persuade men of the fundamental difference between sacrifice and revenge, between judicial system and vengeance, can succeed in bypassing violence.

All this explains why our penetration and demystification of the system necessarily coincides with the disintegration of that system. The act of demystification retains a sacrificial quality and remains essentially religious in character for at least as long as it fails to come to a conclusion—as long, that is, as the process purports to be nonviolent, or less violent than the system itself. In fact, demystification leads to constantly increasing violence, a violence perhaps less "hypocritical" than the violence it seeks to expose, but more energetic, more virulent—and the harbinger of something far worse—a violence that knows no bounds.

JAMES H. CONE (1935–)

*A leading spokesperson for an African American vision of Christian theology, James H.
Cone is currently Charles A. Briggs Distinguished Professor of Systematic Theology at
Union Theological Seminary in New York City, where he has taught since 1965.
Professor Cone is an ordained minister in the African Methodist Episcopal Church,
and he has done significant research as well as extensive teaching not only in African
American theology but also in the theologies of Africa, Asia, and Latin America, as
well as twentieth-century European-American theologies.*

*What is exceptional about Cone's style is its committed tone of confrontation and
compassion. Not only does he identify liberation as the heart of the Christian gospel,
but he also sees blackness as the primary mode of God's presence. For him, as he writes
in the introduction to the newest edition of* Black Theology and Black Power *([1969]
1997), "the God of Moses and of Jesus makes an unqualified solidarity with the
victims, empowering them to fight against injustice." Yet beyond revolution and violence, he also envisions a time when reconciliation will be possible, when the biblical
message of reconciliation will be made "contemporaneous with the black situation in
America," where "black people will bring their new restored image of themselves into
every human encounter," including their encounter with white people.*

Cone's many writings include A Black Theology of Liberation *(1970),* For My
People: Black Theology and the Black Church *(1984),* God of the Oppressed *(1975),*
My Soul Looks Back *(1982),* The Spirituals and the Blues *(1972),* Martin and Mal-
colm and America: A Dream or a Nightmare? *(1991). The following excerpt is from*
God of the Oppressed.

Liberation and the Christian Ethic

JAMES CONE

The black struggle for liberation involves a total break with the white past, "the
overturning of relationships, the transformation of life and then a reconstruction." Theologically, this means that black people are prepared to live according
to God's eschatological future as defined by the reality of Christ's presence in the
social existence of oppressed people struggling for historical liberation. This
perspective informs black people's view of suffering and enables them to know
that white people do not have the last word on black existence.

Because black liberation means a radical break with the existing political and social structures and a redefinition of black life along the lines of black power and self-determination, it is to be expected that white theologians and assorted moralists will ask questions about methods and means. Theologically and philosophically, they want to know whether revolutionary violence can be justified as an appropriate means for the attainment of black liberation. If Black Theology is Christian theology, how does it reconcile violence with Jesus' command to turn the other cheek and to go the second mile (Matt. 5:39)? Is it not true that violence is a negation of the gospel of Jesus Christ?

These are favorite *white* questions, and it is significant that they are almost always addressed to the oppressed and almost never to the oppressors. This fact alone provides the clue to the motive behind the questions. White people are not really concerned about violence in all cases but only when they are the victims. As long as blacks are beaten and shot, they are strangely silent, as if they are unaware of the inhumanity committed against the black community. Why didn't we hear from the so-called nonviolent Christians when black people were *violently* enslaved, *violently* lynched, and *violently* ghettoized in the name of freedom and democracy? When I hear questions about violence and love coming from the children of slave masters whose identity with Jesus extends no further than that weekly Sunday service, then I can understand why many black brothers and sisters say that Christianity is the white man's religion, and it must be destroyed along with white oppressors. What many white people fail to realize is that their questions about violence and Christian love are not only very naïve, but are hypocritical and insulting. When whites ask me, "Are you for violence?" my rejoinder is: "*Whose* violence?" "Richard Nixon or his victims?" "The Mississippi State Police or the students at Jackson State?" "The New York State Police or the inmates at Attica?"

If we are going to raise the question of violence and Christian love, it ought to be placed in its proper theological perspective. Violence is not primarily a theoretical question but a practical question, and it should be viewed in the context of Christian ethics and its relation to divine liberation and the human struggle for freedom in an unjust society. I hope to lay to rest once and for all white people's obscene questions about whether we blacks ought to be violent in the attainment of our freedom.

THE INTERDEPENDENCE OF THEOLOGY AND ETHICS

The ethical question "What am I to do?" cannot be separated from its theological source, that is, what God has done and is doing to liberate the oppressed from slavery and injustice. Thus Christian theology is the foundation of Christian ethics. Theology is the Church's reflection upon the meaning of its faith-claim that God's revelation is identical with the historical freedom of the weak and the helpless. Ethics derived from theology is that branch of the Church's reflection that investigates the implication of faith in divine liberation for Christian life in the world. Formally, Christian theology asks, "Who is God?" and ethics asks, "What must we do?" Although separate questions theoretically, in practice the answer to the theological question about God includes in it the answer to the ethical question about human behavior.

The close connection between theology and ethics is found not only in the current theologies of liberation but also in other theologies as well, even though this point has often been obscured by the influence of Greek philosophy. With the aid of philosophical categories, Christian theologians began to make exorbitant claims about the "universal" character of their discourse, and consequently failed to pay sufficient attention to the danger of divorcing theology from its biblical base. Thus it became easy to minimize the connection between theology and ethics. While the black answer to the God-question focuses on the divine liberation of the oppressed, and thus includes in it God's election of the oppressed for participation with him in the struggle for freedom, other theologies have viewed divine revelation and ethical obedience differently. In the history of Western theology, we seldom find an ethic of liberation derived from the God of freedom, but rather, an ethic of the status quo, derived from Greek philosophy and from the political interests of a church receiving special favors from the state. Sometimes this status-quo ethic was expressed in terms of a philosophical emphasis on reason. At other times, the theme was faith, understood either as assent to propositional truths or as a spiritual relationship with God. Whatever the variation of emphasis on faith and reason, God's revelation was interpreted, more often than not, as consistent with the values of the structures of political oppression. Thus Constantine's participation in the Arian controversy influenced not only the Church's politics but also its theology and the ethical import of that theology. That was why the early Church Fathers could ask about the Son's relation to the Father and later the Holy Spirit's relation to both without connecting the question to the historical freedom of the oppressed. Since the Church and its bishops (during the age of Constantine and thereafter) were not slaves, it did not occur to them that God's revelation in Jesus Christ is identical with the presence of his Spirit in the slave community in struggle for the liberation of humanity. They viewed God in static terms and thus tended to overlook the political thrust of the gospel. This procedure was consistent with the God of Plotinus but not with the God of Moses and Amos. Consequently, the ethics of the fourth-century Fathers differed fundamentally from biblical revelation. Instead of standing unquestionably with the outcasts and downtrodden, as the God of the Bible does, their ethics did more to preserve the status quo than to change it. Whatever else the gospel of Jesus might be, it can never be identified with the established power of the state. Thus whatever else Christian ethics might be, it can never be identified with the actions of people who conserve the status quo. This was the essential error of the early Church. By becoming the religion of the Roman state, replacing the public state sacrifices, Christianity became the opposite of what Jesus intended.

The problem of identifying Christian ethics with the status quo is also found in Augustine and Thomas Aquinas. While they differed regarding the role of faith and reason and theological discourse, they agreed that the slave should not seek to change his civil status through political struggle. According to Augustine, slavery was due to the sinfulness of the slaves. Therefore he admonished "slaves to be subject to their masters . . . ," serving "them with a good-heart and a good-will. . . ." For Thomas, slavery was a part of the natural order of creation. Thus "the slave, in regard to his master, is an instrument. . . . Between a master and his slave there is a special right of domination."

The identification of the will of God with the values of the status quo was not limited to early Christianity and the Middle Ages. In Protestant Christianity, this emphasis is found in Martin Luther's definition of the state as the servant of God. That was why he condemned the Peasant's Revolt, saying that "nothing can be more poisonous, hurtful, or devilish than a rebel." He equated the killing of a rebel with the killing of a mad dog.

An ethic of the status quo is also found in Calvinism and Methodism, despite John Calvin's emphasis on divine sovereignty and John Wesley's *Thoughts on Slavery*. Calvinism seemed especially suited for America with its easy affinity with capitalism and slavery. And Wesley's condemnation of slavery notwithstanding he still appeared to be more concerned about a warm heart than an enslaved body.

Of course, it could be argued that the Church's ethical error in relation to the oppressed and their slavery was due to the historical limitation of thought and that this limitation and its subsequent ethical error did not affect the essential truth of the Church's theology. It is not fair, so runs the argument, for us to stand in the twentieth century, with the benefit of the Enlightenment, Marx, and Fanon, and criticize Luther and Wesley for not being revolutionary in their interpretation and implementation of the gospel.

This argument is only partly valid. It is correct in emphasizing the social determination of ethical discourse in the Church's history. The Church's ethics from its beginnings to the present day has been historically determined by its social and political setting. But the argument is wrong when it suggests that the historical determination of church ethics did not affect the essential truth of church theology. When church theologians, from the time of Constantine to the present, failed to see the ethical import of the biblical God for the liberation of the oppressed, that failure occurred because of defective theology. To understand correctly the Church's ethical mistake, we must see it in connection with a prior theological mistake. The basic problem with theological ethics cannot be solved through a debate of the deliberative, prescriptive, and relational motifs of ethical norms. Neither can it be solved through a discussion of the relative merits of the institutional, operational, and intentional motifs in the implementation of ethical decisions, although these issues are important for Christian ethics. Rather, we must unmask this error by analyzing its theological origin. The matter may be put this way: *Theologians of the Christian Church have not interpreted Christian ethics as an act for the liberation of the oppressed because their views of divine revelation were defined by philosophy and other cultural values rather than by the biblical theme of God as the Liberator of the oppressed.* If American theologians and ethicists had read the Scripture through the eyes of black slaves and their preachers, then they would have created a different set of ethical theories of the "Good." For it is impossible truly to hear the biblical story as told in the songs and sermons of black people without also seeing God as the divine power in the lives of the oppressed, moving them toward the fullness of their humanity. An ethic derived from this God, then, must be defined according to the historical struggle of freedom. It cannot be identified with the status quo.

We cannot say that Luther, Calvin, Wesley, and other prominent representatives of the Church's tradition were limited by their time, as if their ethical judgments on oppression did not affect the essential truth of their theologies. They were wrong ethically because they were wrong *theologically*. They were wrong theologically because they failed to listen to the Bible—with sufficient openness and through the eyes of the victims of political oppression. How ironic it is that he who proclaimed *sola scriptura* as one of the guiding lights if his reformation did not really hear the true meaning of that proclamation. For to hear the message of Scripture is to hear and see the truth of God's liberating presence in history for those who are oppressed by unjust social structures. Luther could not hear God's liberating Word for the oppressed because he was not a victim. He could only see God's liberation in terms of the individual, "religious" oppression of sin and guilt. Any time God is not derived from the biblical theme of liberation of the oppressed, it is to be expected that Christian ethics will be at best indifferent toward the oppressed struggle of freedom. That Luther's ethical error is much more serious than the fact that he lived during the sixteenth century and not the twentieth can be shown through an examination of contemporary American discourse on ethics. If Luther's error were due to the *time* in which he lived, then one would not expect to find similar ethical errors today. But that is just what one does find. Herbert Edwards' essay, "Racism and Christian Ethics in America," shows with unmistakable clarity that white ethicists, from Reinhold Niebuhr to James Gustafson, reflect the racism current in the society as a whole. Here racism appears in the form of *invisibility*. White theologians and ethicists simply ignore black people by suggesting that the problem of racism and oppression is only one social expression of a larger ethical concern. This error in contemporary ethical discourse is no different from Luther's error. It is an ethics of the status quo, primarily derived from an identity with the cultural values of white oppressors rather than the biblical theme of God's liberation of the oppressed. Thus the great theologian Reinhold Niebuhr can speak of black people in terms of "cultural backwardness," and then conclude: "We must not consider the Founding Fathers immoral just because they were slaveholders." What else can this ethical judgment mean than that Niebuhr derived his ethics from white culture and not biblical revelation? Despite slavery, lynchings, sit-ins, and boycotts, white ethicists have not made the problem of racial oppression a central issue in their theological discourse. Most ethicists limit the issue to one or two paragraphs with no more visibility than the problem of stealing a ten-cent bar of candy. And when they do say more, as with Paul Ramsey's *Christian Ethics and the Sit-in*, they spend more time informing black people about the "proper respect for law and order" than in unmasking the systemic order of white injustice. Thus Ramsey says that "simple and not so simple injustice alone has never been a sufficient justification for revolutionary change." This blindness of Christian ethicists is not merely a cultural accident. As with Luther and others in the Western theological tradition, it is due to a *theological* blindness. White ethicists take their cue from their fellow theologians: because white theologians have not interpreted God as the Liberator of the oppressed, it follows that white ethicists would not make liberation the central motif of ethical analysis.

· · · · ·

ETHICS, VIOLENCE, AND JESUS CHRIST

With an authentic ethic of liberation as our point of departure, it is now possible to say a word about violence. Because the oppressed have been victims of mental and physical dehumanization, we cannot make the destruction of humanity, even among oppressors, an end in itself. Such a procedure contradicts the struggle of freedom, the essence of our striving. Our intention is not to make the oppressors the slaves but to transform humanity, or, in the words of Fanon, "set afoot a new man." Thus hatred and vengeance have no place in the struggle for freedom. Indeed, hatred is a denial of freedom, a usurpation of the liberation struggle. The ethic of liberation arises out of love, for ourselves and for humanity. This is an essential ingredient of liberation without which the struggle turns into a denial of what divine liberation means.

However, the radical rejection of hatred and vengeance does not mean that we accept white people's analysis of violence and nonviolence. We are well aware that they derive their analysis of these terms from a theological and political interest that supports the status quo, whereas we must analyze them in accordance with our struggle to be free. We cannot let white rhetoric about nonviolence and Jesus distort our vision of violence committed against black people. Therefore, one of the tasks of the black ethicist is to untangle the confused and much discussed problem of violence and nonviolence and Jesus' relationship to both. At least three points ought to be made. (1) Violence is not only what black people do to white people as victims seek to change the structure of their existence; it is also what white people *did* when they created a society for white people only, and what they *do* in order to maintain it. Violence in America did not begin with the black power movement or with the Black Panther Party. Neither is it limited to the Symbionese Liberation Army. Contrary to popular white opinion, violence has a long history in America. This country was born in violent revolution (remember 1776?), and it has been sustained by the violent extermination of red people and the violent enslavement of black people. This is what Rap Brown had in mind when he said, "Violence is as American as cherry pie."

White people have a distorted conception of the meaning of violence. They like to think of violence as breaking the laws of their society, but that is a narrow and racist understanding of reality. There is a more deadly form of violence, and it is camouflaged in such slogans as "law and order," "freedom and democracy," and "the American way of life." I am speaking of white-collar violence, the violence of Christian murderers and patriot citizens who define right in terms of whiteness and wrong as blackness. These are the people who hire assassins to do their dirty work while they piously congratulate themselves for being "good" and "nonviolent." The assassins are the policemen who patrol our streets, killing our men, women, and children.

I contend, therefore, that the problem of violence is not the problem of a few black revolutionaries but the problem of a whole social structure which outwardly appears to be ordered and respectable but inwardly is "ridden by psychopathic obsessions and delusions"—racism and hatred. Violence is embedded in American law, and it is blessed by the keepers of moral sanctity. This is the core of the problem of violence, and it will not be solved by romanticizing American history, pretending that Hiroshima, Nagasaki, and Vietnam are the first American crimes against humanity. If we take seriously the idea of human dignity, then we know that the annihilation of Indians, the enslavement of Africans, and (Reinhold Niebuhr notwithstanding) the making of heroes out of slaveholders, like George Washington and Thomas Jefferson, were America's first crimes against humankind. And it does not help the matter at all to attribute black slavery to economic necessity or an accident of history. America is an unjust society, and black people have known that for a long time.

(2) If violence is not just a question for the oppressed but *primarily* for the oppressors, then it is obvious that the distinction between violence and non-violence is an illusory problem. "There is only the question of the justified and unjustified use of force and the question of whether the means are proportionate to the ends"; and the only people who can answer the problem are the victims of injustice. It would be the height of stupidity for the victims of oppression to expect the oppressors to devise the means of liberation.

It is important to point out that no one can be nonviolent in an unjust society. The essential fallacy of the much-debated issues of violence versus nonviolence is that the proponents of the latter have merely argued that issue from a perspective that accepted the oppressors' definitions. Too often Christian theologians have made the specious distinction between violence and force. "The state is invested with force; it is an organism instituted and ordained by God, and remains such even when it is unjust; even its harshest acts are not the same thing as the angry or brutal deed of the individual. The individual surrenders his passions, he commits violence." This distinction is false and merely expresses identification with the structures of power rather than with the victims of power. I contend that every one is violent, and to ask, "Are you nonviolent?" is to accept the oppressors' values. Concretely, ours is a situation in which the only option we have is that of deciding whose violence we will support—that of the oppressors or of the oppressed. Either we side with oppressed blacks and other unwanted minorities as they try to redefine the meaning of existence in a dehumanized society, or we take a stand with the President or whoever is defending the white establishment for General Motors and U.S. Steel. There is no possibility of neutrality, the moral luxury of being on neither side. Neither the powers that be nor their victims will allow that! The U.S. government demands support through taxes and the public allegiance to the American flag. The oppressed demand commitment to the struggle of freedom and the willingness to take the risk to create a new humanity. We know that "sometimes [we are] tossed and driven," and "sometimes [we] don't know where to roam." But we've "heard of a city" where "Jesus is the King," and we are struggling "to make it [our] home." Sometimes the city is called heaven, and we speak of it as "crossing the river Jordan" and as the "New Jerusalem." But this vision is the guide to our revolutionary fight to make this world a sign of its coming reality. People who want to join our struggle must relinquish their commitment to the structure of injustice. They cannot be for oppressors and us at the same time.

Of course, I realize that the choice for the oppressed has its own ambiguities. Insofar as we pay taxes and work in the system, are we not on the side of the oppressors? True enough. Well then, what is the difference between Gerald Ford and any black person? The difference is analogous to the distinction between the redeemed sinner and the unredeemed sinner. Ford is the latter, and the oppressed person in struggle of freedom is the former. One recognizes that, despite his participation in it, the world is unjust, and he must be committed to its liberation. The other believes that the world is in good hands, and he enjoys his participation in it. This distinction is crucial, because one participation is by force and the other is voluntary. Thus the hope for the creation of a new society for all is dependent upon those people who know that struggle is the primary means by which a new age will be inaugurated. If they participate in injustice, they know that it is not right, and thus the system must be changed. There will be no change from the system of injustice if we have to depend upon the people who control it and believe that the present order of injustice is the best of all possible societies. It will be changed by the victims whose participation in the present system is against their will. Indeed, while they are participating in it involuntarily, voluntarily they are preparing for its destruction. They are living double lives, one part of which they are seeking to destroy because it contradicts the true self that is being made anew in struggle. Every sensitive black person knows what this means, and it is the source both of our being and not-being. Ethics in this context is a terrible risk, an existential and historical burden that must be borne in the heat of the day. It is this burden that made our ancestors create songs of sorrow and joy. Both realities are combined in this spiritual:

> Nobody knows the trouble I've seen,
> Nobody knows my sorrow.
> Nobody knows the trouble I've seen,
> Glory, Hallelujah!

At Macedonia A. M. E. Church, this spiritual was repeatedly sung as an expression of the people's struggle. Du Bois' "twoness," the American and the Negro, the sorrow and the joy, was present in the very fabric of their existence. But this conflict did not create passivity; it was used by the people as the means of struggle. They put into action the saying that "you got to take what you got and use what you can," and that they did every chance they got. It is this *living* truth embodied in the lives of black people that make the comparison of Ford's predicament with blacks utterly ridiculous. Oppressed blacks and other people of color are the only signs of hope for the creation of a new humanity in America.

From the foregoing analysis of violence and nonviolence, it is obvious that I do not share Martin Luther King, Jr.'s explication of this issue, although I agreed with much of the actual programmatic thrust of his leadership. His dependence on the analysis of love found in liberal theology and his confidence that "the universe is on the side of justice" seem not to take seriously white violence in America. I disagreed with his conceptual analysis of violence versus nonviolence, because his distinctions between these terms did not appear to face head-on the historical and sociological complexities of human existence in a racist society. Thus much of King's writings reflect theological and philosophical discourse that had little to do with his actual creative thinking and acting. The source of the latter is not Gandhi or Bostonian personalism, despite his implied claims to the contrary. King's creative thought and power in the struggle of freedom were found in his black Church heritage. This was the heritage that brought him face to face with agony and despair but also hope and joy that somewhere in the bosom of God's eternity, justice would become a reality "in the land of the free and the home of the brave." This was the source of King's dream and his anticipation that "trouble won't last always." With black sermonic style and rhythm and with theological imagination, he attempted to explicate the content of his vision: "I have a dream," he said at the March on Washington in 1963, "that one day my children will no longer be judged by the color of their skin but by the content of their character." And the night before his assassination in Memphis, he reiterated a similar hope: "I may not get there with you, but I want you to know tonight that we as a people will get to the promised land." The idea that hope is created in the context of despair and oppression is what made King such a creative activist and a great preacher. It is also what makes my theology very similar to King's, despite our apparent difference on violence and nonviolence. For we both recognize that a fight is on and black survival and liberation are at stake. Therefore, we do not need to debate the relative merits of certain academic distinctions between violence and force or violence and nonviolence. The task is what King demonstrated so well in his life and thought, to try to replace inhumanity with humanity.

(3) If violence versus nonviolence is not the issue but, rather, the creation of a new humanity, then the critical question for Christians is not whether Jesus committed violence or whether violence is theoretically consistent with love and reconciliation. We repeat: the question is not what Jesus *did,* as if his behavior in first-century Palestine were the infallible ethical guide for our actions today. We must not ask what he did, but what is he *doing*—and what he did becomes important only insofar as it points to his activity today. To use the Jesus of

history as an absolute ethical guide for people today is to become enslaved to the past, foreclosing God's eschatological future and its judgment on the present. It removes the element of risk in ethical decisions and makes people slaves to principles. But the gospel of Jesus means liberation; and one essential element of that liberation is the existential burden of making decisions about human liberation without being completely sure what Jesus did or would do. This is the risk of faith.

My difficulty with white theologians is their use of Jesus' so-called "non-violent" attitude in the Gospels as primary evidence that the oppressed ought to be nonviolent today. Not only have Rudolf Bultmann and other Form Critics demonstrated that these are historical difficulties in the attempt to move behind the kerygmatic preaching of the early Church to the real Jesus of Nazareth, but the procedure is ethically questionable, especially from white defenders of the status quo. It is interesting that many white scholars are skeptical about the historical validity of practically everything that the Gospels record about Jesus' ministry *except* his political involvement. They are sure that he preached love, which they invariably interpret to mean an acceptance of the political status quo. His gospel, they contend, was spiritual or eschatological but had nothing to do with political, revolutionary struggle. This is a strange form of logic, especially since they are the same scholars who adhere *rigidly* to the form-critical method and also *universally* proclaim that the Kingdom about which Jesus preached included the whole of reality. Why is it that they do not express the same skepticism when dealing with Jesus' politics as they do with everything else? How can they be so sure that Jesus was not violent? Why is it that they say that Jesus preached the Kingdom, an *all-encompassing reality*, but suggest that it had nothing to do with politics? How can they say that the God of Jesus was Yahweh of the Old Testament, but shy away from his political involvement on behalf of the oppressed? How could Jesus be God's representative on earth, and not be concerned about social, economic, and political injustice? I think the answer to these questions is obvious. White theologians' exegesis is decided by their commitment to, and involvement in, the social structures of oppression. They cannot see the radical and political thrust of Jesus' person and work because their vision is committed to the very structures that Jesus despised. They are the contemporary representatives of the scribes and lawyers who cannot recognize the essential fallacy of their perspective.

SHARON WELCH (1940–)

Sharon Welch is a specialist in religion and culture, a form of analysis that bridges the disciplines of theology and ethics. Born in west Texas, she received her doctorate from Vanderbilt University and has taught at Rhodes College, Harvard Divinity School, and the University of Missouri, Columbia. She has also held visiting appointments at Uppsala University and the University of Amsterdam.

Welch's first book, Communities of Resistance and Solidarity: A Feminist Theology of Liberation *(1985), analyzes the epistemic claims of three contemporary religious movements: Latin American liberation theology, black theology, and feminist theology. She utilizes the philosophy of Michel Foucault to describe the significance of the epistemic shift in these religious movements, exploring the ways in which they exemplify an "insurrection of subjugated knowledges," then offering a genealogy of oppression and liberation which leads to a redefinition of "truth" in terms of the political and cultural impact of religious claims about divinity, humanity, and power.*

Her second book, A Feminist Ethic of Risk *(1989), queries the construction of ethical responsibility in contemporary American culture. While many devout Christians ostensibly support an ethic of responsibility and justice, Welch argues that this "ethic of control" actually sustains the nuclear arms race and hampers work for systemic social change. Following Foucault, she argues that one can see the particularity of one's constructions of truth and morality only through critical engagement with traditions which have other constructions of reliable knowledge and responsible action. She gives as an example of this critical engagement a response to the alternative ethic of risk expressed in the activism of African Americans and in the literature of African American women.*

In her latest book, Sweet Dreams in America: Making Ethics and Spirituality Work *(1998), Welch takes up the ethical and spiritual challenges of multiculturalism. She provides an ethic of power, chaos, and social change informed by postmodern philosophy and liberationist political commitments. A key dimension to this view of power is a nondualistic understanding of good and evil, one that offers images of hope to counter cynicism and despair without relying on utopian expectations or millennial dreams of inexorable progress and long-lasting social change.*

The following excerpt is taken from Communities of Resistance and Solidarity, *the foundational text for Welch's revisionist view of ethics and theology.*

Dangerous Memory and Alternate Knowledges

SHARON WELCH

The power and peril of discourse and the constant tendency to elide its pitfalls characterize theology as much as they do the discourse of penology, sexuality, and madness. Within the Christian tradition, radically different understandings of the nature of God, of faith, of sin and redemption are produced by people who rely on the same sources: scripture, doctrine, tradition, and the contemporary life of faith. Some Christian theologians claim that such endless changes in theological discourse can be avoided. They find a secure home for theological discourse in ahistorical or supernatural authorities, either in revelation as found in scripture and doctrine or in the weight and wisdom of tradition. Both authorities are valued and used without acknowledgment that they are characterized by the same tenuousness, contingency, and partiality as the discourse they are presumed to ground.

The methodological difficulties in theology are not often described as part of an elision of discourse. Yet I find in theology signs of such an elision, signs of unease as to the nature of theology, the type of truth-claims it can make, the warrants that establish its importance, the realm to which it refers. These questions do not only stem from the plurality of theologies, each with a different understanding of its status in relation to faith and to other disciplines. Christian theology has been characterized by plurality since its inception. While this plurality of options may not be greater now than at any other time in the past, the self-evidence of theology as a discrete if debatable method with an identifiable or meaningful referent has been shattered.

The nineteenth and twentieth centuries have reflected this "dis-ease" of theology, the loss of an obvious referent and method. As the "death of God"—the loss of an absolute referent as constitutive of human existence—permeated much of Western culture, theology sought either to accommodate itself to secularity by interpreting it as coherent with incarnational faith or to oppose it with a neo-orthodox positivism of revelation.

The "shaking of the foundations" has not stopped, however, with the shaking of the foundations of Christian theism. The twentieth century could just as well be characterized by the shaking of the foundations of humanism and secularity: the increasing fragility of the morality of humanity and of technological, scientific society as manifest in the Nazi holocaust, the nuclear arms race, genocide, poverty, ecological disasters, and the exploitation of scarce resources. As the old certitudes, the old gods, crumble, new ones have risen to take their place:

national socialism in Nazi Germany, the "Christo-fascism" of the moral majority in the United States, the ideology of the national security state. Our era is marked as much by the struggle of competing gods as it is by the death of God.

In the midst of this confusion, the increasingly strong voice of liberation theology, a specific form of ecclesiality and reflection, declares that the problem with Christendom is not that its claims were false or unrealistic, but that it failed to claim enough, to hope enough. Liberation theology is a proclamation of the presence of the God of Exodus, the God of liberation. It is an impassioned critique of society and established religion and theology in the name of justice. Liberation theology exposes the conflictual fabric of traditional Western academic theology; it is forging a new type of discourse that struggles for truth within that power- and ideology-ridden matrix.

COMMUNITIES OF RESISTANCE

The significance of liberation theology lies in its matrix and its content. Its matrix is that of the "*battle* for truth," not just the proclamation of revealed truths. Metz, for example, speaks of the crisis of faith as practical, not intellectual. The fundamental failure of Christianity, as he sees it, is not its inability to deal with the philosophical critiques of theological knowledge offered by the Enlightenment. The failure of Christianity is a failure of practice, a failure to transform the corruption and inhumanity of the world. The failure of Christendom is not a failure of intellectual understanding, but a failure to establish in practice its vision of the human community.

The critique of Christendom by liberation theologians emerges from a specific matrix: the struggle to establish as true in history what has been declared from the perspective of faith as the truth of human being in the world. Liberation theology is not based in the academy, in the study of texts or a specific literature; it is based in actual communities in the concrete experience of women and men struggling to build a new world. Their vision of this new world is forged in the context of a community of faith, a community that appropriates the Christian tradition in the context of political and social struggle.

There is yet another aspect of this matrix that is central to understanding the significance of liberation theologies. The most vital expressions of liberation theology have come from the fringes of the Christian tradition. The primary source for liberation theology is not the intellectual or scholarly theological tradition, but the experience of those who have been excluded from structures of power within society and within the church. Liberation theologians express the voice and experience of women of all races, racial and ethnic minorities, and the poor of the Third World.

The terms used by liberation theologians often belie the revolutionary signif- icance of their knowledge. Their language is that of traditional theology—God, Christ, salvation, sin, grace—but the meanings of these traditional terms are distinctly nontraditional. Liberation theology uses the same symbols that are found in traditional theology, but they are interpreted by different criteria. There may still be exegesis, apologetics, and dogmatics within liberation theol- ogy, but these traditional tasks are all performed within a different horizon— that of resistance to oppression. Merely to state that liberation theology is reflection on practice is to obscure this horizon and to overlook the epistemic shift constitutive of this theology. The reflection of liberation theologians on practice entails a reconsideration of the nature of theological reflection and the identification of a particular sort of practice—resistance to oppression—as the focus of Christian faith and theology.

My claims for liberation theology may appear extravagant. Although the movement is coextensive with a radical or revolutionary political option, and is thus quite different from mainstream Christianity and its politics, it is possible to miss the epistemic challenge of liberation theology. The reason for this is found in the explanations given by liberation theologians themselves of their work. While the constitutive role of practice and commitment to the oppressed is central, many liberation theologians also claim as warrant for their theologi- cal work a traditional source: the revelation of God as found in scripture.

Biblical traditions are important for liberation theologians; study of the scriptures is a central feature of base Christian communities and funds the powerful imagery of preaching in the black church. The political interpretation of their faith cannot, however, be explained solely by the impact of biblical texts. How can the same collection of texts be used to support both a political and an ostensibly apolitical church? I think that the answer lies in who is reading the texts, what community is providing, as Sharon Parks puts it, the point of refer- ence. The determining factor in shaping liberation faith and theology is not the scriptures in themselves, but who is reading the scriptures and why.

Locating the fundamental source of liberation theology in communities of and for the oppressed is of special importance in my work as a feminist theolo- gian of liberation, but it is not totally foreign to the work of other liberation theologians. I do not think that liberation theology offers us the finally definitive reading of the scriptures. What it offers is something that is both more modest and more revolutionary: an interpretation of scriptural traditions (and thus of human being, of history, and of political structures) by those who have not yet named the world—the marginal, the silenced, the defeated.

What follows is both an exposition and an extension of liberation theology and its definition of truth; it is descriptive and constructive. I describe some of the present tendencies of liberation theologians and I construct a method of reflection, a strategy in the battle for truth, that reflects my own social location— white, Western, feminist, middle-class.

Liberation theology is an insurrection of subjugated knowledges and the manifestation of a new episteme. Liberation theology is grounded in a particular activity of the church, not in an exegesis of scripture, in an interpretation of the Christian tradition, or in philosophical questions and concerns. The basis of my reflection is not only the present life of the church, but it is a particular type of church, one that follows not denominational but political divisions. Liberation theology is grounded in churches of and for the oppressed; thus its basis is an explicitly politicized church. This church consists of communities of faith that challenge the existing order of society as being institutionally repressive and unjust.

We find here three ways of identifying liberation theology. It is a theology of and for the present: the present needs of humanity are its primary focus, determining problems addressed and answers given. It is a theology of the church: the activity of ecclesia is its primary source. And it arises from a particular type of ecclesia, one which identifies with the needs of an oppressed group and struggles to end their oppression.

These elements of liberation theology can be more explicitly identified and methodologically elaborated when the method of liberation theology is understood as a genealogy of subjugated knowledges. To identify liberation theology explicitly as an insurrection of subjugated knowledges provides us with a rationale for its central themes: a pretheoretical commitment to the oppressed as the focus of theological reflection and a turn to the practical category of liberation as the criterion of "authentic" Christianity and evidence of the truth of Christianity.

To state that liberation theology is an insurrection of subjugated knowledges means that the discourse of liberation theology represents the resurgence of knowledges suppressed by a dominant theology and a dominant culture. Further analysis involves three elements of genealogy: (1) the preservation and communication of memories of conflict and exclusion; (2) the discovery and exposition of excluded contents and meanings; and (3) the strategic struggle between the subjugated and dominant knowledges.

Dangerous Memory

Like Foucault's genealogies, liberation theology begins with the fact of insurrection, not with an abstract or normative statement that there should be resistance. It begins by recognizing actual challenges to repressive aspects of society and of the institutional church and its theology. Metz describes this aspect of theology as the dangerous memory of conflict and exclusion, and he examines the role of the church as the vehicle of that memory.

The Memory of Suffering

Dangerous memory has two dimensions, that of hope and that of suffering. A striking characteristic of liberation theology is its focus on the memory of suffering. Liberation theology recounts the history of the marginal, the vanquished, and the oppressed. Black theology delineates the meaning of salvation and of a God of love and freedom within the matrix of the denial of freedom to black people, within the matrix of a history of dehumanization through slavery, racism, and repression. James Cone describes the perspective of black theology as follows:

> In all roles the theologian is committed to that form of existence arising from Jesus' life, death, and resurrection. He knows that the death of the man on the tree has radical implications for those who are enslaved, lynched, and ghettoized in name of God and country. In order to do theology from that standpoint, he must ask the right questions. . . . The right questions are always related to the basic question: What has the gospel to do with the oppressed of the land and their struggle for liberation?

Liberation theology does not address the problem of suffering and evil in the abstract, but focuses on concrete memories of specific histories of oppression and suffering. It declares that such suffering matters; the oppression of people is of ultimate concern. Cone points, therefore, to the ultimate significance of racism, arguing that the issue of racism in our time is analogous to the Arian controversy of the fourth century.

> Athanasius perceived quite clearly that if Arius' views were tolerated, Christianity would be lost. But few white churchmen have questioned whether racism was a similar denial of Jesus Christ.

By placing the issue of racism in the forefront, Cone affirms the significance of a particular history of oppression, and demands that the church confront it explicitly. He claims that "racism implies the absence of fellowship and service, which are primary qualities, indispensable marks of the Church. To be racist is to fall outside the definition of the Church."

Black theologians protest the exclusion of black experience from theology and from the life of the church. They claim that the gospel requires the vindication of the poor, the oppressed, and the helpless in society. Black theology is the voice of a particular type of oppression ignored in Western academic theology and in the established churches.

Similar resurgences of particular histories of oppression provide the motive force for the work of both feminist and Latin American theologians. Daly, Ruether, Collins, and Russell denounce the degradation of women in the established churches. They expose the history of women's exclusion from speaking in the church, their exclusion from participation in theology. They challenge traditional definitions of women as evil or weak, definitions that deny the full humanity of women. They trace the history of women's subjugation throughout the Christian tradition, from the misogyny of Genesis through the silencing of women in the early Christian church and the burning of millions of women as witches during the fifteenth, sixteenth, and seventeenth centuries to Barth's definition of women's secondary role in the order of creation. The memory of the church's mutilation, execution, and denigration of women is preserved and exposed by feminist theologians.

The liberation theology done by Latin American theologians is another expression of a dangerous memory of suffering and oppression. The basis of this theology is the identification of part of the church with the poorest and least powerful segments of society—peasants and Indians. The church of the oppressed serves as their vehicle of protest against an economic situation that concentrates wealth in a small percentage of the population and condemns the majority of the people to poverty.

Latin American liberation theologians assert that the suffering of the poor is an indictment of existing economic and political systems. Gutiérrez's theology of liberation contains an extensive critique of the policy of economic development implemented in Latin America by the United States. Miranda also criticizes the capitalist system of private property because of its contribution to the suffering of the poor. Archbishop Romero and many other people of faith have been killed because of their determination to name the suffering around them— to be, in Romero's words, the voice of the voiceless.

Memory as Critique

Liberation theology is based on dangerous memories; it recounts the history of human suffering. These accounts of specific histories of oppression are both descriptions and critiques. They serve as critiques of existing institutions and social structures in two ways. First, they criticize the structure of a society and expose its fallacious claim of universality. A society's claim that its economic or political system represents the interests of all people is discredited by the disclosure of who pays the costs of that system and of the imbalance of benefits and costs. The memory of suffering reminds us that, all too often, economic and political systems benefit the few at the cost of the suffering of many others.

Second, the accounts of oppression criticize Western theology and established religion for their failure to address grave human problems, the problems of racism, sexism, and class struggle. By uncovering the suffering unaddressed and thus tacitly tolerated by established religion, liberation theologians criticize the universal pretensions of that religion and expose it as a religion of and for the middle class. Liberation theologians criticize both the rituals and theologies of middle-class religion, seeing in each an avoidance of concrete forms of human suffering. To proclaim and celebrate in liturgy the reconciliation between God and humanity accomplished in the life of Jesus while ignoring the lack of reconciliation between landowners and peasants, between military and Indians is to deny the ongoing power of the gospel to transform human life.

Just as social problems (such as the torture in many Latin American countries) are not acknowledged in traditional liturgies, so academic theology regards the analysis of such problems as secondary. Its primary task is the disclosure of the universals of faith and their correlation with the ontological structure of existence. The limitation of such an ontological analysis is twofold: specific historical concerns are bracketed, and the experience of certain groups of people is excluded from contributing to or determining that analysis. The first limitation is one of time and focus. The task of theological anthropology is to try to understand the nature of the human as such, the possibility of meaning, and the structures of being that underlie particular manifestations of human life such as justice, injustice, and equality. Liberation theologians challenge philosophical or fundamental theology to show the relevance of this sort of investigation to the life and death problems disclosed in the history of human suffering. This is not to say that such work could never be justified, but only that its value can no longer be considered self-evident.

The second limitation of ontological analysis is that it is based solely in the experience of men of a certain class. Those who write and study theology have been predominantly male and middle-class. Men from lower social strata and women lack the access to education needed to engage in the examination of universal or ontological structures of existence and human being. The only basis for that work has been, therefore, a race-, class-, and sex-specific one.

An emphasis on the history of human suffering leads to the declaration that the experience of these people, and experience of the denial and destruction of their humanity, is as normative for our understanding of humanity as is the experience of the victors in historical struggles. The disclosure of the class-, sex-, and race-specific nature of theology is dangerous in that it protests the arrogance, the pretension of men to speak for all humanity and to attempt to ascertain from their limited basis anything universal about human being.

Another dimension of liberation theologians' critique of society and of religion is their exposure of the disparity between discursive and nondiscursive elements in a culture. They contrast the claim of a social system or religion as expressed in literature, philosophy, and theology (the discursive elements) with the concrete relations of power (the nondiscursive elements) in the social system. An example is the contrast between America's ideals of equality and justice and its continuing practice of racism. A similar example comes from feminist theologians, who point out the juxtaposition of the Renaissance claim to humanitarian ideals and to rationality and the simultaneous social practice of witch-burning.

Critical histories disclose the nonnecessity of the dominant apparatuses of a social system, expose their fragility, and claim that they are attained and maintained only through exclusion and repression. To point to the history of the witch-burnings is to indicate that the silence of women in the church, in medicine, and in the sciences is not a matter of natural law but a matter of the exercise of domination, a power struggle in which women were forcibly excluded.

Similarly, the disclosure of the peasant massacres in the early twentieth century in El Salvador and of the continued resistance of peasants to the economic system which exploits them demonstrates that a system in which a few enjoy economic prosperity and many are poor is not a natural phenomenon but continues to exist only through repression. Memories of struggle against social systems are dangerous; they are witnesses to protests against an order of things that claims to be natural, self-evident, or inevitable.

The Memory of Freedom and Resistance

The dangerous memory expressed in liberation theology is not only a memory of conflict and exclusion as in Foucault's genealogies. It is also a memory of hope, a memory of freedom and resistance. This memory of hope is a significant element of the experience of resistance not treated explicitly by Foucault in his account of genealogy. In order for there to be resistance and the affirmation that is implied in the preservation of the memory of suffering, there must be an experience that includes some degree of liberation from the devaluation of human life by the dominant apparatuses of power/knowledge. Even to resist implies a modicum of liberation and success. Domination is not absolute as long as there is protest against it.

We must be careful here not to reify the existence of resistance, too easily pointing to an undefeatable stratum in human being that always continues to resist. On the contrary, analyses or descriptions of resistance seem to point to something quite different: the contingency of resistance, its frailty, and the possibility and actuality of its being at times obliterated. The fragility of resistance leads me to consider an element of specific histories of oppression that is often mentioned but rarely explained: the paucity of resistance.

Awareness of the scarcity of resistance can be seen in the search by Marxists for a revolutionary proletariat, for the class that becomes conscious of its oppression and then resists. The Frankfurt philosophers Adorno and Horkheimer despaired of ever finding such a class in the industrial West, and Habermas is still looking for a glimmer of resistance shining through the cracks in advanced capitalism.

Martin Jay has described the failure to find a revolutionary subject in the work of the Frankfurt School. Jay finds greater attention is given to universal structures as the historical situation appears less open to revolutionary developments.

> With the shifting of the Institute's emphasis away from class struggle to the conflict between man [sic] and nature, the possibility of a historical subject capable of ushering in the revolutionary age disappeared. That imperative for *praxis*, so much a part of what some might call the Institute's heroic period, was no longer an integral part of its thought.

A similar tension characterizes the work of Jürgen Habermas. Habermas provides an extensive analysis of the legitimation crisis in advanced capitalism, but is unable to locate a revolutionary subject to take advantage of this crisis.

Even in current experiences of resistance, those committed to that resistance are painfully aware of how long the domination has prevailed and how rare the moments of resistance have been. One of the most striking features of women's history is that the suppression of women was accepted for so long as self-evident and natural. The history of blacks in America also reflects this pattern; black history is characterized by an ongoing struggle not only against racism but also against defeatism and a negative self-image, the internalization of oppression by the oppressed.

The rarity of explicit resistance does not mean that resistance is not occurring just because there are no visible signs of it. Foucault reminds us of the multifarious nature of power, stating that we should be watchful for manifestations of resistance more subtle than armed rebellion or active withdrawal from an oppressive system. The paucity of resistance in any form cannot be denied, however, and prevents us from too easily locating resistance in the nature of human being as such. Apparently human dignity, the will to freedom, or whatever it is that resists, can be effectively neutralized or actually destroyed in individuals and in groups of people.

Given the rarity of resistance, a careful examination of its conditions is hardly an idle inquiry. What is it in fact that enables people to resist? What are the historical conditions of resistance and liberation? The important consideration for liberation theologians is not the universal or a priori conditions of resistance, but the historical conditions of struggles against domination. One could identify in a regional ontology the nature of human being and its capacity for meaning, decision, and action, indicating the universal ground of resistance without the understanding of why or how in specific histories those fundamental possibilities are actualized or effaced.

Liberation theology is a preservation of dangerous memory, an account of actual, although rare, instances of resistance and liberation. These accounts are a declaration of the possibility of freedom and justice, and they may be examined in an attempt to understand what enables resistance in specific, historical situations. Experiences of partial liberation, experiences that motivate a continued political struggle for liberation, are discussed at different levels by various theologians. Although the degree of analysis varies, the preservation of a memory of historical, actual liberation is common to all liberation theologies.

Such memories are an affirmation of human dignity. They motivate the political struggle against institutions within society and the church that deny and suppress that dignity. James Cone, for example, describes the liberating impact of Christianity on Afro-American women and men during and after slavery. He states that the religion of a God who affirms the worth of all people was lived despite the ideological interpretations of that religion by those who supported slavery. The black church was the locus of experiences of acceptance, love, and dignity. The power that comes from believing that "God" (that which is ultimate) affirms the importance and value of the lives of slaves prevented black acquiescence to the definition of themselves as sub-human by white slave owners. The various African languages and practices of African religion were suppressed, but the Christian religion served as a vehicle for the memory of suffering. In the church it was possible to voice both despair and the hope for release, a hope grounded in the affirmation already experienced.

> How was it possible for black people to keep their humanity together in the midst of servitude, affirming that the God of Jesus is at work in the world, liberating them from bondage? The record shows clearly that black slaves believed that just as God had delivered Moses and the Israelites from Egyptian bondage, he [sic] also will deliver black people from American slavery. . . . That truth . . . came from a liberating encounter with the One who is the Author of black faith and existence.

Mary Daly describes the interaction of personal and political liberation in the experience of sisterhood. As women share stories of their own lives, a common experience of oppression and of resistance is recognized. This politicizing gives women the courage to persist in resistance, recognizing that their difficulties have not only an individual basis but a social and political basis as well. Fear of moving beyond accepted definitions of behavior is not definitively allayed, but the experience of self-affirmation and hope that comes from the affirmation and community of sisterhood gives courage and enables creative resistance. I, too, interpret the experience of sisterhood as an experience of resistance and liberation, an affirmation of an identity that is different from that imposed by the dominant patriarchal social structures. The experience of resistance is itself a denial of the necessity of patriarchy; it is a moment of freedom, the power to embody momentarily an alternative identity. This affirmation serves as the ground for political resistance to social structures.

Gutiérrez grounds Latin American liberation theology in a similar phenomenon in the Latin American churches. The basis of Latin American liberation theology is the politicization of peasants. The gospel message and the experience of solidarity in base Christian communities gives the peasants a sense of worth and power that counters the definition imposed on them by the church in the past and by their own governments. Gutiérrez writes that the church politicizes the poor by evangelizing.

> . . . the annunciation of the Gospel, precisely insofar as it is a message of total love, has an inescapable political dimension, because it is addressed to people who live within a fabric of social relationships, which, in our case, keep them in a subhuman condition . . . to conscienticize, to politicize, to make the oppressed person become aware that he [sic] is a man [sic] . . . does challenge that privilege [the privilege of the ruling classes].

Metz describes dangerous memory as the remembrance of the process of becoming subjects in the presence of God.[1] The memory of subjectivity is carried by some forms of ecclesia and by certain strands of the biblical tradition such as the Exodus tradition and the promises in the gospels of the kingdom of God. The memory is of a community in which people were freed to claim an identity different from that imposed on them. It is both a memory of past liberation and a motivation for further liberation. It is a memory of resistance and of hope for further resistance.

THE BEARERS OF DANGEROUS MEMORY

The work of liberation theologians is firmly grounded in the reality of oppression and of resistance to oppression. Foucault and many liberation theologians find the impetus for their work in these specific instances of resistance among the oppressed. Their analyses of power and domination do not emerge from mere intellectual curiosity, but from two sources: the fact of resistance, and their own commitment to the oppressed. The attitude of commitment is pretheoretical, the already-given attitude that alternative interpretations and voices claiming oppression should be heard. The philosopher or theologian of resistance then brings the skills of his or her training in analysis and synthesis to bear on the power relations manifest in oppression. The result can be a corpus of work like that of Foucault: an analysis of the concrete mechanisms of exclusion and domination in medicine, penology, the asylum, sexuality. In theology, commitment and reflection have led to works like those of Gutiérrez, Daly, Heyward, and Cone—works that describe specific histories of oppression, criticize the role of the church and theology in that oppression, and offer alternative interpretations of the gospel and ecclesia.

At this stage there is a tension in the articulation of dangerous memories. Often the oppressed either do not resist or their expressions of resistance are more immediate than reflective, taking the form of direct action and symbolic expression. Base Christian communities, the black church, and women's collectives offer numerous examples. Here the form or expression of resistance is often imagistic rather than analytic. It is an expression of protest, hope, and vision that motivates political action.

In the base Christian communities the study of scripture passages that challenge oppression leads to a critique of existing social, political, and economic arrangements.

> They [members of base Christian communities] read the Bible much as medieval and reformation radicals read it, as a critical and subversive document. They find in it a God who sides with the poor and with others despised by society; who, at the same time, confronts the social and religious institutions that are the tools of injustice.

Black theology conceptualizes direct expressions of hope and protest found in spirituals, sermons, and prayers. James Cone analyzes the power of these expressions of faith in the black community's struggle for liberation.

> But when blacks went to church and experienced the presence of Jesus' Spirit among them, they realized that he bestowed a meaning upon their lives that could not be taken away by white folks. That's why folks at Macedonia sang: "A little talk with Jesus makes it right": not that "white is right," but that God had affirmed the rightness of their existence, the

righteousness of their being in the world. That affirmation enabled black people to meet "the Man" on Monday morning and to deal with his dehumanizing presence the remainder of the week, knowing that white folks could not destroy their humanity.

The critical reflection by intellectuals on the symbolic expression and political action of those who are oppressed includes a recognition of the tension implied in theoretical work: it may be either useless or oppressive. The value of a conceptual analysis of powerful systems of action and symbolic reflection is determined by the role that analysis plays in furthering resistance. Its possible oppressiveness lies in what Foucault calls the indignity of speaking for other people. In a conversation between Deleuze and Foucault, Deleuze states:

> In my opinion, you were the first—in your books and in the practical sphere—to teach us something absolutely fundamental: the indignity of speaking for others. We ridiculed representation and said it was finished, but we failed to draw the consequences of this "theoretical" conversion—to appreciate the theoretical fact that only those directly concerned can speak in a practical way on their own behalf.

Foucault responds by referring to prisoners and to what happened when they began to speak for themselves:

> It is this form of discourse which ultimately matters, a discourse against power, the counter-discourse of prisoners and those we call delinquents—and not a theory *about* delinquency.

Gutiérrez recognizes this as well. He sees the value of liberation theology as the opening of theological discourse to include the voices of the oppressed.

> But in the last instance we will have an authentic theology of liberation only when the oppressed themselves can freely raise their voice and express themselves directly and creatively in society and in the heart of the people of God, when they themselves "account for the hope," which they bear, when they are the protagonists of their own liberation.

Respect for the integrity of those who are oppressed is expressed by liberation theologians both in their willingness to learn from symbolic, immediate expressions of hope and protest and in their providing access to communication systems that enable the oppressed to speak for themselves. The *Theology in the Americas* association, a group of liberation theologians and activists, for example, sponsors conferences in which the primary speakers are those who are oppressed. Foucault's political work focuses not on reforming prisons according to his genealogy of the prison, but on providing structures that allow prisoners to speak for themselves and to make changes based on their analysis. In both liberation theology and the work of Foucault there is an ongoing tension between avoiding the indignity of speaking for the oppressed and attempting to respond to their voices by engaging in social and political critique.

NOTE

1. Johann Baptist Metz, *Faith in History and Society: Toward a Practical Fundamental Theology*, trans. David Smith (New York: Seabury Press, 1980), 67. [Original reference.]

SIMONE WEIL (1909–1943)

Simone Weil emblematizes Europe's generation of anger. Her crusade for the worker, her empathy for the marginalized and forgotten led her to punish her own body, to risk her own health, but also to engage in subtle reflection on metaphysical issues that resulted in a string of writings, still widely read and still capable of provocation.

Born in Paris in 1909 into a close-knit, affluent, and agnostic Jewish family, she decided to become a Bolshevik after the Russian Revolution. By the time she entered college, her revolutionary zeal had tempered; she wrote incisive critiques of Marxist thought, although she remained critical of capitalist modes of production, above all, of the suffering they inflicted on workers. From her undergraduate years on, she practiced what she preached: not only did she offer classes to railway, mine, and farm workers free of charge, but she also gave most of her salary, and her nonacademic time, to help workers organize.

She matriculated at the Sorbonne, the most elite of elite institutions in post–World War I France, yet she was far from a "normal" student. She gave herself to the cause of hunger and workers' rights at the same time that she committed herself to chastity, in public and with a stridency that led her classmates to dub her "the Red Virgin."

Her remarkable double life as an intellectual and an activist was etched in the years after her graduation from the Sorbonne. She began teaching in a rural French city, while at the same time organizing and marching with the town's unemployed workers. Fired from her job, she took up teaching philosophy in another rural French community. One of her students took notes of those lectures, which were published decades later as Lectures on Philosophy *(1959). They are now used as college-level textbooks. The next stage of her pedagogical activism led Simone Weil to challenge the French factory system. She quit teaching, lived with the unskilled women workers, and engaged in long stints of fasting. In 1937 Weil left for Spain to fight on behalf of anarchists in the Spanish Civil War, where she proved more adept as a mystic than a soldier, as is evident in her remarkable "Spiritual Autobiography," a chapter in the book* Waiting for God *(1950).*

In 1942 Weil fled from France to America, then back to England, where she worked for the French resistance and also contracted tuberculosis. She died the following year, but not before writing a number of major essays, published posthumously as The Need for Roots *(1949). Among her exemplary works was* The Iliad, or the Poem of Force. *In it she pours forth the interpretation of force as an intrinsic violence that few overcome, yet all should recognize for its apotheosis in the theater of war. Because the Trojan War, which provides the backdrop for the* Iliad, *is the classic projection of war as glory, Weil uses it to demonstrate how war reduces humankind to the level of brute slavery, automatons to instincts that blind and numb, rather than ennoble and elevate, human potential.*

The *Iliad*, or the Poem of Force

SIMONE WEIL

The true hero, the true subject, the center of the *Iliad* is force. Force employed by man, force that enslaves man, force before which man's flesh shrinks away. In this work, at all times, the human spirit is shown as modified by its relations with force, as swept away, blinded by the very force it imagined it could handle, as deformed by the weight of the force it submits to. For those dreamers who considered that force, thanks to progress, would soon be a thing of the past, the *Iliad* could appear as an historical document; for others, whose powers of recognition are more acute and who perceive force, today as yesterday, at the very center of human history, the *Iliad* is the purest and the loveliest of mirrors.

To define force—it is that x that turns anybody who is subjected to it into a *thing*. Exercised to the limit, it turns man into a thing in the most literal sense: it makes a corpse out of him. Somebody was here, and the next minute there is nobody here at all; this is a spectacle the *Iliad* never wearies of showing us:

> . . . *the horses*
> *Rattled the empty chariots through the files of battle,*
> *Longing for their noble drives. But they on the ground*
> *Lay, dearer to the vultures than to their wives.*

The hero becomes a thing dragged behind a chariot in the dust:

> *All around, his black hair*
> *Was spread; in the dust his whole head lay,*
> *That once-charming head; now Zeus had let his enemies*
> *Defile it on his native soil.*

The bitterness of such a spectacle is offered us absolutely undiluted. No comforting fiction intervenes; no consoling prospect of immortality; and on the hero's head no washed-out halo of patriotism descends.

> *His soul, fleeing his limbs, passed to Hades,*
> *Mourning its fate, forsaking its youth and its vigor.*

Still more poignant—so painful is the contrast—is the sudden evocation, as quickly rubbed out, of another world: the faraway, precarious, touching world of peace, of the family, the world in which each man counts more than anything else to those about him.

> She ordered her bright-haired maids in the palace
> To place on the fire a large tripod, preparing
> A hot bath for Hector, returning from battle.
> Foolish woman! Already he lay, far from hot baths,
> Slain by grey-eyed Athena, who guided Achilles' arm.

Far from hot baths he was indeed, poor man. And not he alone. Nearly all the *Iliad* takes place far from hot baths. Nearly all of human life, then and now, takes place far from hot baths.

Here we see force in its grossest and most summary form—the form that kills. How much more varied in its processes, how much more surprising in its effects is the other force, the force that does *not* kill, i.e., that does not kill just yet. It will surely kill, it will possibly kill, or perhaps it merely hangs, poised and ready, over the head of the creature it *can* kill, at any moment, which is to say at every moment. In whatever aspect, its effect is the same: it turns a man into a stone. From its first property (the ability to turn a human being into a thing by the simple method of killing him) flows another, quite prodigious too in its own way, the ability to turn a human being into a thing while it is still alive. He is alive; he has a soul; and yet—he is a thing. An extraordinary entity this—a thing that has a soul. And as for the soul, what an extraordinary house it finds itself in! Who can say what it costs it, moment by moment, to accommodate itself to this residence, how much writhing and bending, folding and pleating are required of it? It was not made to live inside a thing; if it does so, under pressure of necessity, there is not a single element of its nature to which violence is not done.

A man stands disarmed and naked with a weapon pointing at him; this person becomes a corpse before anybody or anything touches him. Just a minute ago, he was thinking, acting, hoping:

> Motionless, he pondered. And the other drew near,
> Terrified, anxious to touch his knees, hoping in his heart
> To escape evil death and black destiny. . . .
> With one hand he clasped, suppliant, his knees,
> While the other clung to the sharp spear, not letting go. . . .

Soon, however, he grasps the fact that the weapon which is pointing at him will not be diverted; and now, still breathing, he is simply matter; still thinking, he can think no longer:

Thus spoke the brilliant son of Priam
In begging words. But he heard a harsh reply:
He spoke. And the other's knees and heart failed him.
Dropping his spear, he knelt down, holding out his arms.
Achilles, drawing his sharp sword, struck
Through the neck and breastbone. The two-edged sword
Sunk home its full length. The other, face down,
Lay still, and the black blood ran out, wetting the ground.

. . . . .

Perhaps all men, by the very act of being born, are destined to suffer violence; yet this is a truth to which circumstance shuts men's eyes. The strong are, as a matter of fact, never absolutely strong, nor are the weak absolutely weak, but neither is aware of this. They have in common a refusal to believe that they both belong to the same species: the weak see no relation between themselves and the strong, and vice versa. The man who is the possessor of force seems to walk through a non-resistant element; in the human substance that surrounds him nothing has the power to interpose, between the impulse and the act, the tiny interval that is reflection. Where there is no room for reflection, there is no room either for justice or prudence. Hence we see men in arms behaving harshly and madly. We see their sword bury itself in the breast of a disarmed enemy who is in the very act of pleading at their knees. We see them triumph over a dying man by describing to him the outrages his corpse will endure. We see Achilles cut the throats of twelve Trojan boys on the funeral pyre of Patroclus as naturally as we cut flowers for a grave. These men, wielding power, have no suspicion of the fact that the consequences of their deeds will at length come home to them—they too will bow the neck in their turn. If you can make an old man fall silent, tremble, obey, with a single word of your own, why should it occur to you that the curses of this old man, who is after all a priest, will have their own importance in the gods' eyes. Why should you refrain from taking Achilles' girl away from him if you know that neither he nor she can do anything but obey you? Achilles rejoices over the sight of the Greeks fleeing in misery and confusion. What could possibly suggest to him that this rout, which will last exactly as long as he wants it to and end when his mood indicates it, that this very rout will be the cause of his friend's death, and, for that matter, of his own? Thus it happens that those who have force on loan from fate count on it too much and are destroyed.

But at the time their own destruction seems impossible to them. For they do not see that the force in their possession is only a limited quantity; nor do they see their relations with other human beings as a kind of balance between unequal amounts of force. Since other people do not impose on their movements that halt, that interval of hesitation, wherein lies all our consideration for our brothers in humanity, they conclude that destiny has given complete license to them, and none at all to their inferiors. And at this point they exceed the measure of the force that is actually at their disposal. Inevitably they exceed it, since they are not aware that it is limited. And now we see them committed irretrievably to chance; suddenly things cease to obey them. Sometimes chance is kind to them, sometimes cruel. But in any case there they are, exposed, open to misfortune; gone is the armor of power that formerly protected their naked souls; nothing, no shield, stands between them and tears.

This retribution, which has a geometrical rigor, which operates automatically to penalize the abuse of force, was the main subject of Greek thought. It is the soul of the epic. Under the name of Nemesis, it functions as the mainspring of Aeschylus' tragedies. To the Pythagoreans, to Socrates and Plato, it was the jumping-off point of speculation upon the nature of man and the universe. Wherever Hellenism has penetrated, we find the idea of it familiar. In Oriental countries which are steeped in Buddhism, it is perhaps this Greek idea that has lived on under the name of Karma. The Occident, however, has lost it, and no longer even has a word to express it in any of its languages: conceptions of limit, measure, equilibrium, which ought to determine the conduct of life, are in the West, restricted to a servile function in the vocabulary of technics. We are only geometricians of matter; the Greeks were, first of all, geometricians in their apprenticeship to virtue.

The progress of the war in the *Iliad* is simply a continual game of seesaw. The victor of the moment feels himself invincible, even though, only a few hours before, he may have experienced defeat; he forgets to treat victory as a transitory thing. At the end of the first day of combat described in the *Iliad*, the victorious Greeks were in a position to obtain the object of all their efforts, i.e., Helen and her riches—assuming of course as Homer did, that the Greeks had reason to believe that Helen was in Troy. Actually, the Egyptian priests, who ought to have known, affirmed later on to Herodotus that she was in Egypt. In any case, that evening the Greeks are no longer interested in her or her possessions:

> *"For the present, let us not accept the riches of Paris;*
> *Nor Helen; everybody sees, even the most ignorant,*
> *That Troy stands on the verge of ruin."*
> *He spoke, and all the Achaeans acclaimed him.*

What they want is, in fact, everything. For booty, all the riches of Troy; for their bonfires, all the palaces, temples, houses; for slaves, all the women and children; for corpses, all the men. They forget one detail, that *everything* is not within their power, for they are not in Troy. Perhaps they will be there tomorrow; perhaps not. Hector, the same day, makes the same mistake:

> For I know well in my entrails and in my hearts,
> A day will come when Holy Troy will perish,
> And Priam, and the nation of Priam of the good lance.
> But I think less of the grief that is in store for the Trojans,
> And of Hecuba herself, and of Priam the king,
> And of my brothers, so numerous and so brave,
> Who will fall in the dust under blows of the enemy,
> Than of you that day when a Greek in his bronze breastplate
> Will drag you away weeping and deprive you of your liberty.
> But as for me, may I be dead, and may the earth have covered me
> Before I hear you cry out or see you dragged away!

At this moment what would he not give to turn aside those horrors which he believes to be inevitable? But at this moment nothing he *could* give would be of any use. The next day but one, however, the Greeks have run away miserably, and Agamemnon himself is in favor of putting to the sea again. And now Hector, by making a very few concessions, could readily secure the enemy's departure; yet now he is even unwilling to let them go empty-handed:

> Set fires everywhere and let the brightness mount the skies
> Lest in the night the long-haired Greeks,
> Escaping, sail over the broad back of ocean. . . .
> Let each of them take home a wound to heal
> . . . thus others will fear
> To bring dolorous war to the Trojans, tamers of horses.

His wish is granted; the Greeks stay; and the next day they reduce Hector and his men to a pitiable condition:

> As for them—they fled across the plain like cattle
> Whom a lion hunts before him in the dark midnight. . . .
> Thus the mighty Agamemnon, son of Atreus, pursued them,
> Steadily killing the hindmost; and still they fled.

In the course of the afternoon, Hector regains the ascendancy, withdraws again, then puts the Greeks to flight, then is repulsed by Patroclus, who has come in with his fresh troops. Patroclus, pressing his advantage, ends by finding himself exposed, wounded and without armor, to the sword of Hector. And finally that evening the victorious Hector hears the prudent counsel of Polydamas and repudiates it sharply:

> *Now that wily Kronos's son has given me*
> *Glory at the ships; now that I have driven the Greeks to the sea,*
> *Do not offer, fool, such counsels to the people.*
> *No Trojan will listen to you; nor would I permit it. . . .*
> *So Hector spoke, and the Trojans acclaimed him. . . .*

The next day Hector is lost. Achilles has harried him across the field and is about to kill him. He has always been the stronger of the two in combat; how much the more so now, after several weeks of rest, ardent for vengeance and victory, against an exhausted enemy? And Hector stands alone, before the walls of Troy, absolutely alone, alone to wait for death and to steady his soul to face it:

> *Alas, were I to slip through the gate, behind the rampart,*
> *Polydamas at once would heap dishonor on me. . . .*
> *And now that through my recklessness I have destroyed my people,*
> *I fear the Trojans and the long-robed Trojan women,*
> *I fear to hear from some one far less brave than I:*
> *"Hector, trusting his own strength too far, has ruined his people." . . .*
> *Suppose I were to down my bossed shield,*
> *My massive helmet, and, leaning my spear against the wall,*
> *Should go to meet renowned Achilles? . . .*
> *But why spin out these fancies? Why such dreams?*
> *I would not reach him, nor would he pity me,*
> *Or respect me. He would kill me like a woman*
> *If I came naked thus. . . .*

Not a jot of the grief and ignominy that fall to the unfortunate is Hector spared. Alone, stripped of the prestige of force, he discovers that the courage that kept him from taking to the shelter of the walls is not enough to save him from flight:

> *Seeing him, Hector began to tremble. He had not the heart*
> *To stay. . . .*
> *. . . It is not for a ewe nor the skin of an ox,*
> *That they are striving, not these ordinary rewards of the race;*
> *It is for a life that they run, the life of Hector, tamer of horses.*

Wounded to death, he enhances his conqueror's triumph by vain supplications:

> *I implore you, by your soul, by your knees, by your parents. . . .*

But the auditors of the *Iliad* knew that the death of Hector would be but a brief joy to Achilles, and the death of Achilles but a brief joy to the Trojans, and the destruction of Troy but a brief joy to the Achaeans.

Thus violence obliterates anybody who feels its touch. It comes to seem just as external to its employer as to its victim. And from this springs the idea of a destiny before which executioner and victim stand equally innocent, before which conqueror and conquered are brothers in the same distress. The conquered brings misfortune to the conqueror, and vice versa:

> A single son, short-lived, was born to him.
> Neglected by me, he grows old—for far from home
> I camp before Troy, injuring you and your sons.

A moderate use of force, which alone would enable man to escape being enmeshed in its machinery, would require superhuman virtue, which is as rare as dignity in weakness. Moreover, moderation itself is not without its perils, since prestige, from which force derives at least three quarters of its strength, rest principally upon that marvelous indifference that the strong feel toward the weak, an indifference so contagious that it infects the very people who are the objects of it. Yet ordinarily excess is not arrived at through prudence or politic considerations. On the contrary, man dashes to it as to an irresistible temptation. The voice of reason is occasionally heard in the mouths of the characters in the *Iliad*. Thersites' speeches are reasonable to the highest degree; so are the speeches of the angry Achilles:

> Nothing is worth my life, not all the goods
> They say the well-built city of Ilium contains. . . .
> A man can capture steers and fatted sheep
> But, once gone, the soul cannot be captured back.

But words of reason drop into the void. If they come from an inferior, he is punished and shuts up; if from a chief, his actions betray him. And failing everything else, there is always a god handy to advise him to be unreasonable. In the end, the very idea of wanting to escape the role fate has allotted one—the business of killing and dying—disappears from the mind:

> We to whom Zeus
> Has assigned suffering, from youth to old age,
> Suffering in grievous wars, till we perish to the last man.

Already these warriors, like Craonne's so much later, felt themselves to be "condemned men."

It was the simplest trap that pitched them into this situation. At the outset, at the embarkation, their hearts are light, as hearts always are if you have a large force on your side and nothing but space to oppose you. Their weapons are in their hands; the enemy is absent. Unless your spirit has been conquered in advance by the reputation of the enemy, you always feel yourself to be much stronger than anybody who is not there. An absent man does not impose the yoke of necessity. To the spirits of those embarking no necessity yet presents itself; consequently they go off as though to a game, as though on holiday from the confinement of daily life.

> Where have they gone, those braggadocio boasts
> We proudly flung upon the air at Lemnos,
> Stuffing ourselves with flesh of horned steers,
> Drinking from cups brimming over with wine?
> As for Trojans—a hundred or two each man of us
> Could handle in battle. And now one is too much for us.

But the first contact of war does not immediately destroy the illusion that war is a game. War's necessity is terrible, altogether different in kind from the necessity of peace. So terrible is it that the human spirit will not submit to it so long as it can possibly escape; and whenever it can escape it takes refuge in long days empty of necessity, days of play, of revelry, days arbitrary and unreal. Danger then becomes an abstraction; the lives you destroy are like toys broken by a child, and quite as incapable of feeling; heroism is but a theatrical gesture and smirched with boastfulness. This becomes doubly true if a momentary access of vitality comes to reinforce the divine hand that wards off defeat and death. Then war is easy and basely, coarsely loved.

But with the majority of the combatants this state of mind does not persist. Soon there comes a day when fear, or defeat or the death of beloved comrades touches the warrior's spirit, and it crumbles in the hand of necessity. At that moment war is no more a game or a dream; now at last the warrior cannot doubt the reality of its existence. And this reality, which he perceives, is hard, much too hard to be borne, for it enfolds death. Once you acknowledge death to be a practical possibility, the thought of it becomes unendurable, except in flashes. True enough, all men are fated to die; true enough also, a soldier may grow old in battles; yet for those whose spirits have bent under the yoke of war, the relation between death and the future is different than for other men. For other men death appears as a limit set in advance on the future; for the soldier death *is* the future, the future his profession assigns him. Yet the idea of men's having death for a future is abhorrent to nature. Once the experience of war makes visible the possibility of death that lies locked up in each moment, our thoughts cannot travel from one day to the next without meeting death's face. The mind is then strung up to a pitch it can stand for only a short time; but each new dawn reintroduces the same necessity; and days piled on days make years. On each one of these days the soul suffers violence. Regularly, every morning, the soul castrates itself of aspiration, for thought cannot journey through time without meeting death on the way. Thus war effaces all conceptions of purpose or goal, including even its own "war aims." It effaces the very notion of war's being brought to an end. To be outside a situation so violent as this is to find it inconceivable; to be inside it is to be unable to conceive its end. Consequently, nobody does anything to bring this end about. In the presence of an armed enemy, what hand can relinquish its weapon? The mind ought to find a way out, but the mind has lost all capacity to so much as look outward. The mind is completely absorbed in doing itself violence. Always in human life, whether war or slavery is in question, intolerable sufferings continue, as it were, by the force of their own specific gravity, and so look to the outsider as though they were easy to bear; actually, they continue because they have deprived the sufferer of the resources which might serve to extricate him.

Nevertheless, the soul that is enslaved to war cries out for deliverance, but deliverance itself appears to it in an extreme and tragic aspect, the aspect of destruction. Any other solution, more moderate, more reasonable in character, would expose the mind to suffering so naked, so violent that it could not be borne, even as memory. Terror, grief, exhaustion, slaughter, the annihilation of comrades—is it credible that these things should not continually tear at the soul, if the intoxication of force had not intervened to drown them? The idea that an unlimited effort should bring in only a limited profit or no profit at all is terribly painful.

> What? Will we let Priam and the Trojans boast
> Of Argive Helen, she for whom so many Greeks
> Died before Troy, far from their native land?
> What? Do you want us to leave the city, wide-streeted Troy,
> Standing, when we have suffered so much for it?

But actually what is Helen to Ulysses? What indeed is Troy, full of riches that will not compensate him for Ithaca's ruin? For the Greeks, Troy and Helen are in reality mere sources of blood and tears; to master them is to master frightful memories. If the existence of an enemy has made a soul destroy in itself the thing nature put there, then the only remedy the soul can imagine is the destruction of the enemy. At the same time the death of dearly loved comrades arouses a spirit of somber emulation, a rivalry in death:

> May I die, then, at once! Since fate has not let me
> Protect my dead friend, who far from home
> Perished, longing for me to defend him from death.
> So now I go to seek the murderer of my friend,

Hector. And death shall I find at the moment
Zeus wills it—Zeus and the other immortals.

It is the same despair that drives him on toward death, on the one hand, and slaughter on the other:

I know it well, my fate is to perish here,
Far from father and dearly loved mother; but meanwhile
I shall not stop till the Trojans have had their fill of war.

The man possessed by this twofold need for death belongs, so long as he has not become something still different, to a different race from the race of the living.

What echo can the timid hopes of life strike in such a heart? How can it hear the defeated begging for another sight of the light of day? The threatened life has already been relieved of nearly all its consequence by a single, simple distinction: it is now unarmed; its adversary possesses a weapon. Furthermore, how can a man who has rooted out of himself the notion that the light of day is sweet to the eyes respect such a notion when it makes its appearance in some futile and humble lament?

I clasp tight your knees, Achilles. Have a thought, have pity for me.
I stand here, O son of Zeus, a suppliant, to be respected.
In your house it was I first tasted Demeter's bread,
That day in my well-pruned vineyard you caught me
And sold me, sending me far from father and friends,
To holy Lemnos; a hundred oxen was my price.
And now I will pay you three hundred for ransom.
This dawn is for me my twelfth day in Troy,
After so many sorrows. See me here, in your hands,
Through some evil fate. Zeus surely must hate me
Who again puts me into your hands. Alas, my poor mother, Laothoe,
Daughter of the old man, Altes—a short-lived son you have borne.

What a reception this feeble hope gets!

Come, friend, you too must die. Why make a fuss about it?
Patroclus, he too has died—a far better man than you are.
Don't you see how handsome I am, how mighty?
A noble father begat me, and I have a goddess for mother.
Yet even I, like you, must some day encounter my fate,
Whether the hour strikes at noon, or evening, or sunrise,
The hour that comes when some arms-bearing warrior will kill me.

To respect life in somebody else when you have had to castrate yourself of all yearning for it demands a truly heartbreaking exertion of the powers of generosity. It is impossible to imagine any of Homer's warriors being capable of such an exertion, unless it is that warrior who dwells, in a peculiar way, at the very center of the power—I mean Patroclus, who "knew how to be sweet to everybody," and who throughout the *Iliad* commits no cruel or brutal act. But then how many men do we know, in several thousand years of human history, who would have displayed such god-like generosity? Two or three? Even this is doubtful. Lacking this generosity, the conquering soldier is like a scourge of nature. Possessed by war, he, like the slave, becomes a thing, though his manner of doing so is different—over him too, words are as powerless as over matter itself. And both, at the touch of force, experience its inevitable effects: they become deaf and dumb.

Such is the nature of force. Its power of converting a man into a thing is a double one, and in its application double-edged. To the same degree, though in different fashions, those who use it and those who endure it are turned to stone. This property of force achieves its maximum effectiveness during the clash of arms, in battle, when the tide of the day has turned, and everything is rushing toward a decision. It is not the planning man, the man of strategy, the man acting on the resolution taken, who wins or loses a battle; battles are fought and decided by men deprived of these faculties, men who have undergone a transformation, who have dropped either to the level of inert matter, which is pure passivity, or to the level of blind force, which is pure momentum. Herein lies the last secret of war, a secret revealed by the *Iliad* in its similes, which liken the warriors either to fire, flood, wind, wild beasts, or God knows what blind cause of disaster, or else to frightened animals, trees, water, sand, to anything in nature that is set into motion by the violence of external forces. Greeks and Trojans, from one day to the next, sometimes even from one hour to the next, experience, turn and turn about, one or the other of these transmutations:

> As when a lion, murderous, springs among the cattle
> Which by thousands are grazing over some vast marshy field . . .
> And their flanks heave with terror; even so the Achaians
> Scattered in panic before Hector and Zeus, the great father.
> As when a ravening fire breaks out deep in a busy wood
> And the wheeling wind scatters sparks far and wide,
> And trees, root and branch, topple over in flames;
> So Atreus' son, Agamemnon, roared through the ranks
> Of the Trojans in flight. . . .

The art of war is simply the art of producing such transformations, and its equipment, its processes, even the casualties it inflicts on the enemy, are only means directed toward this end—its true object is the warrior's soul. Yet these transformations are always a mystery; the gods are their authors, the gods who kindle men's imagination. But however caused, this petrifactive quality of force, two-fold always, is essential to its nature; and a soul which has entered the province of force will not escape this except by a miracle. Such miracles are rare and of brief duration.

. . . . .

The relations between destiny and the human soul, the extent to which each soul creates its own destiny, the question of what elements in the soul are transformed by merciless necessity as it tailors the soul to fit the requirements of shifting fate, and of what elements can on the other hand be preserved, through the exercise of virtue and through grace—this whole question is fraught with temptations to falsehood, temptations that are positively enhanced by pride, by shame, by hatred, contempt, indifference, by the will to oblivion or to ignorance. Moreover, nothing is so rare as to see misfortune fairly portrayed; the tendency is either to treat the unfortunate person as though catastrophe were his natural vocation, or to ignore the effects of misfortune on the soul, to assume, that is, that the soul can suffer and remain unmarked by it, can fail, in fact, to be recast in misfortune's image. The Greeks, generally speaking, were endowed with spiritual force that allowed them to avoid self-deception. The rewards of this were great; they discovered how to achieve in all their acts the greatest lucidity, purity, and simplicity. But the spirit that was transmitted from the *Iliad* to the Gospels by way of the tragic poets never jumped the borders of Greek civilization; once Greece was destroyed, nothing remained of this spirit but pale reflections.

Both the Romans and the Hebrews believed themselves to be exempt from the misery that is the common human lot. The Romans saw their country as the nation chosen by destiny to be mistress of the world; with the Hebrews, it was their God who exalted them and they retained their superior position as long as they obeyed Him. Strangers, enemies, conquered peoples, subjects, slaves, were objects of contempt to the Romans; and the Romans had no epics, no tragedies. In Rome gladiatorial fights took the place of tragedy. With the Hebrews, misfortune was a sure indication of sin and hence a legitimate object of contempt; to them a vanquished enemy was abhorrent to God himself and condemned to expiate all sorts of crimes—this is a view that makes cruelty permissible and indeed indispensable. And no text of the Old Testament strikes a note comparable to the note heard in the Greek epic, unless it be certain parts of the book of

Job. Throughout twenty centuries of Christianity, the Romans and the Hebrews have been admired, read, imitated, both in deed and word; their masterpieces have yielded an appropriate quotation every time anybody had a crime he wanted to justify.

Furthermore, the spirit of the Gospels was not handed down in a pure state from one Christian generation to the next. To undergo suffering and death joyfully was from the very beginning considered a sign of grace in the Christian martyrs—as though grace could do more for a human being than it could for Christ. Those who believe that God himself, once he became man, could not face the harshness of destiny without a long tremor of anguish, should have understood that the only people who can give the impression of having risen to a higher plane, who seem superior to ordinary human misery, are the people who resort to the aids of illusion, exaltation, fanaticism, to conceal the harshness of destiny from their own eyes. The man who does not wear the armor of the lie cannot experience force without being touched by it to the very soul. Grace can prevent this touch from corrupting him, but it cannot spare him the wound. Having forgotten it too well, Christian tradition can only rarely recover that simplicity that renders so poignant every sentence in the story of the Passion. On the other hand, the practice of forcible proselytization threw a veil over the effects of force on the souls of those who used it.

In spite of the brief intoxication induced at the time of the Renaissance by the discovery of Greek literature, there has been, during the course of twenty centuries, no revival of the Greek genius. Something of it was seen in Villon, in Shakespeare, Cervantes, Molière, and—just once—in Racine. The bones of human suffering are exposed in *L'Ecole des Femmes* and in *Phèdre*, love being the context—a strange century indeed, which took the opposite view from that of the epic period, and would only acknowledge human suffering in the context of love, while it insisted on swathing with glory the effects of force in war and politics. To the list of writers given above, a few other names might be added. But nothing the peoples of Europe have produced is worth the first known poem that appeared among them. Perhaps they will yet rediscover the epic genius, when they learn that there is no refuge from fate, learn not to admire force, not to hate the enemy, nor to scorn the unfortunate. How soon this will happen is another question.

PART IV. THE STATE OF VIOLENCE

The State was first this abstract unity that
integrated subaggregates functioning
separately; it is now subordinated to a field
of forces whose flows it co-ordinates and
whose autonomous relations of domination
and subordination it expresses.
—Gilles Deleuze and Félix Guattari,
Anti-Oedipus

IN 1649 CHARLES I WAS TRIED and executed after the Royalist uprising, and the Scots army's invasion of England was successfully crushed by Oliver Cromwell's parliamentarian forces. Two years later, Thomas Hobbes published *Leviathan*, with its sustained critique of what he calls the "injustice" of regicide. *Leviathan* begins with the stated assumption that all men are created equal by nature, whether in body or mind, and that even though there may be one who is deemed stronger than another, yet the weaker possesses enough strength to kill the strongest "either by secret machination, or by confederacy with others that are in the same danger with himself." The same can be said of the relative strength of the mind, "prudence," which is synonymous with experience, and which "equal time equally bestows on all men in those things they equally apply themselves unto." This equality, Hobbes suggests, always and necessarily leads to war or enmity between men when they desire the same things, the chief causes of quarrel being competition, diffidence, and glory. This state of perpetual war characterized by a condition where "every man is enemy to every man" is entailed in the absence of a "common power to keep them all in awe." Such a state is one of "continual fear and danger of violent death, and the life of man, solitary, poor, nasty, brutish, and short."

This continual unrest and conflict can be averted only by means of a covenant whereby each man relinquishes his natural rights to a sovereign. The mechanism of this appointment of a sovereign rests primarily on the nature and sources of fear of violent death: first, the fear of life and property that each feels from the other, that is, the enemy within; and second, the fear of invasion from other societies or states, that is, the enemy without. It is for protection from these sources of danger that each man pledges himself to a sovereign who might be one person or an assembly of persons. This, for Hobbes, is not really consent or accord of men, but "a real unity of them all, in one and the same person, made by a covenant of every man with every man." The covenant is valid, and forms a commonwealth, only if every one of these men becomes subject, that is, consents to relinquishing his right to governing himself to the sovereign on the condition that every other man does the same.

But if the state finds its validation in the promise it holds—the promise of aversion of the perpetual danger of violence in the state of nature, or war, it is also the case that the very existence and maintenance of the state can be brought about by precisely this threat of violence. In other words, the state contains within itself that state of violence which it represses by means of a concomitant violence. For the consent of the subjects does not need to be offered willfully. This consent can also be forced on the subjects if the sovereign is mightier and acquires sovereignty through force, by subjugating others, as in the case of sovereignty by acquisition. Furthermore, like a commonwealth by acquisition, a commonwealth by institution also contains within itself that dormant violence, for even though such a commonwealth is founded on the mutual consent of the subjects, who agree, of their own accord, to invest power and relinquish some of their natural rights to a chosen sovereign, even in this form of commonwealth, such investiture of power is motivated by the fear of such a sovereign, what Hobbes calls "awe." And it is precisely through the fear of the punishment that the subjects might suffer at the sovereign's hands that they constrain their natural passions and their appetites.

If Hobbes talks about state formation as the panacea to the ills of the state of nature, Hannah Arendt, writing about the totalitarian movements of the first half of the twentieth century, suggests that the difference between the totalitarian and other kinds of states is that the totalitarian state does not replace older forms of law with its own sense of legality: "Its defiance of all, even its own positive laws implies that it believes it can do without any consensus iuris whatever, and still not resign itself to the tyrannical state of lawlessness, arbitrariness and fear." Arendt describes totalitarianism as a movement, not a government, and suggests that totalitarianism in power—what she calls the "so-called totalitarian state," which is not really a state but a perpetual movement at approximating the state—uses the state organization for its purposes but never actually becomes the state. That is why there is always a duplication of authority in the duality of the state and the party.

Arendt considers this peculiar form of a state, the totalitarian movement-state, as a symptom of a radical evil that emerged in the twentieth century—an evil so radical that it defies understanding. This radical evil has been "previously unknown to us," Arendt states, and all one can say about it is that "something seems to be involved in modern politics that actually should never be involved in politics as we used to understand it, namely all or nothing." The "all or nothing," this radical evil, appears in totalitarian movements in the form of designs to conquer the world and produce a homogeneous entity, "an undetermined infinity of forms of human living-together"—the all. Alternative to this is the nothing, which can be conceptualized as a "victory of the concentration-camp system," which "would mean the same inexorable doom for human beings as the use of the hydrogen bomb would mean the doom of the human race."

This peculiar historical state-formation, as opposed to other kinds of states, works through violence; it is not an alternative to the violence of the state of nature, but is itself a violent entity, so that it actually becomes that kind of a state which is itself the Hobbesian state of nature, of lawlessness and war. This kind of state is centered on sites of violence: totalitarian domination "stands or falls with the existence of these concentration and extermination camps; for unlikely as it may sound, these camps are the true central institution of totalitarian organizational power." The irrational violence it deploys is not only physical but also psychological; the concentration and extermination camps are used not only for killing off whole sections of the population "like bedbugs," as well as exterminating any memory or trace of them, but also as an experiment in killing off in the victims any sense of humanity or worth, thereby transforming them into "uncomplaining animals."

This radical evil, which posits a situation of all or nothing, Arendt suggests, has "emerged in connection with a system in which all men have become equally superfluous"; with "population and homelessness everywhere on the increase," with the increase of "economically superfluous and socially rootless human masses," the masses in most states have become much "too desperate to retain much fear of death." It is this lack of fear of death that characterizes the sense of superfluousness, for not only the victims but also the murderers in this system come to have no fear of death. In other words, what in the Hobbesian framework was an incentive for state formation—that is, fear of death—has become obsolete; it is the realization of this obsolescence that prompts Arendt to question the demise of totalitarianism: she warns that even though one may have already seen the fall of the totalitarian regimes of the first half of the twentieth century, the totalitarian solutions and their instruments may perhaps have survived "in the form of strong temptations which will come up whenever it seems impossible to alleviate political, social, or economic misery in a manner worthy of man." In other words, what one finds in Arendt is the sense that this change in the material conditions of humanity—the population increase and the social, political, and economic superfluity that humans thus face—has also given rise to a different kind of humanity, which, in turn, means different ways of organizing power. What one is left with is the implicit doubt about whether, with the appearance of this radical evil which has made men superfluous, the very concept of the state as a protector from violent death has become a thing of the past.

While Arendt considers totalitarian regimes as being characterized by "the struggle for total domination of the total population of the earth, the elimination of every competing non-totalitarian reality," Michel Foucault discusses the modern state, with its disciplinary panoptic technologies, as precisely capable of curtailing wayward tendencies in the subject by partitioning and through the disciplinary powers of an omnipresent gaze. This Foucauldian state, though obviously not the historical totalitarian state of Arendt's framework, in fact derives its power from a metaphoric totalitarianism, all-embracing in its reach, all-pervasive in its approach. The figure for this state is the panopticon, an architectural model which has in its center the observer who can oversee everything and everyone—be it a schoolboy, a prisoner, or a madman—isolated in his or her cell, partitioned off from the other inmates, each seen but not seeing.

This panopticon, Foucault intones, is not simply a figure for an institution, but a generalized model for the workings of power, for the entire state system. Moreover, the panopticon is the defining feature of a society in which the "principal elements are no longer the community and public life, but, on the one hand, private individuals and, on the other, the state." Foucault comes to this conclusion by tracing a history of the birth of the prison; its genealogy lies in the medieval form of punishment, that is, the graphic tearing of the body, the wrath of the sovereign inscribed on the body of the culprit. This form of punishment later yielded to the "gentle way in punishment," which continued into the eighteenth century—a punishment that focused on transforming and reintegrating the individual into a socius through public works and introspection.

The gentle way in punishment forms the midstage to the panoptic world. The two figures, or epistemes, for reading this shift are the leper colony and the plague. Whereas the leper and the leper colony manifest the anxieties and the fantasies of a society that disciplines by exclusion, exile, and invisibility, the plague and the will to order which confronts the plague undergird the fantasies of a society where the disciplinary mechanism involves total arrest, integration, and surveillance. And it is this intensified surveillance which characterizes the panopticon. What Foucault also traces by outlining this history of punishment —from a society of spectacle, where an individual body is seen by all, to a society of panopticism, where all are seen by one—is a shift in the emphasis of violence. For whereas the society of spectacle involves graphic violence done to the culprit's body, torture for general edification, the panoptic state sublimates violence onto the noncorporal plane. The subject is constantly being observed, its every move monitored, beaten into shape, disciplined. Whereas the spectacle unifies observers into a body politic, the panopticon cuts the body politic into segments, into individuals.

In the work of Gilles Deleuze and Félix Guattari the Foucauldian opposition of the society of the spectacle versus the panopticon, or despotic power versus the power of the modern state, becomes less an opposition than a continuity. Speaking of tribal societies, Deleuze and Guattari regard cruelty as the founding basis of culture and of cultural memory, whereby the individual becomes a body without organs through the act of cruelty, through initiation rites which mark his body as being "of" a certain culture or a certain tribe. The individual becomes this body without organs because his body loses its apartness from the culture and becomes appropriated by the smooth, taut, nondifferentiated surface of the cultural body without organs: "Cruelty has nothing to do with some ill-defined or natural violence that might be commissioned to explain the history of mankind; cruelty is the movement of culture that is realized in bodies and inscribed on them, belaboring them."

The process through which the cultural body without organs is able to effect miraculation is the practice of cruelty, which, following Nietzsche, Deleuze and Guattari call a "terrible alphabet" that inscribes, cuts, on the individual body, the permanent sign of its appropriation into the cultural body without organs. This marking of the body, this inscription, is what constitutes memory, not of his body or of its biological genesis (since, according to the Nietzschean-Deleuzean-Guattarian framework, man is constituted by an "active faculty of forgetting" or "repression of biological memory"), but a "collective memory" of the word, of language, which pulls the individual to the collective. As such, scarification is a sign not only of belonging but of possession by the community. Indeed, scarification does not simply constitute a memory of the word, but itself is the inscription, or the "writing," which "renders man capable of language, and gives him a memory of the spoken word." In other words, this writing precedes speech, which is made possible only through a prior inscription or cutting into the individual's body, thereby initiating it into the cultural-linguistic body without organs.

This initiation rite is described in terms of a debt system or territorial representation of primary societies. This imparting of a cultural memory to the individual by the socius is neither a contract nor an exchange. Rather, Deleuze and Guattari suggest, there is nothing reciprocal about this relationship; indeed, the whole theater of cruelty and of violence is precisely to "render him capable of alliance, to form him within the debtor-creditor relation, which on both sides turns out to be a matter of memory—a memory straining towards the future." It is as if the "desiring-machine of eye-hand-voice" had "foreseen everything," except for how its own death would come to it from without, in the form of "the blond beasts of prey, a conqueror and master race," the "founders of the state." And this time the primitive territorial machine would find itself and its inscription system "taken into an immense machinery that renders the debt infinite" and precludes, "once and for all, the prospect of a final discharge; the aim now is to make the glance recoil disconsolately from an iron impossibility."

If primitive territorial representation organizes itself around the creditor-debtor relationship by including the individual into its socius through the act of cutting its sign on the body of the individual, thereby making him own the debt of his initiation into the socius, with the advent of the state the creditor-debtor relationship changes such that the debt becomes not only infinite but also internalized. The mark that the primitive man carried on his body as the sign of his debt has now become an internal mark by the process of an inward spiritual-ization, which entails a "repressed cruelty of the animal-man made inward and scared back into himself, the creature imprisoned in the 'state' so as to be tamed": "These are the two aspects of the becoming of the state: its internaliza-tion in a field of increasingly decoded social forces forming a physical system; its spiritualization in a supraterrestrial field that increasingly overcodes, forming a metaphysical system."

These two aspects of the becoming of a state, that is, internalization and spiritualization, are related to two acts: first, the act of territoriality through the fixing of residence, and second, the act of liberation through the abolition of small debts. These two acts, however, entail exactly the opposite of what they seem to entail; as Deleuze and Guattari suggest, these two acts are "euphe-misms" for more sinister designs. The act of fixing residence actually effects a deterritorialization: the earth becomes the "object of a State ownership of prop-erty, or an ownership held by the State's richest servants and officials." This is a deterritorialization because it "substitutes abstract signs for the signs of the earth"; it is a deterritorialization because as opposed to the older systems where the full body of the earth was the body without organs, now, in the new system, the earth's body is deterritorialized and abstracted to the body of the despot.

Likewise, the second act, the abolition of small debts, initiates the relation-ship of an infinite creditor and the infinite debtor, where the debt "becomes a debt of existence, a debt of the existence of the subjects themselves," and which manifests its "infinite relation in the form of the tribute" to the despot. This tribute to the despot is nothing other than "money in the form of taxes that are required for the maintenance of the apparatus of the state." This form of taxa-tion, even when it occurs under the guise of the redistribution of money (taxa-tion on the aristocracy and redistribution to the poor), ends up reinforcing deterritorialization by maintaining the distribution of landed property: "In a word, money—the circulation of money—is the means for rendering the debt infinite."

This despotic state is the "primordial Urstaat, the eternal model of all the State ever wants to be and desires." As Deleuze and Guattari suggest, the state did not evolve through successive stages, but appeared "fully armed, a master-stroke executed all at once" in the form of the despotic state. All later forms and permutations of the state are merely manifestations of this primordial despotic state. But what had characterized the despotic state was its ability to overcode the territorial elements of the earlier primitive socius that it had appropriated for its use. Now, however, the appearance of private property, wealth, commodities, and classes bring about not simply the overcoding, but the "breakdown of codes." In other words, the elements that the despotic state had originally depended on for its sustenance—that is, private property, the formation of distinct classes, and taxation and money—became themselves the cause of its decline.

This decline does not, however, mean the passing of the despotic state into some other form of social government. Indeed, all that happens is that the despotic state enters into a state of "latency" only to "reform itself on modified foundations, in order to spring back more 'mendacious,' 'colder,' and more 'hypocritical' than ever." What happens now, in this new modulation of the despotic state, is the appearance of decoded flows in place of the overcoded flows of the despotic state; in response to the needs of the new permutation of the state, specific new codes must be invented for "flows that are increasingly deterritorialized," thereby "putting despotism in the service of the new class relations." The creditor-debtor relationship now provides the structure not for the relationship between the despot and his people (as in the case of the despotic state), but for the "relationship between the opposed classes." As opposed to the despotic state, the state now does not form the ruling classes; it is itself formed by the ruling classes: "As a machine it no longer determines a social system; it is itself determined by the social system into which it is incorporated in the exercise of its functions."

The English philosopher Thomas Hobbes lived through the breakdown of law and order that took place during the civil war between the parliament, led by Oliver Cromwell, and the Royalist forces, which supported the monarchy of Charles I—a war which ended in 1649 with the defeat of the Royalists and the beheading of Charles I. Hobbes fled with other Royalists to France, where he came under suspicion because of his claim that kings rule not by divine authority, but by virtue of the contract with his subjects. Although he later made peace with the parliamentarians and returned to England, his relationship with the church remained precarious: he was almost burned at the stake for being a heretic; his books were burned at Oxford in 1683. His views exerted a formative influence on later political philosophers like John Locke, Baruch Spinoza, and Jean-Jacques Rousseau.

In Leviathan *(1651) Hobbes begins with the assumption that human beings are, in the state of nature, equal beings, that they are armed with the natural right of defending their life and their possessions, and that they are free to pursue any line of action they deem fit either for defending themselves from threat or for enhancing their happiness. This natural right, however, gives rise to a condition of perpetual war, for all are guided by appetites, by desires, in the attainment of which all are pitted against each other. It is only by means of a social contract, whereby one surrenders one's powers to a sovereign ruler, that the perpetual state of war can be averted; this contract is the basis of civil society.*

Among Hobbes's other works are De Cive *(1642),* De Homine *(1658), and* Behemoth *(1679).*

Leviathan

THOMAS HOBBES

PART II. OF COMMONWEALTH

Chapter 17. Of the Causes, Generation, and Definition of a COMMON-WEALTH

The finall Cause, End, or Designe of men, (who naturally love Liberty, and Dominion over others,) in the introduction of that restraint upon themselves, (in which wee see them live in Common-wealths,) is the foresight of their own preservation, and of a more contented life thereby; that is to say, of getting themselves out from that miserable condition of Warre, which is necessarily consequent (as hath been shewn) to the naturall Passions of men, when there is no visible Power to keep them in awe, and tye them by feare of punishment to the performance of their Covenants, and observation of those Lawes of Nature set down in the foreteenth and fifteenth Chapters.

For the Lawes of Nature (as *Justice, Equity, Modesty, Mercy,* and (in summe) *doing to others, as wee would be done to,*) of themselves, without the terrour of some Power, to cause them to be observed, are contrary to our naturall Passions, that carry us to Partiality, Pride, Revenge, and the like. And Covenants, without the Sword, are but Words, and of no strength to secure a man at all. Therefore notwithstanding the Lawes of Nature, (which every one hath then kept, when he has the will to keep them, when he can do it safely,) if there be no Power erected, or not great enough for our security; every man will and may lawfully rely on his own strength and art, for caution against all other men. And in all places, where men have lived by small Families, to robbe and spoyle one another, has been a Trade, and so farre from being reputed against the Law of Nature, that the greater spoyles they gained, the greater was their honour; and men observed no other Lawes therein, but the Lawes of Honour; that is, to abstain from cruelty, living to men their lives, and instruments of husbandry. And as small Families did then; so now do Cities and Kingdomes which are but greater Families (for their own security) enlarge their Dominions, upon all pretences of danger, and fear of Invasion, or assistance that may be given to Invaders, endeavour as much as they can, to subdue, or weaken their neighbours, by open force, and secret arts, for want of other Caution, justly; and are remembered for it in after ages with honour.

Nor is it the joyning together of a small number of men, that gives them this security; because in small numbers, small additions on the one side or the other, make the advantage of strength so great, as is sufficient to carry the Victory; and therefore gives encouragement to an Invasion. The Multitude sufficient to confide in for our Security, is not determined by any certain number, but by comparison with the Enemy we feare; and is then sufficient, when the odds of the Enemy is not of so visible and conspicuous moment, to determine the event of Warre, as to move him to attempt.

And be there never so great a Multitude; yet if their actions be directed according to their particular judgements, and particular appetites, they can expect thereby no defence, nor protection, neither against a common enemy, nor against the injuries of one another. For being distracted in opinions concerning the best use and application of their strength, they do not help, but hinder one another; and reduce their strength by mutuall opposition to nothing: whereby they are easily, not onely subdued by a very few that agree together; but also when there is no common enemy, they make warre upon each other, for their particular interests. For if we could suppose a great Multitude of men to consent in the observation of Justice, and other Lawes of Nature, without a common Power to keep them all in awe; we might as well suppose all Man-kind to do the same; and then there neither would be, nor need to be any Civill Government, or Common-wealth at all; because there would be Peace without subjection.

Nor is it enough for the security, which men desire should last all the time of their life, that they be governed, and directed by one judgement, for a limited time; as in one battell, or one Warre. For though they obtain a Victory by their unanimous endeavour against a forraign enemy; yet afterwards, when either they have no common enemy, or he that by one part is held for an enemy, is by another part held for a friend, they must needs by the difference of their inter-ests dissolve, and fall again into a Warre amongst themselves.

It is true, that certain living creatures, as Bees, and Ants, live sociably one with another, (which are therefore by *Aristotle* numbred amongst Politicall creatures;) and yet have no other direction, than their particular judgements and appetites; nor speech, whereby one of them can signifie to another, what he thinks expedient for the common benefit: and therefore some man may perhaps desire to know, why Man-kind cannot do the same. To which I answer,

First, that men are continually in competition for Honour and Dignity, which these creatures are not; and consequently amongst men there ariseth on that ground, Envy and Hatred, and finally Warre; but amongst these not so.

Secondly, that amongst these creatures, the Common good differeth not from the Private; and being by nature enclined to their private, they procure thereby the common benefit. But man, whose Joy consisteth in comparing himselfe with other men, can relish nothing but what is eminent.

Thirdly, that these creatures, having not (as man) the use of reason, do not see, nor think they see any fault, in the administration of their common busi-nesse: whereas amongst men, there are very many, that thinke themselves wiser, and abler to govern the Publique, better than the rest; and these strive to reforme and innovate, one this way, another that way; and thereby bring it into Distraction and Civill Warre.

Fourthly, that these creatures, though they have some use of voice, in making knowne to one another their desires, and other affections; yet they want that art of words, by which some men can represent to others, that which is Good, in the likenesse of Evill; and Evill, in the likenesse of Good; and augment, or diminish the apparent greatnesse of Good and Evill; discontenting men, and troubling their Peace at their pleasure.

Fifthly, irrationall creatures cannot distinguish betweene *Injury*, and *Dammage*; and therefore as long as they be at ease, they are not offended with their fellowes: whereas Man is then most troublesome, when he is most at ease: for then it is that he loves to shew his Wisdome, and controule the Actions of them that governe the Common-wealth.

Lastly, the agreement of these creatures is naturall; that of men, is by covenant only, which is Artificiall: and therefore it is no wonder if there be somewhat else required (besides Covenant) to make their Agreement constant and lasting; which is a Common Power, to keep them in awe, and to direct their actions to the Common benefit.

The only way to erect such a Common Power, as may be able to defend them from the invasion of forraigners, and the injuries of one another, and thereby to secure them in such sort, as that by their owne industrie, and by the fruites of the Earth, they may nourish themselves and live contentedly, is, to conferre all their power and strength upon one Man, or upon one Assembly of men, that may reduce all their Wills, by plurality of voices, unto one Will: which is as much as to say, to appoint one man, or Assembly of men, to beare their Person; and every one to owne, and acknowledge himselfe to be Author of whatsoever he that so beareth their Person, shall Act, or cause to be Acted, in those things which concerne the Common Peace and Safetie; and therein to submit their Wills, every one to his Will, and their Judgements, to his Judgment. This is more than Consent, or Concord; it is a reall Unitie of them all, in one and the same Person, made by Covenant of every man with every man, in such manner, as if every man should say to every man, *I Authorise and give up my right of Governing my selfe, to this Man, or to this Assembly of men, on this condition, that thou give up thy Right to him, and Authorise all his Actions in like manner.* This done, the Multitude so united in one Person, is called a COMMON-WEALTH, in latine CIVITAS. This is the Generation of that great LEVIATHAN, or rather (to speake more reverently) of that *Mortall god*, to which wee owe under the *Immortall God*, our peace and defence. For by this Authoritie, given him by every particular man in the Common-Wealth, he hath the use of so much Power and Strength conferred on him, that by terror thereof, he is inabled to forme the wills of them all, to Peace at home, and mutuall ayd against their enemies abroad. And in him consisteth the Essence of the Common-wealth; which (, to define it,) is *One Person, of whose Acts a great Multitude, by mutuall Covenants one with another, have made themselves everyone the Author, to the end he may use the strength and means of them all, as he shall think expedient, for their Peace and Common Defence.*

And he that carryeth this Person, is called SOVERAIGNE, and said to have *Soveraigne Power*; and every one besides, his SUBJECT.

The attaining to this Soveraigne Power, is by two wayes. One, by Naturall force; as when a man maketh his children, to submit themselves, and their children to his government, as being able to destroy them if they refuse; or by Warre subdueth his enemies to will, giving them their lives on that condition. The other, is when men agree amongst themselves, to submit to some man, or Assembly of men, voluntarily, on confidence to be protected by him against all others. This later, may be called a Politicall Common-wealth or Common-wealth by *Institution*; and the former, a Common-wealth by *Acquisition*. And first, I shall speak of a Common-wealth by Institution.

Chapter 18. Of the RIGHTS of Soveraignes by Institution

A *Common-wealth* is said to be *Instituted*, when a *Multitude* of men do Agree, and *Covenant, every one, with every one*, that to whatsoever *Man*, or *Assembly of Men*, shall be given by the major part, the *Right to Present* the Person of them all, (that is to say, to be their *Representative*;) every one, as well he that *Voted for it*, as he that *Voted against it*, shall *Authorise* all the Actions and Judgements, of that Man, or Assembly of men, in the same manner, as if they were his own, to the end, to live peaceably amongst themselves, and be protected against other men.

From this Institution of a Common-wealth are derived all the *Rights*, and *Facultyes* of him, or them, on whom the Soveraigne Power is conferred by the consent of the People assembled.

First, because they Covenant, it is to be understood, they are not obliged by former Covenant to any thing repugnant hereunto. And Consequently they that have already Instituted a Common-wealth, being thereby bound by Covenant, to own the Actions, and Judgements of one, cannot lawfully make a new Covenant, amongst themselves, to be obedient to any other, in any thing whatsoever, without his permission. And therefore, they that are subjects to a Monarchy, and return to the confusion of a disunited Multitude; nor transferre their Person from him that beareth it, to another Man; or other Assembly of men: for they are bound, every man to every man, to Own, and be reputed Author of all, that he that already is their Soveraigne, shall do, and judge fit to be done; so that any one man dissenting, all the rest should break their Covenant made to that man, which is injustice: and they have also every man given the Soveraignty to him that beareth their Person: and therefore if they depose him, they take from him that which is his own, and so again it is injustice. Besides, if he that attempteth to depose his Soveraigne, be killed, or punished by him for such attempt, he is author of his own punishment, as being by the Institution, Author of all his Soveraigne shall do; And because it is injustice for a man to do any thing, for which he may be punished by his own authority, he is also upon that title, unjust.

And whereas some men have pretended for their disobedience to their Soveraigne, a new Covenant, made, not with men, but with God; this also is unjust: for there is no Covenant with God, but by mediation of some body that representeth Gods Person; which none doth but Gods Lieutenant, who hath the Soveraignty under god. But this pretence of Covenant with God, is so evident a lye, even in the pretenders own consciences, that is not onely an act of an unjust, but also of a vile, and unmanly disposition.

Secondly, because the Right of bearing the Person of them all, is given to him they make Soveraigne, by Covenant onely of one to another, and not of him to any of them; there can happen no breach of Covenant on the part of the Soveraigne; and consequently none of his Subjects, by any pretence of forfeiture, can be freed from his Subjection. That he which is made Soveraigne maketh no Covenant with his Subjects beforehand, is manifest; because either he must make it with the whole multitude, as one party to the Covenant; or he must make a severall Covenant with every man. With the whole, as one party, it is impossible; because as yet they are not one Person: and if he make so many severall Covenants as there be men, those covenants after he hath the Soveraignty are voyd, because what act soever can be pretended by any one of them for breach thereof, is the act both of himselfe, and of all the rest, because done in the Person, and by the Right of every one of them in particular. Besides, if any one, or more of them, pretend a breach of the Covenant made by the Soveraigne at his Institution; and others, or one other of his Subjects, or himselfe alone, pretend there was no such breach, there is in this case, no Judge to decide the controversie: it returns therefore to the Sword again; and every man recovereth the right of Protecting himselfe by his own strength, contrary to the designe they had in the Institution. It is therefore in vain to grant Soveraignty by way of precedent Covenant. The opinion that any Monarch receiveth his Power by Covenant, that is to say on Condition, proceedeth from want of understanding this easie truth, that Covenants being but words, and breath, have no force to oblige, contain, constrain, or protect any man, but what it has from the publique Sword; that is, from the untyed hands of that Man, or Assembly of men that hath the Soveraignty, and whose actions are avouched by them all, and performed by the strength of them all, in him united. But when an Assembly of men is made Soveraigne; then no man imagineth any such Covenant to have passed in the Institution; for no man is so dull as to say, for example, the People of *Rome*, made a Covenant with the Romans, to hold the Soveraignty on such or such conditions; which not performed, the Romans might lawfully depose the Roman People. That men see not the reason to be alike in a Monarchy, and in a Popular Government, proceedeth from the ambition of some, that are kinder to the government of an Assembly, whereof they may hope to participate, than of Monarchy, which they despair to enjoy.

Thirdly, because the major part hath by consenting voices declared a Soveraigne; he that dissented must now consent with the rest; that is, be contended to avow all the actions he shall do, or else justly be destroyed by the rest. For if he voluntarily entered into the Congregation of them that were assembled, he sufficiently declared thereby his will (and therefore tacitely covenanted) to stand to what the major part should ordayne: and therefore if he refuse to stand thereto, or make Protestation against any of their Decrees, he does contrary to his Covenant, and therefore unjustly. And whether he be of the congregation, or not; and whether his consent be asked, or not, he must either submit to their decrees, wherein he might without injustice be destroyed by any man whatsoever.

Fourthly, because every Subject is by this Institution Author of all the Actions, and Judgments of the Soveraigne Instituted; it followes, that whatsoever he doth, it can be no injury to any of his Subjects; nor ought he to be by any of them accused of Injustice. For he that doth any thing by authority from another, doth therein no injury to him by whose authority he acteth: But by this Institution of a Common-wealth, every particular man is Author of all the Soveraigne doth; and consequently he that complaineth of injury from his Soveraigne, complaineth of that whereof he himselfe is Author; and therefore ought not to accuse any man but himselfe; no not himselfe or injury; because to do injury to ones selfe, is impossible. It is true that they that have Soveraigne power, may commit Iniquity; but not Injustice, or Injury in the proper signification.

Fifthly, and consequently to that which was sayd last, no man that hath Soveraigne power can justly be put to death, or otherwise in any manner by his Subjects punished. For seeing every Subject is Author of the actions of his Soveraigne; he punisheth another, for the actions committed by himselfe.

And because the End of this Institution, is the Peace and Defence of them all; and whosoever has right to the End, has right to the Means; it belongeth of Right, to whatsoever Man, or Assembly that hath the Soveraignty, to be Judge both of the meanes of Peace and Defence; and also of the hindrances, and disturbances of the same; and to do whatsoever he shall think necessary to be done, both before hand, for the preserving of Peace and Security, by prevention of Discord at home and Hostility from abroad; and, when Peace and Security are lost, for the recovery of the same. And therefore,

Sixthly, it is annexed to the Soveraignty, to be Judge of what Opinions and Doctrines are averse, and what conducting to Peace; and consequently, on what occasions, how farre, and what, men are to be trusted withall, in speaking to Multitudes of people; and who shall examine the Doctrines of all bookes before they be published. For the Actions of men proceed from their Opinions; and in the well governing of Opinions, consisteth the well governing of mens Actions, in order to their Peace, and Concord. And though in matter of Doctrine, nothing ought to be regarded but the Truth; yet this is not repugnant to regulating of the same by Peace. For doctrine repugnant to Peace, can no more be True, than Peace and Concord can be against the Law of Nature. It is true, that in a Common-wealth, where by the negligence, or unskilfullnesse of Governours, and Teachers, false Doctrines are by time generally received; the contrary Truths may be generally offensive: Yet the most sudden, and rough busting in of a new Truth, that can be, does never breake the Peace, but only sometimes awake the Warre. For those men that are so remissely governed, that they dare take up Armes, to defend, or introduce an Opinion, are still in Warre; and their condition not Peace, but only a Cessation of Armes for feare of one another; and they live as it were, in the procincts of battaile continually. It belongeth therefore to him that hath the Soveraigne Power, to be Judge, or constitute all Judges of Opinions and Doctrines, as a thing necessary to Peace, thereby to prevent Discord and Civill Warre.

Seventhly, is annexed to the Soveraignty, the whole Power of prescribing the Rules, whereby every man may know, what goods he may enjoy and what Actions he may doe, without being molested by any of his fellow Subjects: And this is it men call *Propriety*. For before constitution of Soveraigne Power (as hath already been shewn) all men had right to all things; which necessarily causeth Warre: and therefore this Propriety, being necessary to Peace, and depending on Soveraigne Power, is the Act of that Power, in order to the publique peace. These Rules of Propriety (or *Meum* and *Tuum*) and of *Good, Evill, Lawfull,* and *Unlawfull* in the actions of Subjects, are the Civill Lawes, that is to say, the Lawes of each Common-wealth in particular; though the name of Civill Law be now restrained to the antient Civill Lawes of the City of *Rome*; which being the head of a great part of the World, her Lawes at that time were in these parts the Civill Law.

Eightly, is annexed to the Soveraignty, the Right of Judicature; that is to say, of hearing and deciding all Controversies, which may arise concerning Law, either Civill, or Naturall or concerning Fact. For without the decision of Controversies, there is no protection of one Subject, against the injuries of another; the Lawes concerning *Meum* and *Tuum* are in vain; and to every man remaineth, from the Naturall and necessary appetite of his own conservation, the right of protecting himselfe by his private strength, which is the condition of Warre; and contrary to the end for which every Common-wealth is instituted.

Ninthly, is annexed to the Soveraignty, the Right of making Warre, and Peace with other Nations, and Common-wealths; that is to say, of Judging when it is for the publique good, and how great forces are to be assembled, armed, and payd for that end; and to levy mony upon the Subjects, to defray the expenses thereof. For the Power by which the people are to be defended, consisteth in their Armies; and the strength of an Army, in the union of their strength under one Command; which Command the Soveraigne Instituted, therefore hat; because the command of the *Militia*, without other Institution, maketh him that hath it Soveraigne. And therefore whosoever is made Generall of an Army, he that hath the Soveraigne Power is alwayes Generallissimo.

Tenthly, is annexed to the Soveraignty, the choosing of all Councellours, Ministers, Magistrates, and Officers, both in Peace, and Warre. For seeing the Soveraigne is charged with the End, which is the common Peace and Defence; he is understood to have Power to use such Means, as he shall think most fit for his discharge.

Eleventhly, to the Soveraigne is committed the Power of Rewarding with riches, or honour; and of Punishing with corporall, or pecuniary punishment, or with ignominy every Subject according to the Law he hath formerly made; or if there be no Law made, according as he shall judge most to conduce to the encouraging of men to serve the Common-wealth, or deterring of them from doing dis-service to the same.

Lastly, considering what values men are naturally apt to set upon themselves; what respect they look for from others; and how little they value other men; from whence continually arise amongst them, Emulation, Quarrells, Factions, and at last Warre, to the destroying of one another, and diminution of their strength against a Common Enemy; It is necessary that there be Lawes of Honour, and a publique rate of the worth of such men as have deserved, or are able to deserve well of the Common-wealth; and that there be force in the hands of some or other, to put those Lawes in execution. But it hath already been shewn, that not onely the whole *Militia*, or forces of the Common-wealth; but also the Judicature of all Controversies, is annexed to the Soveraignty. To the Soveraigne therefore it belongeth also to give titles of Honour; and to appoint what Order of place, and dignity, each man shall hold; and what signes of respect, in publique or private meetings, they shall give to one another.

These are the Rights, which make the Essence of Soveraignty; and which are the markes, whereby a man may discern in what Man, or Assembly of men, the Soveraigne Power is placed, and resideth. For these are incommunicable, and inseparable. The Power to coyn Mony; to dispose of the estate and persons of Infant Heires; to have præemption in Markets; and all other Statute Prærogatives, may be transferred by the Soveraigne; and yet the Power to protect his Subjects be retained. But if he transferre the *Militia*, he retains the Judicature in vain, for want of execution of the Lawes: Or if he grant away the Power of raising Mony; the *Militia* is in vain: or if he give away the government of doctrines, men will be frighted into rebellion with the feare of Spirits. And so if we consider any one of the said Rights, we shall presently see, that the holding of all the rest, will produce no effect, in the conservation of Peace and Justice, the end for which all Common-wealths are Instituted. And this division is it, whereof it is said, *a Kingdome divided in it selfe cannot stand*: For unlesse this division precede, division into opposite Armies can never happen. If there had not first been an opinion received of the greatest part of *England*, that these Powers were divided between the King, and the Lords, and the House of Commons, the people had never been divided, and fallen into this Civill Warre; first between those that disagreed in Politiques; and after between the Dissenters about the liberty of Religion; which have so instructed men in this point of Soveraigne Right, that there be few now (in *England*), that do not see, that these Rights are inseparable, and will be so generally acknowledged, at the next return of Peace; and so continue, till their miseries are forgotten; and no longer, except the vulgar be better taught than they have hitherto been.

And because they are essentiall and inseparable Rights, it follows necessarily, that in whatsoever words any of them seem to be granted away, yet if the Soveraigne Power it selfe be not in direct termes renounced, and the name of Soveraigne no more given by the Grantees to him that Grants them, the Grant is voyd: for when he has granted all he can, if we grant back the Soveraignty, all is restored, as inseparably annexed thereunto.

This great Authority being Indivisible, and inseparably annexed to the Soveraignty, there is little ground for the opinion of them, that say of Soveraigne Kings, though they be *singulis majores*, of greater Power than every one of their Subjects, yet they be *Universis minores*, of lesse power than them all together. For if by *all together*, they mean not the collective body as one person, the *all together*, and *every one*, signifie the same; and the speech is absurd. But if by *all together*, they understand them as one Person (, which person the Soveraigne bears,) then the power of all together, is the same with the Soveraigne power; and so again the speech is absurd: which absurdity they see well enough, when the Soveraignty is in an Assembly of the people; but in a Monarch they see it not; and yet the power of Soveraignty is the same in whosoever it be placed.

And as the Power, so also the Honour of the Soveraigne, ought to be greater, than that of any, or all the Subjects. For in the Soveraignty is the fountain of Honour. The dignities of Lord, Earle, Duke, and Prince are his Creatures. As in the presence of the Mater, the Servants are equall, and without any honour at all; So are the Subjects, in the presence of the Soveraigne. And though they shine some more, some lesse, when they are out of his sight; yet in his presence, they shine no more than the Starres in presence of the Sun.

But a man may here object, that the condition of Subjects is very miserable; as being obnoxious to the lusts, and other irregular passions of him, or them that have so unlimited a power in their hands. And commonly they that live under a Monarch, think it the fault of Monarchy; and they that live under the government of Democracy, or other Soveraign Assembly, attribute all the inconvenience to that forme of Common-wealth; whereas the Power in all formes, if they be perfect enough to protect them is the same; not considering that the estate of Man can never be without some incommodity or other; and that the greatest, that in any form of Government can possibly happen to the people in generall, is scarce sensible, in respect of the miseries, and horrible calamities, that accompany a Civill Warre; or that dissolute condition of masterlesse men, without subjection to Lawes, and a coërcive Power to tye their hands from rapine, and revenge: nor considering that the greatest pressure of Soveraign Governours, proceedeth not from any delight, or profit they can expect in the dammage, or weakening of their Subjects, in whose vigor, consisteth their own strength and glory; but in the restiveness of themselves, that unwillingly contributing to their own defence, make it necessary for their Governours to draw from them what they can in time of Peace, that they may have means on any emergent occasion, or sudden need, to resist, or take advantage of their Enemies. For all men are by nature provided of notable multiplying glasses, (that is their Passions and Self-love,) through which every little payment appeareth a great grievance; but are destitute of those prospective glasses, (namely Morall and Civill Science,) to see a farre off the miseries that hang over them, and cannot without such payments be avoyded.

. . . . .

Chapter 20. Of Dominion PATERNALL, and DESPOTICALL

A *Common-*WEALTH *by Acquisition,* is that, where the Soveraigne Power is acquired by Force; and it is acquired by force, when men singly, or many together by plurality of voyces, for fear of death, or bonds, do authorise all the actions of that Man, or Assembly, that hath their lives and liberty in his Power.

And this kind of dominion, or Soveraignty, differeth from Soveraignty by Institution, onely in this, That men who choose their Soveraigne, do it for fear of one another, and not of him whom they Institute: But in this case, they subject themselves, to him they are afraid of. In both cases they do it for fear: which is to be noted by them, that hold all such Covenants, as proceed from fear of death, or violence, voyd: which if it were true, no man, in any kind of Common-wealth, could be obliged to Obedience. It is true, that in a Common-wealth once Instituted, or acquired, Promises proceeding from fear of death, or violence, are no Covenants, nor obliging, when the thing promised is contrary to the Lawes; But the reason is not, because it was made upon fear, but because he that promiseth, hath no right in the thing promised. Also, when he may lawfully performe, and doth not, it is not the Invalidity of the Covenant, that absolveth him, but the Sentence of the Soveraigne. Otherwise, whensoever a man lawfully promiseth, he unlawfully breaketh; but when the Soveraigne, who is the Actor, acquitteth him, then he is acquitted by him that extorted the promise, as by the Author of such absolution.

But the Rights, and Consequences of Soveraignty, are the same in both. His Power cannot, without his consent, be Transferred to another: He cannot Forfeit it: He cannot be Accused by any of his Subjects, of Injury: He cannot be Punished by them: He is Judge of what is necessary for Peace; and Judge of Doctrines: He is Sole Legislator; and Supreme Judge of Controversies; and of the Times, and Occasions of Warre, and Peace: to him it belongeth to choose Magistrates, Counsellours, Commanders, and all other Officers, and Ministers; and to determine of Rewards, and Punishments, Honour, and Order. The reasons whereof, are of the same which are alledged in the precedent Chapter, for the same Rights, and consequences of Soveraignty by Institution.

Dominion is acquired two wayes: by Generation, and by Conquest. The right of Dominion by Generation, is that, which the Parent hath over his Children; and is called PATERNALL. And is not so derived from the Generation, as if therefore the Parent had Dominion over his Child because he begat him; but from the Childs Consent, either expresse, or by other sufficient arguments declared. For as to the Generation, God hath ordained to man a helper: and there be alwayes two that are equally Parents: the Dominion therefore over the Child, should belong equally to both; and he be equally subject to both, which is impossible; for no man can obey two Masters. And whereas some have attributed the dominion to the Man onely, as being of the more excellent Sex; they misreckon in it. For there is not always that difference of strength or prudence between the man and the woman, as that the right can be determined without Warre. In Common-wealths, this controversie is decided by the Civill Law: and for the most part, (but not alwayes) the sentence is in favour of the Father; because for the most part Common-wealths have been erected by the Fathers, not by the Mothers of families. But the question lyeth now in the state of meer Nature; where there are supposed no lawes of Matrimony; no Lawes for the Education of Children; but the Law of Nature, and the naturall inclination of the Sexes, one to another, and to their children. In this condition of meer Nature, either the Parents between themselves dispose of the dominion over the Child by Contract; or do not dispose thereof at all. If they dispose thereof, the right passeth according to the Contract. We find in History that the *Amazons* Contracted with the Men of the neighbouring Countries, to whom they had recourse for issue, that the issue Male should be sent back, but the Female remain with themselves: so that the dominion of the Females was in the Mother.

If there be no Contract, the Dominion is in the Mother. For in the condition of meer Nature, where there are no Matrimoniall lawes, it cannot be known who is the Father, unlesse it be declared by the Mother: and therefore the right of Dominion over the Child dependeth on her will, and is consequently hers. Again, seeing the Infant is first in the power of the Mother, so as she may either nourish, or expose it, if she nourish it, it oweth its life to the Mother; and is therefore obliged to obey her, rather than any other; and by consequence the Dominion over it is hers. But if she expose it, and another find, and nourish it, the Dominion is in him that nourisheth it. For it ought to obey him by whom it is preserved; because preservation of life being the end, for which one man becomes subject to another, every man is supposed to promise obedience, to him, in whose power it is to save, or destroy him.

If the Mother be the Fathers subject, the Child, is in the Fathers power: and if the Father be the Mothers subject, (as when a Soveraigne Queen marrieth one of her subjects,) the Child is subject to the Mother; because the Father also is her subject.

If a man and a woman, Monarches of two severall Kingdomes, have a Child, and Contract concerning who shall have the Dominion of him, the Right of the Dominion passeth by the Contract. If they contract not, the Dominion followeth the Dominion of the place of his residence. For the Soveraigne of each Country hath Dominion over all that reside therein.

He that hath the Dominion over the Child, hath dominion also over the Children of the Child; and over their Childrens Children. For he that hath dominion over the person of a man, hath Dominion over all that is his; without which, Dominion were but a Title, without the effect.

The Right of Succession to Paternall Dominion, proceedeth in the same manner, as doth the Right of Succession to Monarchy; of which I have already sufficiently spoken in the precedent Chapter.

Dominion acquired by Conquest, or Victory in war, is that which some Writers call DESPOTICALL, from Δεπότης, which signifieth a *Lord*, or *Master*; and is the Dominion of the Master over his Servant. And this Dominion is then acquired to the Victor, when the Vanquished, to avoyd the present stroke of death, covenanteth either in expresse words, or by other sufficient signes of the Will, that so long as his life, and the liberty of his body is allowed him the victor shall have the use thereof, at his pleasure. And after such Covenant made, the Vanquished is a SERVANT, and not before: for by the word *Servant* (whether it be derived from *Servire*, to Serve, or from *Sevare*, to Save, which I leave to Grammarians to dispute) is not meant a Captive, which is kept in prison, or bonds, till the owner of him that took him, or bought him of one that did, shall consider what to do with him: (for such men, (commonly called Slaves,) have no obligation at all; but may break their bonds, or the prison; and kill, or carry away captive their Master, justly:) but one, that being taken, hath corporall liberty allowed him; and upon promise not to run away, nor to do violence to his Master, is trusted by him.

It is not therefore the Victory, that giveth the right of Dominion over the Vanquished, but his own Covenant. Nor is he obliged because he is Conquered; that is to say, beaten, and taken, or put to flight; but because he commeth in, and submitteth to the Victor; nor is the Victor obliged by an enemies rendring himselfe, (without promise of life,) to spare him for this his yeelding to discretion; which obliges not the Victor longer, than in his own discretion he shall think fit.

And that which men do, when they demand (as it is now called) *Quarter*, (which the Greeks called Ζωγρία, *taking alive*,) is to evade the present fury of the Victor, by Submission, and to compound for their life, with Ransome, or Service: and therefore he that hath Quarter, hath not his life given, but deferred till farther deliberation; For it is not in yeelding on condition of life, but to discretion. And then onely is his life in security, and his service due, when the Victor hath trusted him with his corporall liberty. For Slaves that work in Prisons, or Fetters, do it not of duty, but to avoyd the cruelty of their task-masters.

The Master of the Servant, is master also of all he hath; and may exact the use thereof; that is to say, of his goods, of his labour, of his servants, and of his children, as often as he shall think fit. For he holdeth his life of his Master, by the covenant of obedience; that is, of owning, and authorising whatsoever the Master shall do. And in case the Master, if he refuse, kill him, or cast him into bonds, or otherwise punish him for his disobedience, he is himselfe the author of the same; and cannot accuse him of injury.

In summe the Rights and Consequences of both *Paternall* and *Despoticall* Dominion, are the very same with those of a Soveraigne by Institution; and for the same reasons: which reasons are set down in the precedent Chapter. So that for a man that is Monarch of divers nations, whereof he hath, in one the Soveraignty by Institution of the people assembled, and in another by Conquest, that is by the Submission of each particular, to avoyd death or bonds; to demand of one Nation more than of the other, from the title of Conquest, as being a Conquered Nation, is an act of ignorance of the Rights of Soveraignty. For the Soveraigne is absolute over both alike; or else there is no Soveraignty at all; and so every man may Lawfully protect himselfe, if he can, with his own sword, which is the condition of war.

By this it appears, that a great Family if it be not part of some Common-wealth, is of it self, as to the Rights of Soveraignty, a little Monarchy; whether that Family consists of a man and his children; or of a man and his servants; or of a man, and his children, and servants together: wherein the Father or Master is the Soveraigne. But yet a Family is not properly a Common-wealth; unlesse it be of that power by its own number, or by other opportunities, as not to be subdued without the hazard of Warre. For where a number of men are manifestly too weak to defend themselves united, every one may use his own reason in time of danger, to save his own life, either by flight, or by submission to the enemy, as hee shall think best; in the same manner as a very small company of souldiers, surprised by an army, may cast down their armes, and demand quarter, or run away, rather than be put to the sword. And thus much shall suffice; concerning what I find by speculation, and deduction, of Soveraigne Rights, from the nature, need, and designes of men, in erecting of Common-wealths, and putting themselves under Monarchs, or Assemblies, entrusted with power enough for their protection.

Let us now consider what the Scripture teacheth in the same point. To *Moses*, the children of *Israel* say thus. *Speak thou to us, and we will heare thee; but let not God speak to us, lest we dye* (Exod 20.19). This is absolute obedience to *Moses*. Concerning the Right of Kings, God himself by the mouth of Samuel, saith, *This shall be the Right of the King you will have to reigne over you. He shall take your sons, and set them to drive his Chariots, and to be his horsemen, and to run before his chariots; and gather in his harvest; and to make his engines of War, and Instruments of his chariots; and shall take your daughters to make perfumes, to be his Cookes, and Bakers. He shall take your fields, your vine-yards, and your olive-yards, and give them to his servants. He shall take the tyth of your corne and wine, and give it to the men of his chamber, and to his other servants. He shall take your man-servants, and your maid-servants, and the choice of your youth, and employ them in his businesse. He shall take the tyth of your flocks; and you shall be his servants* (1 Sam 8.11, 12, etc.). This is absolute power, and summed up in the last words, *you shall be his servants*. Againe, when the people heard what power their King was to have, yet they consented thereto, and say thus, *We will be as all other nations, and our King shall judge our causes, and goe before us, to conduct our wars* (1 Sam 8.19, etc.). Here is confirmed the Right that Soveraignes have, both to the *Militia*, and to all *Judicature*; in which is conteined as absolute power, as one man can possibly transferre to another. Again, the prayer of King *Salomon* to God, was this. *Give to thy servant understanding, to judge thy people, and to discerne between Good and Evill* (1 Kgs 3.9). It belongeth therefore to the Soveraigne to bee *Judge*, and to præscribe the Rules of *discerning Good* and *Evill*: which Rules are Lawes; and therefore in him is the Legislative Power. *Saul* sought the life of *David*; yet when it was in his power to slay *Saul*, and his Servants would have done it, *David* forbad them, saying, *God forbid I should do such an act against my Lord, the anoynted of God* (1 Sam 24.9). For obedience of servants St. *Paul* Saith, *Servants obey your masters in All things*, (Col 3.20) and, *Children obey your Parents in All things* (Col 3.22). There is simple obedience in those that are subject to Paternall, or Despoticall dominion. Again, *The Scribes and Pharisees sit in Moses chayre and therefore All that they shall bid you observe, that observe and do* (Matt 23.2, 3). There again is simple obedience. And St. *Paul, Warn them that they subject themselves to Princes, and to those that are in Authority, and obey them* (Titus 3.2). This obedience is also simple. Lastly, our Saviour himselfe acknowledges, that men ought to pay such taxes as are by Kings imposed, where he sayes, *Give to Cæsar that which is Cæsars*; and payed such taxes himselfe. And that the Kings word, is sufficient to take any thing from any Subject, when there is need; and that the King is Judge of that need: For he himselfe, as King of the Jewes, commanded his Disciples to take the Asse, and Asses Colt to carry him into *Jerusalem*, saying, *Go into the Village over against you, and you shall find a shee Asse tyed, and her Colt with her, unty them, and bring them to me. And if any man ask you, what you mean by it, Say the Lord hath need of them: And they will let them go* (Matt 21.2, 3). They will not ask whether his necessity be a sufficient title; nor whether he be judge of that necessity; but acquiesce in the will of the Lord.

To these places may be added also that of *Genesis, You shall be as Gods, knowing Good and Evill* (Gen 3.5). And verse II. *Who told thee that thou wast naked? Hast thou eaten of the tree, of which I commanded thee thou shouldest not eat?* For the Cognisance of Judicature *of Good* and *Evill*, being forbidden by the name of the fruit of the tree of Knowledge, as a triall of *Adams* obedience; The Divel to enflame the Ambition of the woman, to whom that fruit already seemed beautifull, told her that by tasting it, they should be as Gods, knowing *Good* and *Evill*. Whereupon having both eaten, they did indeed take upon them Gods office, which is Judicature of Good and Evill; but acquired no new ability to distinguish between them aright. And whereas it is sayd, that having eaten, they saw they were naked; no man hath so interpreted that place, as if they had been formerly blind, and saw not their own skins: the meaning is plain, that it was then they first judged their nakednesse (wherein it was Gods will to create them) to be uncomely; and by being ashamed, did tacitely censure God himselfe. And thereupon God saith, *Hast thou eaten, etc.* as if he should say, doest thou that owest me obedience, take upon thee to judge of my Commandements? Whereby it is cleerly, (though Allegorically) signified, that the Commands of them that have the right to command, are not by their Subjects to be censured, nor disputed.

So that it appeareth plainly, to my understanding, both from Reason, and Scripture, that the Soveraigne Power, whether placed in One Man, as in Monarchy, or in one Assembly of men, as in Popular, and Aristocraticall Common-wealths, is as great, as possibly men can be imagined to make it. And though of so unlimited a Power, men may fancy many evill consequences, yet the consequences of the want of it, which is perpetuall warre of every man against his neighbour, are much worse. The condition of man in this life shall never be without Inconveniences; but there happeneth in no Common-wealth any great Inconvenience, but what proceeds from the Subjects disobedience, and breach of those Covenants, from which the Common-wealth hath its being. And whosoever thinking Soveraigne Power too great, will seed to make it lesse; must subject himselfe, to the Power, that can limit it; that is to say, to a greater.

The greatest objection is, that of the Practise; when men ask, where, and when, such Power has by Subjects been acknowledged. But one may ask them again, when, or where has there been a Kingdome long free from Sedition and Civill Warre. In those Nations, whose Common-wealths by forraign warre, the Subjects never did dispute of the Soveraigne Power. But howsoever, an argument for the Practise of men, that have not sifted to the bottom, and with exact reason weighed the causes, and nature of Common-wealths, and suffer daily those miseries, that proceed from the ignorance thereof, is invalid. For though in all places of the world, men should lay the foundation of their houses on the sand, it could not thence be inferred, that so it ought to be. The skill of making, and maintaining Common-wealths, consisteth in certain Rules, as doth Arithmetique and Geometry; not (as Tennis-play) on Practise onely: which Rules, neither poor men have the leisure, nor men that have had the leisure, have hitherto had the curiosity, or the method to find out.

The German-born American political philosopher Hannah Arendt was born to a wealthy Jewish family. She studied philosophy at the University of Marburg with luminaries such as Martin Heidegger, Karl Jaspers, and Edmund Husserl, writing a dissertation on St. Augustine's concept of love. In 1924 the eighteen-year-old Arendt enrolled in a course taught by Heidegger, who was thirty-five at the time, married, and father of two sons. They began an affair, which ended, albeit temporarily, in 1933, around the time Heidegger joined the Nazi Party and had been appointed the rector of Albert-Ludwigs University at Freiburg. Arendt had just moved to Paris to escape Nazi terrorism. In that same year Arendt wrote to Heidegger accusing him of anti-Jewish acts on campus; this letter was their last correspondence until after World War II, when they reconciled and resumed a friendship.

Arendt escaped to America in 1941, shortly before the Nazi occupation of France. In America she held an array of offices: research director of the Conference on Jewish Relations (1944–1946); chief editor of Schocken Books (1946–1948); and executive director of Jewish Cultural Reconstruction (1949–1952). In 1963 she received an academic appointment at the University of Chicago (1963–1967); she later taught at the New School for Social Research.

Her three volumes of The Origins of Totalitarianism *(1951) deal with anti-Semitism, with imperialism, and with the terror systems of Nazi Germany and Soviet communism. She argues that totalitarianism, as a particularly twentieth-century phenomenon, arises out of the void left by the withering of the traditional nation-state—a withering which is not manifested in the imperial world-system. Arendt's work is marked not only by her unrelenting criticism of Nazi Germany but also by a critique of European Jews, who, she argues, were complicit in their persecution, a subject she takes up in her controversial* Eichmann in Jerusalem *(1961), wherein she reports on the trial of Adolf Eichmann as a war criminal. The book excited considerable controversy, first because she portrays Eichmann not as an out-of-the-ordinary monster, but simply as an opportunistic bureaucrat whose everyday activities included rounding up Jews for extermination, and second because she concludes that the Jews of Europe ultimately "sold themselves."*

Her other titles include On the Human Condition *(1958),* On Revolution *(1963), and* On Violence *(1970).*

The Origins of Totalitarianism

HANNAH ARENDT

When a movement, international in organization, all-comprehensive in its ideological scope, and global in its political aspiration, seizes power in one country, it obviously puts itself in a paradoxical situation. The socialist movement was spared this crisis, first, because the national question—and that meant the strategical problem involved in the revolution—had been curiously neglected by Marx and Engels, and, secondly, because it faced governmental problems only after the First World War had divested the Second International of its authority over the national members, which everywhere had accepted the primacy of national sentiments over international solidarity as an unalterable fact. In other words, when the time came for the socialist movements to seize power in their respective countries, they had already been transformed into national parties.

This transformation never occurred in the totalitarian, the Bolshevik, and the Nazi movements. At the time it seized power the danger to the movement lay in the fact that, on one hand, it might become "ossified" by taking over the state machine and frozen into a form of absolute government, and that, on the other hand, its freedom of movement might be limited by the borders of the territory in which it came to power. To a totalitarian movement, both dangers are equally deadly: a development toward absolutism would put an end to the movement's interior drive, and a development toward nationalism and frustrate its exterior expansion, without which the movement cannot survive. The form of government the two movements developed, or, rather, which almost automatically developed from their double claim to total domination and global rule, is best characterized by Trotsky's slogan of "permanent revolution" although Trotsky's theory was no more than a socialist forecast of a series of revolutions, from the antifeudal bourgeois to the anti-bourgeois proletarian, which would spread from one country to the other. Only the term itself suggests "permanency," with all its anti-anarchistic implications, and is, strictly speaking, a misnomer; yet even Lenin was more impressed by the term than by its theoretical content. In the Soviet Union, at any rate, revolutions, in the form of general purges, became a permanent institution of the Stalin regime after 1934. Here, as in other instances, Stalin concentrated his attacks on Trotsky's half-gotten slogan precisely because he had decided to use this technique. In Nazi Germany, a similar tendency toward permanent revolution was clearly discernible though the Nazis did not have time to realize it to the same extent. Characteristically enough, their "permanent revolution" also started with the liquidation of the party faction which had dared to proclaim openly the "next stage of the revolution" and precisely because "the Fuehrer and his old guard knew that the real struggle had just begun." Here, instead of the Bolshevik concept of permanent revolution, we find the notion of a racial "selection which can never stand still" thus requiring a constant radicalization of the standards by which the selection, *i.e.*, the extermination of the unfit, is carried out. The point is that both Hitler and Stalin held out promises of stability in order to hide their intention of creating a state of permanent instability.

There could have been no better solution for the perplexities inherent in the co-existence of a government and a movement, of both a totalitarian claim and limited power in a limited territory, of ostensible membership in a comity of nations in which each respects the other's sovereignty and claim to world rule, than this formula stripped of its original content. For the totalitarian ruler is confronted with a dual task which at first appears contradictory to the point of absurdity: he must establish the fictitious world of the movement as a tangible working reality of everyday life, and he must, on the other hand, prevent this new world from developing a new stability; for a stabilization of its laws and institutions would surely liquidate the movement itself and with it the hope of eventual world conquest. The totalitarian ruler must, at any price, prevent normalization from reaching the point where a new way of life could develop— one which might, after a time, lose its bastard qualities and take its place among the widely differing and profoundly contrasting ways of life of the nations of the earth. The moment the revolutionary institutions became a national way of life (that moment when Hitler's claim that Nazism is not an export commodity or Stalin's that socialism can be built in one country, would be more than an attempt to fool the nontotalitarian world), the totalitarianism would lose its "total" quality and become subject to the law of the nations, according to which each possesses a specific territory, people, and historical tradition which relates it to other nations—a plurality which *ipso facto* refutes every contention that any specific form of government is absolutely valid.

Practically speaking, the paradox of totalitarianism in power is that the possession of all instruments of governmental power and violence in one country is not an unmixed blessing for a totalitarian movement. Its disregard for facts, its strict adherence to the rules of a fictitious world, becomes steadily more difficult to maintain, yet remains as essential as it was before. Power means a direct confrontation with reality, and totalitarianism in power is constantly concerned with overcoming this challenge. Propaganda and organization no longer suffice to assert that the impossible is possible, that the incredible is true, that the insane consistency rules the world; the chief psychological support of totalitarian fiction—the active resentment of the status quo, which the masses refused to accept as the only possible world—is no longer there; every bit of factual information that leaks through the iron curtain, set up against the ever-threatening flood of reality from the other, nontotalitarian side, is a greater menace to totalitarian domination than counterpropaganda has been to totalitarian movements.

The struggle for total domination of the total population of the earth, the elimination of every competing nontotalitarian reality, is inherent in the totalitarian regimes themselves; if they do not pursue global rule as their ultimate goal, they are only too likely to lose whatever power they have already seized. Even a single individual can be absolutely and reliably dominated only under global totalitarian conditions. Ascendancy to power therefore means primarily the establishment of official and officially recognized headquarters (or branches in the case of satellite countries) for the movement and the acquisition of a kind of laboratory in which to carry out the experiment with or rather against reality, the experiment in organizing a people for ultimate purposes which disregard individuality as well as nationality, under conditions which are admittedly not perfect but are sufficient for important partial results. Totalitarianism in power uses the state administration for its long-range goal of world conquest and for the direction of the branches of the movement; it establishes the secret police as the executors and guardians of its domestic experiment in constantly transforming reality into fiction; and it finally erects concentration camps as special laboratories to carry through its experiment in total domination.

I. THE SO-CALLED TOTALITARIAN STATE

. . . . .

What strikes the observer of the totalitarian state is certainly not its monolithic structure. On the contrary, all serious students of the subject agree at least on the co-existence (or the conflict) of a dual authority, the party and the state. Many, moreover, have stressed the peculiar "shapelessness" of the totalitarian government. Thomas Masaryk saw early that "the so-called Bolshevik system has never been anything but a complete absence of system"; and it is perfectly true that "even an expert would be driven mad if he tried to unravel the relationships between Party and State" in the Third Reich. It has also been frequently observed that the relationship between the two sources of authority, between state and party, is one of ostensible and real authority, so that the government machine is usually pictured as the powerless facade which hides and protects the real power of the party.

All levels of the administrative machine in the Third Reich were subject to a curious duplication of offices. With a fantastic thoroughness, the Nazis made sure that every function of the state administration would be duplicated by some party organ: the Weimar division of Germany into states and provinces was duplicated by the Nazi division into *Gaue* whose borderlines, however, did not coincide, so that every given locality belonged, even geographically, to two altogether different administrative units. Nor was the duplication of function abandoned when, after 1933, outstanding Nazis occupied the official ministries of the state; when Frick, for instance, became Minister of the Interior or Guerthner Minister of Justice. These old and trusted party members, once they had embarked upon official nonparty careers, lost their power and became as uninfluential as other civil servants. Both came under the factual authority of Himmler, the rising chief of the police, who normally would have been subordinate to the Minister of the Interior. Better known abroad has been the fate of the old German Foreign Affairs Office in the Wilhelmstrasse. The Nazis left its personnel nearly untouched and of course never abolished it; yet at the same time they maintained the prepower Foreign Affairs Bureau of the Party, headed by Rosenberg, and since this office had specialized in maintaining contacts with Fascist organizations in Eastern Europe and the Balkans, they set up another organ to compete with the office in the Wilhelmstrasse, the so-called Ribbentrop Bureau, which handled foreign affairs in the West, and survived the departure of its chief as Ambassador to England, that is, his incorporation into the official apparatus of the Wilhelmstrasse. Finally, in addition to these party institutions, the Foreign Office received another duplication in the form of an ss Office, which was responsible "for negotiations with all racially Germanic groups in Denmark, Norway, Belgium, and the Netherlands." These examples prove that for the Nazis the duplication of offices was a matter of principle and not just an expedient for providing jobs for party members.

The same division between a real and an ostensible government developed from very different beginnings in Soviet Russia. The ostensible government originally sprang from the All-Russian Soviet Congress, which during the civil war lost its influence and power to the Bolshevik party. This process started when the Red Army was made autonomous and the secret political police reestablished as an organ of the party, and not of the Soviet Congress; it was completed in 1923, during the first year of Stalin's General Secretaryship. From then on, the Soviets became the shadow government in whose midst, through cells formed by Bolshevik party members, functioned the representatives of real power who were appointed and responsible to the Central Committee in Moscow. The crucial point in the later development was not the conquest of the Soviets by the party, but the fact that "although it would have presented no difficulties, the Bolsheviks did not abolish the Soviets and used them as the decorative outward symbol of their authority."

The co-existence of an ostensible and a real government therefore was partly the outcome of the revolution itself and preceded Stalin's totalitarian dictatorship. Yet while the Nazis simply retained the existing administration and deprived it of all power, Stalin had to revive his shadow government, which in the early thirties had lost all its functions and was half forgotten in Russia; he introduced the Soviet constitution as the symbol of the existence as well as the powerlessness of the Soviets. (None of its paragraphs ever had the slightest practical significance for life and jurisdiction in Russia.) The ostensible Russian government, utterly lacking the glamour of tradition so necessary for a facade, apparently needed the sacred halo of written law. The totalitarian defiance of law and legality (which "in spite of the greatest changes . . . still [remain] the expression of a permanently desired order") found in the written Soviet constitution, as in the never-repudiated Weimar constitution, a permanent background for its own lawlessness, the permanent challenge to the nontotalitarian world and its standards whose helplessness and impotence could be demonstrated daily.

Duplication of offices and division of authority, the co-existence of real and ostensible power, are sufficient to create confusion but not to explain the "shapelessness" of the whole structure. One should not forget that only a building can have a structure, but that a movement—if the word is to be taken as seriously and as literally as the Nazis meant it—can have only a direction, and that any form of legal or governmental structure can be only a handicap to a movement which is being propelled with increasing speed in a certain direction. Even in the prepower stage the totalitarian movements represented those masses that were no longer willing to live in any kind of structure, regardless of its nature; masses that had started to move in order to flood the legal and geographical borders securely determined by the government. Therefore, judged by our conceptions of government and state structure, these movements, so long as they find themselves physically still limited to a specific territory, necessarily must try to destroy all structure, and for this willful destruction a mere duplication of all offices into party and state institutions would not be sufficient. Since duplication involves a relationship between the facade of the state and the inner core of the party, it, too, would eventually result in some kind of structure, where the relationship between party and state would automatically end in a legal regulation which restricts and stabilizes their respective authority.

As a matter of fact, duplication of offices, seemingly the result of the party state problem in all one-party dictatorships, is only the most conspicuous sign of a more complicated phenomenon that is better defined as multiplication of offices than duplication. The Nazis were not content to establish *Gaue* in addition to the old provinces, but also introduced a great many other geographical divisions in accordance with the different party organizations: the territorial units of the SA were neither co-extensive with the *Gaue* nor with the provinces; they differed, moreover, from those of the SS and none of them corresponded to the zones dividing the Hitler Youth. To this geographical confusion must be added the fact that the original relationship between real and ostensible power repeated itself throughout, albeit in an ever-changing way. The inhabitant of Hitler's Third Reich lived not only under the simultaneous and often conflicting authorities of competing powers, such as the civil services, the party, the SA, and the SS; he could never be sure and was never explicitly told whose authority he was supposed to place above all others. He had to develop a kind of sixth sense to know at a given moment whom to obey and whom to disregard.

· · · · ·

To be sure, totalitarian dictators do not consciously embark upon the road to insanity. The point is rather that our bewilderment about the anti-utilitarian character of the totalitarian state structure springs from the mistaken notion that we are dealing with a normal state after all—a bureaucracy, a tyranny, a dictatorship—from our overlooking the emphatic assertions by totalitarian rulers that they consider the country where they happened to seize power only the temporary headquarters of the international movement on the road to world conquest, that they reckon victories and defeats in terms of centuries or millennia, and that the global interests always overrule the local interests of their own territory. The famous "Right is what is good for the German people" was meant only for mass propaganda; Nazis were told that "Right is what is good for the movement," and those two interests did by no means always coincide. The Nazis did not think that the Germans were a master race, to whom the world belonged, but that they should be led by a master race, as should all other nations, and that this race was only on the point of being born. Not the Germans were drawn of the master race, but the SS. The "Germanic world empire," as Himmler said, or the "Aryan" world empire, as Hitler would have put it, was in any event still centuries off. For the "movement" it was more important to demonstrate that it was possible to fabricate a race by annihilating other "races" than to win a war with limited aims. What strikes the outside observer as a "piece of prodigious insanity" is nothing but the consequence of the absolute primacy of the movement not only over the state, but also over the nation, the people, and the positions of power held by the rulers themselves. The reason why the ingenious devices of totalitarian rule, with their absolute and unsurpassed concentration of power in the hands of a single man, were never tried out before, is that no ordinary tyrant was ever mad enough to discard all limited and local interests—economic, national, human, military—in favor of a purely fictitious reality in some indefinite distant future.

. . . . .

One of the important differences between a totalitarian movement and a totalitarian state is that the totalitarian dictator can and must practice the totalitarian art of lying more consistently and on a larger scale than the leader of a movement. This is partly the automatic consequence of swelling the ranks of fellow-travelers, and is partly due to the fact that unpleasant statements by a statesman are not as easily revoked as those of a demagogic party leader. For this purpose, Hitler chose to fall back, without any detours, on the old-fashioned nationalism which he had denounced many times before his ascent to power; by posing as a violent nationalist, claiming that National Socialism was not an "export commodity," he appeased Germans and non-Germans alike and implied that Nazi ambitions would be satisfied when the traditional demands of a nationalist German foreign policy—return of territories ceded in the Versailles treaties, *Anschluss* of Austria, annexation of the German-speaking parts of Bohemia—were fulfilled. Stalin likewise reckoned with both Russian public opinion and the non-Russian world when he invented his theory of "socialism in one country" and threw the onus of world revolution on Trotsky.

Systematic lying to the whole world can be safely carried out only under the conditions of totalitarian rule, where the fictitious quality of everyday reality makes propaganda largely superfluous. In their prepower stage the movements can never afford to hide their true goals to the same degree—after all, they are meant to inspire mass organizations. But, given the possibility to exterminate Jews like bedbugs, namely, by poison gas, it is no longer necessary to propagate that Jews are bedbugs; given the power to teach a whole nation the history of the Russian Revolution without mentioning the name of Trotsky, there is no further need for propaganda against Trotsky. But the use of the methods of carrying out the "ideologically utterly firm"—whether they have acquired such firmness in the Comintern schools or the special Nazi indoctrination centers—even if these goals continue to be publicized, on such occasions it invariably turns out that the mere sympathizers never realize what is happening. This leads to the paradox that "the secret society in broad daylight" is never more conspiratory in character and methods than after it has been recognized as a full-fledged member of the comity of nations. It is only logical that Hitler, prior to his seizure of power, resisted all attempts to organize the party and even the elite formations on a conspiratory basis; yet after 1933 he was quite eager to help transform the ss into a kind of secret society. Similarly, the Moscow-directed Communist parties, in marked contrast to their predecessors, show a curious tendency to prefer the conditions of conspiracy even where complete legality is possible. The more conspicuous the power of totalitarianism the more secret becomes its true goals. To know the ultimate aims of Hitler's rule in Germany, it was much wiser to rely on his propaganda speeches and *Mein Kampf* than on the oratory of the Chancellor of the Third Reich; just as it would have been wiser to distrust Stalin's words about "socialism in one country," invented for the passing purposes of seizing power after Lenin's death, and to take more seriously his repeated hostility to democratic countries. The totalitarian dictators have proved that they knew only too well the danger inherent in their pose of normality; that is, the danger of a true nationalist policy or of actually building socialism in one country. This they try to overcome through a permanent and consistent discrepancy between reassuring words and the reality of rule, by consciously developing a method of always doing the opposite of what they say. Stalin has carried his art of balance, which demands more skill than the ordinary routine of diplomacy, to the point where a moderation in foreign policy or the political line of the Comintern is almost invariably accompanied by radical purges in the Russian party. It was certainly more than coincidence that the Popular Front policy and the drafting of the comparatively liberal Soviet constitution were accompanied by the Moscow Trials.

. . . . .

Totalitarian regimes are not afraid of the logical implications of world conquest even if they work the other way around and are detrimental to their own peoples' interests. Logically, it is indisputable that a plan for world conquest involves the abolition of differences between the conquering mother country and the conquered territories, as well as the difference between foreign and domestic politics, upon which all existing nontotalitarian institutions and all international intercourse are based. If the totalitarian conqueror conducts himself everywhere as though he were at home, by the same token he must treat his own population as through he were a foreign conqueror. And it is perfectly true that the totalitarian movement seizes power in much the same sense as a foreign conqueror may occupy a country which he governs not for its own sake but for the benefit of something or somebody else. The Nazis behaved like foreign conquerors in Germany when, against all national interests, they tried and half succeeded in converting their defeat into a final catastrophe for the whole German people; similarly in case of victory, they intended to extend their extermination politics into the ranks of "racially unfit" Germans.

A similar attitude seems to have inspired Soviet foreign policy after the war. The cost of its aggressiveness to the Russian people themselves is prohibitive: it has foregone the great postwar loan from the United States which would have enabled Russia to reconstruct devastated areas and industrialize the country in a rational, productive way. The extension of Comintern governments throughout the Balkans and the occupation of large Eastern territories brought no tangible benefits, but on the contrary strained Russian resources still further. But this policy certainly served the interests of the Bolshevik movement, which had spread over almost half of the inhabited world.

Like a foreign conqueror, the totalitarian dictator regards the natural and industrial riches of each country, including his own, as a source of loot and a means of preparing the next step of aggressive expansion. Since this economy of systematic spoliation is carried out for the sake of the movement and not of the nation, no people and no territory, as the potential beneficiary, can possibly set a saturation point to the process. The totalitarian dictator is like a foreign conqueror who comes from nowhere, and his looting is likely to benefit nobody. Distribution of the spoils is calculated not to strengthen the economy of the home country but only as a temporary tactical maneuver. For economic purposes, the totalitarian regimes are as much at home in their countries as the proverbial swarms of locusts. The fact that the totalitarian dictator rules his own country like a foreign conqueror makes matters worse because it adds to ruthlessness an efficiency which is conspicuously lacking in tyrannies in alien surroundings. Stalin's war against the Ukraine in the early thirties was twice as effective as the terrible bloody German invasion and occupation. This is the reason why totalitarianism prefers quisling governments to direct rule despite the obvious dangers of such regimes.

The trouble with totalitarian regimes is not that they play power politics in an especially ruthless way, but that behind their politics is hidden an entirely new and unprecedented concept of power, just as behind their *Real politik* lies an entirely new and unprecedented concept of reality. Supreme disregard for immediate consequences rather than ruthlessness; rootlessness and neglect of national interests rather than nationalism; contempt for utilitarian motives rather than unconsidered pursuit of self-interest; "idealism," *i.e.*, their unwavering faith in an ideological fictitious world, rather than lust for power—these have all introduced into international politics a new and more disturbing factor than mere aggressiveness would have been able to do.

Power, as conceived by totalitarianism, lies exclusively in the force produced through organization. Just as Stalin saw every institution, independent of its actual function, only as a "transmission belt connecting the party with the people" and honestly believed that the most precious treasures of the Soviet Union were not the riches of its soil or the productive capacity of its huge manpower, but the "cadres" of the party (*i.e.*, the police), so Hitler as early as

1929 saw the "great thing" of the movement in the fact that sixty thousand men "have outwardly become almost a unit, that actually these members are uniform not only in ideas, but that even the facial expression is almost the same. Look at these laughing eyes, this fanatical enthusiasm and you will discover . . . how a hundred thousand men in a movement become a single type." Whatever connection power had in the minds of Western man with earthly possessions, with wealth, treasures, and riches, has been dissolved into a kind of dematerialized mechanism whose every move generates power as friction or galvanic currents generate electricity. The totalitarian division of states into Have and Have-not countries is more than a demagogic device; those who make it are actually convinced that the power of material possessions is negligible and only stands in the way of development of organizational power. To Stalin constant growth and development of police cadres were incomparably more important than the oil in Baku, the coal and ore in the Urals, the granaries in the Ukraine, or the potential treasurers of Siberia—in short the development of Russia's full power arsenal. The same mentality led Hitler to sacrifice all Germany to the cadres of the ss; he did not consider the war lost when German cities lay in rubble and industrial capacity was destroyed, but only when he learned that the ss troops were no longer reliable. To a man who believed in organizational omnipotence against all mere material factors, military or economic, and who, moreover, calculated the eventual victory of his enterprise in centuries, defeat was not military catastrophe or threatened starvation of the population, but only the destruction of the elite formations which were supposed to carry the conspiracy for world rule through a line of generations to its eventual end.

The structurelessness of the totalitarian state, its neglect of material interests, its emancipation from the profit motive, and its nonutilitarian attitudes in general have more than anything else contributed to making contemporary politics well-nigh unpredictable. The inability of the nontotalitarian world to grasp a mentality which functions independently of all calculable action in terms of men and material, and is completely indifferent to national interest and the well-being of its people, shows itself in a curious dilemma of judgment: those who rightly understand the terrible efficiency of totalitarian organization and police are likely to overestimate the material force of totalitarian countries, while those who understand the wasteful incompetence of totalitarian economics are likely to underestimate the power potential which can be created in disregard to all material factors.

. . . . .

Above the state and behind the facades of ostensible power, in a maze of multiplied offices, underlying all shifts of authority and in a chaos of inefficiency, lies the power nucleus of the country, the superefficient and super-competent services of the secret police. The emphasis on the police as the sole organ of power, and the corresponding neglect of the seemingly greater power arsenal of the army, which is characteristic of all totalitarian regimes, can still be partially explained by the totalitarian aspiration to world rule and its conscious abolition of the distinction between a foreign country and a home country, between foreign and domestic affairs. The military forces, trained to fight a foreign aggressor, have always been a dubious instrument for civil-war purposes; even under totalitarian conditions they find it difficult to regard their own people with the eyes of a foreign conqueror. More important in this respect, however, is that their value becomes dubious even in time of war. Since the totalitarian ruler conducts his policies on the assumption of an eventual world government, he treats the victims of his aggression as though they were rebels, guilty of high treason, and consequently prefers to rule occupied territories with police, and not with military forces.

Even before the movement seizes power, it possesses a secret police and spy service with branches in various countries. Later its agents receive more money and authority than the regular military intelligence service and are frequently the secret chiefs of embassies and consulates abroad. Its main tasks consist in forming fifth columns, directing the branches of the movement, influencing the domestic policies of the respective countries, and generally preparing for the time when the totalitarian ruler—after overthrow of the government or military victory—can openly feel at home. In other words, the international branches of the secret police are the transmission belts which constantly transform the ostensibly foreign policy of the totalitarian state into the potentially domestic business of the totalitarian movement.

. . . . .

Neither dubious nor superfluous is the political function of the secret police, the "best organized and the most efficient" of all government departments, in the power apparatus of the totalitarian regime. It constitutes the true executive branch of the government through which all orders are transmitted. Through the net of secret agents, the totalitarian ruler has created for himself a directly executive transmission belt which, in distinction to the onion-like structure of the ostensible hierarchy, is completely severed and isolated from all other institutions. In this sense, the secret police agents are the only openly ruling class in totalitarian countries and their standards and scale of values permeate the entire texture of totalitarian society.

From this viewpoint, it may not be too surprising that certain peculiar qualities of the secret police are general qualities of totalitarian society rather than peculiarities of the totalitarian secret police. The category of the suspect thus embraces under totalitarian conditions the total population; every thought that deviates from the officially prescribed and permanently changing line is already suspect, no matter in which field of human activity it occurs. Simply because of their capacity to think, human beings are suspects by definition, and this suspicion cannot be diverted by exemplary behavior, for the human capacity to think is also a capacity to change one's mind. Since, moreover, it is impossible ever to know beyond doubt another man's heart—torture in this context is only the desperate and eternally futile attempt to achieve what cannot be achieved—suspicion can no longer be allayed if neither a community of values nor the predictabilities of self-interest exist as social (as distinguished from merely psychological) realities. Mutual suspicion, therefore, permeates all social relationships in totalitarian countries and creates an all-pervasive atmosphere even outside the special purview of the secret police.

In totalitarian regimes provocation, once only the specialty of the secret agent, becomes a method of dealing with his neighbor which everybody, willingly or unwillingly, is forced to follow. Everyone, in a way, is the *agent provocateur* of everyone else; for obviously everybody will call himself an *agent provocateur* if ever an ordinary friendly exchange of "dangerous thoughts" (or what in the meantime have become dangerous thoughts) should come to the attention of the authorities. Collaboration of the population in denouncing political opponents and volunteer service as stool pigeons are certainly not unprecedented, but in totalitarian countries they are so well organized that the work of specialists is almost superfluous. In a system of ubiquitous spying, where everybody may be a police agent and each individual feels himself under constant surveillance; under circumstances, moreover, where careers are extremely insecure and where the most spectacular ascents and falls have become everyday occurrences, every word becomes equivocal and subject to retrospective "interpretation."

The most striking illustration of the permeation of totalitarian society with secret police methods and standards can be found in the matter of careers. The double agent in nontotalitarian regimes served the cause he was supposed to combat almost as much as, and sometimes more than, the authorities. Frequently he harbored a sort of double ambition: he wanted to rise in the ranks of the revolutionary parties as well as in the ranks of the services. In order to win promotion in both fields, he had only to adopt certain methods which in a normal society belong to the secret daydreams of the small employee who depends on seniority for advancement: through his connections with the police, he could certainly eliminate his rivals and superiors in the party, and through his connections with the revolutionaries he had at least a chance to get rid of his chief in the police. If we consider the career conditions in present Russian society, the similarity to such methods is striking. Not only do almost all higher officials owe their positions to purges that removed their predecessors, but promotions in all walks of life are accelerated in this way. About every ten years, a nationwide purge makes room for the new generation, freshly graduated and hungry for jobs. The government has itself established those conditions for advancement which the police agent formerly bid to create.

This regular violent turnover of the whole gigantic administrative machine, while it prevents the development of competence, has many advantages: it assures the relative youth of officials and prevents a stabilization of conditions which, at least in time of peace, are fraught with danger for totalitarian rule; by eliminating seniority and merit, it prevents the development of the loyalties that usually tie younger staff members to their elders, upon whose opinion and good will their advancement depends; it eliminates once and for all the dangers of unemployment and assures everyone of a job compatible with his education. Thus, in 1939, after the gigantic purge in the Soviet Union had come to an end, Stalin could note with great satisfaction that "the Party was able to promote to leading posts in State or Party affairs more than 500,000 young Bolsheviks." The humiliation implicit in owing a job to the unjust elimination of one's pre-decessor has the same demoralizing effect that the elimination of the Jews had upon the German professions: it makes every jobholder a conscious accomplice in the crimes of the government, their beneficiary whether he likes it or not, with the result that the more sensitive the humiliated individual happens to be, the more ardently he will defend the regime. In other words, this system is the logical outgrowth of the Leader principle in its full implications and the best possible guarantee for loyalty, in that it makes every new generation depend for its livelihood on the current political line of the Leader which started the job-creating purge. It also realizes the identity of public and private interests, of which defenders of the Soviet Union used to be so proud (or, in the Nazi version, the abolition of the private sphere of life), insofar as every individual of any consequence owes his whole existence to the political interest of the regime; and when this factual identity of interest is broken and the next purge has swept him out of office, the regime makes sure that he disappears from the world of the living. In a not very different way, the double agent was identified with the cause of the revolution (without which he would lose his job), and not only with the secret police; in that sphere, too, a spectacular rise could end only in an anonymous death, since it was rather unlikely that the double game could be played forever. The totalitarian government, when it set such conditions for promotions in all careers as had previously prevailed only among social outcasts, has effected one of the most far-reaching changes in social psychology. The psychology of the double agent, who was willing to pay the price of a short life for the exalted existence of a few years at the peak, has necessarily become the philosophy in personal matters of the whole post-revolutionary generation in Russia, and to a lesser but still very dangerous extent, in postwar Germany.

This is the society, permeated by standards and living by methods which once had been the monopoly of the secret police, in which the totalitarian secret police functions. Only in the initial stages, when a struggle for power is still going on, are its victims those who can be suspected of opposition. It then embarks upon its totalitarian career with the persecution of the objective enemy, which may be the Jews or the Poles (as in the case of the Nazis) or so-called "counter-revolutionaries"—an accusation which "in Soviet Russia . . . is established . . . before any question as to [the] behavior [of the accused] has arisen at all"—who may be people who at any time owned a shop or a house or "had parents or grandparents who owned such things," or who happened to belong to one of the Red Army occupational forces, or were Russians of Polish origin. Only in its last and fully totalitarian stage are the concepts of the objective enemy and the logically possible crime abandoned, the victims chosen completely at random and, even without being accused, declared unfit to live. This new category of "undesirables" may consist, as in the case of the Nazis, of the mentally ill or persons with lung and heart disease, or in the Soviet Union, of people who happen to have been taken up in that percentage, varying from one province to another, which is ordered to be deported.

This consistent arbitrariness negates human freedom more efficiently than any tyranny ever could. One had at least to be an enemy of tyranny in order to be punished by it. Freedom of opinion was not abolished for those who were brave enough to risk their necks. Theoretically, the choice of opposition remains in totalitarian regimes too; but such freedom is almost invalidated if committing a voluntary act only assures a "punishment" that everyone else may have to bear anyway. Freedom in this system has not only dwindled down to its last and apparently still indestructible guarantee, the possibility of suicide, but has lost its distinctive mark because the consequences of its exercise are shared with completely innocent people. If Hitler had had the time to realize his dream of a General German Health Bill, the man suffering from a lung disease would have been subject to the same fate as a Communist in the early and a Jew in the later years of the Nazi regime. Similarly, the opponent of the regime in Russia, suffering the same fate as millions of people who are chosen for concentration camps to make up certain quotas, only relieves the police of the burden of arbitrary choice. The innocent and the guilty are equally undesirable.

The change in the concept of crime and criminals determines the new and terrible methods of the totalitarian secret police. Criminals are punished; undesirables disappear from the face of the earth; the only trace which they leave behind is the memory of those who knew and loved them, and one of the most difficult tasks of the secret police is to make sure that even such traces will disappear together with the condemned man.

. . . . .

The truth of the matter is that totalitarian leaders, though they are convinced that they must follow consistently the fiction and the rules of the fictitious world which were laid down during their struggle for power, discover only gradually the full implications of this fictitious world and its rules. Their faith in human omnipotence, their conviction that everything can be done through organization, carries them into experiments which human imaginations may have outlined but human activity certainly never realized. Their hideous discoveries in the realm of the possible are inspired by an ideological scientificality which has proved to be less controlled by reason and less willing to recognize factuality than the wildest fantasies of prescientific and prephilosophical speculation. They establish the secret society which now no longer operates in broad daylight, the society of the secret police or the political soldier or the ideologically trained fighter, in order to be able to carry out the indecent experimental inquiry into what is possible.

The totalitarian conspiracy against the nontotalitarian world, on the other hand, its claim to world domination, remains as open and unguarded under conditions of totalitarian rule as in the totalitarian movements. It is practically impressed upon the coordinated population of "sympathizers" in the form of a supposed conspiracy of the whole world against their own country. The totalitarian dichotomy is propagated by making it a duty for every national abroad to report home as though he were a secret agent, and by treating every foreigner as a spy for his home government. It is for the practical realization of this dichotomy rather than because of specific secrets, military and other, that iron curtains separate the inhabitants of a totalitarian country from the rest of the world. Their real secret, the concentration camps, those laboratories in the experiment of total domination, is shielded by the totalitarian regimes from the eyes of their own people as well as from all others.

For a considerable length of time the normality of the normal world is the most efficient protection against disclosure of totalitarian mass crimes. "Normal men don't know that everything is possible," refuse to believe their eyes and ears in the face of the monstrous, just as the mass of men did not trust theirs in the face of a normal reality in which no place was left for them. The reason why the totalitarian regimes can get so far toward realizing a fictitious, topsy-turvy world is that the outside nontotalitarian world, which always comprises a great part of the population of the totalitarian country itself, indulges also in wishful thinking and shirks reality in the face of real insanity just as much as the masses do in the face of the normal world. This common-sense disinclination to believe the monstrous is constantly strengthened by the totalitarian ruler himself, who makes sure that no reliable statistics, no controllable facts and figures are ever published, so that there are only subjective, uncontrollable, and unreliable reports about the places of the living dead.

Because of this policy, the results of the totalitarian experiment are only partially known. Although we have enough reports from concentration camps to assess the possibilities of total domination and to catch a glimpse into the abyss of the "possible," we do not know the extent of character transformation under a totalitarian regime. We know even less how many of the normal people around us would be willing to accept the totalitarian way of life—that is, to pay the price of a considerably shorter life for the assured fulfillment of all their career dreams. It is easy to realize the extent to which totalitarian propaganda and even some totalitarian institutions answer the needs of the new homeless masses, but it is almost impossible to know how many of them, if they are further exposed to a constant threat of unemployment, will gladly acquiesce to a "population policy" that consists of regular elimination of surplus people, and how many, once they have fully grasped their growing incapacity to bear the burdens of modern life, will gladly conform to a system that, together with spontaneity, eliminates responsibility.

In other words, while we know the operation and the specific function of the totalitarian secret police, we do not know how well or to what an extent the "secret" of this secret society corresponds to the secret desires and the secret complicities of the masses in our time.

III. TOTAL DOMINATION

. . . . .

What runs counter to common sense is not the nihilistic principle that "everything is permitted," which was already contained in the nineteenth-century utilitarian conception of common sense. What common sense and "normal people" refuse to believe is that everything is possible. We attempt to understand elements in present or recollected experience that simply surpass our powers of understanding. We attempt to classify as criminal a thing which, as we all feel, no such category was ever intended to cover. What meaning has the concept of murder when we are confronted with the mass production of corpses? We attempt to understand the behavior of concentration-camp inmates and ss-men psychologically, when the very thing that must be realized is that the psyche *can* be destroyed even without the destruction of the physical man; that, indeed, psyche, character, and individuality seem under certain circumstances to express themselves only through the rapidity or slowness with which they disintegrate. The end result in any case is inanimate men, *i.e.*, men who can no longer be psychologically understood, whose return to the psychologically or otherwise intelligibly human world closely resembles the resurrection of Lazarus. All statements of common sense, whether of a psychological or sociological nature, serve only to encourage those who think it "superficial" to "dwell on horrors."

If it is true that the concentration camps are the most consequential institution of totalitarian rule, "dwelling on horrors" would seem to be indispensable for the understanding of totalitarianism. But recollection can no more do this than can the uncommunicative eyewitness report. In both these genres there is an inherent tendency to run away from the experience; instinctively or rationally, both types of writer are so much aware of the terrible abyss that separates the world of the living from that of the living dead, that they cannot supply anything more than a series of remembered occurrences that must seem just as incredible to those who relate them as to their audience. Only the fearful imagination of those who have been aroused by such reports but have not actually been smitten in their own flesh, of those who are consequently free from the bestial, desperate terror which, when confronted by real, present horror, inexorably paralyzes everything that is not mere reaction, can afford to keep thinking about horrors. Such thoughts are useful only for the perception of political contexts and the mobilization of political passions. A change of personality of any sort whatever can no more be induced by thinking about horrors than by the real experience of horror. The reduction of a man to a bundle of reactions separates him as radically as mental disease from everything within him that is personality or character. When, like Lazarus, he rises from the dead, he finds his personality or character unchanged, just as he had left it.

Just as the horror, or the dwelling on it, cannot affect a change of character in him, cannot make men better or worse, thus it cannot become the basis of a political community or party in a narrower sense. The attempts to build up a European elite with a program of intra-European understanding based on the common European experience of the concentration camps have foundered in much the same manner as the attempts following the First World War to draw political conclusions from the international experience of the front generation. In both cases it turned out that the experiences themselves can communicate no more than nihilistic banalities. Political consequences such as postwar pacifism, for example, derived from the general fear of war, not from the experiences in war. Instead of producing a pacifism devoid of reality, the insight into the structure of modern wars, guided and mobilized by fear, might have led to the realization that the only standard for a necessary war is the fight against conditions under which people no longer wish to live—and our experiences with the tormenting hell of the totalitarian camps have enlightened us only too well about the possibility of such conditions. Thus the fear of concentration camps and the resulting insight into the nature of total domination might serve to invalidate all obsolete political differentiations from right to left and to introduce beside and above them the politically most important yardstick for judging events in our time, namely, whether they serve totalitarian domination or not.

· · · · ·

The real horror of the concentration and extermination camps lies in the fact that the inmates, even if they happen to keep alive, are more effectively cut off from the world of the living than if they had died, because terror enforces oblivion. Here, murder is as impersonal as the squashing of a gnat. Someone may die as the result of systematic torture or starvation, or because the camp is overcrowded and superfluous human material must be liquidated. Conversely, it may happen that due to a shortage of new human shipments the danger arises that the camps become depopulated and that the order is now given to reduce the death rate at any price. David Rousset called his report on the period in a German concentration camp "*Les Jours de Notre Mort*," and it is indeed as if there were a possibility to give permanence to the process of dying itself and to enforce a condition in which both death and life are obstructed equally effectively.

It is the appearance of some radical evil, previously unknown to us, that puts an end to the notion of developments and transformations of qualities. Here, there are neither political nor historical nor simply moral standards but, at the most, the realization that something seems to be involved in modern politics that actually should never be involved in politics as we used to understand it, namely all or nothing—all, and that is an undetermined infinity of forms of human living-together, or nothing, for a victory of the concentration-camp system would mean the same inexorable doom for human beings as the use of the hydrogen bomb would mean the doom of the human race.

There are no parallels to the life in the concentration camps. Its horror can never be fully embraced by the imagination for the very reason that it stands outside of life and death. It can never be fully reported for the very reason that the survivor returns to the world of the living, which makes it impossible for him to believe fully in his own past experiences. It is as though he had a story to tell of another planet, for the status of the inmates in the world of the living, where nobody is supposed to know if they are alive or dead, is such that it is as though they had never been born. Therefore all parallels create confusion and distract attention from what is essential. Forced labor in prisons and penal colonies, banishment, slavery, all seem for a moment to offer helpful comparisons, but on closer examination lead nowhere.

$$. \ . \ . \ . \ .$$

The incredibility of the horrors is closely bound up with their economic uselessness. The Nazis carried this uselessness to the point of open anti-utility when in the midst of the war, despite the shortage of building material and rolling stock, they set up enormous, costly extermination factories and transported millions of people back and forth. In the eyes of a strictly utilitarian world, the obvious contradiction between these acts and military expediency gave the whole enterprise an air of mad unreality.

This atmosphere of madness and unreality, created by an apparent lack of purpose, is the real iron curtain which hides all forms of concentration camps from the eyes of the world. Seen from outside, they and the things that happen in them can be described only in images drawn from a life after death, that is, a life removed from earthly purposes. Concentration camps can very aptly be divided into three types corresponding to three basic Western conceptions of a life after death: Hades, Purgatory, and Hell. To Hades correspond those relatively mild forms, once popular even in nontotalitarian countries, for getting undesirable elements of all sorts—refugees, stateless persons, the asocial, and the unemployed—out of the way; as DP camps, which are nothing other than camps for persons who have become superfluous and bothersome, they have survived the war. Purgatory is represented by the Soviet Union's labor camps, where neglect is combined with chaotic forced labor. Hell in the most literal sense was embodied by those types of camp perfected by the Nazis, in which the whole of life was thoroughly and systematically organized with a view to the greatest possible torment.

$$. \ . \ . \ . \ .$$

The films which the Allies circulated in Germany and elsewhere after the war showed clearly that this atmosphere of insanity and unreality is not dispelled by pure reportage. To the unprejudiced observer these pictures are just about as convincing as snapshots of mysterious substances taken at spiritualist séances. Common sense reacted to the horrors of Buchenwald and Auschwitz with the plausible argument: "What crime must these people have committed that such things were done to them!"; or, in Germany and Austria, in the midst of starvation, over-population, and general hatred: "Too bad that they've stopped gassing the Jews"; and everywhere with the skeptical shrug that greets ineffectual propaganda.

If the propaganda of truth fails to convince the average person because it is too monstrous, it is positively dangerous to those who know from their own imaginings what they themselves are capable of doing and who are therefore perfectly willing to believe in the reality of what they have seen. Suddenly it becomes evident that things which for thousands of years the human imagina-tion had banished to a realm beyond human competence can be manufactured right here on earth, that Hell and Purgatory, and even a shadow of their per-petual duration, can be established by the most modern methods of destruction and therapy. To these people (and they are more numerous in any large city than we like to admit), the totalitarian hell proves only that the power of man is greater than they ever dared to think, and that man can realize hellish fantasies without making the sky fall or the earth open.

These analogies, repeated in many reports from the world of the dying, seem to express more than a desperate attempt at saying what is outside the realm of human speech. Nothing perhaps distinguishes modern masses as radically from those of previous centuries as the loss of faith in a Last Judgment: the worst have lost their fear and the best have lost their hope. Unable as yet to live without fear and hope, these masses are attracted by every effort which seems to promise a man-made fabrication of the Paradise they had longed for and the Hell they had feared. Just as the popularized features of Marx's classless society have a queer resemblance to the Messianic Age, so the reality of concentration camps resem-bles nothing so much as medieval pictures of Hell.

The one thing that cannot be reproduced is what made the traditional con-ceptions of Hell tolerable to man: the Last Judgment, the idea of an absolute standard of justice combined with the infinite possibility of grace. For in the human estimation there is no crime and no sin commensurable with the ever-lasting torments of Hell. Hence the discomfiture of common sense, which asks: What crime must these people have committed in order to suffer so inhumanly? Hence also the absolute innocence of the victims: no man ever deserved this. Hence finally the grotesque haphazardness with which concentration-camp victims were chosen in the perfected terror state: such "punishment" can, with equal justice and injustice, be inflicted on anyone.

In comparison with the insane end-result—concentration-camp society— the process by which men are prepared for this end, and the methods by which individuals are adapted to these conditions, are transparent and logical. The insane mass manufacture of corpses is preceded by the historically and politically intelligible preparation of living corpses. The impetus and what is more important, the silent consent to such unprecedented conditions are the products of political disintegration, which suddenly and unexpectedly made hundreds of thousands of human beings homeless, stateless, outlawed, and unwanted, while millions of human beings were made economically superfluous and socially burdensome by unemployment. This in turn could only happen because the Rights of Man, which had never been philosophically established but merely formulated, which had never been politically secured but merely proclaimed, have, in their traditional form, lost all validity.

The first essential step on the road to total domination is to kill the juridical person in man. This was done, on the one hand, by putting certain categories of people outside the protection of the law and forcing at the same time, through the instrument of denationalization, the nontotalitarian world into recognition of lawlessness; it was done, on the other, by placing the concentration camp outside the normal penal system, and by selecting its inmates outside the normal judicial procedure in which a definite crime entails a predictable penalty. Thus criminals, who for other reasons are an essential element in concentration-camp society, are ordinarily sent to a camp only on completion of their prison sentence. Under all circumstances totalitarian domination sees to it that the categories gathered in the camps—Jews, carriers of diseases, representatives of dying classes—have already lost their capacity for both normal and criminal action.

. . . . .

To the amalgam of politicals and criminals with which concentration camps in Russia and Germany started out, was added at an early date a third element which was soon to constitute the majority of all concentration-camps inmates. This largest group has consisted ever since of people who had done nothing whatsoever that, either in their own consciousness or the consciousness of their tormenters, had any rational connection with their arrest. In Germany, after 1938, this element was represented by masses of Jews, in Russia by any groups which, for any reason having nothing to do with their actions, had incurred the disfavor of the authorities. These groups, innocent in every sense, are the most suitable for thorough experimentation in disfranchisement and destruction of the juridical person, and therefore they are both qualitatively and quantitatively the most essential category of the camp population. This principle was most fully realized in the gas chambers which, if only because of their enormous capacity, could not be intended for individual cases but only for people in general. In this connection, the following dialogue sums up the situation of the individual: "For what purpose, may I ask, do the gas chambers exist?"—"For what purpose were you born?" It is this third group of the totally innocent who in every case fare the worst in the camps. Criminals and politicals are assimilated to this category; thus deprived of the protective distinction that comes of their having done something, they are utterly exposed to the arbitrary. The ultimate goal, partly achieved in the Soviet Union and clearly indicated in the last phases of Nazi terror, is to have the whole camp population composed of this category of innocent people.

· · · · ·

While the classification of inmates by categories is only a tactical, organizational measure, the arbitrary selection of victims indicates the essential principle of the institution. If the concentration camps had been dependent on the existence of political adversaries, they would scarcely have survived the first years of the totalitarian regimes. One only has to take a look at the number of inmates at Buchenwald in the years after 1936 in order to understand how absolutely necessary the element of the innocent was for the continued existence of the camps. "The camps would have died out if in making its arrest the Gestapo had considered only the principle of opposition," and toward the end of 1937 Buchenwald, with less than 1,000 inmates, was close to dying out until the November pogroms brought more than 20,000 new arrivals. In Germany, this element of the innocent was furnished in vast numbers by the Jews after 1938; in Russia, it consisted of random groups of the population which for some reason entirely unconnected with their actions had fallen into disgrace. But if in Germany the really totalitarian type of concentration camp with its enormous majority of completely "innocent" inmates was not established until 1938, in Russia it goes back to the early thirties, since up to 1930 the majority of the concentration-camp population still consisted of criminals, counterrevolutionaries, and "politicals" (meaning, in this case, members of deviationist factions). Since then there have been so many innocent people in the camps that it is difficult to classify them—persons who had some sort of contact with a foreign country, Russians of Polish origin (particularly in the years 1936 to 1938), peasants whose villages for some economic reason were liquidated, deported nationalities, demobilized soldiers of the Red Army who happened to belong to regiments that stayed too long abroad as occupation forces or had become prisoners of war in Germany, etc. But the existence of a political opposition is for a concentration-camp system only a pretext, and the purpose of the system is not achieved even when, under the most monstrous terror, the population becomes more or less voluntarily co-ordinated, i.e., relinquishes its political rights. The aim of an arbitrary system is to destroy the civil rights of the whole population, who ultimately become just as outlawed in their own country as the stateless and homeless. The destruction of a man's rights, the killing of the juridical person in him is a prerequisite for dominating him entirely. And this applies not only to special categories such as criminals, political opponents, Jews, homosexuals, on whom the early experiments were made, but to every inhabitant of a totalitarian state. Free consent is as much an obstacle to total domination as free opposition. The arbitrary arrest which chooses among innocent people destroys the validity of free consent, just as torture—as distinguished from death—destroys the possibility of opposition.

Any, even the most tyrannical, restriction of this arbitrary persecution to certain opinions of a religious or political nature, to certain modes of intellectual or erotic social behaviour, to certain freshly invented "crimes," would render the camps superfluous, because in the long run no attitude and no opinion can withstand the threat of so much horror; and above all it would make for a new system of justice, which, given any stability at all, could not fail to produce a new juridical person in man, that would elude the totalitarian domination. The so-called "*Volksnutzen*" of the Nazis, constantly fluctuating (because what is useful today can be injurious tomorrow), and the eternally shifting party line of the Soviet Union which, being retroactive, almost daily makes new groups of people available for the concentration camps, are the only guaranty for the continued existence of the concentration camps, and hence for the continued total disfranchisement of man.

The next decisive step in the preparation of living corpses is the murder of the moral person in man. This is done in the main by making martyrdom, for the first time in history, impossible: "How many people here still believe that a protest has even historic importance? This skepticism is the real masterpiece of the ss. Their great accomplishment. They have corrupted all human solidarity. Here the night has fallen on the future. When no witnesses are left, there can be no testimony. To demonstrate when death can no longer be postponed is an attempt to give death a meaning, to act beyond one's own death. In order to be successful, a gesture must have social meaning. There are hundreds of thousands of us here, all living in absolute solitude. That is why we are subdued no matter what happens."

The camps and the murder of political adversaries are only part of organized oblivion that not only embraces carriers of public opinion such as the spoken and written word, but extends even to the families and friends of the victim. Grief and remembrance are forbidden. In the Soviet Union a woman will sue for divorce immediately after her husband's arrest in order to save the lives of her children; if her husband chances to come back, she will indignantly turn him out of the house. The Western world has hitherto, even in its darkest periods, granted the slain enemy the right to be remembered as a self-evident acknowledgment of the fact that we are all men (and *only* men). It is only because even Achilles set out for Hector's funeral, only because the most despotic governments honored the slain enemy, only because the Romans allowed the Christians to write their martyrologies, only because the Church kept its heretics alive in the memory of men, that all was not lost and never would be lost. The concentration camps, by making death itself anonymous (making it impossible to find out whether a prisoner is dead or alive), robbed death of its meaning as the end of a fulfilled life. In a sense they took away the individual's own death, proving that henceforth nothing belongs to him and he belongs to no one. His death merely set a deal on the fact that he had never really existed.

This attack on the moral person might still have been opposed by man's conscience which tells him that it is better to die a victim than to live as a bureaucrat of murder. Totalitarian terror achieved its most terrible triumph when it succeeded in cutting the moral person off from the individualist escape and in making the decisions of conscience absolutely questionable and equivocal. When a man is faced with the alternative of betraying and thus murdering his friends or of sending his wife and children, for whom he is in every sense responsible, to their death; when even suicide would mean the immediate murder of his own family—how is he to decide? The alternative is no longer between good and evil, but between murder and murder. Who could solve the moral dilemma of the Greek mother, who was allowed by the Nazis to choose which of her three children should be killed?

Through the creation of conditions under which conscience ceases to be adequate and to do good becomes utterly impossible, the consciously organized complicity of all men in the crimes of totalitarian regimes is extended to the victims and thus made really total. The ss implicated concentration-camp inmates—criminals, politicals, Jews—in their crimes by making them responsible for a large part of the administration, thus confronting them with the hopeless dilemma whether to send their friends to their death, or to help murder other men who happened to be strangers, and forcing them, in any event, to behave like murderers. The point is not only that hatred is diverted from those who are guilty (the *capos* were more hated than the ss), but that the distinguishing line between persecutor and persecuted, between the murderer and his victim, is constantly blurred.

Once the moral person has been killed, the one thing that still prevents men from being made into living corpses is the differentiation of the individual, his unique identity. In a sterile form such individuality can be preserved through a persistent stoicism, and it is certain that many men under totalitarian rule have taken and are each day still taking refuge in this absolute isolation of a personality without rights or conscience. There is no doubt that this part of the human person, precisely because it depends so essentially on nature and on forces that cannot be controlled by the will, is the hardest to destroy (and when destroyed is mostly easily repaired).

The methods of dealing with this uniqueness of the human person are numerous and we shall not attempt to list them. They begin with the monstrous conditions in the transports to the camps, when hundreds of human beings are packed into a cattle-car stark naked, glued to each other, and shunted back and forth over the countryside for days on end; they continue upon arrival at the camp, the well-organized shock of the first hours, the shaving of the head, the grotesque camp clothing; and they end in the utterly unimaginable tortures so gauged as not to kill the body, at any event not quickly. The aim of all these methods, in any case, is to manipulate the human body—with its infinite possibilities of suffering—in such a way as to make it destroy the human person as inexorably as do certain mental diseases of organic origin.

· · · · ·

The killing of man's individuality, of the uniqueness shaped in equal parts by nature, will, and destiny, which has become so self-evident a premise for all human relations that even identical twins inspire a certain uneasiness, creates a horror that vastly overshadows the outrage of the juridical-political person and the despair of the moral person. It is this horror that gives rise to the nihilistic generalizations which maintain plausibly enough that essentially all men alike are beasts. Actually the experience of the concentration camps does show that human beings can be transformed into specimens of the human animal, and that man's "nature" is only "human" insofar as it opens up to man the possibility of becoming something highly unnatural, that is, a man.

After murder of the moral person and annihilation of the juridical person, the destruction of individuality is almost always successful. Conceivably some laws of mass psychology may be found to explain why millions of human beings allowed themselves to be marched unresistingly into the gas chambers, although these laws would explain nothing else but the destruction of individuality. It is more significant that those individually condemned to death very seldom attempted to take one of their executioners with them, that there were scarcely any serious revolts, and that even in the moment of liberation there were very few spontaneous massacres of ss men. For to destroy individuality is to destroy spontaneity, man's power to begin something new out of his own resources, something that cannot be explained on the basis of reactions to environment and events. Nothing then remains but ghastly marionettes with human faces, which all behave like the dog in Pavlov's experiments, which all react with perfect reliability even when going to their own death, and which do nothing to react. This is the real triumph of the system: "The triumph of the ss demands that the tortured victim allow himself to be led to the noose without protesting, that he renounce and abandon himself to the point of ceasing to affirm his identity. And it is not for nothing. It is not gratuitously, out of sheer sadism, that the SS men desire his defeat. They know that the system which succeeds in destroying its victim before he mounts the scaffold . . . is incomparably the best for keeping a whole people in slavery. In submission. Nothing is more terrible than these processions of human beings going like dummies to their death. The man who sees this says to himself: 'For them to be thus reduced, what power must be concealed in the hands of the masters,' and he turns away, full of bitterness but defeated."

. . . . .

The uselessness of the camps, their cynically admitted anti-utility, is only apparent. In reality they are more essential to the preservation of the regime's power than any of its other institutions. Without concentration camps, without the undefined fear they inspire and the very well-defined training they offer in totalitarian domination, which can nowhere else be fully tested with all of its most radical possibilities, a totalitarian state can neither inspire its nuclear troops with fanaticism nor maintain a whole people in complete apathy. The dominating and the dominated would only too quickly sink back into the "old bourgeois routine"; after early "excesses," they would succumb to everyday life with its human laws; in short, they would develop in a direction which all observers counseled by common sense were so prone to predict. The tragic fallacy of all these prophecies, originating in a world that was still safe, was to suppose that there was such a thing as one human nature established for all time, to identify this human nature with history, and thus to declare that the idea of total domination was not only inhuman but also unrealistic. Meanwhile we have learned that the power of man is so great he really can be what he wishes to be. . . .

What totalitarian ideologies therefore aim at is not the transformation of the outside world or the revolutionizing transmutation of society, but the transformation of human nature itself. The concentration camps are the laboratories where changes in human nature are tested, and their shamefulness therefore is not just the business of their inmates and those who run them according to strictly "scientific" standards; it is the concern of all men. Suffering, of which there has been always too much on earth, is not the issue, nor is the number of victims. Human nature as such is at stake, and even though it seems that these experiments succeed not in changing man but only in destroying him, by creating a society in which the nihilistic banality of *homo homini lupus* is consistently realized, one should bear in mind the necessary limitations to an experiment which requires global control in order to show conclusive results.

Until now the totalitarian belief that everything is possible seems to have proved only that everything can be destroyed. Yet, in their effort to prove that everything is possible, totalitarian regimes have discovered without knowing it that there are crimes which men can neither punish nor forgive. When the impossible was made possible it became the unpunishable, unforgivable absolute evil which could no longer be understood and explained by the evil motives of self-interest, greed, covetousness, resentment, lust for power, and cowardice; and which therefore anger could not revenge, love could not endure, friendship could not forgive. Just as the victims in the death factories or the holes of oblivion are no longer "human" in the eyes of their executioners, so this newest species of criminals is beyond the pale even of solidarity in human sinfulness.

It is inherent in our entire philosophical tradition that we cannot conceive of a "radical evil," and this is true both for Christian theology, which conceded even to the Devil himself a celestial origin, as well as for Kant, the only philosopher who, in the word he coined for it, at least must have suspected the existence of this evil even though he immediately rationalized it in the concept of a "perverted ill will" that could be explained by comprehensible motives. Therefore, we actually have nothing to fall back on in order to understand a phenomenon that nevertheless confronts us with its overpowering reality and breaks down all standards we know. There is only one thing that seems to be discernible: we may say that radical evil has emerged in connection with a system in which all men have become equally superfluous. The manipulators of this system believe in their own superfluousness as much as in that of all others, and the totalitarian murderers are all the more dangerous because they do not care if they themselves are alive or dead, if they ever lived or never were born. The danger of the corpse factories and holes of oblivion is that today, with populations and homelessness everywhere on the increase, masses of people are continuously rendered superfluous if we continue to think of our world in utilitarian terms. Political, social, and economic events everywhere are in a silent conspiracy with totalitarian instruments devised for making men superfluous. The implied temptation is well understood by the totalitarian common sense of the masses, who in most countries are too desperate to retain much fear of death. The Nazis and the Bolsheviks can be sure that their factories of annihilation which demonstrate the swiftest solution to the problem of over-population, of economically superfluous and socially rootless human masses, are as much of an attraction as a warning. Totalitarian solutions may well survive the fall of totalitarian regimes in the form of strong temptations which will come up whenever it seems impossible to alleviate political, social, or economic misery in a manner worthy of man.

One of the most famous twentieth-century French philosophers and historians, Michel Foucault was educated at the École Normale Supérieure and began his career as a philosopher and psychologist, conducting research at hospitals and writing extensively on mental illnesses, the outcome of which was Madness and Civilization *(1965). He taught at several institutions internationally before being appointed professor at the prestigious Collège de France.*

Foucault's work, which ranges from critiques of psychiatric practices to structuralist challenges to epistemology—particularly about the existence and construction of human subjectivity and about academic disciplines, practices, and production of knowledge—has made it impossible to theorize anything credibly without at least acknowledging these challenges. One of the most important contributions of Foucault's work is his suggestion that historical epochs are ordered and structured by epistemes which regulate what can or cannot be articulated at that historical juncture. He demonstrates how data, facts, *and* methodologies *are themselves products, effects produced by the ways in which power organizes the world through discourse. In other words, data, facts, and claims to objectivity are invested with power relations and allegiances. They are not preexistent entities awaiting identification or discovery. Foucault undertakes this questioning via a shift of emphasis from the interiority of the subject to discourse and practices, which seek to effect a normalization or disciplining of the subject in an attempt to maintain the relationships of power, and to show how subjects constitute themselves through discourse and practices.*

Subjectivity, for Foucault, is part of a larger nexus of texts, institutions, and discursive practices. Methodologically, what this means is a shift away from the primacy of concepts which approximate reality, to archaeology and genealogy. The first refers to a method whereby the interpreter undertakes to uncover the ways in which epistemes organize a given text, be it social or literary, so that textual analysis entails teasing out the complexities within a text. The second method involves a reconstruction of the origins and evolution of discursive practices within a nexus of power relations. This archaeological-genealogical method foregrounds the necessity of reading a given text within its historical context, that is, within the networks of power that produce that text.

Among Foucault's other works are The Order of Things *(1966),* The Archaeology of Knowledge *(1969), and the three-volume* The History of Sexuality *(1976–1988).*

Discipline and Punish: The Birth of the Prison

MICHEL FOUCAULT

PART II. PUNISHMENT

Chapter 2. The Gentle Way in Punishment

The art of punishing, then, must rest on a whole technology of representation. The undertaking can succeed only if it forms part of a natural mechanics. "Like the gravitation of bodies, a secret force compels us ever towards our well-being. This impulsion is affected only by the obstacles that laws oppose it. All the diverse actions of man are the effects of this interior tendency." To find the suitable punishment for a crime is to find the disadvantage whose idea is such that it robs forever the idea of a crime of any attraction. It is an art of conflicting energies, an art of images linked by association, the forgoing of stable connections that defy time: it is a matter of establishing the representation of pairs of opposing values, of establishing quantitative differences between the opposing forces, of setting up a complex of obstacle-signs that may subject the movement of the forces to a power relation. "Let the idea of torture and execution be ever present in the heart of the weak man and dominate the feeling that drives him to crime." These obstacle-signs must constitute the new arsenal of penalties, just as the old public executions were organized around a system of retaliatory marks. But in order to function, they must obey several conditions.

1. They must be as unarbitrary as possible. It is true that it is society that defines, in terms of its own interests, what must be regarded as a crime: it is not therefore natural. But, if punishment is to present itself to the mind as soon as one thinks of committing a crime, as immediate a link as possible must be made between the two: a link of resemblance, analogy, proximity. "The penalty must be made to conform as closely as possible to the nature of the offence, so that fear of punishment diverts the mind from the road along which the prospect of an advantageous crime was leading it." The ideal punishment would be transparent to the crime that it punishes; thus, for him to contemplate, it will be infallibly the sign of the crime that it punishes; and for him who dreams of the crime, the idea of the offence will be enough to arouse the sign of the punishment. This is an advantage for the stability of the link, an advantage for the calculation of the proportions between crime and punishment and the quantitative reading of interest; it also has the advantage that, by assuming the form of a natural sequence, punishment does not appear as the arbitrary effect of a human power: "To derive the offence from the punishment is the best means of

proportioning punishment to crime. If this is the triumph of justice, it is also the triumph of Liberty, for then penalties no longer proceed from the will of the legislator, but from the nature of things; one no longer sees man committing violence on man." In analogical punishment, the power that punishes is hidden.

The reformers proposed a whole panoply of penalties that were natural by institution and which represented in their form the content of the crime. Take Vermeil, for example: those who abuse public liberty will be deprived of their own; those who abuse the benefits of law and the privileges of public office will be deprived of their civil rights; speculation and usury will be punished by fines; theft will be punished by confiscation; "vainglory" by humiliation; murder by death; fire-raising by the stake. In the case of poisoner, "the executioner will present him with a goblet the contents of which will be thrown into his face; thus he will be made to feel the horror of his crime by being offered an image of it; he will then be thrown into a cauldron of boiling water." Mere day-dreaming? Perhaps. But the principle of a symbolic communication was clearly formulated by Le Peletier, when in 1791 he presented the new criminal legislation: "Exact relations are required between the nature of the offence and the nature of the punishment"; he who has used violence in his crime must be sentenced to hard labour; he who has acted despicably will be subjected to infamy.

Despite cruelties that are strongly reminiscent of the tortures of the Ancien Régime, a quite different mechanism is at work in these analogical penalties. Horror is not opposed to horror in a joust of power; it is no longer the symmetry of vengeance, but the transparency of the sign to that which it signifies; what is required is to establish, in the theatre of punishments, a relation that is immediately intelligible to the senses and on which a simple calculation may be based: a sort of reasonable aesthetic of punishment. "It is not only in the fine arts that one must follow nature faithfully; political institutions, at least those that display wisdom and permanence, are founded on nature." The punishment must proceed from the crime; the law must appear to be a necessity of things; and power must act while concealing itself beneath the gentle force of nature.

2. This complex of signs must engage with the mechanics of forces: reduce the desire that makes the crime attractive; increase the interest that makes the penalty be feared; reverse the relation of intensities, so that the representation of the penalty and its disadvantages is more lively than that of the crime and its pleasures. There is a whole mechanics, therefore, of interest, of its movement, of the way that one represents it to oneself, and of the liveliness of this representation. "The legislator must be a skillful architect who knows how to employ all the forces that may contribute to the solidity of the building and reduce all those that might ruin it."

There are several ways of achieving this. "Go straight to the source of evil."

Smash the mainspring that animates the representation of the crime. Weaken the interest that brought it to birth. Behind the offences of the vagabond, there is laziness; that is what one must fight against. "One will not succeed by locking beggars up in filthy prisons that are more like cesspools"; they will have to be forced to work. "The best way of punishing them is to employ them." Against a bad passion, a good habit; against a force, another force, but it must be the force of sensibility and passion, not that of armed power. "Must one not deduce all penalties from this principle, which is so simple, so appropriate and already well known, namely, to choose them in that which is most subduing for the passion that led to the crime committed?"

Set the force that drove the criminal to the crime against itself. Divide interest, use it to make the penalty something to be feared. Let the punishment irritate it and stimulate it more than the crime was able to flatter it. If pride led to the committing of a crime, let it be hurt, let the punishment disgust it. Shameful punishments are effective because they are based on the vanity that was at the root of the crime. Fanatics glory both in their opinions and in the tortures that they endure for them. Let us, therefore, set against fanaticism the proud obstinacy that sustains it: "Reduce it with ridicule and shame; if one humiliates the proud vanity of fanatics before a great crowd of spectators, one may expect happy effects from this punishment." It would be quite useless, on the other hand, to impose physical pain on them.

Reanimate the useful, virtuous interest that has been so weakened by the crime. The feeling of respect for property—for wealth, but also for honour, liberty, life—this the criminal loses when he robs, calumniates, abducts, or kills. So he must be taught this feeling once again. And one will begin by teaching it to him for his own benefit; one will show him what it is to lose the freedom to dispose as one wishes of one's own wealth, honour, time, and body, so that he may respect it in others. The penalty that forms stable and easily legible signs must also recompose the economy of interests and the dynamics of passion.

3. Consequently, one must use a temporal modulation. The penalty transforms, modifies, establishes signs, arranges obstacles. What use would it be if it had to be permanent? A penalty that had no end would be contradictory: all the constraints that it imposes on the convict and of which, having become virtuous once more, he would never be able to take advantage, would be little better than torture; and the effort made to reform him would be so much trouble and expense lost by society. If incorrigibles there be, one must be determined to eliminate them. But, for all the others, punishment can function only if it comes to an end. This analysis was accepted by the Constituent Assembly: the code of 1791 lays down the death penalty for traitors and murderers; all other penalties must have an end (the maximum is twenty years).

But above all the role of duration must be integrated into the economy of the penalty. In its very violence, the public execution tended to have the following result: the more serious the crime, the shorter the punishment. Duration certainly intervened in the old system of penalties; days at the pillory, years of banishment, hours spent dying on the wheel. But it was a time of ordeal, not of concerted transformation. Duration must now facilitate the proper action of the punishment: "A prolonged succession of painful privations, sparing mankind the horror of torture, has much more effect on the guilty party than a passing moment of pain. . . . It constantly renews in the eyes of the people that witness it the memory of vengeful laws and revives in all the moments of a salutary terror." Time is the operator of punishment.

But the delicate mechanism of the passions must not be constrained in the same way or with the same insistence when they begin to improve; the punishment should diminish as it produces its effects. It may well be fixed, in the sense that it is determined for all, in the same way, by law, but its internal mechanism must be variable. In the bill put before the Constituent Assembly, Le Peletier proposed a system of diminishing penalties: a convict condemned to the most serious penalty would be subjected to the "*cachot*" (manacles on hands and feet, darkness, solitude, bread and water) only during the first stage of his imprisonment; he would be allowed to work first two then three days a week. After two thirds of his sentence had been served, he could pass to the "*géne*" (a cell with light, chains around the waist, solitary work for five hours a day, but with other prisoners on the other two days; this work would be paid and would enable him to improve his daily fare). Lastly, when he approached the end of his sentence, he could pass to the normal prison régime: "He will be allowed each day to meet other prisoners for work in common. If he prefers, he will be able to work alone. He will pay for his food from what he earns from his work."

4. For the convict, the penalty is a mechanics of signs, interests, and duration. But the guilty person is only one of the targets of punishment. For punishment is directed above all at others, at all the potentially guilty. So these obstacle-signs that are gradually engraved in the representation of the condemned man must therefore circulate rapidly and widely; they must be accepted and redistributed by all; they must shape the discourse that each individual has with others and by which crime is forbidden to all by all—the true coin that is substituted in people's minds for the false profits of crime.

For this, everyone must see punishment not only as natural, but in his own interest; everyone must be able to read in it his own advantage. There must be no more spectacular, but useless penalties. There must be no secret penalties either; but punishment must be regarded as a retribution that the guilty man makes to each of his fellow citizens, for the crime that has wronged them all—

penalties that are constantly placed before citizens' eyes, and which "bring out the public utility of common and particular *movements.*" The ideal would be for the convict to appear as a sort of rentable property: a slave at the service of all. Why would society eliminate a life and a body that it could appropriate? It would be more useful to make him "serve the state in a slavery that would be more or less extended according to the nature of his crime"; France has all too many impracticable roads that impede trade; thieves who obstruct the free circulation of goods could be put to rebuilding the highways. Far more telling than death would be "the example of a man who is ever before one's eyes, whom one has deprived of liberty and who is forced to spend the rest of his days repairing the loss that he has caused society."

In the old system, the body of the condemned man became the king's property, on which the sovereign left his mark and brought down the effects of his power. Now he will be rather the property of society, the object of a collective and useful appropriation. This explains why the reformers almost always proposed public works as one of the best possible penalties; in this, they were supported by the *Cahiers de doléances*: "Let those condemned to penalties short of death be put to the public works of the country for a time proportionate to their crimes." Public work meant two things: the collective interest in the punishment of the condemned man and the visible, verifiable character of the punishment. Thus the convict pays twice, by the labour he provides and by the signs that he produces. At the heart of society, on the public squares or highways, the convict is a focus of profit and signification. Visibly, he is serving everyone; but, at the same time, he lets slip into the minds of all the crime-punishment sign: a secondary, purely moral, but much more real utility.

5. Hence a whole learned economy of publicity. In physical torture, the example was based on terror: Physical fear, collective horror, images that must be engraved on the memories of the spectators, like the brand on the cheek or shoulder of the condemned man. The example is now based on the lesson, the discourse, the decipherable sign, the representation of public morality. It is no longer the terrifying restoration of sovereignty that will sustain the ceremony of punishment, but the reactivation of the code, the collective reinforcements of the link between the idea of crime and the idea of punishment. In the penalty, rather than seeing the presence of the sovereign, one will read the laws themselves. The laws associated a particular crime with a particular punishment. As soon as the crime is committed, the punishment will follow at once, enacting the discourse of the law and showing that the code, which links ideas, also links realities. The junction, immediate in the text, must be immediate in acts. "Consider those first movements in which the news of some horrible act spreads through out towns and country-side; the citizens are like men who see lightning

falling about them; everyone is moved by indignation and horror. . . . That is the moment to punish the crime: do not let it slip by; hasten to prove it and judge it. Set up scaffolds, stakes, drag out the guilty man to the public squares, summon the people with great cries; you will then hear them applaud the proclamation of your judgments, as the proclamation of peace and liberty; you will see them run to these terrible spectacles as to the triumph of the laws." Public punishment is the ceremony of immediate recoding.

The law is re-formed: it takes up its place on the side of the crime that violated it. The criminal, on the other hand, is detached from society; he leaves it. But not in those ambiguous festivals of the Ancien Régime in which the people inevitably took part, either in the crime or in the execution, but in a ceremony of mourning. The society that has rediscovered its laws has lost the citizen who violated them. Public punishment must manifest this double affliction: that a citizen should have been capable of ignoring the law and that one should have been obliged to separate oneself from a citizen. "Associate the scaffold with the most lugubrious and most moving ceremonies; let this terrible day be a day of mourning for the nation; let the general sorrow be painted everywhere in bold letters. . . . Let the magistrate, wearing black, funeral crépe, announce the crime and the sad necessity of a legal vengeance to the people. Let the different scenes of this tragedy strike all the senses, stir all gentle, honest affections."

· · · · ·

The duration that makes the punishment effective for the guilty is also useful for the spectators. They must be able to consult at each moment the permanent lexicon of crime and punishment. A secret punishment is a punishment half wasted. Children should be allowed to come to the places where the penalty is being carried out; there they will attend their classes in civics. And grown men will periodically relearn the laws. Let us conceive the places of punishment as a Garden of the Laws that families would visit on Sundays. "I propose that, from time to time, after preparing people's minds with a reasoned discourse on the preservation of the social order, on the utility of punishment, men as well as boys should be taken to the mines and to the work camps and contemplate the frightful fate of these outlaws. Such pilgrimages would be more useful than the pilgrimages made by the Turks in Mecca." . . . Long before he was regarded as an object of science, the criminal was imagined as a source of instruction. Once one made charitable visits to prisoners to share in their sufferings (the seventeenth century had invented or revived this practice); now it was being suggested that children should come and learn how the benefits of the law are applied to crime—a living lesson in the museum of order.

6. This will make possible in society an inversion of the traditional discourse of crime. How can one extinguish the dubious glory of the criminal? This was a matter of grave concern to the lawmakers of the eighteenth century. How can one silence the adventures of the great criminals celebrated in the almanacs, broadsheets, and popular tales? If the recording of punishments is well done, if the ceremony of mourning takes place as it should, the crime can no longer appear as anything but a misfortune and the criminal as an enemy who must be re-educated into social life. Instead of those songs of praise that turn the criminal into a hero, only those obstacle-signs that arrest the desire to commit the crime by the calculated fear of punishment will circulate in men's discourse. The positive mechanics will operate to the full in the language of every day, which will constantly reinforce it with new accounts. Discourse will become the vehicle of the law: the constant principle of universal recoding. The poets of the people will at last join those who call themselves the "missionaries of eternal reason"; they will become moralist. . . .

. . . This, then, is how one must imagine the punitive city. At the crossroads, in the gardens, at the side of roads being repaired or bridges built, in workshops open to all, in the depths of mines that may be visited, will be hundreds of tiny theatres of punishment. Each crime will have its law; each criminal his punishment. It will be a visible punishment, a punishment that tells all, that explains, justifies itself, convicts: placards, different-coloured caps bearing inscriptions, posters, symbols, texts read or printed, tirelessly repeated the code. Scenery, perspectives, optical effects, *trompe-l'oeil* sometimes magnify the scene, making it more fearful than it is, but also clearer. From where the public is sitting, it is possible to believe in the existence of certain cruelties which, in fact, do not take place. But the essential point, in all these real or magnified severities, is that they should all, according to a strict economy, teach a lesson: that each punishment should be a fable.

There is a whole new arsenal of picturesque punishments. "Avoid inflicting the same punishments," said Mably. The idea of a uniform penalty, modulated only according to the gravity of the crime is banished. To be more precise: the use of imprisonment as a general form of punishment is never presented in these projects for specific, visible, and "telling" penalties. Imprisonment is envisaged, but as one among other penalties; it is the specific punishment for certain offences, those that infringe the liberty of individuals (such as abduction) or those that result from an abuse of liberty (disorder, violence). It is also envisaged as a condition to enable certain punishments to be carried out (forced labour, for example). But it does not cover the whole field of penalty with its duration as the sole principle of variation. Or rather, the idea of penal imprisonment is explicitly criticized by many reformers. Because it is incapable of corresponding to the specificity of crimes. Because it has no effect on the public. Because it is useless, even harmful, to society: it is costly, it maintains convicts in idleness, it multiplies their vices. Because the execution of such a penalty is difficult to supervise and because there is a risk of exposing prisoners to the arbitrary will of their guards. Because the job of depriving a man of his liberty and of supervising him is an exercise of tyranny. "You are demanding that there should be monsters among you; and if these odious men existed, the legislator ought perhaps to treat them as murderers." Prison as the universal penalty is incompatible with this whole technique of penalty-effect, penalty-representation, penalty-general function, penalty-sign and discourse. It is obscurity, violence, and suspicion. "It is a place of darkness in which the citizen's eye cannot count the victims, in which consequently their number is lost as an example . . . whereas, if without multiplying crimes, one could multiply the example of punishment, one would succeed at last in rendering them less necessary; indeed, the obscurity of the prison becomes a subject of defiance for the citizens; they easily suppose that great injustices are committed. . . . There is certainly something wrong when the law, which is made for the good of the multitude, instead of arousing its gratitude, continually arouses its discontent."

The idea that imprisonment might as it does today cover the whole middle ground of punishment, between death and light penalties, was one that the reformers could not arrive at immediately.

· · · · ·

[For the reformers the central question was:] where exactly did the penalty apply its pressure, gain control of the individual? Representations: the representations of his interests, the representations of his advantages and disadvantages, pleasure and displeasure; and, if the punishment happens to seize the body, to apply techniques to it that are little short of torture, it is because it is—for the condemned man and for the spectators—an object of representation. But what instrument did not act on the representations? Other representations, or rather couplings of ideas (crime-punishment, the imagined advantage of crime-disadvantage perceived in the punishments); these pairings could function only in the element of publicity: punitive scenes that established them or reinforced them in the eyes of all, a discourse that circulated, brought back into currency at each moment the complex of signs. The role of the criminal in punishment was to reintroduce, in the face of crime and the criminal code, the real presence of the signified—that is to say, of the penalty which, according to the terms of the code, must be infallibly associated with the offence. By producing this signified abundantly and visibly, and therefore reactivating the signifying system of the code, the idea of crime functioning as a sign of punishment, it is with this coin that the offender pays his debt to society. Individual correction must, therefore, assure the process of redefining the individual as subject of law, through the reinforcement of the systems of signs and representations that they circulate.

The apparatus of corrective penalty acts in a quite different way. The point of application of the penalty is not the representation, but the body, time, everyday gestures and activities; the soul, too, but in so far as it is the seat of habits. The body and the soul, as principles of behaviour, form the element that is now proposed for punitive intervention. Rather than on an art of representations, this punitive intervention must rest on a studied manipulation of the individual: "I have no more doubt of every crime having its cure in moral and physical influence . . . ," so, in order to decide on punishments, one "will require some knowledge of the principles of sensation, and of the sympathies which occur in the nervous system." As for the instruments used, these are no longer complexes of representation, reinforced and circulated, but forms of coercion, schemata of constraint, applied and repeated. Exercises, not signs: time-tables, compulsory movements, regular activities, solitary meditation, work in common, silence, application, respect, good habits. And ultimately, what one is trying to restore in his technique of correction is not so much the juridical subject, who is caught up in the fundamental interests of the social pact, but the obedient subject, the individual subjected to habits, rules, orders, an authority that is exercised continually around him and upon him, and which he must allow to function automatically in him. There are two quite distinct ways, therefore, of reacting to the offence: one may restore the juridical subject of the social pact, or shape an obedient subject, according to the general and detailed form of some power.

All this would no doubt amount to little more than a speculative difference— for in each case it is a question of forming obedient individuals—if the penalty of "coercion" did not bring with it certain crucial consequences. The training of behaviour by a full time-table, the acquisition of habits, the constraints of the body imply a very special relation between the individual who is punished and the individual who punishes him. It is a relation that not only renders the dimension of the spectacle useless: it excludes it. The agent of punishment must exercise a total power, which no third party can disturb; the individual to be corrected must be entirely enveloped in the power that is being exercised over him. Secrecy is imperative, and so too is autonomy, at least in relation to this technique of punishment: it must have its own functioning, its own rules, its own techniques, its own knowledge; it must fix its own norms, decide its own results. There is a discontinuity, or in any case a specificity, in relation to the legal power that declares guilt and fixes the general limits of punishment. These two consequences—secrecy and autonomy in the exercise of the power to punish—are unacceptable for a theory and a policy of penalty that has two aims in view: to get all citizens to participate in the punishment of the social enemy and to render the exercise of the power to punish entirely adequate and transparent to the laws that publicly define it. Secret punishments and punishments not specified in the legal code, a power to punish exercised in the shadows according to criteria and with instruments that elude control—this was enough to compromise the whole strategy of the reform. After the sentence, a power was constituted that was reminiscent of the power exercised in the old system. The power that applied the penalties now threatened to be as arbitrary, as despotic, as the power that once decided them.

In short, the divergence is the following: punitive city or coercive institution? On the one hand, a functioning of penal power, distributed throughout the social space; present everywhere as scene, spectacle, sign, discourse; legible like an open book; operating by a permanent recodification of the mind of the mind of the citizens; eliminating crime by those obstacles placed before the idea of crime; acting invisibly and uselessly on the "soft fibres of the brain," as Servan put it. A power to punish that ran the whole length of the social network would act at each of its points, and in the end would no longer be perceived as a power of certain individuals over others, but as an immediate reaction of all in relation to the individual. On the other hand, a compact functioning of the power to punish: a meticulous assumption of responsibility for the body and the time of the convict, a regulation of his movements and behaviour by a system of authority and knowledge; a concerted orthopaedy applied to convicts in order to reclaim them individually; an autonomous administration of this power that is isolated both from the social body and from the judicial power in the strict sense. The emergence of the prison marks the institutionalization of the power to punish, or, to be more precise: will the power to punish (with the strategic aim adopted in the late eighteenth century, the reduction of popular illegality) be better served by concealing itself beneath a general social function, in the "punitive city," or by investing itself in a coercive institution, in the enclosed space of the "reformatory"?

In any case, it can be said that, in the late eighteenth century, one is confronted by three ways of organizing the power to punish. The first is the one that was still functioning and which was based on the old monarchical law. The other two both refer to a preventive, utilitarian, corrective conception of a right to punish that belongs to society as a whole; but they are very different from one another at the level of the mechanisms they envisage. Broadly speaking, one might say that, in monarchical law, punishment is a ceremonial of sovereignty; it uses the ritual marks of the vengeance that it applies to the body of the condemned man; and it deploys before the eyes of the spectators an effect of terror as intense as it is discontinuous, irregular, and always above its own laws, the physical presence of the sovereign and of his power. The reforming jurists, on the other hand, saw punishment as a procedure for requalifying individuals as subjects, as juridical subjects; it uses not marks, but signs, coded sets of representations, which would be given the most rapid circulation and the most general acceptance possible by citizens witnessing the scene of punishment. Lastly, in the project for a prison institution that was then developing, punishment was seen as a technique for the coercion of individuals; it operated methods of training the body—not signs—by the traces it leaves, in the form of habits, in behaviour; and it presupposed the setting up of a specific power for the administration of the penalty. We have, then, the sovereign and his force, the social body and the administrative apparatus; mark, sign, trace; ceremony, representation, exercise; the vanquished enemy, the juridical subject in the process of requalification, the individual subjected to immediate coercion; the tortured body, the soul with its manipulated representations, the body subjected to training. We have here the three series of elements that characterize the three mechanisms that face one another in the second half of the eighteenth century. They cannot be reduced to theories of law (though they overlap with such theories), nor can they be identified with apparatuses or institutions (though they are based on them), nor can they be derived from moral choices (though they find their justification in morality). They are modalities according to which the power to punish is exercised: three technologies of power.

The problem, then, is the following: how is it that, in the end, it was the third that was adopted? How did the coercive, corporal, solitary, secret model of the power to punish replace the representative, scenic, signifying, public, collective model? Why did the physical exercise of punishment (which is not torture) replace, with the prison that is its institutional support, the social play of the signs of punishment and the prolix festival that circulated them?

PART III. DISCIPLINE

Chapter 3. Panopticism

Bentham's *Panopticon* is the architectural figure of . . . [disciplinary exclusion, confinement. and surveillance.] We know the principle on which it was based: at the periphery, an annular building; at the centre, a tower; this tower is pierced with wide windows that open onto the inner side of the ring; the peripheric building is divided into cells, each of which extends the whole width of the building; they have two windows, one on the inside, corresponding to the windows of the tower; the other, on the outside, allows the light to cross the cell from one end to the other. All that is needed, then, is to place a supervisor in a central tower and to shut up in each cell a madman, a patient, a condemned man, a worker, or a schoolboy. By the effect of backlighting, one can observe from the tower, standing out precisely against the light, the small captive shadows in the cells of the periphery. They are like so many cages, so many small theatres, in which each actor is alone, perfectly individualized and constantly visible. The panoptic mechanism arranges spatial unities that make it possible to see constantly and to recognize immediately. In short, it reverses the principle of the dungeon; or rather of its three functions—to enclose, to deprive of light, and to hide—it preserves only the first and eliminates the other two. Full lighting and the eye of the supervisor capture better than darkness, which ultimately protected. Visibility is a trip.

To begin with, this made it possible—as a negative effect—to avoid those compact, swarming, howling masses that were to be found in places of confinement, those painted by Goya or described by Howard. Each individual, in his place, is securely confined to a cell from which he is seen from the front by the supervisor; but the side walls prevent him from coming into contact with his companions. He is seen, but he does not see; he is the object of information, never a subject in communication. The arrangement of his room, opposite the central tower, imposes on him an axial visibility; but the divisions of the ring, those separated cells, imply a lateral invisibility. And this invisibility is a guarantee of order. If the inmates are convicts, there is no danger of a plot, an attempt at collective escape, the planning of new crimes for the future, bad reciprocal influences; if they are patients, there is no danger of contagion; if they are madmen, there is no risk of their committing violence upon one another; if they are schoolchildren, there is no copying, no noise, no chatter, no waste of time; if they are workers, there are no disorders, no theft, no coalitions, none of those distractions that slow down the rate of work, make it less perfect, or cause accidents. The crowd, a compact mass, a locus of multiple exchanges, individualities merging together, a collective effect, is abolished and replaced by a collection of separated individualities. From the point of view of the guardian, it is replaced by a multiplicity that can be numbered and supervised; from the point of view of the inmates, by a sequestered and observed solitude.

Hence the major effect of the Panopticon: to induce in the inmate a state of conscious and permanent visibility that assures the automatic functioning of power. So to arrange things that the surveillance is permanent in its effects, even if it is discontinuous in its action; that the perfection of power should tend to render its actual exercise unnecessary; that this architectural apparatus should be a machine for creating and sustaining a power relation independent of the person who exercises it; in short, that the inmates should be caught up in a power situation of which they are themselves the bearers. To achieve this, it is at once too much and too little that the prisoner should be constantly observed by an inspector: too little for what matters is that he knows himself to be observed; too much, because he has no need in fact of being so. In view of this, Bentham laid down the principle that power should be visible and unverifiable. Visible: the inmate will constantly have before his eyes the tall outline of the central tower from which he is spied upon. Unverifiable: the inmate must never know whether he is being observed at any one moment; but he must be sure that he may also be so. In order to make the presence or absence of the inspector unverifiable, so that the prisoners, in their cells, cannot even see a shadow, Bentham envisioned not only Venetian blinds on the windows of the central observation hall, but, on the inside, partitions that intersected at the hall at right angles and, in order to pass from one quarter to another, not doors but zig-zag openings; for the slightest noise, a gleam of light, a brightness in a half-opened door would betray the presence of the guardian. The Panopticon is a machine for dissociating the see/being seen dyad: in the peripheric ring, one is totally seen, without ever being seeing; in the central tower, one sees everything without ever being seen.

It is an important mechanism, for it automatizes and disindividualizes power. Power has its principle not so much in a person as in a certain concerted distribution of bodies, surfaces, lights, gazes; in an arrangement whose internal mechanisms produce the relation in which individuals are caught up. The ceremonies, the rituals, the marks by which a sovereign's surplus power was manifested are useless. There is a machinery that assures dissymmetry, disequilibrium, difference. Consequently, it does not matter who exercises power. Any individual, taken almost at random, can operate the machine: in the absence of the director, his family, his friends, his visitors, even his servants. Similarly, it does not matter what motive animates him: the curiosity of the indiscreet, the malice of a child, the thirst for knowledge of a philosopher who wishes to visit this museum of human nature, or the perversity of those who take pleasure in spying and punishing. The more numerous those anonymous and temporary observers are, the greater the risk for the inmate of being surprised and the greater his anxious awareness of being observed. The Panopticon is a marvellous machine which, whatever use one may wish to put it to, produces homogeneous effects of power.

A real subjection is born mechanically from a fictitious relation. So it is not necessary to use force to constrain the convict to good behaviour, the madman to calm, the worker to work, the schoolboy to application, the patient to the observation of the regulations. Bentham was surprised that panoptic institutions could be so light: there were no more bars, no more chains, no more heavy locks; all that was needed was that the separations should be clear and the openings well arranged. The heaviness of the old "houses of security," with their fortress-like architecture, could be replaced by the simple, economic geometry of a "house of certainty." The efficiency of power, its constraining force have, in a sense, passed over to the other side—to the side of its surface of application. He who is subjected to a field of visibility, and who knows it, assumes responsibility for the constraints of power; he makes them play spontaneously upon himself; he inscribes in himself the power relation in which he simultaneously plays both roles; he becomes the principle of his own subjection. By this very fact, the external power may throw off its physical weight; it tends to the non-corporal; and, the more it approaches this limit, the more constant, profound, and permanent are its effects: it is a perpetual victory that avoids any physical confrontation and which is always decided in advance.

Bentham does not say whether he was inspired, in his project, by La Vaux's menagerie at Versailles: the first menagerie in which the different elements are not, as they traditionally were, distributed in a park. At the centre was an octagonal pavilion which, on the first floor, consisted of only a single room, the king's *salon*; on every side large windows looked out onto seven cages (the eighth side was reserved for the entrance), containing different species of animals. By Bentham's time, this menagerie had disappeared. But one finds in the programme of the Panopticon a similar concern with individualizing observations with characterization and classification, with the analytical arrangement of space. The Panopticon is a royal menagerie; the animal is replaced by man, individual distribution by specific grouping, and the king by the machinery of a furtive power. With this exception, the Panopticon also does the work of a naturalist. It makes it possible to draw up differences: among patients, to observe the symptoms of each individual, without the proximity of beds, the circulation of miasmas, the effects of contagion confusing the clinical tables; among school-children, it makes it possible to observe performances (without there being any imitation or copying), to map aptitudes, to assess characters, to draw up rigorous classifications, and, in relation to normal development, to distinguish "laziness and stubbornness" from "incurable imbecility"; among workers, it makes it possible to note the aptitudes of each worker, compare the time he takes to perform a task, and if they are paid by the day, to calculate their wages.

So much for the question of observation. But the Panopticon was also a laboratory; it could be used as a machine to carry out experiments, to alter behaviour, to train or correct individuals. To experiment with medicines and monitor their effects. To try out different punishments on prisoners, according to their crimes and character, and to seek the most effective ones. To teach different techniques simultaneously to the workers, to decide which is the best.

To try out pedagogical experiments.... [T]he Panopticon functions as a kind of laboratory of power. Thanks to its mechanisms of observation, it gains in efficiency and in the ability to penetrate into men's behaviour; knowledge follows the advances of power, discovering new objects of knowledge over all the surfaces on which power is exercised....

It is polyvalent in its applications; it serves to reform prisoners, but also to treat patients, to instruct schoolchildren, to confine the insane, to supervise workers, to put beggars and idlers to work. It is a type of location of bodies in space, of distribution of individuals in relation to one another, of hierarchical organization, of disposition of centers and channels of power, of definition of the instruments and modes of intervention of power, which can be implemented in hospitals, workshops, schools, prisons. Whenever one is dealing with a multiplicity of individuals on whom a task or a particular form of behavior must be imposed, the panoptic schema may be used. It is—necessary modifications apart—applicable "to all establishments whatsoever, in which, within a space not too large to be covered or commanded by buildings, a number of persons are meant to be kept under inspection" (although Bentham takes the penitentiary house as his prime example, it is because it has many different functions to fulfill—safe custody, confinement, solitude, forced labour, and instruction).

In each of its applications, it makes it possible to perfect the exercise of power. It does this in several ways: because it can reduce the number of those who exercise it, while increasing the number of those on whom it is exercised. Because it is possible to intervene at any moment and because the constant pressure acts even before offences, mistakes, or crimes have been committed. Because, in these conditions, its strength is that it never intervenes, it is exercised spontaneously and without noise, it constitutes a mechanism whose effects follow from one another. Because, without any physical instrument other than architecture and geometry, it acts directly on individuals; it gives "power of mind over mind." The panoptic schema makes any apparatus of power more intense: it assures its economy (in material, in personnel, in time); it assures its efficacy by its preventative character, its continuous functioning, and its automatic mechanisms. It is a way of obtaining from power "in hitherto unexampled quantity," "a great and new instrument of government . . . ; its great excellence consists in the great strength it is capable of giving to *any* institution it may be thought proper to apply it to." . . .

Furthermore, the arrangement of this machine is such that its enclosed nature does not preclude a permanent presence from the outside: we have seen that anyone can come and exercise in the central tower the functions of surveillance, and that, this being the case, he can gain a clear idea of the way in which the surveillance is practiced. In fact, any panoptic institution, even if it is as vigorously closed as a penitentiary, may without difficulty be subjected to such irregular and constant inspections: and not only by the appointed inspectors, but also by the public; any member of society will have the right to come and see with his own eyes how the schools, hospitals, factories, prisons function. There is no risk, therefore, that the increase of power created by the panoptic machine may degenerate into tyranny; the disciplinary mechanism will be democratically controlled, since it will be constantly accessible "to the great tribunal committee of the world." This Panopticon, subtly arranged so that an observer may observe, at a glance, so many different individuals, also enables everyone to come and observe any of the observers. The seeing machine was once a sort of dark room into which individuals spied; it has become a transparent building in which the exercise of power may be supervised by society as a whole.

The panoptic schema, without disappearing as such or losing any of its properties, was destined to spread throughout the social body; its vocation was to become a generalized function. The plague-stricken town provided an exceptional disciplinary model: perfect, but absolutely violent; to the disease that brought death, power opposed its perpetual threat of death; life inside it was reduced to its simplest expression; it was, against the power of death, the meticulous exercise of the right of the sword. The Panopticon, on the other hand, has a role of amplification; although it arranges power, although it is intended to make it more economic and more effective, it does so not for power itself, nor for the immediate salvation of a threatened society: its aim is to strengthen the social forces—to increase production, to develop the economy, spread education, raise the level of public morality; to increase and multiply.

How is power to be strengthened in such a way that, far from impeding progress, far from weighing upon it with its rules and regulations, it actually facilitates such progress? What intensificator of power will be able at the same time to be a multiplicator of production? How will power, by increasing its forces, be able to increase those of society instead of confiscating them or impeding them? The Panopticon's solution to this problem is that the productive increase of power can be assured only if, on the one hand, it can be exercised continuously in the very foundations of society, in the subtlest possible way, and if, on the other hand, it functions outside these sudden, violent, discontinuous forms that are bound up with the exercise of sovereignty. The body of the king, with its strange material and physical presence, with the force that he himself deploys or transmits to some few others, is at the opposite extreme of this new physics of power represented by panopticism; the domain of panopticism is, on the contrary, the whole lower region, that region of irregular bodies, with their details, their multiple movements, their heterogeneous forces, their spatial relations; what are required are mechanisms that analyse distributions, gaps, series, combinations, and which use instruments that render visible, record, differentiate, and compare: a physics of a rational and multiple power, which has its maximum intensity not in the person of the king, but in the bodies that can be individualized by these relations. At the theoretical level, Bentham defines another way of analysing the social body and the power relations that traverse it; in terms of practice, he defines a procedure of subordination of bodies and forces that must increase the utility of power while practising the economy of the prince. Panopticism is the general principle of a new "political anatomy" whose object and end are not the relations of sovereignty but the relations of discipline.

The celebrated, transparent, circular cage, with its high tower, powerful and knowing, may have been for Bentham a project of a perfect disciplinary institution; but he also set out to show how one may "unlock" the disciplines and get them to function in a diffused, multiple, polyvalent way throughout the whole social body. These disciplines, which the classical age had elaborated in specific, relatively enclosed places—barracks, schools, workshops—and whose total implementation had been imagined only at the limited and temporary scale of a plague-stricken town, Bentham dreamt of transforming into a network of mechanisms that would be everywhere and always alert, running through society without interruption in space or in time. The panoptic arrangement provides the formula for this generalization. It programmes, at the level of an elementary and easily transferable mechanism, the basic functioning of a society penetrated through and through with disciplinary mechanisms.

There are two images, then, of discipline. At one extreme, the discipline-blockage, the enclosed institution, established on the edges of society, turned inwards towards negative functions: arresting evil, breaking communications, suspending time. At the other extreme, with panopticism, is the discipline-mechanism: a functional mechanism that must improve the exercise of power by making it lighter, more rapid, more effective, a design of subtle coercion for a society to come. The movement from one project to the other, from a schema of exceptional discipline to one of a generalized surveillance, rests on a historical transformation: the gradual extension of the mechanisms of discipline throughout the seventeenth and eighteenth centuries, their spread throughout the whole social body, the formation of what might be called in general, the disciplinary society. . . .

But this extension of the disciplinary institutions was no doubt only the most visible aspect of various, more profound processes.

1. *The functional inversion of the disciplines.* At first, they were expected to neutralize dangers, to fix useless or disturbed populations, to avoid the inconveniences of over-large assemblies; now they were being asked to play a positive

role, for they were becoming able to do so, to increase the possible utility of individuals. Military discipline is no longer a mere means of preventing looting, desertion or failure to obey orders among the troops; it has become a basic technique to enable the army to exist, not as an assembled crowd, but as a unity that derives from this very unity an increase in its forces; discipline increases the skill of each individual, co-ordinates these skills, accelerates movements, increases fire power, broadens the fronts of attack without reducing their vigour, increases the capacity for resistance, etc. The discipline of the work-shop, while remaining a way of enforcing respect for the regulations and authorities, of preventing thefts or losses, tends to increase aptitudes, speeds, output, and therefore profits; it still exerts a moral influence over behaviour, but more and more it treats actions in terms of their results, introduces bodies into a machinery, forces into an economy. When, in the seventeenth century, the provincial schools or the Christian elementary schools were founded, the justifications given for them were above all negative: those poor who were unable to bring up their children left them "in ignorance of their obligations: given the difficulties they have in earning a living, and themselves having been badly brought up, they are unable to communicate a sound upbringing that they themselves never had"; this involves three major inconveniences: ignorance of God, idleness (with its consequence drunkenness, impurity, larceny, brigandage), and the formation of those gangs of baggers, always ready to stir up public disorder and "virtually to exhaust the funds of the Hôtel-Dieu." Now, at the beginning of the Revolution, the end laid down for primary education was to be, among other things, to "fortify," to "develop the body," to prepare the child "for a future in some mechanical work," to give him "an observant eye, a sure hand, and prompt habits." The disciplines function increasingly as techniques for making useful individuals. Hence their emergence from a marginal position on the confines of society, and detachment from the forms of exclusion or expiration, confinement or retreat. Hence the slow loosening of their kinship with religious regularities and enclosures. Hence also their rooting in the most important, most central, and most productive sectors of society. They become attached to some of the great essential functions: factory productions, the transmission of knowledge, the diffusion of aptitudes and skills, the war-machine. Hence, too, the double tendency one sees developing throughout the eighteenth century to increase the number of disciplinary institutions and to discipline the existing apparatuses.

2. *The swarming of disciplinary mechanisms.* While, on the one hand, the disciplinary establishments increase, their mechanisms have a certain tendency to become "de-institutionalized," to emerge from the closed fortresses in which they once functioned, and to circulate in a "free" state; the massive, compact

disciplines are broken down into flexible methods of control, which may be transferred and adapted. Sometimes the closed apparatuses add to their internal and specific function a role of external surveillance, developing around themselves a whole margin of lateral controls. Thus, the Christian School must not simply train docile children; it must also make it possible to supervise the parents, to gain information as to their way of life, their resources, their piety, their morals. The school tends to constitute minute social observatories that penetrate even to the adults and exercise regular supervision over them: the bad behaviour of the child, or his absence, is a legitimate pretext, according to Demia, for one to go and question the neighbours, especially if there is any reason to believe that the family will not tell the truth; one can then go and question the parents themselves to find out whether they know their catechism and the prayers, whether they are determined to root out the vices of their children, how many beds there are in the house, and what the sleeping arrangements are; the visit may end with the giving of alms, the present of a religious picture, or the provision of additional beds. Similarly, the hospital is increasingly conceived of as a base for the medical observation of the population outside; after the burning down of the Hôtel-Dieu in 1772, there were several demands that the large buildings, so heavy and so disordered, should be replaced by a series of smaller hospitals; their function would be to take in the sick of the quarter, but also to gather information, to be alert to any endemic or epidemic phenomena, to open dispensaries, to give advice to the inhabitants, and to keep the authorities informed of the sanitary state of the region.

One also sees the spread of disciplinary procedures, not in the form of enclosed institutions, but as centres of observation disseminated throughout society. Religious groups and charity organizations had long played their role of "disciplining" the population. For the Counter-Reformation to the philanthropy of the July monarchy, initiatives of this type continued to increase; their aims were religious (conversion and moralization), economic (aid and encouragement to work), or political (the struggle against discontent or agitation). . . . .

3. *The state-control of the mechanisms of discipline.* In England, it was private religious groups that carried out, for a long time, the functions of social discipline in France, although a part of this role remained in the hands of parish guilds or charity associations, another—and no doubt the most important part —was very soon taken over by the police apparatus. . . .

But, although the police as an institution were certainly organized in the form of state apparatus, and although this was certainly linked directly to the centre of political sovereignty, the type of power that exercises, the mechanisms it operates, and the elements to which it applies them are specific. It is an apparatus that must be coextensive with the entire social body and not only by the extreme limits that it embraces, but by the minuteness of the details it is concerned with . . . : the infinitely small [elements] of political power.

And in order to be exercised, this power had to be given the instrument of permanent, exhaustive, omnipresent surveillance, capable of making all visible, as long as it could itself remain invisible. It had to be like a faceless gaze that transformed the whole social body into the field of perception: thousands of eyes posted everywhere, mobile attentions ever on the alert, a long, hierarchized network. . . . And this unceasing observation had to be accumulated in a series of reports and registers; throughout the eighteenth century, an immense police text increasingly covered society by means of a complex documentary organization. And, unlike the methods of judicial or administrative writing, what was registered in this way were forms of behaviour, attitudes, possibilities, suspicions—a permanent account of individuals' behaviour. . . .

The organization of the police apparatus in the eighteenth century sanctioned a generalization of the disciplines that became co-extensive with the state itself. Although it was linked in the most explicit way with everything in the royal power that exceeded the exercise of regular justice, it is understandable why the police offered such slight resistance to the rearrangement of the judicial power; and why it has not ceased to impose its prerogatives upon it, with ever-increasing weight, right up to the present day; this is no doubt because it is the secular arm of the judiciary; but it is also because, to a far greater degree than the judicial institution, it is identified by reason of its extent and mechanisms, with a society of the disciplinary type. Yet it would be wrong to believe that the disciplinary functions were confiscated and absorbed once and for all by a state apparatus.

"Discipline" may be identified neither with an institution nor with an apparatus; it is a type of power, a modality for its exercise, comprising a whole set of instruments, techniques, procedures, levels of application, targets; it is a "physics" or an "anatomy" of power, a technology. And it may be taken over either by "specialized" institutions (the penitentiaries or "houses of correction" of the nineteenth century), or by institutions that use it as an essential instrument for a particular end (schools, hospitals), or by pre-existing authorities that find in it a means of reinforcing or reorganizing their internal mechanisms of power (one day we should show how intra-familial relations, essentially in the parents-children cell, have become "disciplined," absorbing since the classical age external schemata, first educational and military, then medical, psychiatric, psychological, which have made the family the privileged locus of emergence for the disciplinary question of the normal and the abnormal), or by apparatuses that have made discipline their principle of internal functioning (the disciplinarization of the administrative apparatus from the Napoleonic period), or finally by state apparatuses whose major, if not exclusive, function is to assure that discipline reigns over society as a whole (the police).

On the whole, therefore, one can speak of the formation of a disciplinary society in this movement that stretches from the enclosed disciplines, a sort of social "quarantine," to an indefinitely generalizable mechanism of "panopticism." Not because the disciplinary modality of power has replaced all the others; but because it has infiltrated the others, sometimes undermining them, but serving as an intermediary between them, linking them together, extending them, and above all making it possible to bring the effects of power to the most minute and distant elements. It assures an infinitesimal distribution of power relations. . . .

The formation of the disciplinary society is connected with a number of broad historical processes—economic, juridico-political, and, lastly, scientific—of which it forms part.

1. Generally speaking, it might be said that the disciplines are techniques for assuring the ordering of human multiplicities. It is true that there is nothing exceptional or even characteristic in this: every system of power is presented with the same problem. But the peculiarity of the disciplines is that they try to define in relation to the multiplicities a tactics of power that fulfills three criteria: firstly, to obtain the exercise of power at the lowest possible cost (economically, by the low expenditure it involves; politically, by its discretion, its low exteriorization, its relative invisibility, the little resistance it arouses); secondly, to bring the effects of this social power to their maximum intensity and to extend them as far as possible, without either failure or interval; thirdly, to link this "economic" growth of power with the output of the apparatuses (educational, military, industrial, or medical) within which it is exercised; in short, to increase both the docility and the utility of all the elements of the system. This triple objective of the disciplines corresponds to the well-known historical conjuncture. One aspect of this conjuncture was the large demographic thrust of the eighteenth century; an increase in the floating population (one of the primary objects of discipline is to fix; it is an anti-nomadic technique); a change of quantitative scale in the groups to be supervised or manipulated (from the beginning of the seventeenth century to the eve of the French Revolution, the school population had been increasing rapidly, as had no doubt the hospital population; by the end of the eighteenth century, the peace-time army exceeded 200,000 men). The other aspect of the conjuncture was the growth in the apparatus of production, which was becoming more and more extended and complex; it was also becoming more costly and its profitability had to be increased. The development of the disciplinary methods corresponded to these

two processes, or rather, no doubt, to the new need to adjust their correlation. Neither the residual forms of feudal power nor the structures of the administrative monarchy, nor the local mechanism of supervision, nor the unstable, tangled mass they all formed together could carry out this role: they were hindered from doing so by the irregular and inadequate extension of their network, by their often conflicting functioning, but above all by the "costly" nature of the power that was exercised in them. It was costly in several senses: because directly it cost a great deal to the Treasury; because the system of corrupt offices and farmed-out taxes weighed indirectly, but very heavily, on the population; because the resistance it encountered forced it into a cycle of perpetual reinforcement; because it proceeded essentially by levying (levying on money or products by royal, seigniorial, ecclesiastical taxation; levying on men or time by *corvées* of press-ganging, by locking up or banishing vagabonds). The development of the disciplines marks the appearance of elementary techniques belonging to a quite different economy: mechanisms of power which, instead of proceeding by deduction, are integrated into the productive efficiency of the apparatuses from within, into the growth of this efficiency, and into the use of what it produces. For the old principle of "levying-violence," which governed the economy of power, the disciplines substitute the principle of "mildness-production-profit." These are the techniques that make it possible to adjust the multiplicity of men and the multiplication of the apparatuses of production (and this means not only "production" in the strict sense, but also the production of knowledge and skills in the school, the production of health in the hospitals, the production of destructive force in the army).

In this task of adjustment, discipline had to solve a number of problems for which the old economy of power was not sufficiently equipped. It could not reduce the inefficiency of mass phenomena: reduce what, in a multiplicity, makes it less manageable than a unity; reduce what is opposed to the use of each of its elements and of their sum; reduce everything that may counter the advantages of number. That is why discipline fixes; it arrests or regulates movement; it clears up confusion; it dissipates compact groupings of individuals wandering about the country in unpredictable ways; it establishes calculated distributions. It must also master all the forces that are formed from the very constitution of an organized multiplicity; it must neutralize the effects of counter-power that spring from them and which form a resistance to the power that wishes to dominate it: agitations, revolts, spontaneous organizations, coalitions—anything that may establish horizontal conjunctions. Hence the fact that the disciplines use procedures of partitioning and verticality, that they introduce, between the different elements at the same level, as solid separations as possible, that they define compact hierarchical networks, in short, that they oppose to the intrinsic, adverse force of multiplicity the technique of the continuous, individualizing pyramid. They must also increase the particular utility of each element of the multiplicity, but by means that are the most rapid and the least costly, that is to say, by using the multiplicity itself as an instrument of this growth. Hence, in order to extract from bodies the maximum time and force, the use of those overall methods known as time-tables, collective training, exercises, total and detailed surveillance. Furthermore, the disciplines must increase the effect of utility proper to the multiplicities, so that each is made more useful than the simple sum of its elements: it is in order to increase the utilization effects of the multiple that the disciplines define tactics of distribution, reciprocal adjustment of bodies, gestures and rhythms, differentiation of capacities, reciprocal co-ordination in relation to apparatuses or tasks. Lastly, the disciplines have to bring into play the power relations, not above but inside the very texture of the multiplicity, as discreetly as possible, as well articulated on the other functions of these multiplicities and also in the least expensive way possible: to this correspond anonymous instruments of power, coextensive with the multiplicity that they regiment, such as hierarchical surveillance, continuous registration, perpetual assessment, and classification. In short, to substitute for a power that is manifested through the brilliance of those who exercise it, a power that insidiously objectifies those on whom it is applied; to form a body of knowledge about these individuals, rather than to deploy the ostentatious signs of sovereignty. In a word, the disciplines are the ensemble of minute technical inventions that make it possible to increase the useful size of multiplicities by decreasing the inconveniences of the power which, in order to make them useful, must control them. A multiplicity, whether in a workshop or a nation, an army or a school, reaches the threshold of a discipline when a relation of the one to the other becomes favourable.

If the economic take-off of the West began with the techniques that made possible the accumulation of capital, it might perhaps be said that the methods of administering the accumulation of men made possible a political take-off in relation to the traditional, ritual, costly, violent forms of power, which soon fell into disuse and were superseded by a subtle, calculated technology of subjection. In fact, the two processes—the accumulation of men and the accumulation of capital—cannot be separated; it would not have been possible to solve the problem of the accumulation of men without the growth of an apparatus of production capable of both sustaining them and using them; conversely, the techniques that made the cumulative multiplicity of men useful accelerated the accumulation of capital. At a less general level, the technological mutations of the apparatus of production, the division of labour and the elaboration of the disciplinary techniques sustained an ensemble of very close relations. Each makes the other possible and necessary; each provides a model for the other. The disciplinary pyramid constituted the small cell of power within which the separation, coordination and supervision of tasks was imposed and made efficient; and analytical partitioning of time, gestures, and bodily forces constituted an operational schema that could easily be transferred from the groups to be subjected to the mechanisms of production; the massive projection of military methods onto industrial organization was an example of this modelling of the division of labour following the model laid down by the schemata of power. But, on the other hand, the technical analysis of the process of production, its "mechanical" breaking-down, were projected onto the labour force whose task it was to implement it: the constitution of those disciplinary machines in which the individual forces that they bring together are composed into a whole and therefore increased is the effect of this projection. Let us say that discipline is the unitary technique by which the body is reduced as a "political" force at the least cost and maximized as a useful force. The growth of a capitalist economy gave rise to the specific modality of disciplinary power, whose general formulas, techniques of submitting forces and bodies, in short, "political anatomy," could be operated in the most diverse political régimes, apparatuses, or institutions.

2. The panoptic modality of power—at the elementary, technical, merely physical level at which it is situated—is not under the immediate dependence or a direct extension of the great juridico-political structures of a society; it is nonetheless not absolutely independent. Historically, the process by which the bourgeoisie became in the course of the eighteenth century the politically dominant class was masked by the establishment of an explicit, coded, and formally egalitarian juridical framework, made possible by the organization of a parliamentary, representative régime. But the development and generalization of disciplinary mechanisms constituted the other, dark side of these processes. The general juridical form that guaranteed a system of rights that were egalitarian in principle was supported by these tiny, everyday, physical mechanisms, by all those systems of micro-power that are essentially non-egalitarian and asymmetrical that we call the disciplines. And although, in a formal way, the representative régime makes it possible, directly or indirectly, with or without relays, for the will of all to form the fundamental authority of sovereignty, the disciplines provide, at the base, a guarantee of the submission of forces and bodies. The real, corporal disciplines constituted the foundation of the formal, juridical liberties. The contract may have been regarded as the ideal foundation of law and political power; panopticism constituted the technique, universally widespread, of coercion. It continued to work in depth on the juridical structures of society, in order to make the effective mechanisms of power function in opposi-

tion to the formal framework that it had acquired. The "Enlightenment," which discovered the liberties, also invented the disciplines.

In appearance, the disciplines constitute nothing more than an infra-law. They seem to extend the general forms defined by law to the infinitesimal level of individual lives; or they appear as methods of training that enable individuals to become integrated into these general demands. They seem to constitute the same type of law on a different scale, thereby making it more meticulous and more indulgent. The disciplines should be regarded as a sort of counter-law. They have the precise role of introducing insuperable asymmetries and excluding reciprocities. First, because discipline creates between individuals a "private" link, which is a relation of constraints entirely different from contractual obligation; the acceptance of a discipline may be underwritten by contract; the way in which it is imposed, the mechanisms it brings into play, the non-reversible subordination of one group of people by another, the "surplus" power that is always fixed on the same side, the inequality of position of the different "partners" in relation to the common regulation, all these distinguish the disciplinary link from the contractual link, and make it possible to distort the contractual link systematically from the moment it has as its content a mechanism of discipline. We know, for example, how many real procedures undermine the legal fiction of the work contract: workshop discipline is not the least important. Moreover, whereas the juridical systems define juridical subjects according to the universal norms, the disciplines characterize, classify, specialize; they distribute along a scale, around a norm, hierarchize individuals in relation to one another, and, if necessary, disqualify and invalidate. In any case, in the space and during the time in which they exercise their control and bring into play the asymmetries of their power, they effect suspension of the law that is never total, but is never annulled either. Regular and institutional as it may be, the discipline, in its mechanism, is a "counter-law." And, although the universal juridicism of modern society seems to fix limits on the exercise of power, its universally widespread panopticism enables it to operate, on the underside of the law, a machinery that is both immense and minute, which supports, reinforces, multiplies the asymmetry of power and undermines the limits that are traced around the law. The minute disciplines, the panopticisms of every day may well be below the level of emergence of the great apparatuses and the great political struggles. But, in the genealogy of modern society, they have been, with the class domination that traverses it, the political counterpart of the juridical norms according to which power was redistributed. Hence, no doubt, the importance that has been given for so long to the small techniques of discipline, to those apparently insignificant ticks that it has invented, and even to those "sciences" that give it a respectable face; hence the fear of abandoning them if one cannot find any substitute; hence the affirmation that they are at the very foundation of society, and an element in its equilibrium, whereas they are a series of mechanisms for unbalancing power relations definitively and everywhere; hence the persistence in regarding them as the humble, but concrete form of every mortality, whereas they are a set of physico-political techniques.

To return to the problem of legal punishments, the prison with all the corrective technology at its disposal is to be resituated at the point where the codified power to punish turns into a disciplinary power to observe; at the point where the universal punishments of the law are applied selectively to certain individuals and always the same ones; at the point where the redefinition of the juridical subject by the penalty becomes a useful training of the criminal; at the point where the law is inverted and passes outside itself, and where the counter-law becomes the effective and institutionalized content of the juridical forms. What generalizes the power to punish, then, is not the universal consciousness of the law in each juridical subject; it is the regular extension, the infinitely minute web of panoptic techniques.

3. Taken one by one, most of these techniques have a long history behind them. But what was new, in the eighteenth century, was that, by being combined and generalized, they attained a level at which the formation of knowledge and the increase of power regularly reinforced one another in a circular process. At this point, the disciplines crossed the "technological" threshold. First the hospital, then the school, then, later, the workshop were not simply "reordered" by the disciplines; they became, thanks to them, apparatuses such that any mechanism of objectification could be used in them as an instrument of subjection, and any growth of power could give rise in them to possible branches of knowledge; it was this link, proper to the technological systems, that made possible within the disciplinary element the formation of clinical medicine, psychiatry, child psychology, educational psychology, the rationalization of labour. It is a double process, then: an epistemological "thaw" through a refinement of power relations; a multiplication of the effects of power through the formation and accumulation of new forms of knowledge. . . .

In the Middle Ages, the procedure of investigation gradually superseded the old accusatory justice, by a process initiated from above; the disciplinary technique, on the other hand, insidiously and as if from below, has invaded a penal justice that is still, in principle, inquisitorial. All the great moments of extension that characterize modern penalty—the problematization of the criminal behind his crime, the concern with a punishment that is a correction, a therapy, a normalization, the division of the act of judgment between various authorities that are supposed to measure, assess, diagnose, cure, transform individuals—all this betrays the penetration of the disciplinary examination into the judicial inquisition.

What is now imposed on penal justice as its point of application, its "useful" object, will no longer be the body of the guilty man set up against the body of the king; nor will it be the juridical subject of an ideal contract; it will be the disciplinary individual. The extreme point of penal justice under the Ancien Régime was the infinite segmentation of the body of the regicide: a manifestation of the strongest power over the body of the greatest criminal, whose total destruction made the crime explode into its truth. The ideal point of penality today would be an indefinite discipline: an interrogation without end, an investigation that would be extended without limit to a meticulous and ever more analytical observation, a judgment that would at the same time be the constitution of a file that was never closed, the calculated leniency of a penalty that would be interlaced with the ruthless curiosity of an examination, a procedure that would be at the same time the permanent measure of a gap in relation to an inaccessible norm and asymptotic movement that strives to meet in infinity. The public execution was the logical culmination of a procedure governed by the Inquisition. The practice of placing individuals under "observation" is a natural extension of a justice imbued with disciplinary methods and examination procedures. Is it surprising that the cellular prison, with its regular chronologies, forced labour, its authorities of surveillance and registration, its experts in normality, who continue and multiply the functions of the judge, should have become the modern instrument of penalty? Is it surprising that prisons resemble factories, schools, barracks, hospitals, which all resemble prisons?

The French philosopher Gilles Deleuze was a prolific writer with an immense, wide-ranging influence on the humanities and social sciences, an influence so profound that Michel Foucault asserted that the twentieth century could be called Deleuzian. Deleuze studied at the Sorbonne, where he eventually taught philosophy before moving to the University of Lyons. After the strikes of May 1968, which disrupted both higher education and civilian life in Paris and led to the collapse of Charles de Gaulle's government, Deleuze became a magnetic force, lecturing at the university established in the working-class suburb of Vincennes. He retired from teaching in 1987 when his health began to fail; on November 7, 1995, suffering from a deteriorating respiratory illness, he committed suicide by flinging himself from his window.

The French psychoanalyst and philosopher Félix Guattari was also known as an antipsychoanalyst and antiphilosopher. He had studied psychoanalysis with Lacan and was a member of the Freudian School of Paris. Along with Deleuze, he was also an active member of the antipsychiatry group Centre d'Initiative pour de Nouveaux Espaches de Liberte. He was a member of the French Communist Party but was expelled because he opposed the 1956 Soviet invasion of Hungary. A dedicated social activist, he played an instrumental role in the May 1968 upheavals. Toward the end of his life, he actively supported France's environmental-protection movement and ran, unsuccessfully, in the regional elections as a Green Candidate. He died of a heart attack in 1992.

Deleuze's and Guattari's Anti-Oedipus: Capitalism and Schizophrenia *(1983) is internationally acclaimed to be one of the most influential post–May 1968 texts. It is a text that abounds in neologisms and intracontinental references in broaching a radical critique of the capitalist world system. Deleuze and Guattari argue that the logic of capitalism is not only internally schizophrenic but has also had the effect of generalizing a condition of schizophrenia, so that schizophrenia becomes a category through which to analyze capitalism. What they detail is a process of dehumanization and de-individualization that is implicit in their claim that individuals in the world of constant production, which characterizes capitalism, are machines perpetually coupling and decoupling with each other to form other machines. Thus, individuals, social institutions, art and literature, technology, scientific theories, intellectual production are all themselves machines, forming the larger machinery of capital.*

In the world system of the capitalist machine, desire is what has the most subversive potential. And it is here that their antipsychoanalytic tendencies show through: desire is not simply predicated on a lack of an object that the subject strives to incorporate, but has the power to throw into disarray the established world system. Paying a tribute to this text, Foucault asserted that the anti-Oedipal is not simply a theory but a practice, a "life-style"; Anti-Oedipus *thus demonstrates how to combat fascism, not only the historical fascism of Hitler and Mussolini but also the fascism within every human being.*

Savages, Barbarians, and Civilized Men

GILLES DELEUZE AND FÉLIX GUATTARI

1. THE INSCRIBING SOCIUS

If the universal comes at the end—the body without organs and desiring production—under the conditions determined by an apparently victorious capitalism, where do we find enough innocence for generating universal history? Desiring-production also exists from the beginning: there is desiring-production from the moment there is social production and reproduction. But in a very precise sense it is true that precapitalist social machines are inherent in desire: they code it, they code the flows of desire. To code desire—and the fear, the anguish of decoded flows—is the business of the socius. As we shall see, capitalism is the only social machine that is constructed on the basis of decoded flows, substituting for intrinsic codes an axiomatic of abstract quantities in the form of money. Capitalism therefore liberates the flows of desire, but under the social conditions that define its limit and the possibility of its own dissolution, so that it is constantly opposing with all its exasperated strength the movement that drives it toward this limit. At capitalism's limit the deterritorialized socius gives way to the body without organs, and the decoded flows throw themselves into desiring-production. Hence it is correct to understand retrospectively all history in the light of capitalism, provided that the rules formulated by Marx are followed exactly.

First of all, universal history is the history of contingencies, and not the history of necessity. [It provides] ruptures and limits, and not continuity. For great accidents were necessary, and amazing encounters that could have happened elsewhere, or before, or might never have happened, in order for the flows to escape decoding and, escaping, to nonetheless fashion a new machine bearing the determinations of the capitalist socius. Thus the encounter between private property and commodity production presents itself as two quite distinct forms of decoding, by privatization and by abstraction. Or, from the view point of private property itself, the encounter between flows of convertible wealth owned by capitalists and a flow of workers possessing nothing more than their labor capacity (here again, two distinct forms of deterritorialization). In a sense, capitalism has haunted all forms of society, but it haunts them as their terrifying nightmare, it is the dread they feel of a flow that would elude their codes. Then again, if we say that capitalism determines the conditions and the possibility of a universal history, this is true only insofar as capitalism has to deal essentially with its own limit, its own destruction—as Marx says, insofar as it is capable of self-criticism (at least to a certain point: the point where the limit appears, in the very movement that counteracts the tendency). In a word, universal history is not only retrospective; it is also contingent, singular, ironic, and critical.

The earth is the primitive, savage unity of desire and production. For the earth is not merely the multiple and divided object of labor, it is also the unique, indivisible entity, the full body that falls back on the forces of production and appropriates them for its own as the natural or divine precondition. While the ground can be the productive element and the result of appropriation, the Earth is the great unengendered stasis, the element superior to production that conditions the common appropriation and utilization of the ground. It is the surface on which the whole process of production is inscribed, on which the forces and means of labor are recorded, and the agents and the products distributed. It appears here as the quasi cause of production and the object of desire (it is on the earth that desire becomes bound to its own repression). The *territorial machine* is therefore the first form of socius, the machine of primitive inscription, the "megamachine" that covers a social field. It is not to be confused with technical machines. In its simplest, so-called manual forms, the technical machine already implies an acting, a transmitting, or even a driving element that is nonhuman, and that extends man's strength and allows for a certain disengagement from it. The social machine, in contrast, has men form its parts, even if we view them *with* their machines, and integrate them, internalize them in an institutional model at every stage of action, transmission, and motricity. Hence the social machine fashions a memory without which there would be no synergy of man and his (technical) machines. The latter do not in fact contain the conditions for the reproduction of their process; they point to the social machines that condition and organize them, but also limit and inhibit their development. It will be necessary to await capitalism to find a semiautonomous organization of technical production that tends to appropriate memory and reproduction, and thereby modifies the forms of the exploitation of man; but as a matter of fact, this organization presupposes a dismantling of the great social machines that preceded it.

The same machine can be both technical and social, but only when viewed from different perspectives: for example, the clock as a technical machine for measuring uniform time, and as a social machine for reproducing canonic hours and for assuring order in the city. When Lewis Mumford coins the word "megamachine" to designate the social machine as a collective entity, he is literally correct (although he limits its application to the barbarian despotic institution): "If, more or less in agreement with Reuleaux's classic definition, one can consider the machine to be the combination of solid elements, each having its specialized function and operating under human control in order to transmit a movement and perform a task, then the human machine was indeed a true machine." The social machine is literally a machine, irrespective of any metaphor, inasmuch as it exhibits an immobile motor and undertakes a variety of interventions: flows are set apart, elements are detached from a chain, and portions of the tasks to be performed are distributed. Coding the flows implies all these operations. This is the social machine's supreme task, inasmuch as the apportioning of production corresponds to extractions from the chain, result-ing in a residual share for each member, in a global system of desire and destiny that organizes the productions of production, the productions of recording, and the productions of consumption. Flows of women and children, flows of herds and of seed, sperm flows, flows of shit, menstrual flows: immobile motor, the earth, is already a social machine, a megamachine, that codes the flows of production, the flows of means of production, of producers and consumers: the full body of the goddess Earth gathers to itself the cultivable species, the agricul-tural implements, and the human organs.

Meyer Fortes makes a passing remark that is joyous and refreshingly sound: "The circulation of women is not the problem. . . . A woman circulates of herself. She is not at one's disposal, but the juridical rights governing progenitor are determined for the profit of a specific person." We see no reason in fact for accepting the postulate that underlies exchangist notions of society; society is not first of all a milieu for exchange where the essential would be to circulate or to cause to circulate, but rather a socius of inscription where the essential thing is to mark and to be marked. There is circulation only if inscription requires or permits it. The method of the primitive territorial machine is in this sense the collective investment of the organs; for flows are coded only to the extent that the organs capable respectively of producing and breaking them are themselves encircled, instituted as partial objects, distributed on the socius and attached to it. A mask is such an institution of organs. Initiation societies compose the pieces of a body, which are at the same time sensory organs, anatomical parts, and joints. Prohibitions (see not, speak not) apply to those who, in a given state or on a given occasion, are deprived of the right to enjoy a collectively invested organ. The mythologies sing of organs—partial objects and their relations with a full body that repels or attracts them: a vagina riveted on the woman's body, an immense penis shared by the men, an independent anus that assigns itself a body without an anus. A Gourma story begins: "When the mouth was dead, the other parts of the body were consulted to see which of them would take charge of the burial. . . ." The unities in question are never found in persons, but rather in *series* which determine the connections, disjunctions, and conjunctions of organs. That is why fantasies are group fantasies. It is the collective investment of the organs that plugs desire into the socius and assembles social production and desiring-production into a whole on the earth.

Our modern societies have instead undertaken a vast privatization of the organs, which corresponds to the decoding of flows that have become abstract. The first organ to suffer privatization, removal from the social field, was the anus. It was the anus that offered itself as a model for privatization, at the same time as money came to express the flows' new state of abstraction. Hence psychoanalytic remarks concerning the anal nature of monetary economy provide a relative truth. But the "logical" order is the following: the substitution of abstract quantity for the coded flows; the resulting collective disinvestment of the organs, on the model of the anus; the constitution of private persons as individual centers of organs and functions derived from the abstract quantity. One is even compelled to say that, while in our societies the penis has occupied the position of a detached object distributing lack to the persons of both sexes and organizing the Oedipal triangle, it is the anus that in this manner detaches it, it is the anus that removes and sublimates the penis in a kind of *Aufhebung* ("sublimation") that will constitute the phallus. Sublimation is profoundly linked to anality, but this is not to say that the latter furnishes a material to be sublimated, for want of another use. Anality does not represent a lower requiring conversion to a high. It is the anus itself that ascends on high, under the conditions (which we must analyze) of its removal from the field, conditions that do not presuppose sublimation, since on the contrary it is sublimation in its entirety that is anal; moreover, the simplest critique of sublimation is the fact that it does not by any means rescue us from the shit (only the mind is capable of shitting). Anality is all the greater once the anus is disinvested. The libido is indeed the essence of desire; but when the libido becomes abstract quantity, the elevated and disinvested anus produces the global persons and the specific egos that serve this same quantity as unites of measure. Artaud expresses it well: the "dead rat's ass suspended from the ceiling of the sky," whence issues the daddy-mommy-me triangle, "the uterine mother-father of a frantic anality," whose child is only an angle, this "kind of covering eternally hanging on something that is the self."

The whole of Oedipus is anal and implies an individual overinvestment of the organ to compensate for its collective disinvestment. That is why the commentators most favorable to the universality of Oedipus recognize nonetheless that one does not encounter in primitive societies any of the mechanisms or any of the attitudes that make it a reality in our society. No superego, no guilt. No identification of a specific ego with global persons—but group identifications that are always partial, following the compact, agglutinated series of ancestors, and the fragmented series of companions and cousins. No anality—although, or rather because, there is a collectively invested anus. What remains then for the making of Oedipus? Is the structure but an unrealized potentiality? Are we to believe that a universal Oedipus haunts all societies, but exactly as capitalism haunts them, *that is to say*, as the nightmare and the anxious foreboding of what might result from the decoding of flows and the collective disinvestment of organs, the becoming-abstract of the flows of desire, and the becoming-private of the organs?

The primitive territorial machine codes flows, invests organs, and marks bodies. To such a degree that circulating—exchanging—is a secondary activity in comparison with the task that sums up all the others: marking bodies, which are the earth's products. The essence of the recording, inscribing socius, insofar as it lays claim to the productive forces and distributes the agents of production, resides in these operations: tattooing, excising, incising, carving, scarifying, mutilating, encircling, and initiating. Nietzsche thus defined the "*morality of mores* . . . —the labor performed by man upon himself during the greater part of the existence of the human race, his entire *prehistoric* labor"; a system of evaluations possessing the force of law concerning the various members and parts of the body. Not only is the criminal deprived of organs according to a régime (*ordre*) of collective investments; not only is the one who has to be eaten, eaten according to social rules as exact as those followed in carving up and apportioning a steer; but the man who enjoys the full exercise of his rights and duties has his whole body marked under a régime that consigns his organs and their exercise to the collectivity (the privatization of the organs will only begin with "the shame felt by man *at the sight of* man"). For it is a bounding act—that the organs be hewn into the socius, and that the flows run over its surface—through which man ceases to be a biological organism and becomes a full body, an earth, to which his organs become attached, where they are attracted, repelled, miraculated, following the requirements of socius. Nietzsche says: it is a matter of creating a memory for man; and man, who was constituted by means of an active faculty of forgetting (*oubli*), by means of a repression of biological memory, must create an *other* memory, one that is collective, a memory of words (*paroles*) and no longer a memory of things, a memory of signs and no longer of effects. This organization, which traces its signs directly on the body, constitutes a system of cruelty, a terrible alphabet: "Perhaps indeed there was nothing more fearful and uncanny in the whole prehistory of man than his *mnemotechnics*. . . . Man could never do without blood, torture, and sacrifices when he felt the need to create a memory for himself; the most dreadful sacrifices and pledges . . . the most repulsive mutilations . . . the cruelest rites of all the religious cults . . . one has only to look at our former codes of punishments to understand what effort it costs on this earth to breed a 'nation of thinkers'!"

Cruelty has nothing to do with some ill-defined or natural violence that might be commissioned to explain the history of mankind; cruelty is the movement of culture that is realized in bodies and inscribed on them, belaboring them. That is what cruelty means. This culture is not the movement of ideology: on the contrary, it forcibly injects production into desire, and conversely, it forcibly inserts desire into social production and reproduction. For even death, punishment, and torture are desired, and are instances of production (compare the history of fatalism). It makes men or their organs into the parts and wheels of the social machine. The sign is a position of desire; but the first signs are the territorial signs that plant their flags in bodies. And if one wants to call this inscription in naked flesh "writing," then it must be said that speech in fact presupposes writing, and that it is this cruel system of inscribed signs that renders man capable of language, and gives him a memory of the spoken word.

. . . . .

6. THE BARBARIAN DESPOTIC MACHINE

The founding of the despotic machine or the barbarian socius can be summarized in the following way: a new alliance and direct filiation. The despot challenges the lateral alliances and the extended filiations of the old community. He imposes a new alliance system and places himself in direct filiation with the deity: the people must follow. A leap into a new alliance, a break with the ancient filiation—this is expressed in a strange machine, or rather a machine of the strange whose locus is the desert, imposing the harshest and the most barren of ordeals, and attesting to the resistance of an old order as well as to the validation of the new order. The machine of the strange is both a great paranoiac machine, since it expresses the struggle with the old system, and already a glorious celibate machine, insofar as it exalts the triumph of the new alliance. The despot is the paranoiac: there is no longer any reason to forego such a statement, once one has freed oneself from the characteristic familialism of the concept of paranoia in psychoanalysis and psychiatry, and provided one sees in paranoia a type of investment of a social formation. And new perverse groups spread the despot's invention (perhaps they even fabricated it for him), broadcast his fame, and impose his power in the towns they found or conquer. Wherever a despot and his army pass, doctors, priests, scribes, and officials are part of the procession. It might be said that the ancient complementarity has shifted to form a new socius: no longer the bush paranoiac and the encampment or village perverts, but the desert paranoiac and the town perverts.

In theory the despotic barbarian formation has to be conceived of in terms of an opposition between it and the primitive territorial machine: the birth of an empire. But in reality one can perceive the movement of this formation just as well when one empire breaks away from a preceding empire; or even when there arises the dream of a spiritual empire, wherever temporal empires fall into decadence. It may be that the enterprise is primarily military and motivated by conquest, or that it is primarily religious, the military discipline being converted into internal asceticism and cohesion. It may be that the paranoiac himself is either a gentle creature or a raging beast. But we always rediscover the figures of this paranoiac and his perverts, the conqueror and his elite troops, the despot and his bureaucrats, the holy man and his disciples, the anchorite and his monks, Christ and his Saint Paul. Moses flees from the Egyptian machine into the wilderness and installs his new machine there, a holy ark and a portable temple, and gives his people a new religious-military organization. In order to summarize Saint John the Baptist's enterprise, one author declares: "John attacks at its foundation the central doctrine of Judaism, the doctrine of the alliance with God through a filiation that goes back to Abraham." There is the essential: every time the categories of new alliance and direct filiation are mobilized, we are talking about the imperial barbarian formation or the despotic machine. And this holds true whatever the context of this mobilization, whether in a relationship with preceding empires or not, since throughout these vicissitudes the imperial formation is always defined by a certain type of code and inscription that is in direct opposition to the primitive territorial codings. The number of elements in the alliance makes little difference: new alliance and direct filiation are specific categories that testify to the existence of a new socius, irreducible to the lateral alliances and the extended filiations that declined the primitive machine. It is this force of projection that defines paranoia, this strength to start again from zero, to objectify a complete transformation: the subject leaps outside the intersections of alliance-filiation, installs himself at the limit, at the horizon, in the desert, the subject of a deterritorialized knowledge that links him directly to God and connects him to the people. For the first time, something has been withdrawn from life and from the earth that will make it possible to judge life and to survey the earth from above: a first principle of paranoiac knowledge. The whole relative play of alliances and filiations is carried to the absolute in this new alliance and this direct filiation.

It remains to be said that, in order to understand the barbarian formation, it is necessary to relate it not to other formations in competition with it temporally and spiritually, according to relationships that obscure the essential, but to the savage primitive formation that it supplants by imposing its own rule of law, but that continues to haunt it. It is exactly in this way that Marx defines Asiatic production: a higher unity of the State establishes itself on the foundations of the primitive rural communities, which keep their ownership of the soil, while the State becomes the true owner in conformity with the apparent objective movement that attributes the surplus product to the State, assigns the productive forces to it in the great projects undertaken, and makes it appear as the cause of the collective conditions of appropriation. The full body as socius has ceased to be the earth, it has become the body of the despot, the despot himself or his god. The prescriptions and prohibitions that often render him almost incapable of acting make of him a body without organs. *He* is the sole quasi cause, the source and fountainhead and estuary of the apparent objective movement. In place of mobile detachments from the signifying chain, a detached object has jumped outside the chain; in place of flow selections, all the flows converge into a great river that constitutes the sovereign's consumption: a radical change of régimes in the fetish or the symbol. What counts is not the person of the sovereign, nor even his function, which can be limited. It is the social machine that has profoundly changed: in place of the territorial machine, there is the "megamachine" of the State, a functional pyramid that has the despot at its apex, an immobile motor, with the bureaucratic apparatus as its lateral surface and its transmission gear, and the villagers at its base, serving as its working parts. The stocks form the object of an accumulation, the blocks of debt become an infinite relation in the form of the tribute. The entire surplus value of code is an object of appropriation. This conversion crosses through all the syntheses: the synthesis of production, with the hydraulic machine and the mining machine; the synthesis of inscription, with the accounting machine, the writing machine, and the monument machine; and finally the synthesis of consumption, with the upkeep of the despot, his court, and the bureaucratic caste. Far from seeing in the State the principle of a territorialization that would inscribe people according to their residence, we should see in the principle of residence the effect of a movement of deterritorialization that divides the earth as an object and subjects men to the new imperial inscription, to the new full body, to the new socius. "They come like fate, . . . they appear as lightning appears, too terrible, too sudden."

The death of the primitive system always comes from without; history is the history of contingencies and encounters. Like a cloud blown in from the desert, the conquerors are there: "In some way that is incomprehensible to me they have pushed right into the capital, although it is a long way from the frontier. At any rate, here they are; it seems that every morning there are more of them. . . . Speech with the nomads is impossible. They do not know our own language." But this death that comes from without is also that which was rising from within: the general irreducibility of alliance to filiation, the independence of the alliance groups, the way in which they serve as a conducting element for the political and economic relations, the system of primitive rankings, the mechanism of surplus value—all these already prefigured despotic formations and caste hierarchies. And how does one distinguish the way in which the primitive community remains on its guard with respect to its own institutions of chieftainship, and exorcizes or strait-jackets the image of the possible despot whom it threatens to secrete from within, from the way in which it binds up the symbol—a symbol that has become derisory—of a former despot who thrust himself upon the community from the outside long ago? It is not always easy to know if one is considering a primitive community that is repressing an endogenous tendency, or one that is regaining its cohesion as best it can after a terrible exogenous adventure. The wave of alliances is ambiguous: are we still on this side of the new alliance, or already beyond it, having fallen back, as it were, into a this-side-of that is residual and transformed? (Related question: what is the feudal system?) We are only able to fix the precise moment of the imperial formation as that of the new exogenous alliance, not only in the place of former alliances, but *in relation to them.*

This new alliance is something altogether different from a treaty or a contract. What is suppressed is not the former régime of lateral alliances and extended filiations, but merely their determining character. They subsist, more or less modified, more or less harnessed by the great paranoiac, since they furnish the material of surplus value. In point of fact, that is what forms the specific character of Asiatic production: the autochthonous rural communities subsist, and continue to produce, inscribe, and consume; in effect, they are the State's sole concern. The wheels of the territorial lineage machine subsist, but are no longer anything more than the working parts of the State machine. The objects, the organs, the persons, and the groups retain at least a part of their intrinsic coding, but these coded flows of the former régime find themselves overcoded by the transcendent unity that appropriates surplus value. The old inscription remains, but is bricked over by and in the inscription of the State. The blocks subsist, but have become encasted and embedded bricks, having only a controlled mobility. The territorial alliances are not replaced, but are merely allied with the new alliance; the territorial filiations are not replaced, but are merely affiliated with the direct filiation. It is like an immense right of the first-born over all filiations, an immense right of the wedding night over all alliances. The filiative stock becomes the object of an accumulation in the other filiation, while the alliance debt becomes an infinite relation in the other alliance. It is the entire primitive system that finds itself mobilized, requisitioned by a superior power, subjugated by new exterior forces, put in the service of other ends; so true is it, said Nietzsche, that what is called the evolution of a thing is "a succession of more or less profound, more or less mutually independent processes of subduing, plus the resistances they encounter, the attempts at transformation for the purpose of defense and reaction, and the results of successful counteractions."

It has often been remarked that the State commences (or recommences) with two fundamental acts, one of which is said to be an act of territoriality through the fixing of residence, and the other, an act of liberation through the abolition of small debts. But the State operates by means of euphemisms. The pseudo territoriality is the product of an effective deterritorialization that substitutes abstract signs for the signs of the earth, and that makes the earth itself into the object of a State ownership of property, or an ownership held by the State's richest servants and officials. (There is no great change, *from this point of view*, when the State no longer does anything more than guarantee the private property of a ruling class that becomes distinct from the State.) The abolition of debts, when it takes place, is a means of maintaining the distribution of land, and a means of preventing the entry on stage of a new territorial machine, possibly revolutionary and capable of raising and dealing with the agrarian problem in a comprehensive way. In other cases where a redistribution occurs, the cycle of credits is maintained, in the new form established by the State— money. For without question, money does not begin by serving the needs of commerce, or at least it has no autonomous mercantile model. The despotic machine holds the following in common with the primitive machine, it confirms the latter in this respect: the dread of decoded low-flows of production, but also mercantile flows (*flux marchands*) of exchange and commerce that might escape the State monopoly), with its tight restrictions and its plugging of flows. When Etienne Balazs asks why capitalism wasn't born in China in the thirteenth century, when all the necessary scientific and technical conditions nevertheless seemed to be present, the answer lies in the State, which closed the mines as soon as the reserves of metal were judged sufficient, and which retained a monopoly or a narrow control over commerce (the merchant as functionary).

The role of money in commerce hinges less on commerce itself than on its control by the State. Commerce's relationship with money is synthetic, not analytical. And money is fundamentally inseparable, not from commerce, but from taxes as the maintenance of the apparatus of the State. Even where dominant classes set themselves apart from this apparatus and make use of it for the benefit of private property, the despotic tie between money and taxes remains visible. Basing himself on the research of Edouard Will, Michel Foucault shows how, in certain Greek tyrannies, the tax on aristocrats and the distribution of money to the poor are a means of bringing the money back to the rich and a means of remarkably widening the régime of debts, making it even stronger, by anticipating and repressing any reterritorialization that might be produced by the economic givens of the agrarian problem. (As if the Greeks had discovered in their own way what the Americans rediscovered after the New Deal: that heavy taxes are good for business.) In a word, money—the circulation of money —is the means for rendering the debt infinite. And that is what is concealed in the two acts of the State: the residence or territoriality of the State inaugurates the great movement of deterritorialization that subordinates all the primitive filiation to the despotic machine (the agrarian problem); the abolition of debts or their accountable transformation initiates the duty of an interminable service to the State that subordinates all the primitive alliances to itself (the problem of debts). The infinite creditor and infinite credit have replaced the blocks of mobile and finite debts. There is always a monotheism on the horizon of despotism: the debt becomes a *debt of existence*, a debt of the existence of the subjects themselves. A time will come when the creditor has not yet lent while the debtor never quits repaying, for repaying is a duty but lending is an option—as in Lewis Carroll's song, the long song about the infinite debt:

> A man may surely claim his dues:
> But, when there's money to be lent,
> A man must be allowed to choose
> Such times as are convenient.

The despotic State, such as it appears in the purest conditions of "Asiatic" production, has two correlative aspects: on the one hand it replaces the territorial machine, it forms a new deterritorialized full body; on the other hand it maintains the old territorialities, integrates them as parts or organs of production in the new machine. It is perfected all at once because it functions on the basis of dispersed rural communities, which are like pre-existing autonomous or semiautonomous machines from the viewpoint of production; but from this same viewpoint, it reacts on them in producing the conditions for major work projects that exceed the capacities of the separate communities. What is produced on the body of the despot is a connective synthesis of the old alliances with the new, and a disjunctive synthesis that entails an overflowing of the old filiations into the direct filiation, gathering all the subjects into the new machine. The essential action of the State, therefore, is the creation of a second inscription by which the new full body—immobile, monumental, immutable—

appropriates all the forces and agents of production; but this inscription of the State allows the old territorial inscriptions to subsist, as "bricks" on the new surface. And finally, from this appropriation there results the way in which the conjunction of the two parts is implemented and the respective portions are distributed to the higher proprietary unity and to the propertied communities, to the overcoding process and to the intrinsic codes, to the appropriated surplus value and to the usufruct put into use, to the State machine and to the territorial machines. As in Kafka's "The Great Wall of China," the State is the transcendent higher unity that integrates relatively isolated subaggregates, functioning separately, to which it assigns a development in bricks and a labor of construction by fragments. Scattered partial objects hang on the body without organs. No one has equaled Kafka in demonstrating that the law had nothing to do with a natural, harmonious, and immanent totality, but that it acted as an eminent formal unity, and *reigned accordingly over pieces and fragments* (the wall and the tower). Hence the State is not primeval, it is an origin or an abstraction, it is the original abstract essence that is not to be confused with a beginning. "We think only about the Emperor. But not about the present one; or rather we would think about the present one if we knew who he was or knew anything definite about him. . . . [The people] do not know what emperor is reigning, and there exist doubts regarding even the name of the dynasty. . . . Long-dead emperors are set on the throne in our villages, and one that only lives in song recently had a proclamation of his read out by the priest before the altar."

As for the subaggregates themselves, the primitive territorial machines, they are the concrete itself, the concrete base and beginning, but their segments here enter into relationships corresponding to the essence; they assume precisely this form of bricks that ensures their integration into the higher unity, and their distributive operation, consonant with the great collective designs of this same unity: major work projects, extortion of surplus value, tributes, generalized servitude. Two inscriptions coexist in the imperial formation, and mutually adjust insofar as the one is imbricated into the other, but the new inscription cements the whole and brings producers and products into relations with itself (they do not need to speak the same language). The imperial inscription countersects all the alliances and filiations, prolongs them, makes them converge into the direct filiation of the despot with the deity, and the new alliance of the despot with the people. All the coded flows of the primitive machine are now forced into a bottleneck, where the despotic machine overcodes them. *Overcoding* is the operation that constitutes the essence of the State, and that measures both its continuity and its break with the previous formations: the dread of flows of desire that would resist coding, but also the establishment of a new inscription that overcodes, and that makes desire into the property of the sovereign, even though he be the death instinct itself. The castes are inseparable from this overcoding, and imply the existence of dominant "classes" that do not yet manifest themselves as classes, but are merged with a State apparatus. Who is able to touch the full body of the sovereign? Here we have a problem of castes. It is overcoding that impoverishes the earth for the benefit of the deterritorialized full body, and that on this full body renders the movement of debt infinite. It is a measure of Nietzsche's force to have stressed the importance of such a movement that begins with the founders of States, these artists with a look of bronze, creating "an oppressive and remorseless machine," erecting before any perspective of liberation an ironclad impossibility. This "infinitivation" cannot be understood exactly as Nietzsche would have it—that is, as a consequence of the interplay of ancestors, profound genealogies, and extended filiations; rather, when these are short-circuited, abducted by the new alliance and direct filiation, *then* the ancestor—the master of the mobile and finite blocks—finds himself dismissed by the deity, the immobile organizer of the bricks and of their infinite circuit.

. . . . .

8. THE URSTAAT

The city of Ur is the point of departure of Abraham or the new alliance. The State was not formed in progressive stages; it appears fully armed, a master stroke executed all at once; the primordial *Urstaat*, the eternal model of everything the State wants to be and desires. "Asiatic" production, with the State that expresses or constitutes its objective movement, is not a distinct formation; it is the basic formation, on the horizon throughout history. There comes back to us from all quarters the discovery of imperial machines that preceded the traditional historical forms, machines characterized by State ownership of property, with communal possession bricked into it, and collective dependence. Every form that is more "evolved" is like a palimpsest: it covers a despotic inscription, a Mycenaean manuscript. Under every Black and every Jew there is an Egyptian, and a Mycenaean under the Greeks, and an Etruscan under the Romans. And yet their origin sinks into oblivion, a latency that lays hold of the State itself, and where the writing system sometimes disappears. It is beneath the blows of private property, then of commodity production, that the State witnesses its decline. Land enters into the sphere of private property and into that of commodities. *Classes* appear, inasmuch as the dominant classes are no longer merged with the State apparatus, but are distinct determinations that make use of this transformed apparatus. At first situated adjacent to communal property, then entering into the latter's composition or conditioning it, then becoming more and more a determining force, private property brings about an internalization of the creditor-debtor relation in the relations of opposed classes.

But how does one explain both this latency into which the despotic State enters, and this power with which it re-forms itself on modified foundations, in order to spring back more "mendacious," "colder," and more "hypocritical" than ever? It is both oblivion and return. On the one hand, the ancient city-state, the Germanic commune, and feudalism presuppose the great empires, and cannot be understood except in terms of the Urstaat that serves as their horizon. On the other hand, the problem confronting these forms is to reconstitute the Urstaat insofar as possible, given the requirements of their new distinct determinations. For what do private property, wealth, commodities, and classes signify? They signify *the breakdown of codes*, that is, the appearance, the surging forth of now decoded flows that pour over the socius, crossing it from one end to the other. The State can no longer be content to overcode territorial elements that are already coded, it must invent specific codes for flows that are increasingly deterritorialized, which means: putting despotism in the service of the new class relations; integrating the relations of wealth and poverty, of commodity and labor; reconciling market money and money from revenues; everywhere stamping the mark of the Urstaat on the new state of things. And everywhere, the presence of the latent model that can no longer be equaled, but that one cannot help but imitate. The Egyptian's melancholy warning to the Greeks echoes through history: "You Greeks will never be anything but children!"

This special situation of the State as a category—oblivion and return—has to be explained. To begin with, it should be said that the primordial despotic State is not a historical break like any other. Of all the institutions, it is perhaps the only one to appear fully armed in the brain of those who institute it, "the artists with a look of bronze." That is why Marxism didn't quite know what to make of it: it has no place in the famous five stages: primitive communism, ancient city-states, feudalism, capitalism, and socialism. *It is not one formation among others, nor is it the transition from one formation to another.* It appears to be set back at a remove from what it transects and from what it resects, as though it were giving evidence of another dimension, a cerebral ideality that is added to, superimposed on the material evolution of societies, a regulating idea or principle of reflection (terror) that organizes the parts and the flows into a whole. What is transected, supersected, or overcoded by the despotic State is what comes before —the territorial machine, which it reduces to the state of bricks, of working parts henceforth subjected to the cerebral idea. In this sense the despotic State is indeed the origin, but the origin as an abstraction that must include its differences with respect to the concrete beginning. We know that myth always expresses a passage and a divergence (*un écart*). The primitive territorial myth of the beginning expressed the divergence of a characteristically intense energy— what Marcel Griaule called "the metaphysical part of mythology," the vibratory spiral—in relation to the social system in extension that it conditioned, passing back and forth between alliance and filiation. But the imperial myth of the origin expresses something else: the divergence of this beginning from the origin itself, the divergence of the extension from the idea, of the genesis from the order and the power (the new alliance), and also what repasses from filiation to alliance, what is taken up again by filiation. Jean-Pierre Vernant shows in this way that the imperial myths are not able to conceive a law of organization that is immanent in the universe: they need to posit and internalize this difference between the origin and the beginnings, between the sovereign power and the genesis of the world; "the myth constitutes itself within this distance, it makes it into the very object of its narrative, retracing the avatars of sovereignty down through the succession of generations to the moment when a supremacy, this time definitive, puts an end to the dramatic elaboration of the *dunesteia*." So that in the end one no longer really knows what comes first, and whether the territorial machine does not in fact presuppose a despotic machine from which it extracts the bricks or that it segments in its turn.

In a certain sense it is necessary to say as much in regard to what comes after the primal State, in regard to what is resected by this State. It supersects what comes before, but resects the formations that follow. There too it is like an abstraction that belongs to another dimension, always at a remove and struck by latency, but that springs back and returns stronger than before in the later forms that lend it a concrete existence. A protean State, yet there has never been but one State, and hence the variations, all the variants of the new alliance, fall nevertheless under the same category. For example, feudalism not only presupposes an abstract despotic State that it divides into segments according to the régime of its private property and the rise of its commodity production, but the latter induce in return the concrete existence of a *feudal state in the proper sense of the term*, where the despot returns as the absolute monarch. For it is a double error to think that the development of commodity production is enough to bring about feudalism's collapse—on the contrary, this development reinforces feudalism in many respects, offering the latter new conditions of existence and survival—and that feudalism of itself is in opposition to the State, which on the contrary, as the feudal State, is capable of preventing commodities from introducing the decoding of flows that *alone* would be ruinous to the system under consideration. And in more recent examples, we have to go along with Wittfogel when he shows the degree to which modern capitalist and socialist States take on the characteristic features of the primordial despotic State. As for democracies, how could one fail to recognize in them the despot who has become colder and more hypocritical, more calculating, since he must himself count and code instead of overcoding the accounts? It is useless to compose the list of differences after the manner of conscientious historians: village communes here, industrial societies there, and so on. The differences could be determining only if the despotic State were one concrete formation among others, to be treated comparatively. But the despotic State is the abstraction that is realized—in imperial formations, to be sure—only as an abstraction (the overcoding eminent unity). It assumes its immanent concrete existence only in the subsequent forms that cause it to return under other guises and conditions. Being the common horizon for what comes before and what comes after, it conditions universal history only provided it is not on the outside, but always off to the side, the cold monster that represents the way in which history is in the "head," in the "brain" —the Urstaat.

Marx recognized that there was indeed a way in which history proceeded from the abstract to the concrete: "the simple categories are the expression of relations within which the less developed concrete may have already realized itself before having posited the more many-sided connection or relation which is mentally expressed in the more concrete category; while the more developed concrete preserves the same category as a subordinate relation." The State was first this abstract unity that integrated subaggregates functioning separately; it is now subordinated to a field of forces whose flows it co-ordinates and whose autonomous relations of domination and subordination it expresses. It is no longer content to overcode maintained and imbricated territorialities; it must constitute, invent codes for the decoded flows of money, commodities, and private property. It no longer of itself forms a ruling class or classes; it is itself formed by these classes, which have become independent and delegate it to serve their power and their contradictions, their struggles and their compromises with the dominated classes. It is no longer the transcendent law that governs fragments; it must fashion as best it can a whole to which it will render its law immanent. It is no longer the pure signifier that regulates its signifieds; it now appears behind them, depending on the things it signifies. It no longer produces an overcoding unity; it is itself produced inside the field of decoded flows. As a machine it no longer determines a social system; it is itself determined by the social system into which it is incorporated in the exercise of its function. In brief, it does not cease being artificial, but it becomes concrete, it "tends to concretization" while subordinating itself to the dominant forces. The existence of an analogous evolution has been demonstrated for the technical machine, when it ceases to be an abstract unity or intellectual system reigning over separate subaggregates to become a relation that is subordinated to a field of forces operating as a concrete physical system.

But isn't this tendency to concretization in the social or technical machine precisely the movement of desire? Again and again we come upon the monstrous paradox: the State is desire that passes from the head of the despot to the hearts of his subjects, and from the intellectual law to the entire physical system that disengages or liberates itself from law. A State desire, the most fantastic machine for repression, is still desire—the subject that desires and the object of desire. Desire—such is the operation that consists in always stamping the mark of the primordial Urstaat on the new state of things, rendering it immanent to the new system insofar as possible, making it interior to this system. As for the rest, it will be a question of starting again from zero: the founding of a spiritual empire there where forms exist under which the State can no longer function as such in the physical system. When the Christians took possession of the Empire, this complementary duality reappeared between those who wanted to do everything possible to reconstruct the Roman world, and the purists, who wanted a fresh start in the wilderness, a new beginning for a new alliance, a rediscovery of the Egyptian Urstaat. What strange machines those were that cropped up on columns and in tree trunks! In this sense, Christianity was able to develop a whole set of paranoiac and celibate machines, a whole string of paranoiacs and perverts who also form part of our history's horizon and people our calendar. These are the two aspects of a becoming of the State: its internalization in a field of increasingly decoded social forces forming a physical system; its spiritualization in a supraterrestrial field that increasingly overcodes, forming a metaphysical system. The infinite debt must become internalized at the same time as it becomes spiritualized. The hour of bad conscience draws nigh; it will also be the hour of the greatest cynicism, "that repressed cruelty of the animal-man made inward and sacred back into himself, the creature imprisoned in the 'state' so as to be tamed. . . ."

IN THIS SECTION WE WILL DEAL WITH the relationship between violence and its representation. Throughout we will ask not only about this relationship but also about the uses and abuses of this representation. What effect do stories of violence and domination have in the "real world"? Do such stories always have a regressive, adverse effect, reinscribing violence and aggression even as they narrate its occurrence? Or can representation of violence be used effectively to counteract violence?

Some of the questions concern our own deepest identity. Is the subject of violence so fascinating and alluring that we get entranced by its magic even while we claim to disavow it? Is talking about violence tantamount to doing violence? Or is it possible that talking about violence, ad nauseum, literally becomes so nauseating that we necessarily distance ourselves from it, thereby affecting, so to say, a "cure"? It is these and related questions that the selections in this section address.

Although the image of totalitarianism depicted by Hannah Arendt in part IV seems to be unremittingly deceptive and destructive, artists from within the former U.S.S.R. paint a different portrait. Dealing with the relationship between the artist and society, André Breton and Leon Trotsky disavow the totalitarian regime of the U.S.S.R., but at the same time they posit against it a more authentic form of communism that could be liberatory. Art is the key, and they see art as bringing about a revolution that would free not only art and the artist, but also, through their freedom, ensure a more encompassing freedom, by way of a more complete and radical reconstruction of society.

In the very beginning of their manifesto, Breton and Trotsky point to the plight of "world civilization, united in its historic destiny, reeling under the blows of reactionary forces armed with the entire arsenal of modern technology." It is in response to this violence enacted by "reactionary forces" on "world civilization" that Breton and Trotsky put forth their agenda of changing the existing state of affairs.

Breton and Trotsky suggest that any creative activity, philosophical, scientific or artistic, "brings about an objective enriching of culture." It is this creative fountain that they perceive as being under siege, due to the "ever more widespread destruction of those conditions under which intellectual creation is possible." Furthermore, they see in this destructive trend, "an increasingly manifest degradation not only of the work of art but also of the specifically 'artistic' personality"—a degradation that manifests itself in the disappearance, under Hitler's regime and in totalitarian U.S.S.R., of "all those artists whose work expressed the slightest sympathy for liberty." They describe this situation as a "twilight hostile to every sort of spiritual value . . . a twilight of filth and blood."

Yet at the same time that this creative fountain is under siege in these regimes, it becomes the source of creativity that also contains within itself the transformational impulse: "The opposition of writers and artists is one of the forces which can usefully contribute to the discrediting and overthrow of regimes which are destroying, along with the right of the proletariat to aspire to a better world, every sentiment of nobility and even of human dignity."

What is particular to Breton and Trotsky's version of the communist revolution is that this revolution is "not afraid of art" and that it realizes that the role of the artist in a decadent capitalist society is determined by the conflict between the individual and various social forms that are hostile to him. Because of this role, the artist is the "natural ally of revolution." The manifesto writers claim "complete freedom for arts," because it is in the arts and in the creative impulse that they see the possibility of changing the world, disgorging from it both violence and degeneration. They end with a note of advice to artists and intellectuals, to all those who see themselves "threatened with the loss of their right to live and continue working." They suggest that artists and intellectuals should come together and raise a collective voice against the present state of affairs: "Independent revolutionary art must now gather its forces for the struggle against reactionary persecution. It must proclaim aloud its right to exist."

While representation of violence has a complex relationship to artistic freedom within a socialist or communist polity, it is no less complex, and complicated, in the colonized regions of Asia, Africa—and the Americas. Michael Taussig addresses the colonial situation and the economic venture that lay at the heart of the representation of violence in Colombia. What Taussig's exploration of the workings of the colonial machinery in Putumayo discloses is the dual role of representation, its power to wreak violence as well as to heal.

In discussing the colonial situation during the Putumayo rubber boom, Taussig suggests that colonial narrators relished stories of Indians' acts of violence and cannibalism. They used them to foster a culture of terror that was integral to the maintenance of the colonies and of the debt-peonage system whereby the colonizers could extract labor from the Indian subjects in order to make the colonial enterprise profitable and worth maintaining. This culture of terror flourished through the dissemination of stories of violence perpetrated by Indians, stories which laid hold of the colonial imagination and made it "a diseased imagination." Seeing everywhere attacks by Indians, conspiracies, uprisings, and treachery, in order to save themselves from these fancied perils, "they killed, and killed without compassion." This dialectic of terror involved not only the terror that the colonizers felt of the Indians—a terror mediated by the muchachos, who gave back as stories to the whites the same phantoms that the whites had in their brains—but also the violence and savagery that the colonizers heaped on the Indians in response to their perceived fear. "What stands out," observes Taussig, "is the mimesis between the savagery attributed to the Indians by the colonists and the savagery perpetrated by the colonists in the name of what Julio Cesar Arana called civilization, meaning business."

Taussig refers to these stories of Indian savagery circulating among the whites as phantoms, as figments of the colonial imagination. In all the time he spent with the Indians, he never heard or overheard stories remotely approaching these ghoulish tales "spun with such fiendish and melodramatic aesthetic pleasure derived from fear and mystery."

So what was the point of these stories? What powerful purpose did they serve? As Taussig demonstrates, the representation of violence became "a phantasmic social force," a "high-powered medium of domination," which, during the Putumayo rubber boom, was integral to the establishment and maintenance of the debt-peonage system which facilitated the trade in white commodities for India rubber.

In other words, through a strange twist of logic, these stories became an efficient means of cost-effectiveness. The market value of such stories derives as follows: if such stories portrayed Indians as brutal and violent, other stories portrayed those very same Indians as intractable, from whom one could not extract a hard day's work without the threat of violence. And it is through these tales of terror that the colonizers were able to mobilize a counterterror on the Indians: in response to these stories, the colonizers wreaked havoc on the Indian subjects.

And so while on one level Taussig's argument points toward the abuses of representations of violence, yet on another level his project also uncovers the benefits of such representation, which inspires not only terror but also healing. Taussig's project, which is based on the representation of violence and terror during the Putumayo rubber boom, is about counter-representation. Counter-representation is a strong form of contrarian logic. It seeks to overturn the "obvious" representation, to desensationalize terror, and so to promote "the long-awaited demythification and reenchantment of Western man in a quite different confluence of self and otherness," one which heals through subtle interpretation, through sensitive writing, and, above all, through nuanced representation.

Kristine Stiles also promotes nuanced representation. She is an artist and art historian renowned for her systematic examination of destruction and violence in art. Through exploring the many meanings of shaved heads and marked bodies, she demonstrates how cultures of trauma reveal more than the violence, the trauma, at the core of their most visible artifacts or representations. Her purpose is to use trauma to examine some of the deeper contradictions and paradoxes of identity that are bound up with images, especially images that contort and deform their subjects, as do shaved heads and marked bodies. Physical pain does not exhaust the social outrage that leads to its infliction, for at the very least one should try to understand, in Stiles's words, "the reciprocal ways in which different languages, cultural representations, social and political institutions, and races and sexualities comprise identity." In an assertion that harkens back to Catharine MacKinnon, yet moves through multiple registers beyond the law, Stiles claims that the violence perpetrated on outlawed women is masculine in nature. "Organization by hierarchy makes all conceptual organization subject to man," Hélène Cixous and Catherine Clément write, and that organization "is located in the logocentric orders that guarantee the masculine order a rationale equal to history itself."

In a particularly brilliant comparison of the suffering that totalitarian norms inflict in Romania, with the silenced demeanor of incest survivors, Kristine Stiles looks at two figures whose mental self-images project the scars of pain even more than do their bodily deficits. "As a signifier for the charged complexity of Romanian national identity, the tattoo brands Dan Perjovschi's body with the arbitrary geographical identity agreed upon by governments, and it displays the ambiguous psychological allegiances such boundaries inevitably commit to the mind. His action-inscription also conveys some of the content of the accreted spaces of Romanian suffering and guilt, guilt that Perjovschi addressed when he explained that in Romania, where both prisoners and citizens alike habitually were transformed into perpetrators, guilt and innocence intermingle inseparably. And he asked, 'Who may point a finger?' " Similarly, the psychiatrist Judith Lewis Herman describes the process by which incest victims are silenced and made to become complicit in their own abuse: "Terror, intermittent reward, isolation, and enforced dependency may succeed in creating a submissive and compliant prisoner. But the final step in the psychological control of the victim is not completed until she [/he] has been forced to violate her [/his] own moral principles and to betray her [/his] basic human attachments. Psychologically, this is the most destructive of all coercive techniques, for the victim who has succumbed loathes herself [/himself]. It is at this point, when the victim under duress participates in the sacrifice of others, that she [/he] is truly 'broken.' "

Like Stiles, Osama bin Laden emblematizes bodies that are marked for destruction. He is not concerned to study their pain, but to multiply their destruction for the relief of his own pain. Bin Laden targets collective bodies of evil, which is to say, the entire infidel world, and commits himself to their destruction, but he does so in the name of moral purity—and he does so through the modern media, with a finesse that no rogue state has heretofore mastered. The key to understanding bin Laden's message is to grasp the disconnection he perceives between his adopted homeland, Saudi Arabia, and his spiritual lodestone, the Qur'an. The former has betrayed the latter. The infidel flourishes in the birthplace of Islam. The protectors of Islam have become its worst enemies; the Saudis are no longer believers but infidels, but both the infidel Saudis and their Crusader cohorts, the United States and Israel, are marked through the power of the fatwa, and not just any fatwa but an online fatwa that claims to have religious sanction and therefore to convey moral authority, at least for the devout Muslims who are his target audience. The fatwa is included here from an Internet site, and salient commentary is provided by Roland Jacquard, a French strategic expert and consultant on terrorism. Jacquard's book, *In the Name of Osama Bin Laden: Global Terrorism and the Bin Laden Brotherhood*, was a bestseller in France before being translated into English and widely circulated in the United States and Great Britain. It makes clear and compelling what most observers have missed: the radical engagement with options for representation in the Information Age. Without understanding bin Laden's intensive use of modern media to wage his jihad, or war of cleansing, it is impossible to grasp why since September 11, 2001, he has become the primary icon of terror for most Westerners (at the same time that he remains the symbol of hope for many marginalized in the current world system). Jacquard's book became renowned even before September 11, since he "predicted" the longterm influence that bin Laden would have due to his skillful use of self-representation on global satellite television and other electronic outlets.

It is a long way from Trotsky's and Breton's aesthetic optimism to Taussig's documentary interpellations. It may seem still further a leap from Stiles's deft analysis of trauma as cultural expression to bin Laden's culture of mediated terror. But the final exercise of representing violence has to be the most difficult; it is an exercise of good that remains shadowed by evil, sometimes trumped as itself the evil even when it attempts to be the good. This paradox of understanding and engagement is embodied by nongovernmental organizations (NGOS), which hope not to manage violence, but still to mitigate its worst effects. The foremost of such NGOS is perhaps Médecins Sans Frontières (MSF), or Doctors without Borders.

If this volume is to breathe hope into the good exercise of violence, then it must come through NGOS, like MSF, that wage a different kind of jihad, or cleansing war, than bin Laden's. MSF was founded in 1971 by a small group of French doctors who believed that all people have the right to medical care regardless of race, religion, creed, or political affiliation, and that the needs of these people supersede respect for national borders. It was the first NGO to both provide emergency medical assistance and publicly bear witness to the plight of the populations they served. It won the 1999 Nobel Peace Prize for its extraordinary efforts, yet it, too, is caught in the trap of representation-misrepresentation of goals and efforts. The final selection of *On Violence* explores both the prospects and the problems that mark the labor of MSF. Its members, according to Elliott Leyton, emblematize the best of ongoing initiatives to channel and redirect violence, yet they cannot separate themselves from the limits of an imperfect, less-than-morally-pure Western civilization.

It is the paradox of violence that its representation pervades all levels of national and international life, not reducing hope, but making those who are agents of hope keenly aware of the many obstacles that daunt them not just in their labor but also in the way that their labor is perceived by different audiences. No reform is possible without self-reform, as Stiles reaffirms. The goal remains, to quote Taussig, "to create counterrepresentations and counterdiscourses—deflectional, oppositional modes of arresting and diverting the flow of fear"—while also building chains of providence to match, and overlap, the chains of violence.

The French poet, critic, novelist, essayist, and cofounder of surrealism, André Breton graduated from the Lycée Chaptal in 1912 and began medical studies at the Sorbonne in 1913. During World War I, he was drafted for service and assisted in the treatment of patients suffering from mental disorders as a result of war. Breton's writings show a marked interest in mental disorders—an interest he had picked up as a result of his war-time experience. Toward the end of the war, he began to participate actively in literary and intellectual society, joining the dadaists and in 1919 founding the review Littérature in collaboration with Louis Aragon and Philippe Soupault. His involvement with dada evolved into the surrealist movement, which found its first major articulation in Breton's 1924 Manifeste du surréalisme. Although surrealism had begun primarily as an aesthetic movement, during the upheaval of the 1930s it became heavily politicized. Breton joined the Communist Party, but diverged from the party in 1935. During the Nazi occupation of France, Breton escaped to America, but returned to France in 1946.

The communist theorist and activist, Leon Trotsky featured prominently in the Russian Revolutions of 1905 and October 1917. Trotsky was first drawn to Marxism when he moved to Nikolayev in 1896 to finish school and came into contact with an underground socialist group. He was arrested in 1898 for revolutionary activity as a result of his work with the South Russian Worker's Union and was sent to Siberia after spending some time in prison. He escaped in 1902 and landed shortly thereafter in London, where he resumed revolutionary activity. He returned to Russia in 1905, but was again tried for anti-tsarist activity in 1906, again exiled to Siberia, and again escaped, this time settling in Vienna, before moving to Switzerland and Paris. Because of his antiwar position, he was expelled from Spain and France, so he moved to the United States in 1917 to join Nikolai Bukharin at his newspaper, Novy mir (New World). After the Russian Revolution of 1917, Trotsky joined the Bolshevik Party and collaborated with Vladimir Lenin in defeating proposals for a joint government with the Mensheviks and the Socialist Revolutionaries. He subsequently became foreign commissar of the Soviet government, resigning after the Treaty of Brest-Litovsk and becoming war commissar in order to build a new Red Army. In the scramble for Lenin's succession, Josef Stalin took over the leadership, and Trotsky was exiled from the Soviet Union in 1929. After living for periods in Turkey, France, and Norway, he finally settled in Mexico, where he was axed to death by a Spanish communist.

Breton's and Trotsky's collaboration on the manifesto in this volume came when Breton visited Trotsky in Mexico in 1938. Breton had been inspired by Trotsky's biography of Lenin to write a review of the book in La révolution surréaliste in 1925; in the review he *extolled communism as the sole means of providing the kind of revolution that would permit the spiritual revolution that Breton looked to for human emancipation. For Breton and the surrealists, Trotsky had become, especially after their disillusionment with communism, the figure most associated with the revolution of humanity and with the liberty of mind and spirit, in opposition to repressive fascist and communist regimes.*

Manifesto: Towards a Free Revolutionary Art

ANDRÉ BRETON AND LEON TROTSKY

We can say without exaggeration that never has civilization been menaced so seriously as today. The Vandals, with instruments that were barbarous, and so comparatively ineffective, blotted out the culture of antiquity in one corner of Europe. But today we see world civilization, united in its historic destiny, reeling under the blows of reactionary forces armed with the entire arsenal of modern technology. We are by no means thinking only of the world war that draws near. Even in times of "peace," the position of art and science has become absolutely intolerable.

Insofar as it originates with an individual, insofar as it brings into play subjective talents to create something which brings about an objective enriching of culture, any philosophical, sociological, scientific, or artistic discovery seems to be the fruit of a precious *chance*, that is to say, the manifestation, more or less spontaneous, of necessity. Such creations cannot be slighted, whether from the standpoint of general knowledge (which interprets the existing world), or of revolutionary knowledge (which, the better to change the world, requires an exact analysis of the laws which govern its movement). Specifically, we cannot remain indifferent to the intellectual conditions under which creative activity take place, nor should we fail to pay all respect to those particular laws which govern intellectual creation.

In the contemporary world we must recognize the ever more widespread destruction of those conditions under which intellectual creation is possible. From this follows of necessity an increasingly manifest degradation not only of the work of art but also of the specifically "artistic" personality. The regime of Hitler, now that it has rid Germany of all those artists whose work expressed the slightest sympathy for liberty, however superficial, has reduced those who still consent to take up pen or brush to the status of domestic servants of the regime, whose task it is to glorify it on order, according to the worst possible aesthetic conventions. If reports may be believed, it is the same in the Soviet Union, where Thermidorean reaction is now reaching its climax.

It goes without saying that we do not identify ourselves with the currently fashionable catchword: "Neither fascism nor communism!" a shibboleth which suits the temperament of the Philistine, conservative and frightened, clinging to the tattered remnants of the "democratic" past. True art, which is not content to play variations on ready-made models but rather insists on expressing the inner needs of man and of mankind in its time—true art is unable *not* to be revolutionary, *not* to aspire to a complete and radical reconstruction of society. This it must do, were it only to deliver intellectual creation from the chains which bind it, and to allow all mankind to raise itself to those heights which only isolated geniuses have achieved in the past. We recognize that only the social revolution can sweep clear the path for a new culture. If, however, we reject all solidarity with the bureaucracy now in control of the Soviet Union, it is precisely because, in our eyes, it represents not communism but its most treacherous and dangerous enemy.

The totalitarian regime of the U.S.S.R., working through the so-called "cultural" organizations it controls in other countries, has spread over the entire world a deep twilight hostile to every sort of spiritual value. A twilight of filth and blood in which, disguised as intellectuals and artists, those men steep themselves who have made of servility a career, of lying for pay a custom, and of the palliation of crime a source of pleasure. The official art of Stalinism mirrors with a blatancy unexampled in history their efforts to put a good face on their mercenary profession.

The repugnance which this shameful negation of the principles of art inspires in the artistic world—a negation which even slave states have never dared carry so far—should give rise to an active, uncomprising condemnation. The *opposition* of writers and artists is one of the forces which can usefully contribute to the discrediting and overthrow of regimes which are destroying, along with the right of the proletariat to aspire to a better world, every sentiment of nobility and even of human dignity.

The communist revolution is not afraid of art. It realizes that the role of the artist in a decadent capitalist society is determined by the conflict between the individual and various social forms that are hostile to him. This fact alone, insofar as he is conscious of it, makes the artist the natural ally of revolution. The process of *sublimation*, which here comes into play, and which psychoanalysis has analyzed, tries to restore the broken equilibrium between the integral "ego" and the outside elements it rejects. This restoration works to the advantage of the "ideal of self," which marshals against the unbearable present reality all those powers of the interior world, of the "self," which are *common to all men* and which are constantly flowering and developing. The need for emancipation felt by the individual spirit has only to follow its natural course to be led to mingle its stream with this primeval necessity: the need for the emancipation of man.

The conception of the writer's function that the young Marx worked out is worth recalling. "The writer," he declared, "naturally must make money in order to live and write, but he should not under any circumstances live and write in order to make money. The writer by no means looks at his work as a *means*. It is an *end in itself* and so little a means in the eyes of himself and of others that if necessary he sacrifices his existence to the existence of his work. . . . *The first condition of the freedom of the press is that it is not a business activity.*" It is more than ever fitting to use this statement against those who would regiment intellectual activity in the direction of ends foreign to itself, and prescribe, in the guise of so-called "reasons of State," the themes of art. The free choice of these themes and the absence of all restrictions on the range of his explorations—these are possessions that the artist has a right to claim as inalienable. In the realm of artistic creation, the imagination must escape from all constraint and must, under no pretext, allow itself to be placed under bonds. To those who would urge us, whether for today or for tomorrow, to consent that art should submit to a discipline which we hold to be radically incompatible with its nature, we give a flat refusal, and we repeat our deliberate intention of standing by the formula: *complete freedom for art.*

We recognize, of course, that the revolutionary State has the right to defend itself against the counterattack of the bourgeoisie, even when this drapes itself in the flag of science or art. But there is an abyss between these enforced and temporary measures of revolutionary self-defense and the pretension to lay commands on intellectual creation. If, for the better development of the forces of material production, the revolution must build a *socialist* regime with centralized control, to develop intellectual creation an *anarchist* regime of individual liberty should from the first be established. No authority, no dictation, not the least trace of orders from above! Only on a base of friendly cooperation, without the constraint from outside, will it be possible for scholars and artists to carry out their tasks, which will be more far-reaching than ever before in history.

It should be clear by now that in defending freedom of thought we have no intention of justifying political indifference, and that it is far from our wish to revive a so-called "pure" art which generally serves the extremely impure ends of reaction. No, our conception of the role of art is too high to refuse it an influence on the fate of society. We believe that the supreme task of art in our epoch is to take part actively and consciously in the preparation of the revolution. But the artist cannot serve the struggle for freedom unless he subjectively assimilates its social content, unless he feels in his very nerves its meaning and drama and freely seeks to give his own inner world incarnation in his art.

In the present period of the death agony of capitalism, democratic as well as fascist, the artist sees himself threatened with the loss of his right to live and continue working. He sees all avenues of communication choked with the debris of capitalist collapse. Only naturally, he turns to the Stalinist organizations, which hold out the possibility of escaping from his isolation. But if he is to avoid complete demoralization, he cannot remain there, because of the impossibility of delivering his own message and the degrading servility which these organizations exact from him in exchange for certain material advantages. He must understand that his place is elsewhere, not among those who with unshaken fidelity bear witness to this revolution, among those who, for this reason, are alone able to bring it to fruition, and along with it the ultimate free expression of all forms of human genius.

The aim of this appeal is to find a common ground on which may be reunited all revolutionary writers and artists, the better to serve the revolution by their art and to defend the liberty of that art itself against the usurpers of the revolution. We believe that aesthetic, philosophical, and political tendencies of the most varied sort can find here a common ground. Marxists can march here hand in hand with anarchists, provided both parties uncompromisingly reject the reactionary police-patrol spirit represented by Joseph Stalin and by his henchman, Garcia Oliver.

We know very well that thousands on thousands of isolated thinkers and artists are today scattered throughout the world, their voices drowned out by the loud choruses of well-disciplined liars. Hundreds of small local magazines are trying to gather youthful forces about them, seeking new paths and not subsidies. Every progressive tendency in art is destroyed by fascism as "degenerate." Every free creation is called "fascist" by the Stalinists. Independent revolutionary art must now gather its forces for the struggle against revolutionary persecution. It must proclaim aloud its right to exist. Such a union of forces is the aim of the *International Federation of Independent Revolutionary Art* that we believe it is now necessary to form.

We by no means insist on every idea put forth in this manifesto, which we ourselves consider only a first step in the new direction. We urge every friend and defender of art, who cannot but realize the necessity for this appeal, to make himself heard at once. We address the same appeal to all those publications of the left-wing which are ready to participate in the creation of the International Federation and to consider its task and its methods of action.

When a preliminary international contract has been established through the press and by correspondence, we will proceed to the organization of local and national congresses on a modest scale. The final step will be the assembling of a world congress that will officially mark the foundation of the International Federation.

Our aims:

The independence of art—for the revolution;

The revolution—for the complete liberation of art!

An Australian-born symbolic anthropologist who also pursues work in performance theory, Michael Taussig is a prolific, impressive, and influential postcolonial theorist who writes with passion, sometimes bordering on obsessiveness. His formative field-work in South America led to his first major monograph, The Devil and Commodity Fetishism in South America *(1980). Invoking both Walter Benjamin and Karl Marx to speak on behalf of the plantation workers and miners of South America (to whom the book is dedicated), Taussig demonstrates how the symbolic representation of goods, or commodity fetishism, is an unstable ploy of capitalism that can have as its counter-point magical rites wherein either the Virgin Mary or the Devil or both can be invoked against the colonial captains of industry, the exploiters of the native underclass who produce both wealth and magic.*

In subsequent works, such as Shamanism, Colonialism, and the Wild Man: A Study in Terror and Healing *(1987),* The Nervous System *(1992), and* The Magic of the State *(1997), Taussig attempts to show how shock or surprise can destabilize dominant myths, creating new memories that channel opposition to the existing order. As he notes in* The Nervous System, *his project is "to radically rethink what it means to take an example or use some new symbolic theories or systems while also trying to remain 'nervous' about them, hoping to undermine the lust for order that provokes us all, including down under symbolic anthropologists of the post-colonial disorder."*

Shamanism, Colonialism, and the Wild Man:
A Study in Terror and Healing
MICHAEL TAUSSIG

THE IMAGE OF THE AUCA

Cast as an ethnographic and geographical report, Robuchon's book has been compiled and edited by the able hand of one of Arana's closest associates, Carlos Rey de Castro, the Peruvian consul of Manaos, the foremost port during the Amazon rubber boom. His ingenuity was equal to the task. In his own work, *Los pobladores del Putumayo*, he set out to further Peruvian (and hence Arana's) claims to the disputed stretches of the Putumayo and its indigenous inhabitants by claiming the latter as descendants of the *orejones* of the sacred Incan capital of

Cuzco, far away in the Andean mountains (Casement argued a similar case in his beautiful and moving article for *The Contemporary Review* in which he depicted the Indians as in but not of the forest). But that was not all. In 1909 Rey de Castro tried to wheedle maps and notes out of Captain Whiffen when they met in Manaos in the presence of Julio César Arana.

Whiffen was on his way back to England where reports were flying that the company was up to no good. "I showed him the notes and my draft maps," Whiffen informed the Select Committee on Putumayo. "He was very interested in it all. He informed me that he had edited Robuchon's book on the country in question, and that he would like to have my notes in hand, to treat in the same way as he treated Robuchon's notes."

A few months later Arana met with Whiffen in Paris at the Nouvelle Hôtel where they had lunch. Arana asked him his opinions about Hardenburg's revelations of atrocities in *Truth*. He was anxious to know if Whiffen had been approached by *Truth* in order to provide further condemnation. Two weeks later they dined at the Café Royal in London, on which occasion Whiffen informed Arana that he had to prepare a report for the Foreign Office. They drank champagne all evening. Arana suggested they stop off at the Motor Club. The next morning Whiffen's recollection was none too clear. It seemed that Arana had asked him how much money he would require to write a report for the Peruvian government. Whiffen told him his expenses had been £1,400 and started to copy down what Arana dictated to him. It was in Spanish and Whiffen's Spanish, he later admitted under cross-examination by the Select Committee, was very poor. When Arana asked for the paper Whiffen got suspicious and tore it up. "I thought he had laid some trap for me," he told the Select Committee. They were still drinking champagne.

Later on in Arana's letter to the shareholders of the Peruvian Amazon Company this written statement of Whiffen's appeared in English. Someone got hold of the pieces and stuck them together, a collage of the original. The words "one thousand pounds" were stuck in the wrong place. The Spanish pronoun *mis* was missing from one page and placed on another. It was grotesque. It was banal. Whiffen was supposed to have written that he was willing to write a report for the Peruvian government saying he had *not* seen any irregularities in the Putumayo.

Certainly his book, which came out a little later, contained no mention of ill-treatment of Indians by the rubber company—although there was a deep brooding, malevolent tone throughout, the tone of the primal, the forest ill at ease. "My expenses were £1,400," ended his note. "But I am agreeable and will receive £1,000 as compensation—nothing else." And the last two words appeared forged, presumably by Arana or at his bidding.

It was from such dexterous hands that Eugenio Robuchon's Putumayan notes and photographs emerged in book form—no less than 20,000 copies of which, so it was said, were printed by Arana in Lima in 1907. And it was from this book that Casement extracted the notion of the *chupe del tabaco* as a ritual in which the Indians formulated terrible vows of vengeance against the whites— the same ritual that the whites were said to have used to bind Indians to debt-peonage and to the collection of rubber.

Doubtless many different fingers could be stuck into the tobacco pot and sucked. Many were the orations it facilitated. The one about itself, now that the white man has been added to the circle, is still going on.

It was Don Crisóstomo Hernández who wrought to perfection the colonial meta-ritual of the *chupe*, or rather, as in so many things about the Putumayo rubber boom, it was the story about Don Crisóstomo that was so perfect in this regard, the story about his stories—which were so compelling that, for the assemblies of Huitoto captains sitting with him, orating around the tobacco pot, there was nought else to do but unanimously agree to his proposals.

Moreover, stories about the *chupe del tabaco* could be as mystically powerful as those related around it; in particular the story related by Rocha that brought the *chupe* into the very center of the charmed circle of cannibalism itself. Wildly extravagant and melodramatic, it certainly rings true, not necessarily regarding the cannibalism in question but regarding the poetics of fear and astonishment that I know from listening to colonists swapping yarns of the forest and its people. My mind goes back, for instance, to a night I spent in 1978 in a tiny store by the Rió San Miguel, an affluent of the Putumayo and maybe 150 miles upstream from where Rocha was absorbed in his tales of terror while the slow chit-chat of frogs croaking entranced the jungle night. Where I was, so many years later, the hardened men of the forest talked to each other for hours of stories they had heard about being lost in the forest, stories of its dangerous animals and its fearsome spirits such as the *espanta*, with her hair down to the ground and her long white breasts, a spirit so frightening that, on seeing her, all consciousness is lost. But never in all my nights with Indians in the foothills did I hear or overhear stories like these, spun with such fiendish and melodramatic aesthetic pleasure derived from fear and mystery.

Traven wrote in *The March to the Monteria* about a Chamula Indian from the highlands of Chiapas, Mexico, who went down into the jungle, the first step to enslavement as a lumberjack in debt-peonage in the mahogany industry. "All along the way the People he consulted told him the most terrifying stories about the jungle," wrote Traven.

These people, however, had never been in the jungle themselves; they had not even approached the thicket at the outer edges. All of them re-counted merely what others had seen or lived through.

But the various stories related to Celso all contributed, without exception, to inspire in him a terrific fear of the vast jungle. Nobody really cared whether Celso perished in the jungle or not. The narrations were made mostly to enjoy the changing expressions of an interested listener, to pass the time away, and to get excited over one's story. Ghost stories, tales of spooks, are not told at night to make someone desist from crossing the cemetery if that is his road home. They are told to spend a pleasant evening by watching with delight the terror-stricken faces of one's audience.

Now a march through the jungle is by no means a holiday hike. The facts came very close to the terrifying narrations of its terrors. . . .

Such is Traven's story. And he, too, went down into the mahogany forests. Joaquin Rocha tells us, presumably as he was told, that

all the individuals of the nation that has captured the prisoner retire to an area of the bush to which women are absolutely prohibited, except one who acts a special role. Children are also rigorously excluded. In the center, a pot of cooked tobacco juice is placed for the pleasure of the men, and in a corner seated on a little bench and firmly bound is the captive.

Clasping each others' arms, the savages form a long line, and to the sound of drums advance dancing very close to the victim. They retreat and advance many times, with individuals separating to drink from the pot of tobacco. Then the drum stops for the dancing cannibals, and so that the unfortunate victim can see how much he is going to lose by dying, the most beautiful girl of the tribe enters, regally attired with the most varied and brilliant feathers of the birds of these woods. The drum starts again, and the beautiful girl dances alone in front of and almost touching him. She twists and advances, showering him with passionate looks and ges-tures of love, turning around and repeating this three or four times. She then leaves, terminating the second act of this solemn occasion. The third act follows with the same men's dance as before, except that each time the line of dancers approaches the prisoner, one of the men detaches himself and declaims something like this: "Remember when your people killed Jatijiko, man of our nation whom you couldn't take prisoner because he knew how to die before allowing himself to be dragged in front of your people? We are going to take vengeance of his death in you, you coward, who doesn't know how to die in battle like he did." Or else: "Remember when you and your people surprised my sister Jifisino bathing, captured her and while alive made a party of her flesh and tormented her until her last breath? Do you remember? Now you god-cursed man we are going to devour you alive and you won't die until all traces of your bloody flesh have disappeared from our mouths."

Following this is the fourth and last act of the terrifying tragedy. One by one the dancers come forward, and with his knife each one cuts a slice of meat off the prisoner, which they eat half roasted to the sound of his death rattle. When he eventually dies, they finish cutting him up and continue roasting and cooking his flesh, eating him to the last little bit.

NARRATIVE MEDIATION: EPISTEMIC MURK

It seems to me that stories like these were indispensable to the formation and flowering of the colonial imagination during the Putumayo rubber boom. "Their imagination was diseased," wrote the Peruvian judge Rómulo Paredes in 1911, referring to the rubber station employees about and from whom he obtained 3,000 handwritten pages of testimony after four months in the forest, "and they saw everywhere attacks by Indians, conspiracies, uprisings, treachery etc.; and in order to save themselves from these fancied perils . . . they killed, and killed without compassion."

Far from being trivial daydreams indulged in after work was over, these stories and the imagination they sustained were a potent political force without which the work of conquest and of supervising rubber gathering could not have been accomplished. What is crucial to understand is the way these stories functioned to create through magical realism a culture of terror that dominated both whites and Indians.

The importance of this colonial work of fabulation extends beyond the nightmarish quality of its contents. Its truly crucial feature lies in the way it creates an uncertain reality out of fiction, giving shape and voice to the formless form of the reality in which an unstable interplay of truth and illusion becomes a phantasmic social force. All societies live by fiction taken as real. What distinguishes cultures of terror is that the epistemological, ontological, and otherwise philosophical problem of representation—reality and illusion, certainty and doubt—becomes infinitely more than a "merely" philosophical problem of epistemology, hermeneutics, and deconstruction. It becomes a high-powered medium of domination, and during the Putumayo rubber boom this medium of epistemic and ontological murk was most keenly figured and thrust into consciousness as the space of death.

The managers lived obsessed with death, Rómulo Paredes tells us. They saw danger everywhere. They thought solely of the fact that they lived surrounded by vipers, tigers, and cannibals. It was these ideas of death, he wrote, that constantly struck their imagination, making them terrified and capable of any action. Like children they had nightmares of witches, evil spirits, death, treason, and blood. The only way they could live in such a terrifying world, he observed, was to inspire terror themselves.

SOCIOLOGICAL AND MYTHIC MEDIATION: THE MUCHACHOS

If it was the telling of tales that mediate this inspiration of terror, then it behooves us to inquire a little into the group of people who mediated this mediation; namely, the corps of Indian guards trained by the company and known as the *muchachos de confianza*, the "trusted boys." For in Rómulo Paredes's words, they were "constantly devising executions and continually revealing meetings of Indians 'licking tobacco' [the *chupe*]—which meant an oath to kill white men—imaginary uprisings that never existed, and other similar crimes." What is at stake here is in many ways the linchpin of the company's control, namely, the typical colonial ploy of using indigenous culture in order to exploit it. But, of course, things are never quite so simple. Even the manipulators have a culture and, moreover, culture is not so easily "used."

Mediating as semicivilized and semirational Indians between the savages of the forest and the whites of the rubber camps, the *muchachos* embodied the salient differences of the class and caste system in the rubber boom. Cut off from their own kind, whom they persecuted and betrayed and in whom they often inspired envy and hatred, and now classified as semicivilized and dependent on the whites for food, arms, and goods, the *muchachos* typified all that was savage in the colonial mythology of savagery—because they were in the perfect social and mystic space to do so. Not only did they embellish fictions that stoked the fires of white paranoia, they also embodied the brutality that the whites feared, created, and tried to harness to their own ends. The *muchachos* traded their colonially created identity as savages for their new colonial status as civilized Indians and guards. As Paredes noted, they placed at the disposal of the whites "their special instincts, such as sense of direction, scent, their sobriety, and their knowledge of the forest." Just as they brought rubber from the wild Indians of the forest, so the whites also brought the *auca*-like savage "instincts" of the Indian *muchachos*.

Yet, unlike rubber, these savage instincts were manufactured from the whites' imaginations. All the *muchachos* had to do to receive their rewards was to objectify and through stories give back to the whites the phantoms lying dormant in colonial culture. Given the centuries of Incan and Spanish colonial mythology concerning the *auca* and the wild man, and given the implosion of this mythology in the contradictory social being of the *muchachos*, this was a simple task. The *muchachos'* stories were but fragments of a more encompassing one that constituted them as objects in a colonial discourse rather than its authors.

The debt-peonage established by the Putumayo rubber boom was more than a trade in white commodities for india rubber. It was also a trade in fictitious realities, pivoted on the *muchachos* whose storytelling bartered betrayal of Indian realities for the confirmation of colonial fantasies.

THE "ILLIMITABLE DELIRIUM"

Joaquin Rocha's man-eating tale ends not with the death of the prisoner but with his being eaten "to the last little bit," ingesting him so as to incorporate his strength and augment one's war magic, as Konrad Preuss wrote was the case with Huitoto cannibalism, or to degrade him, as Captain Whiffen was told. If the torture practiced by modern states, as in Latin America today, is any guide, these motives by no means preclude one another. Nor does proof of these frequently disputed contentions necessarily lie in the eating. For now, as Captain Whiffen writes, "when the orgy of blood and gluttony is over, the warriors must *dance*"—and do so for eight days to what he describes as the gloomy rolling of drums, breaking off every now and again from the dance to stir great troughs of liquid with the forearms of dead enemies. With intoxication, the captain tells us, their songs become shrieks, demoniacal and hellish. "But the scene defies description," he notes with humility, and with wisdom, too, for tucked eighty pages away in the quiet eddy of a footnote he mentions that "I never was present at a cannibal feast. The information comes from Robuchon's account, checked by cross-questioning the Indians with whom I came in contact."

"It is," he nevertheless goes on to write in the mainstream of his narrative, "a mad festival of savagery."

> The naked men are wildly excited; their eyes glare, their nostrils quiver, but they are not drunk. The naked women abandon themselves to the movement of the dance; they scream their chorus to the tribal dance-song; but they are not lewd. There is about it an all-pervading illimitable delirium. The wild outburst affects even the stranger in their midst. Forgotten cells in his brain react to the stimulus of the scene. He is no longer apart, alien in speech and feeling. He locks arms in the line of cannibals, sways in rhythm with them, stamps as solemnly, and sings the meaningless words as fervently as the best of them. He has bridged an age of civilization, and returned to barbarism in the debased jetsam of the riverbanks. It is the strange fascination of the Amazons.

And in that other rubber belt of King Leopold's Congo, toiling slowly upstream "on the edge of a black and incomprehensible frenzy" a dozen years before Captain Whiffen was locking arms, swaying with cannibals, entering the delirium, returning to barbarism, another Englishman, Joseph Conrad's storyteller, the sailor Marlow, also bridged an age, if not the very genesis, of civilization: "they howled and leaped, and spun, and made horrid faces; but what thrilled you was just the thought of their humanity—like yours—the thought of your remote kinship with this wild and passionate uproar."

> "And you say you saw the Indians burnt?" the consul-general asked Augustus Walcott, who had been born in the Caribbean island of Antigua twenty-three years before.
> "Yes."
> "Burnt alive?"
> "Alive."
> "How do you mean? Describe this?"
> "Only one I see burnt alive."
> "Well, tell me about that one."
> "He had no work, 'caucho,' he ran away and he kill a 'muchacho,' a boy, and they cut off his two arms and his legs by the knee and they burn his body . . . they drag the body and they put plenty of wood and set fire to it, and throw the man on it."
> "Are you sure he was still alive—not dead when they threw him on the fires?
> "Yes, he did live. I'm sure of it—I see him move—open his eyes, he screamed out."

There was something else that the consul-general could not understand, and he called Walcott back to explain what he meant by saying "because he told the Indians that we was Indians too, and eat those—." What he meant was that the rubber station manager, Señor Normand, "to frighten the Indians told them that the negroes were cannibals, and a fierce tribe of cannibals who eat people, and that if they did not bring in rubber these black men would be sent to kill and eat them." "This is what he meant to say," added Casement. "Señor Normand had so described the Barbados men on bringing them among the Andokes Indians, in order to terrify the Indians."

James Mapp (who said that he, unlike other people, never saw or heard of Señor Aguero killing Indians for food for his dogs) told the consul-general he had seen Hilary Quales bite pieces out of four Indians. They were hanging with their arms twisted behind their backs for about three hours and Quales was playing with them, swinging them by the legs with Aguero, the station manager, looking on. He bit the little toe off one man and spat it on the floor. He bit the others in the calves and thighs. Aguero was laughing.

"Have you seen Aguero kill Indians?" the consul-general asked Evelyn Batson in the rubber collecting depot of La Chorrera.

"No, Sir; I haven't seen him kill Indians—but I have seen him send *muchachos* to kill Indians. He has taken an Indian man and given him to the *muchachos* to eat, and they have a dance off it."

"Did you see that?"

"Yes, Sir; I seen that."

"You saw the man killed?"

"Yes, Sir. They tied him to a stake and they shot him, and they cut off his head after he was shot and his feet and hands, and they carried him about in the section—in the yard—and they carries them up and down singing, and they carries them to their houses and dances. . . . They carries off the pieces of him, and they pass in front of the manager's house with these—his feet and his arms and his head, and they took them to their own house."

"How do you know they ate them?"

"I heard that they ate them. I have not witnessed it, sir, but I heard the manager Señor Aguero, tell that they ate this man."

"The manager said all this?"

"Yes, Sir, he did."

Katenere was a famous rebel chief whose wife was kidnapped by the rubber company. He tried to free her and was shot dead by the *muchachos* sent by Evelyn Batson.

"What did they do with the body of Katenere?" the consul-general asked Batson. "Did they bury it?"

"Yes, Sir. Zellada [the acting manager] cut his head off, and his feet and hands—they put these in the grave along with the body."

"Did they show these members to everyone in the station?"

"Yes, Sir; the head they put in the river til the manager come, that the manager could see it."

Katenere had escaped from gathering rubber. He captured weapons and shot dead Arana's brother-in-law. He was counted, says Casement, "a brave man and a terror to the Peruvian rubber-workers." Imagined terror made men do terrible things, as Judge Rómulo Paredes observed. In hunting down Katenere, the display was spectacular and—as with the dismembering of his body—it was focused on the head. James Chase was on one of these hunts, and the consul-general summarized what he said about it.

At the next house they reached they caught four Indians, one woman and three men. Vasquez, who was in charge, ordered one of the *muchachos* to cut this woman's head off. He ordered this for no apparent reason that James Chase knows of, simply because "he was in command, and could do what he liked." The *muchacho* cut the woman's head off; he held her by the hair of her head, and flinging her down, hacked her head off with a machete. It took more than one blow to sever the head—three or four blows.

Her remains were left on the path, as were the severed heads and truncated bodies of other people caught in this raid; Kateners's child, decapitated for crying, and a woman, an adolescent boy, and three adult men—all for walking too slowly. The company men were walking very fast because they were a bit frightened thinking of the Indians pursuing them.

In assuming the character of the cannibals who pursued them, as much if not more in their fantasies than when they were pursuing Indians to gather rubber, the whites seemed oblivious to the tale that the Indians would *not* eat them. At least that's what Casement and Judge Paredes were separately informed. A rubber gatherer familiar for many years with the Huitotos and their language told the judge that the Indians felt repugnance toward the civilized, whom they called the *gemuy comuine*, kinsmen of the monkey, whose nauseating smell precluded their being eaten, dead or alive. "The only case of cannibalism I became acquainted with during my mission in the Putumayo," avowed the judge, "was that ordered by the civilized themselves."

Perhaps it was their smell that made their orders to eat people that much more compelling? For in those stories recently heard by some anthropologists in the northernmost extremity of what was then Arana's territory, it is said by Indians that the whites in the rubber company were immune to Indian sorcery. It could not enter them because they, the whites, smelled so bad. That was why the legendary revolt of Yarocamena failed. At least that's what some say. But the interpreting of such things is perhaps better left alone. For these Histories of Punishment and the Danger are for sorcerers only. Indeed, so I've been told, it's from the interpreting of such stories that sorcerers gain their evil power.

THE COLONIAL MIRROR OF PRODUCTION

The yarns of seamen have a direct simplicity, the whole meaning of which lies within the shell of a cracked nut. But Marlow was not typical (if his propensity to spin yarns be excepted), and to him the meaning of an episode was not inside like a kernel but outside, enveloping the tale which brought it out only as a glow brings out a haze, in the likeness of one of those misty halos that sometimes are made visible by the spectral illumination of moonshine.

I hope by now it is obvious why I chose what may have seemed a strange point of departure—the mediation of terror through narration, and the problem that raises for effective counter-representations. I hope it will later also be obvious why I have to push on to work through the ways that shamanic healing in the *upper* reaches of the Putumayo, like the culture of terror, also develops its force from the colonially generated wildness of the epistemic murk of the space of death.

What began for me as a seaman's yarn aimed at cracking open the shell of other seamen's yarns to reveal their meaning—the tales of Rocha, Whiffen, Hardenburg, Casement, and so on, and the yarns their yarns were based upon—ended up like Marlow's, whose meaning lay outside, enveloping the tale that brought it out as a glow brings out a haze. Meaning was elusive. Doubt played havoc with certainty. Perspectives were as varied as they were destructive of one another. The real was fictional and the fictional was real and the haziness brought out by the glow could be as powerful a force for terror as it could be for resistance. In such a world of control, clarity itself was deceptive, and attempts to explain the terror could barely be distinguished from the stories contained in those explanations—as if terror provided only inexplicable explanations of itself and thrived by so doing.

For me the problem of interpretation grew ever larger until I realized that this problem of interpretation is decisive for terror, not only making effective counterdiscourse so difficult but also making the terribleness of death squads, disappearances, and torture all the more effective in crippling of peoples' capacity to resist. The problem of interpretation turned out to be an essential component of what had to be interpreted, just as resistance was necessary for control. Deeply dependent on sense and interpretation, terror nourished itself by destroying sense. This the Putumayo texts about terror faithfully reproduced.

Particularly wanting in this regard was the hard-bitten appeal to the logic of business, to the rationality of market logic, viewing the terror as a means chosen for cost-effectiveness. In making sense this view heightened the situation's hallucinatory quality. Cost-effectiveness and "scarcity" could be computed any which way, and if rationality suggested killing off the labor supply within a few years it was no less a sport to kill and torture Indians as to work them. Ostensibly a means of increasing production, the torture of Indians was also an end in itself and the region's most enduring product. In these outposts of progress the commodity fetishism portrayed by Karl Marx acquired a form that was both fantastic and brutal. Here, where labor was not free or capable of being turned into a commodity, it was not merely rubber and European trade goods that were subject to fetishization. More important still was the fetishization of the debt of debt-peonage that these commodities constellated and in which the entire imaginative force, the ritualization and viciousness, of colonial society was concentrated. A gigantic piece of make-believe, the debt was where the gift economy of the Indian meshed with the capitalist economy of the colonist. It was here in this strategically undetermined zone of exchange where the line between war and peace is always so fine that the conditions were laid for an enormity of effort no less imaginative than it was cruel and deadly. Indeed, it was in the cultural elaboration of death and the death-space that the fine line between peace and war was maintained. They see death everywhere, wrote the Peruvian judge Rómulo Paredes, in speaking of the rubber company employees. They think solely of the fact that they live surrounded by vipers, tigers, and cannibals. Their imaginations are constantly struck by the idea of death as figured by these images of the wild and the only way they could live in such a world, he thought, after his tour through the area, was by themselves inspiring terror.

> The shrill voices of those who give orders
> Are full of fear like the squeaking of
> Piglets awaiting the butcher's knife, as their fat arses
> Sweat with anxiety in their office chairs. . . .
> Fear rules not only those who are ruled, but
> The rulers too.

Thus wrote Brecht in exile in 1937, pondering a companion's response after a visit to the Third Reich, who, when asked what really ruled there, answered, Fear. Given the immense power of the regime, its camps and torture cellars, its well-fed policemen, Brecht asked, why do they fear the open world?

In modern times this culture of terror depends upon primitivism, and the revolutionary poet will appeal to the magic of primitiveness to undermine it too.

> But their Third Reich recalls
> The House of Tar, the Assyrian, that mighty fortress
> Which according to the legend, could not be taken by an army, but
> When one single distinct word was spoken inside it
> Fell to dust.

And if there was anything to that notion of Benjamin's and T. W. Adorno's concerning the resurgence of primitivism along with the fetishism of commodities (think for a moment of Adam Smith's invisible hand as the modern version of animism), then it was in the theater of racist cruelty on the frontier uniting wildness with civilization that the fetish force of the commodity was fused with the phantoms of the space of death, to the dazzling benefit of both. I am thinking here not of steady incremental steps toward progress but of sudden eruptions of whitening the dark zones at the margins of the developing nations where the commodity met the Indian and appropriated through death the fetish power of the savagery created by the spellbinding of the European. Here the Putumayo is but a figure for a global stage of development of the commodity fetish; think also of the Congo with its rubber and ivory, of the enslavement of the Yaquis for the sisal plantations of the Yucatan in Mexico, of the genocidal bloodletting in tragic Patagonia—all around the same time.

The new science of anthropology was no less a manifestation of the modernist fascination with the primitive, and in this it was in tandem with the new artistry: Flaubert's realism and the sensual exoticism of his Egypt/Carthage, Rimbaud's season in hell where the pagan blood returns and the disordered mind becomes sacred, Yeats's sixteenth-century Moorish anti-self ("this is our modern hope"), Conrad's modernizing heart of darkness, Richard Huelsenbeck beating "negro rhythms" for Dada evenings in the Cabaret, Voltaire in Zurich at the time of World War I (we were like birds in a cage surrounded by lions, said Hugo Ball), Apollinaire's Paris evening turning to dawn:

> You walk toward Auteuil, you walk home on foot
> To sleep among your fetishes from Oceanic and Guinea
> They are all Christ in another form and of another faith . . .

And if Casement slept with his fetishes "colored like the very tree-trunks they fitted among like spirits of the woods" in a dreamy world that pictured Huitotos and all upper Amazonian Indians as naturally gentle and docile, Captain Whiffen could write an entire book under the spell of a nature that displayed its human inhabitants as well as its animal and plant life as innately wild and vengeful, nasty and thrillingly so. Against these views the inland mariner Alfred Simon portrayed the primitive as that plenitude of flitting shadowiness of possible anything betraying all the opposite traits of character (except, perhaps, servility) that not only constituted the wild Indian but also constituted the misty essence of wildness on which terror seized. If the commodity fetishism of Marx meant a wild oscillation between things and phantoms, then these figures of wildness caught that relationship with a precision no less binding than the stocks with which the terror pinned down its object, only to watch it writhe and die.

Of course there was some safety in numbers, even though they were diminishing. Rocha quoted anonymous authority in putting the number of Huitotos at a quarter a million. Others gave other figures and there was a magical number of thirty thousand Huitotos dead or fled between 1900 and 1910—numbers that were wild guesses but unacknowledged as such. Proffered the reader as implicit signs of control and order, gestures of expertise in tricky terrain, these numbers oozed epistemic tranquility as the measure of horror and provided a stolid ambience of reality, a back-stiffening jolt of certainty, awful as it might be, before steaming into the hermeneutic swamp of Putumayo terror and its explanation.

Casement said that if offered decent terms of trade the Indians would work rubber without torture, while Barbadian overseers, Rocha, and the U.S. consul of Iquitos were not all that sure. They doubted you could get an Indian to work intensively for long in any "system," just as Casement himself had said earlier when he was responsible for getting work done by indigenous people in the Congo. It was an intangible, teasing, and even deadly issue—work motivation and the evaluation of the worth and meaning of trade goods for forest people. It was the central problem involved in the industrialization of Europe, too; a compacted nugget of the history of civilization that lay at the very heart of the debt-peonage relationship and the meaning of its torture. It is not the sort of thing that is going to run away with an explanation, either then or now.

An unacknowledged uncertainty also constituted the morass of ideas, images, hunches, and feelings about the likelihood of an Indian uprising. Against the views of some of the overseers, Casement confidently and lucidly asserted that revolt was unlikely for this, that, and the other socio-logical reasons. Yet in other places in his report he provided ample signs of its occurrence. Joaquin Rocha's book likewise created an unacknowledged medley of possibilities, at one point asserting that the whites had nothing to fear while at another saying their lives hung by a thread. Reasoning confounded itself in this situation. The search for law and order led to unacknowledged disorder. The blithe confidence of tone in the reports totally belied the uncertainty of their contents wherein the politically crucial feature of the situation was the way the standoff between terror and uncertainty created more of the same.

"The Phraseology of Conquest" was one of the subheadings in the introduction of the published account of the hearings held by the British Parliamentary Select Committee on Putumayo. The Committee members were perplexed as they sifted the sands of contrary meanings and plots associated with the words *conquistar* and *reducir*, conquest and reduce. In addition to the effort to bring an Englishman's words to bear on a sly Latin like Julio César Arana, who equated conquest with doing business and cannibalism with a distaste for trading, the Select Committee had before it wildly different versions of the history of conquest—a notably mythological subject in its authority and appeal as was nicely brought out when a letter from the British consul of Iquitos, read to the baffled Committee, explained that the conquest of the Indians of Peru was like the conquest of Britain by Romans. On the one hand the Committee was presented with a picture of the conquest of the Putumayo as opening with death and destruction and closing with meek submission and trading. On the other hand was Casement's history of smooth-talking, seductive traders who used Western commodities to woo the Indians, "grown-up children," into an act of colonial pederasty and then into the bonds of slavery—for some reason not called slavery but dissimulated as "debt-peonage."

The source of the Committee's perplexity with "The Phraseology of Conquest" did not simply lie in habits of legal nitpicking or the inevitable methodological problem for anthropology of translating one culture's forms into another's. Beyond those considerations was the active social role played by perplexity with which Joaquin Rocha observed the "deforming of good speech" and the failure to observe "the propriety" of terms. Yet on it went, day in and day out, a deformation of this, a failure of that, disorder writ large in the elusive opacity of social institutions that juggled floggings with ritualized displays of double-entry bookkeeping, and gift-giving rituals of exchange with no less ritualized practices of business—parodies of capitalist theatricality on the equatorial line. Were the rubber gatherers traders or slaves or debts? Could a person be a debt? Why were the "payments"—or were they "advances"?—forced onto Indians ("I want a black dog!")? Why was there so much cruelty?

There is an image swimming into focus here, an image of the Indian in the stocks. The stocks hold the body tight, at least its head and its arms. Perhaps the rubber station manager and his employees are watching from the veranda. They are, so it has been said, the jaguars and the thunder of commodities. Perhaps some of them are wondering when their turn will come to be fixed in the stocks. But for the moment the jaguar and the thunder are free. It is the Indian who is fixed tight. Yet all around in the forest nothing is fixed. The rain is beating. The water drips off the shining leaves in the dark forest. Rivulets form into streams and rivers gather force to form the muddy Amazon swirling past the Italian marble and Polish prostitutes of rubber-rich Manaos where Arana and Rey de Castro tried to bribe Whiffen for his ethnological notes and photographs. He accepts. He doesn't accept. Onward swirls the river to the sea close by where Columbus's boats met the heaving chop of the currents on the Orinoco, one of the four rivers of Paradise, onward to New York and to Europe where Whiffen gets drunk on champagne, signs a note declaring the Putumayo a paradise and then tears it to pieces. But the note is pieced together, disjointedly as it turns out, like the collages mocking representation with presentation that the Cubists were inventing to replace visual illusion by mental illusion, not far from the hotel where Arana and Whiffen were lunching, after which Whiffen wrote his book without a mention of the torture and killing of the Indians he studied. He may as well not have ripped the note into pieces, over in Europe where everything is fixed and nothing is fixed and where a British Parliamentary Select Committee is trying to get to the bottom of "The Phraseology of Conquest." Little makes sense. Little can be pinned down, only the Indian in the stocks being watched. And we are watching the watched so that with our explanation we can pin them down and then pin down the real meaning of terror, putting it in the stocks of explanation. Yet in watching in this way we are made blind to the way that terror makes mockery of sense-making, how it requires sense in order to mock it, and how in that mockery it heightens both sense and sensation.

If terror thrives on the production of epistemic murk and metamorphosis, it nevertheless requires the hermeneutic violence that creates feeble fictions in the guise of realism, objectivity, and the like, flattening contradiction and systematizing chaos. The image of the Putumayo here is not so much the smoothly vicious horror of the vortex, which is the title of Eustacio Rivera's novel of Putumayo rubber and savagery, but rather the world frozen in death-dealing, as (in the story) when Don Crisóstomo, who held savages spellbound with the magic of his oratory, grasped for his gun in the frenzy of his death throes so as to die killing—the ultimate *tableau vivant*.

Here time stood still in the endless movement between banality and melodrama reproducing the terror represented. In Casement's rendition the Barbadian overseers' testimony comes across as emotionless and unamazing—zombies adrift in a dream world, we did this, then we did that—so different in its distanced remoteness from the histrionic testimony published by Hardenburg which included much material from Iquitos newspapers.

In both modes of representation, the banal and the melodramatic, there is the straining to express the inexpressible, what at one stage is the struggle on the stage of Putumayan truth was dismissed as "fantastic credibility." Fantastic it was; its very credibility made it so, went the retort—pointing to both magical (fantastic) realism (credibility) and to Brecht's *Verfremdungseffekt*, his "alienation effect" aimed at the alienating alienation, making the everyday strange and the credible fantastic. Perhaps either of these modes of representation, the magically real or the Brechtian, would have succeeded better in transmitting and transforming the hallucinatory reality of Putumayo terror than Casement's Foreign Office's authoritarian realism of Hardenburg's lavish melodrama. But it was the latter two forms that were selected out by the political culture for the task at hand; they were deemed truth, factual, reportage, nonfictional, and as such they may have achieved much. We will never really know.

But the question remains whether the banality and the melodrama were only part of the act of representing or whether they were in the events represented. We shake ourselves clear. We insist on the distinction between reality and depictions of it. But the disturbing thing is that the reality seeped through the pores of the depiction and by means of such seepage continued what such depictions were meant only to be about.

So it was with the stories circulating during the Putumayo rubber boom in which the colonists and rubber company employees not only feared themselves but created through narration fearful and confusing images of savagery, images that bound colonial society together through the epistemic murk of the space of death. The terror and tortures they devised mirrored the horror of the savagery they both feared and fictionalized.

Moreover, when we turn to the task of creating counterrepresentations and counterdiscourses—deflectional, oppositional modes of arresting and diverting the flow of fear—we need to pause and take stock of the ways that the accounts reproduced by Hardenburg and by Casement, accounts that were critical in intention, were similarly fictionalized and aestheticized, drawing upon and fortifying the very same rituals of the colonizing imagination to which men succumbed when torturing Indians. In their imaginative heart these critiques were complicit with what they opposed.

From the accounts of Casement and Timerman it is also obvious that torture and terror are ritualized art forms and that, far from being spontaneous, sui generis, and an abandonment of what are often called the values of civilization, such rites of terror have a deep history deriving power and meaning from those very values.

In Whiffen's case the sensuous interpenetration of opposites is orgiastically enshrined, as when he writes of succumbing to the illimitable delirium of savagery in the cannibal dance, against which he defines civilization. Father Gaspar, the Capuchin missionary, likewise finds holiness vividly wrought where it confronts the signs of the underworld as in the lugubrious crypts formed by the rotting tree trunks closing off the rivers and in the inhabitants of those crypts. On encountering what he called new and savage tribes in the forest his first act was to exorcize the demon who had held sway there for so long. The words of his exorcizing spell came from the pope. But where did his power come from? From God, or from the evil exorcized? His was a faith no less dependent on the anti-self than that of the most brutal *conquistador*.

What stands out here is the mimesis between the savagery attributed to the Indians by the colonists and the savagery perpetrated by the colonist in the name of what Julio César Arana called civilization, meaning business.

The magic of mimesis lies in the transformation wrought on reality by rendering its image. In a postmodern age we are increasingly familiar with this "magic" and no longer think of it as only "primitive." In the notion of the changes effected in the world by carving and dancing with the spirit's mask, in the naming and the singing of one's enemy, in weaving into the magical cloth the image of the wildness as *auca* so as to tease and gain control over it—in all of this we see clearly how the word "magic" magically contains both the art and the politics involved in representation, in the rendering of objecthood. In the colonial mode of production of reality, as in the Putumayo, such mimesis occurs by a colonial mirroring of otherness that reflects back onto the colonists the barbarity of their own social relations, but as imputed to the savagery they yearn to colonize. The power of this colonial mirror is ensured by the way it is diabolically constructed through storytelling, as in the colonial lore retold by Captain Whiffen, Joaquin Rocha, and Robuchon's ever-active ghost, among others, concerning cannibalism and the inevitability with which the wild strives to consume as well as to distinguish difference. And what is put into discourse through the artful storytelling of the colonists is the same as what they practiced on the bodies of Indians.

Tenaciously embedded in this artful practice is a vast and vastly mysterious Western history and iconography of evil exemplified by the imagery of the inferno and the savage, which in turn is indissolubly welded to images of paradise and the good. We hear the voice of Timerman, we see the torturer and the victim coming together. "We victims and victimizers," he writes, "we're part of the same humanity, colleagues in the same endeavor to prove the existence of ideologies, feelings, heroic deeds, religions, obsessions. And the rest of humanity, what are they engaged in?"

Post-Enlightenment European culture makes it difficult if not impossible to draw apart the veil of the heart of darkness without either succumbing to its hallucinatory quality or losing that quality. Fascist poetics succeed where liberal rationalism self-destructs. But what might point a way out of this impasse is precisely what is so painfully absent from the Putumayo accounts, namely the narrative mode of the Indians themselves. It is the ultimate anthropological conceit, anthropology in its highest, indeed redemptive, moment, rescuing the "voice" of the Indian from the obscurity of pain and time. From the represented shall come that which overturns the representation.

But this very same anthropology tells us that we cannot take our place in the charmed circle of men orating through the night around the tobacco pot, chewing coca. It is said that the stories about the rubber boom are dangerous, "histories of punishment" meant only for sorcerers who, in interpreting such histories, gain evil power. There is no place for us here, and anthropology, the science of man, confounds itself in its very moment of understanding the natives' point of view.

The lesson? Before there can be a science of man there has to be the long-awaited demythification and re-enchantment of Western man in a quite different confluence of self and otherness. Our way lies upstream, against the current, upriver near the foothills of the Andes where Indian healers are busy healing colonists of the phantoms assailing them. There in the jointness of their construction across the colonial divide the healer desensationalizes terror so that the mysterious side of the mysterious (to adopt Benjamin's formula) is indeed denied by an optic that perceives the everyday as impenetrable, the impenetrable as everyday. This is another history not only of terror, but of healing as well. (It is not meant for sorcerers, so far as I know.)

An artist and art historian, Kristine Stiles is internationally recognized for her work on
performance and experimental art, as well as her studies of destruction, violence, and
trauma in art. Having earned her doctorate in 1987 from the University of California,
Berkeley, she currently teaches in the department of art history at Duke University. She
is the co-author, with Peter Selz, of the highly acclaimed Theories and Documents of
Contemporary Art: A Sourcebook of Artists' Writings *(1996), and she is the author of*
three forthcoming books: Uncorrupted Joy: Art Actions, History, and Social Value,
Correspondence Course: Selected Letters of Carolee Schneemann, An Epistolary
History of Art and Culture, *and* Concerning Consequences: Manifestations of
Survival in Cultures of Trauma through Performance Art and Photography.

Her doctoral dissertation offered the first systematic examination of destruction
and violence in art, and her work on cultures of trauma, epitomized in an article
excerpted below, continues to refine and redefine the issues and arguments surround-
ing the representation of violence.

Shaved Heads and Marked Bodies:

Representations from Cultures of Trauma

KRISTINE STILES

A multitude of representations and cultural productions emanate from social
and political events located in, and imprinted with, trauma, the ancient Greek
word for wound. These images and attendant behaviors constitute the aggregate
visual evidence of the "cultures of trauma," a phrase I want to introduce to
denote traumatic circumstance that is manifest in culture, discernible at the
intersection of aesthetic, political, and social experience. While research in trau-
matogenesis has proliferated during the past two decades, few have examined
the cultural formations that result from, and bear illustrative witness to, the
impact on world societies of the ubiquitous wounds of trauma. Meditating on
the history of trauma, British psychiatrist Michael R. Trimble observed that its
"etiology and pathogenesis . . . remains *invisible*" (my emphasis). Yet, however
invisible its origin and development, I maintain that the cultural signs of trauma
are *highly visible* in images and actions that occur both within the conventional

boundaries of visual art and in the practices and images of everyday life. This essay explores two of these sites: shaved heads and marked bodies.

Trauma may be defined concisely as "an emotional state of discomfort and stress resulting from (unconscious and conscious) memories of an extraordinary, catastrophic experience" that shatter "the survivor's sense of invulnerability to harm." War, with its institutions and practices, is a ubiquitous source of trauma. But the genesis of trauma is not limited to the effects of war since the abuse of bodies destroys identity and leaves results parallel to war and its consequences. For several centuries trauma was diagnosed as neurosis. But the term "post-traumatic neurosis," used to describe the symptoms of shell-shocked World War I veterans, was changed to "post-traumatic stress disorder" (PTSD) in the 1970s when the symptoms of Korean and Vietnam War veterans began to be diagnosed as stress. This diagnosis refers to a heterogeneous group of causes with a homogeneous set of behaviors: disassociation, loss of memory coupled with repetitive, intrusive, and often disguised memories of the original trauma, rage, addictive disorders, somatic complaints, vulnerability, guilt, isolation, alienation, detachment, reduced responsiveness, inability to feel safe or to trust, and numbing. Causes include war, shock, concentration camp experiences, rape, incest, sexual abuse, racism, shocks related to natural disasters or accidents, prolonged periods of domination as in hostage and prisoner-of-war situations, and the brutal psychological conditions perpetrated by some religious cults. I do not want to suggest that the omnipresence of trauma means that all traumatic experiences are the same. But if one considers the genocide of Cambodians, Indians and Pakistanis, Bosnians, the Kurds, or blacks in the United States, or the cultural influence of the "disappeared" among Argentinians, Chileans, and El Salvadorans, or the Boat People of Vietnam and Haiti, or the effects of the Chinese Cultural Revolution, then the occurrence and advance of trauma is staggering and global. Indeed, the world's some 40 million refugees, most of whom are women and children, offer a material image of trauma. If I were to identify the capitals of the cultures of trauma, they would be such places as the second-largest city in Pakistan or the third-largest city in Malawi, both of which are refugee camps!

At the nexus of the cultures of trauma is the highly celebrated new world order, which, I think, did not begin with the fall of the Berlin Wall in 1989, but with the ethos of the Holocaust and nuclear age. The epoch of the Cold War and its aftermath might be understood as an age of trauma whose threats increase exponentially, especially with the grim reality of the thriving global business in weapon-grade plutonium and enriched uranium contraband and such nuclear-industry disasters as Three Mile Island (1975) and Chernobyl (1986). In this regard, the U.S. response to the so-called rape of Kuwait was perhaps as much an excuse to dismantle Iraq's nuclear-weapons capacity as it was to restore Kuwait's sovereignty. Where such continuous peril exists, trauma is constant. The task is to undermine its invisibility. For its concealed conditions, its silences, are the spaces in which the destructions of trauma multiply.

My past research attended to the impact of destruction in the formation of works that grew out of violent experience. In particular, I studied the use artists made of their bodies as the primary signifying material of visual art performances, actions removed from the context and history of theater. While certain antecedents in futurism, dada, the Bauhaus, and surrealism exist for this historically specific phenomenon, it developed as a viable independent visual art medium in Japan, Europe, and the United States in the 1950s and, I think, must be correlated directly to the corporeal threat experienced by populations living in the geographical spaces most terrorized with destruction. The actualization of destruction in performative works of art was a cultural sign, I suggested, a *techne* for making one's life into an aesthetic coefficient of survival. Such art not only bore witness to various survival strategies by converting invisible trauma into a representation, but, more immediately, into a presentation. Simultaneously representational and pre-sensational, this art offered an alternative paradigm for cultural practices, one that appended the traditional metaphorical mode of communication, based on a viewing subject and an inanimate object, to a paradigm of exchange, based in the connectedness implied by metonymy. In this model, the human body held the potential for an exchange between individual subjectivities.

While I concentrated on the unprecedented physical and material violence and destruction that artists used, paradoxically, as the creative means for making art, that research was confined generally to the topic of war. Typically, although not exclusively, questions related to the interconnection between sexuality, identity, and violence I filter through that lens. Now my work examines the shared symptoms that result from the interrelated causes of trauma in war and sexual violence. This work poses such questions as: what are the visual codes of trauma and how does an understanding of these representations facilitate knowledge of the cultural effects of trauma? Such questions are not, however, concerned with the history, methodology, or therapeutic aims associated with either the research or practice of art therapy, practice that involves the treatment of individual cases. Nor does it engage in a psychoanalytic analysis of individual works of art. Rather, I seek to map the behavioral symptoms identified with trauma onto cultural representations and actions produced in conditions where trauma occurs. For I reason that the heterogeneity of traumatic causes that results in a homogeneity of symptoms may equally produce a heterogeneous body of images and actions that can function as homogeneous representations of trauma.

This study explores how visual responses to trauma may assist peoples of diverse individual, social, and political experiences in arriving at a shared language from which to construct different cultural, social, and political institutions and practices. In seeking to identify a shared body of visual representations of trauma, I have no lingering desire for holistic humanism or any need to attempt the constitution of false homogeneous communities. Rather, the goal is to acknowledge the growth and development of global networks of information-sharing systems and shared ecological concerns, and to reclaim for visual art the powerful role it is capable of playing in the development of a global humanitarian discourse of humane concern—a role threatened by the disempowering conditions of the economies and markets of art and usurped by cynical denials of art's contemporary efficacy by many theorists of postmodernism. Identifying the visual results of cultures of trauma may hasten development of shared cultural terms through which to address disparate cultural events. Transforming visual representations into textual analysis may increase insight into, and compassion for, suffering, which is the first and necessary stage for reform.

This essay considers two sites within the cultures of trauma. Shaved heads is a representation that refers both to an image and a style resulting from a wide variety of social and political experiences outside of the context of the visual arts. Marked bodies is a representation that pertains to the performative paradigm that developed within the visual arts, an aesthetic practice that I believe is rooted deeply in cultures of trauma in accordance with larger political frames of destruction and violence.

In one instance, the community gathered in French towns and villages to shear the woman's head with animal clippers and then smear the sign of the swastika in soot on her bald forehead. The citizens judged her a "horizontal collaborator" for having sex with German soldiers during World War II. Denigrated and denounced as a whore, she was even stripped naked sometimes before being paraded through town, a token of the "emblematic territories, defamations, arid controls of war." She remained solitary amidst the molesting, persecuting assembly, exiled in a particularly sordid historical moment in a throng of her countrymen and women.

Horizontal collaborators served as metonymic signifiers for the "vertical collaborators" who, under the Vichy government, maintained an upright appearance while they capitulated to the Germans, raised their hands in the Nazi salute, and welcomed "the New Europe" into their beds. These women with shaved heads were used as communal purgatives, scapegoats for the French who themselves had whored for jobs in Germany, for extra food, and for peacetime amenities, especially during the years 1940 to 1943. In 1944 and 1945, photographers Robert Capa and Carl Mydan documented the terrible brutality to women accused of sexual collaborations with the Germans; and Marcel Ophuls included documents of one such incident in the town of Clermont-Ferrand in his 1969 film *The Sorrow and the Pity*. Female collaborators whose crimes were not sexual were not treated with the same kind of corporeal violations as the horizontal collaborators, whose primary sedition was to have slept with the enemy. The ritual scrutiny by French communities of the intimate affairs and bodies of "their" women suggests that these women's crime was vulvic, the vaginal betrayal of the patrimonial body of the State. The assault on, and psychological domination of, the female body and the photographic and filmic records, "taken" or "shot," of her display on communal viewing stands all typify physical and scopic aggression linked to sexuality, especially sanctioned in the "theater of war." War condones and ritualizes the destruction and occupation of territories and bodies. Marked as properly owned by the community, the shaved head confirms feminist's observations that wars are fought for, among other things, privilege to the bodies of women.

The visual discourse of the phallocratic order may be seen in the shaved female head, the site where rule by the phallus joins power to sexuality. Phallic rule is fundamental in cultures of trauma and forms the nexus between war and sexual abuse, a site where assaults on the body and identity produce similar traumatic symptoms. In his important new book *Shattered Selves: Multiple Personality in a Postmodern World*, political theorist James M. Glass argues that the justification for taking women issues from the same "perversion of power and the arrogance of patriarchal assumptions over the possession of women" that result in incest and other kinds of sexual abuse. He concludes that "to the extent that power moves beyond its ordered field and beyond its respect for the lives and bodies of others, it is not much different from political forms of power which define sovereignty as the infliction of harm, the punishment of bodies, and the depletion of life."

Nowhere is this conjunction more agonizing than in the testimony of Bok Dong Kim, a Korean military "comfort woman" (*jugun ianfu*), one of the many Asian women abducted for sexual service during World War II by the Imperial Army under the name of the Japanese emperor. Kim testified about war crimes against women on June 15, 1993, at the Center for Women's Global Leadership during the International Conference on Human Rights in Vienna. She explained that after her body was unable to continue to provide sexual services for as many as fifty soldiers a day, her blood was used in transfusions for the wounded. The comfort woman provided the furniture of sex, and her body, when broken, became a mere blood bag from whose veins the life of one woman was drained into the health of many men. The ferocity of her experience is unbearable and related to the pornography now being made of the rapes of Bosnian women conquered as territory, possessed, and displayed.

Hélène Cixous and Catherine Clément, French feminist theorists, identify the "intrinsic connection . . . between the philosophical, the literary . . . and the phallocentric"—which, they argue, is a bond "constructed on the premise of woman's abasement [and] subordination of the feminine to the masculine order." Shaved heads signify humiliation, a visual manifestation of a supralineal condition of domination and power that joins war and violence to the abuses of rule by the phallus. The doctrine of male hegemony is global and founded in the texts of organized world religions. In the Judeo-Christian tradition, this instrument is the Bible:

> I want you to know that the head of every man is Christ; the head of a woman is her husband; and the head of Christ is the Father. Any man who prays or prophesies with his head covered brings shame upon his head. Similarly, any woman who prays or prophesies with her head uncovered brings shame upon her head. It is as if she had had her head shaved. Indeed, if a woman will not wear a veil, she ought to cut off her hair. If it is shameful for a woman to have her hair cut off or her *head shaved*; it is clear that she ought to wear a veil. A man, on the other hand, ought not to cover his head, because he is the image of God and the reflection of his glory. Woman, in turn, is the reflection of man's glory. Man was not made from woman but woman from man. Neither was man created for woman but woman for man. For this reason a woman ought to have a sign of submission on her head, because of the angels. (I Corinthians 2:1–16; emphasis added)

The above citation from the New Testament is anticipated in the Old Testament:

> The Lord said: Because the daughters *of* Zion are haughty, and walk with necks outstretched, ogling and mincing as they go, their anklets tinkling with every step, *the Lord shall cover the scalps* of *Zion's daughters* with *scabs*, and *the Lord shall bare their heads*. On that day the Lord will do away with the finery of the anklets, sunbursts, and crescents; the pendants, bracelets, and veils; the headdresses, bangles, cinctures, perfume boxes, and amulets; the signet rings, and the nose rings; the court dresses, wraps, cloaks, and purses; the mirrors, linen tunics, turbans, and shawls. Instead of perfume there will be stench, instead of the girdle, a rope, and for the coiffure, *baldness*; for the rich gown, a sackcloth skirt. Then, instead of

beauty: Your men will fall by the sword, and your champions, in war; her gates will lament and mourn, as the city sits desolate on the ground. (Isaiah 3:16–26; emphasis added)

This passage recasts the theme of women's culpability in the original fall from grace. Here the vanity and narcissism with which she is charged is cited as the source for the demise of men by the sword in war. He shall check her haughty and seductive ways, the Lord God, who shall mete punishment upon her body in the form of scabs, stench, and baldness.

The French were not alone in shaving the heads of women who slept with the enemy. Similar proprietary national interests, rights, and rites regarding the sexuality of German women were recorded by Bertolt Brecht in his poem entitled "Ballade von der 'Judenhure' Marie Sanders" (Ballad of Marie Sanders, the Jew's Whore, 1934–36). Brecht wrote that Marie Sanders, a woman from Nuremburg, was "driven through the town in her slip, round her neck a sign, her hair all shaven. . . ." Her crime was to have slept with a Jew.

In yet another context, African American novelist Ishmael Reed summons the specter of a shaved head in his book *Reckless Eyeballing*. This time, however, the image refers to the war between the races. Advocating shaving the heads of black feminist writers whom he accuses of collaborating with white feminists, Reed growls, "They deserve what they get. Cut off their hair. . . ." Reed charges black feminists with acting on behalf of white men in whose name white feminists serve to emasculate black men: "To turn the afro man into an international scapegoat . . . showing black dudes as animalistic sexual brutes." Reed's rage lives in the "colonialist program" identified by Frantz Fanon in which "the woman [is given] the historic mission of shaking up the man," a strategy described by Gayatri Spivak as "brown women saved by white men from brown men." Reed detested any association with the architects of colonization, white men, whom he labeled "the biggest cannibal, [who] have cannibalized whole civilizations, they've cannibalized nature they'd even cannibalize their own mothers."

Reed's diatribe, coupled with his misogynistic advice to shave black women's heads, offers a multifarious view of the convoluted manifestations of rule by the phallus. Kinship, race, or national identity, for Reed, resolves the question of sexual access to female bodies, and entry into them is determined by war, colonization, enslavement, incest, and rape. Here the Bible offers instruction, complete with shaved heads:

> *Marriage* with a *Female Captive*. When you go out to war against your enemies and the Lord, your God, delivers them into your hand, so that you take captives, if you see a comely woman among the captives and become so enamored of her that you wish to have her as wife, you may take her

home to your house. But before she may live there, she must shave her head and pare her nails and lay aside her captive's garb. After she has mourned her father and mother for a full month, you may have relations with her, and you shall be her husband and she shall be your wife. However, if later on you lose your liking for her, you shall give her her freedom, if she wishes it; but you shall not sell her or enslave her, since she was married to you under compulsion. (Deuteronomy 21:10–14)

The doctrine of privileged right to women, especially "comely" women, mandated in Deuteronomy has chilling social reverberations in Reed's text. But it also has demoralizing parallels in cultural practices. For example, the 1973 film *Soylent Green*, directed by Richard Fleischer, depicts a ravaged and famine-ridden chaotic New York in the year 2022, a warlike environment where every luxury from strawberry jam to "comely" women is guarded jealously. Beautiful women are assigned to apartments as "furniture" and provided for only as long as the incoming male tenant agrees to continue to rent them or, in the language of Deuteronomy: if you later on lose your liking for her, you shall give her her freedom. Moreover, Thorn West (Charlton Heston) refers to Shirl (Leigh Taylor-Young) as a "hell of a piece of furniture" and "like a grapefruit," both metaphors interchangeable with the ways in which the actual bodies of the comfort women, mentioned earlier, were used as furniture and nutrient. But while women are without question the majority of those who suffer the rule of the phallus, the fact does not abrogate the reality that men, too, may be, and are, abased in phallocracy. Few more striking and unpredictable examples of such men exist in this constellation than the skinhead.

Skinheads derived their look, in part, from an identification with "West Indian immigrants and the white working class," James Ridgeway explains, in his horrifying history of the rise of a new white racist culture. Dick Hebdige adds that it was "those values conventionally associated with white working-class culture which had been eroded and by that time were rediscovered embedded in [the black musical culture of] ska, reggae, and rocksteady." Prevented from participating in white male power and privilege because of their class and lack of education, skins adapted an appearance of marginality with respect to Western systems of power. They also condensed a stunning array of differing cultural and political sites and meanings into an image. The result was a representation of absolute brute force signified by the shaved head but also by such articles of clothing as black army-surplus combat boots and camouflage gear. Skins visualized interconnected networks of brutality ordinarily categorized as different culture ills: These include the hardened countenance of the military man, under whose sign society contracts death; the veneer of the outlaw, or prisoner of ball, chain, and spiked collar, whose transgressions bar him from the privilege to kill; the demented, dangerous, unpredictable mental patient, shaved and lobotomized; an image of ravaged diseased bodies, radiated and suffering; and, finally, the debased aspect of the concentration camp Jew, the ultimate picture of oppression. The image of the skinhead contains the powerful and the abject, the oppressor and the oppressed, the killer and the killed. Skins would seem to differ from the women with shaved heads cited above because they appear to be the agents in the reconstruction of their own identity. To a certain degree they are. But agency depends upon a more complex set of relations that involve not only personal will but social forces. Thus, the constitution of an image—like that of the skins—that is aimed at vitiating the threat of helplessness and powerlessness succeeds better in betraying and reinforcing the locus of its identity in the trauma of that threat.

Toni Morrison addresses this seeming paradox when she points out how the United States is simultaneously a "nation of people who decided that their world view would combine agendas for individual freedom [and the] mechanism for devastating racial oppression." Morrison thus demonstrates how such apparent paradoxes are better understood as the reciprocal ways in which different languages, cultural representations, social and political institutions, and races and sexualities comprise identity. Morrison's deconstruction of this intertextuality offers further access to the links shared by black Ishmael Reed and white skinheads. "The Africanist character" she writes, becomes a "surrogate" who "enables . . . whites, to think about themselves . . . to know themselves as not enslaved, but free; not repulsive, but desirable; not helpless, but licensed and powerful; not history-less, but historical; not damned, but innocent; not a blind accident of evolution, but a progressive fulfillment of destiny."

Skinheads live contradiction. Their social experience is to be enslaved, repulsive, helpless, damned, and to belong to the very group who has a history and a promise of fulfillment in which they cannot share. This paradox is also the foundation for the anger that incited the dispossessed French in World War II, for Reed's rage, and for the skins' lethal frustration, a fury that takes its revenge upon the bodies of the women proclaimed their own. This delusion of possession helps to explain why the image of a happy coupling between a white woman and a black man is described in a 1981 Aryan Nation flyer as "the ultimate abomination." For if nothing else belongs to the British or American (French/German/Japanese/African/Serbian/Iraqi) skinhead, if he is socially fucked by other men, he alone will fuck her white (black/brown/yellow/red) body. The vicious retaliation of the skinhead unfolds within the epistemological spaces ensured by white male hegemony, a phallic rule in which his virility becomes merely a caricature unmasking the reality of his impotence, a lack derived from the fact that he actually cohabitates the same disempowered spaces of women and all other dominated peoples. His inadequacy sustains his obsession with white supremacy where, fortified by emblematic images of superiority and power, he attempts to exercise his deprived authority.

All of these shaved heads inhabit the visual memory of culture, a memory of the history of war, domination, and colonization across whose pages bodies reach back to the Old and New Testaments and forward to the white power of skinheads, the youth paramilitary arm of ultraconservative groups whose theology is based on Scripture and who act out of a belief in their divine right to be on the top, where power and sexual abuse fire the cultures of trauma. "Organization by hierarchy makes all conceptual organization subject to man," Cixous and Clément write, and that organization "is located in the logocentric orders that guarantee the masculine order a rationale equal to history itself."

In the performance "Test of Sleep" Amalia (Lia) Perjovschi, Romanian artist, covers her body with white paint over which she inscribes a complex sequence of symbols resembling hieroglyphic marks, untranslatable signs, a visual language that she then animates with gestures deployed in silence—hand, arm, leg, and full-body signals enacted in her home before her husband, the only witness. Perjovschi's principal means of communication, beyond the direct but silent, intimate liaison with her husband, artist Dan Perjovschi, is through photographs, documents that he—as husband, collaborator, and beholder—recorded. Her action took place in 1988, one of the darkest years of Romanian captivity under the autocratic totalitarianism of Nicolae and Elena Ceausescu, who were assassinated December 25, 1989. In 1993, in Timisoara, site of the revolution, Eastern European artists gathered for the performance festival, Europe Zone East. Dan Perjovschi's action was to sit silently while the word "Romania" was tattooed on his upper left forearm.

While shaved heads provided visual access and insight into the linkage between power and sexuality that contributes to the construction of cultures of trauma, Lia and Dan Perjovschi's marked bodies enunciate the silence that is a rudiment of trauma and a source of the destruction of identity. Silence was maintained efficiently by the Romanian secret police, the Securitate, which enforced Ceausescu's crushing control. In large measure, that organization was successful through the sheer force of rumor, hearsay that numbered the Securitate, with its system of informers, at one in six Romanian citizens. No one remained above suspicion. Fear and secrecy resulted in the effective supervision of all aspects of Romanian life. Stealth was augmented by reports of reprisals against challenges to authority, threats that were invigorated by actual punishments. Extreme even among nations of the former Soviet bloc, Romanians endured their conditions in isolation. Preventing its citizens from travel, the government retained Romanian passports and politically sequestered the nation from exchange with most of the world. Romania resembled a concentration camp, especially in the 1980s when Lia and Dan Perjovschi (both born in 1961) were in their twenties.

While such coercion was the most obvious process by which Romanians were traumatized into obedience, a double bind, comprised of intense nationalism coupled with economic shortage, incapacitated the people into perceiving themselves as absolutely dependent upon a government that they could not criticize without being labeled unpatriotic. This paradoxical predicament reinforced what Katherine Verdery, a U.S. anthropologist specializing in Romanian culture, calls the "symbolic-ideological" discourse in Romania, a discourse that utilizes "the Nation ... as a master *symbol*." Romanian debates over national identity rose to a fever pitch in the 1980s, especially, with the programmatic decimation of Romanian traditional life, the destruction of villages, and the relocation of peasants and workers into the bleak cityblock houses, all of which were part of Ceausescu's massive relocation and urbanization project that followed his 1971 visit to North Korea, China, and North Vietnam when he inaugurated "a 'mini-cultural revolution,' with renewed emphasis on socialist realism." The ambitious reconstruction of Romanian cities included the erection of high-rise apartment complexes in an idiosyncratic and hybrid Korean-Chinese style imitative of the International style. In the redevelopment of Bucharest, especially between 1984 and 1989, some 50,000 people lost their Beaux Arts and Victorian homes to the unrivaled, infamous, architectural complex leading to the vulgar Casa Poporlu-lui, House of the People, funded by Romanian taxes at the expense of all other civic, social, industrial, and agricultural projects. Like its historical antecedents, Ceausescu's building campaign was aimed at a monolithic representation of power through which to arouse awe and complete compliance. An effective means of social control, its sterility mirrored the repression of interior life.

But questions related to Romanian national identity did not originate in Ceausescu's regime. They reside deep in Romanian history and consciousness, both of which have been split for centuries between the philosophical and teleological worldviews of the Occident and the Orient, as well as along the geographical political exigencies of North-South and East-West. Romanians trace their bipolarity to the occupation in A.D. 106–107 of the Roman emperor Trajan, who invaded the ancient lands of the Carpatho-Danubian people, the Geto-Dacians. Since Neolithic times the Gateo of the lower Danube and the Dacians of the Carpathian Mountains had inhabited what is now modern Romania. Such divisions make Romanians especially vulnerable to psychological fragmentation and contribute to the renowned "distrust of all the cherished notions . . . of progress and history" that is "characteristic" of Balkan peoples, according to Andrei Codrescu, a Romanian, expatriate poet living in the United States. The historic rupture of Romanian national identity was reinforced in, and is echoed by, the shattering of personal identity under Ceausescu. In this regard, Verdery has recognized a "social schizophrenia" among Romanians that she has described as an ability to experience a "real meaningful and coherent self only in relation to the enemy party."

Artist Ion Bitzan, an admired professor of art at Nicolae Grigorescu Academia de Arta in Bucharest, provides a special example of this schism. Bitzan, born in 1924, lived through Stalin, Gheorghiu-Dej, and Ceausescu. Under Stalin, Bitzan learned as a student, that transgression was impossible. He remembered the painful "unmaskings" (his term) during which students denounced each other and their professors, denunciations accompanied by obligatory applause, the same obligatory applause required at the very mention of Stalin's name. His terror was so deep, he remembered, that he felt "guilty for being human" and was afraid of "being an enemy of the party, an enemy of the State, an enemy of the Soviet Union."

In 1964, one of Bitzan's paintings was selected for inclusion in the Venice Biennale. A social realist work of "a lorrie filled with wheat, a field worker, and a red flag in the corner," the socialist subject and style, like the applause, was mandated. But Bitzan felt his work was "perfect" because he had composed it precisely according to the rules for the Golden Section. When he traveled to Venice to attend the Biennale, however, he saw the assemblages and collages of Robert Rauschenberg, the American artist who received first prize at that Biennale. Bitzan returned to Romania confused, disturbed, and embarrassed by his art. He felt himself to be a provincial outsider and was humiliated by the very painting of which he had been so proud. Three years later, Bitzan also began to make collages and constructions, and to fabricate exquisite handmade papers on which he wrote in a flowing and elegant but secret, unreadable personal language. He created these works, however, only in the privacy of his studio. In public, Bitzan continued to paint in a socialist realist style. Like many Romanian artists, he capitulated to Ceausescu's frequent requests to paint "Him" or "Her" —the terms Romanians used for Nicolae and Elena. For his compliance, Bitzan earned money, prestige in the Art Academy, and the right to travel. He "sold" himself, he insisted, "but only for an hour or so a day when I worked on their pictures." After that he turned the canvases of Him or Her—emblems of his repression—to the wall and began his secret life. In telling this story for the first time, in his own words Bitzan became "ashamed" and left the room. I too felt shame. My interview had perpetrated the familiar form of an interrogation. Before contributing to and witnessing Bitzan's shame, I had been sheltered from understanding the interview form of discourse as a persecuting interrogative.

Bitzan's private collages, hand-made papers, artist's books, and indecipherable texts are all a microcosm of the conflict that characterized Romanian artists' conduct, their need to invent alternative languages and to make hidden private works. Verdery's observation about Romanians' "social schizophrenia" is related to Bitzan's experience. Comments by a number of Romanians confirm her view. Alexandra Cornilescu, a linguist from Bucharest University, noted that survival in Romania depends upon "hedging." Hedging means that one cultivates the ability to live multiple lives. Romanians learned to say one thing and mean something else, to speak in layered code impenetrable to informers, often even confusing to friends, to use their eyes and gestures as if they were words. Or, as Andrei Codrescu confessed, "I lie in order to hide the truth from morons." "Repressive discourse," Cornilescu continued, "gradually developed towards a rigid inventory of permissible topics; religion, non-dogmatic philosophy or political theories, poverty, prisons, concentration camps, political dissidents, unemployment, sex, etc., were, as many taboo topics, unmentionable and, largely, unmentioned in repressive discourse."

Nothing is more pernicious in the "discourse of fear" than the problem identified by Cornilescu when she writes that in Romania, "If an object/person/phenomenon is not named, then it does not exist." With the word "Romania" emblazoned on the surface of his body, Dan Perjovschi staked the authenticity of his existence on a name. His tattoo divulges the dependence of his identity upon his country, a territory marked by centuries of uncertainty and the challenged, manipulated, and traumatized conditions in which he and his fellow Romanians lived. But his tattoo is also an indeterminate sign signifying the synchronicity of a visible wound and a mark of honor. A symbol of resistance and icon of marginality, it is a signature of capture, a mask that both designates and disguises identity. As a signifier for the charged complexity of Romanian national identity, the tattoo brands Dan Perjovschi's body with the arbitrary geographical identity agreed upon by governments, and it displays the ambiguous psychological allegiances such boundaries inevitably commit to the mind. His action-inscription also conveys some of the content of the accreted spaces of Romanian suffering and guilt, guilt that Perjovschi addressed when he explained that in Romania, where both prisoners and citizens alike habitually were transformed into perpetrators, guilt and innocence intermingle inseparably. And he asked, "Who may point a finger?" Similarly, psychiatrist Judith Lewis Herman describes the process by which incest victims are silenced and made to become complicit in their own abuse: "Terror, intermittent reward, isolation, and enforced dependency may succeed in creating a submissive and compliant prisoner. But the final step in the psychological control of the victim is not completed until she [/he] has been forced to violate her [/his] own moral principles and to betray her [/his] basic human attachments. Psychologically, this is the most destructive of all coercive techniques, for the victim who has succumbed loathes herself [/himself]. It is at this point, when the victim under duress participates in the sacrifice of others, that she [/he] is truly 'broken.' "

Only recently have such experiences begun to be verbalized in Romanian discourse. Cornilescu explains that in the media, terms such as "survival," "nightmares," and "shock therapy" appear increasingly as metaphors describing the past and referring to the current transitional period. Such words comprise the languages of trauma and provide new textual evidence of the stress that punctuates the Romanian imagination.

But Romanian silences must be understood in the context of silences that result from terror threatened by the situation and its perpetrator(s), from the repressed silences shielding victims from the pain of memory, and from the *robotization* that results from chronic captivity. These silences represent only some of a host of traumatic silences. All these conditions lead to what many researchers describe as the "conspiracy of silence," a complex environment that culminates in the silence remembered by Holocaust, incest, and rape survivors. Herman proposes that the shame, fear, and horror that traumatized victims experience, leading to silence, is augmented by public denial of trauma and even by the behavior of mental health professionals, who sometimes treat those who "listen too long and too carefully to traumatized patients" as *"contaminated"* (my emphasis).

Romanians feel contaminated. This emotion is embedded in journalistic metaphors that refer to Romania as a "dead" or "diseased body," an "organism . . . undergoing some form of therapy . . . severe pain . . . nightmares," and in need of "shock therapy." Such "therapy" is administered in a collage created by Romanian artist Ion Grigorescu, born in 1946. In a 1986 black and white photo-montage, overpainted and decorated with collage elements in gold foil, Grigorescu depicted himself as St. George slaying a dragon. Entitling the work *Bine si Rau* (Good and Evil), Grigorescu montaged two photographs of himself together to create a composite image of a conqueror and a vanquished. In the image, Grigorescu appears to leap over a figure who bends over a large boulder. The vaulting Grigorescu plunges a huge wooden stake through the bent figure's back, killing the "dragon" that turns out to be simply another image of himself. Driving the stake into his own back, Grigorescu spills his own blood; it gushes from his self-inflicted wound, the life fluid of a body that spurts out and pours over the rock that breaks his fall. Set against the backdrop of a landscape image and around this striking scene, the murder takes place in what appears to be a room, an architectural space created when the artist drew faint lines of ink that traced the perspectival space of a box. In gold ink on one of the room's transparent walls, he painted a half-figure who, reclined on a pillow, wails from the pain inflicted by a foot and leg that is clad in Roman centurion sandals and that stomps on his stomach. At the top of the picture and outside of the architectural space, Grigorescu collaged a small scale that he cut out of gold metallic paper, a symbol of judgment that suspends from the sky.

In the image, Grigorescu collapsed self-sacrifice into the martyrdom of Romania. Visually comparing his suffering to that of the sacrificed Christian, he also summoned the forces of Christianity necessary to vanquish the predator, a tyrant that he slayed in the same manner required to rid the world of the mythic Romanian terror, Dracula: by plunging a stake through the heart. But Grigorescu drives the stake through his own heart, dashing its evil and shedding his blood on the rock that suggests St. Peter's Church. The recollection of Roman dress and Roman Catholic faith draws the Occident into this dramatic scene of violence. Internal repression and external invasion commingle across the territories of power, faith, self-sacrifice, violence, guilt, and martyrdom. These complex threads weave through Grigorescu's image of pain as visual witness to a conflict in which all are implicated. Inside individual subjectivity, and outside that being in the social and political world of competing ideologies and teleologies, Grigorescu confesses his own culpability. Such a representation gains even more force as an authentic image of Romanian social and psychological experience when considered in light of the observation that Romanians "resist anything that resembles the construction of state power [yet] simultaneously . . . live with internalized expectations of a state that is paternalistic, that frees them of the necessity to take initiative or worry about their pay checks, hospital bills, pensions, and the like. They simultaneously blame the state for everything and expect the state to resolve everything [in an] . . . amalgam of accusation and expectation."

Grigorescu's collage is made even more compelling by the fact that these photographs are self-portraits of a performative action the artist undertook in private to prepare this work. His private ritual suggests an exorcism of self undertaken in secret, stealth demanded by the political exigencies of 1986, the year of the work's making. Such hidden performances recall other actions Grigorescu did before the gaze only of his own camera. A self-portrait of 1975, for example, features another striking image of the martyred artist, this time with a crown of thorns encircling his neck. Another self-portrait shows the artist with an elongated neck over which is superimposed the image of the Egyptian King Tut's renowned coffin. In another series of auto-portraits, Grigorescu created body actions in his own living quarters. One series entitled *The Tongue* (ca. 1973–75) pictures only the anatomical feature of a mouth, teeth, and tongue that is gaping wide in a clear invocation of a scream.

The choking, silently screaming, entombed self-image offers other representations of Romanian self-recrimination, guilt, anger, futility, and suffering. "Sufferance" was a term Cornilescu also used in her discussion of textual practices in the contemporary Romanian press. Suffering cohabits the silences that, as literary theorist Elaine Scarry argues, "actively destroy" language, a process that brings about "an immediate reversion to a state anterior to language."

In "Test of Sleep," Lia Perjovschi conjures that anterior state. As the apparatus of the dream condenses and displaces meaning, so Romanian silence registered existence as somnambulant. "Everyone in Romania silently calls out loudly," Lia said. "I wanted to draw attention to that inner life, to make it possible for people to understand it without words." Even the title of her action—"Test of Sleep"—offers textual access to the blocked layers of the performative unconscious available in sleep. Sanda Agalidi, a Romanian artist and expatriate living in the United States, has also summoned the idea of sleep in relation to Romanian social reality. She writes about the "determined will" necessary to maintain aspects of the estranged self, to create an "alternative language"—for "as the words awaken," the "bad world falls asleep." In both artists' metaphors, the silence of sleep parallels repression but also approximates a space within which a different language may be formed, a language that Lia described as the "discrete communication" she enacted in "Test of Sleep." Mikhail Bakhtin, a victim of Stalin's despotism, might have compared her corporeal narrative to the heteroglossia of the oppressed who long to speak for themselves. For he observed that all social life is an ongoing struggle between the attempt of power to impose a uniform language and the attempt of those below to speak in their own dialects (heteroglossia). The struggle between the multiplicity of internal voices and the monolithic voice of external authority breeds trauma.

Many theorists of postmodernism celebrate schizophrenia, or decentered fragmentation, as the cultural sign of postmodern political resistance to holistic models of self and society associated with the hegemony of the humanist paradigm. My personal experience, knowledge of Romania and scholarship all support different conclusions. For such theories fail as viable theoretical constructs when called upon to address the actual experiences of Romanians. Recently conclusions similar to my own have been argued eloquently by James M. Glass, who believes that the textual critique of postmodern resistance to *unicity* is not only "naive" but "dangerous." These theories collapse before the *actual* conditions that real people with multiple personalities suffer; and they cannot account for, or move toward, healing the terrible incapacitating fragmentation and the agonizing internal struggle for unity without which it is impossible to survive and function. Glass asks, "Is it not equally as important to understand

and interpret the world from the point of view of the victims themselves?" Scarry approaches this question from a slightly different position. She insists that trauma sometimes causes so much suffering that "the person in pain is . . . bereft of the resources of speech . . . [so] that the language for pain should sometimes be brought into being by those who are not themselves in pain but who speak on behalf of those who are." Yet while trauma may be so severe that victims might require someone other than themselves to speak, recovery depends upon victims speaking for themselves.

Mute, but gesturing, Lia wrote the language of internal spaces on the surface of her body, words that—although reversed and unreadable—narrated her private suffering. Speechless and immobile, his body imprinted by another man with an inscription, Dan documented the interdependence of the psyche, identity, and ideology in history. The Perjovschis' art provides ocular witness to, and gestural voice for, the prolonged psychological, intellectual, and physical oppression that transformed Romania into a culture of trauma. Through their signifying bodies, they suggest means to express "the corporal threat in social and political experience [and] the inexorable human link between subject and subject." In such performances, the body and its languages may transform victimization into personal agency. "Write yourself," Cixous declared. "Your body must make itself heard."

"The systematic study of psychological trauma depends on the support of a political movement," Herman has argued, a movement "powerful enough to legitimate an alliance between investigators and patients to counteract the ordinary social processes of silencing and denial." Lia and Dan Perjovschi contribute to such an alliance by producing cultural signs that convert invisible pain into images able to be shared with, and scrutinized by, the public. Such actions impart the visual language of survivors and, however specific to Romania, remain paradigmatic of the kinds of representations found in cultures of trauma.

Analysis of the regularization of trauma is pressing and may advance understanding of its human consequences. Marked bodies and shaved heads visualize the aggregate forms of suffering. Should we learn to recognize them, we may reform. But I am not optimistic.

This entry includes two subsections: the first, a long excerpt from Osama bin Laden on his rationale for jihad, and the second a brief commentary on his media savvy from a French expert on terrorism.

Much has been written and discussed and conjectured about Osama bin Laden, especially since September 11, 2001. Yet almost no one has commented on the function of bin Laden as a telelectronic phantom of the Information Age. His representation as the custodian of "legitimate" violence for aggrieved Muslims is central to his effectiveness as a hero for some, a terrorist for others. It is this less often acknowledged aspect of bin Laden, that Roland Jacquard, a Lebanese-born French expert on terrorism, highlights in his bestselling book, In the Name of Osama Bin Laden: Global Terrorism and the Bin Laden Brotherhood.

Taken together, the two texts excerpted here underscore the paradox of bin Laden as a product of the current age, who redefines violence even as he looms large as one of its central agents.

Osama bin Laden is a middle-aged Saudi businessman turned terrorist. A son of one of Saudi Arabia's wealthiest families, he became the coordinator of an international terrorist network believed to be responsible for numerous deadly attacks against American and Western targets, including the September 11 attacks on Washington and New York City. It was from Afghanistan that bin Laden formed the terrorist Al-Qaeda ("the base") organization in 1988, with operatives around the world. It remained quiescent, however, until 1998, when bin Laden announced the establishment of the International Islamic Front for Holy War against Jews and Crusaders, an umbrella organization linking Islamic extremists in scores of countries from Morocco to Indonesia. On its establishment, the group issued a religious edict: "The ruling to kill the Americans and their allies, civilians, and the military, is an individual duty for every Muslim who can do it in any country in which it is possible to do it, in order to liberate al-Aqsa Mosque and the Holy Mosque from their grip and in order for their armies to move out of all the lands of Islam, defeated, and unable to threaten any Muslim. This is in accordance with the words of Almighty God, and 'fight the pagans all together as they fight you all together' (Q 2:193), and 'fight them until there is no more tumult or oppression, and there prevail justice and faith in God'" (Q 8:39).[1]

Both these Qur'anic dicta, taken out of context, have their basis in his 1996 document, projected as a fatwa or juridical decree, which stands as the foundational statement for both his worldview and the directives of Al-Qaeda. It is not only that bin Laden legitimates violence but he does so from a special perch that justifies his holy war, that is to say, a war of purifying or cleansing the Muslim community of its filth, in this case, the infidelity of the Saudis paired with that of their coordinates, the United States and Israel. Bin Laden sought to bolster his own authority with reference to a recognized religious scholar, but the importance of his fatwa is its radical move to legalize the killing of noncombatants, a move that most Muslim scholars would disavow. The basis for bin Laden's argument is the seamless weaving together of scriptural dicta with early Islamic history and transposing both into the context of contemporary warfare. He could be dismissed as a jingoistic psychopath except that he projects a representation of himself as virtuous and his enemy as vile that resonates with many Muslims throughout Asia, Africa, and the Arab world, a resonance that is only enhanced by his skillful use of media, including the World Wide Web.

NOTE

1. See Bruce Lawrence, ed., *Messages to the World: The Statements of Osama bin Laden* (London and New York: Verso, 2005), 61.

Declaration of War Against the Americans Occupying the Land of the Two Holy Places: Expel the Polytheists from the Arabian Peninsula (August 23, 1996)

OSAMA BIN LADEN

A Letter from Sheikh Osama bin Muhammad bin Laden to his Muslim Brothers across the world, and particularly those in the Arabian Peninsula. . . .

It is no secret to you, my brothers, that the people of Islam have been struck by oppression, hostility and injustice by the Jewish-Christian alliance and their supporters. This shows our enemies' belief that Muslims' blood is the cheapest and their property and wealth is merely loot. Your blood has been spilt in Palestine and Iraq, and the horrific image of the massacre in Qana in Lebanon [April 1996] is still fresh in people's minds. The massacres that have taken place in Takijistan, Burma, Kashmir, Assam, the Philippines, Fatani, Ogadin, Somalia, Eritrea, Chechnya and Bosnia-Herzegovina send shivers down our spines and stir up our passions. All this has happened before the eyes and ears of the world, but the clear imperial arrogance of America, under the cover of the immoral United Nations, has prevented the dispossessed from arming themselves.

So the people of Islam realised that they were the fundamental target of the hostility of the Jewish-Crusader alliance, and all the false propaganda about the supposed rights of Islam was abandoned in the face of the attacks and massacres committed against Muslims everywhere, the latest and most serious of which—the greatest disaster to befall the Muslims since the death of the Prophet Muhammad, prayers and peace be upon him—is the occupation of the Land of the Two Holy Sanctuaries [Saudi Arabia], cornerstone of the Islamic world, place of revelation, source of the Prophetic mission, and home of the Noble Ka'ba where Muslims direct their prayers. Despite this, it was occupied by the armies of the Christians, the Americans and their allies. There is no strength or power save in God.

I meet you today in the midst of this gloomy scenario, but also in light of the tremendous, blessed awakening that has swept across the world, and particularly the Islamic world. After the scholars of Islam underwent an enforced absence enforced due to the oppressive Crusader campaign led by America in the fear that these scholars will incite the Islamic Umma against its enemies, in the same way as the pious scholars of old—God bless their souls—like Ibn Taymiyya and al-'Izz bin 'Abd al-Salam, this Crusader-Jewish alliance undertook to kill and arrest the righteous scholars and hardworking preachers. May God sanctify whom He wishes! They killed the holy warrior Sheikh 'Abdallah 'Azzam, they arrested Sheikh Ahmed Yassin at the scene of the Prophet's, prayers and peace be upon him, night journey to the seven heavens, and they killed the holy warrior Sheikh 'Omar 'Abd al-Rahman in America, as well as arresting—on the advice of America—a large number of scholars, preachers and the youth in the Land of the Two Holy Sanctuaries. The most prominent of these were Sheikh Suleiman al-'Auda and Sheikh Safar al-Hawali and their brothers.

This injustice was inflicted on us, too, as we were prevented from talking to Muslims and were hounded out of Saudi Arabia to Pakistan, Sudan and then Afghanistan. That is what led to this long absence of mine, but by the grace of God there became available a safe base in Khurasan, high in the peaks of the Hindu Kush, the very same peaks upon which were smashed, by the grace of God, the largest infidel military force in the world, and on which the myth of the great powers perished before the cries of the holy warriors: God is greatest!

And today, in the same peaks of Afghanistan we work to do away with the injustice that has befallen our Umma at the hands of the Judeo-Crusader alliance, especially after its occupation of the place of the Prophet's, prayers and peace be upon him, night journey [Jerusalem], and its appropriation of the land of the Two Holy Sanctuaries [Saudi Arabia]. We pray to God that He might bless us with victory—He is our protector and is well capable of doing so.

And so here we are today, working and discussing with each other to find ways of rectifying what has happened to the Islamic world generally and the Land of the Two Holy Sanctuaries in particular. We need to study the appropriate paths to take in order to restore things to good order, and to restore people their rights after the considerable damage and harm inflicted on their life and religion. This has afflicted every section of society, whether civilian or military or security personnel, whether employees or merchants, young or old, university students, graduates or the unemployed, who now represent a broad section of society numbering hundreds of thousands. The situation in the Land of the Two Holy Sanctuaries has begun to resemble a huge volcano that is about to explode and destroy the unbelief and corruption, wherever it comes from. The two explosions in Riyadh [November 1995] and Khobar [June 1996] are merely warning signs pointing to this destructive torrent which is produced by bitter repression, the terrible injustice, and the humiliating poverty that we see today.

People are struggling even with the basics of everyday life, and everyone talks with no compunction about economic recession, price inflation, mounting debts and prison overcrowding. Low-income government employees talk to you about debts in the tens or hundreds of thousands of riyals, whilst complaining that the riyal's value is declining dramatically. Domestic debts owed by the government to its citizens have reached 340 billion riyals, and are rising daily due to usurious interests, let alone all the foreign debt. People are wondering: are we really the biggest source of oil in the world? They feel that God is bringing this torture upon them because they have not spoken out against the regime's injustice and illegitimate behaviour, the most prominent aspects of which being its failure to rule in accordance with God's law, its depriving of legal rights to its servants, its permitting the American occupiers into the Land of the Two Holy Sanctuaries, and its arresting of righteous scholars—inheritors of the Prophet's legacy—and unjustly throwing them in prison. The regime has desecrated its legitimacy through many of its own actions, the most important being:

1. Its suspension of the rulings of the shari'a [Islámic law] and replacement of them with man-made laws, and its entering a bloody confrontation with the righteous scholars and pious youth. May God sanctify whom He pleases!

2. Its inability to protect the Land and its allowing the enemies of God to occupy it for years in the form of the American Crusaders who have become the principal reason for all aspects of our country's disastrous predicament.

The voices of the shadows have spoken up, their eyes uncovering the veil of injustice, and their noses smelling the stench of corruption. The voices of reform have spoken up, calling for the situation to be put right: they have sent petitions, testimonies and requests for reform. In the year 1411 AH, at the time of the Gulf War [1990–91], a petition was sent to the king with around 400 signatures calling for reform in the country, but he made a mockery of them by completely ignoring their advice, and the situation went from bad to worse.

Brother Muslims in the Land of the Two Holy Sanctuaries, does it make any sense at all that our country is the biggest purchaser of weapons from America in the world and America's biggest trading partner in the region, while at the very same time as the Americans are occupying the Land of the Two Holy Sanctuaries and supporting—with money, arms and manpower—their Jewish brothers in the occupation of Palestine and their murder and expulsion of Muslims there? Depriving these occupiers of the huge returns they receive from their trade with us is a very important way of supporting the jihad against them, and we expect you to boycott all American goods.

Men of the radiant future of the Umma of Muhammad, prayers and peace be upon him, raise the banner of jihad up high against the Jewish-American alliance that has occupied the holy places of Islam! God told His Prophet, prayers and peace be upon him: "He will not let the deeds of those who are killed for His cause come to nothing; for He will guide them and put them in a good state and admit them into the Garden that He has made known to them." And the Prophet, prayers and peace be upon him, said: "There are one hundred levels in Heaven that God has prepared for the holy warriors who have died for Him, between two levels as between the earth and the sky." And the *al-Jami' al-Sahih* says that the Prophet, prayers and peace be upon him, said: "The best martyrs are those who stay in the battle line and do not turn their faces away until they are killed. They will have the highest level of Heaven, and their Lord will look kindly upon them. When your Lord looks kindly upon a slave in the world, He will not hold him to account." And he said: "The martyr has a guarantee from God: He forgives him at the first drop of his blood and shows him his seat in Heaven. He decorates him with the jewels of faith, marries him to the pure virgins of paradise, protects him from the torment of the grave, keeps him safe on the day of judgement, places a crown of dignity on his head with the finest rubies in the world, marries him to seventy two of the pure virgins of paradise and intercedes on behalf of seventy of his relatives," as related by Ahmad al-Tirmidhi through a strong chain of reference.

I say to the youth of Islam who have waged jihad in Afghanistan and Bosnia-Herzegovina, with their financial, spiritual, linguistic and scholarly resources, that the battle is not yet over. I remind them of what Gabriel said to the Prophet, prayers and peace be upon him, after the battle of Ahzab [627]: "When the Messenger of God, prayers and peace be upon him, departed to Medina and laid down his sword, Gabriel came to him and said: 'You have laid down your sword?' By God, the angels have not yet laid down their swords. Get up and go with whoever is with you to the Bani Qurayza, and I will go ahead of you to shake their fortresses and strike fear into them." So Gabriel went off, accompanied by his pageant of angels, the Prophet, prayers and peace be upon him, along with holy warriors and helpers." This is as it was told by al-Bukhari.

I say to our Muslim brothers across the world: your brothers in the Land of the Two Holy Sanctuaries and Palestine are calling for your help and asking you to share with them in the jihad against the enemies of God, your enemies the Israelis and Americans. They are asking you to defy them in whatever way you possibly can, so as to expel them in defeat and humiliation from the holy places of Islam. God Almighty has said: "If they seek help from you against persecution, it is your duty to assist them" (Q 8:72).[1]

Cavalry of Islam, be mounted! This is a difficult time, so you yourselves must be tough. You should know that your coming-together and co-operation in order to liberate the holy places of Islam is the right step towards unification of the world of the Umma under the banner of God's unity. At this point we can only raise our palms humbly to ask God Almighty to provide good fortune and success in this matter.

Lord, bless your slave and messenger Muhammad, prayers and peace be upon him, and also his family and companions. Our final prayer is praise to God, Lord of the worlds.

Your brother in Islam,
Osama bin Muhammad bin Laden

NOTE

1. Bin Laden leaves out both the first part of the verse, which refers to the emigrants (muhajirun), and also the final part, which reads: "except against people with whom you have a treaty: God sees all that you do."

As powerful as is the rhetoric of bin Laden, it would not have had success, even as propaganda, without his nimble use of modern media, especially Al-Jazeera television but also the Internet. In the following passage, Roland Jacquard analyzes the under-side of modernity that made possible the representation of violence now so reflexively associated with bin Laden and Al-Qaeda.

In the Name of Osama Bin Laden:

Global Terrorism and the Bin Laden Brotherhood

ROLAND JACQUARD

Electronic message services on the Internet can contribute to the jihad and allow a subversive network to communicate in real time, to exchange documents, photos, videos, and graphics, with absolute anonymity. Respect for a few basic security measures makes the circulation of information almost impossible to tap into even for the most effective secret services. Dozens of electronic message service providers, such as Hotmail and Yahoo! in the United States and Liberty-surf in Europe, make it possible to set up an Internet address in a few minutes, without revealing one's identity, or by using a false name, and to stop using it after one message has been sent or received. It is not even necessary to have one's own phone line or even a computer in order to communicate. The flourishing of Internet cafes throughout the world, especially in developing countries, makes tracking Internet users even more difficult. Cities like Cairo and Pesha-war already have dozens of Internet cafes, and electronic message services are accessible there by cellular telephone, as they are in Uganda and Thailand. Terrorists, in fact, no longer need to meet face to face. For a dollar each, from Internet cafes or business centers in hotels in Jakarta, San Francisco, and Johan-nesburg, the members of an "action cell" can communicate person to person for fifteen minutes, using pseudonyms in an anonymous forum, and exchange information about an attack before disappearing into their respective hiding places. If they consider it useful, they could confirm their decisions with en-crypted messages sent through message services in private, in order to outwit the webmasters in charge of supervising websites, who are supposed to keep a vigilant eye on the content of public conversations, although they seem prin-cipally concerned with eliminating pedophile matters.

Using the Internet, a terrorist armed with topographical details about a public place in Rabat or Riyadh gathered in preparation for an attack, could send to the terrorist entrusted with setting the bomb, who might still be in hiding in Manila or Toronto, a short video recorded with an amateur camera setting out precisely the path to follow to avoid the security services and surveillance cameras and where to place the explosive charge. Three-dimensional imaging software could make it possible to have a relief view of the site of an attack in order to organize the commando's retreat. Commercially available cameras connected to the telephone network and the Internet, adopting the concept of webcam sites, could allow terrorists to maintain continuous surveillance of their target with no human intervention other than the original setting up of a camera hooked up to a portable computer and a modem in an apartment facing the target.

Jihad's new weapons, already held by Osama bin Laden, are not only offensive weapons. They also belong to the panoply of means of communication and the surveillance of private life evoked in George Orwell's *1984*: "Big Brother is watching you."

Elliott Leyton is a renowned Canadian anthropologist, who earned his Ph.D. from the University of Toronto and now teaches at Memorial University in St. John's, Newfoundland. Leyton traveled to central Africa to document the labor of the most renowned emergency medical team, Médecins Sans Frontières (MSF); he worked closely with a seasoned international photojournalist, Greg Locke, to produce a poignant profile, not just of MSF, but of all those who work in emergency-aid situations. Leyton makes reference to the Rwandan catastrophe, which is also cited in the introduction to this volume, so it is fitting in many ways to make the last link in this effort to evoke not only violence but also its causes, consequences, and consolations the work of MSF in Rwanda.

Touched by Fire: Doctors without Borders in a Third World Crisis

ELLIOTT LEYTON

MSF

MSF was founded in France in 1971, when the radicalism of the 1960s had temporarily transformed the consciousness of an entire generation in the western world. A group of disillusioned French doctors and journalists returned to Paris from a Red Cross mission to the Biafran War and created Médecins Sans Frontières/Doctors Without Borders. MSF would quickly become the world's largest private, independent emergency medical relief organization, charged with speaking out against human-rights violations and providing medical assistance wherever it is needed. The Canadian branch was founded in 1991, and since then several hundred Canadians have worked in dozens of countries around the world. Worldwide, MSF has six major sections: Holland, France, Belgium, Switzerland, Spain, and Luxembourg. Thirteen nations including Canada have affiliate status—Canada being funded and administered primarily from Holland.

The name of Médecins Sans Frontières (and the anglicized Doctors Without Borders) is an unfortunate linguistic capitulation to the prestige of physicians in the modern world. Perhaps for reasons of public relations, it explicitly states that this is an organization of M.D.s. In fact, MSF is much more than that: it is nurses, not doctors, who do much of the actual hands-on medical work; it is water and sanitation specialists, nutritionists, and epidemiologists who make the largest contribution to public health; and it is logisticians and administrators, plumbers and radio operators, lawyers, mechanics, and accountants who ensure that the essential medicines, food, petrol, personnel, vehicles, water bladders, and tools are delivered to those in the heart of the emergency. Inside the organization, this equality of contribution is implicitly recognized in the universal absence of titles and the routine use of first names—practices that discourage that social distancing, that lack of intimacy and work-team harmony, that disincentive to cooperate inherent in the use of reminders of the outside world's status hierarchy.

Inside MSF, the informal prestige hierarchy is based less on what its members do—less on the fine distinctions of rank the world makes between doctors and nurses, logisticians and administrators—than on where they have served. Arriving at a new station or in a new country, they introduce themselves the way abused Yanomamo wives sometimes compare scalp scars—with a perverse pride in the catalogue of what they have endured, and where. "I worked in the Ivory Coast for twelve months, in Afghanistan, then in the bloody mess in Bosnia," says one as she walks for the first time through the up country Rwandan MSF station door and proffers her credentials. The longer the list and the more dangerous the locations, the more prestige will implicitly be hers. Distinctions are also made according to the length of time served. The ten-year veteran, Martin, admits he sometimes feels profoundly different from short-termers who sign up for a month in an emergency but maintain their comfortable lives at home.

In unstressed times, MSF recruits its people through conventional means, cautiously matching persons to niches—thus a mechanical engineer in civilian life becomes a water and sanitation specialist, or perhaps an administrator. But in times of crisis, people can be hurriedly recruited, as with one MSF legend, a tattooed giant with purple hair who had run a biker bar in Montreal. Virtually plucked from a street in Paris, he found himself on a plane to Malawi to organize the construction of a cholera camp, a task he accomplished with celebrated discipline and *élan*.

THE ECSTASY OF MORAL CLARITY

"The world can afford a humanitarian ideal."
—MSF country manager

What is the point of MSF? It cannot possibly help all those in need; indeed, it cannot even offer aid to the majority. Moreover, what help it can provide is often negated by the ugly reality that many of its patients will later be murdered by the warlords, or die from hunger, disease, or AIDS.

It is indeed caught in a terrible and cruel dilemma. There is no way for it to be certain that its decisions are the right ones: only time and leisurely analysis can reveal that, and these are luxuries MSF does not have. MSF emergency response teams can only do what they understand the best—rapidly assess a situation and act immediately. Yet in acting quickly, mistakes are made, resources squandered: that is the price that must be paid.

The point of MSF has nothing to do with whether it can save the world—it cannot possibly hope to do so. Its social legitimacy can perhaps be best understood through an analogy with the philosophy that precipitated the abolition of capital punishment throughout the civilized western world. That philosophy did not capture the imagination of the world because it stated that kidnappers and murderers had any claim to humanity, or even any right to live. Rather, it did so as a solemn declaration that *there has been enough killing*. Thus, the state protects the tawdry life of a killer not out of respect for his person, but to maintain a social principle—that the state has no more right to take a life than does any individual. In this way, the doctrine of the sanctity of life can universally be maintained.

The work of MSF is a similar declaration that we struggle to be civilized. The world can afford a humanitarian ideal, and it cannot afford the brutalization that comes with indifference to catastrophe. However powerful the wish may be to deny it, each nation is part of this planet; and each political, cultural, and economic act reverberates throughout the world. Moreover, MSF is relatively cheap. These are no bloated careerist bureaucrats: they sleep on foam mats and eat a meal or two a day, they live only for their work and save little or nothing, they bring credit to our tainted civilization and its grievous history of world war, brutal imperialism, and mass extermination.

MSFers are often seen as the reckless "cowboys" of the international aid movement because they help first and ask questions later. Indeed, their occasionally shrill and sanctimonious style makes many enemies. Yet if they see their action has been inappropriate or misguided, they will reverse their decisions. They are not gripped by that bureaucratic paralysis that makes the United Nations so universally despised—perching ineffectually in the best hotels and restaurants, their thumbs in their collective fundament, as a genocide or plague unfolds. When MSF sees hunger, disease, or mass murder, they witness it for the world, and they do whatever they can to assuage it.

They do not retreat in fearful impotence as does so much of the international community. Many of the Rwandans who were slaughtered in the spring of 1994 remained in the capital city despite the obvious danger, because they had a tragically misplaced confidence in the UN. When Human Rights Watch/Africa later asked the few survivors why they had remained when they might have fled to safety, "they replied that they had not been able to imagine the UN troops standing by while Rwandans were massacred." In fact, it took the UN six months to redeploy after it had pulled its tiny, underarmed, and ineffectual force out of the country; six months during which the genocide was completed; six months for member nations to haggle with one another to maximize the political profit they might reap from the venture. Near the end of the extermination, *one* UN monitor was actually placed in Rwanda, but "she remained alone for two months, a single person to attempt to discourage and investigate abuses for a population of some five million people. Until late August, she had no vehicle, no communications equipment, and no computer."

MSF has a knack for stepping on the toes of others in the aid industry, and it jeers unmercifully at the aid circus's parade of leather-lined and air-conditioned luxury four-wheel-drives ferrying the recipients of preposterous European salaries from luxury hotel to expensive restaurant. Neither is MSF there to deliver some coercive mandate, demanding religious or political conversion in return for western food and medicine—as a century of missionaries and imperial rivals have done and continue to do. Nor is it there to further the political aims of some rancid political power, anxious to consolidate or enlarge its domain. Certainly MSFers are not there *for* crude, self-serving reasons: their ascetic style —a few hundred dollars a month plus room and board, sleeping in tents or rented rooms, eating where and what they can—lies largely outside the careerist syndrome. Their ecstatic fulfilment comes instead *from* what they do, and what the doing does to them, and for us.

The twentieth century's enthusiastic participation in the twin apocalypses of world war and genocide destroyed what simple faith western civilization had in its morality and its heroes. What can there be left to believe in after reading the Nazis' instructions to their killing squads in Eastern Europe, reminding them that when machine-gunning groups of villagers, it is essential to aim low enough to ensure the children are hit? In the modern world, only fools—religious fundamentalists, demagogues of all stripes, the naive, and the uneducated—still proclaim that there is such a thing as honour in public or private affairs.

Indeed, in the great literature of our time the protagonist has come to be an *anti*-hero, one who by definition lacks the admirable attributes of nobility of mind and spirit, a life marked by action or purpose. Our new hero is a kind of depressed failure, and the essence of his being is anguish, self-doubt, and distrust of society. Symptomatic of our mentality, the novelist Graham Greene, in *A Burnt-Out Case*, used a sycophantic charlatan to romanticize the motives of Querry, a jaded and heartsick European working in a leper colony in Zaire: "You want to know what makes him [Querry] tick? I am sure that it is love, a completely selfless love without the barrier of colour or class."

The distrust is so deeply rooted that should a Dr. Albert Schweitzer expend his substance in some African bush hospital, or a Mother Teresa devote her life tending to the poor of Calcutta, an industry will surely be created to damage their repute. As soon as they become cultural icons, a counter-attack will be mounted: now it will be "discovered" that their methods and goals are authoritarian, even ethnocentric and eccentric, and therefore worthless. Should people devote their lives to caring for the children of the poor, it may even be hinted, or assumed, or expected, that they are also pedophiles abusing their charges. Such is the spirit of the times, as enervating as the corruption it exposes.

Indeed, it sometimes appears as if the media assume that everyone lies, and nothing is as it appears to be. Under the headline "PHOTOS THAT LIE," the Canadian journal of record reminds us that "some famous historical shots" were fakes, and asks with ill-concealed delight: "Remember that famous photo of the sailor dipping the nurse on VI Day? It was posed. Ditto the equally renowned shot of two lovers kissing in a Paris street. The raising of the flag at Iwo Jima did happen, but not the way it was pictured. The Marines had already put up a flag, but raised a second, bigger one because they thought it would look better. Now, be truthful. Are you disappointed?"

This focused cynicism is as it should be, for if the world runs on fear and greed, much of it is built on a tissue of lies. Indeed, too few perceive the ethical wilderness that shapes their lives. There is, however, a truth too often concealed in modern commentary—and it is concealed somewhere between the ancient and nonsensical claims that supermen advanced to save the world on behalf of Christianity and Civilization, and the equally noxious assumption that since humans are profoundly flawed they must all therefore be utterly corrupt. In some persons and institutions, there can be a congruence between self-serving desires and the needs of suffering humanity. Perhaps a craving for adventure, a need for a legitimizing sense of accomplishment, a dash of moral superiority, an ascetic sense of self-denial, can have positive consequences?

When the rapes and massacres, the plagues, the famines, the floods, or the droughts erupt anywhere in the world, the world stands still. MSF does not. It can place its emergency medical teams and equipment anywhere in the world within twenty-four hours. In the opinion of one thoughtful Third World medical practitioner, MSF's genius is that "they are 'smoke jumpers,' and their job is putting out fires rather than preventing them. In times of disaster, the big divisions are slow moving up into the line, but MSF can get there in time to give first aid when it counts."

In the crisis zone, MSFers act as if they do not care that they are taking terrible risks; or that in helping one they may unintentionally assist another who is less deserving; or whether aid is or is not "a good investment." They go about their business with that single-minded energy that accompanies a clear sense of purpose. It is what they know how to do; it is worth doing; and they do it better than almost anyone else.

Working for MSF liberates them as human beings, freeing them from the triviality of personal woes and the mindless-ness of modern life. Focusing utterly on their acts, they give witness to the abominations in the world and treat its survivors. They dig the latrines, they ferry pure water, they treat the mutilated, the starved, and the pestilent. They make few distinctions between the innocent and the guilty and so perform a kind of righteous penance for the machinations of racist imperialism. In acting thus, their personal dilemmas dissolve and their identities fuse. Through their healing gifts of medicine and emotional connection, they achieve a kind of heart-pounding ecstasy.

Writing from Zaire, an M.D. describes his life and his beloved MSF: "An approaching war. Machine guns, military, mercenaries, and rebels. In the middle of nowhere 150,000 refugees from Rwanda create a camp on the road in a village named Tingi Tingi. Out of guilt, out of fear, out of collective hysteria, they fled the rebels' attack on their previous camp near Bukavu and headed west instead of east. They walked 500 km through the forest, their feet mangled, eating roots and stems and now they are here. I spend several hours a day rounding on the most severe cases. In a tent, on the ground, in the mud of the rainy season, 30 starving children and their desperate mothers. Nasogastric tubes to force feed the feeble. IV lines and injections to fight bacterial fires and the shock of diarrheal dehydration. The ubiquitous red plastic mugs and plates of feeding centres. Déjà vu. They stare at you, these little ones with bodies like frogs and little monkeys. No flesh. They never smile. And when you return later, several have gone. Without a whisper."

Late one night in December 1996, in Nairobi airport's departure lounge, we prepare to quit Africa and MSF for good. The three of us sit across the aisle from a breathtakingly beautiful woman: she has an utterly serene face and confidently makes direct and fearless eye contact. We notice the MSF stickers on each other's hand luggage, and she tells us she has spent six years in medical work with MSF— mostly in Sierra Leone, but this last month in Rwanda's emergency. She is going home to the Netherlands for a visit: she has not been with her family for the last eight Christmases, and in any case she needs a break from her beloved Africa. "I love Holland, too, but it is hard to leave your friendships here," she explains. We wish each other good luck getting on the plane in Kenya, and then again the following morning when disembarking in Amsterdam. She has the regal air of someone at peace with herself and in charge of her own life.

The hardest thing is not to arrive, but to leave MSF. When you leave, you lose all contact with the centre of the world, with one another, with the suffering, and with yourself. You are out of the loop, no longer part of the sweaty action or the gripping flow of news. Now you will be deprived of the brief romances and the warm friendships that come from sharing so much tension, deprivation, and hard work. Suddenly, and cruelly, all the loving arms and comforting cheeks will be torn from your shoulders and your life. If you are lucky, you may get a Christmas card—perhaps to memorialize this double death that is the loss of intimacy and the reacquisition of conventional life. No wonder they return again and again, these MSFers.

For our part, we merely sense that we have been jettisoned, like empty canisters. Once home in Newfoundland, we are informed that MSF maintains a sophisticated psychological support team for those who have returned from the field. "Call collect, at any time you feel the need," they tell us. One month later, sensing that some terrible Rwandan wound has opened in my soul, I decide to ask them for help. Following their instructions, I call collect. The husband of the physician who runs the support team answers the telephone and I identify myself. "Elliott somebody?" I hear him saying to another man. "Never heard of him." He refuses the call and abruptly hangs up. The grating buzz of the disconnected line underscores this new emptiness, and reminds us that we are alone again.

PART III. THE INSTITUTION OF VIOLENCE: THREE CONNECTIONS

Familial

Legal

Religious

PART IV. THE STATE OF VIOLENCE

PART V. THE REPRESENTATION OF VIOLENCE

raneens, no. 64–65 (July–December 1993). Reprinted by permission of Paul Vieille and *Peuples Mediterraneens*.

Osama bin Laden, "Declaration of War against Americans Occupying the Land of the Two Holy Places," in *Messages to the World: The Statements of Osama bin Laden*, ed. Bruce Lawrence (London and New York: Verso, 2005), 24–30. Reprinted by permission of Verso. Sequel from Roland Jacquard, *In the Name of Osama Bin Laden: Global Terrorism and the Bin Laden Brotherhood* (Durham, N.C.: Duke University Press, 2002), 156–57. Reprinted by permission.

Elliott Leyton, *Touched by Fire: Doctors without Borders in a Third World Crisis* (Toronto: McClelland and Stewart, 1998), 57–58, 187–98. Reprinted by permission of McClelland and Stewart Ltd.

banking, Marx's discussion of, 73–77

Bard, Morton, 257

battered wives: Gordon's discussion of, 217–18; Martin's discussion of, 255–59

begging laws, Marx's discussion of, 64–65

being-for-an-other, Hegel's concept of, 34

being-for-self: Hegel's concept of, 28–33; utility and, 34

being-in-and-for-itself, Hegel's concept of, 34

Benjamin, Walter, 220, 268–85, 503, 514

Bentham, Jeremy, 455–61

biblical traditions: culture of trauma and, 527–29; Hobbes's discussion of, 413–15; liberation theology and, 365; Weil's discussion of, 389–90

Biehl, Amy, 1

Bine si Rau, 535–36

bin Laden, Osama, portrayal of Islam by, 495–96, 539–44

Bin Laden Brotherhood, media visibility of, 545–46

Bitzan, Ion, 533–34

Black Boy, 211–12

black nationalism, Malcolm X's discussion of, 148–56

Black Panther Party, 357

black power movement, liberation theology and, 352, 357

black theology, 356–61, 367, 372, 374

Black Theology and Black Power, 351–61

body, culture of trauma and role of, 524–38

body organs, social privatization of, 475–78

Bolshevism, 498; Arendt's discussion of, 417–18, 420–22

bonded legal interpretation: death sentences and, 307–11; legal interpretation as, 302–3

Book of Rites, 335

Bosnia-Herzegovina, U.N actions in, 323–24

Bourdieu, Pierre, 8; legacy of, 188–89; on modes of domination, 190–98, 334; on precapitalist and capitalist societies, 106

bourgeoisie: discipline as mechanism of, 468–71; Engels's discussion of, 44–46; family violence and, 252–54; Fanon's discussion of, 84–87; Gramsci's discussion of, 172–76; Marx's discussion of, 68

Brecht, Bertolt, 514, 528

Breitman, George, 144

Breton, André, 492–93, 498–502

Breuer, Josef, 226

Bronstein, Lev Davidovich, 164, 178n.2

Brown, Rap, 357

Brownmiller, Susan, 287, 290

Brown v. Board of Education, 156n.1

Bukharin, Nikolai, 167, 498

bureaucracy: duplication of, in totalitarian state, 420–22; secret police in totalitarian states and role of, 428–32

Burnt-Out Case, A, 550

Cadorna, Luigi, 178n.1

Cadornism, Gramsci's discussion of, 163–65, 178n.1

Calvin, John, 354–55

cannibalism, colonial imagination concerning, 505–21

Capa, Robert, 526

Capital, 39; excerpts from, 63–77; labor discussed in, 43–52

capitalism: Bourdieu's cultural competence principle and, 192–98; colonialism and, 84–100; Deleuze's and Guattari's discussion of, 472–85; disciplinary mechanisms in, 465–71; educational system and, 80–81; Engels's discussion of, 22–23, 43–52; history and, 23–26; pre-capitalism and, 106; primitive accumulation of, 20–22; role of artist in, 492–93, 500–502; socius and, 473–78; subordination of labor to, 63–

77; in underdeveloped countries, 97–100; Urstaat model and, 487–89. *See also* industrial capitalism

capital punishment: Benjamin's discussion of, 274–75; Cover's views on, 292, 306–11; judicial independence and, 307–11

career conditions, secret police in totalitarian states and, 428–32

caste systems: international politics and status of, 325–26; power relations and, 205–10; as substitutionary sacrifice, 338–39

Ceausescu, Nicolae, 531–33

Central Africa, violence in, 2

Cervantes, Miguel de, 390

Césaire, Aimé, 89–91

Charcot, Jean-Martin, 226

Charles I (king of England), 392

children's welfare, feminist influence in, 247–54

China: human rights violations in, 327; production forces in, 481–85; substitutionary sacrifice in, 335

Christian Ethics and the Sit-in, 356

Christianity: elision of discourse in, 363–76; ethics and, 352–56; Freud's discussion of, 228–33; liberation theology's critique of, 351–61, 364–65; Malcolm X's discussion of, 151–56; paranoia in, 489; role of law in, 262–67; violence in history of, 356–61; Weil's discussion of, 389–90

chupe del tabaco ritual, 505–7

church: as artificial group, 228–33; liberation theology and role of, 366–76; separation of Church and state and, 168–76; violence institutionalized in, 221–23

civilization, Gandhi's discussion of, 102–3, 106–7, 111–14

Civilization and Its Discontents, 226

civil rights: concentration camps and destruction of, 438–41; conscription

and, 273–74; Malcolm X's discussion of, 147–56; power relations and, 207–10; social control theory and, 249–54. *See also* human rights

civil society, Gramsci's discussion of, 163–65, 168–76

Cixous, Hélène, 495, 527, 538

class structure: battered wives and, 255–59; Benjamin's discussion of, 271–73; Bourdieu's discussion of, 189–98; Engels's discussion of, 56–61; Fanon's discussion of, 84–87; Gramsci's discussion of, 159–65; labor strikes and, 278–85; liberation theology's critique of, 369–70; Marx on creation of, 63–68; power relations and, 205–10; role of State and, 170–76; social control theory and, 249–54; Urstaat model and, 485–89; Williams's discussion of, 183. *See also* bourgeoisie; middle class

Clément, Catherine, 495, 527

Code of Criminal Procedure (India), 263

Codrescu, Andrei, 533–34

coercion: discipline as mechanism of, 468–71; punishment as, 450–55

Cohen, Hermann, 282–85

Cold War: culture of trauma and, 523–24; violence during, 3

"collective man," Gramsci's discussion of, 166–67

colonialism: capitalist mode of production and, 21–22; cultural fabulism of, 507–8; culture of terror fostered by, 493–94, 503–21; Fanon's discussion of, 5–6, 8, 23–26, 79–100; international context of, 93–100; primitive accumulation of capitalism and, 70–77; truth expropriated by, 82–84; violence and, 80–100. *See also* decolonization

"comfort women," 526–27

commodity fetishism, colonialism and, 513–21

commodity production, capitalism and, 43–52

common sense, totalitarianism and, 432–43

commonwealth, Hobbes on formation of, 399–403; forcible acquisition, 409–15; sovereignty of monarch vs., 403–9

communism: Breton's and Trotsky's involvement with, 498–99; Gramsci's involvement in, 158; Marx's contributions to, 62–63; role of artist in, 492–93, 500–502

Communist Manifesto, 56, 62–63

Communities of Resistance and Solidarity: A Feminist Theology of Liberation, 362–76

community: Engels's discussion of, 43–52, 54–61; role of vengeance in, 340–50

competition, Engels's discussion of, 50–52

compromise, decolonization and, 85–87

concentration camps: anti-utilitarianism of, 435; arbitrary selection process in, 438–41; predominance of innocent victims in, 437–38; understanding of totalitarianism through, 433–43

Cone, James H., 6, 221–22, 351–61; on black theology, 367, 372, 374–75

conflict: colonialism and, 88–100; non-violent resolution of, 277–85

Congress of Racial Equality (core), 143, 153

Congress (U.S.), Malcolm X's criticism of, 144–56

Conrad, Joseph, 510

conscience, destruction by concentration camps, 439–41

consciousness: Hegel's discussion of, 28–33; utility and, 33–34

consent, rape and role of, 287–91

conspiracy, totalitarian use of, 423–24

constitutional law: institutional violence and, 307–11; rebellion as foundation for, 295–98; violence and, 281–85

control, fantasy and, 210–13

Cornilescu, Alexandra, 534–35, 537

correction, punishment as apparatus for, 451–55

counter-representations of terror, 494, 513–21

Cover, Robert M., 220, 292–313

creativity, totalitarianism and destruction of, 492–93

crime and criminals: Foucault on punishment of, 445–55; mass murder in context of, 433–43; totalitarian concepts of, 420–31

Crimean War, Engels's discussion of, 51–52

criminal sentencing: judicial interpretation and, 303–13; violence in context of, 296–98

Croce, Benedetto, 168

Cromwell, Oliver, 392

cruelty, cultural basis for, 396–98, 478

Cuban Missile Crisis, 3

culture: as accumulation of capital, 192–98; cruelty as principle of, 396–98; discursive vs. nondiscursive elements of, 370; Gramsci's discussion of, 175–76, 182–83; Hegel's discussion of, 36–38; religion and, 362; of trauma, 495, 522–38; Williams's discussion of, 184–87. *See also* Western culture

dadaism, 498

Daly, Mary, 368, 373

dangerous memory, liberation theology and, 367–76

Darwin, Charles, 241, 269

Dawes Plan, 130, 142n.2

death: absolute freedom as, 19–20; colonial obsession with, 507–8; impersonality in concentration camps of, 434–43; lack of fear of, 394; martyrdom and, 293–98; self-consciousness and, 29–33; Weil's discussion of, 385–90. *See also* capital punishment

death penalty. *See* capital punishment

debt: Bourdieu's discussion of, 195–98;

colonial debt-peonage systems and, 504–9, 514–21; impact on human rights of, 328; Marx's discussion of, 72–77; primitive organizations and role of, 396–97; State role in administration of, 482–85

Décadence de la Liberté, 172–73

Declaration on the Granting of Independence to Colonial Countries and Peoples, 318

decolonialization: advancement of human rights and, 317–18; compromise and, 85–87; Fanon's discussion of, 79–100

deference, power relations and, 203–10

Deleuze, Gilles, 375, 391, 395–98; philosophical legacy of, 472–73; socius concept of, 473–78

democracy, Urstaat model and, 487–89

Democratic Party, Malcolm X's criticism of, 144–56

desire: Hegel's self-consciousness and, 28–33; production and, 473–78; State and role of, 489

despotic state: decline of, 397–98; Hobbes's discussion of, 409–15; socius and role of, 478–85; Urstaat model and, 487–89

Deutsche-Französische Jahrbucher, 62

Devil and Commodity Fetishism in South America, The, 503

Dickens, Charles, 245–46

disarmament, Hitler's opposition to, 130–42

discipline, Foucault's discussion of, 455–71; functional inversion of, 461–62; mechanisms for, 462–63

discourse, theology and role of, 363–76

disguise and anonymity, Scott's discussion of, 201

division of labor, Hegel's discussion of, 20

divorce, as institutional violence, 4–5, 218–21, 262–67

domination and subordination: Bourdieu's discussion of, 190–98, 334; criminal sentencing and, 303–4; Engels's discussion of, 56–61; hegemony and, 184–87; Hobbes's discussion of, 410–15; legal interpretations of, 302; power relations and, 203–10; rape and, 287–91; representation of violence as tool for, 494; Scott's discussion of, 107, 199; social control theory and, 249–54; totalitarian goal of total domination, 432–43

Domination and the Arts of Resistance, 199–213

double-consciousness, racism and, 212–13

Drei Bekenntnisse, 128

Du Bois, W. E. B., 212, 359

Dühring, Eugen, Engels's critique of, 22, 39–61, 86

Durkheim, Emile, 194–95

Dworkin, Ronald, 310

Eastern Europe, revolution in, 318–19

East India Company, Marx's discussion of, 71

Eastland, James, 156n.1

economics: black nationalist philosophy of, 151–56; disciplinary mechanisms in, 465–71; Engels's discussion of, 58–61; Gramsci's discussion of, 162–65; human rights and, 327–28; international politics and human rights and, 325–26; in totalitarian state, 425–26

Edict of the State and Towns of Holland, 65

education: Bourdieu's discussion of, 192–98; capitalism and, 80–81; Foucault on discipline within, 462–71; Gramsci's discussion of, 158; punishment as source of, 450–55; role of State in, 166–67

Edward VI (king of England), legislation on beggars, 64

Frank, Leo, 308

Frankfurt School, 249; scarcity of resistance and, 371

fraud, Benjamin's discussion of, 277–85

freedom: arbitrary negation in totalitarianism of, 430–32; Benjamin's discussion of, 274–75; memory of, 370–76; violence and, 18–26

French Penal Code, slave conditions and, 21

French Revolution: Engels's discussion of, 44–52, 60–61; Gramsci's discussion of, 166–67, 171–76, 178n.3

Freud, Anna, 301–2

Freud, Sigmund: on artificiality of groups, 228–33; on identification, 236–40; on morphology of groups, 233–36; on primal hordes and group behavior, 241–44; violence and theories of, 216–22, 226

fugitive slave laws, role of judiciary in, 292

Future of an Illusion, 226

Gandhi, Indira, 264–65

Gandhi, Mohandas K., 4–6, 13; on brute force, 116–20; on civilizations, 102–3, 105–7; comparison of Italy and India, 115–16; Gramsci's discussion of, 105–6, 159; Indian Home Rule advocated by, 110–23; legacy of, 110–11; on passive resistance, 121–26

Gandhi, Rajiv, 265

Gelles, Richard, 218, 256–59

gender: power relations and, 209–10; rape and role of, 287–91

genealogy, violence and, 6–7

Germany: Hitler on fate of, 130–42; Nationalist Right in, 159

gifts, Bourdieu's discussion of, 195–98

Girard, René, 8–9, 221, 334

Glass, James M., 537–38

Gordon, Linda, 217–18, 245–54

government: domestic and foreign policies, 175–76; family structure and role of, 250–54; feminism and Marxism and, 287–91; Gramsci's discussion of, 161–68, 170–76; Hegel's discussion of, 35–38; Hitler's view of, 104–6, 129–42; Hobbes's discussion of sovereignty within, 406–9; judicial independence, 305–6; law and, 169–70; Malcolm X's criticism of, 104, 144–56; ostensible vs. real, in totalitarian states, 421–22; religion and, 177–78; secret police in totalitarian regimes of, 427–32; sociology and political science concerning, 167–68. *See also* commonwealth, Hobbes on formation of

Graham, Billy, 153

Gramsci, Antonio, 105–6; hegemony discussed by, 165–68; on national societies, 176–78; politics and warfare discussed by, 159–65; on separation of powers, 168–76; on the State, 170–76; trial and imprisonment of, 158; Williams's discussion of, 182–87

Greek culture: Engels's discussion of, 56–61; substitutionary sacrifice in mythology, 335–36, 341–42; Weil's discussion of, 223, 377–90

Greene, Graham, 550

Griaule, Marcel, 487

grief, concentration camps and destruction of, 439–41

Grigorescu, Ion, 535–37

Group Psychology and the Analysis of the Ego, 226–44

groups: Freud on artificiality in, 228–33; morphology of, 233–36; primal horde in relation to, 241–44

Guattari, Félix, 390, 395–98; philosophical legacy of, 472–73; socius concept of, 473–78

guilt, Foucault on punishment and, 448–55

Gulf War, human rights and, 321–24

Gustafson, James, 356

Habermas, Jürgen, 371

habitus, Bourdieu's discussion of, 189–98

Halévy, Daniel, 172–73

Harris poll, on domestic violence, 256–58

Hart, H. L. A., 299

hatred, ethic of liberation and, 356–61

Hebdige, Dick, 529

Hebrews, Weil's discussion of, 389–90

Hegel, G. F. W.: on absolute freedom and terror, 33–38; Bourdieu's discussion of, 190–98; duelist analysis of, 210–13; excerpts from work of, 28–38; French Revolution and, 18; lordship and bondage metaphor of, 18–20, 24, 28–33; philosophical legacy of, 27; on the State, 171–76; on violence, 5

hegemony: Gramsci's discussion of, 165–68; Scott's discussion of, 200–213; separation of power and, 168–76; Williams's discussion of, 182–87

Heidegger, Martin, 416

Heisenberg effect, Scott's discussion of, 206–10

Henry VIII (king of England), legislation on beggars, 63–64

Herman, Judith Lewis, 495, 534–35, 538

Heroes of Their Own Lives, 245

heroism: of nongovernmental workers, 550–53; Weil's discussion of, 223, 377–90

hidden transcript, Scott's concept of, 107, 199–213

hierarchies: Bourdieu's discussion of, 193–98; Gramsci's discussion of, 160–65; morphology of groups and, 233–36; in primitive societies, 338–39

historiography, capitalism and, 23–26

history: colonialism and, 83–84; critique of violence and, 284–85; Engels's discussion of, 48–61; Foucault's discussion of, 444; of labor legislation, 63–68; of private property, 43–52; universal, 473–78; Urstaat model and, 487–89; violence in context of, 18–26, 357–61

Hitler, Adolf, 6, 8, 102; Arendt's discussion of, 417–18, 425–26, 430–31; career of, 127–28; Gramsci's discussion of, 177–78; nationalism of, 423–24; on violence, 104–6

Hobbes, Thomas, 194–95, 391, 394, 399–415

Hochschild, Airlie, 203

Hoggart, Richard, 208

homosexuality, Oedipus complex and, 238–40

Horkheimer, Max, 371

horror, Foucault on punishment and, 446–55

humanism, erosion of foundations for, 363–64

humanitarian assistance: liberation theology and, 366–76; morality of, 548–53; sovereignty and, 320–21

human nature: concentration camps as laboratories on, 439–43; primal horde concept of Freud and, 241–44; violence as intrinsic to, 4–5, 220–21

human rights: concentration camps and destruction of, 438–41; decolonialization and, 317–18; economic agenda and, 327–28; formation of commonwealth and, 403–9; Gulf War and violation of, 321–24; information flow and, 328–29; instruments and institutions for, 315–17; international politics and, 324–26; new world order and, 315–29; obstacles to, 319–29; restrictions on meaning of, 326–27; revolution and, 318–19; sovereignty as obstacle to, 319–21; U.N. role in protection and advancement of, 326, 330–32; weapons and war and, 329

human sacrifice, as substitution for violence, 336–40

Husserl, Edmund, 416

Hutu genocide, death toll from, 1, 14n.1. *See also* Rwanda genocide

hypnosis, Freud's discussion of, 243–44

identification, Freud's discussion of, 236–40

ideology: Bourdieu's discussion of, 193–98; hegemony and, 183–87; of punishment, 297–98; violence and, 8

Il Belluzzi, 170

Iliad, or the Poem of Force, The, 223, 377–90

Illustrated Weekly of India, 267

imperialism: capitalism and, 97–100; territorial machine of, 479–85

incest, silence of victims of, 495, 534–35

India: Ayodhya mandir/Babri masjid dispute in, 265–67; caste system in, 206–10; Gandhi's advocacy of home rule for, 111–23; Gramsci's discussion of, 159; Muslim-Muslim and Muslim-Hindu violence in, 2, 5, 265–67; Muslim Personal Law in, 218–21, 263–67; Muslim Women's Bill in, 266–67

Indians. *See* indigenous populations

indigenous populations: in colonial imagination, 87–100, 514–21; colonial torture and coercion of, 513–21; culture of terror concerning, 493–94, 503–7; Marx's discussion of, 71–77; violence and, 91–93. *See also* tribal societies

individualism: Benjamin's critique of violence and, 271–85; concentration camps and destruction of, 439–43; group behavior and, 241–44; Hegel's self-consciousness and, 34–38

industrial capitalism, Marx's discussion of, 69–77

information flow, human rights and, 328–29

ingratiation, power relations and, 203–10

Injustice: The Social Bases of Obedience and Revolt, 199

innocent people, predominance in concentration camps of, 437–38

institutional context of violence, 216–23; discipline as tool in, 462–71; human rights and, 315–17; legal interpretation and, 300–302; state formation and, 392–98

intellectuals, Gramsci's discussion of, 158

international credit system, Marx's discussion of, 72–77

international politics, human rights and, 324–26

International Women's Decade, 263

Internet, coverage of bin Laden on, 544–46

intervention, in theory of social control, 249–54

In the Name of Osama Bin Laden: Global Terrorism and the Bin Laden Brotherhood, 539

Iraq: national sovereignty issues facing, 324; U.N. role in, 320–21

Ireland, Gramsci's discussion of, 160

Islam: bin Laden's interpretations of, 495–96, 539–44; in India, 2, 5; violence in, 218–21, 262–67

Israel, lack of U.N. action against, 321–24

Italy: Gandhi's discussion of, 115–16; Hitler on fate of, 134–42

Jacobin movement, Gramsci's discussion of, 166–67, 172, 178n.3

Jacquard, Roland, 495–96, 539–46

James, William, 4, 13

James I (king of England), 64–65

Janeway, Elizabeth, 246

Jaspers, Karl, 416

Jay, Martin, 371

Jefferson, Thomas, 358

Joke, The, 210

judicial system: concentration camps as erasure of, 437–41; criminal sentencing and interpretations by, 303–13; death sentences imposed by, 306–11; Hobbes on sovereignty of, 406–9, 413–15; independence from government, 304–6; institutional violence and role of, 262–67, 300–302; interpretation as practical

judicial system (*continued*)
    activity of, 298–99; latent role factors in, 304–6; passive acquiescence in, 292; sacrifice compared to, 342–50; vengeance deflected through, 341–50
Justice Accused: Antislavery and the Judicial Process, 292
justification of means, violence and, 280–85

Kafka, Franz, 484
Kant, Immanuel, 190, 273, 443
Kardiner, Abram, 212
Kennedy, John F., 3
khadi, Gandhi's advocacy of, 110
Khan, Muhammad Ahmad, 262–67
Khrushchev, Nikita, 3
Kim, Bok Dong, 526–27
King, Martin Luther, Jr., 110, 360
kings, Hobbes's defense of rights of, 392–93, 403–9
Ku Klux Klan, 143, 156n.1
Kundera, Milan, 210
Kurdish rebellion, U.N. role in, 320–21
Kuwait, Iraqi invasion of, 321–24, 524

labor: capitalism and exploitation of, 72–77; colonial coercion of, 513–21; Engels's discussion of, 43–52, 57–61; Hegel's discussion of, 20; history of legislation on, 63–68; Marx's discussion of, 20–22, 63–68; militancy and, 89–100; property ownership and, 43–52. *See also* organized labor
Lakoff, Robin, 204–10
land cultivation, Engels's discussion of, 55–61
Landwehr system, Engels's discussion of, 49–50
La révolution surréaliste, 498
Last Judgment, loss of faith in, 436
Latin American theology, genealogy of, 368–76
law: Benjamin's critique of violence and, 270–85; Bourdieu's discussion of, 193–98; Christian ethics and role of, 354–56; Cover's discussion of, 293–98; discipline as mechanism of, 467–71; Gramsci's discussion of, 169–70; institutionalization of violence in, 218–21, 262–67, 292–98, 357–61; military law, Benjamin's discussion of, 273–74; nonviolent conflict resolution and, 277–85; police violence as form of, 275–76; punishment and role of, 449–55; rape and role of, 289–91
Lawrence, Bruce B., 219–21
Le Chapelier, Isaac, 21, 68–68
L'Ecole des Femmes, 390
Lectures on Philosophy, 377
legal contract, violence and, 276–77
legal interpretation: as bonded interpretation, 302–3; criminal sentencing and, 303–13; death sentence and, 306–11; institutional violence and, 300–302; judicial independence and, 304–6; as judiciary activity, 298–99; limits of, 311–13; violence as context for, 293–98
legal rights: labor's right to, 271–73; Malcolm X's discussion of, 149–56; military law and, 273–74; Shah Bano divorce case as example of, 262–67
legislation: Gramsci's discussion of, 176–78; labor legislation, history of, 63–68
Lenin, Vladimir, 164, 178n.2, 417, 498
Les Jours de Notre Mort, 434
Leviathan, 392–93, 399–415
Lévy-Bruhl, Lucien, 338
Leyton, Elliott, 6, 8, 13, 497, 549–53
liberal theory: separation of Church and state and, 168–76; on violence, 6–9
liberation theology: communities of resistance and, 364–65; dangerous memory and, 367–76; evolution of discourse in, 364; genealogy of resistance in, 366–76; memory of freedom and resistance in, 370–76; racism and, 351–61; as social critique, 368–70

libido, Freud's discussion of, 227–28; group structures, 229–36

linguistics, power relations and, 204–10

literacy, Bourdieu's discussion of, 192–98

literature, Williams's discussion of, 182–87

Littérature, 498

Little Entente, Gramsci's discussion of, 159

Locke, Greg, 547

Lorenz, Konrad, 301–2

love: ethic of liberation and, 357–61; Freud's discussion of, 227–28; morphology of groups and, 234–36

Lowie, Robert, 342–43

Luther, Martin, 354–56

Luxemburg, Rosa, 161–62, 165

Machiavelli, Niccolò, 170, 177–78

MacKinnon, Catherine, 7, 15n.5, 219–21, 286–91, 495

Madness and Civilization, 444

Maistre, Joseph de, 337

Malaparte, Curzio, 173

Malaysia, political activism in, 314

Malcolm X, 6, 13, 102; legacy of, 143–44; on violence and reciprocity, 103–7

Malcolm X Speaks: Selected Speeches and Statements, 143–44

Malinowski, Bronislaw, 342–43

Manicheanism: colonialism and, 83–84; Fanon's discussion of, 92–93; violence and, 8

manufactured consent, Hegel's discussion of, 19

manufacturing, Marx's discussion of, 72–77

March to the Monteria, The, 505–7

market forces, media reporting on violence and, 2

Mark of Oppression, The, 212

Markovic, Mihailo, 12–13

marriage: battered wives and role of, 255–59; rape in, 288–91; substitutionary sacrifice in, 339; violence in, 7, 217–18

Martin, Dorothy (Del), 7, 217–18, 255–59

martyrdom: in concentration camps, 439–41; legal interpretation and, 294–98

Marx, Karl: Arendt's discussion of, 417; Engels and, 39, 43–53, 62–63; Gramsci's discussion of, 171–76; on industrial capitalism, 69–77; political activism and legacy of, 62–63; on state role in production, 480; Taussig and, 503; on violence, 5–6, 20–22; on wage labor, 63–68; working-class revolution and, 18; on writers' role in revolution, 501

Marxism: feminism and, 287–91; Gramsci's involvement in, 158; Hitler's discussion of, 135–42; scarcity of resistance and, 371; social control theories and, 249; Trotsky's involvement in, 498; Urstaat model and, 486–89; Weil's critique of, 377; Williams's discussion of, 182–87

Marxism and Literature, 180

Masaryk, Thomas, 419

McEvoy, James III, 257–58

Médecins San Frontières (MSF), 496–97, 547–53

Media, 336–37

mediation: Hegel's lord-bondsman metaphor concerning, 30–33; in primitive societies, 346–50; of terror, in colonial narratives, 507–8, 513–21

Mein Kampf, 127–28, 177–78, 424

melancholia, Freud's discussion of, 239–40

memory: concentration camps and destruction of, 439–41; as critique, 368–70; cultural memory, 396–98; as dangerous memory, 367–76; of freedom and resistance, 370–76

Merck, Mandy, 15n.5

Methodism, 354

Metz, Johann Baptist, 364, 367, 373
middle class, Fanon's discussion of, 94–100
military structures and militarism: as artificial group, 228–33; colonialism and, 80–100; economic power and, 23; Engels's discussion of, 46–52; Foucault on discipline within, 461–62; Gramsci's discussion of, 159–65; Hobbes's discussion of, 407–9, 413–15; military law, 273–74; secret police vs., 427–32; violence and collapse of, 7–8
mimesis, colonial representation of savagery and, 504–21
misogyny, culture of trauma and, 528–38
monarchy, Hobbes's discussion of, 403–9
money, role in commerce of, 482–85
Moore, Barrington, Jr., 199
morality: concentration camps and destruction of, 439–41; humanitarian aid and role of, 548–53
Morrison, Toni, 530
motherhood, Hobbes on power of, 410–15
muchachos de confianza, colonial creation of, 508–9
Muhammad Speaks, 143
multiculturalism, Welch's discussion of, 362
Muslim Mosque, Inc., 151
Muslim Personal Law, 218–21, 263–67
Muslim Women's Bill (India), 267
Muzaffar, Chandra, 220–21, 314, 330–32; on human rights, 315–29
Mydan, Carl, 526
mythical violence: Benjamin's discussion of, 280–85; sociological mediation of, 508–9

National Association for the Advancement of Colored People (NAACP), 151–56
National Commission on the Causes and Prevention of Violence, 257

national debt, Marx's discussion of, 72–77
nationalism: Fanon's discussion of, 79–100; international context of, 93–100; Romanian totalitarianism and, 531–38; sovereignty issues and, 324; totalitarianism and, 417, 423–24
national societies, Gramsci's discussion of, 176–78
Nation of Islam, 143–44
natural law: commonwealth formation and, 400–403; Hobbes on distribution of power in, 410–15; violence and, 7, 269–85
natural theory of violence, 7
nature, man's domination of, 53–61
Nazism: Arendt's experiences with, 416–18; concentration camps as tool of, 434–41; destruction of art by, 499–502; dual authority of state and party in, 419–22; Hitler's defense of, 104–6, 127–28, 140–41; role of secret police in, 430–32
Need for Roots, The, 377
negativity, of absolute freedom, 36–38
Nervous System, The, 503
neurosis: Freud's discussion of, 216–18, 226; Oedipus complex and, 237–40; trauma as, 523
neutrality, fallacy of, 358–61
New International Economic Order (NIEO), 328
New International Information Order (NIIO), 328–29
New Left, social control theory and, 249
news media: coverage of bin Laden by, 544–46; coverage of nongovernmental organizations by, 550–53; Shah Bano divorce case and role of, 265–67; violence reporting by, 1–2
Niebuhr, Reinhold, 356, 358
Nietzsche, Friedrich: on cultural body, 396; Freud's discussion of, 242; morality of mores of, 477–78, 482

"nightwatchman" metaphor, Gramsci's use of, 168–76

"Nomos and Narrative," 292

nongovernmental organizations, violence and role of, 496–97, 547–53

nonreciprocity, of power relations, 206–10

nonviolence: conflict resolution and, 277–85; ethic of liberation and, 356–61; Gandhi's advocacy of, 102–3, 105–7, 110; injustice and fallacy of, 358–61; Malcolm X's discussion of, 144–56

normality, as defense against totalitarianism, 431–32

Novy mir, 498

Obedience to Authority, 300–302

objectivity, self-consciousness and, 33–34

Oedipus complex: Freud's discussion of, 236–40; privatization of organs and, 476–78

ontological analysis, limitations of, 369–70

Ophuls, Marcel, 526

order and disorder, 292

Ordinance of 13 July 1777, 65–68

organized labor: Benjamin's discussion of, 271–73; Gramsci's discussion of, 164–65

Origins of Totalitarianism, The, 416–43

Outline of a Theory of Practice, 188–98

overcoding, State and role of, 484–85

overdetermination, Bourdieu's concept of, 191

Ovesey, Lionel, 212

Oxford University Extra-Mural Delegacy, 180

pain: cultures of trauma and, 495; legal interpretations of, 298–99; martyrdom and, 293–98

Pakistani-Indian hostilities, 2

Palestinian state, United Nations and, 320–24

panic, Freud's discussion of, 230–33

panopticon, Foucault's concept of, 395–96, 455–71

paranoia, despotism and, 478–85

Paredes, Rómulo, 507–9, 514

Parsons, Talcott, 248–49

passive resistance: Gandhi's discussion of, 121–26; Gramsci's discussion of, 159; Hitler's discussion of, 139–42

patriarchal relationships: battered wives and role of, 255–59; Hobbes's discussion of, 415–19; judicial power and, 342–43; marriage as example of, 217–18; rape as example of, 219–21

patriotism, Gandhi's discussion of, 115–16

peasantry: Engels's discussion of, 54–61; Fanon's discussion of, 84–87; Marx's discussion of, 65–68

"People of Color, The," 246–47

performance, power relations and, 203–10

Perjovschi, Amalia (Lia), 531, 537–38

Perjovschi, Dan, 531, 534, 538

permanent revolution: Gramsci's discussion of, 166–67, 178n.3; Trotsky's concept of, 417

permanent vengeance, in primitive cultures, 342–50

permanent visibility, Foucault's concept of, 456–71

Peruvian culture, colonial interpretations of, 503–7

petitioning, Gandhi's discussion of, 119–20

phallocratic order, culture of trauma and, 525–38

Phèdre, 390

Phenomenology of Spirit, excerpts from, 28–38

Plakaat laws, 65

plane crashes, death toll from, 1

Plato, 227

Plotinus, 353–54

Pokorny, Alex D., 259

police: as disciplinary institution, 463–64; institutionalized violence and, 275–76; in totalitarian state, 427–32

political economy: Engels's discussion of, 40–52; Marx's critique of, 63–77; role of discipline in, 466–71

political parties, in totalitarian states, 419–22, 429–32

political theory: art and, 501–2; concentration camps and limits of, 433–43; feminist movement and, 373; Gramsci's discussion of, 105–6, 159–64; of Hobbes, 400–403; revolution and rebellion and, 295–98; Scott's discussion of, 107, 199–200; sociology and, 167–68; war of maneuver vs. war of position in, 165–68

Popular Manual, 167–68

positivism: Benjamin's discussion of, 270; Gramsci's discussion of, 169–70

post-traumatic stress disorder, evolution of, 523

power: acting and, 203–10; Bourdieu's discussion of, 188, 193–98; culture of trauma and, 526–38; discipline as, 461–71; forcible acquisition of, 409–15; formation of commonwealth and, 402–3; Hegel's lord-bondsman metaphor concerning, 31–33; Hobbes on constitution of, 403–15; panopticonism as perfection of, 456–71; punishment as form of, 453–55; rape as displacement of, 287; Scott's discussion of, 201–13; of secret police, 427–32; totalitarianism and paradox of, 418–19, 424–26; violence and, 13–14; of the weak, 246–54

praxis: Gramsci's discussion of, 158–78; Hobbes's discussion of, 415

Preuss, Konrad, 509

primitive accumulation of capital, Marx's discussion of, 20–22, 70–77

primitive societies: Engels's discussion of, 43–52; modernist fascination with, 515–21; vengeance and violence in, 335–50

primitivism, political hegemony and, 175–76

prison: Foucault's discussion of, 395–96, 445–71; inversion of law in, 470–71; panoptic mechanism of, 455–71; uselessness of, as punishment, 451–52

Prison Notebooks, 158–78

private property, commodity production and, 473–78

production: Asiatic, 480–85; capitalist modes of, 67–68; colonial mirror of, 512–21; commodity, 43–52

professionalization of social work, social control theory and, 249–54

proletariat: Marx on creation of, 63–68; scarcity of resistance in, 371

property: convicts as, 449; force as foundation of, 42–61; Islamic law regarding, 262–67

psychoanalysis: Freud's discussion of, 227–28; morphology of groups and, 234–36

public opinion: on domestic violence, 255–58; on violence, 357

public transcript: power relations and, 212–13; Scott's discussion of, 200–213

punishment: Benjamin's discussion of, 274–75; Foucault's discussion of, 395–96, 445–71; randomness in totalitarian state of, 430–32; vengeance as, 343–50; violence in context of, 296–98. *See also* discipline

Putumaya rubber industry, 504–21

Qur'an, bin Laden's interpretation of, 539–44

Racine, Jean, 390

racism: bias in violence reporting due to, 1; liberation theology and, 351–61, 367–70; Malcolm X's discussion of, 103–7,

Salt March, 110–11
savagery, colonial representation of, 504–21
scapegoat theory (Girard), 334
Scarry, Elaine, 293–94
Schopenhauer, Arthur, 234–36
science: Bourdieu's discussion of, 189, 194–98; panopticon as tool of, 458–71; totalitarian subversion of, 431–32
Scotland, deprivation of rights in, 20–21
Scott, James, 6, 107; on domination, 200–213; political theories of, 199–200
secondary rules and principles: institutional violence and, 312–13; of legal interpretation, 299–302
secrecy, Foucault on punishment and, 446–55
secret police, in totalitarian state, 427–32
secularity, erosion of foundations for, 363–64
segregation, Malcolm X's discussion of, 104, 144–56
self-consciousness: absolute freedom and, 33–38; Hegel's discussion of, 18–19, 28–33
self-determination, liberation theology and, 352
self-love: family violence and, 216–18; morphology of groups and, 234–36
self-rule (swaraj), Gandhi's concept of, 110–23
separation of powers, hegemony and, 168–76
servitude: colonialism and, 81–82; Engels's discussion of, 42–52; Hegel's discussion of, 31–33
Sex and Character, 209–10
sexism, liberation theology's critique of, 369–70
sexuality: culture of trauma and, 525–38; Freud's discussion of, 227–28; identification and, 238–40; morphology of groups and, 235–36; primal horde

behavior and, 242–44; violence and, 7, 15n.5, 287–91
Shahabuddin, Syed, 266–67
Shah Bano divorce case, 4–5, 219–21, 262–67
Shakespeare, William, 390
Shamanism, Colonialism, and the Wild Man: A Study in Terror and Healing, 503–21
Shariat Law, 264–67
Shattering the Myth: Islam Beyond Violence, 262
shaved heads, culture of trauma and symbolism of, 525–38
Shaw, Nate, 208–10
Shouri, Arun, 267
silence, culture of trauma and role of, 531–38
sisterhood, liberation of, 373
skinhead movement, culture of trauma and, 529–31
slavery: Bourdieu's discussion of, 188, 196–98; Christian ethics concerning, 354–56; Engels's discussion of, 22–23, 40–52, 58–61; Fanon's discussion of, 24; judicial system and, 292; Marx's discussion of, 21–22, 70; power relations and, 208–10; as punishment, 449; Scott's discussion of, 200–213
social change: art as agent for, 268; black nationalism as agent for, 152–56; Freud's discussion of, 240–44; liberation theology's advocacy for, 368–70; punishment as agent for, 449–55; role of discipline in, 465–71; Williams's discussion of, 106
social codes: institutionalization of violence and, 300–302; punishment and role of, 452–53; secret police and role of, 428
social control: capitalism and, 474–78; contrition and shame as tools for, 296–98; disciplinary mechanisms for, 464–71; family violence and, 245–54;

Gramsci's social conformism as, 166–
67; punishment as form of, 449–55;
religion as tool for, 353–56

social cooperation, for constitutional
violence, 309–11

socialism: Arendt's discussion of, 417; in
underdeveloped countries, 96–100

social work, feminist influence in, 247–54

sociology: Bourdieu's discussion of, 189–
98; Gramsci's discussion of, 167–68;
mediation of mythic violence in, 508–
9; of power relations, 204–10; of totalitarian states, 429–32

socius, history and concept of, 473–78

Sorrow and the Pity, The, 526

soul, Weil's discussion of, 385–90

Soupault, Philippe, 498

South Asia, transnational violence in, 2

sovereignty: forcible acquisition of, 409–
15; formation of commonwealth and,
402–3; Hobbes's discussion of, 403–9;
human rights as threat to, 319–21;
national, 324

Soviet Union: artists in, 492–97; concentration camps in, 434–41; destruction of art in, 499–502; dual authority
of state and party in, 420–22; expan-
sionist foreign policy of, 424–26; formation of, 178n.2; purges in, 429–32;
revolution in, 417; role of secret police
in, 430–32

Soylent Green, 529

spirit, as absolute freedom, 34–38

stability, totalitarian promise of, 417–18

Stalin, Joseph, 178n.2, 417, 420–22, 424–
26, 498, 502

Stark, Rodney, 257–58

State: disciplinary mechanisms in, 463–
71; domestic and foreign policies, 175–
76; family structure and role of, 250–
54; feminism and Marxism and, 287–
91; forcible formation of, 403–9;
Foucault's concept of, 395–96; Gramsci's discussion of, 161–68, 165–68,

170–76; Hegel's discussion of, 35–38;
Hitler's view of, 104–6, 129–42;
Hobbes's discussion of, 392–93;
institutional formation of, 403–9;
institutionalization of violence in,
392–98; internalization and spiritualization of, 397–98; judicial independence, 305–6; law and, 169–70; Malcolm X's criticism of, 104, 144–56;
party's authority in, 419–22; production and role of, 480–85; religion and,
177–78; role of art in, 480–85, 501–2;
sociology and political science concerning, 167–68; territoriality of, 482–
85; totalitarianism and, 393–94, 417–
43; Urstaat model of, 485–89. *See also*
commonwealth, Hobbes on formation
of; government

Statute of Charles V, 65

Statute of Labourers, 66

Stern, Herbert, 304–6

Stevens, Wallace, 292

Stiles, Kristine, 494–95, 522–38

strikes: as class struggle, 278–85; labor's
right to, 271–73

structure of feeling, Williams's concept
of, 180–87

Student Nonviolent Coordinating Committee (SNCC), 151–52, 292

subjectivity: Foucault's discussion of,
444; violence and, 7

subjugated knowledges: liberation theology and, 366–76; Welch's discussion
of, 362

sublimation, art and role of, 500–502

substitutionary sacrifice, prevention of
violence and, 334–50

"superman," Nietzsche's concept of,
242

Supreme Court, constitutional role of,
309–11

surrealism, 498

surveillance, Foucault's panopticon as
tool for, 455–56

on human rights of, 316–17; information flow policies of, 328–29; instruments and institutions for human rights in, 315–17; Malcolm X's discussion of, 150–51; restrictions on human rights by, 326–27; restructuring proposals for, 330–32; Rwanda mission of, 549–50; Security Council structure, 326; sovereignty issues and, 319–21, 324; weapons and warfare policies of, 329

United Nations Conference on Trade and Development (UNCTAD), 328

United States: culture of trauma in, 530–31; Gulf War and, 321–24; judicial interpretation in, 309–11; national sovereignty and superpower status of, 324; restrictions on meaning of human rights in, 326–27; violence in history of, 357–61

United States v. Tiede, 304–6

Universal Declaration of Human Rights, 220–21; advancement of human rights and, 315–17; restrictions on meaning of human rights in, 326–27

universality, absolute freedom and, 34–38

Urstaat model of state, 485–89

utility: consciousness and, 33–34; disciplinary mechanisms for increase of, 465–71

vengeance: freedom and, 356–61; Girard on cyclical nature of, 334; replacement of judicial power with, 342–50; substitutionary sacrifice as freedom from, 339–40

Vietnam War, violence during, 3

Villon, François, 390

violation, Williams's discussion of, 181–82

violence: battered wives and patterns of, 255–59; Benjamin's critique of, 268–85; Bourdieu's discussion of, 188, 196–98; Christianity and, 356–61; contextual

influences on, 1–2, 9–10; culture of trauma and, 522–38; death penalty as interpretive act of, 306–11; discipline as mechanism for, 467–71; ethics and, 356–61; family violence, 216–18, 245–54; Fanon's discussion of, 5–6, 8, 23–26, 79–100; Gandhi's discussion of, 102–3; history and, 18–26; Hitler's discussion of, 104–6; illegitimacy of power obtained by, 409–15; institutional context of, 216–23; international context of, 93–100; of legal acts, Cover's discussion of, 293–98; legal interpretation and generation of, 300–302; legal structures for, 218–21, 271–85; libido and, 227–28; Malcolm X's discussion of, 103–4, 144–56; modern theories on, 1–3, 5–9; nongovernmental organizations and, 496–97, 547–53; police and institutionalization of, 275–76; policies for ending, 12–14; post-Cold War legacy of, 3–5; predictable patterns of, 12; product-process dichotomy in, 11–12; racism and, 356–61; religious structures for, 221–23; representation of, 492–97; state institutionalization of, 392–98; substitutionary sacrifice for prevention of, 334–50; totalitarianism and, 393–94; Weil's discussion of, 223, 377–90; Williams's discussion of, 106, 181–82; Wright's discussion of, 211–12

Violence and the Sacred, 334

Violent Home, The, 256, 259

voting rights, Malcolm X's discussion of, 144–56

wage labor. *See* labor

wages, Marx's discussion of, 63–68

Waiting for God, 377

warfare: capitalism and, 74–77; colonialism and, 88–100; culture of trauma and, 524–38; Engels's discussion of, 6, 23, 48–52; Gramsci's discussion of,

warfare (*continued*)
105–6, 159–65; Hobbes's discussion of, 400–403, 406–9; human rights violations and, 329; modern fear of, 434; Weil's discussion of, 223, 377–90

Warith Deen (son of Elijah Muhammad), 143

Washington, George, 358

weakness, power and, 246–54

wealth: cultural capital as, 192–98; Fanon on redistribution of, 25–26; industrial capitalism and, 69–77

weapons: Engels's discussion of, 46–52; human rights violations and, 329; Malcolm X's discussion of, 155–56

weapons of mass destruction, U.N. inspectors and, 323–24

Weber, Max, 193–94

Weil, Simone, on divine discourse, 223, 377–90

Weininger, Otto, 209–10

Welch, Sharon, 221–22, 362–76

welfare recipients, jurisdictional theory concerning, 292

welfare state, social control theory and, 251–54

Wesley, John, 354–55

Western culture: economic agenda in, 327–28; liberation theology's critique of, 369–70; restrictions on meaning of human rights in, 326–27; violence theories in, 7–9, 11–12

will: absolute freedom and, 34–38; rape and role of, 288–91

Williams, Raymond, 106; legacy of, 180; on Marxism and literature, 182–87

wisdom, fear and, 18–26

women: culture of trauma and violence against, 525–38; domestic violence against, 216–18, 245–54; in India, legal status of, 262–67; international politics and status of, 324–26; legal violence against, 4–5, 218–21, 262–67; liberation theology as voice for, 364–65; MacKinnon's discussion of violence against, 287–91; scarcity of resistance among, 371

work: Hegel's discussion of, 20, 32–33; Marx on conditions of, 21–22, 63–68; transformation of violence into, 24–25

Workers' Educational Association, 180

world domination, totalitarian obsession with, 422–26

World War I, Hitler's discussion of, 130–42

Wretched of the Earth, The, 23–26

Wright, Richard, 211–12

Zakaria, Rafiq, 267

Zuccolo, Ludovico, 170

BRUCE B. LAWRENCE is the Nancy and Jeffrey Marcus
Humanities Professor of Religion at Duke University. He is
the author and editor of numerous books, including *The
Qur'an: A Biography* (2007), *Messages to the World: The
Statements of Osama Bin Laden* (2005), *New Faiths, Old Fear:
Muslims and Other Asian Immigrants in American Religious
Life* (2002), *Shattering the Myth: Islam beyond Violence* (1998),
and *Defenders of God: The Fundamentalist Revolt against the
Modern Age* (1989).

AISHA KARIM is an assistant professor of English at
St. Xavier University.

. . . . .

Library of Congress Cataloging-in-Publication Data
On violence : a reader / edited by Bruce B. Lawrence and
Aisha Karim.
p. cm.
Includes bibliographical references and index.
ISBN-13: 978-0-8223-3756-0 (cloth : alk. paper)
ISBN-13: 978-0-8223-3769-0 (pbk. : alk. paper)
1. Violence.   I. Lawrence, Bruce B.   II. Karim, Aisha
B105.V505 2007
179.7—dc22 2007019209